HUMAN ADAPTABILITY

THIRD EDITION

HUMAN ADAPTABILITY

AN INTRODUCTION TO ECOLOGICAL ANTHROPOLOGY

EMILIO F. MORAN

Westview
PRESS

A Member of the Perseus Books Group

Find us on the World Wide Web at www.westviewpress.com.

Westview Press books are available at special discounts for bulk purchases in the United
States by corporations, institutions, and other organizations. For more information,
please contact the Special Markets Department at the Perseus Books Group, 2300
Chestnut Street, Suite 200, Philadelphia, PA 19103, call (800) 255-1514, or e-mail
special.markets@perseusbooks.com.

Designed by Trish Wilkinson
Set in 10 point Adobe Garamond

Library of Congress Cataloging-in-Publication Data
Moran, Emilio F.
    Human adaptability : an introduction to ecological anthropology / Emilio F.
Moran. — 3rd ed.
        p.   cm.
    Includes bibliographical references and index.
    ISBN-13: 978-0-8133-4367-9 (pbk. : alk. paper)
    ISBN-10: 0-8133-4367-4 (pbk. : alk. paper) 1. Human beings—Effect of
environment on. 2. Adaptation (Physiology) I. Title.
GF51.M58 2008
304.2—dc22   2007036237

10 9 8 7 6 5 4 3 2 1

To

Carlos Coimbra Jr.	Jonathan Hill
Ricardo Santos	Peter Little
Eduardo Neves	Mahir Saul
Eduardo Brondizio	Maria de Lourdes Villar
Andrea Siqueira	Janette Rawlings
Fabio de Castro	Nicholar Shorr
Maria Clara da Silva-Forsberg	Stefano Fiorini
Mateus Batistella	Geoff Childs
Celia Futemma	Lisa Cliggett
Maria Angelica Toniolo	Brian Donahoe
Francisco Gurri	Bret Ruby
Nora Haenn	Martha Balshem
Andreas Massing	Katherine Dettwyler

and many other past students, now colleagues, always friends and scholars—and always an inspiration to me in trying to understand human-environment interactions. Thanks!

I dedicate this book to all of you!

CONTENTS

———————— PART ONE ————————

ENVIRONMENTAL ANTHROPOLOGY
History, Theory, and Method

———————————— PART TWO ————————————

STUDIES OF HUMAN ADAPTABILITY

——————————— PART THREE ———————————

URBAN SUSTAINABILITY

ILLUSTRATIONS

Figures

PREFACE TO THE THIRD EDITION

Widespread use of this book's earlier editions among environmental specialists in ecology, medical sciences, public health, geography, and anthropology has encouraged me to prepare a third edition. The first edition presented a systems approach that sought to overcome disciplinary biases restricting the development of holistic research and theory building. Over the years, readers have told me the book has contributed to this important task. I hope this new edition will continue to play a role in conceptualizing research and formulating our growing understanding of the multiple levels of adaptation under the increasingly rapid conditions of global environmental change.

In focusing on mechanisms of human adaptability, this book integrates findings from ecology, physiology, social anthropology, and geography around a set of problems or constraints posed by human habitats. This problem-oriented approach lends itself to the integration of data and at the same time orients the researcher toward answering the question, How do humans adapt, mitigate, accommodate, and respond to environmental changes?

The place of environmental studies in anthropology reflects the changing interests of the discipline as well as trends in society at large (Siniarska and Dickinson 1996). In the past twenty years some trends appear to favor disciplinary integration while other trends seem to exacerbate its fragmentation. This book is committed to multidisciplinary integration and to ensuring that our methods and theories speak to concerns of people who seek to achieve a workable and sustainable resource use system.

LOCAL AND REGIONAL
ANALYSIS IN GLOBAL CONTEXT

One of the jewels in the practice of anthropology has always been its attention to the ethnographic detail of a village or community. More than simply a favored form of doing research, this became the only way we expected anthropological research to be carried out. This preference fit well with a desire to provide a holistic picture of human society, and it helped ecologically oriented anthropologists measure the relevant variables with some degree of completeness.

Or so we thought. This preference has become increasingly questionable as we have become more aware that the single village fails to adequately represent the range of variation present within even a limited region. Localized studies provide insights into family structure, subsistence strategies, labor inputs, health and nutritional status, flow of energy, socialization, and cultural institutions. Studies at this level, however, cannot address issues of origin and social evolution, economic development, demography, history, or political economy. These issues require a different type of research method emphasizing historical, geographic, economic, and political change over time and space (Moran 1990:286; Moran and Ostrom 2005). Studies based on a single village should not be expected to represent the range present in any population, and the construction of theory is set back by the unreliability of generalizing from single-site data. Even the most isolated human population and its immediate environment maintains a fluid set of relationships with other communities, opening it up to demographic, economic, and cultural exchange that over time alters the constitution of those same communities. Ellen demonstrated how this works itself out in the Moluccas (1990) and in a number of other ethnographic cases. Earlier, Rappaport (1968:226) had commented how, in retrospect, he had found the Maring local populations to be ephemeral through time and that the regional population would have been a more appropriate unit of study. A growing number of scholars have begun to consider local case studies in a regional context (Turner 2005; Aber and Foster 2004; Moran and Ostrom 2005).

This trend toward regional analysis gained further focus with the development of what has come to be known as human dimensions research. What is new in this approach is a concern for the cumulative impact of human action at a global scale (Lubchenco 1998). Research in this new multidisciplinary field concerns human activities that alter the earth's environment, the driving forces or causes of these activities, the consequences of environmental change for human societies, and human responses to the expectation or experience of global change. Such research takes place at scales from local to global. It began with trying to understand causes, consequences, and responses to climate change events or its probability (for example, sea level rise, El Niño forecasts). It has also focused on impacts of climate change, on impacts of land use and land cover change on biodiversity, and on issues such as urban sustainability and globally significant resources such as water and energy (NRC 1992, 1994, 1998a, 1999a,b; Tillman 1999).

Human dimensions research has already made a significant contribution to global change research by convincing the biogeochemical research community that research on global issues must address regionally scaled processes. Global models have provided valuable insights into aggregate change processes, but at this scale human processes are not salient enough to be captured—at least not with our current social science tools or data. What is most evident to environmental social scientists is that human communities vary greatly in how they use resources, including among the highly industrialized countries. Less industrialized countries show even more variability in resource use. There are gigantic differences, for example, in per capita energy and materials consumption between China and Japan, and within each of these two countries. Tropical deforestation may be driven by population growth in Indonesia, but in Brazil it is more a product of tax breaks and subsidies given to cattle ranchers. Research on the human dimensions of global change tries to explain the patterns of changes taking place in terms of forces that act globally, regionally, and locally (Steffen et al. 2004).

These environmental changes will only continue in the twenty-first century. Major climate change cannot be safely relegated to the future (for example, carbon dioxide in the atmosphere has doubled). Climate change is here, and we are experiencing its impact. The demands of an additional 3–5 billion people by 2050 will alter land cover, water availability and quality, and social systems beyond what we can imagine. Environmental anthropology, environmental geography, human ecology, and environmental social science have a lot to contribute to addressing these challenges.

ABOUT THE NEW EDITION

The third edition follows the format of earlier editions, since readers have found it useful over the years. The text has been updated and revised throughout. There are also some new features in this edition:

- A new chapter on urban sustainability (Chapter 10) addresses the growing urbanization of the human population worldwide, and the growing concern with the sustainability, or unsustainability, of our cities.
- A new chapter on methods of spatial analysis (Chapter 4) describes the latest approaches in spatially explicit techniques, now widely used across the natural and social sciences.
- Chapters on history and theory from previous editions have been tightened and updated into one integrative chapter (Chapter 2).
- Global environmental change issues as they affect particular ecosystems have been enhanced throughout the volume.
- This edition provides greater attention to the role of gender in human adaptability research, reflecting the growth in attention to this dimension across the social sciences.
- New sections at the end of each chapter provide websites that give access to material relevant to the text, the biomes under discussion, and ways to get involved with environmental issues. The suggested readings at the end of each chapter have been completely updated.
- Readers have told me that they appreciate my balanced approach to physiological and cultural adaptation, so I have maintained and wherever possible strengthened that balance.

- The jargon-free writing of earlier editions has been maintained with a view toward making this volume even more accessible to the general reader.
- The bibliography has been expanded to reflect the rapidly growing literature in this area of study, providing the reader with what remains the most comprehensive bibliography on the subject.

The third edition is designed to serve as a textbook in a variety of courses, as a reference book for professionals, and as a book that gives the general public access to the integrative science of human-environment interactions research. As a textbook, it will be useful in courses in ecological anthropology, public health, environmental social science, cultural geography, human biology, and cultural ecology and in core courses surveying major approaches to the study of human society. It will also be useful in interdisciplinary courses on human ecology, global environmental change, the environmental social sciences, and environmental science. A glossary is provided at the end of the book to assist readers with selected technical terms. Terms that are defined in the glossary appear in boldface type the first time they appear in the text.

The material is presented in three parts. Part 1 (Chapters 1–4) introduces the history, methods, and principal concepts relevant to the study of human adaptability. Part 2 (Chapters 5–9) synthesizes studies of human adaptability to ecosystems in arctic, high altitude, arid, grassland, and tropical moist forest areas. Crucial constraints in each ecosystem are identified (for example, extreme cold) and responses analyzed (for example, characteristics of clothing and peripheral blood flow to the extremities). In each of these chapters I try to make readers aware of the state of knowledge on how global change impacts these ecosystems and the directions research is taking in each biome. Part 3 (Chapter 10) focuses on the new, rapidly growing field of urban ecology and sustainability, treated as an anthropogenic biome or ecosystem. This has been recognized by the National Science Foundation, which several years ago began funding two urban long-term ecological research sites, one at Phoenix, Arizona, the other at Baltimore, Maryland, to understand the interactions of people and the built environment as an integrated whole.

The current excitement in the environmental social sciences comes from the reintegration of disciplines, not their fragmentation. We should be less concerned with the fragmentation of any single discipline and more with our capacity to work with scientists in other fields. Anthropology can only remain vital if its various subfields maintain their intimacy with the theories and methods of other disciplines, if it jointly continues to address questions of importance to the human condition, and with a firm voice rejects any form of discourse that reduces our ability to contribute to the scientific study of the human species in its environmental context.

The preparation of the third edition required the assistance of many. Vonnie Peischl, Paula S. Dias, Jessica Chelekis, Anthony Cak, and Kelsey Scroggins devoted countless hours to proofing the manuscript, looking up references, websites, illustrations, and obtaining permissions. I am profoundly grateful for their contributions and friendship. Vonnie Peischl in particular helped steer both the second and editions to press with her remarkable skill and competence. I wish to thank the anonymous reviewers who provided suggestions, many of which have been incorporated into this third edition. Despite all this assistance, I alone am responsible for any deficiencies in the book.

Emilio F. Moran

ACRONYMS

ASDR	age-specific death rate
ASFR	age-specific fertility rate
BAT	brown adipose tissue
BMR	basal metabolic rate
CAP	Central Arizona project
CDR	crude death rate
CEC	cation exchange capacity
CIAT	Centro Internacional de Agricultura Tropical
CPR	common-pool resources
DBH	diameter at breast height
DEM	digital elevation model
DTM	digital terrain model of relief
ENSO	El Niño Southern Oscillation
GCM	global circulation model
GECHS	Global Environmental Change and Human Security
GLP	Global Land Project
GFR	general fertility rate
GIS	geographic information systems
GRR	gross reproductive rate
IBP	International Biological Program
IDB	international database
IDGEC	Institutional Dimensions of Global Environmental Change
IGBP	International Geosphere Biosphere Program
IIASA	International Institute of Applied Systems Analysis
IIAT	Instituto Interamericano de Agricultura Tropical
IITA	International Institute of Tropical Agriculture
IMR	infant mortality rate
IPCC	Intergovernmental Panel on Climate Change
IRRI	International Rice Research Institute
IT	industrial transformation

IV	importance value
LTER	long-term ecological research
LUCC	Land Use and Land Cover Change core project
MAB	Man and the Biosphere Program
MSS	multispectral scanner
NASA	National Aeronautics and Space Administration
NICHD	National Institute for Child Health and Human Development
NOAA	National Oceanic and Atmospheric Administration
NSF	National Science Foundation
RMR	resting metabolic rate
SCDR	standardized crude death rate
TFR	total fertility rate
TM	Landsat Thematic Mapper
UV	ultraviolet

PART

ONE

ENVIRONMENTAL ANTHROPOLOGY

History, Theory, and Method

Photo by E. Moran

1

PEOPLE IN ECOSYSTEMS

The study of human adaptability focuses on functional and structural features of human populations that facilitate coping with and transforming the physical environment, particularly under conditions of environmental change and stress. All around us we see evidence of global-scale environmental change and its local and regional manifestations. Global climate change, exacerbated by emissions of earth-warming gases, has been associated with the growing severity and frequency of extreme events such as storms, drought cycles, and flooding associated with El Niño and La Niña events. The Greenland and antarctic ice sheets are melting at a surprising pace (Hassol 2004). Climate change and the loss of biodiversity worldwide due to deforestation, fragmentation, and economic development not only threaten us with the loss of this accumulated genetic bank but constitute a globally scaled experiment with the structure and function of the biosphere (Walker et al. 1999; NRC 1999a; Steffen et al. 2004). The challenge is all the greater given the difficulties in distinguishing between human-induced changes and, for example, natural decadal climatic variability (Hulme et al. 1999). Demand is growing for a refined understanding of the environmental changes we are experiencing, of the consequences to human populations, and of the scale and magnitude of the adaptations different populations must make in order to adapt to or mitigate these changes. Human populations are amazingly adaptable. This chapter and Chapters 3–4 present major theoretical and methodological concepts relevant to the study of adaptability. Chapter 2 outlines the historical development of **environmental anthropology**.[1]

Contemporary studies of human adaptability reflect a growing interaction between the social and the biological sciences (Harrison and Morphy 1998; Gutman et al. 2004; Goodchild and Janelle 2004; Moran and Ostrom 2005; Moran 2006). **Cultural ecology** and **ethnoecology** were earlier forms of this research, in which the concepts and methods of the biological sciences played a less central role. Most of the research in human ecology in the disciplines of anthropology, geography, and sociology was of this kind until the early 1970s. These social and cultural approaches to the study of human adaptability have enriched our understanding of coping behaviors. Nevertheless, a full explanation of human adaptability must integrate the physiological aspects of our responses with a solid understanding of the physical environment in which our behavior takes place. This is particularly true today given the growing practice of team-based multidisciplinary research required by the study of environmental change at scales from local to regional to global (NRC 1999a; Turner 2005; Moran and Ostrom 2005).

The integration of social and biological approaches to the study of adaptability was facilitated by acceptance of the **ecosystem** concept (see review of this history in Moran 1990; Golley 1992). This concept, derived from the study of biological ecology, views all organisms as part of ecological systems and subject to the same physical laws. Within this framework, human beings can be seen as third-order **consumers** in a food chain, or the interaction between two human populations can be considered **mutualistic.** The ecosystem approach makes it possible to apply a greater body of data to explanatory models of human behavior than is possible from a strictly social or cultural approach.

In this chapter, we will consider the ecosystem concept and the distinction between **adaptation** and **adjustment.** While the concept of evolutionary adaptation is relevant to the understanding of human adaptability, most research with human populations has found that nongenetic forms of adaptability are more common. Genetic adaptation involves changes in gene frequencies that confer reproductive advantage to the population in a particular environment. It is a response to prevailing environmental circumstances and may lower the population's capacity to adjust to future changes in its environment. It also tends to restrict the population to types of habitat in which it has a reproductive advantage. The human species is characterized by a marked degree of **phenotypic** plasticity. As a result, the interaction between environment and **genotype** brings about variations (adjustments) in behavior and morphology to adjust the organism to those conditions. These adjustments occur at the individual level, although they may be shared by the whole population living in a given habitat. In other words, the human species is generalized and adjusts itself to new circumstances by physiological as well as social and/or cultural means, and in so doing transforms the environment. Few corners of the earth have escaped being transformed by humans, and even some "pristine" places are the product of millennia-old changes brought on by our ancestors (Redman 1999; Redman et al. 2004; Diamond 2005).

The other central concept examined in this chapter, the ecological system or ecosystem, describes the interaction between living and nonliving components of a given habitat. While it is possible to view the whole biosphere as an ecosystem for some purposes, scientists have found it useful to divide the biosphere into smaller and more homogeneous biogeographical regions, or **biomes.** Such biomes represent a given set of climatic, floral, and faunal characteristics. While species may differ between continents, the type of **biota** across biomes will manifest commonalities resulting from the adaptation and adjustment to similar ecological conditions. Terrestrial and aquatic ecosystems respond to stress in similar ways: reduced biodiversity, altered primary and secondary productivity, increased disease prevalence, reduced efficiency of nutrient cycling, increased dominance of exotic species, and increased presence of smaller, shorter-lived opportunistic species (Rapport and Whitford 1999).

Although the interdependence of biological organisms was recognized during the nineteenth century, the ecosystem concept was not articulated until 1935, when A. G. Tansley proposed it to explain the dynamic aspects of populations and communities. An ecosystem includes "all the organisms in a given area, interacting with the physical environment, so that a flow of energy leads to a clearly defined trophic structure, biotic diversity and material cycles" (E. Odum 1971:8).

Ecosystems are said to be self-maintained and self-regulating, an assumption that has affected ecosystem studies but has been questioned recently by biologists and anthropologists. The concept of **homeostasis,** once defined as the tendency for biological systems to resist change and to remain in a state of equilibrium (E. Odum 1971:34), led to an overemphasis on static considerations and to an evaluation of man's role as basically disruptive. Later, Vayda (1974), Slobodkin (1968, 1974), and Bateson (1963) defined homeostasis as the maintenance of system properties (while others, for example, emphasize resilience [Holling 1973]). Recent ecosystem studies have emphasized, instead, the emergent properties of complex systems as characteristic of ecosystems (Levin 1998).

The cybernetic quality of ecosystems leads naturally to the use of systems analysis, which begins with a holistic model of the components and interrelations of an ecosystem—essentially a qualitative and descriptive process that anthropologists find useful. However, it then proceeds to simplify these complex interactions so that it can quantitatively study the behavior of both the whole and particular parts of an ecological system (E. Odum 1971:276–292).

Systems theory provides a broad framework for analyzing empirical reality and for cutting across disciplinary boundaries. Nonetheless, system approaches rely on other theories and develop measurements based on criteria other than those suggested by the system itself. Essentially, systems theory is a perspective that resembles anthropological holism: a system is an integral whole and no part can be understood apart from the entire system. Early studies focused on closed systems, understood through the negative feedbacks that maintain functional equilibrium. Later system analyses dealt with open systems reflecting positive feedback, nonlinear oscillating phenomena, and the purposive behavior of human actors. Such purposiveness is unevenly and differentially distributed, leading to conflict over goals and to system behavior reflecting the internal distribution of power. More recent stochastic approaches use dynamic modeling approaches such as STELLA (Constanza et al. 1993) and intelligent agent-based models such as SWARM and SUGARSCAPE (Epstein and Axtell 1996; Grimm et al. 2006; Walker et al. 2006; Parker et al. 2003). The former is an ecosystem type model, whereas the latter simulates "intelligent agent's behavior" based on principles of artificial intelligence (Deadman 1999; LeBars et al. 2005; Macy and

Willer 2002). The study of complex adaptive systems recognizes the nonlinear nature of systems and assumes that the complexity associated with a system is simply an emergent phenomenon of the local interactions of the parts of the system (Openshaw 1994, 1995; Epstein and Axtell 1996; Langton 1997; DeAngelis and Gross 1992).

Clifford Geertz, influenced by his reading of Dice (1955), Marston Bates (1953), and Eugene Odum (1971), was perhaps the first anthropologist to argue for the ecosystem as a viable unit of analysis in cultural anthropology. In his *Agricultural Involution* (1963), Geertz used the ecosystem concept to stress that a historical perspective helps explain Indonesia's economic stagnation as largely a result of the economic patterns established during the era of Dutch colonialism.

For purposes of this volume, the ecosystem can be subdivided into the three components that structure it: **energy, matter,** and **information.** Energy flows into ecosystems and is converted into vegetal biomass, which in turn sustains animals and humans. Chemical energy makes possible the conversion of matter from organic to inorganic forms and the cycle of essential nutrients in ecosystems. Information makes possible control over rates of flow, changes in ecosystem structure and function, and overall adaptability to both internal and external conditions. In studying adaptability, it is most convenient to begin with humans' response to **constraints** imposed by their habitat.

HUMAN ADAPTABILITY AS A RESPONSE TO CONSTRAINTS

The study of human adaptability tends to emphasize the plasticity of human response to any environment. Its use of a broad database that includes physiological, behavioral, and cultural adjustments to environmental change circumvents sterile debates over whether cultural or biological studies provide the most useful tools for studying interactions between humans and their environments. The human adaptability approach deals with the specific problems faced by inhabitants of various ecosystems. It focuses on how human populations, as they interact with each other and their environment, attempt to accommodate themselves to specific environmental problems, change the environment to make it more usable, and, in turn, how they are changed by these reciprocal dynamics. The approach gives agents (people) a lively role as decisionmakers in changing, adjusting, and transforming the physical environment, without overlooking the fact that the agents are changed in the process. Every constraint also represents an opportunity. For example, aridity constrains the practice of rain-fed agriculture, but it reduces fungi and mold which cause severe damage in humid areas. Likewise, arid lands are commonly less constrained by nutrient-poor soils than are humid areas. Nevertheless, it still stands to reason that limited access to water is the most constraining feature of arid regions.

Focusing on problems presented by environments does not imply abandoning the study of entire biomes. However, the data available is still fragmentary, and re-

TABLE 1.1 Limiting Factors of Representative Biomes

Biome	*Characteristics*
Arctic zones	Extreme and prolonged low temperatures Light/dark seasonal cycles Low biological productivity
High altitudes	Low oxygen pressure, or hypoxia Nighttime cold stress Low biological productivity High neonate mortality
Arid lands	Low and uncertain rainfall High rates of evaporation Low biological productivity
Grasslands	Prolonged dry season Cyclical drought Herd size and composition
Humid tropics	Great diversity of species High rainfall Secondary succession Solar radiation

searchers have experienced difficulty in analyzing these broad units. Some scientists divide a biome into species for study, while others deal with the specific behavior of populations and communities. The approach used in this book identifies clearly defined limiting factors, **stresses,** or problems that elicit human responses—transforming the source of the stress whenever possible (Balée and Erickson 2006) and not just adjusting to it. Problems such as extreme cold, low biological productivity, and water scarcity demand adjustment by organisms. Human agents must move nutrients to infertile areas and irrigate areas where water is scarce. The question is, Under what conditions do agents decide that the effort is justified or possible? Table 1.1 summarizes the major constraints of a number of ecosystems that will be studied in Chapters 5–9.

Focusing on a problem allows the researcher to get away from the debate over the appropriate unit of analysis (individual, population, or ecosystem) and initially requires the researcher to consider all levels of response to the problem. For example, extreme and continuing stress may elicit a coping response of irreversible physiological change during the individual's developmental period **(developmental adjustments).** Acclimatory forms of physiological response, on the other hand, facilitate the adjustment of individuals after the developmental period and are reversible **(acclimatory**

adjustment). Perhaps the most common forms of adjustment are behavioral, social, and cultural **(regulatory adjustments).** Regulatory adjustments are more flexible than developmental or acclimatory adjustments because they involve less commitment from the physical organism, and can be acquired promptly by learning from others.

A problem approach permits the inclusion of these multilevel responses to a particular problem—for example, cold stress. It also facilitates the conceptualization of the research by suggesting **hypotheses** to be tested and knowledge to be sought. During the investigation, focusing on specific problems helps keep the study on track by continuous testing of the hypotheses proposed. In the analysis stage, the focus on specific problems helps guide the interpretation of data. Lees and Bates (1990) suggest that one can focus on, for example, a dam building project, a development project, or a drought to study the entirety of human responses to an unprecedented or precipitating event in a manner similar to what I propose in the study of ecosystem constraints. This approach is comparable to geographers' efforts to understand human responses to natural hazards (White 1974). For these approaches to have theoretical benefit, classes of events must be clustered to ensure their potential for comparison, generalization, and theory building.

Adaptation and Adjustment

Adaptation is at the heart of the ecological approach. Organisms, human and nonhuman, respond to the structural and functional characteristics of their environment. Adaptations result from exposure to physical and chemical factors, from interaction with other species, and from the interaction of individuals within the same species. Evolutionary change through the mechanism of natural selection involves individuals with one type of adaptation being replaced by those with another. This type of **genetic** or **evolutionary adaptation** involves a slow adjustment to environmental change and is studied at the level of populations. Importantly, humans and animals have the capability for maladaptation. Since many animals, including the human species, are capable of learning from others, and since social learning is an important mechanism for rapid adaptation to changing circumstances, maladaptive behaviors can also be transmitted (Eder 1987; Laland and Williams 1998).

Individuals respond to changes in their environment by morphological and functional adjustments. For example, dental defects can mirror environmental, nutritional, or psychological stress experienced by individuals and populations. Dental enamel hypoplasia refers to a deficiency in enamel thickness that anthropologists use to assess when the individual or the population has experienced a severe stress such as undernutrition or infection (Goodman et al. 1984; Cook and Buikstra 1980; Goodman and Rose 1990; Gurri 1997). Fluctuations in adult height (as evidenced by average height at maturity) also reflect environmental factors, such as food availability and disease exposure throughout the growth period (see Chapter 3). Ricklefs (1973:56) differentiates between regulatory, acclimatory, and developmental adjustments. All three types operate by a process known as negative **feedback,** which seeks to maintain a stable relationship between the organism and the surroundings. To be effective, a response must be of the proper magnitude and occur at a time and rate that is appropriate in relation to the stimulus that elicited the adjustment.

Regulatory responses occur rapidly and reflect an organism's physiological and behavioral flexibility. Virtually all behavior is a form of regulatory response that maintains a stable relationship to the environment or makes adjustments to changes in that environment. Cultural **strategies** of clothing and shelter are regulatory mechanisms that enhance human survival and comfort in a variety of environments.

Acclimatory responses take longer to come into operation because they require a change in organismic structure. They occur when an external stimulus is present for a sufficient amount of time. They are usually reversible when the situation that produced the organismic change ends. For example, muscle enlargement resulting from physical exercise is reversed when a more sedentary life is resumed (Maud and Foster 2006).

Developmental responses are not reversible and occur during an individual's growth and development. They occur as the organism adjusts to the environmental conditions prevalent during the developmental period. But people in different regions (for example, high mountains) may respond differently to the constraints of those biomes (Beall 2001; Beall et al. 2002; Beall 2006). During this developmental period, human organisms have the ability to mold themselves to prevalent environmental conditions **(phenotypic plasticity).** For example, a child growing at high altitudes may develop larger lungs and chest capacity to adjust to low oxygen conditions. After the developmental period, a nonnative will be unable to achieve a larger chest cavity. Developmental adjustments are of limited value for short-term environmental adjustments, but provide a more flexible adjustment to prevalent conditions than does genetic change. The developmental flexibility of the human population provides a rapid mechanism for improving survival chances and enhancing reproduction, more so than genetic change accumulated over several generations (Ricklefs 1973:60).

The Ecosystem Concept

The ecosystem is a fundamental ecological unit that comprises associated species of living organisms in a nonliving physical environment and the structural and functional relationships among them. The ecosystem approach as a way to organize knowledge has had its ups and downs. Following a rapid rise to popularity in the late 1960s, it was heavily criticized in the 1980s. But it has made a strong comeback at the start of the twenty-first century. The NSF-funded Center for Ecological Analysis and Synthesis at the University of California–Santa Barbara (www.nceas.ucsb.edu) has advanced productive use of the ecosystem concept in ecological analysis. Integrative centers, such as the Abess Center for Ecosystem Science and Policy at the

University of Miami (www.cesp.miami.edu), are built around this integrative concept. The concept has been expanded to include the integration of spatial analysis and the consideration of spatial as well as temporal changes in the structure and function of the ecosystem (Goodchild and Janelle 2004). In the study of human adaptability, the ecosystem is the total situation in which adaptability occurs. Because human populations have spread throughout the earth, this adaptability varies a great deal. A population in a specific ecosystem adjusts to environmental conditions in ways that reflect both present and past conditions. A desert population that has existed in that environment for several millennia will differ significantly in its responses to desert conditions from a population that migrated there only in the past generation. A population that has existed longer in a particular environment is more likely than a recently settled population to have developed physiological and even genetic characteristics for coping with environmental constraints, such as hypoxia. The more recent inhabitants will have physiological and cultural adjustments attuned to another environment. Adjusting to the new environment may take several generations, and the final result may or may not resemble the adjustments of the original inhabitants. This is particularly true when native populations are available. The newcomers may borrow some of the practices of the original inhabitants in order to achieve a satisfactory adjustment to their new habitat (Moran et al. 2002a).

The above scenario suggests that human adaptability can proceed along various paths. In the absence of borrowing and **diffusion** of ideas, the population may develop new forms of adjustment and landscape transformation. If the new adjustment pattern conflicts with previous practices and yet provides a workable solution that does not threaten the survival and well-being of the individual or group, some form of compromise may emerge. If the exposure to stress is continual, physiological change of a permanent kind (developmental adjustment) may provide a more adequate adjustment than regulatory forms. The human body is able to adapt by genetic, physiological, and behavioral and cultural means. These various levels of adjustment enhance adaptability through a flexible hierarchy of response.

Human adaptability, therefore, refers to ecological success as measured by demographic, energetic, or nutritional criteria. Demographic criteria often used include (1) a balance between natality and mortality, (2) morbidity or incidence of disease, and (3) the population's rate of reproduction. Energetic criteria can be relative or absolute. Relative **energetic efficiency** indicates the adequacy of a technology. Efficient subsistence technologies are sustainable at low levels of population density. In the past total energy was considered indicative of success (White 1959), but this privileged powerful economic systems that may not be sustainable over the long term. Nutrition (Nina Etkin 1994, 2006; Dufour 1987, 1988) provides a good index of adaptability, since food consumption reflects knowledge of resources, ability to exploit them, and capacity to achieve a given level of work capacity. Health measures go hand in hand and interact closely with nutritional indices in ways that make separate analysis difficult (Gurri 1997). However, all these criteria are only indexes of adaptability and do not constitute a firm measure of **fitness** (reproductive success). The more adapted a species is in its environment, the greater the opportunity for individuals to survive and reproduce and then occupy the territory. Defining energetic failure or inefficiency and nutritional inadequacy is easier than determining reproductive success. Overpopulation raises numerous questions about the adequacy of reproductive fitness as an index of human adaptation. China discouraged couples from having more than one child because of the dangers of overpopulation, and its phenomenal economic development in the past decade can be taken as a measure, among others such as lower infant mortality, of greater fitness rather than less. This remains an important discussion in the study of adaptability. Maud and Foster (2006) provide an updated approach to physiological assessment of human fitness focusing on the general population using blood lactate, respiratory and heart rate markers, pulmonary gas exchange, body composition, and joint range of motion. This is an important way to think of fitness beyond evolutionary reproductive fitness.

MODELING

The complexity and multiplicity of factors that impinge on human adjustment to environment mandate a simplification of the overall situation. To this end, we turn to representations of real-world situations, or **models,** that facilitate comprehension of complex ecosystems. A model simplifies reality and reflects processes that may be involved in producing the observed facts. Once relevant processes have been identified, we infer other possibly related facts. These facts can then be observed and/or measured. Next, we check our predictions against the real world and assess the accuracy of our simplified representation. The model may be modified in accordance with our new observations and then retested to see whether it now more accurately represents and predicts real behaviors found in the system. A model, in other words, is evaluated in terms of its ability to predict correctly other new facts about the system (Lave and March 1975). Because it provides a systematic development of conjectures, tests, and validations that help us explain and appreciate how systems work, modeling is a major tool in the natural and social sciences.

To date, modeling risk has not equaled the same degree of sophistication as has modeling uncertainty (Haftka et al. 2006), but progress has been made in evaluating public risk preferences (Ananda and Herath 2005). Modeling can take place at any one of a number of scales of analysis, and each is appropriate for addressing different questions. During the 1980s and early 1990s considerable effort was invested in developing individual-based models. These models make more realistic assumptions than state-based and ecosystem-scaled models; nonetheless, models aim to advance a theoretical understanding of the whole rather than an appreciation of the parts (Grimm et al. 1999; Lomnicki 1999; Lorek and Sonnenschein 1999; Parker et al. 2003). However, understanding the behavior of individuals may be necessary to understand community dynamics, persistence, and other properties that provide stability and/or regulation to populations (Grimm et al. 1999; Uchmanski 1999; DeAngelis and Mooij 2005). These shifts mirror shifts in microeconomics, evolutionary ecology, and a concern with how and why individuals make decisions, including the differences in, for example, the migration intentions of men and women, reflecting differences in gender roles (DeJong 2000). There is a need also to reconcile the perspectives of agency and structure in human environment studies (Chowdhury and Turner 2006). A focus limited to agency or structural constraints can result in erroneous characterizations of processes, as compared to an approach that takes advantage of both.

Boundaries: Closed and Open Systems

In defining a model's boundaries, the researcher must delimit the field, usually based on the issue or problem investigated. Modeling ecosystems that include people is particularly thorny. To cope with the complexity, ecologists and social scientists deal with systems as if they were closed. A **closed system** is bounded for heuristic reasons and is treated as if it were unaffected by forces outside the system.

Although this approach has allowed many scientists to deal with complex data, it is more realistic to view most living systems as open to outside forces. While a closed system is maintained by internal cycling of materials, an **open system** requires constant inputs from outside the system to maintain it. In ecological systems everything is ultimately interconnected and everything ultimately feeds back on itself (Miller 1975:77). This interconnectedness helps preserve the system because of cybernetic characteristics; **cybernetic systems** are those that maintain control and adaptability by information feedback.

The thermoregulatory functioning of the human body is a good illustration of how feedback operates (see Figure 1.1). In the presence of warm temperatures or vigorous exercise, sensory devices send messages to the brain, and the brain, in turn, brings on a sweating response. The evaporation of sweat cools the skin. The skin sensors feel the cooling and send new information to decrease sweating (negative feedback). When a system is overloaded—when conditions are beyond the tolerance capacity of the organism or system—the system goes out of control and positive feedback takes over. Such a response can either permit reorganization to occur and a new adaptive response to emerge, or it may mean death or breakdown.

The interest in holism has been closely associated with the development of **general systems theory** and the study of **complex adaptive systems** (von Bertalanffy 1968; Buckley 1968; Holling 1973, 1986; Constanza et al. 1993; Levin 1998; Lansing 2003). The systems approach is a way of thinking, an approach to problem solving. It provides a systematic approach to treating groups of interacting, interdependent parts linked by exchanges of matter, energy, and information. Before powerful computers were available, efforts to describe the behavior of complex systems were limited to simple linear systems of algebraic or differential equations. However, the behavior of

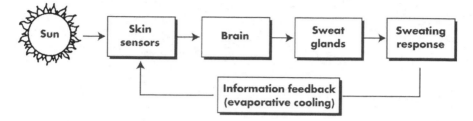

FIGURE 1.1 Cybernetics and Feedback

Negative feedback allows the system to self-correct and adjust to changing conditions.

complex systems is markedly nonlinear, and sometimes discontinuous or even chaotic (Rosser 1991; Constanza et al. 1993; Levin 1998; Lansing 2003). Approaches such as discrete choice models offer theory and method for understanding the probability of an individual selecting a resource as a function of the attributes of that resource and other available resources (Cooper and Millspaugh 1999).

Modelers may be tempted to simplify reality to the point of static equilibrium. Both ecologists (Slobodkin 1974; Holling 1973) and social scientists (Buckley 1967; Friedman 1974) have pointed out that the equilibrium models that came so easily in the past are not so reliable or useful as once thought. A more viable and realistic notion is to conceptualize human societies as complex adaptive systems (Lansing 2003). The study of complex adaptive systems is a subset of nonlinear dynamical systems. Recent studies have focused on the properties of self-organizing systems. For example, biologists and some ecologists see natural selection as the only source of order in the biological world. Social scientists have focused on the emergence of new properties from local interactions (Ostrom 2005). Closed systems have been characterized by minimal linkages with the rest of the world and a minimum internal capacity for change. Open systems, on the other hand, emphasize that internal flows are capable of significantly changing the internal components of the system. Information flows about the state of the outside world lead to feedback loops that do not return the system to equilibrium, but rather lead it along new paths that improve its adjustment to changing conditions. Modelers must deal with how change occurs instead of aiming at elegant models that do not represent the survival demands faced by living organisms.

An interesting recent debate has centered on the self-organization of ecosystems. Any ecosystem contains hundreds of species interacting with each other and their abiotic environment. Not all of these interactions have the same strength or direction, and the first-order interactions that structure the system may be confined to a small number of biotic and abiotic variables that make up the template (Southwood 1977) or matrix that allows much of the rest of the system to "come along for the ride" (Carpenter and Leavitt 1991; Cohen 1991; Holling 1992). The latter are affected by the ecosystem but do not seem to have a measurable impact. The role of these keystone species may only become apparent under particular conditions that trigger their key structuring functions at some magnitude of change or disturbance.

Advantages of Modeling

Modeling can be utilized at any phase of a study, but it is particularly useful in the preliminary stages of an investigation. At this point, it helps identify knowledge gaps and formulate relationships to be investigated. Narrowing down objectives is crucial for most investigations, given the limited resources and time available. During data-gathering stages, modeling can be helpful in monitoring the gradual accumulation of data and in identifying those compartments with sufficient data (Evans et al. 2005a).

Simulation at the intermediate phases of research may be helpful in testing the model's accuracy in representing the situation under study. Simulation refers to a technique for solving and studying problems by following a model's changes over time. It is one of the most useful techniques available for studying complex systems. A simulation model attempts to represent system functioning in a way that reproduces *dynamic* interactions between system components. Simulations are useful in planning for optimum changes in a system (Constanza and Voivnov 2004). This may avoid those disheartening discoveries that much of the data gathered were inappropriate for a workable model and that other data are still required. At the end of the data-gathering period, a wide range of techniques for analysis and simulation are available, such as agent-based models (Epstein and Axtell 1996; Axelrod 1997; Parker et al. 2003), ecosystem dynamic models such as STELLA (Hannon and Ruth 1997), and complex biogeochemical models such as NASA-CASA (Potter et al. 1998).

Another advantage of modeling is that systemic relationships rather than detailed content receive special attention (Evans et al. 2001). In addition, the investigator is not bound to modeling only one type of information. If agricultural, climatic, and social variables are relevant, they can be included in the model. Their inclusion may be vital if the model is to adequately represent the structure and function of the system. Regardless of the topic of investigation or the level of a model's complexity, the parts of a system are always linked by flows of energy, matter, and information. These flows connect the components of ecosystems, and they must be understood if we are to understand the structure and function of ecosystems and human adaptability within those systems.

ENERGY

Modeling in ecological analyses is most often used to represent flows of energy, matter, or both. Since the writings of Leslie White (1943, 1959) and Fred Cottrell (1955), the social sciences have been aware of the relationship between humankind's social complexity and its harnessing of energy. Because energy refers to the ability to do work, it is important to know what units to use in computing the energy harnessed or released by an organism. Energy can be expressed as joules, BTUs, watt-hours, foot-pounds, and **kilocalories.** The kilocalorie (kcal) is the unit most commonly used in human ecological studies. It is defined as the amount of heat required to raise the temperature of one kilogram (that is, one liter) of water 1°C at a temperature of 15°C. This unit has wide applicability and is commonly used in nutrition, physics, and chemistry. Some scientists have advocated the use of the joule as a unit because kcal cannot be defined with sufficient accuracy for certain physical purposes. A joule is, however, an inconvenient unit to use because it is very small: 1 kilocalorie equals 4,184 joules. Since many of the energy studies that involve human populations are based on nutritional assessments, the kilocalorie remains the most convenient unit (Durnin 1975:10).

How energy is stored and how it performs work are best described by the **laws of thermodynamics.** The first law states that energy is neither created nor destroyed. It may change form, go from one place to another, or be degraded into less usable forms. The second law is closely related to the first and states that part of energy involved in doing work is lost as heat to the surrounding environment. Thus there is a constant degradation of energy. This leads to an increase in **entropy** (disorder) in ecological systems. In open systems, such as those in the biosphere, entropy occurs as heat and waste continuously drain off, while the system's order is maintained by a constant inflow of potential energy from the sun (see Figure 1.2). The earth, therefore, is an open system with respect to solar energy. Over any appreciable period, the amount of energy received from the sun is roughly equal to the energy lost by the earth to outer space. This balance permits the earth to maintain its heat balance. Without the energy balance, the earth would heat up or cool down, and biological systems would experience lethal climatic changes (Murdoch 1971:2). The dramatic increase in the emission of earth-warming gases has been the subject of intense study since the 1990s and has resulted in accurate simulations of expected climatic anomalies (some of them already evident to climate forecasters) and extreme events with a doubling of CO_2. However, a tripling of CO_2 is not out of the question, and simulations of what such a tripling might imply have yet to be developed because of the difficulty of imagining how biological organisms might respond to such high levels of CO_2 (NRC 1999a; Watson et al. 1998; Moran 2006).

Solar energy not absorbed by plants, either because it is of the wrong wavelength or because of plant efficiency, is radiated outward from earth or participates in differential heating of the earth through reflection and transmission from the earth's cloud cover. This is referred to as heat energy. It warms the earth, heats the atmosphere, drives the water cycle, and provides currents of air and water (R. L. Smith 1974:30). Because of differences in the angle of the earth and other factors, temperature differences cause winds. When surface water is heated, some of it evaporates, and this vapor is transported by the wind over land where it may fall as either rain or snow.

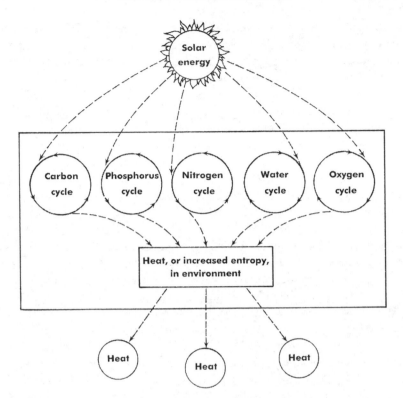

FIGURE 1.2 Closed and Open Cycles in the Biosphere

We can treat a system as closed for analytical purposes, but systems are open and have inputs from outside the "closed" system. *Source:* Adapted from G. Tyler Miller, *Living in the Environment* (Belmont, CA: Wadsworth, 1975).

Water and wind are forms of natural energy that can be harnessed and transformed to stored or potential energy (as, for example, when water is restrained behind a dam) or they can be used directly (as in the case of wind-generated grist mills).

Solar energy is stored in the form of living biomass as well as fossil fuels (for example, coal, oil, gas). Fossil fuels are formed by a lengthy process of organic accumulation and decomposition under conditions of heat and pressure (Odum and Odum 1976:28). The use of fossil fuels in our time has obscured the fact that it is still the sun that powers our ecological systems. Significantly, our use of that accumulated energy source exceeds the speed at which the processes of nature can create it.

The energy converted and stored in plant **biomass** becomes available to other organisms of the ecosystem. (Biomass refers to the mass of living organisms in a given area or population, may be expressed in calorie terms or in weight units, and may

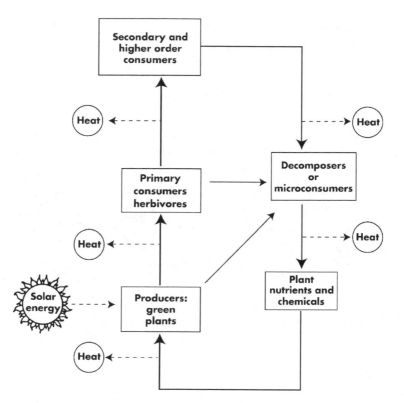

FIGURE 1.3 A Simplified Food Web

Solid lines represent movement of matter; unshaded lines indicate flow of energy.

refer to the total mass or to a portion, as in plant biomass, livestock biomass, and so forth.) The energy stored in plant biomass powers a series of organisms in what has been described as a food chain. A food chain is a simple summary of who-eats-whom. In nature, however, the situation is not a simple chain but a complex network of **trophic** (feeding) relationships, referred to as a food web (Figure 1.3). At each step in a food chain or food web, energy is lost as heat because of the expenditure of energy within the food-chain process (the second law of thermodynamics). Thus an increasing loss of potential energy passes from plants to higher organisms. This loss of energy can be visualized as a pyramid that represents trophic relations in the system. Figure 1.4 is one such pyramid and illustrates the dramatic declines in biomass and number of organisms.

An ecosystem represents the interrelations between living and nonliving components. The living portion is made up of green plants (**producers**), consumers (**herbivores** and **carnivores**), and **decomposers.** The nonliving portion includes the

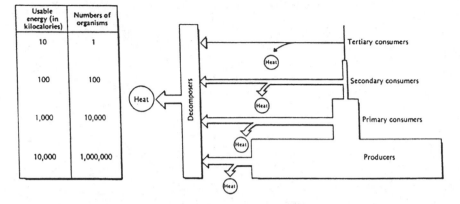

Usable energy (in kilocalories)	Numbers of organisms
10	1
100	100
1,000	10,000
10,000	1,000,000

FIGURE 1.4 An Ecological Pyramid Used to Describe Trophic Levels

Because of the steady decrease in usable energy, both energy and numbers of organisms decrease from producer organisms to higher-order consumers.

solar energy that drives the entire system, organic and inorganic substances, and physical factors such as temperature, light, wind, humidity, and rainfall. The characteristics of a given ecosystem are a function of the interaction of all these factors.

MATTER

The work of plants in converting energy from the sun into energy that can be used by other organisms for growth and development would not be possible without the availability of organic and inorganic materials that provide both mechanical support and nutrients essential for life. While energy flows continually in and out of systems, matter essentially cycles from one state to another. There has been a tendency to speak of **cycles of matter** as closed cycles. This is an oversimplification, since elements cross ecosystems boundaries. Carried by the atmosphere, water, or other mechanical means and leaving in similar ways, elements make their way from one area to another (see Figure 1.5).

Thirty to forty elements are required for the maintenance of life. Some are required in large amounts (for example, carbon, nitrogen, oxygen, and hydrogen), others in minute doses. The cycles of materials on the earth involve pathways that take elements from organic to inorganic forms and back again. For instance, nitrogen is released from animal remains by decomposers, later recombined in its elemental form by nitrogen-fixing organisms in the soil, and then utilized by plants in synthesizing protoplasm. These cycles continue whether human beings are present or not. However, human activity affects material flows in such a way that, in an in-

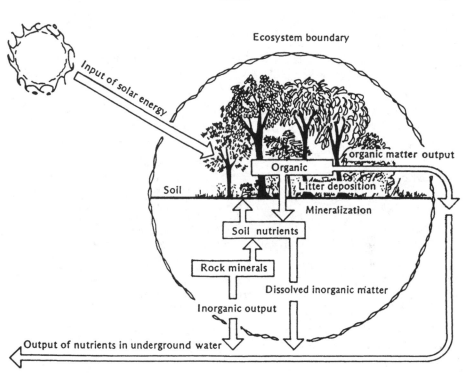

Ecosystem boundary

Input of solar energy

organic matter output

Organic

Litter deposition

Soil

Mineralization

Soil nutrients

Rock minerals

Dissolved inorganic matter

Inorganic output

Output of nutrients in underground water

FIGURE 1.5 Flow and Storage of Matter in a Terrestrial Ecosystem

creasing number of cases, the components of the natural system cannot cycle materials fast enough, and toxic accumulations result.

How plants use elements and how human beings enter into these processes illustrate cycles of matter. As with energy, plant producers are the key element in the material exchange cycles. Human populations have helped control these cycles of matter. For example, contour planting and terracing alter water and sedimentary cycles by controlling erosion and delaying the runoff of water and minerals suspended in it. Multistoried cropping, which positions plants of different heights in close proximity, helps control nutrient leaching, uses sunlight efficiently, and increases net yield. In managing plants, people often test the limits of plant tolerance and soil productivity. Sometimes failure results but in other cases, unexpected advantages—as when a plant taken to another continent thrives in the absence of its natural enemies under soil and climatic conditions similar to those of its native habitat (for example, rubber, *Hevea brasiliensis*, when taken to Malaysia at the turn of the nineteenth century, escaped some of the diseases that affect it in its native Amazonian habitat and has subsequently thrived in Asia).

INFORMATION

How information flows and is transformed is significant to an analysis of how matter and energy are transformed and work is achieved (Adams 1974:21). The effect of cognition on human value structures and the effect of those values, in turn, on the implementation of controls over natural processes have not always been empirically determined. Some authors argue that such controls are responses to systemic states (Rappaport 1968), while others emphasize the role of individual choice making (Bennett 1969). The growing fields of environmental psychology and cognitive anthropology address the ways in which culture, values, and information influence the behavior of human populations toward the environment (Gardner and Stern 1996; Kempton et al. 1996).

In the interest of formulating theories that can adequately deal with the interrelations between social, cultural, and environmental variables, several authors have advocated that structural analyses of communication, meaning, and cognition be combined with energetic and/or other forms of ecological research (Alland 1975; Adams 1974). Similarly, Rappaport discusses how ritual can act as a cybernetic switch that automatically adjusts the relationship between a population and its resources. According to Rappaport, ritual reduces ambiguity by putting complex analogic information and more/less information into simple digital signals (that is, a switch). In general, religious ritual affirms group values and asks individuals to abandon their selfishness and take on the social good. Ritual is an expensive cultural investment, but it pays off by providing unequivocal information of value for adaptability.

Mackay (1968a:204) suggests that semantic questions can be included in information theory only when senders and receivers are thought of as goal-directed, self-adaptive systems. According to this view, an organism requires a certain repertoire of acts and has a selective process that is organized according to the current state of the environment. Constant work must be done to update the informational system in a logical sense. If one defines information as logical work that orients the organism toward better coping behaviors, then information can be measured. What is measured is not an amount of something learned, but the establishment of logical relations (structure). In this view of information, both perception and evaluation are neatly included in the model. Human systems are self-organizing—able to receive inputs of new information and develop characteristic organizing sequences as a result of combining new and old information. Since the environment manifests consistent and recurrent features, an individual having a set of perceived conditions can use the notion of probability in deciding which routine is most likely to be successful (Mackay 1968b:363–364).

A number of authors have questioned the assumption that humans act according to the principles of probability. According to van Heerden (1968:20), it was Laplace who extended the concept of probability to events in which the card game types of

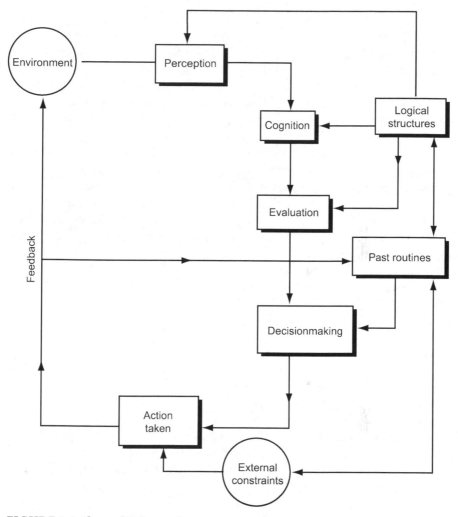

FIGURE 1.6 Flow of Information

Information flow is seen as an organizing feedback that attunes the organism to environmental and social conditions. External restraints may refer to social pressure put on the individual by the social group that steers the person in a course other than that decided on individually. Each action taken becomes part of the past routines that will constrain choice.

selection do not apply. Some argue that human choices respond to empirical experience, that is, if it worked in the past, try it again; if it did not, try something else (van Heerden 1968:45). Others suggest that the choices are made from a limited set of options, usually those that have occurred in the most recent past and that express the least uncertainty about outcomes (Slovic et al. 1974).

Figure 1.6 presents a more realistic view of how information flows through a human cognitive system. There is sensory reception of signals and symbols, some of which are ignored and some of which are perceived, depending on the sensory quality of the information and its fit with current logical structures that result from linguistic and cultural categorization. This allows for several possible interpretations, ambiguity, and new reorderings. When a perceived stimulus does not fit neatly into categories, the cognitive domain may develop structured analyses of the stimulus so that it can create hypotheses and assign meaning to the information acquired. After this occurs, the information is processed and put into the realm of information-for-decision—consideration of whether the stimulus is first- or second-hand information, whether it elicits an immediate response, or whether it is meant to be stored as a subroutine until certain conditions elicit it. For example, someone who reads that drinking animal blood is not a satisfactory way of coping with thirst in the desert because the metabolic requirements of processing are higher than the liquid ingested, might store that information. Later, such second-hand information might be employed in decisionmaking should one be stranded in a desert with a small water supply.

ECOSYSTEMS AND GLOBAL CHANGE

Ecosystems have always experienced change and disturbance, but the rates and magnitudes of change at local, regional, and global scales have grown in recent years. Regional and local climate and geomorphology set the stage for the self-organizing processes that establish persistent self-repeating patterns that result in a recognizably structured and functioning ecosystem. However, recent studies support the notion that only a small set of self-organizing processes are critical in forming the overall behavior of ecosystems and that these represent sets of relationships that dominate a given range of spatial and temporally scaled processes (Holling 1992). When global change comes about, it may not lead to gradual incremental change in ecosystems but to sudden and extensive transformation. Because a smaller set of processes structure ecosystems, such as shifts in precipitation, temperature, or landscape changes such as massive deforestation, changes are more likely to be from forest to grassland or grassland to semiarid desert (Holling 1973; Walker et al. 1981), as control of key ecosystem processes will shift from one set of organizing interactions and variables to another set. Diversity in ecosystems matters because it is the diversity of overlapping interactions that defines a system's resilience (Baskin 1994).

A similar transformation is taking place in social systems. Global media, international labor flows, the spread of infectious diseases (from less developed to developed nations) and chronic diseases (from developed to developing nations), and the global economy are transforming concepts of community, culture, and society (Moran 2006). Food and famine are no longer local problems. International interventions are routine but still mediated through local, regional, and national institutions caught up in a web of politics (Messer 1996; Moran 1982b). Nongovernmental organizations have sprouted worldwide, some local and others international in scope. Their behavior seems to be associated with various state failures to deliver needed resources and access to people. Likewise, they threaten to undermine the relations of people to government agencies and could ultimately affect their long-term vulnerability to global actors likely to benefit from weak states (C. Smith 1996).

Put together, the process of globalization has the potential to threaten human ecosystems in ways and at scales not currently imaginable. Likewise, they have the potential to be self-correcting and (when adequately informed about negative outcomes from current action) to change in order to ensure the survival of the system and the interest of its components. But this says little about who will be victims of the survival of the core of the system. As we study human ecology, we must keep in mind the multiscale impacts of people on environment, and vice versa, in order to adequately assess the consequences of actions and understand the scope of processes. Throughout the following chapters you will find discussions of how global environmental changes are affecting human populations in various biomes and how the science of the human dimensions of global change is being carried out.

SUGGESTED READINGS AND USEFUL WEBSITES

The *American Journal of Human Biology* (www.humbio.org/journal.html) regularly publishes articles of interest on human adaptability. The Program for Man and the Biosphere also has a website of interest: www.mabnetamericas.org/home2.html. In 1988 the International Geosphere Biosphere Program (IGBP), which began as an international global change program focusing on climate and atmospheric change, invited social scientists to participate in this global effort and has an excellent website (www.igbp.kva.se/secretar.html) providing links to other scientific programs, such as the Past Global Changes Program (PAGES) for understanding long-term climate changes (www.pages.unibe.ch), of particular interest to archeologists, paleoecologists, and paleontologists; the Analysis, Integration, and Modeling of the Earth System program (AIMES) for global modeling and global change (www.aimes .ucar.edu); the Global Land project for studying coupled human-land environment systems (www.globallandproject.org); and the Integrated History and Future of People on Earth program (IHOPE) for reconstructing human history and environmental change (www.aimes.ucar.edu/activities/ihope.shtml).

The Anthropology and Environment section of the American Anthropological Association (www.eanth.org/index.php) provides resources for those interested in anthropology and environment (www.eanth.org/onlineresources2.php?resource =programs.php), as well as links to other available online resources (www.eanth.org/ onlineresources2.php). More general anthropological resources can be found at the Anthro.net (www.anthro.net/index.html), Anthrotech (http://vlib.anthrotech.com), and Anthropology Resources on the Internet (www.anthropologie.net) websites. The

Anthropological Index Online (http://lucy.ukc.ac.uk/AIO.html) also serves as a database for searching anthropological and environmental research articles. The Intute: Social Sciences website (www.intute.ac.uk/socialsciences/environmental sciences) and the Social Sciences Research Network (www.ssrn.com/sein/index.html) serve as gateways to other Internet resources on environmental social sciences.

The Social Science Working Group of the Society for Conservation Biology (www.conbio.org/WorkingGroups/SSWG) and the Research Committee on Environment and Society RC24 of the International Sociological Association (www .isa-sociology.org/rc24.htm) link together researchers working on conservation issues within the social sciences, particularly sociology. Additional theory and research can be found at the website for Research Resources for the Social Sciences (www .socsciresearch.com). The H-Environment website (www.h-net.org/~environ), part of H-NET, the Humanities and Social Sciences Online initiative, provides resources for human-environment research, especially from a political and historical perspective. Additionally, the Society for Applied Anthropology (www.sfaa.net) offers resources for human-environment study.

Through the leadership of the International Social Sciences Council, programs such as the International Human Dimensions Program (IHDP) (www.uni-bonn.de/ ihdp) have emerged with specific research topics such as institutions (www.ihdp .uni-bonn.de/html/projects/i-idgec.html), human security (www.ihdp.uni-bonn.de/ html/projects/i-gechs.html), industrial transformation (www.vu.nl/ivm/research/ ihdp-it, www.ihdp.uni-bonn.de/html/projects/i-it.html), and urbanization (www .ihdp.uni-bonn.de/html/projects/i-urbanisation.html). Other topics that the IHDP has now spawned are the study of institutional dimensions of global environmental change (IDGEC) (www2.bren.ucsb.edu/~idgec), land-ocean interactions in the coastal zone (www.loicz.org), and the above noted Global Land Project (www .globallandproject.org).

The journal *Human Ecology* (http://maxweber.hunter.cuny.edu/anthro/ecology .html) publishes a wide range of articles concerning the interaction between people and environment, while the Society for Human Ecology (www.societyfor humanecology.org) links researchers examining human-environment interactions from an ecological perspective. Additionally, the *Journal of Cultural Geography* (www.geog.okstate.edu/users/culture/culture.htm) and the journal *Theory, Culture, and Society* (http://tcs.sagepub.com) are useful resources for human-environment study. At the National Academy of Sciences, several committees and websites emphasize human-environment interactions, including the Committee on the Human Dimension of Global Change (www7.nationalacademies.org/hdgc), the Committee on Human Factors (www7.nationalacademies.org/bcsse/Committee_on_Human _Factors.html), and an overview of global change research (http://dels.nas.edu/ globalchange).

Also, useful materials are available from the Center for International Earth Science Information Network (www.ciesin.org) at Columbia University, which provides information on the study of social, natural, and informational sciences, especially on information and spatial data management. It also includes a manual for social scientists introducing them to remote sensing and discusses many resources on the study of population, while the Forum on Science and Innovation for Sustainable Development provides an overview of research on climate change and sustainability (http://sustainabilityscience.org).

NOTE

1. Terms in boldface are defined in the glossary.

Charles Robert Darwin (1809–1882)
Portrait by Hon. John Collier (1881)
Courtesy of Linnean Society of London

2

THEORIES OF
HUMAN-HABITAT
INTERACTION

Contemporary theories about human effects on the environment and the environment's effects on them are only intelligible in light of the historical roots of such theories. Modern notions of homeostasis reflect ancient concerns and assumptions about the order of nature, just as our current fascination with chaos theory reflects a contemporary jaundiced view of the social order, also reflected in the discourses about postmodernity. Some authors' gloomy view of the potential for development in the tropics reflects a long tradition of environmental determinism that sees some regions of the world as ecologically bound to backwardness and others to progress. Every society has philosophical or mythological explanations about the natural world and humans' place in it. Through these explanations, a society articulates individuals' behavior and their survival requirements.

This chapter begins with a survey of the major Western intellectual currents up to the 1950s and then considers theories that were predominant in the second half of the twentieth century and are current today. Three main themes help organize the theories: environmental determinism, which postulates the determining effect of nature on human society and **culture;** cultural determinism, which views nature as a mere backdrop and sees cultural context as the only way to understand our place in nature; and human adaptation and evolution, which are driven by the dynamic interaction of people and environment. These themes represent three points on the intellectual spectrum. One view overemphasizes the influence of environment, while another overemphasizes the role of human culture. The third view bridges the gap between the other two. The deterministic themes conceptualize human-environment interactions as mainly unidirectional rather than systemic, and they emphasize stages rather than processes (Orlove 1980). Environmental determinism offers the clearest example of this type of unidirectional, stage-oriented explanation.

ENVIRONMENTAL DETERMINISM

Determinism is a broad term referring to explanations that assign one factor a dominating influence over the whole system. From Greco-Roman times through the early part of the twentieth century, scientific theories stressed single-factor explanations to the neglect of the complex interactions of biological systems. Environmental deterministic theories also rationalized political dominance. The format of all such theories was essentially the same: a "temperate" or "balanced" climate, ethnocentrically defined, is responsible for the virtuous qualities of those who inhabit an area. As a result, they are destined to rule and control the lesser domains where populations are more lethargic, less courageous, and less intelligent. Roughly, then, a predominant or technologically superior position indicates that those with power are innately superior. This superiority is produced by favorable geoclimatic conditions. Ironically, the locus of the "temperate climes" or "middle latitudes" has shifted from the balmy Mediterranean to the cooler regions of western Europe as world power has shifted over the centuries.

Greek, Roman, and Arab Theories

The original Greek geoclimatic theories arose from observations of nature and society. At the heart of their argument was their own political power and the role that their strategic location in the Mediterranean played in acquiring and maintaining such power. Writers rose to the task by explaining that the "middle latitudes" (that is, Greece) were most conducive to favorable cultural developments because there humans were subject to an ideal proportion of the basic four elements (fire, water, earth, air). A tropical climate was believed to foster idleness and resignation (Thomas 1925:227), while the climate of Greece, with its seasonal changes, balanced exposure to the elements and thus was the most conducive to progress. These ideas, which were endorsed by Hippocrates, Aristotle, and other major figures of ancient Greece, set a trend that was followed by the Romans.

Roman writers confidently cited geoclimatic reasons for Roman world conquest. Cicero attributed this success to Rome's strategic location. Like Greek authors before him, Vitrivius identified the optimal location as midway between the two extremes of hot and cold. He pointed to Rome's dominance as proof of the correctness of his judgment. In a similar vein, Tacitus viewed Germanic tribes as strong but disorganized savages. Pliny argued that Rome's location was so salutary to human development that "the manner of the people are gentle, the intellect clear, the genius fertile and capable of comprehending every part of nature. They have formed empires which has never been done by the remote nations" (Pliny in Thomas 1925:38).

Preserved in Christian monasteries and Arab centers of scholarship, the human environment theories of classical times survived the turmoil that followed the breakdown of Roman rule (Castaglioni 1958). Environmental and astrological explanations, which were derived from classical speculation, dominated medieval science.

Theoretical contributions by Arabs elaborated on classical theories. The Arab conception of the human-environment relationship was twofold. An astrological explanation considered humans to be part of the cosmos, with their character and outlook determined by the ruling stars of their environment. The other part was a purely geographical explanation based on climatic considerations (Alavi 1965:68). Elaborating on the geographical explanation, the Arab scholar al-Mas'udi discussed the importance of water, natural vegetation, and topography in determining the sites of human settlement. He also correlated the climate to the humors of the body, showing how a certain climate gives rise to humoral imbalance and thus to particular virtues or vices (Alavi 1965:69–70).

> The Arabs preferred life in an open countryside, where the air was pure, wholesome and free from epidemics, and where there was refinement of intelligence and strength of body; for intelligence, they thought, was produced in the same way as fresh air. The Arabs are, therefore, marked by strength of resolution, wisdom and physical fitness. They take care of those whom they take under their protection, they are distinguished in acts of charity and possess good intelligence, for these qualities are produced by the purity of environment. (al-Mas'udi in Alavi 1965:70)

Arab scholars preserved and translated the Greco-Roman classics and added some of their own interpretations to the texts. As a result, when the classics were read in twelfth- and thirteenth-century Europe, it was with the addition of commentaries by Arab and Jewish scholars from Cordoba, Seville, Toledo, Baghdad, and Damascus.

Theories of the Renaissance and the Eighteenth Century

With the discovery of the East Indies and the New World, Europeans were thrust into contact with cultures and environments that differed from their own. Among the adventurers, missionaries, and merchants of those days were naturalists and curious travelers; their accounts of the strange habitats and ways of native Asians and Americans stimulated an intellectual interest in explaining cultural and environmental differences.

A new boldness, based on the discoveries of the natural sciences, fostered secular explanations for similarities and differences in plant and animal forms. As information on new environments continued to spread, writers of the Renaissance began to question Greco-Roman theories on the relationship between environment and human character. With a growing awareness of the oversimplifications in classical conceptions, Renaissance writers raised many questions, including whether climate had the same influence on all living things. The role of human culture in buffering the impact of environment on society began to be appreciated, and the scope of possible explanations for similarities and differences in human populations was greatly expanded.

In the eighteenth century, climatic influences again became the focus of deterministic explanations. Bodin and Montesquieu, among others, reaffirmed the ancient notion that the middle latitudes are superior environments. (This time France was shown to be ideally located and predisposed for greatness!) Climate was strongly associated with physical and moral character. Theories were secularized as the role of religion and astrology was deemphasized. Generalizations were rampant: whole regions were treated as uniform, and nations were seen as drawn together by the action of dominant civilizations.

Nineteenth- and Twentieth-Century Theories

In the late nineteenth century, efforts to organize archaeological and **ethnological** data led to an attempt to illuminate the processes by which human cultural history changes. The notion that many cultures with similar artifacts and customs can be grouped by geographic location was seized on by geographers and then **ethnographers.** They believed that the interrelation between groups and their habitats produced specific kinds of cultural traits.

Friedrich Ratzel (1844–1904), a scholar with broad ethnographic interests who founded anthropogeography, emphasized the primacy of **habitat** in bringing about cultural diversity (Helm 1962:630). In his view, human society reacts to nature as any animal to its habitat. He explained human cultural evolution as spurred by conflicts over territory among migrating peoples. His thesis thus centered on group **migration,** which promotes the diffusion of cultural traits (Harris 1968:383). While diffusion may produce divergence in the original traits, Ratzel also believed that migratory peoples usually "hold fast to their natural conditions of existence [i.e., culture]" (quoted in Thomas 1925:140).

Ratzel pointed out that the "natural boundaries" created by topography and location give definition, distinction, coherence, and unity to such entities as political units. Similar locational conditions give rise to similar political models, as, for example, in all island societies (Thomas 1925:163). Yet geographic diversity within a nation's territory can produce a variety of effects: "mountains produce isolation and cultural stability, while lowlands promote racial and cultural mixture and migration . . . topography that promotes isolation and overexuberant flora [as in tropical forests] inevitably produces political and cultural stagnation" (quoted in Thomas 1925:165).

The environmental determinist trend continued in the twentieth century with the work of geographers Ellsworth Huntington (1915) and Griffith Taylor (1951). Huntington's chief concern was to ascertain the bearing of various climatic, seasonal, and weather conditions on human efficiency. According to this view, humans, when confronted with an environmental challenge, always take the path of least effort, for example, herding cattle in dry areas rather than farming and irrigating the land.

Huntington believed that variations in temperature and humidity were beneficial, provided they were not taken to extremes. He eventually postulated what he came to regard as an ideal climate for maximum human efficiency: moderate seasonal changes, average humidity, and abundant storms. Huntington formulated his generalizations as if climate were the only important factor.[1] Variants of this form of determinism are still expounded today, tempered, however, by a clearer awareness of the complex factors that may be involved in any human-habitat situation.

These deterministic theories, however, misuse inductive reasoning. The inductive approach requires observing the facts and then forming a generalization that fits all the observed facts. Determinists may formulate a generalization first and then set out to prove it with an unclear methodology and an inadequate sample. Selective sampling led to confirmation of many deterministic generalizations. At a time when little was known about the workings of the physical world, the broad scope of these generalizations was striking.

CULTURAL DETERMINISM: NATURE AS A LIMITING FACTOR

Unlike environmental deterministic theories that emphasize nature's influence on human behavior and institutions, cultural deterministic theories view nature as a static factor or backdrop, and human history and culture as shaping observable features in human communities. Some authors tie the idea of limiting factors to cultural determinism. The notion of limiting factors was most clearly stated by Justus Liebig around 1840. His contribution, known as the law of the minimum, explained that organisms are limited by the factor in most limited supply. When the principle is extended to include the limiting effect of one thing on the rest of the system, we have a broadly encompassing concept of wide applicability. For example, nutrients like nitrogen and phosphorus may be rapidly leached from the soil under some management practices and account for declines in yield, fallow cycles, and even crop choices.

In the late eighteenth century Thomas Malthus attempted to show the earth's limitations as an abode for human beings. He was not interested in how environment molds culture or in how human cultures have modified the environment. According to Malthus, all living things have a tendency to increase geometrically if they have enough food. However, once good soils have been put into production, populations find increasing difficulty in providing enough food for their rapidly growing numbers. Disease, war, famine, and other forms of population control enter to reduce the pressure on resources. His views influenced Darwin and many other nineteenth-century scholars and continue to have relevance today. The notion of Spaceship Earth with limitations on the resources needed to support our exponentially growing human population has its roots in the insights of Malthus.

Franz Boas (1858–1942) proposed a different view of environmental limitations—**historical possibilism**—in which nature circumscribes the possibilities for humans, but historical and cultural factors explain what is actually chosen. Boas rejected the idea that the environment is a primary molder of culture (Boas 1896:901–908) and sought explanations for cultural differences in the cultural history of a people. Boas came to this position after initially accepting the environmental deterministic views of his day, as expressed by Buckle and Ritter. He was also influenced by Adolf Bastian (1826–1905), the well-traveled German ethnographer who saw variation in geographical conditions as the basic source of cultural variations. When Boas went to Baffin Island to study the Eskimos, he did so "with a strong presumption in favor of the primacy of geographical factors in the life of the Eskimo" (Harris 1968:265). Boas's account, *The Central Eskimo* (1964), is a lucid portrayal of life in the arctic, stressing the interrelationship between geographical and cultural factors. Thereafter, however, Boas gave environment only a perfunctory role in his work. For Boas, people use what they want in the environment, and it is such cultural decisions, not the physical world, that dictate the direction of cultural change (Bennett 1976:165). Ethnological inquiry began for him with the perceptions, interests, wants, and actions of humans as conditioned by their social milieu. The Boasian approach set out to correct environmental determinism, but ended up as strongly culturally deterministic.

In *The Mind of Primitive Man* (1963), Boas pointed out that the environment furnishes the material people use to shape and develop the artifacts of daily life as well as their theories, beliefs, and customs (Thomas 1925:278). While granting that the environment has a general influence, Boas criticized the one-sided notion that the same type of environment will, in a given stage of culture, produce the same results everywhere. He noted that Eskimo subsistence was based on hunting and fishing, while the Siberian Chukchi made a living through breeding reindeer. At the opposite climatic extreme, the African Hottentot follow a pastoral life, while the Bushmen rely on hunting in a semitropical environment (Thomas 1925:279). Boas and his students pointed out that customs originating in one habitat can be perpetuated by "cultural inertia" after the group has moved to a new location in which the custom is no longer appropriate. Examples cited are the expensive and complicated tents of the Chukchi—a survival from the time when they were permanent dwellers on the coast (Goldenweiser 1937:446–447).

Boas's emphasis on the particular circumstances of a population led him to fruitless efforts at explaining cultural similarities and differences. Boas, like Francis Bacon before him, glorified the inductive method as a means to correcting the lack of data behind scientific doctrine (Harris 1968:287). He demanded careful collection of data, suspension of generalization, critical analysis of materials, and conservative excursions into theory. While his followers denied the existence of a Boasian school, they did share a certain common ground. Regarding the environment, their approach was a reaction to environmental determinism and therefore iconoclastic in character. Lowie (1883–1957), for one, in his *Culture and Ethnology* (1917) set out to disprove the environmental deterministic notions that "culture reaches its highest stages in temperate regions"; that the concept of liberty is directly correlated with altitude; and that island inhabitants are accomplished seafarers. Lowie argued that under the same geographical conditions, radically different cultures have developed. As examples, he pointed to the differences between the native cultures of North

America and the modern civilization that quickly arose in that same environment. He sought to tighten his argument by studying racially and culturally related populations (the Hopi and the Navaho) within comparable environments. Although they occupied similar regions in the Southwest, their cultures, Lowie showed, were markedly different. Lowie attempted to demonstrate that the availability of a resource does not predispose a population to use it; North American Indians did not domesticate the buffalo, nor did the Eskimo the reindeer.

Goldenweiser saw the environment as a static force and culture as the dynamic element that shapes the use of natural resources. He also suggested (compare Ferndon 1959) that man changes the natural environment (for example, turning forests into cultivated fields) and, as a result, makes his own environment instead of being determined by it (Goldenweiser 1937:452–453). As we will see later, this view (that people do not adapt to environment but modify their environment to suit them) has returned under what some scholars have named historical ecology, emphasizing historical context and agency (Balée 1998; Balée and Erickson 2006).

Lowie, Wissler, and others developed the cultural area approach that divides continents into culture areas based on shared linguistic characteristics and a mixed bag of cultural traits. This emphasis on shared traits was based on the strong assumption that diffusion may have occurred and can be traced to the work of the German and British diffusionists and, more immediately, to the work of Wissler (1870–1947). Wissler had noted that maps of geological and ecological features matched areas of cultural features. From this observation he postulated the diffusionist **age-area concept.** According to this principle, traits tend to diffuse outward in all directions from their point of origin. The more widely distributed a trait is from its origin, the older it is. Environment in this scheme is seen as an inert configuration that passively sets limits on cultural development (Wissler 1926).

Kroeber (1876–1960), like other anthropologists of his day, subscribed to the Boasian credo that the physical environment is acted on by human culture. However, unlike the other Boasians, Kroeber completely subordinated the individual to his cultural milieu. Kroeber elaborated this idea in his notion of the superorganic in culture: in all cultures the individual is subordinated to the cultural pattern and is an agent of inevitable cultural forces. This view implies that a scientific understanding of historical processes and social evolution is impossible.

In his 1939 book *Cultural and Natural Areas of Native North America*, Kroeber briefly departed from his usual approach and followed the scheme proposed by Wissler. Kroeber organized his descriptive material into regional categories developed from data on subsistence systems, habitat characteristics, and population densities. In this work, he momentarily admitted that "no culture is wholly intelligible without reference to . . . environmental factors with which it is in relation, and which condition it" (Kroeber 1939:205). He gave extensive examples of how environmental factors limit and define such cultural practices as maize farming, population concentration, and tribal and linguistic boundaries.

Kroeber's approach in *Cultural and Natural Areas* can be likened to that of his contemporary, British geographer-anthropologist C. D. Forde (1902–1973). Both of them emphasized the need for collecting ecological data and viewed such data as potentially valuable in explaining cultural similarities. Forde, for example, after summarizing the history of economic systems in relation to ecology and social organization, concluded that neither an evolutionary sequence of economic stages nor the nature of the subsistence base will explain the changes in culture (Forde 1934). He therefore warned against racial, geographical, and economic determinism (Minshull 1970:18). Economic and social activities, he concluded, are products of the long, but largely unpredictable, processes of cultural accumulation and integration.

Kroeber's conclusions in *Cultural and Natural Areas* resemble Forde's in *Habitat, Economy, and Society* (1934). Kroeber's fleeting use of techno-environmental explanation then ended, and he turned his idea of culture area increasingly toward notions of diffusion and areas of culture origins. In regard to his earlier culture-environment explorations, he became baffled: "The interaction of culture and environment becomes increasingly complex when followed out. And this complexity makes generalization unprofitable, on the whole. In each situation or area, different natural factors are likely to be impinging on culture with different intensity" (1939:205).

Despite this inability and/or unwillingness to deal with irregularities in human-environment interaction, Kroeber's *Cultural and Natural Areas* formed the backdrop of the cultural ecological approach proposed soon after by Julian Steward. Although Kroeber rejected the idea that modes of subsistence are causally and functionally related to social structure, the comprehensiveness of his effort remains impressive.

HUMAN ADAPTATION TO ENVIRONMENT

The Humoral Doctrine

The adaptationist view of human-environment interactions is rooted in Greco-Roman scientific concepts and can be traced to attempts to cure disease and achieve a healthful balance. Disease was considered a disturbance of the body's natural harmony. According to Hippocrates (460–375 BC), everything on the earth and in the universe is made up of four elements—air, earth, water, and fire—that had analogs in the human body as the four humors—blood, phlegm, black bile, and yellow bile. When the four humors are in balance, the body enjoys health. Air was thought to be represented in the body by blood, both being hot and moist; fire by yellow bile (hot and dry); water by phlegm (cold and moist); and earth by black bile (cold and dry). This theory, known as the humoral doctrine, contributed to the development of environmental deterministic theories and strongly influenced the development of soil theory, chemistry, and agriculture (Glacken 1967:12). In addition, the humoral doctrine has influenced psychological and physiological research on the influence of climate on the body.

Alternative notions of human adaptation were rare throughout the Middle Ages and the Renaissance. The few that were suggested linked diseases with environmental conditions. For example, José de Acosta (1539–1600) noted that individuals who traveled into high altitudes experienced mountain sickness, but those who lived there permanently seemed to have adjusted to the altitude (Leake 1964:4).

Evolutionary Sequences: Eighteenth-Century Views

During the eighteenth century natural historians, concerned with human progress, formulated evolutionary sequences that attempted to explain human society in terms of increased human control over nature. One of these figures, Turgot (1727–1781), foreshadowed the cultural ecological approach of Julian Steward. In *Universal History*, Turgot interpreted the band organization of hunters as a response to the necessity of pursuing game over vast areas. Such pursuit resulted, in turn, in the dispersal and diffusion of peoples and ideas. On the other hand, where easily domesticated species were present, a pastoral way of life with greater population concentrations and greater control over resources might emerge.

During this period, the Scottish School (an intellectual elite in Scotland in the eighteenth century) tried to correlate social organization with **subsistence.** A major figure of this school was historian William Robertson. His landmark *History of America* (1777) discusses the conditions for cultural similarities around the world. Robertson believed that cultural similarities are evidence of independent invention, arguing that similarities between the resource bases of two groups would lead to similar adaptive responses:

> The character and occupations of the hunter in America must be little different from those of the Asiatic, who depend for subsistence on the chase. A tribe of savages on the banks of the Danube must nearly resemble one upon the Plains washed by the Mississippi. Instead of presuming from the similarities that there is any affinity between them, we should only conclude that the disposition and manners of men are formed by their situation and arise from the state of society in which they live. (Robertson 1777:652, quoted in Harris 1968:34)

Whenever Robertson encountered a seemingly nonadaptive trait, he explained that the group borrowed the trait, despite its nonadaptiveness, from neighbors with whom it had previous contact. Thus Robertson dealt with two of the major research questions in cultural ecology: diffusion versus innovation and adaptive versus maladaptive cultural behavior.

The Scottish School included such writers as Adam Smith (1723–1790), Adam Ferguson (1723–1816), David Hume (1711–1776), and James Millar (1735–1801), who examined the evolution of complex societies and the cultural and materialistic forces that lead to social stratification (Voget 1975:90). These men looked at the interrelation of cultural units, especially those involved in the economics of a society, rather than the evolution of ideas per se. Adam Smith emphasized the division of labor as basic to understanding the increasing complexities of a modern nation (Voget 1975:78). Ferguson and Millar attempted to correlate various institutions, such as land tenure, marriage, and slavery, to the subsistence base found in various cultures. In so doing, they tried to correct some of the distorted accounts and explanations of primitive life by utilizing a variety of data sources and by avoiding racial and ethnocentric ideas about primitive "nature" or "intellect" (Harris 1968:29–31).

Millar and others also identified control over resources and accumulation of economic surplus as accounting for differing institutions. Their writings show a growing awareness that any explanation of cultural diversity must consider a broad range of factors. They do not use single-factor deterministic explanations, nor do they overemphasize individual choice, cultural determinism, or the purposeful movement of nature toward "progress" and higher civilization. Turgot and the Scottish philosophers emphasized adaptation from one subsistence mode to another.

Buffon (1707–1788) and Cuvier (1769–1832) emphasized the functional interrelations of living things and the relevance of past living forms for an understanding of the present. Buffon thought that change in an environment had little impact on the structures of individual living things. Lamarck (1744–1829), on the other hand, suggested that change could occur in individual morphology during a creature's lifetime as an adjustment to environmental change and that these changes could then be passed on, and intensified, through inheritance (Leake 1964:5).

Darwin's Theory of Evolution

The nineteenth century was the heyday of the naturalists. The similarities and differences in living organisms impressed them and stimulated their search for explanations. Charles Darwin's (1809–1882) contributions to ecological theory are particularly notable. Darwin found inspiration for his theory of evolution in the works of Charles Lyell and Thomas Malthus (1766–1834). Darwin took a copy of Lyell's *Principles of Geology* (1830) with him on his HMS *Beagle* voyage and confided in his diary that it "altered [his] whole tone of mind." Through Lyell's account of the geological record, Darwin saw an alternative to the narrow biblical timescale and was impressed by the relationship between environmental change and modifications in biological forms. Malthus's *An Essay on the Principle of Population* (1798) influenced Darwin with its idea that the natural trend of the human population was to increase unless stopped by disease, war, or famine. Darwin extended this notion to plant and animal populations.

Darwin's synthesis appeared in 1859 as *On the Origin of Species by Means of Natural Selection.* Darwin begins by assuming that all living things are related and that the diversity of species results from a continual branching out. Such branching is a product of the process known as natural selection. According to this principle, organisms most fit to survive and reproduce in a given environment will outreproduce less adapted organisms; species not adapted to current environmental conditions will be reduced to insignificant numbers and possible extinction.

Evolution includes what may be termed *mechanisms of continuity* and *mechanisms of variation* (Alland 1973:4). Mechanisms of continuity provide stability in nature, while mechanisms of variation are the product of chance and provide the variability in species that allows new solutions to be available when environmental changes occur. If **biological evolution** reflected only the process of adaptation to environment, it would be a static, nonevolutionary process. For evolutionary change to occur, there must be random changes in species that are not responses to current needs but under given circumstances give an advantage to individuals that share the trait in a population.

Darwin's view of natural selection is easily misunderstood. The Lamarckian idea that organisms improve themselves by their own efforts and that they pass on these advantages to their offspring appeals to common sense and to the notion that evolution travels along a progressive path (Gould 1980:76). However, species do not evolve in this manner. The specter of Lamarck in evolutionary theory can be traced to his central notion that organisms respond to felt needs. Lamarck's ideas are relevant to the notion of specific evolution as proposed by Sahlins and Service (1960) and to Steward's emphasis on adaptive processes in local environments (1955a). Selection acts on unoriented variation and changes result from reproductive success. Darwinian theory's power derives from its complexity, from its refusal to be a mechanistic theory driven by environmental determinism (Gould 1980:81) or purpose. It is less appealing than Lamarck's theory because it presents us with a universe devoid of intrinsic meaning or direction. As Rappaport notes (1984), human beings have to invent culture and ritual "to give meaning to a world devoid of meaning." Lamarck's theory, while failing to explain how species evolve, suggests instead how human cultural evolution occurs. In this realm we can expect rapid acquisition of adaptive traits through ideological and behavioral change and its transmission through socialization. Technological change and cultural change work in Lamarckian ways, and they have unleashed a rate of change inconceivable in the slower, undirected process of natural selection.

Modern Evolutionary Theory

Modern evolutionary theory and genetics have put to rest the simplistic notions of determinism. The functions and forms of organisms can be understood only through careful accounts of complex interactions. This is best expressed in the contrast between genotype and phenotype. Genotype refers to the hereditary potential of an organism. Phenotype, on the other hand, is the product of the interaction between the genotype and the organism's environment. Some species tolerate a minimum of environmental change and exhibit a minimum of phenotype variation (that is, highly specialized species). Bacteria tolerate only minute differences in habitat temperature. The human species, by contrast, manifests great phenotypic variations and can tolerate a wide range of environmental conditions (that is, we are a generalized species).

The basic elements of evolutionary theory include the following: (1) all populations are capable of genetic variation through the mechanisms of mutation and recombination, (2) all populations seek to increase their numbers exponentially until restricted by environmental constraints, (3) under a given set of environmental circumstances, the best-adapted phenotypes in a population will be selected for, and (4) the effect of the environment on the genotype is indirect. Adaptive changes in all organisms, including human beings, are mediated by the genetic hereditary material passed on from generation to generation. "The evolutionary fitness of the particular combination of hereditary traits embodied in an organism is largely determined by interaction of the organism with its environment during its lifetime" (Ricklefs 1973:69). Since more fit individuals who possess the best-adapted traits must replace a population, evolutionary change is always slow. Thus a population often reflects earlier conditions and is always changing—just as the environment is always changing (Levins 1968:11).

Biological adaptation is seldom perfect and is opposed by numerous factors. Among these are mutations and **gene flow,** evolutionary opportunity, physical limits, problems of allocation, and changing environments (Ricklefs 1973:71–73). No matter how well adapted a population may be, new random mutations occur and are introduced into a population, leading to change. The history of an organism limits future changes, so that major changes in anatomy are rare and may take millennia. The range of adaptation is also limited by the properties of the natural world, which cannot be easily altered either. Adaptation is essentially a compromise. The results are seldom the best, but represent solutions to conflicting priorities. If they are to be advantageous and selected, they must increase fitness over cost (Levins 1968:35). Adaptation is never perfect because environments are always changing, and populations must constantly readjust to the new environmental conditions. Since biological change is slow, populations are rarely in perfect adaptation to their present situation, except in rare cases of long-term environmental stability.[2]

Evolutionary ecology has developed vigorously since the 1980s (for example, Winterhalder and Smith 1981; E. A. Smith 1991; Boyd and Richerson 1985; Durham 1990). The attention that it gives to the great complexity of the environment distinguishes it from earlier forms of sociobiology. The latter tends to be general (for example, kin selection, sexual selection, sex-ratio manipulation) and best for addressing interspecific, comparative research. However, for those with an interest in the exceptional plasticity and diversity of behavior within a species, an evolutionary ecological approach is more appropriate. It is more concerned with why diversity of behavioral outcomes occurs, and less with how such adaptations effectively address the needs of species or individuals. For the latter, an adaptationist or functional approach is still more appropriate.

CULTURAL ECOLOGY:
COMPARISON IN HUMAN-ENVIRONMENT RESEARCH

Julian Steward's early writings broke with both environmental and cultural determinism by emphasizing the use of the comparative method to test causal connections between **social structure** and modes of subsistence. Steward's approach was a **functionalist** one, concerned with the operation of a variable in relation to a limited set of variables, not in relation to an entire social system. Unlike the British functionalists who emphasized the role of institutions in the maintenance of structural equilibrium at a given point in time (they employed a **synchronic** approach), Steward limited his scope to one system. However, his interest in evolution led him to study change in time and across societies (he used a **diachronic** approach). Steward's functionalism was not so much concerned with equilibrium as with change.

Steward's cultural ecological approach involves both a problem and a method. The problem is to test whether adjusting to their environment requires specific behaviors by human societies or whether there is considerable latitude (Steward 1955a:36). The method consists of three procedures: (1) to analyze the relationship between subsistence system and environment, (2) to analyze the behavior patterns associated with a given subsistence technology, and (3) to ascertain the extent to which the behavior pattern entailed in a given subsistence system affects other aspects of culture (Steward 1955a:40–41). In short, the cultural ecological approach postulates a relationship between environmental resources, subsistence technology, and the behavior required to bring technology to bear on resources.

The crucial element in Steward's approach is neither nature nor culture but resource utilization. The reasons for this are clear: food and shelter are immediate and urgent needs in all societies, and patterns of work at a given level of technology are limited in their ability to exploit resources. The approach is best illustrated by his study of the western Shoshoni.

The Shoshoni inhabited the Great Basin of North America, a semiarid land with widely dispersed resources. The Shoshoni were hunter-gatherers with simple tools and relied heavily on grass seeds, roots, and berries. Steward showed how almost every resource could best be exploited by individuals—except rabbits and antelope, which required seasonal group hunting. Each fall the Shoshoni gathered pine nuts that were stored for the long, cold winter. Although they formed larger population concentrations during the winter, they did not form stable social units because pine nuts were not available in the same places each year, and groups had to remain fluid to adequately exploit the basin. Thus subsistence requirements produced fluid and fragmentary social units that lacked distinct patterns of leadership.

To Steward, the Shoshoni presented an extreme case of the environment limiting the workable options available to a culture. Steward hypothesized that the immediate impact of environment on behavior decreased as technological complexity improved the human capacity to modify the environment. He suggested that in complex societies, social factors may be more important in explaining change than subsistence technology or environment (Steward 1938:262).

Steward's research strategy is even more striking against its historical backdrop. Until Steward's time, human-environment theories either dealt in broad generalities lacking a firm grounding in empirical research or emphasized lists of cultural traits. Cultural ecology emphasized analyzing social interactions, recording movements, timing work activities, and so forth. Through such research, it was possible to delimit the field of study and arrive at cause and effect relationships.

In an earlier study (1936), Steward compared hunter-gatherers in varied environments. The groups chosen for study lived in territorially based bands and were characterized by patrilocal residence, patrilineal descent, and **exogamous** marriage. The environmental determinist approach had long been baffled by the social similarities between groups as different as the Kalahari Bushmen, the Australian aborigines, and the rain forest pygmies. Steward showed that the ecological parallels between these groups were low population density, reliance on foot transportation, and the hunting of scattered nonmigratory animals. The need to know the resources of a territory anchored each population to it. Their limited means of transportation reduced the range that could be effectively exploited and favored the maintenance of low densities. Although his conclusion was not totally correct, Steward motivated others to study the interactions of hunter-gatherers with their habitats. The results of some of those studies are discussed in the next section.

Steward has been criticized because his approach is difficult to operationalize in the field and because it assigns primacy to subsistence behaviors. The focus on subsistence is essential to the cultural ecological approach. There are cases when other factors may have far greater control over a social system, and over the years Steward expanded the scope of cultural ecology to include political, religious, military, and aesthetic features of culture (1955a:93). Geertz (1963) concluded in his study of Indonesian agriculture that historical and political factors are part of the total environment to which populations adapt and must not be dismissed as secondary. Rappaport, a few years later, showed how ritual can play a central role in the maintenance of a society's balance with resources (1968).

While revolutionary in his emphasis on human environment interactions, Steward slighted several variables that could well affect the adaptive behavior of human groups. For instance, he had little to say regarding the influence of demographic makeup, epidemiology, and competition with other groups in a given area, or human physiological adaptations (Vayda and Rappaport 1976). More serious is the charge that the comparative approach cannot yield cause and effect relationships. Vayda and Rappaport question whether correlations between adaptations and cultural traits can be translated into causes and effects (Vayda and Rappaport 1976:14). Steward never followed a clear statistical sample, and his correlations left out cases in which the correlation did not hold. Steward usually succeeded in demonstrating functional relationships, but not in establishing causality. More than anyone before him, Steward delimited the field of human-environment interaction by emphasizing behavior, subsistence, and technology. The weaknesses of this approach became apparent within a decade and spawned other research strategies.

APPLICATIONS OF THE CULTURAL ECOLOGICAL METHOD

In the 1950s scholars began using the cultural ecological method to study old and new problems. Those following the Stewardian style of cultural ecology tend to utilize a culturally defined human population as their unit of study, focus on cultural rather than biological adaptations, and acknowledge a direct debt to Julian Steward (Netting 1968:11).[3] The method of cultural ecology has been applied to the study of hunter-gatherers, preindustrial farmers, pastoralists, and contemporary rural societies.

Hunter-Gatherers

Cultural ecological research has led to a revision of our understanding of hunter-gatherers. Earlier they were viewed as populations at the mercy of unpredictable resources, constantly under threat of starvation, and primarily concerned with subsistence. Field research since the time of Steward has demolished that simplistic notion. A rich variety of social forms, complex adjustments to neighbors and resources, and, in some cases, a life of relative leisure and security have been revealed. Important in this respect are *Man the Hunter* (R. E. Lee and DeVore 1968), *Hunters and Gatherers Today* (Bicchieri 1972), and the work of the Harvard Kalahari Research Group (R. E. Lee and DeVore 1976; Yellen 1977; Bentley 1985). Excellent reviews are also provided by Cashdan (1989), Burch and Ellanna (1994), and Erlandson (1994). For an updated overview, see Barnard (2004).

These new interpretations of hunter-gatherers resulted from data on labor time and the weighed yields from hunter-gatherer efforts. Important, too, were improved data on the prehistoric distributions of hunter-gatherers. Such investigation showed hunter-gatherers present in most of the habitable globe in 10,000 BC and concentrated in areas that later supported agricultural populations. By 1900, however, their range had contracted to marginal areas, and their way of life was threatened with extinction. Most ethnographic research was conducted under these later conditions, and it comes as no surprise that the first impressions suggested an impoverished way of making a living (Lee and DeVore 1968:5).

Since hunting and gathering is essentially a subsistence mode, it was an attractive topic for cultural ecologists. Steward had formulated his classic comparison of patrilineal bands using hunter-gatherers as samples. Because these populations maintain intimate contact with their habitat, the interaction between nature and humans is explicit among them. Hunter-gatherers also form relatively small groups, so quantifying relevant variables is more feasible among them than among larger groups, such as those in terrace-irrigation societies.

Although the hunting and gathering way of life is flexible and complex, it is still possible to make some generalizations. Hunter-gatherers appear to live in small groups and to be fairly mobile. They operate in territories but do not appear to have closed social systems. From the very beginning, reciprocal visiting and marriage alliances appear to have operated to form larger breeding and linguistic communities than those found in small, localized bands. Males hunting and females gathering wild plants fan out from base camps and bring back foodstuffs that are shared by all. Because mobility is important, personal property is kept to a minimum and egalitarian conditions predominate. Generally groups are kept small to prevent deterioration of the primary producers (plants) or game depletion. Bands, however, are flexible in size and can adjust to the fluctuating availability of food sources. Variations in the food supply seem to have encouraged the development of reciprocal visiting and food sharing with guests. Conflict is generally avoided, and fission (partitioning of the group) is a common response to social friction when it arises.

In the past twenty years important new insights have come from the use of optimal foraging theory (Winterhalder and Smith 1981; E. A. Smith 1983; Stephens and Krebs 1986). Because the environment has a large stochastic component, risk minimizing seems to have been a prominent feature of hunter-gatherer adaptation (Winterhalder and Smith 1981). Models have been developed that relate specific constraints and benefits to patterns of food sharing which have allowed researchers to examine the evolutionary origins of food sharing (Binford 1985; Winterhalder 1986). Whereas early foraging models ignored risk, later ones were able to show that food sharing among relatively few individuals achieved a considerable gain in food security (Winterhalder 1986; Kaplan and Hill 1985). If the mechanisms that support food sharing are undermined, hunter-gatherers will become more vulnerable and less able to persist in their way of life.

From this basic social outline, specific cultural features are likely to have developed in response to the particular conditions of a habitat or the history of a population. W. Suttles (1968), for example, has pointed out that the fishermen of the Northwest Pacific Coast of North America may have started as nomadic bands but were led into surplus accumulation, stable settlement, and larger population concentrations in response to the abundance of the salmon supply.[4]

Preindustrial Cultivators

The cultural ecological literature on cultivators is even more extensive than the literature on hunter-gatherers. All the subfields of anthropology have attempted to explain the origins of agriculture and contemporary worldwide patterns of food production. Writings on farming societies that preceded the development of cultural ecology dealt only briefly with farming behavior and production. When the farming methods of preindustrial peoples were discussed, they were often unfavorably compared with modern agricultural methods. The comparison also pitted tropical cultivators against temperate cultivators and assigned a higher value to the latter's emphasis on grain crops and domestic animals. The revision of the anthropological view of agricultural societies and productivity began with the work of Harold Conklin (1954, 1957, 1961) among the Hanunóo of the Philippines.[5] What he discovered was an intricate agricultural system based on shifting agriculture that exhibited sound agronomic management and achieved high levels of productivity per unit of labor spent. Shifting agriculture refers to a mode of cultivation in which fields are cropped for fewer years than they are allowed to remain fallow.[6]

Geertz (1963) demonstrated that two models dominated Indonesian agricultural systems. He showed how traditional shifting agriculture in the outer islands imitated the natural forest vegetation. The system only supported low population but was also low in labor costs. The other model, the complex irrigated rice paddy system of the inner islands, was described by Geertz as a response to the historical and cultural experience of colonialism, as ever greater amounts of labor were spent to sustain the demands of a colonial power.

While the development of agriculture has been commonly associated with the diffusion of sophisticated tools from a few centers of cultural innovation (Childe 1951), the new cultural ecological research has pointed out that intensive cultivation often was practiced with rudimentary tools. Netting (1968) described the complex **intercropping** practice of the Kofyar of northern Nigeria and showed that it was very efficient, even though the group lacked draft animals and modern farming technology. Farming practices have thus been interpreted as adjustments to the particular ecological situation in which a group finds itself (Carneiro 1957; Conklin 1957; Moran 1993b; Sanchez and Buol 1975).

Cumulative evidence has begun to show that the move from extensive shifting cultivation to a more intensive labor system only occurs when increasing population density puts too much pressure on current resources (Boserup 1965; Clarke 1966). A study that supports this view showed that a given area of irrigated land could support fourteen times as many families as it could with shifting agriculture—but only with a great increase in labor cost (Palerm 1968). Opposite views have been aired by Bronson (1972, 1975), Moerman (1968), Geertz (1963), and Rawski (1972). Bronson argued that cultivators may seek to invest labor for prestige, even at the expense of labor efficiency (1972). Moerman emphasized that social rewards or values may influence preferences in labor utilization (1968). Geertz convincingly showed that intensification can also result from political domination and colonial exploitation (1963). Or producers may seek to improve their exchange rates and income (Rawski 1972). The debate is far from concluded, and readers may wish to join research efforts that may someday give us a clearer view of the processes of agricultural intensification.

An overview of the works relevant to the cultural ecology of farming societies reveals that the direction of studies is toward more sophisticated data collecting and increased concern with the processes of decisionmaking among cultivators, as well as the use of economic anthropology and cultural ecology—evident in the work of

A. Johnson (1971, 1974), Bennett (1969), Moran (1981), McCay Acheson (1987), and Netting (1981, 1993) to name but a few. A new branch of ecological analysis within anthropology—systems ecology—will be discussed later in this chapter. In the new millennium a clearer understanding of the relationship between land use and land cover change will be demanded (Meyer and Turner 1992).

Pastoralists

Cultural ecologists have revised some hallowed assumptions regarding pastoralist societies, as seen in the reinterpretation of the east African cattle complex. The cattle complex refers to dominant cultural values among east African pastoralists that allegedly lead to inefficient and irrational use of cattle. According to the original interpretation (Herskovits 1926), the peculiar characteristics of the east African cattle complex (for example, the herdsman's strong attachment to cattle) represent an irrational use of cattle, rather than for economic or social purposes.

Cultural ecological and economic analyses have substantially changed this view. East African devotion to cattle keeping and to maximizing the number of cattle are now seen as an effective utilization of a biome that is marginal for agriculture and where pastures scattered over a large territory are subject to periodic **drought.** Rainfall is low and unpredictable and diseases can decimate cattle herds in very little time (Ford 1977:146–149). Cattle, though they do not provide the bulk of subsistence in normal times, are an important insurance factor in bad times and crucial to the nomadic pattern of settlement followed by these human groups. Evans-Pritchard (1940) gave a detailed analysis of how the environment of the Nuer determines most aspects of their culture. The cycle of seasonal migrations determines the settlement pattern, the sociopolitical role of segmentary lineages, and the social relations. Gulliver (1955) discussed how the differences in the habitat of the Jie and the Turkana affected their herding practices, their practice of agriculture vis-à-vis herding, their seasonal migrations, and their inheritance patterns.

Schneider (1957, 1970, 1974) presented convincing arguments for the adaptiveness of the east African pastoralist pattern. The Turu, for example, aim at converting their agricultural surplus into cattle, which are less subject to climatic vagaries and can reproduce themselves, thus yielding interest on the Turus' initial investment. Ultimately cattle wealth, like money, is sacrificed in favor of social status. In periods of grain scarcity, however, cattle provide a major food source (Dyson-Hudson and Dyson-Hudson 1969). Even the apparently uneconomic practice of maximizing herd size rather than quality has been shown to be an appropriate adjustment to local conditions. Spencer (1965) pointed out that during dry spells a large percentage of the herd will die, so the more cattle units a man owns during normal times, the better off he is. Cyclical droughts force the east African herder to maximize because he can seldom, if ever, optimize his production. Before he can reach an optimum herd size, another dry spell decimates his herd (see Figure 2.1).

FIGURE 2.1 Pastoralist Youth Milking Camels, Ariaal Rendille, Northern Kenya
Courtesy of Elliot Fratkin

Several studies address the interaction between pastoralists and cultivators, as well as historical explanations for changing relationships between the two groups (Barth 1969). A crucial work in this vein is Barth's analysis of the relations between ethnic groups in north Pakistan (1956). Barth tried to show that the economic and political organization of neighboring ethnic groups is best understood in terms of the niche concept, "the place of [each] group in the total environment, its relation to resources, and competitors" (Barth 1956:10–79). Barth showed that the niches occupied by three neighboring groups (Pathans, Gujars, and Kohistanis) reflected adjustments to the habitats occupied by each, as well as their changing relations over time. While two groups could use an area with equal effectiveness, a group with greater military strength could drive the other one to a different area and force it to adjust to a different set of resources. The merit of Barth's study lies in his careful blending of historical data with ecological concepts and cultural data. In a study among the Persian Basseri (1961), Barth provided an excellent analysis of the cyclical shifts between pastoralism and agriculture. Populations turn to farming on the basis of the success or failure of pastoralist activities, and there appears to be a new exodus from pastoralist societies in the direction of farming communities (see Lees and Bates 1977 for a contrasting view).

Edgerton (1965, 1971) made a key contribution to the study of pastoralist-farming adaptations as part of a large collaborative effort known as the Culture and Ecology of East Africa Project. Instead of traditional behavioral observation and ecological data collection, the study made heavy use of psychological testing and other projective techniques in combination with the collection of life histories and inter-viewing. This approach to cultural ecology is significant because in trying to under-stand the locus and mechanisms of adaptation, it focuses on adjustments by both individuals and the culturally defined group.[7]

Edgerton's research among four east African tribal groups (the Hehe, the Kamba, the Pokot, and the Sebei) searched for covariance in the attitudes of pastoralists and farmers who exploited highland and valley resources with different subsistence modes. He sought to explain "how and why farmers and pastoralists became differ-ent" (Edgerton 1971:294). He predicted that the attitudes, values, and personality characteristics of farmers and pastoralists would vary because of differences in their subsistence mode. However, he found that individual responses were more likely to express past environments than present ones—a finding he explained by suggesting that the environment exercises a causal influence on attitudes that operate over a period of years. Although an environment may change overnight, the attitudes de-veloped in response to it adjust more slowly. Edgerton concluded that a person's tribe or culture was dominant over his subsistence mode; persons of different subsis-tence modes (farmers and pastoralists) of one tribe were more alike than were per-sons of the same subsistence mode (farmers) from the four tribes. Nevertheless, he also found impressive differences between farmers and pastoralists—for example, open versus closed emotions, direct versus indirect action, social cohesion versus so-cial negativism. Edgerton believes these differences can be traced back to the envi-ronment.[8] Each milieu makes different demands on its inhabitants, who are thus subject to different constraints. In time, the individual adopts a set of attitudes and values appropriate to his environment, and even his personality type is affected. The conclusions of such studies suggest that culture is the result of situation-specific ad-justments, reflecting the interaction of people adapting to particular environmental circumstances, by particular technological means, at a given point in their history.

> Culture, as such, does not adapt. The process of adaption can only be studied through the close examination of individual action and specific items of behav-ior. . . . [T]he grand schemes of cultural evolution may be seen as an epiphenome-non to the process of ecological adaptation; similarly, I think it is reasonable to see ecological adaptation as a generalized statement of the process of individual adap-tive acts. (Goldschmidt in Edgerton 1971:303)

Modern Farmers

To date, cultural ecologists have concentrated on tribal and peasant groups. How-ever, more anthropologists are considering complex societies as a research focus. Bennett's pioneering studies in this area (1969, 1976) reflect his ability as a practi-tioner and his program for a policy-oriented cultural ecology.

Bennett attempts to show that controls over resources can be rational choices and are not necessarily culturally embedded patterns, contrary to studies of tribal societies

(Rappaport 1968; Nietschmann 1973). The Amish impose constraints on consumption and the use of modern machinery. These taboos are designed, according to Bennett, to shield the Amish from what they perceive to be corruption in the majority culture. A number of these restrictions prohibit the use of environmentally damaging techniques, including chemical fertilizers, powered implements, and pesticides. The Amish obtain substantially lower crop yields than their neighbors, but because of their simpler consumption standards and low-cost technology, they are able to live at a higher economic level than non-Amish neighbors who have comparably small tracts of land (Bennett 1976:277).

The communal Hutterites, farming the low-productivity northern plains of Canada, exercise similar controls over individual consumption but use a full range of sophisticated technological implements and support a larger number of people than the Amish could. Their communal lifestyle generates some of the benefits of economies of scale (which reduce the cost per unit of production as a result of large-scale operations) and more efficient use of farm equipment. Both the Hutterites and the Amish separate themselves from the outside culture, but they have different economic arrangements, social organization, and population density.

ECOLOGICAL ANTHROPOLOGY

Dissatisfaction with the research approach of cultural ecology led some scholars to search for new theories, new data-collecting techniques, and new analytical tools. The major influence on this new approach came from general (or biological) ecology. The ecosystem concept provided a conceptual framework more satisfactory to some scientists than the behavior–social structure equation stressed by Steward. Little and Morren succinctly expressed the strategy: "We are concerned with those cultural and biological responses, factors, processes and cycles that affect or are directly connected with the survival, reproduction, development, longevity or spatial positions of people. This set of questions rather than the traditional division of scientific labor defines the subject matter" (1976:5).

Roy Rappaport and Andrew Vayda gave the strongest impetus to an ecosystem approach in the field of anthropology. They preferred the term "ecological anthropology," reasoning that the emphasis on culture suggested by the term "cultural ecology" obscures the applicability of principles from biological ecology to the study of human adaptation (Vayda and Rappaport 1976:20–21). Given that humans are but one species in nature, subject to the same laws as other species, use of the principles, methods, and analytical tools of the ecological sciences would advance our understanding of our own species. Vayda and Rappaport believed that anthropologists should not hesitate to adopt biological units (such as population, community, and ecosystem) as units of study since this allows a more comprehensive approach to ecological studies. Even the topics of research can be couched in terms that make sense across both disciplines. Vayda and Rappaport point out that ecologists have shared various areas of interest with anthropology: ways of defining territorial rights, ways of establishing group identity, and mechanisms for establishing buffer zones. All these can be viewed ecologically as regulating behavior or serving a homeostatic function. A wealth of information is required to test ecological hypotheses, and no single researcher can expect to gather it all. Their fieldwork in Papua New Guinea as part of a large interdisciplinary team studying war in that region led Vayda and Rappaport to see the value of ecosystem as an integrator of work across ecology, geography, and anthropology (Vayda and Rappaport 1976:23).

Vayda's study relating warfare in New Guinea to population fluctuations, changes in man-to-resource ratios, and the competition of different highland clans for gardens and pigs is a notable example of the ecological approach (Vayda 1974, 1976). Rappaport, working in the same region, was more concerned with how ritual serves to regulate (1) the size of the pig herd, (2) the frequency of warfare, (3) the availability of horticultural land within reasonable walking distance of the village, (4) the length of the fallow cycle, and (5) the military strength and alliances of a tribe and the likelihood that it will hold on to its claimed territory.[9] Rappaport is not really concerned with the individual decisions of the Tsembaga Maring as they see their pig herd increase to the point that it becomes a threat to the human ecological system. Rather, he finds that the system "senses" the increased burden of having too many pigs. When a system threshold is reached, the elders call for a ritual pig slaughter. The ritual reduces the number of pigs and facilitates the creation of alliances between neighboring groups. Warfare follows, and it serves to distribute the population over the landscape and return the system to a state of equilibrium.

Bennett has criticized Rappaport's approach for its use of biological analogies, but concedes that Rappaport's study is important "as a concrete demonstration of the fact that the behavior of men toward each other, as well as toward Nature, is part of ecosystems" (1976:182). The major difference between Rappaport and Bennett lies in the former's emphasis on the fact that the systemic nature of the feedback loops can be found in culturally patterned behavior, such as the ritual-warfare complex. Bennett agrees that such patterned behavior may indeed be pervasive in technologically simple cultures. However, he argues that if this fact is always taken as a given, the role of individual decisionmaking can be overlooked. Such decisionmaking, he feels, plays a greater role in the technologically complex cultures of our day. Today human decisions about the use of the environment are predicated on institutional and technological considerations.

Bennett found the distinction between cultural ecology and the ecosystem approach artificial. The choice of one approach over the other depended for him on the size and complexity of the group under study. Among small tribes with primitive technologies, the ecosystem approach can be employed since the human-environment interactions in such tribes tend to be embedded in cultural traditions (Rappaport 1968). On the other hand, in larger, complex, and technologically advanced cultures, institutions and technology have created a distance between the population and its environment. Studies of modern societies must investigate these institutions and the processes of decisions that affect nature and humans. In these contexts, Bennett argues, the ecosystem approach does not work well because it cannot research the dynamic processes of institutions and the conscious processes of choice among alternatives due to the complexity of the systems. This was one of the leading reasons for the move away from an ecosystem approach in the 1980s, when actor-based approaches became dominant. However, the development in the late 1990s and early 2000s of agent-based modeling permits the analysis of complex systems and the behavior of individual agents in spatially explicit landscapes (Evans et al. 2001; Deadman et al. 2004; Parker et al. 2003, among others).

Rappaport's study (1968) raises questions about the utility of the homeostasis concept. As used by Rappaport, homeostatis is equivalent to equilibrium—a view shared by some biological ecologists and reminiscent of the Greco-Roman search for order in nature. Equilibrium models pay attention to how cultural practices help maintain human populations in a stable relationship with their environment. This view, the prototype of neofunctionalism, has drawbacks. It views the current state of the system as the norm and overemphasizes the functions of negative feedback to the neglect of the dynamics of change accelerated by positive feedback. In addition, it tends to preclude the possibility that behaviors might be maladaptive—as they surely are in certain situations (Alland 1975; Eder 1987).

Adaptation to environment is, however, not a simple matter of negative feedback. System correction through negative feedback operates most effectively at lower levels. Higher levels operate at a more general level where ambiguity and vagueness permit constant reinterpretation and restructuring of system properties as responses to perturbations. Homeostasis and **dynamic equilibrium** do not imply changelessness. On the contrary, they require constant adjustment of system parts and even some change in structure (in response to perturbations) (Rappaport 1977:169). In other words, while systems have lower-order mechanisms geared to maintain stability, they also have higher-level, less specialized responses that can reorder the system to ensure its survival.

There are problems in how the ecosystem concept was used: a tendency to reify the ecosystem and give it properties of a biological organism; an overemphasis on energetic flows and measurement of calories; a tendency for models to ignore time and structural change (and overemphasize homeostasis); a tendency to neglect the role of the individual; a lack of clear criteria for defining boundaries of systems; and level shifting between field study and analysis of data (see Moran 1990 for a review of these problems). Problems of reification have been addressed in recent years by an emphasis on how individuals modify the environment instead of simply adapting to a reified nature (Balée 1998; Crumley 1994; Boster 1983). Few scholars today would suggest that measuring energy flow ought to be a central concern of ecosystem studies. Concerns have shifted to nutrient cycling, decisionmaking, system complexity, and loss of biodiversity (Jordan 1987; NRC 1999a; National Science Board 1989; Levin 1998; Lansing 2003). Studies now focus on historical factors and even whole schools of thought in regard to historical ecology, environmental history, environmental geography, and other spin-offs. The role of individuals and households has also received attention (Lees and Bates 1990; Wilk 1990; Rindfuss et al. 2003; Chowdhury and Turner 2006). Researchers are challenged by how to determine boundaries for their research, but more sophisticated approaches have been proposed, such as historically variant graded boundaries (Ellen 1990; Allen 1988).

No one should expect the ecosystem perspective to resolve our questions about human adaptation. Biological and behavioral scientists will have to cooperate closely to generate an integrated study of people in ecosystems (cf. Moran and Ostrom 2005). Future studies are likely to be most fruitful when they integrate the general systems approach with the study of how actors develop their own individual strategies. There is no reason why both perspectives cannot be used, and researchers have already begun to balance concern for the individual with concern for the population. One way to overcome the tendency toward static equilibrium models would be to study how populations adapt to certain kinds of stress. By studying individuals' response to hazards, we can answer such questions as, Who responds? Does stress lead to changes in the structuring of the population? Are cultural patterns changed? How do people perceive the severity of the stress to which they are responding? How does the human population adjust to termination of the stress? These questions are more likely to be productive in outlining systemic interrelations in populations experiencing changing situations than in those with stable situations (cf. Lees and Bates 1990; Vayda 1983; for an analysis using a nonhomeostatic perspective, see McCabe 2004).

ETHNOECOLOGICAL AND COGNITIVE APPROACHES

A different approach to the study of human-environment relations grew out of developments in sociolinguistics. This general approach has been termed ethnoscience, and it studies cultural perceptions of the world and how people order those perceptions through language (see Sturtevant 1964). Ethnoscience has given rise to subfields dealing with specific cultural domains, such as ethnobotany, ethnozoology, and ethnoecology. Ethnoecological research aims for a better understanding of how people perceive their environment and how they organize these perceptions (Frake 1961, 1962). This approach assumes that "taxonomies of native terms either comprise in themselves standards of ethnoecology or provide the information necessary for inferring ethnoecology" (Vayda and Rappaport 1976:18). For two decades researchers emphasized the cognitive, rather than the behavioral, aspects of cultural study. By uncovering the organizing principles behind native **taxonomies** (the system of classification used by natives of a given society), ethnoecologists claimed that it was possible to overcome the tendency to impose an outsider's a priori structures on the data (Nazarea 1999; Boster 1984). In the 1990s the approach became more behavioral, while maintaining a strong link to the rise of cognitive sciences. There are now sophisticated studies showing how cognition affects our use of the environment (Kempton 1993; Kempton et al. 1995; Berlin 1992; Nazarea 1998; Behrens 1989; Boster 1984; Barrera-Bassols et al. 2006). These studies tend to rely on survey research methods, key informant field interviews, and examination of environmental variables such as varieties of crops and plants. A particularly exciting set of studies connects ethnoecology to the preservation of native knowledge in the face of global forces of cultural homogenization (Plotkin 1993; Posey and Balée 1989; Denevan and Padoch 1987; Redford and Padoch 1992; Balée 1994; Brondizio 2007).

Data collection in the ethnoecological tradition aims at eliciting native terms for plants, animals, insects, soil types, and so forth. An effort is made to deal exhaustively with the distinctive criteria that are used to make up the labels that go with things and to relate the terms within one domain to each other. This should lead to the development of taxonomies or a hierarchical arrangement of terms according to levels of generality. Items are assigned to the taxonomy on the basis of how their distinguishing features contrast with one another. From these contrasts, it is possible to arrive at which features are considered important and which are not (see Figure 2.2 for an example of a taxonomy derived in this manner).

The ethnoecological approach operationalizes the seemingly obvious fact that what people know about the environment and how they categorize that information will affect what they do to their environment. This approach helps identify variables that are amenable to empirical investigation—variables that must be identified early on by the fieldworker (Plotkin 1993; Posey and Balée 1989; Denevan and Padoch 1987; Redford and Padoch 1992; Balée 1994). However, knowledge is not synonymous with behavior, and even populations with millenarian experience in a habitat, such as the Tzetzal Maya of Chiapas, Mexico, use multiple criteria such as size of trees, humidity, soil characteristics, and species composition in making decisions on use of habitats—something that could be missed by researchers who pay overly zealous attention to how natives name features of their environment (Casagrande 2004). A couple of recent approaches promise to offer new insights emphasizing history and political economy.

HISTORICAL ECOLOGY

This approach, which bridges the social sciences and the humanities, offers valuable insights to scholars from all disciplines interested in global environmental change. History represents the recent record of evolution, except that the historical record, compared with the longer record of evolution, tends to be more detailed, more nuanced, and closer to contemporary conditions. It offers provocative insights into alternatives to our current environmental dilemma. Global models tend to be coarse in scale, lacking anything like an adequate representation of human variability and real biotic differences. One of the current and most exciting areas of research is the collaboration of paleoclimatologists, archeologists, and historians in reconstructing the record of the past 300 years, and eventually of the past 6,000 years (C. D. Johnson

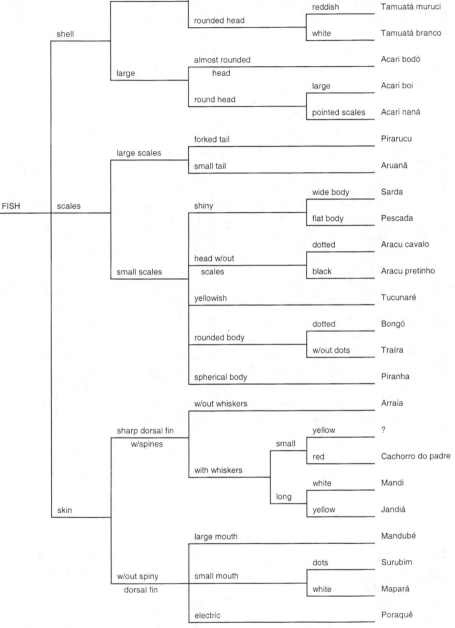

FIGURE 2.2 A Fish Taxonomy from the Amazon Estuary

Source: Emilio Moran and Fábio de Castro, field notes.

et al. 2005). See end of Chapter 1 for websites of PAGES, AIMES, and IHOPE, which address current research on long-term human-environment interactions.

Landscape history (Crumley 1994:6) refers to the study of changing landscapes over time and in space. Human beings adapt to (and bring about) modifications in ecosystems—and have done so for thousands, if not millions, of years. Historically informed environmental analysis is necessary to correct the misperception that past environments were pristine and that human impact on the earth is recent (Jacobsen and Firor 1992; Redman et al. 2004b; Redman 1999; Diamond 2005). Hardly any spot on earth is unaffected by human action. Humans have changed all landscapes, in positive and negative ways. This record of human environmental impact reflects the choices we have made, and their consequences, providing a view of alternatives much richer than a focus on the present would ever provide—choices to avoid and alternatives to be taken. Historical ecology brings together ethnography, archeology, history, and paleoscience to address environmental issues at regional and global scale (Crumley 1994). To date, the marriage of environmental history with historical ecology has not been consummated (Winterhalder 1994). The former, coming from the discipline of history, has a reluctance to theorize, while the latter sees itself as a research program that emphasizes agency and historical context. This problem could be resolved by greater interaction, given the desire of some environmental historians to ally themselves with ecological anthropological theory (Wooster 1984). Focusing together on a given historical problem or landscape is likely to be the way forward.

Balée and Erickson (2006) suggest that historical ecology is a new research program. This strategy is distinct from landscape ecology in focusing on how human beings bring about changes in landscapes. They take a very strong position that there are no pristine environments. As soon as humans enter an environment, it is made into a human landscape and modified by human actions for human objectives. They argue that human beings do not adapt to the physical conditions of the environment by adjusting their population size and settlement size to environmental conditions. Rather, they propose that humans transform those constraints into negligible analytical phenomena (Balée and Erickson 2006:4) through transformation of soils, drainage, cropping practices, and so on. Further, they dismiss cultural ecology, ecosystem ecology, adaptationist approaches, and systems ecology because they "ultimately deny human agency" in positively changing the environment over time (Balée and Erickson 2006:4). While there is value in emphasizing how local populations modify an environment to achieve their goals (Balée 1998), it is an overstatement to say that all adaptationist approaches deny human agency, as we have seen earlier in this chapter.

POLITICAL ECOLOGY

One current and popular theoretical approach used by environmentally oriented anthropologists and geographers is that of political ecology. A couple of years ago the section on cultural ecology of the Association of American Geographers, for example, was renamed the section on cultural and political ecology (cf. Jarosz 2004). Human ecologists have become increasingly aware that power relations affect human uses of the environment. As environmental movements exert pressure on political bodies, corporations, and institutions, there is a renewed awareness of the potential value of human ecology in influencing policy and understanding the future of how humans impact the environment (Brosius 1999; Greenberg and Park 1994).

Studies with a political ecological bent are reinterpreting our understanding of hunter-gatherers (Wilmsen 1989), pastoralists (McCay and Acheson 1987; Bromley 1992), agriculturalists (Sheridan 1988), and urban-industrial populations (Heynen et al. 2006a,b). We now recognize the long interaction of foragers with larger systems and their complex adaptation and accommodation to this unequal relationship. In some cases, foragers have chosen to artfully pose as primitives, while in others they have abandoned their mode of production in favor of agriculture. Some agricultural populations, facing potential enslavement by powerful neighbors, have deculturated into small bands of foragers that stay one step ahead of slavers (Balée 1994; Gomes 1988).

Few if any places in the world today are untouched by global forces such as climate change, capitalism, media, and the United Nations (Braudel 1973; Wolf 1982, 1999; Blaikie and Brookfield 1987; Rappaport 1993). Those who engage in environmental analysis cannot ignore the ways these relationships of local to global systems lead to particular outcomes (Moran 1982b). As Bates and Lees have put it:

> While historical change and external influence might once have been regarded as annoying distractions or distortions of indigenous systems, they are now the focus of attention. (1996:2)

Political ecology bears great affinity with political economy, as both explore the role of power relations in affecting human uses of the environment, particularly the impact of capitalism on developing societies (Brosius 1997, 1999; Gezon 1999; Kottak 1999; Harvey 1973). Unlike political economy (with its focus on class relations), political ecology is centered on how capitalism ravages the environment and human-habitat relations (Peet and Watts 1994; Rappaport 1993; Lansing 1991; Johnson 1995). Political ecology has a tendency to privilege the local scale as more desirable than other scales, often viewing larger scales as oppressing the local, and this "local trap" can lead to major analytical errors (Brown and Purcell 2005). As a relatively new approach, political ecology still lacks a robust theory or a settled paradigm (Biersack 1999). The above noted scale preference is just one of several philosophical and theoretical traps that remain to be solved. It could develop closer to the concerns of the environmental social sciences (Crumley 1994; Bates and Lees 1996) or to critical theory and cultural studies (Biersack 1999; Peet and Watts 1996).

At present, the bulk of political ecological analysis has stayed well within the concerns of the social sciences and distant from the physical and biological sciences in its data collection and methods of research. It has been more concerned with cultural and political critique, and rarely presents a substantive body of environmental data as part of the analysis of political ecology. In short, it has been stimulating on the political side but less substantive on the environmental side. Vayda and Walters (1999) take issue with the dominant role claimed for political and political-economic influences in advance of the research (Bryant and Bailey 1997) instead of empirically examining a broader set of factors in which the outcome of what is most important is not known in advance. Gezon (1997, 1999), among others espousing political ecology, focuses on examining how people engage politically in contesting access to resources, but only rarely presents environmental data on the contested resources. Vayda and Walters (1999:170) argue that ignoring the biological data can lead to unwarranted conclusions about the primacy of political influences. This may be a sign of political ecology's newness as a field and of scholars' felt need to address environmental concerns and other political causes. But if its results cannot be integrated with efforts at understanding human dimensions of global change, conservation biology, environmental NGOs, and other local and regional agencies engaged in environmental protection, it may be marginal to the policy world it wishes to influence. The best course for political ecologists is to join biophysical scientists in examining together the complex forces at play. As with any other complex adaptive system, human ecosystem outcomes are nonlinear, have emergent properties, and can be remarkably counterintuitive. Political ecology, as well as other ecologies used by environmental social scientists, need to seek new ways to integrate knowledge and advance understanding of the complexities inherent in ecological systems.

POLITICAL ECONOMY AND HUMAN ADAPTABILITY

From the 1950s to the 1970s human adaptability research was strongly influenced by social concerns of the time: the cold war, the rise of the new evolutionary synthesis, the beginning of environmental concern, and the study of cybernetics. The cold war provided ample funding for the International Biological Program and for Human Adaptability concerns (Huss-Ashmore and Thomas 1997:296–297) and funding gave priority to work performance and adaptability to climatic extremes. Many ecosystem studies were funded by the Atomic Energy Commission, including the response of various ecosystem to gamma radiation. The evolutionary synthesis started with assumptions about the genetic predispositions of populations and ended up emphasizing the plasticity of human populations. The early environmental movement led to the rise of ecosystem ecology, ecosystem design, and computer simulations of ecosystems. These earlier studies made important contributions and pointed to a host of new concerns: access to health and nutrition, cultural and social variables, and concern with the role of macropolitical forces on local populations' adaptability.

Consequently a new paradigm in biocultural anthropology has arisen that is informed by political economic concerns. Human adaptability is affected by poverty, access to land, access to health and nutritional resources, differing access to resources due to gender and age, and the relations of social sectors to dominant economic and political interests (Goodman and Leatherman 1998). Heat, cold, hypoxia, and disease are still important in human adaptability research, but access to cash plays no less important a role in bringing about or coping with environmental stressors. Study of environmental conditions needs to include features of the local and extralocal political economy in order to fully understand the life chances of human populations.

This new perspective on human adaptability research is concerned with local to global linkages; historical contingencies that can be deciphered from local, regional, and global histories; human populations as active agents in the construction of their environments, including forms of resistance, accommodation, adjustment, and transformation in the modes of production and reproduction; and ideology and knowledge as not only scientists but as the people that are the subject of study (Goodman and Leatherman 1998:20).

In the past, many anthropologists treated the environment as if it were cognitively neutral. This is patently not the case, given the human capacity to imbue the world with meaning and define what is stressful in their responses. These cultural meanings need to be integrated into future examinations of how people adapt through studies of mental mapping of environmental parameters (Huss-Ashmore and Thomas 1997:304). This is a rapidly developing process, given the speed of change experienced by contemporary populations. In this sense, spatially explicit histories provide a useful counterpoint to the tendency to see change as homogeneously spreading across societies, rather than having spatially specific ways of affecting human communities because of differences in power, ethnicity, and wealth.

SUGGESTED READINGS AND USEFUL WEBSITES

The History of Science Society (www.hssonline.org), including its publications *Isis* and *Osiris* (www.hssonline.org/society/isis/mf_isis.html), the American Society for Environmental History (www.aseh.net), including its journal *Environmental History* (www.aseh.net/publications/environmental-history), the European Society for Environmental History (http://eseh.org), the Forest History Society (www.foresthistory .org/index.html), including its journal, *Environmental History* (www.foresthistory .org/Publications/EH/index.html), and the Museum of the History of Science at the University of Oxford (UK) (www.mhs.ox.ac.uk) all provide discussions and resources concerning the history and development of science. Other journals and resources include *Environment and History* (www.erica.demon.co.uk/EH.html), the Environmental Studies Association of Canada (www.thegreenpages.ca/portal/esac), including its journal *Rhizome* (www.thegreenpages.ca/portal/esac/publications/index.html), the Association for the Study of Literature and Environment (www.asle.umn.edu), and the Environmental History Resources website (www.eh-resources.org). Additionally, W. Kovarik at Radford University provides an interactive timeline of the history of environmental research (www.runet.edu/~wkovarik/envhist).

Many books detail the history and development of ecology and environmentalism and provide interesting insights and summaries, including *Ecology in the Twentieth Century: A History* by Bramwell (1989); *A History of the Ecosystem Concept in Ecology: More Than the Sum of the Parts* by Golley (1993); *An Entangled Bank: The Origins of Ecosystems Ecology* by Hagen (1992); *The Background of Ecology: Concept and Theory* by McIntosh (1985); *The State of Nature: Ecology, Community, and American Social Thought, 1900–1950* by Mitman (1992); and *Nature's Economy: A History of Ecological Ideas* by Worster (1994). Additionally, the Ecology WWW page (www.people.fas.harvard.edu/~brach/Ecology-WWW.html) provides an exhaustive list of links to practically every aspect of ecological history and research.

There has been a revival of interest in Charles Darwin and Alfred Russell Wallace, who share the honor of discovering the concept of natural selection and its role in evolution. Readers will want to consult recent biographies of each man and his times, including numerous recent and new works that have been published on the life of Darwin and his theories (Browne 2007; Quammen 2007; Eldredge 2005; Herbert 2005; Wilson 2003, 2005; Mayr 1991) and on the life of Wallace (Shermer 2006; Slotten 2006; Berry 2002; Camerini 2001). The websites The Complete Works of Charles Darwin Online from the University of Cambridge (http://darwin-online .org.uk) and the Alfred Russell Wallace Page by C. H. Smith at Western Kentucky University (www.wku.edu/~smithch/index1.htm) provide detailed biographies, lists of publications, and accessible manuscripts. Several works by these authors, including Darwin's *The Origin of Species by Means of Natural Selection* and Bates's *The Naturalist on the River Amazon* are available for free download at Project Gutenberg (www.gutenberg.org). Stephen Jay Gould's volumes on natural history provide enjoyable reading on Darwinian theory and its complexities (for example, Gould 1977, 1980, 1981, 1983, 1995, 1998, 1999, 2000a,b, 2002a,b, 2003a,b).

Other key figures in biology and ecology include Linnaeus, who developed the taxonomic classification system that is universally used (see the Linnean Society of London web page: www.linnean.org); Alexander von Humboldt, who was one of the first researchers to consider relationships between organisms and their environments (Sachs 2006); Arthur Tansley, who coined the term "ecosystem" and founded the *Journal of Ecology* (Godwin 1957, 1958, 1977); Henry Chandler Cowles, who pioneered research on ecological succession at the Indiana dunes at the southern end of Lake Michigan (Cowles 1899); Frederick Clements, who explored the relationships between organisms in communities and the concept of ecological succession (Clements 1905, 1907, 1916, 1920, 1928); Raymond Lindeman, who developed the notion of trophic relationships between organisms in food webs (Lindeman 1942); G. Evelyn Hutchinson, who pioneered modern limnology (Hutchinson 1953, 1957, 1967, 1975, 1979, 1993); Eugene P. and Howard T. Odum, who played key roles in developing systems ecology and biogeochemistry (E. Odum 1971; H. Odum 1971; Odum and Odum 1976; Odum 1983; Odum 2004) and wrote popular textbooks on ecology—*Fundamentals of Ecology* (Odum and Barrett 2004); and Gene E. Likens and F. Herbert Bormann, who pioneered watershed studies at the Hubbard Brook Experimental Forest in New Hampshire (Likens et al. 1970; Likens and Bormann 1995). As ecology has grown in popularity, several figures in ecology and the environmental movement have moved into the public sphere, including Aldo Leopold (*A Sand County Almanac*, 1949), Paul Ehrlich (*The Population Bomb*, 1968), Rachel Carson (*Silent Spring*, 1962), and Edward O. Wilson (Wilson 1967, 1979, 1992, 2002, 2005).

Additional useful books include *Ecological-Evolutionary Theory: Principles and Applications* by Lenski (2005); *An Introduction to Cultural Ecology* by Sutton and Anderson (2004); *Human Adaptive Strategies: Ecology, Culture, and Politics* by Bates (2001); *People and Forests* edited by Gibson et al. (2000a); *Environmentalism and Cultural Theory: Exploring the Role of Anthropology in Environmental Discourse* by Milton (1996); *Redefining Nature: Ecology, Culture, and Domestication* edited by Ellen and Fukui (1996); and *Cultural Ecology* by Netting (1977).

The books *Political Ecology* edited by Zimmerer and Bassett (2003), *Critical Political Ecology: The Politics of Environmental Science* by Forsyth (2002), *Political Ecology: A Critical Introduction* by Robbins (2004), and *Political Ecology: Science, Myth, and Power* edited by Stott and Sullivan (2000) offer insights into political ecology research and theory. The peer-reviewed *Journal of Political Ecology* (http:// jpe.library.arizona.edu), supported by the Political Ecology Society (PESO) (http:// jpe.library.arizona.edu/eco-1.htm), includes many articles on the interaction of political economy and environment. The Cultural and Political Ecology Specialty Group (CAPE) of the Association of American Geographers also addresses cultural and political ecology issues (www.stetson.edu/artsci/cape), as does the Center for Political Ecology (CPE) (www.centerforpoliticalecology.org/index.html).

NOTES

1. Reviews of the determinist tradition in geography are found in Minshull (1970:100–118) and Sprout and Sprout (1965).

2. Readers will find stimulating discussions of evolutionary theory in Levins (1968), Bajema (1971), and Lewontin (1968). The journal *Evolution* is particularly recommended.

3. This section on cultural ecological applications owes a great deal to Netting (1974a and especially 1977). Readers seeking greater detail are urged to consult Netting's work and the articles in Bates and Lees (1996).

4. This brief discussion does not do justice to the large number of workers involved and the data they generated on this ancient subsistence mode. Readers are encouraged to consult the sources previously mentioned (R. B. Lee 1968, 1969; Lee and DeVore 1968, 1976; W. Suttles 1968), as well as the works of Woodburn among the Hadza (1968); Damas (1968) and Laughlin (1963) on Eskimos; Peterson (1975) and Yengoyan (1968, 1976) on Australian aborigines; Flannery (1968) on the prehistoric bands

of the Tehuacan valley; Bishop among the Ojibwa (1970) of Hudson Bay; and Yellen in the Kalahari (1977).

5. The British functionalists produced valuable studies during the 1930s and 1940s that included excellent descriptions of agricultural systems (see Richards 1939). However, their efforts to fit the data into equilibrium models limited the cultural ecological value of these studies. Equilibrium models are discussed in the next chapter.

6. Shifting agriculture is a dominant land preparation technique in 30 percent of the world's cultivable soils, especially those covered by tropical forests. It is also known as swidden, slash-and-burn, milpa, and citemene (Conklin 1963). Citemene is an adaptation to soil conditions, limited vegetation, and low labor areas of central Africa (Allan 1965). Citemene includes clearing an area larger than will be cultivated and piling the vegetation into a restricted area. When fallow periods are reduced, the amount of vegetation is inadequate for a good burn, and added areas must be cleared.

7. Statistically analyzed data from Edgerton's work is available in the 1971 volume.

8. This is somewhat surprising given the relatively scant attention paid by Edgerton (1971) to ecological data gathering and reporting. However, Porter (1965), as a geographer, may have provided such data for the project.

9. More details on the Tsembaga Maring studies by Rappaport can be found in Chapter 9 of this volume and in Rappaport's ethnographic accounts (1968, 1984).

Photo from ACT Photo Collection, Indiana University

3

FUNDAMENTAL CONCEPTS
AND METHODS

The methodology of human ecology is firmly rooted in the human and the natural sciences. Investigations must consider ecosystem interactions, human physiological responses to environmental stresses, and sociocultural adjustments. Chapter 1 presented a brief overview of the role of energy-matter-information flows between system components, or **state variables.** This chapter begins with a discussion of ecosystem relationships that examines population ecology, primary production, and the importance of soils in plant productivity. It continues with aspects of human biology, including physiological responses (thermoregulation, biological rhythms, and work capacity), growth and development, and nutrition and disease, including a discussion of gender differences. This chapter and the next focus on methodological approaches, including an integrated study of population, soils, human biology, and information theory, that are not part and parcel of the training received by environmental social scientists. A discussion of remote sensing (using digital satellite data) and geographic information systems (**GIS**) techniques applicable to contemporary human-environment studies is included in Chapter 4. These techniques are not yet common among ecologists or social scientists (except for geographers) but are growing in usefulness across the social and biological sciences.

ECOSYSTEM RELATIONSHIPS

Population and Environment

Ecosystems are heuristic units that help us carry out holistic (whole or integrative) ecological research on given problems. They do not represent a real physical unit, and they are sometimes too complex as units of analysis for individual research questions. Biological research commonly focuses on the organism, the population, or the community. Ecological research primarily studies populations. To understand the subject of human ecology, we need to familiarize ourselves with the measurement of population characteristics. Although not all the measures discussed in this section are used in this book, they will be introduced. Numerous comprehensive treatments of population ecology and demography are readily available, some of which are recommended at the end of the chapter.

A **population** is a group of individuals of the same species that occupy a given area and breed with each other. Populations are units through which energy flows, matter cycles, and information is transmitted. Since they are self-regulating, they help ecosystems adjust to environmental fluctuations. Maintaining flexibility is an important strategy of most living systems. Populations respond to changes in the environment by physiological and behavioral adjustments and, less often, by genetic adaptation. The strategy is to change only what is necessary to maintain flexibility for future environmental changes. Intrapopulation variability enhances this flexibility and stability. Through variability the population can maintain individuals with different genetic and behavioral capability whose resources may become crucial under conditions of environmental change.

It is important to understand the factors that impinge on population structure and process. Basically a population can increase, decrease, or remain stable. Birth and death are of primary importance in these processes. **Migration,** for most contemporary populations, is more important than fertility and mortality in population and environment studies (NRC 1999a). In some cases, the general figures on births and deaths may be broken down into age-specific rates (for example, the birth rate for fifteen- to nineteen-year-old women) or such rates may be related to socio-economic factors (for example, race- or education-specific birth rates). Breaking down the general figures on death, birth, and migration may reveal more information on the factors that determine a given growth pattern in the population under study. Table 3.1 lists important measures in the study of mortality and **fertility** and the formulas appropriate to estimating each rate.

Populations grow geometrically: their potential growth follows a typically exponential pattern. This ideal situation seldom occurs, and the balance between **birth** and **death rates** (the rate of natural increase) determines the actual growth of populations. If births equal deaths, there is no growth. When this situation occurs, the population is said to be stationary. If there is an excess of births over deaths, a situation of exponential growth exists (the population is said to be expanding at a compound interest rate). When the rate of natural increase is 1 percent, population will double in seventy years. At a 2 percent rate of natural increase population will double in thirty-five years, and a 3 percent rate will achieve it in only twenty-three years. A negative rate of natural increase means that the population is declining and traditionally has been taken as an indicator of maladaptation and potential extinction. In most contemporary societies this is patently not the case. On the contrary, the leading industrial societies have close to stationary or negative growth rates (for example, Japan, Germany, Italy, Spain, Sweden) as a result of dramatic decline in mortality, declining

TABLE 3.1 The Principal Measures of Mortality and Fertility

Measure	Formula [a]
1. Crude death rate (CDR)	$k\left(\dfrac{D}{P}\right)$
2. Age-specific death rate (ASDR)	$k\,\dfrac{Di}{Pi}$
3. Infant mortality rate (IMR)	$k\,\dfrac{Do}{B}$
4. Crude birth rate (CBR)	$k\,\dfrac{B}{P}$
5. Crude rate of natural increase	$k\,\dfrac{B-D}{P}$
6. General fertility rate (GFR)	$k\,\dfrac{B}{F15\text{--}44}$
7. Age-specific fertility rate (ASFR)	$k\,\dfrac{Bi}{Fi}$
8. Total fertility rate (TFR)	$5\,\Sigma\,ASFRi$
9. Gross reproduction rate (GRR)	$5\,\Sigma\,ASFR_{Fi}$
10. Net reproduction rate (NRR)	$\Sigma\,(ASFR_{Fi})\left(\dfrac{5Lx}{1_o}\right)$

[a] k equals 1,000
  D equals number of deaths
  P equals population at the midpoint in the year
  i equals the age-group interval
  o equals dead under the age of one year
  B equals number of live births
  F equals number of females
  Σ equals sum total
  $\dfrac{5Lx}{1_o}$ equals mortality rate for cohort

fertility, later marriage, and longer lifespans. Wealthy countries attract migrants, and they are renewed genetically and culturally by international flows of labor. Nevertheless, European societies remain concerned with their below-replacement levels of total fertility (Lutz et al. 2003).

Given the great potential for exponential growth of human populations, it is surprising how long their population remained low. Since a female can become pregnant roughly between the ages of fifteen and forty-five, it is theoretically possible for an individual female to produce forty offspring. In actuality, social and cultural practices drastically reduce that number. Many populations do not wean a child from the mother's breast for a period of up to five years. In some populations (with low caloric intakes) this might inhibit ovulation and reduce **fecundity** (the capacity to reproduce). During this period cultural practices also may restrict sexual intercourse. These two practices alone reduce the reproductive potential of females from over forty offspring to about nine. If life expectancy were less than forty-five years, the number of births would be further reduced. Infant mortality would reduce the number to a mere two or three per woman. Even if these mechanisms to reduce potential fertility were inoperative, cultural practices like infanticide, delayed marriage, and celibacy could also play a role in reducing population.

The exponential rates of growth in some populations appear to result primarily from a drastic reduction in morbidity and mortality, especially infant mortality. Reductions in adult mortality have increased life expectancy and the number of years women can participate in reproduction. Shortened periods of breast-feeding and elimination of postpartum taboos on sexual intercourse have further limited factors that in the past effectively reduced the rate of natural increase. Today this role is played primarily by contraceptive techniques. The use of reversible methods (such as the pill, the IUD, and hormonal implants) and irreversible methods (such as male and female sterilization) have permitted major declines in total female fertility (Siqueira et al. 2007).

Because death occurs only once, it is a useful measure of population that is readily available and accurate. Several measures of mortality are commonly used: the crude death rate (CDR), age-specific death rate (ASDR), standardized crude death rate (SCDR), and infant mortality rate (IMR). The crude death rate is the number of deaths per 1,000 people per year. It is calculated by taking the population at midyear (the number of people in January and December) and dividing by two in order to eliminate variations resulting from factors such as births, deaths, and migration. The range for the CDR varies between a low of about 5 per 1,000 to a high of about 30 per 1,000.

Age-specific death rates mirror a population more accurately because they can reflect population-specific differentials in age structure. For example, Taiwan's crude death rate is 5 per 1,000 while that of the United States is 9 per 1,000. Does this mean that Taiwan really has a lower death rate? Not exactly; the lower rate results from the fact that the population of Taiwan is very young, and young people have a generally low death rate after age one. In other words, older or stable populations tend to have a higher CDR than younger populations. To get a more accurate picture of the status of a population, it is useful to rely on age-specific death rates. ASDR is calculated by taking the number of deaths in each age-group and dividing by the population at midyear of each age-group (for example, in five-year intervals, from age zero to four, five to nine, and so forth). However, such data may be unavailable among some populations of interest to anthropologists and geographers, and in these cases the only approximation possible may be CDR.

Because the age structure of a population has a pronounced effect on the CDR, a technique of standardization has been devised. In standardization, two populations are compared by using one population's age structure as the standard or constant. Any book on demography will discuss the derivation of this adjusted death rate, which is too complex for inclusion in this brief discussion. (See suggestions for additional reading at the end of the chapter.)

Infant mortality is a useful demographic measure, in that children under one year are susceptible to environmental stresses and experience unusually high mortality. Sources of very early infant deaths (in the first month of life) tend to be congenital defects, birth injuries, prematurity, and other factors beyond the control of normal health practices. Subsequent infant deaths tend to result from infectious disease, malnutrition, and so on. Neonate deaths have some relation to the mother's condition during pregnancy and during the birth process. Subsequent deaths reflect the overall living conditions of the population. Infant mortality (IMR) is calculated by taking the number of deaths occurring among children under one year of age and dividing by the number of live births in the year per 1,000 persons. Rates vary anywhere from a low of about 2 or 3 (on the Isle of Man and in Jersey, UK, respectively) to a high of 144 per 1,000 (Afghanistan). Higher rates may be found among local populations, particularly those still undergoing epidemiological transition after contact with western diseases and those lacking in adequate medical care (for example, Amazonian native Americans; Coimbra 1988, 1989; Santos 1991). These measures (CDR, ASDR, SCDR, and IMR) can give useful information about mortality in the absence of unusual sources of fluctuations, such as epidemics, famine, and seasonal fluctuations. Disease epidemics can have a major local effect on a population's structure, as evidenced in the age structure long after the epidemics subside. The same is true of famine, whether it results from natural hazards or from political blockading of food movement across frontiers. Populations that depend on a single crop for their subsistence are sensitive to market fluctuations and crop blights (for example, the Irish potato famine). Chronic exposure to endemic diseases (for example, malaria) and chronic malnutrition are also reflected in the population structure, particularly in childhood.

Several sociological factors affect death rates: age, sex, marital status, social status, and occupation. Age is the most important factor coloring mortality. The human mortality curve is U-shaped. Rates are high in the first year of life, decline rapidly and remain low through middle age, and then rise rapidly with old age (the definition of which varies according to the life expectancy of a population). Nevertheless, the shape of the mortality curve is the same whether life expectancy is thirty-two or seventy-five years. Sex also accounts for differences in mortality. Males have higher age-specific death rates than females. Surprisingly, the gap between male and female rates actually increases with a rise in living standards and sedentarization. Married people appear to have lower mortality than single, widowed, or divorced people. Social status and occupation affect death rates as a result of differential work demands, nutritional level, settlement pattern density, and overall living standards (Moran 1995).

Fertility measures are also necessary in the study of population ecology. Fertility can occur many times and is heavily influenced by intermediate variables (intrinsic factors), such as age-specific participation in sexual unions, frequency of intercourse during unions, use of contraceptive techniques, and gestation variables (fetal mortality). Figure 3.1 summarizes these and other interactions relevant to the structure of populations.

Several measures of fertility are commonly used: the crude birth rate (CBR), general fertility rate (GFR), age-specific fertility rate (ASFR), and total fertility rate (TFR). The crude birth rate is estimated by taking the number of live births per year divided by the population at midyear per 1,000 people. The highest recorded CBR is 60 per 1,000 for a Hutterite population. The lowest CBR is that of Germany, the Czech Republic, and Italy with 9 per 1,000. However, CBR, like CDR, is significantly affected by the population's age structure. A young population will have a higher CBR than older or more stable populations, especially if the population has high numbers of persons in their late teens and early twenties.

The general fertility rate (GFR) is a more accurate measure than the CBR because it includes only women during childbearing years. It is measured by taking the number of live births in a year and dividing this figure by the number of women between the ages of fifteen and forty-four, per 1,000 people. Such a breakdown may not be available for some populations. Another measure that seeks to overcome the limitations of the CBR is the age-specific fertility rate. It is estimated by taking the number of live births per age-group divided by the number of women in that age-group per 1,000. As with death rates, the bith rates may be standardized for the purpose of interpopulation comparisons. The importance of age-specific rates is revealed by the fact that 50–60 percent of all births occur to women between the ages of twenty and twenty-nine. Differences exist between populations according to marriage patterns and age at the time of marriage.

The total fertility rate serves to estimate completed family size by giving the total number of children a woman would have in a lifetime if the age-specific rates were continued indefinitely through the reproductive years. However, this rate does not take into account the effect of infant or maternal mortality. A modified form of this measure is the gross reproductive rate (GRR), which refines TFR by including only

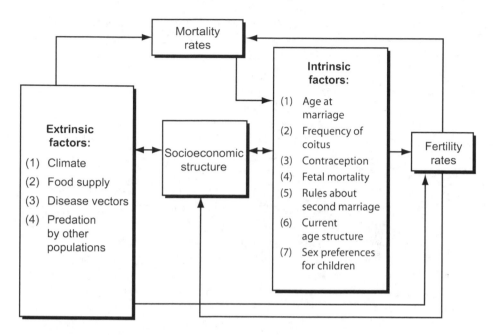

FIGURE 3.1 The Complex Interactions Between Extrinsic and Intrinsic Factors
These interactions result in given rates of mortality and fertility in human populations.

the number of female births; it gives the average number of daughters a cohort of 1,000 would bear if all these women survived through their reproductive years. But the GRR, like the TFR, does not control for mortality. Consequently another measure—the net reproductive rate (NRR)—is preferable. NRR is the number of daughters a cohort of new female babies would bear given the continuation of a fixed fertility schedule and a fixed mortality schedule. When mortality rates are low, NRR and GRR will be close; but when mortality rates are high, they will differ. The fertility curve by age has an inverted U-shape: low in the mid to late teens, highest for women in their twenties, then declining slowly until menopause. Social and cultural practices have a marked effect on fertility rates but not on this general pattern.

To sum up, then, population size and distribution are affected by intrinsic and extrinsic factors (see Figure 3.1). Extrinsic factors operate from outside the population and include climate, predation, and food supply. Intrinsic factors are internally generated—social class, occupation, age at marriage, contraceptive practices, sex preferences in children, and dietary allocation within households. Moreover, the well-being of a population is significantly affected by its relations with other populations. Interactions between populations can take a variety of forms: cooperation, mutualism, commensalism, amensalism, and a variety of competitive forms. In cooperation the two populations favor the well-being of each other but do not depend on each other for survival, as they do in mutualism. In commensalism one population remains relatively unaffected by its interaction with the other, while in amensalism one population actually inhibits the growth and survival of the other. In competition individuals or populations vie for resources.

Forms of intraspecific competition (for example, territoriality) are also significant in population size and distribution. Territorial size tends to vary with habitat. For example, where food or water is scarce, the size of the territory tends to be larger. Organisms also require a certain amount of personal space. Denied it, they experience stress and a set of bodily reactions, usually referred to as general adaptation syndrome. If the syndrome persists, it may result in declining reproductive capacity or death. Increased population density brings increased social density and frequent intrusions on personal space. Although social stress is not an important regulator of human population size, it does have numerous negative effects that involve physiological and behavioral consequences, which can, in turn, lead to individual and offspring marginality. In most stratified societies the lower classes have higher rates of infant and adult mortality, limited access to resources, and an inadequate food supply. These factors affect mortality, morbidity, and fertility rates.

No single factor can be said to predominate at all times and in all places in population regulation. Moreover, the human population seems to have lost any biological homeostatic mechanism for population regulation—if it ever had one. Factors such as drought, war, and disease may come into play at any time and form the subject for much human ecological research. The role played by social and cultural factors in the regulation of population requires further exploration. An emergent field of anthropological demography promises to fill this gap (Kertzer and Fricke 1997), but the number of people with this training remains small, as is also true of population geography. Most demographers are economists and sociologists, and they rarely consider the physical environment in their analyses (see NRC 2005a for a survey of recent research on population and environment by multidisciplinary teams of social scientists and natural scientists).

SOILS AND PLANT PRODUCTIVITY

The crucial biological organisms in nature are the green plants, which convert diffuse solar energy into concentrated energy in the form of plant biomass. Plant growth and production depend on a number of factors, including temperature, water availability, soil nutrients, and soil texture. Human utilization of plants depends on the plants producing a net yield. Because energy transfers are inherently inefficient, plants must absorb and convert far more energy than they can yield. A major portion of this energy goes into keeping the plant alive so that it can reproduce. These processes of energy transfer, usually called **respiration,** always involve a loss of energy or heat. This

TABLE 3.2 Net Primary Production and Plant Biomass of Major World Ecosystems

	Net Primary Productivity Unit Area in Dry g/m²/yr		Net Primary Production (10⁹ dry tons)	Biomass/Unit Area (dry kg/m²)		World Biomass (10⁹ dry tons)
	Range	*Mean*		*Range*	*Mean*	
Tropical rain forest	1,000–5,000	2000	40.0	6–80	45.0	900.00
Tropical savannas	200–2,000	700	10.5	0.2–15	4.0	60.0
Temperate grasslands	150–1,500	500	4.5	0.2–5	1.5	14.0
Tundra/Alpine	10–400	140	1.1	0.1–3	0.6	5.0
Semiarid	10–250	70	1.3	0.1–4	0.7	13.0
True desert	0–10	3	0.07	0–0.02	0.02	0.5

Source: Adapted with permission of Macmillan Publishing Co., Inc., from Robert H. Whittaker, *Communities and Ecosystems* (New York: Macmillan, 1970). Copyright © 1970 Robert H. Whittaker.

loss is significant because only the difference between the total energy assimilated by the plant (its **gross primary production)** and its respiration requirements becomes available to people. Human populations are particularly concerned with this balance, which is referred to as **net primary production.** The more complex the ecosystem is, the greater the portion of gross primary production or overall plant growth that will be invested in maintenance, and the smaller the proportion that will be available as net yield. Table 3.2 illustrates the range of variation in net primary production of the major ecosystems (discussed in Part 2 of this volume). The difference in production and productivity results from basic constraints present in each area—lack of water in deserts and extreme cold in tundras, for example. Soil characteristics also play a role in the productive potential of ecosystems. Soils represent the interphase between aboveground and belowground components of the biosphere (Wardle 2002), and soil conditions and processes mediate community structure and ecosystem functioning. Part of this dynamic is the feedback between plants and the soil medium operating through pathways involving soil physical properties, biogeochemical processes, and soil fauna (Ehrenfeld et al. 2005). Rising levels of carbon dioxide in the atmosphere influence carbon-nitrogen interactions. Reich and colleagues (2006) suggest that the response to elevated carbon dioxide may be smaller at low (relative to high) soil nitrogen levels, and elevated carbon dioxide may then influence soil nitrogen processes that regulate nitrogen availability to plants. These responses could constrain the capacity of terrestrial ecosystems to acquire and store carbon under rising carbon dioxide levels. The global soil carbon reservoir is very large, on the order of 1,500 Gt (gigatons) of carbon (1 Gt = 1012 kg of C), is dynamic on a decadal time scale, and is highly sensitive to both climate and human disturbance. At present, soil carbon is a source of atmospheric carbon dioxide in the tropics and a sink in northern latitudes, but global warming and melting permafrost in the tundra and arctic regions is expected to reverse this; the very large amount of carbon locked in permafrost may be released in the near future (Amundson 2001).

The study of how human populations use plants is intimately tied to the nature of the **soils** in which plants grow. Temperature, rainfall, and other climatic factors are just as important, and there is little humans can do to manage or control these forces of nature. On the other hand, soils can be and often are managed by human groups who have acquired sophisticated knowledge over time. Most populations (particularly farmers) possess ethnoecological expertise about soils (**ethnopedology**; compare WinklerPrins and Barrera-Bassols 2004; Barrera-Bassols et al. 2006) and their characteristics (Conklin 1957; Moran 1981; Moran et al. 2000; Behrens 1989; Lu et al. 2002).

Soil is a dynamic medium that is constantly forming and undergoing transformation. Soils are distinguishable from bedrock and unconsolidated debris by their relatively high content of organic matter, an abundance of roots and soil organisms, and the presence of clearly distinguishable layers, or **horizons** (Buckman and Brady 1969:34). Soils may vary within short distances owing to variations in surface, slope, weathering conditions, and the impact of plant activity. For example, soils originating from chemically basic **parent material** (bedrock) will have a pH close to neutral (7.0), while those originating from acid bedrock will tend to be acid. Soils on steep slopes will be shallower than those on gentler slopes if the steep slopes are not covered by vegetation capable of breaking the impact of water, wind, and light.

The field investigator with interests in agricultural activities or water control, for example, should note a soil's texture, structure, color, the depth of its humus layer, the vegetation that grows on it, and the horizons that it presents. For a description of a minimum data set on soils to collect for either agrarian studies or comparative research, see Nicholaides and Moran (1995). **Soil texture** refers to the arrangement of soil particles. **Soil structure** is influenced by soil texture and chemical status, the plant cover, the soil microorganisms present, soil management, and climatic conditions.

Soil color is an important indicator of various characteristics but is not a foolproof indicator of soil type. Red shale or sandstone may yield red-colored soil even though the oxidation of iron is not the major weathering process. Anyone interpreting the nature of the soil must use color in conjunction with broader knowledge of the weathering factors in a given climatic zone. In temperate regions dark-colored soils are high in organic matter. In the tropics, however, dark clays may be poor in organic matter. Bright red and yellow soils in the tropics may suggest high levels of iron oxides, but they also indicate good drainage and aeration—both important factors to consider in interpreting plant performance and in planning management approaches in an area. In poorly drained areas where oxygen is deficient, reduced iron yields bluish gray colors; good drainage leads to the oxidation of iron, which produces red colors.

Because chemical weathering, slope, and other influences vary at different depths, distinctive layers or horizons develop in most soils. These horizons, when taken as a group, form what is known as a **soil profile,** which expresses the types of processes experienced by the soil in the past and indicates the factors important to the use of that soil in the future. Profiles are two-dimensional slices through a soil. Soils, in general, have four major horizons: an organic or O horizon and three mineral horizons (A, B, and C).

Of all the horizons, the organic layer is the most critical for plant growth (see Figure 3.2). This layer usually contains a disproportionately large portion of the total humus in a soil. **Humus** is highly **colloidal,** a factor that promotes retention of water and nutrients and facilitates exchange of bases (Buckman and Brady 1969:144). Organic matter is also responsible for the loose, friable quality of productive soils. It is the source of phosphorus, sulfur, and nitrogen inputs. Organic matter increases the capacity of soils to hold water and provides most of the sustenance for soil microorganisms. The majority of domesticated plants rely primarily on this humic layer for nutrition (Buckman and Brady 1969:7). This is why most soil sampling for agricultural purposes takes place in the top few inches of soil (often called the plow layer). Soil organic matter can be managed, and populations practicing agriculture intensively have traditionally done so (Wolf and Snyder 2003; Netting 1993). They may move leaves from forest areas to fields, transfer muck from canals to intensively cultivated gardens, or manage mulch to increase organic matter in soils.

The mineral horizons of soil are characterized by lesser concentrations of organic matter and varied particulate structure. The A horizon is richer in organic matter than B or C. It is also characterized by the presence of granular, platy, or crumb structures. The B horizon is characterized by alluvial concentrations of silicates, clay, iron, and aluminum and by the development of blocky, prismatic, or columnar structures. The C horizon lies above the consolidated bedrock and has even larger particulate matter. It is the zone of transition between the B horizon and the bedrock proper.

Soil sampling may involve core sampling or profile sampling. In core (or surface) sampling, a soil sample is taken to a depth of between ten and twenty centimeters. Since this is the zone from which most domesticated plants obtain their nutrients, core sampling is the method commonly used to assess the soil nutrients available to

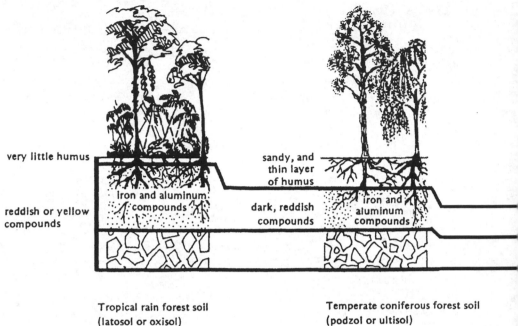

very little humus

reddish or yellow compounds

iron and aluminum compounds

sandy, and thin layer of humus

dark, reddish compounds

iron and aluminum compounds

Tropical rain forest soil
(latosol or oxisol)
wet, warm climate

Temperate coniferous forest soil
(podzol or ultisol)
wet, cool climate

plants. The sample is taken with the use of a core sampler. A single soil sample consists of fifteen to twenty cores collected randomly in an area. A zigzag pattern is usually followed. The cores that make up a single soil sample are deposited in a bag and thoroughly mixed before being sent for laboratory analysis. Each sample should be numbered and described in terms of where it was taken, what vegetation was in the area, what texture the soil had, what the color was (using available color charts such as Munsell color charts), and what the past use of the soil was (if known). Any other remarkable features (for example, drainage problems and slope) should also be noted.

Profile sampling involves using a soil auger to obtain one to three meters of soil to provide a fairly comprehensive cross-section of soil horizons applicable to the study of land use, such as tree farming or the cultivation of plants with deep taproots. This type of sampling aims to establish the various horizons and their characteristics. As the auger is turned, each layer is laid out on a sheet of plastic or other material in the order in which it was extracted. Each horizon is then described in terms of the same information that is noted in core sampling descriptions. Such descriptions help assess the alternatives open to cultivators.

FIGURE 3.2 Three Characteristic Soil Profiles

Note the differences in the depth of the organic horizon, coloration, and mineral content.

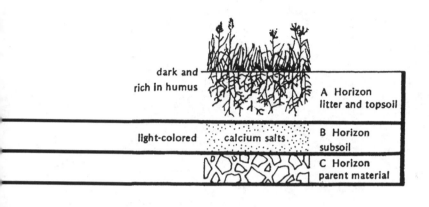

dark and rich in humus

A Horizon
litter and topsoil

light-colored — calcium salts

B Horizon
subsoil

C Horizon
parent material

Grassland soil
(chernozem or mollisol)
semi-dry climate

Knowledge of soil properties is useful when ecological investigation includes a focus on human management of land resources. A system of classification can help group soils that share natural properties. Native systems of classifying soils exist in many human groups. Over 4,000 years ago, the Chinese developed one that was based on color and structural characteristics (Steila 1976:64). The Hanunóo of the Philippines used vegetative cover criteria (Conklin 1957:39), while the Kekchi Maya of Guatemala used color, texture, drainage, and root content, as well as vegetational criteria (Carter 1969). The following chapters refer to a system of soil classification based on soil genesis and characteristics in the B horizon. Most folk classification systems, in contrast, are based on surface or plow layer characteristics and speak more directly to the current appropriateness of a soil to management practices. Agronomists' interest in soil classification differs from those who are interested in management. The latter, like folk taxonomists, are more interested in the A and O horizons than in B and C.

Each order of soils is characterized by diagnostic features (see Table 3.3). **Oxisols,** for example, are characterized by a clay or argillic horizon and by the presence of high proportions of iron and aluminum oxides, the latter having resulted from **leaching**

TABLE 3.3 Soil Orders According to the Comprehensive Classification

Order	Formative Syllable	Derivation	Meaning	Diagnostic Features	Older Equivalents
1. Entisol	ent	Coined syllable	Recent soil	Very weak or no profile development	Regosols, lithosols, alluvial, some low humic gley
2. Vertisol	ert	Latin: *verto*, turn	Inverted soil	Self-mulching; expanding lattice clays; subhumid to arid climates	Grumusol, regur, black cotton, tropical black clays, smonitza, some alluvial
3. Inceptisol	ept	Latin: *inceptum*, beginning	Inception, or young soil	Weak profile development but no strong illuvial horizon; cambic horizon present	Brown forest, subarctic brown forest, tundra, ando, and some lithosols, regosols, and humic gley
4. Aridisol	id	Latin: *aridus*, dry	Arid soil	Soils of arid regions; often have natric, calcic, gypsic, or salic horizons	Desert, red desert, sierozem, reddish brown, solonchak, some regosols, and lithosols
5. Mollisol	oll	Latin: *mollis*, soft	Soft soil	Thick, dark A_1 horizon; usually develops under grassy vegetation	Chernozem, brunizem (prairie), chestnut, reddish prairie, some humic gley, rendzinas, brown, reddish chestnut, and brown forest soils
6. Spodosol	od	Greek: *spodos*, wood ash	Ashy (podzol) soil	Illuvial horizon shows accumulation of iron and organic collodids; weak to strongly cemented pan	Podzols, brown podzolic, groundwater podzols

7. Alfisol	alf	Coined syllable	Pedalfer (alfe) soil	Argillic horizon of relatively high base saturation (>35%); usually under boreal or deciduous broadleaf forest	Noncalcic brown, gray-wooded; many planosols, some half-bog soils
8. Ultisol	ult	Latin: *ultimus*, last	Ultimate (of leaching)	Argillic horizon of low base saturation (<35%); plinthite often present; humid climate; usually forest or savanna vegetation	Red-yellow podzolic, reddish-brown lateritic, rubrozem, some gley and groundwater laterites
9. Oxisol	ox	French: *oxide*, oxide	Oxide soils	Argillic horizon very high in iron and aluminum oxides	Latosols and most groundwater laterites
10. Histosol	ist	Greek: *histos*, tissue	Tissue (organic) soils	Organic surface horizon (>30% organic matter) more than 6 inches thick	Bog and some half-bog soils

Source: After *Soil Classification: A Comprehensive System* (1960; Soil Conservation Service, 1964).

due to intense weathering of soil silica. Although oxisols present favorable structural conditions for plant growth, such soils are relatively acidic (low pH) and may contain aluminum levels that are toxic to some plants. Manioc, cowpeas, and other crops grow well in oxisols, while corn and beans grow poorly. **Alfisols,** on the other hand, are less acidic, richer in nutrients, and present more favorable conditions for agriculture. In order to choose crops that are appropriate to soil conditions, human populations must distinguish among soils and relate soils to crop management. This requires that they devise a system for categorizing soils.

The distribution of major soil orders affects what forms of agriculture are possible and what levels of productivity can be achieved. Since soils are the product of the weathering of rock materials, climatic conditions play a crucial role in the formation of soils and in their characteristics. Thus oxisols are dominant in wet, humid areas, **mollisols** are characteristic of temperate grasslands, and alfisols are common in boreal or deciduous forests.

Table 3.4 illustrates the worldwide distribution of soils. Although pockets of unexpected soil types may be found anywhere, the association of soil orders with ecosystem types is remarkable. Tundra regions are dominated by inceptisols, **deserts** by aridisols, temperate **grasslands** by mollisols, tropical **savannas** by ultisols, and **tropical rain forests** by oxisols. This close association suggests that the soil component needs to be considered in any study of human adaptability to ecosystems, if for no other reason than to understand ecosystem structure and plant productivity. Note, too, that the areal significance of soil types is highly variable (see Table 3.4). **Aridisol** soils, which present high salt levels and high concentrations of other minerals, are the most extensive. Some of these soils can become productive if water is provided in adequate and regular amounts. **Inceptisols** rank second in extent and are also problematic for farming uses. These are soils with rocky, gravelly horizons still in process of development. The third most abundant of the ten categories of soils includes fertile, easily workable soils. This suggests that farming populations must locate areas of land with the best possible soils. Then they need to ensure soil conservation to avoid degradation and loss of productivity (Sonneveld and Keyzer 2003; Ovuka 2000). Over a quarter of the world's agricultural land has been damaged—an area corresponding to one-tenth of the earth's surface (Liniger and Schwilch 2002). Mountainous regions are particularly vulnerable to degradation. Location of productive land requires knowledge of soil characteristics and their effective management. Knowledge of soils, plant productivity, and population ecology would not be helpful in the study of human adaptation unless they were integrated into larger schemes. Increasingly, agroecological (Clements and Shrestha 2004) and other approaches that take into account biological interactions in the soil need to be used to maintain soil productivity under the growing pressure to produce food for billions of people (Shiyomi and Koizumi 2001; Gliessman 2001; Giampietro 2004; Cardon and Gage 2006). There is a clear need to move away from current technologies based on fossil fuels and agrochemicals, in

TABLE 3.4 Areal Significance of Soil Orders

	% of Total World Soils[a]	*Rank (according to total area)*
Entisols	12.5	4
Vertisols	2.1	9
Inceptisols	15.8	2
Aridisols	19.2	1
Mollisols	9.0	6
Spodosols	5.4	8
Alfisols	14.7	3
Ultisols	8.5	7
Oxisols	9.2	5
Histosols	0.8	10

[a]An additional 2.8 percent of the total includes ice fields and unclassified lands.

Source: Donald Steila. © 1976 *The Geography of Soils*. Englewood Cliffs, NJ: Prentice-Hall.

favor of a system in which complex biotic interactions is the key technology (Shiyomi and Koizumi 2001). The management of nitrogen fertilizers is receiving growing attention while we wait for more biological approaches to food production (Mosier et al. 2004).

PHYSIOLOGICAL RESPONSES

The human body responds rapidly to external changes in the environment, particularly shifts in temperature and light (response to a decrease in energy will be discussed later in a section on growth and development). We often measure these physiological responses to assess whether adaptation or acclimatization has occurred.

Human Thermoregulation

An important aspect of human adaptability is our self-regulating temperature control. The average body temperature of a human falls between 36.5 and 37.5°C. Prolonged periods when body temperature goes as low as 24°C or as high as 45°C can be fatal. The body maintains heat balance through two chief avenues of heat exchange: heat production as a by-product of metabolic processes and heat loss to the environment. Heat may be gained or lost through conduction, convection, or radiation. A fourth avenue for heat loss is evaporation. Conduction refers to the flow of heat from one object to another by direct contact—as between two bodies in contact with each other. Convection refers to the exchange of heat between a gas or liquid and an object—as between a person and the ambient air. Radiation is the transfer of heat from one object to a cooler one—as in a hand touching snow or ice. Evaporation is the loss of heat by vaporization of sweat from the skin surface or of moisture from the respiratory passages.

Understanding the human thermoregulatory system requires understanding how heat is produced. The minimum level of metabolic activity of the body during complete rest and after fasting twelve hours is known as the **basal metabolic rate** (BMR). Resting metabolic rate (RMR), which is taken after four hours at rest, runs a little higher than BMR but is often used interchangeably. An average value for young adult males is about forty kcals of heat per square meter of body surface per hour.[1] Heat also may be produced by the dynamic action of food, especially protein; by increased muscle tone and shivering; and by chemical **thermogenesis.** Shivering can increase heat production two to three times above BMR, and strenuous exercise about five times. Heat loss by convection, conduction, radiation, and evaporation depends on (1) the transfer of heat from the core or interior of the body to the surface; (2) the body composition, especially fatty deposits; and (3) the proportion of surface area to weight of the body. Considerable differences can exist between individual thermal responses to environment (Zhang et al. 2001; Van Marken Lichtenbelt et al. 2004; Havenith 2001), mediated by height, weight, subcutaneous fat, clothing, level of activity, and insulation.

The circulatory system is the chief source of heat within the body. Blood flowing through deep body organs picks up heat and can channel it either to the core or to the surface. This is accomplished chiefly by **vasoconstriction** and **dilation** of vessels (arteriovenous capillaries) at the surface, which can change the rate of blood flow to the surface by as much as 30 percent. Direct heat conduction also occurs but is slower. When the body is exposed to cold, the **body core** shrinks and the **shell** (limbs, skin, fat, and other peripheral structures) expands as peripheral blood vessels constrict. Heat is passed on largely by conduction. The opposite occurs during exposure to heat. In adaptation to cold, two mechanisms are particularly relevant to heat transfer: countercurrent heat exchange and cold-induced vasodilation. In countercurrent heat exchange, heat is conserved by the precooling of blood flowing to the periphery, while heat is added to blood flowing to the interior of the body. This exchange is supplemented by cold-induced vasodilation (or peripheral blood flow), which is a protective cyclic response. It refers to the spontaneous rewarming of fingers and toes during cold exposure as specialized vessels dilate. It provides protection to vulnerable parts of the body, like the fingers.

During the course of normal human growth, a number of morphological and physiological changes (particularly changes in height, weight, and surface area) take place that influence temperature regulation. The infant is poorly protected against cold stress because of a low BMR, inadequate subcutaneous fat deposition, poorly developed muscular tissue, small size, and high rate of heat loss. Consequently infants are protected by nonshivering thermogenesis. This form of heat production is related to the presence of **brown adipose tissue,** which is found not only in infants up to one year but also in cold-acclimatized adults. Infants are able to elevate their metabolism by 170 percent over BMR. Cold temperatures also affect infant growth. In experiments, children raised at temperatures two degrees Celsius cooler and fed the same diet as a control group experienced smaller weight gains. This reflects a diversion of calories from storage or growth to heat production aimed at maintaining temperature at normal levels. Clothing plays a very important role in thermal responses of the human body, particularly in mediating environmental transitions between hot and cold via moisture absorption capacity and evaporation (Li and Yi 2005; Ghaddar et al. 2003). The thermal environment offered by a building can also play a key role. Inside a crowded building with no air-conditioning and limited circulation of heat and moisture, considerable heat stress can occur in the human body (Kang et al. 2001). Designing buildings to handle crowded human conditions that maximize air circulation can result in reduced thermal stress for occupants (Li and Yi 2005; Ghaddar et al. 2003).

Circadian Rhythms

The casual observer, without devices to measure the timing characteristics of behavior, is unlikely to identify biological rhythms, yet they are pervasive in nature. All levels of biological integration—from ecosystem to population to individuals, organs, and cells—show rhythms with diverse frequencies (Pati 2004). Gross features of a daily cycle, however, can be noted. Daily rhythm, or **circadian rhythm,** indicates that the period during which these features appear is approximately, though not exactly, twenty-four hours in length. Circadian rhythms have been identified in single-cell animals such as amoebas and paramecia and are universal to living things (Chapple 1970:24; Takahashi et al. 2001). With the aid of measuring devices, the activity rhythm of living organisms (the occurrence of physical activity, its onset, duration, and cutoff) is directly observable, as are the major physiological and biochemical functions of the body. A chemical thermometer reveals the circadian path of body temperature—higher at midday, lower in the morning and at nighttime. Blood sugar, liver glycogen, white corpuscle counts, adrenal activity, RNA and DNA synthesis, cell division, and drug-specific sensitivities also have been shown to follow circadian rhythms. Considerable progress has been made in understanding the molecular foundations of circadian rhythms (Sehgal 2004). How this timing apparatus is adjusted to coordinate human physiology and the changing environment has received growing attention. Cellular metabolic states appear to link physiologic perception of environment to the circadian oscillatory apparatus (Rutter et al. 2002; compare Refinetti 2006). The field of chronobiology has attracted scholarly interest across levels of biological organization (Pati 2004). A newborn lacks a fully developed nervous system and so cannot fully manifest circadian periodicities. Not until the sixth week of life do differences between day and night begin to appear in the infant's rhythm, and the typical pattern seen in the adult does not develop until one year. Similar rhythmical change is manifested in body temperature rhythm.

Given the universality and constant properties of circadian rhythms, it seems reasonable to assume that the total amount of activity and inactivity is constant for the individual animal. Duration of activity and duration of inactivity are under the control of remarkably accurate biological clocks. When an animal is barred from its required activity, compensatory increases in activity need to be taken to restore the balance between activity and inactivity. Biological clocks help synchronize the organism to the changing properties of the environment (Chapple 1970:26; Rutter et al. 2002).

Experiments that expose animals to continuous dark or light have shown that circadian rhythms are innate and repetitive. In other words, the rhythm is endogenous. The organism anticipates each stage of adaptation, reacting in advance in terms of its own internal organization. It is always prepared, allowing it to survive. Given the existence of these various rhythms, there must be ways of setting each clock to the external environment.

Three synchronizers have been identified in connection with biological clocks: light, temperature, and social interaction. Light is the primary clock setter and affects all species. It is the only synchronizer that is well understood. The pineal body, a small, somewhat conical body situated behind the third ventricle of the brain, translates light energy into a fundamental secretion, melanin, which acts directly on the hypothalamus (the autonomic correcting center) to maintain body rhythm. Temperature is important for clock setting in some species, but in most species circadian rhythms are temperature-compensated: significant alterations in rhythms occur only when the limits of thermoequilibrium have been breached. Interaction rhythms of animals are presumed to be part of the clock setting; animals adjust their periodicities in response to other animals with which they interact.

Just as light, temperature, and social interaction can set a biological clock, they also can desynchronize it. When circadian rhythms are desynchronized, the individual can suffer serious damage. Radical disorganization of endocrine activity can lead to rapid growth of tumors, greater susceptibility to disease, and even death. In studies conducted in the arctic, light emerged as the most significant factor in the biological clock of arctic Indians. In winter, the Indians followed regular routines; in summer, irregular ones. Excretion of potassium and other nutrients was out of phase in winter (there were dramatic changes in the excretion of these nutrients), even though interactional patterns were normal (Chapple 1970:28). Above the Arctic Circle, daylight changes dramatically with the seasons. In late June the sun never sets but moves 360 degrees around the horizon. In late December the sun never comes above the horizon. Under these conditions light does not act as a synchronizer of human physiology. Clearly documented studies suggest that vitamin D autosynthesis declines in winter, resulting in lowered intestinal capacity to absorb calcium, thus rendering the Eskimo, or Inuit, hypocalcemic for part of the year (see Chapter 5 for more details on Inuit physiology).

Work Capacity

Human survival often depends on the ability of individuals to perform muscular work under given environmental conditions. The human species possesses a flexible system that is capable of both continuous hard work and sudden bursts of intense activity. The work capacity of individuals is usually assessed by measuring the ability to transfer oxygen from lungs to muscle and to utilize oxygen. This measurement is called the maximum aerobic capacity, or VO_2 max. Among all populations measured, there is a dramatic decline in VO_2 max with age, possibly the result of decreased activity levels. There is also a progressive decline in protein metabolism of 3.5 percent per decade (Short et al. 2004). With progressively intensified muscular effort, VO_2 max can be increased up to 20 percent. This effect takes place irrespective of age with regard to muscle protein synthesis, and can reverse the effects of aging (Short et al. 2004). Subsistence-oriented populations have a higher VO_2 max than urban populations due to greater physical exertion. Low aerobic capacity is strongly associated with cardiovascular and metabolic disease, a result of the sedentary lifestyles common among contemporary urban populations (Wisloff et al. 2005). Both genetic and nongenetic factors are involved in determining the range of **work (aerobic) capacity** (Chapple 1970:455–456). (Studies of twins show that genetic factors help to account for over 80 percent of the variance in VO_2 max.)

When it is not feasible to carry out field measurements, energy expenditure can be estimated through time and motion studies that use a stopwatch and a tally counter. This technique records activities and types of body movement over time. Someone who is measuring planting behavior records how many times per minute the body bends over, what sort of hand motion the planting requires, rest periods, and the weight, age, and sex of the workers. These data are then used to estimate energy expenditure by consulting calorimetric studies of the various types of motions recorded per unit of time (Edholm 1967). New techniques in physiological assessment of human fitness have been developed, such as near-infrared spectrophotometry, blood lactate, and respiratory and heart rate markers (Maud and Foster 2006). Kinesiology and sports physiology have advanced the field of human physiological measurement, including field measurement.

Work and Diet

Human physiological functioning requires calories provided on a regular basis to make up for the calories spent on body maintenance, physical activity, growth, and reproduction. The cost of body maintenance is usually measured by taking the basal metabolic rate of the individual at rest (RMR). The procurement of food and other activities add to this cost, in accordance with the exertion involved. While the energy requirements of the body vary according to activity, and to a lesser extent according to body size and climate, ecosystems vary in their ability to produce energy per unit of labor invested in obtaining that energy. A useful (though crude) index for measuring the relative efficiency of a foraging strategy is to take the number of person-days of work and divide it by the number of person-days of consumption. Among the !Kung San (see Chapter 7), the efficiency rate is about 25 percent, while among New Guinea horticulturalists it is 10 percent (Harrison et al. 1977:402).

Among the many activities of the human population, probably none influences the structure and function of social groupings more than the procurement of food. Human populations have long exhibited an intimate knowledge of their habitat—what is edible and what is not, what is available in drought and what emerges from the ground with the first rains. In the previous chapter we noted that this knowledge has been of interest to ethnoecologists. For some populations, eating insects makes all the difference in a diet that otherwise would be marked by fat and protein deficiencies. Kalahari desert and Amazon tribal peoples alike consume insects, as do Australian aborigines and some populations of western Africa. This practice was likely widespread in the past. If toxic plants have properties that make them desirable and a process can be found to detoxify them, these plants may become key staples. The best-known illustration of this is the domestication of manioc *(Manihot esculenta)*. Through soaking and heating, the toxic cyanogenetic acid is destroyed, and the **carbohydrate-rich** flour of manioc can then be safely consumed. Remarkable yields, in excess of ten tons per hectare, have been noted (Moran 1973, 1976; Dufour 1990).

Preparation, storage, and consumption of food reveal remarkable practices that enhance the nutritional value of the food. Many fermented foods have high vitamin B and mineral value and expand the range of available nutrients. Soaking and boiling maize in alkali (lime, lye, wood ash) water enhances its food value by increasing the availability of niacin and protein in the content of the manufactured tortilla. However, not all food practices are adaptive. Food taboos in many cases appear to deprive segments of the population of foods that they particularly need. In parts of Brazil in decades past, children with gastroenteritis were not given liquids for fear of causing further diarrhea, which only exacerbated dehydration. Bottle-feeding infants has led to a decline in breast-feeding in areas where access to protein-rich bottle formulas is not easy and where water quality may exacerbate gastrointestinal distress in infants (Dettwyler 1994). This has resulted in caloric and protein deficiency and high infant mortality rates.

Until relatively recent times, most populations experienced periods of food scarcity. When able to supply themselves with enough calories, hunter-gatherers seem to have achieved an adequate balance in diet. The uncertainty of the hunt was balanced by the more secure harvesting of seeds, roots, and other plant materials when available. The cultivator has a more secure food supply, but it is seasonally variable and may be inadequate for heavy farm work. Harrison and colleagues (1977:416) noted dramatic weight loss during periods of heavy work and low caloric intake. Farming populations sometimes have an inadequate supply of high-quality protein and fat. Mixed agropastoral economies and those that combine marine/riverine resources with horticulture represent responses to the problem of securing a balanced diet of protein, fat, and carbohydrates.

Human populations have great metabolic flexibility. Comparing the average dietary intake of Britons, Bikuyn, Eskimos, and Bulador Islanders exposes correlations between the food supplying the bulk of the calories and the health status of the group. The proportion of fats and carbohydrates ingested varies significantly among populations. However, all ingest a minimum of protein, fat, and carbohydrates—except the Eskimos, who lacked access to carbohydrates until recent years. Protein, carbohydrates, and fats have important metabolic functions. The **amino acids** that form part of the ingested protein are necessary for tissue repair and growth, as well as for the synthesis of special proteins. Fat provides insulation and caloric storage. Carbohydrates are the main substance in body energy balance. Both protein and fat can be broken down into energy-producing carbohydrates. High carbohydrate intake can make up for deficiencies in fat intake up to a point. Foods supplying animal protein tend to have higher biological value because they have a more complete set of essential amino acids than do vegetable proteins. Most populations satisfy amino acid requirements by a combined diet of animal and vegetable proteins (Harrison et al. 1977:404). Modern populations living in cities have more access to food but differ in their ability to purchase it, and food habits can result in serious metabolic and disease disorders (Temple and Wilson 2006).

SOCIOCULTURAL REGULATORY ADJUSTMENTS

Cultural adjustments include a broad repertoire of knowledge about nature, including knowledge of house construction, clothing styles, subsistence technology, and ritual. Social adjustments mainly include forms of social and economic organization. In conjunction, these adjustments provide flexible yet infinitely variable adjustments to changes in the habitat and changes in relations with other human groups.

Cultural adjustments to climatic conditions occur mainly through knowledge about housing, clothing, and technology that enhances individual cooling or heating. House form, which is constrained but not determined by available materials, represents a compromise between behavioral, religious, and other values of the environment. The Eskimo winter dwelling is a good illustration of the role of climate in house form. A deep entrance pit and a long tunnel permit the gradual heating of cold air that enters the home. The dome design enhances surface area exposed to sun and reduces the drag resistance to wind. Bodily heat and oil lamps serve to maintain a cozy temperature inside the dwelling, and overheating is prevented by manual central air vents.

Housing in dry, hot regions presents a different sort of problem. The goal here is to reduce human heat production and heat gains resulting from radiation and convection. Thick-walled construction is used among sedentary peoples to slow down heat buildup. This type of construction also provides a warm dwelling when temperatures drop in the evening. Nomadic populations depend on ventilation to reduce heat gains. In hot areas, cooking occurs outside the dwelling to reduce heat gains, while in cold areas it occurs inside. Clothing follows much the same pattern as housing.

Religion and cosmology can affect the form, layout, and location of houses. The height of a house, the size of the rooms, and the meaning of house parts may be related to elaborate cosmological interpretations. The special underground houses for menstruating women among the Nez Perce Indians make no sense apart from their religious and therefore social significance.

The settlement patterns of the human population reflect adjustments to both the distribution of resources and associated social and cultural factors. Marriage patterns influence the residential pattern, and available materials and climatic factors influence the type of house form and the proximity between dwellings. In desert areas semisubterranean or highly overlapping houses (for example, pueblos in the southwestern United States) cut down on the surface area exposed to the hot sun and reduce interior heating. In most cases, patterns of residence and marriage are likely to be supportive of this pattern of house construction, rather than contradictory. The predominant subsistence strategy is significantly related to the pattern of settlement: nomadic populations build makeshift structures or carry their housing on their animals, while agricultural peoples are more sedentary.

One topic that has long interested anthropologists is the organization of social groups into units of production. Each type of social organization represents a strategy for subsistence. Flexible forms of social organization have been noted among hunter-gatherers in the arctic, in the Great Basin of North America, and in the Kalahari Desert of Africa. Units tend to be based on **bilateral** affiliation—they trace their descent through males and females—and are of variable composition seasonally. Various **quasi-kin** mechanisms are used to enlarge the cooperative group that individuals have access to. This is accomplished by reciprocal visiting, patterned resource sharing, intermarriage, and patterned trade between groups with differential access to resources. Resource sharing is enhanced by patterns of generalized reciprocity. The hunter-gatherer strategy depends on maintaining the primary productivity of the group's territory. Work effort and population are kept low when the group is optimally adjusted to the resources. Since there is no hierarchical allocation of prestige, effort is not spent on overproduction for the purpose of redistribution and prestige seeking. On the contrary, gift giving is frequent and accumulation is eschewed. The hunter-gatherer strategy would not remain viable without controls over population size and mechanisms that lead to **group fissioning** when densities reach a threshold level.

When small local groups are linked together by ties of marriage, blood, and shared territory, a tribal form of **social organization** results. Tribes are not significantly different from the more atomized bands just described, except that they represent an adjustment to the presence of aliens. This unity, which is elicited by an outside force, may lead to the formation of more complex forms of organization, or ranked societies. Such societies represent a significant departure from the egalitarian hunter-gatherer structure and of some horticultural societies. Prestige is differentially shared in ranked societies, as is access to resources. The chief is far above his fellows and has the power, usually enforced by the military elite under him, to enforce payment of tribute, allocate privilege, and organize systems of redistribution. The chief's position of prestige and power is assured by generous redistribution among the population at large of goods taken from them.

Forms of redistribution are tied to other aspects of a society. Among some populations, conspicuous display of wealth may be a way of redistributing wealth and food, as well as a means of improving social status. Among New Guinea populations, for example, yam feasts function to redistribute production, elevate status, and gain allies for warfare and raiding. The warfare complex is crucial to the maintenance of appropriate man-to-land ratios and to the stability of the system. Particularly in areas subject to natural hazards, such as forest fires, flood, or drought, these forms of redistribution enhance survival by rewarding industrious individuals who produce surpluses. When disaster strikes, such surpluses may be sufficient to prevent famine among the population. Populations practicing redistribution have been more successful in the long run than those lacking it.

The emergence of markets, or "negative reciprocity," as a context for the redistribution of goods marked a significant change in social organization. Individuals could climb the social hierarchy by manipulating the flow of goods into the market, by creating artificial pricing, and by creating demand for unnecessary products. Although these activities are not necessarily associated with markets, there is little doubt that the ideal model of supply-and-demand market pricing is but a neat heuristic device for studying economics. It bears little resemblance to real situations, except as an approximation.

Health and Gender

A topic of growing interest in the study of human adaptability addresses gender differences in access to resources and in female and child mortality. In some societies an excess of female and child mortality has been tied to social, economic, and cultural determinants (S. Li et al. 2004). In China, this has been connected to discrimination against female children and a preference for sons, exacerbated by government-guided family planning regulations. In other countries, the problem may be a lack of adequate medical attention during childbirth (Maimbolwa et al. 2003), or a gap between traditional birth attendants and the women served (Rööst et al. 2004). In rural Guatemala, women follow moralistic and fatalistic views in handling obstetric complications and experience maltreatment and discrimination at the hospital (Rööst et al. 2004). Complications of pregnancy and childbirth are the leading cause of death among women of reproductive age in developing countries (Tinker 2000). Malnutrition contributes to this situation, based on a gap in food intake and labor expenditures, and cultural expectations of allocating the best food to males (Tinker 2000). Scholars have noted, for example, the thinness of young women relative to young men in rural Maharashtra, India. Villagers identified four responsible factors: expectation of early marriage and early isolation from their families and villages resulted in young women not eating adequately; marriage increased the workload of young women as they were assigned the heaviest household chores as well as farm work; young women had no financial autonomy or freedom of movement and were denied access to supplementary food available to young men; and young women felt responsible for their household's health and success. This led to further anxiety and loss of appetite and health (Chorghade et al. 2006).

On the other hand, there is ample evidence for higher rates of suicide and premature death due to coronary heart disease, violence, accidents, and drug and alcohol abuse among males (Moller-Leimkuhler 2003). These vulnerabilities are rising, particularly among younger men. Traditional views of masculinity seem to be associated with this higher male vulnerability promoting maladaptive coping strategies— emotional inexpressiveness, reluctance to seek help, and search for solutions in drugs and alcohol. Growing risk proneness seems to exist where males perceive a reduction in social role opportunities and social exclusion due to transformations in the economy in areas such as Eastern Europe and Russia in the aftermath of the dissolution of the Soviet Union (Moller-Leimkuhler 2003). Economic and social inequality affect both genders and leads to worsening health, including the commodification of the body, and to markets for organs and body parts as individuals trade their long-term health for short-term benefit (Nguyen and Peschard 2003; Rhoades 2000).

INFORMATION AND DECISIONS: TOWARD ACTOR-BASED APPROACHES

In Chapter 1, some elementary principles of information flow in self-regulating systems were introduced. A significant trend of the 1980s and 1990s was a shift away from ecosystem models and toward individual or actor-based models. This shift went along with interests in microeconomics, evolutionary ecology, and a rise in individualism and self-interest, as well as other approaches that privilege the individual over the community and the ecosystem (Bodenhorn 2000; Gaines and Gaines 2000). While the individual has always been the object of research and observation in human and evolutionary studies, ecosystem approaches tend to aggregate individual information because of an interest in higher units of analysis and in how these units operate (NRC 2005b). Evolutionary ecology, optimal foraging theory, and microeconomics are interested in *why* individuals make the decisions they do. The preference is to highlight the variability of individuals in a system in order to understand the origin of particular traits or behaviors (for example, food sharing), rather than focus on the dynamic equilibrium of whole systems. Both approaches are necessary to address the full panoply of questions of interest to human ecology and the human dimensions of global change. These are now seen as processes occurring at different levels of analysis, linked by complex articulations across scales that remain to be investigated.

Research in psychology has yielded some valuable observations on how a self-organizing system develops and functions. If stored information and past routines are simple and small in number, groping can be effective in decisionmaking. The organism goes through its repertoire of activities until the proper response is elicited (Mackay 1968b:363). Although groping is used by people and can result in new and inventive solutions to problems, it is largely ineffective. This is particularly true if the situation is complex or the social or physical environment changes rapidly and unpredictably. If regularity (i.e., redundancy) can be established in the statistical structure of a situation, then one can save time by the use of "imitative organizers" or control sequences based on the statistical characteristics of redundant phenomena (Mackay 1968b:363). These allow the organism to induce the correct adaptive response without major investments in groping. Groping and control sequences assume that one knows in advance the range of options available and constraints present, but this is seldom realistic. Human systems are self-organizing—they are able to receive inputs of new information and develop characteristic organizing sequences as a result of new and old information.

The human informational system probably works at various levels, depending on the level of difficulty in making choices. Decisions can be made in a climate of certainty, uncertainty, or risk. Certainty exists when one can predict what will happen in the period relevant to the decision. Uncertainty describes a situation in which one cannot specify the probability of outcomes. Risk refers to situations where one can specify the probability distribution of several possible outcomes (Levin and Kirkpatrick 1975:106).

Under conditions of certainty about a situation (for example, at breakfast I have a choice between cereal and eggs, with coffee in either case), a set of simple rules or pathways may be followed in arriving at a decision. As certainty decreases and there is a greater possibility of inappropriate or maladaptive choices, increasingly complex logic and structure must be used to help sift the information and allow for decision-making under conditions of risk and uncertainty. Solutions may be elicited from the use of simulation, probability, and judgment heuristics—nonprobabilistic methods that make use of consensus between knowledgeable people. Effective research tools for dealing with conditions of risk have not achieved the sophistication of those dealing with uncertainty. Both areas offer fallow ground for new contributions, given the paucity of analytical tools available and the importance of this aspect of human systems (Levin and Kirkpatrick 1975:529–530). Theories of risk management are increasingly applied to issues in environmental social science, such as how pastoral groups manage risk in a hazardous physical environment (Bollig 2006; McCabe 2004).

Methods developed in microeconomics and in the field of management and decision theory can be usefully applied to the problem of choosing from different possible courses of action (Rapport and Turner 1977). One who has too many choices in a given set of circumstances may be immobilized by indecision. Thus a typical response of information flow systems is to have complex rules to simplify the number of options. Over time, social scientists have presented a variety of theories that seek to give primacy to one factor or another. For many years the assumption behind the behavior of economic man—maximization of expected utility—has been dominant. Much of the behavior has been simplified so that economists can focus on aspects of behavior that advance the interests of business, households, and so forth. However, both theorists and fieldworkers have seriously attacked those assumptions. The key assumption—the decisionmaker's objective is maximization of expected utility—is useful for analysis but does not represent the actual behavior of actors.

Critics have shown that economic man sometimes seeks to maximize noneconomic interests, such as prestige (Cancian 1972; Schneider 1974), or simply tries to minimize risk and uncertainty (Johnson 1971). Leibenstein, in his book *Beyond Economic Man* (1976), calls for an overhaul of economic theory taking into account selective rationality—choice making that reflects a compromise between what one might do in the absence of constraints and what one does when they are present. One's preference reflects social, cultural, and psychological standards of behavior that may conflict with the calculus of maximization. Similar theories have been proposed by business psychologists (March and Simon 1958; Lindblom 1964; Cyert and March 1963) and geographers (Heijnen and Kates 1974; Slovic et al. 1974). These studies emphasize that decisionmakers do not necessarily maximize utility, but aim instead at *satisfactory* solutions to problems—often invoking simplified "programs" that lack the complete knowledge often assumed in economic analysis (see also Ostrom 1998; Gigerenzer and Selten 2002). Linking economic theory and rational choice to selective rationality is attracting interest across the social sciences (Boudon 2003; Miller 2005; Ostrom 2005). A particularly intriguing new area is one that examines how contracts are made. Legal enforcement alone cannot ensure that contracts work in cooperative ventures. Even state intervention in legal enforcement has a limited role. More effective results come about when parties negotiate incomplete contracts that emphasize renegotiation and rely on enforcement through informal mechanisms, such as reputation, repeated dealing between parties, and norms of reciprocity (Scott 2006). This view of law as socially engaged helps us understand not only the behavior of traditional populations but also effective contemporary legal contracts through the use of "smart heuristics" (Udehn 2002; Gigerenzer and Selten 2002; Schwartz 2000).

To integrate relevant information flows into matter-energy models, we must be able to assign a logic to human acts. This logic is derived from the sorts of decision models just described. A new generation of intelligent agent-based models (Grimm et al. 2006) offers exciting opportunities to grow social systems through rule-based iterative approaches that take advantage of artificial intelligence (Epstein and Axtell 1996; Xu and Li 2002).

The next chapter introduces methods and techniques of spatial analysis being used across the biological and social sciences to integrate data in a spatially explicit fashion.

SUGGESTED READINGS AND USEFUL WEBSITES

The Population Association of America (www.popassoc.org), the Population Reference Bureau (www.prb.org/DataFind/datafinder7.htm), and the Census Bureau (www.census.gov/ipc/www/idbnew.html) have useful websites with downloadable materials on demographic methods and population studies. The CIESIN website provides downloadable data and material on demographics in the United States (www.ciesin.org/datasets/us-demog/us-demog-home.html). USAID works in a variety of worldwide areas on studies of health and demographics (www.usaid.gov/our_work/global_health). The National Center for Health Statistics at the CDC provides information and data on health in the United States (www.cdc.gov/nchs). Also see the book by Haining (1993), *Spatial Data Analysis in the Social and Environmental Sciences*, for information about conducting research in a spatially defined framework. The most useful handbook of methods for demography is Siegel and Swanson's *The Methods and Materials of Demography*.

The journal *BioScience* and its association of biological scientists have excellent materials at their website on ecological processes (www.aibs.org/bioscience), as do the journals *Ecology* (http://esapubs.org/esapubs/journals/ecology.htm), *Ecological Applications* (http://esapubs.org/esapubs/journals/applications.htm), and *Frontiers in Ecology and the Environment* (www.frontiersinecology.org) from the Ecological Society of America (www.esa.org/publications). The National Center for Ecological Analysis and Synthesis (www.nceas.ucsb.edu) and the newer National Evolutionary Synthesis Center in the North Carolina research triangle area (www.nescent.org) also have excellent research materials and data on ecological and evolutionary processes. The journal *Ecology and Society* (formerly *Conservation Ecology*) provides open-access published research results from an international perspective (www.ecology andsociety.org). The website of Ecoinformatics.org (www.ecoinformatics.org) serves to synthesize ecological research and computer modeling simulations to enhance understanding of basic ecological processes.

Several excellent books detail ecological processes, including *Climate Change* by Cowie (2007); *Ecology: From Individuals to Ecosystems* by Begon et al. (2005); *Conservation Biology* by Pullin (2002); *Essentials of Ecology* by Townsend et al. (2002); *Ecology: Principles and Applications* by Chapman and Reiss (1998); and *Biogeochemistry: An Analysis of Global Change* by Schlesinger (1997). The Scientific Committee on Problems of the Environment (SCOPE) offers a series of titles related to various environmental research topics, including environmental monitoring, toxicology, biogeochemical cycling, and global change (www.icsu-scope.org).

The Environmental Change Institute at the University of Oxford (www.eci.ox .ac.uk) and the National Institute for Global Environmental Change (NIGEC) (http://nigec.ucdavis.edu) also provide detailed information about environmental research and global change. Additional environmental resources from a variety of environmental biomes can be found through the American Long-Term Ecological Research Network, which supports continued study of twenty-six different sites in North America, the Caribbean, and Antarctica (www.lternet.edu).

Further information on soils can be found at the National Resources Conservation Service of the US Department of Agriculture (www.soils.usda.gov), including spatial data of soil distributions (http://soildatamart.nrcs.usda.gov). The website Science of Soils provides links to a variety of resources on soils and soil research (http://hintze -online.com/sos/soils-online.html). Additionally, many journals cover topics and research related to soil ecology, including *Earth and Environmental Science* (www .springerlink.com/content/102032), the *Soil Science Society of America Journal* (www.scijournals.org), *Applied Soil Ecology* (www.elsevier.com/wps/product/cws _home/524518), and *Soil Biology and Biochemistry* (www.elsevier.com/locate/ soilbio). The Soil Science Society of America (www.soils.org) offers several other soil-related journals (www.scijournals.org). Other academic and research societies related to soils include the Soil Ecology section of the ESA (www.esa.org/soilecology) and the Soil Ecology Society (www.wcsu.edu/ses/ses.html).

The books *Fundamentals on Soil Ecology* by Coleman et al. (2004), *Soils, Land, and Food* by Wild (2003), and *Environmental Soil Chemistry* by Sparks (2002) describe many aspects of soil ecology.

The journal *Forest Ecology and Management* (www.elsevier.com/locate/foreco) offers insightful research articles related to forest topics. The books *Ecology of Woodlands and Forests* by Thomas and Packham (2007) and *Forest Ecology* by Barnes et al. (2001) thoroughly overview forests worldwide, including soils, climate, and forest uses. The US Forest Service (www.fs.fed.us) and the Forest Ecology Branch of the USGS (www.nwrc.usgs.gov/about/feb/frst_eco.htm) offer research and information related to forests. Internationally, the Center for International Forestry Research (CIFOR) (www.cifor.cgiar.org) unites researchers from a variety of different areas. Its list of online journals offers a variety of resources that appeal to forest-based research (www.cifor.cgiar.org/Library/JournalGateways). At the larger landscape level, the journal *Landscape Ecology* (www.springerlink.com/content/103025) from the International Association for Landscape Ecology (www.landscape-ecology.org) also discusses forestry and spatial-related issues.

NOTE

1. The international standard of joules can be calculated by multiplying the kcal by 4.19 = kj (kilojoules).

Photo by E. Moran

4

ENVIRONMENTAL CHANGE
AND SPATIAL ANALYSIS

In this chapter we explore the application of spatial analysis to environmental research and the study of environmental change. We will pay special attention to human dimensions of global environmental change (an emergent interdisciplinary field), spatial analysis using remotely sensed data and geographic information systems (GIS), experimental methods, and the study of institutions within a spatially explicit context. These areas have developed spatially explicit data requirements, spatial modeling, and other spatial analytical ways of examining the human-environment nexus.

There is a growing awareness of people's increasing vulnerability to hurricanes, floods, tornadoes, and drought. Some of these events are a product of climate change, exacerbated by carbon dioxide and methane emissions and consequent global warming. People become even more vulnerable when they engage in poor land use practices or do not enforce building regulations (as discovered in the aftermath of Hurricane Andrew in the Miami area), allow building in hazard-prone areas (for example, close to beaches), and when property values rise in areas subject to decade-to-century long extreme climate events (hurricanes along the Gulf of Mexico, and cycles of flood in the American Southwest and the Mississippi floodplain). Climate change has increased the vulnerability of human population to new and reemergent diseases (see Figure 4.1).

Climate change and variability can lead to changes in the spatial occurrence of poverty and disease. The 1993 floods in the American Midwest were associated with several epidemics. In Milwaukee heavy rains overwhelmed the sanitation system, leading to a Cryptosporidium outbreak that affected 400,000 people and caused more than 100 deaths. In the desert American Southwest, intense rains provided a supply of food for rodents, following a six-year drought that had reduced rodent predators. A tenfold increase in rodents led to transmission of a "new" disease— hantavirus pulmonary syndrome—with a fatality rate of 50 percent.

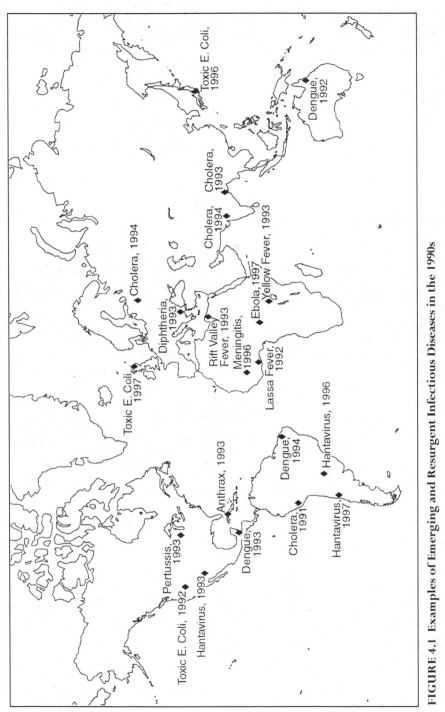

FIGURE 4.1 Examples of Emerging and Resurgent Infectious Diseases in the 1990s

Climate change and international flows of labor and food have resulted in the resurgence of many infectious diseases, made all the more difficult to control by antibiotic-resistant strains. *Source: Adapted from P. R. Epstein, "Climate, Ecology, and Human Health," Consequences 3, no. 2 (1997): 3–19.*

The biggest anthropogenic causes of global change are energy use and land use (Steffen et al. 2004; Lambin and Geist 2006). The use of fossil fuels accounts for over 70 percent of the rise in atmospheric carbon dioxide. Since World War II the human population has grown exponentially, as has the expansion of agricultural land use. Research on land management practices shows that overexploitation of common pool resources—the tragedy of the commons—is not inevitable (Ostrom et al. 1999; McCay and Acheson 1987). Rather, the tragedy is a product of human communities' failure to govern access to resources, monitor their condition, and enforce sanctions (Ostrom 1990, 2005; Moran and Ostrom 2005). Cultural traditions, legal rules (and their enforcement), land tenure and its distribution, and other factors impact how land can be used and by whom (Nagendra 2002).

THE CHALLENGE OF SCALE AND LEVELS OF ANALYSIS

The attention that the research community and policy circles are giving to the human dimensions of global environmental change offers a rare opportunity to environmental social scientists. For the first time, policymakers and the physical science community acknowledge humans' central place in environmental modification (Vitousek et al. 1997; Peck 1990) and thus implicitly accept what anthropology and other social sciences may say about it. Solutions to contemporary environmental problems will require the integration of experimental and theoretical approaches at a variety of levels of analysis, from local to global (Levin 1998). For participation in the contemporary debates over human impact on global environments, ecosystem models and ecosystem theory are fundamental (Moran 1990). This does not mean abiding by notions of equilibrium, fixation on calories, energy flow models, and functionalism. Rather, it means understanding the nature of complex systems that link the atmosphere to the geosphere and to the living components of our planet (the biosphere). These systems are tied by complex cycles of matter, energy, and information. An environmental anthropology lacking the ecosystem approach would be largely irrelevant to the debates over the processes of global environmental change—possibly the most important research agenda for the twenty-first century (Lubchenco 1998)

Contemporary environmental anthropology builds on the past experience of scholars who studied human interaction with the environment, but it must go beyond those approaches. Human-environment research for the twenty-first century must add refined approaches that permit analysis of global environmental changes and their underlying local and regional dynamics (Moran and Ostrom 2005). This poses a major challenge to research methods, as all researchers must employ generally agreed-on ways of selecting sample communities or sites and collecting data across highly variable sites, despite significant differences in environment, culture, economy, and history (Moran and Brondizio 2001).

No single approach will be adequate to the complex tasks ahead. Past approaches that emphasized equilibrium and predictability and were necessary to test null hypotheses do not serve this research agenda well because they hide the dynamic processes of ecosystems, as well as patches within ecosystems. Dynamic, stochastic ecosystem models are necessary to address global environmental change (Xu and Li 2002; Walker et al. 2006). Environmental social scientists need to use such approaches to engage, for example, ecosystem restoration (Mitsch and Day 2004; Pietsch and Hasenauer 2002), biodiversity (Tillman 1999; Nagendra 2001; Wätzold et al. 2006), agroecology (Vandermeer 2003; Wojtkowski 2004), and deforestation (Skole and Tucker 1993; Kaimowitz and Angelsenn 1998; Lambin and Geist 2006).

A tool ecological anthropologists and other human-environment scientists will need to use is geographic information systems (**GIS**) and the techniques of satellite remote sensing. Remote sensing from satellite platforms such as the National Oceanographic and Atmospheric Administration (NOAA)'s AVHRR sensor, the National Aeronautics and Space Administration (NASA)'s Landsat **thematic mapper (TM),** and the French SPOT satellite provides information of considerable environmental richness for local, regional, and global analysis (NRC 1998a; Conant 1978, 1990; Moran and Brondizio 1998; Brondizio 2007). For analyzing global processes of large continental areas such as the entire Amazon basin, NOAA's **AVHRR** is the most appropriate satellite sensor. Its resolution is coarser, but it offers daily coverage. More recently, MODIS, a midrange resolution satellite with 250 meter spatial resolution that provides daily coverage, has been used and connected to satellites capable of finer resolution (Wessels et al. 2004; Anderson et al. 2005; Morton et al. 2005; Hansen et al. 2002a,b). Although designed primarily for meteorology, it has been profitably employed to monitor vegetation patterns over very large areas. Because of its coarse scale, social scientists to date have made little use of AVHRR data.

Available since 1972, data from Landsat's multispectral scanner (**MSS**) is relatively inexpensive and has been used by a number of anthropologists. The pioneering work of Francis Conant (1978) and Priscilla Reining (1973) depended on this data. Use of MSS data is still valuable for studying relatively dichotomous phenomena such as forest/nonforest cover and establishing a historical account of land cover change in a particular region. Before 1972, remotely sensed data came from aerial photographs (Vogt 1974).

A significant advance took place in 1984 with the launch of the Landsat thematic mapper (TM) sensor that improved the spatial resolution from the 80 meters of MSS to 30 meters. It also included three visible spectrum channels and four infrared spectrum channels. This satellite has allowed anthropologists to make detailed studies of land cover changes in some of the most difficult landscapes known: the Amazon basin and the Ituri forest of central Africa (Brondizio 2007, 1996; Moran et al. 1994a, 2002a; Moran and Brondizio 2001; Wilkie 1994). Discrimination between age classes of secondary growth vegetation was achieved for the first time using satellite data (Moran et al. 1994a, 1996), as well as discrimination between subtle palm-based agroforestry management and flooded forest in the Amazon estuary (Brondizio et al. 1994, 1996), erosion in Madagascar (Sussman et al. 1994), and intensification in indigenous systems (Guyer and Lambin 1993; Behrens et al. 1994).

These recent advances required careful attention to issues of scale, both temporal and spatial. Research questions and methods often are scale-specific. In earlier work, Moran (1984, 1990) pointed out that many debates on Amazonian cultural ecology were, at least in part, generated by the use of different levels and scales of analysis. Appreciation for scaling issues has increased as the challenge of integrating data and models from different disciplines and different temporal and spatial scales becomes necessary with the growth of global environmental change studies (Walsh et al. 1999; Wessman 1992:175). Bioecological data, coming as it often does from study of individual organisms, must be connected to regional and global scales. Complex spatial variations and nonlinearities across landscapes occur that challenge facile extrapolations from local scale to more inclusive scales (Green et al. 2005a). The points of articulation between different scales of analysis challenge our narrow disciplinary approaches and require new strategies for acquiring and interpreting data (Walsh et al. 1999; Wessman 1992:175).

The precision of regional analysis depends on the quality of the sampling at local level. Detailed local-level sampling is far from common in traditional remote sensing. Much of what goes for "ground truthing" is visual observation of classes such as dense forest or cropland, without detailed examination of land use history, vegetation structure, and composition. The long-standing anthropological bias for understanding local-level processes, when combined with the use of analytical tools capable of scaling up and down, helps advance land use/land cover change research and articulation between differently scaled processes. Ecosystem research has historically presented challenges to multiscalar analyses because ecosystems can be conceptualized at any number of scales.

Environmental social science is capable of contributing to these multiply scaled analyses, with its strength remaining at the local to regional scale. Wessman (1992:180) has called for studies that link ground observations to regional and global scales to take full advantage of the detailed data available at different scales. A number of these research efforts are continuing, but many have paid scant attention to the human dimension. Extrapolation of ecosystem research to regional and global scale has been hindered in the past by difficulties in observing large-scale spatial heterogeneity. Remote sensing linked to ground-based studies provides the most promising tools for understanding ecosystem structure, function, and change. The capacity to detect long-term change in ecosystems can be enhanced by analysis of image texture, combined with spatial statistics that permit analysis of stand structure from satellite data (Wessman 1992:189). A summary of research in the social sciences on issues of scale can be found in Gibson et al. (2000b). The multiscale strategy proposed here is not a programmatic statement, but rather a well-tested research strategy used by multidisciplinary teams at the Anthropological Center for Training and Research on Global Environmental Change at Indiana University. Readers may wish to consult our website at www.indiana.edu/~act for updates regarding ongoing studies of the human dimensions of global environmental change at our center and at other centers on the human dimensions, through our Enviro-Links webpage (www.indiana.edu/~act/enviro.shtml, see also www.cipec.org offers for access to other websites).

HUMAN ADAPTABILITY TO GLOBAL ENVIRONMENTAL CHANGE

There is no more compelling research agenda in the environmental social sciences than the study of the human dimensions of global environmental change (NRC 1999a). This agenda began to be formulated in 1992 with the National Research Council's book *Global Environmental Change: Understanding the Human Dimensions* (NRC 1992). Research on global change has focused on climate change, biodiversity, pollution, and international environmental agreements driven by a growing awareness of global impacts such as accumulation of earth-warming gases, the appearance of an ozone hole changing the amount of ultraviolet (UV) radiation people receive, and documented glacier meltdowns. The impacts of global change on human societies are expected to intensify in the twenty-first century. Current trends are expected to have cumulative effects on the atmosphere and climate change (NRC 1998b; Hunter 1999; Potter 1999). "Human dimensions research addresses the workings of social systems that manage environmental resources—markets, property rights regimes, treaties, legal and informal norms, and so forth—and the potential to modify those institutions through policy and thus to mitigate global change or increase adaptive capability" (NRC 1999a:5; see Janssen et al. 2006 for a review of the growing community addressing human dimensions of global environmental change).

In 1992 the following issues were identified as needing urgent attention and research priority:

1. Understanding land use and land cover changes
2. Understanding the decisionmaking process
3. Designing policy instruments and institutions to address energy-related problems
4. Assessing impacts, vulnerability, and adaptation to global changes
5. Understanding population-environment interactions

A great deal was accomplished in the following years, focusing on the causes, consequences, and responses of human populations to global environmental change (for a summary of accomplishments and sources, see NRC 1999a). Notable advances occurred in the study of land use and land cover change, the topic the research community was most ready to address (Gutman et al. 2004; Moran and Ostrom 2005; NRC 2005a) for understanding human responses to climate events (NRC 1999b; Moran et al. 2006; Galvin et al. 2001; Gutmann 2000). Human dimensions of global change became an important priority at the National Science Foundation (NSF), NOAA, NASA, and the Social Science and Population Program at the National Institute for Child Health and Human Development (NICHD). Two centers for the study of the human dimensions of global environmental change were created—the Center for the Study of Institutions, Population, and Environmental Change at Indiana University (www.indiana.edu/~cipec) and the Center for Integrated Study of the Human Dimensions of Global Change (www.epp.cmu.edu/global_change/center) at Carnegie Mellon University, both with support from the National Science Foundation.

New priorities position the environmental social sciences at the center of research on global change. There is growing evidence that socioeconomic uncertainties are greater than biophysical uncertainties, for example, in the study of climate impacts (NRC 1999b:1). Major changes in the global atmosphere come from human activities such as deforestation and energy consumption. Studies showing that the tragedy of the commons is not inevitable but the product of how humans organize themselves to respond to perceived threats to their well-being further strengthen the case for the importance of the environmental social sciences. Since 1992, the field has evolved and a new set of research priorities for the first decade of the twenty-first century have been identified:

1. Understanding the social determinants of environmentally significant consumption (NRC 1997a; Moran 2006)
2. Understanding the sources of technological change (www.ihdp.uni-bonn.de)
3. Making climate predictions more relevant and accurate (NRC 1999b)
4. Improving the response of human populations to environmental surprises
5. Understanding the conditions favoring institutional success or failure in resource management (Ostrom 1998, 2005)
6. Linking land use and land cover dynamics to population processes, especially the role of human migration (LUCC 1999; NRC 2005b; Moran and Ostrom 2005)
7. Improving our understanding of human decisionmaking (Moran et al. 2006)
8. Advancing capacity to make social science data **spatially explicit** (NRC 1998a; Goodchild and Janelle 2004)[1]

In order to advance the current state of knowledge, there is a need to engage all of the social sciences in multidisciplinary research, jointly with each other and with the biophysical sciences. In this enterprise, environmental anthropology has much to offer.

Anthropologists and geographers bring two main contributions to the analysis of global change. First, both are committed to understanding local differences.

When looking at a satellite image, for instance, they search for land use patterns associated with socioeconomic and cultural processes coming from local populations. Consequently they strive to find the driving forces behind land use differences and come up with land use classifications that are meaningful in socio-economic and cultural terms.

A second important contribution is related to data collection and methods. Anthropologists, sociologists, and human geographers using satellite images want to reveal the living human reality behind land cover classes. Such a perspective requires methods that link local environmental differences to human behavior (Rindfuss et al. 2003; Moran and Brondizio 1998, 2001). Environmental social scientists take pride in their fieldwork, and they can harness this interest to make important contributions to advancing the state of spatially explicit social science (Moran and Ostrom 2005; Walsh and Crews-Meyer 2002).

Since 1972 earth-orbiting satellites have provided valuable data for the study of the human dimensions of global change. Human ecologists have shown how different land uses affect the rate of secondary succession after tropical deforestation at local (Moran et al. 1994a,b; Brondizio et al. 1994; Moran and Brondizio 1998; Batistella 2001; Futemma 2000; Forsberg 1999; Toniolo 2004) and regional scales (Behrens et al. 1994; Sussman et al. 1994; Brondizio and Moran, in preparation).

THE USE OF REMOTE SENSING AND GIS IN THE SOCIAL SCIENCES

It is hard to imagine trying to engage the human dimensions of global environmental change without the availability of earth-orbiting satellites capable of providing time-series data on features such as soils, vegetation, moisture, urban sprawl, and water-covered areas (Campbell 1987; Lillesand et al. 2004; Jensen 2005, 2007; McCoy 2005; NRC 1998a; 2005b), or studying impacts of climatic variability on populations (Galvin et al. 2001; Gutmann 2000; Moran et al. 2006). Environmental social scientists have enjoyed increasing opportunities since the launch of Landsat 1 in 1972, complemented later with improved sensors and spatial resolution (Landsat 7 was launched successfully in 1999), the French SPOT satellites with still better resolution, and most recently a new generation of commercial satellites such as IKONOS with 1–5 meter resolution (see Table 4.1 for a comparison of other satellites and resolutions available) (Batistella et al. 2004).

The use of GIS to overlay data layers in spatially explicit ways added to this powerful set of techniques (Aronoff 2005; Campbell and Sayer 2003; Goodchild 2003; Goodchild and Janelle 2004; Okabe 2006; Steinberg and Steinberg 2006). Spatial analysis using GIS had its earliest anthropological use as part of site identification and analysis by archaeologists (Johnson et al. 2005). GIS is an essential tool in the environmental analysis tool kit, and is also widely used by environmental NGOs, urban planners, and scientists in the natural and social sciences (Hesse-Biber and Leavy 2006; Greene and Pick 2006; Evans et al. 2005a).

TABLE 4.1 Comparison of the Spatial, Spectral, and Temporal Resolution of the Main Remote Sensing Platforms Available

Satellite	Sensor	Spectral resolution	Spatial resolution	Temporal resolution
AQUA	MODIS			
	AIRS			
	CERES			
CBERS 1	CCD Sensor			
	IRMSS			
	WFI			
CBERS 2	CCD Sensor			
	IRMSS			
	WFI			
EROS A1	CCD Sensor			
EROS B1	CCD-TDI Sensor			
IKONOS 2	PAN & MULTI.			
LANDSAT 5	MSS			
	TM			
LANDSAT 7	ETM+			
QUICKBIRD	QUICKBIRD			
SPOT 2	HRV			
SPOT 4	HRVIR			
	VEGETATION			
SPOT 5	HRG			
	HRS			
	VEGETATION 2			
TERRA	ASTER			
	MODIS			
	CERES			

Legend:

Spectral resolution	Spatial resolution	Temporal resolution
11–36 bands	0–2 m	daily
8–10 bands	3–10 m	2–5 days
4–7 bands	11–30 m	6–20 days
0–3 bands	31–100 m	More than 21 days
	More than 101 m	

Source: Batistella et al. 2004.

Remote sensing techniques have elicited interest among environmental anthropologists. For example, Conklin (1980) used aerial photography in his *Ethnographic Atlas of Ifugao*. He integrated ethnographic and ecological data to show land use zones from the perspective of the local population (compare the review of aerial photo usage in anthropology in Lyons et al. 1972; Vogt 1974). The use of satellite remote sensing in anthropology started in the 1970s, with Reining (1973) studying

Landsat's MSS images to locate individual Mali villages in Africa and Conant (1978) examining Pokot population distribution. After spatial resolution was improved in 1984 with the Landsat TM sensor, more researchers began using this tool (see Conant 1990 for an overview).

Analysis of land use intensification is one of the most promising topics addressed by anthropologists using remote sensing and GIS tools (Behrens 1990). In Nigeria, Guyer and Lambin (1993) used remote sensing combined with ethnographic research to study agricultural intensification, demonstrating the potential of remote sensing to address site-specific ethnographic issues within a larger land use perspective. A special issue of *Human Ecology*, September 1994, was dedicated to regional analysis and land use in anthropology. There was substantial agreement among the articles about the importance of local-level research to inform land use analysis at the regional scale. This conclusion was reinforced in an issue of *Cultural Survival Quarterly* (1995) dedicated to showing the connection between local knowledge and remote sensing, GIS, and mapping tools. The growing use of remote sensing in the social sciences is addressed in *People and Pixels: Linking Remote Sensing and Social Science* (NRC 1998a), including the work of environmental anthropologists (Moran and Brondizio 1998; Sever 1998).

The use of spatial data in analysis presents a number of challenges. Scale persists as a problem, even at the basic level of terminology (Green et al. 2005b). In cartography the term "large scale" refers to detailed resolution, while in anthropology "large scale" refers to a large study area and loss of ethnographic detail. Another basic problem is the interplay between absolute and relative scales, which can result in confusion in modeling ecological processes. This challenge is being addressed by landscape ecology. Many scholars are using landscape ecology methods to better understand land use dynamics, and spectral analysis is being refined to work at the local level with more detailed requirements. In order to continue solving the challenges posed by multiscalar research on global change, social scientists must develop research methods that are explicitly multiscale and capable of nesting data and sampling strategy in such a way that scaling up or down is feasible and integral to the research strategy (see part 3 in Moran and Ostrom 2005:127–214 for a discussion of methods linking remote sensing, GIS, and social science; also NRC 1998a). Use of these techniques requires training and familiarity with the technical requirements of different sensors, sources of variability, and whether comparison is of one area across time or of several areas at one point in time. The representation of space and time in a GIS is complex. Evans and colleagues (2005b) provide a detailed and user-friendly introduction to the handling of spatially explicit data. One of the key decisions in spatially explicit analysis is whether to use raster or vector data (Bolstad 2005; Lo and Yeung 2002, cited in Evans et al. 2005b). Raster data are more suitable to certain kinds of modeling such as cellular automata and agent-based modeling because raster data structures simplify the process of integrating and overlaying data sets. Figure 4.2 provides an example of the spatial representation of a village, with some cells underrepresenting the spatial extent of the village and other cells overrepresenting the spatial extent of the village.

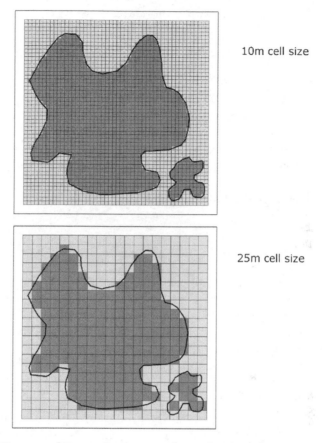

10m cell size

25m cell size

FIGURE 4.2 Vector and Raster Representations of a Hypothetical Village at Different Cell Sizes

Source: Evans et al., "Modeling Land-Use/Land-Cover Change: Exploring the Dynamics of Human-Environment Relationships," in *Seeing the Forest and the Trees: Human-Environment Interactions in Forest Ecosystems,* edited by E. F. Moran and E. Ostrom (Cambridge, MA: MIT Press, 2005), p. 172.

The finer scale of 10 meters provides a better fit. The choice of one over the other ultimately depends on how best to link human behavior to landscape outcomes and on how fine an analysis is necessary.

The Method of Multilevel Analysis of Land Use/Cover Change

Multilevel research can start at any scale of analysis; hence, sampling at one level may need to be aggregated to a higher level or disaggregated to lower levels.[2] This requires paying attention to levels of analysis without subordinating scales. Land use/cover analysis provides us with a setting for the study of levels of analysis that connects human behavior in relation to economic forces and management strategies with ecological aspects of land cover.

We can conceptualize multilevel analysis of land use/cover change as built on a structure of four integrated levels of research: landscape/regional level; vegetation class level; farm/household level; and soil level (Figure 4.3). The conceptual model relies on a nested sampling procedure that produces data that can be scaled up and down independently or in an integrated fashion. The integration of multitemporal, high-resolution satellite data with local data on economy, management, land use history, and site-specific vegetation/soil inventories aims to make it possible to understand ecological and social dimensions of land use at local scale and link them to regional and global scales of land use.

Household / Farm or Local Level of Analysis

Data collection at the farm/household level can include a variety of internal and external aspects of this unit of analysis (Netting et al. 1995; Moran 1995). It is important to collect local data so that it can be aggregated with that of larger populations in which households are nested. For instance, demographic data on household composition (including sex and age) can be aggregated to the population level to construct a demographic profile of the population, but only if the data is collected in such a way that standard intervals of five years are used (Moran 1995). Another important set of data that is collected at this level and can be aggregated at higher levels is related to subsistence economy. It is fundamental for the analysis of land use to understand resource use, economic strategies, market relationships, labor arrangements, and time allocation in productive and nonproductive activities. At this level, it is important to cover the basic dimensions of social organization, such as settlement pattern, labor distribution, resource use, and kinship (see Netting et al. 1995 for a three-level approach to collecting social organization data relevant to land use; and Brondizio 2007 for a more recent analysis).

In land use analysis, decisions must be made about the boundaries of a population. In general, geographic boundaries are associated with a variety of factors, such as land tenure, landscape features, ethnic history, administrative boundaries, and inheritance. An analysis based on local information and maps, images, and aerial photographs can provide more reliable information than either one alone. These boundaries change over time, sometimes in a dramatic fashion that can affect the behavior of populations and how the data are reported (Ellen 1990).

Concern with global change means that data collection at the local level must be capable of aggregation to higher levels of analysis, both in geographical and database formats. **Georeferencing** the household, farm boundaries, and agriculture and fallow fields may be achieved through the use of **global positioning system** (GPS) de-

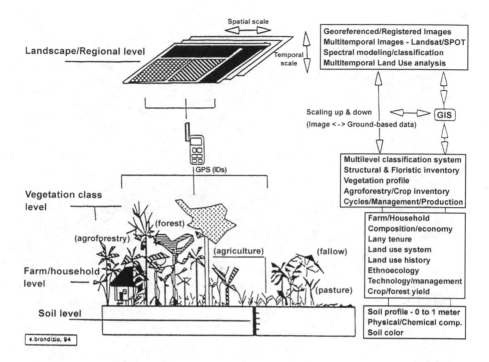

FIGURE 4.3 Method of Multilevel Analysis of Land Use / Land Cover Change

The study of global change requires consideration of multiple levels of analysis and appropriately scaled methods and variables. *Source*: E. F. Moran and E. S. Brondizio, "Land-Use Change After Deforestation in Amazônia," in *People and Pixels: Linking Remote Sensing and Social Science* (Washington, DC: National Academy Press, 1998), p. 101.

vices. These are small units that permit locating any point on the planet within a few meters (see Figure 4.4). The level of precision will vary depending on a number of factors, such as the quality of the GPS receiver. Current accuracies achieved with a GPS are acceptable for most types of land use analysis, and submeter accuracies are rarely necessary. Data collected at this level can inform the next research phase. For instance, information on the distribution of activities throughout the year, the agricultural calendar, and production can highlight the best time for future fieldwork.

Vegetation mapping has implications for understanding the impact of land use practices on land cover. Basic vegetation parameters need to be included so they can inform mapping at the landscape level. In general, vegetation structure, including height, ground cover, **basal area**, density of individuals, **DBH** (diameter at breast height), and floristic composition are important data to be collected. These data inform the interpretation of satellite digital data, provide clues to the characteristics of

FIGURE 4.4 Researchers with GPS on Hand

Teaching Brazilian students to use global positioning system (GPS) devices to locate a precise position in the field during data collection in the Amazon. Photo by Scott Hetrick.

vegetation following specific types of disturbance, and take into account the spatial arrangement of vegetation cover. Remote sensing has considerable potential in vegetation analysis because it enables wide-area, nondestructive, real-time data acquisition (Inoue 2003; Loris and Damiano 2006). The applications are also important in estimating aboveground carbon stocks, relevant to effective reports on Kyoto Protocol requirements (Patenaude et al. 2005) to reduce human-induced emissions of carbon dioxide by at least 5 percent below levels of 1990 by 2012. To do so, countries must estimate carbon stocks in 1990 and any changes since that date, whether through afforestation, reforestation, or deforestation (Patenaude et al. 2005). The applications to monitoring and predicting severe drought also have grown in sophistication (Boken et al. 2005).

In terms of satellite data interpretation, the definition of structural parameters to differentiate vegetation types and environmental characteristics, such as temperature and humidity, is particularly important. Structural differences provide information that can be linked to the image's **spectral** data. Floristic composition, although important, is less directly useful in interpreting spectral responses, but it may have to be considered depending on research questions. Environmental factors, such as soil humidity, soil color, and topographic characteristics, also are associated with spectral responses of vegetation cover. For example, at the farm level, vegetation structure is the main parameter used to evaluate the impact of human management practices, though floristic composition can be relevant. Some plant species are excellent indicators of soil type which are, in turn, associated with given management practices. Farmers commonly use the presence of given species to judge a soil. For instance, the presence of *Imperata brasiliensis* may be a sign of low soil pH in parts of the Amazon estuary (Brondizio et al. 1994). This kind of ethnoecological knowledge is site specific, and such local knowledge does not extrapolate well to landscape, regional, or global analysis.

To determine representative sampling sites of a study area's land cover, four types of information need to be aggregated: vegetation classification, ethnoecological information of resource use, composite satellite images, and classified image/land use/cover maps of the area. Based on the analysis of these data, one can decide how sampling can best be distributed in the area to inform both the image classification (land use/cover map) and the structural-floristic variability of vegetation classes. In selecting a site to be a representative sample of a vegetation type or class, one needs to consider the size of the area and its spatial location on the image. The spatial distribution of the vegetation class must also be taken into account to avoid clustering of the samples and biased information about the vegetation structure and floristic composition. With the use of a GPS device, geographical coordinates of the sampled area are obtained as part of the inventory. If possible, the area should be located on a hard copy of the georeferenced image at the site, to avoid confusion and ensure precision of the GPS information. However, it is in the laboratory, using more precise methods of georeferencing, that the site will be definitively incorporated into the image file. A nested data set on land use history and vegetation inventory can be related through GPS-derived coordinates to a multitemporal image, allowing complex analysis of land use trajectories and regrowth history at site, local, and landscape levels.

Information on land use history is important not only in defining sampling areas of anthropogenic vegetation (for example, fallow and managed forest), but also in verifying that natural vegetation has not been affected or used in the past. For instance, it is important to know whether a savanna has been burned, and if so, with what frequency; or if a particular forest plot has been logged, which species were taken and when the clearing event took place. Land use and management history are more detailed in areas directly subjected to management (for example, agroforestry), since management and technology determine the structure and composition of the site. In these areas, estimates and actual measurements of production are critical for analyzing the importance of the activity on a broader land use and economic context. More importance should be given to the spatial arrangements of planted species and their life cycles as part of the inventory. This area has been neglected in past environmental anthropology research and needs to be addressed by working closely with spatially oriented scientists such as environmental geographers and ecologists.

Vegetation regrowth and agricultural production analyses are limited in their usefulness without information about soil characteristics. Soil analysis should always be associated with vegetation cover analysis; soils should be collected at inventoried vegetation, agroforestry, and crop sites of known land use history and management and georeferenced to the image through a GPS device (Moran et al. 2002a). Ethnoecological interviews can elucidate many soil characteristics. Taxonomic classification of soil types based on color, granulometry, and fertility help identify the major soil types and their distribution with relative reliability. Folk classification can then be cross-checked and compared with systematic soil analyses. Soil analyses should include both chemical (pH, P, K, Ca, etc.) and textural (sand, clay, silt) analyses and permit the aggregation of data to regional levels (Nicholaides and Moran 1995).

Landscape and Regional Level of Analysis

The landscape/regional level provides a more aggregated picture of management practices and driving forces shaping a particular land use/cover at subregional scale. At this level, long-term environmental problems can be more easily identified and predicted than at farm or household scales (Booth 1989; Skole and Tucker 1993; Brondizio and Moran in preparation). This level integrates information from vegetation class, soil, and farm/household levels (Adams and Gillespie 2006). However, landscape level data also informs important characteristics of local-level phenomena that are not measurable at the site-specific scale. For instance, information about the heterogeneity and patchiness of the vegetation is an important parameter to include in site-specific secondary succession analysis, but it can only be observed at the landscape level.

There are four major steps in landscape-level research: (1) understanding the ecological and socioeconomic nature of the features of interest in land use/cover analysis, (2) identifying the extent and frequency of features of interest that can inform the appropriate spatial and temporal scales of analysis, (3) progressively increasing sampling, depending on the emergence of important variables, a process that landscape ecologists call using an adaptive approach (Turner et al. 1989) and that bears some resemblance to what Vayda calls "progressive contextualization" (1983), and

(4) considering the empirical methods needed for checking map accuracy, change detection, and projections and/or predictions, especially when associated with land use planning.

Satellite data are the most important for analysis at the landscape/regional level. However, it is always associated with other sources, such as radar images, aerial photography, and thematic and topographic maps. Anthropologists in the past left this kind of work to others, but today a growing number of anthropologists are developing these skills and making useful contributions to the analysis of satellite images (Behrens 1994, 1990; Moran et al. 1994a, 2002a; Brondizio et al. 1994, 1996, 2002; Moran and Brondizio 1998, 2001; Tucker and Southworth 2005; Nyerges and Green 2000). The digital analysis of satellite images may be divided in four parts: preprocessing, spectral analysis, classification, and postprocessing. During preprocessing one needs to define an image subset, georeference it to available maps and coordinate systems, and register it to other images available if multitemporal analysis is desired. The georeferencing accuracy depends on the quality of the maps, availability of georeferenced coordinates collected during fieldwork, and the statistical procedure used during georeferencing (Jensen 1996). A georeferenced image has a grid of geographical coordinates and is crucial for relating landscape data to site-specific data. When multitemporal analysis is desired, images from different dates need to be registered pixel to pixel, creating a composite image that provides a temporal change dimension at the pixel level, thus allowing the analysis of spectral trajectories related to change in land use. For instance, in a two-date image (for example, two images that are five years apart), one can quantify the change during regrowth of secondary vegetation or a shift in crops grown in that five-year period with considerable accuracy, including statistics for the change in area for each vegetation type or class.

Digital analysis provides the flexibility to use a variety of scales to analyze parameters and to define sampling procedures, depending on the land use/cover pattern and extent of the study area. In general, one can work at the landscape or regional scale (for example, the whole Landsat or SPOT image, 185 by 185 kilometer areas for Landsat images) while staying in close association with local scale processes (for example, image subsets of a watershed) to help the selection of sampling areas that will inform the image about specific spectral and spatial characteristics of land use/cover classes.

By taking a hybrid approach during image classification and processing, one can integrate unsupervised and supervised classification procedures. A hybrid approach allows one to develop an analysis of spectral patterns present in the image, in conjunction with ground information, and to arrive at spectral signature patterns which account for detailed differentiation of land use/cover features. In this fashion, a conceptual spectral model can be developed in which the features of interest can be incorporated. The model considers the reflection and absorption characteristics of the physical components that comprise each feature. For instance, in a Landsat TM image, the model attempts to account for chlorophyll absorption in the visible bands of the spectrum, for mesophyll reflectance in the near-infrared band, and for both plant and soil water absorption in the mid-infrared bands (Mausel et al. 1993; Brondizio et al. 1996). The integration of those spectral features with field data on vegetation height, basal area, density, and dominance of species can be used to differentiate stages of secondary regrowth (Moran et al. 1994a). The analysis of spectral statistics derived from unsupervised clustering and from areas of known features and land use history allows the development of representative statistics for supervised classification of land use/cover.

Classification accuracy analysis requires close association with fieldwork. Accuracy may decrease as spatial variability increases. Thus ground-truth sampling needs to increase in the same proportion. In this case, the use of a GPS device is necessary to provide reliable ground-truth information, whereas in areas with low spatial heterogeneity visual spot-checking may be enough. Accuracy check of a time series of satellite images for an area requires the analysis of vegetation characteristics and interviews about the history of a specific site with local people, so it is possible to accurately relate past events with present aspects of land cover (Mausel et al. 1993; Brondizio 2005, 2007).

Integration of data at these scales is an interactive process during laboratory analysis of images and field data, and during fieldwork (Moran and Brondizio 1998; Meyer and Turner 1994). Advanced data integration and analysis is achieved using GIS procedures that integrate layers of spatial information with georeferenced databases of socioeconomic and ecological information. Georeferencing of the database to maps and images must be a consideration from the very beginning of the research so that appropriate integration and site-specific identification are compatible. Data on household/farm and vegetation/soil inventory need to be associated with specific identification numbers that georeference it to images and maps so that integrated associations can be derived. For instance, the boundaries of a farm property may compose a land tenure layer that overlaps with a land use/cover map. These two layers may be overlapped with another layer that contains the spatial distribution of households. Each household has a specific identification that relates it to a database with socioeconomic, demographic, and other information. In another layer, all the sites used for vegetation and soil inventory can be associated with a database containing information on floristic composition, structural characteristics, and soil fertility, which will also relate to land use history.

Global Level of Analysis

The 1990s saw the rapid development of approaches variously called integrated assessment modeling, GCMs (global circulation models), and other approaches at a biosphere level of analysis. Some of these have even managed to focus on the human impacts on the earth system (compare Weyant et al. 1996). GCMs were developed first and lacked a human dimension. They were largely concerned with climate and atmospheric processes, using a very aggregated scale of analysis that made even large-scale units, such as national boundaries, not always relevant to understanding differences, say, in rates of energy consumption. However, a new generation of models has emerged in the past few years that has relevance for environmental social scientists. These are a vast improvement from the pioneering work of the Club of Rome models that appeared in the early 1970s in *Limits to Growth* (Meadows et al. 1972). Despite the many problems with this early effort, it introduced important concepts like feedback, overshoot, and resource limits to everyday discourse and scientific debate. The next attempt came from the International Institute of Applied Systems Analysis (IIASA) in Austria, with its Finite World model examining global energy flows (Häfele 1980). This attempt was broadly criticized in the scientific community and little happened until the first Intergovernmental Panel on Climate Change (IPCC) published its initial assessment in 1990. New generation models benefited from the progress made by GCMs, growing evidence of the global nature of environmental problems, and the democratization of computer technology through its wide availability (Alcamo et al. 1998:262). The next step was clear: both social and physical aspects of the world system had to be coupled in so-called integrated assessment models. Most global modeling groups today acknowledge that progress on the accuracy and predictability of modeling efforts at this scale will require a simultaneous effort to link them to regionally scaled models that can improve the quality of the spatial resolution and to the role of human drivers in global change.

One of the more sophisticated models to date is known as IMAGE 2 (Alcamo et al. 1998). It was the first global integrated model with geographic resolution, an important feature that permits improved representation of global dynamic processes, including feedback and rapid, efficient testing against new data. It is composed of two fully linked systems of models (see Figure 4.5): a socioeconomic system model (on top), and an earth system model (at bottom). The socioeconomic model is elaborated for twenty-four regions of the world, whereas the earth system (or ecosystem/atmospheric) model is spatially explicit on a 0.5-degree grid scale. The terrestrial environmental model simulates changes in global land cover on a grid scale based on climatic and economic factors. The atmosphere-ocean model computes the build-up of greenhouse gases and aerosols and the resulting impact on average temperature and precipitation. Factors such as population change, economic change, and technical change are particularly important in the terrestrial model—and the ones most in need of good-quality regional data to inform the grid-based model. To date, few environmental social scientists have engaged this community of global modelers' efforts, forcing the modelers to make estimates based on very coarse national-scale statistics rather than derived from more refined regional studies. This is an important new direction for environmental anthropologists, given the importance of global simulation models on policies such as carbon trading, setting emission ceilings for carbon dioxide by the beginning of the twenty-first century, and debt-for-nature swaps. The main participants in these exercises have been economists who rely on the use of optimizing utility functions, rather than the less than optimal, more realistic behavior of human populations, whether in the First or Third World.

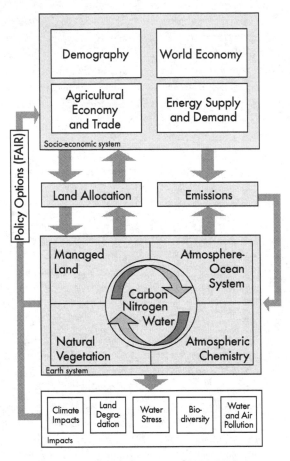

FIGURE 4.5   Flow Diagram of IMAGE 2.4

Source: Adapted from Alcamo et al., *Global Change Scenarios of the 21st Century: Results from IMAGE 2.4 Model* (Oxford: Elsevier, 1998).

The relevance of regionally informed approaches to global models becomes evident when we begin to design a classification system of vegetation types and of land use classes as a first step toward a classification of land use/cover. This can be achieved through bibliographies and databases of the study area, analysis of satellite images, fieldwork observation, and ethnoecological interviews with local inhabitants. Different levels of organization are required to define a vegetation cover of a region. In general, levels are organized to fit a specific scale of analysis into the phytogeographical arrangement and into the land use types present in the area. In other words, one starts with a more aggregated level of major dominant classes (first) adequate to a regional scale and proceeds with increased detail at the next sublevel (second) to inform more detailed scales. For instance, the first level may include major vegetation covers such as forest, secondary succession, and savanna. In the second, more detailed level, forest is subdivided into open forest and closed forest, secondary succession into old secondary succession and young secondary succession, and savanna into grassland savanna and woodland savanna. At the third level of this classification system, still more detailed information needs to be included to account for the variability of vegetation required at this local scale. So, a new subdivision of the forest class may include a third structural variation of the former two and/or a floristic variation of them, such as a forest with a dominant tree species. The importance of developing a detailed classification key is crucial to inform the land use/cover analysis at the landscape level, as well as the sampling distribution at the site-specific level.

EXPERIMENTAL APPROACHES IN THE SOCIAL SCIENCES

A combination of experimental, laboratory, and field methods can refine ecological study of land use/land cover change and many other aspects of research on human adaptability. Limited use of this mix of methods took place in the IBP Human Adaptability Program. The development of experimental economics and spatially explicit experiments permits sophisticated testing of ideas, as well as modeling decision-making in ways unimaginable just a decade ago. But experimental approaches have been resisted by the anthropological community, despite valuable results already obtained by experimental economics (V. Smith 1982, who later got the Nobel Prize for his work advancing this approach; see also Camerer 1998, 2003), experiments in natural resource management on issues of common property and institutions (Ostrom et al. 1994), and experimental social sciences (Evans et al. 2006; Bousquet et al. 2002; Goldstone and Janssen 2005). Experiments in the study of institutions are discussed in the final section of this chapter.

The use of production experiments as a complement to other field approaches and amenable to the traditions of cultural ecology is illustrated in the following example (for more details, see Brondizio 1996). Four different producers and eight different sites were selected to measure açaí *(Euterpe oleracea)* production during the 1994 harvest season. Açaí is a palm that produces highly valued fruit for local populations in the Amazon estuary. Site selection was accomplished based on socioeconomic considerations and agroforestry and ecological characteristics. At each site a 25x25 meter plot was marked with a rope that served as a fence to remind the local producer to restrict the area for the experiment's purpose. A subplot of 10x10 meters was set up inside the plot and marked in the same way. Subplot location was based on a stratified random selection.

In the large plots (25x25 m) a complete inventory of all tree individuals (DBH = 10 cm) and all açaí individuals was collected for species identification, DBH, total height, and the number of açaí stems per clump. All açaí bunches were subsequently weighed. In the small plots (10x10 m) all açaí clumps and respective stems were labeled to account for production at the individual level; the number of bunches per stem was counted; and the spatial location of each clump was mapped.

Each producer was trained and oriented to proceed with the experiment, and a notebook was prepared and used by the producer to record information during the harvesting season. The orientation involved a clear statement of the goals of the experiment, how to use the scales for weighing, and how to take appropriate notes concerning weight of bunches, fruits, and baskets, as well as account for the number of trees and bunches harvested. Most of the time the research team was present to measure the harvest in all the sites.

The unmanaged floodplain forest contained forty-four significant tree species for which detailed data were collected, while the number of species in açaí agroforestry varied from eleven to twenty-eight. There is a clear change in the concentration of economic valuable species. The **importance value** of açaí agroforestry areas is dominated by the açaí palm, with an importance value up to 0.72, whereas other forest species have importance values generally of 0.05 or less. Açaí palm also dominated the unmanaged floodplain forest in the study area, but its naturally occurring importance value was only 0.22. Forty-three additional forest species were present with importance values generally less than 0.05. Vegetation composition declined not only in terms of tree species diversity but also in the number of individuals per species. The more managed the floodplain forest, the fewer the number of species with diameters above 10 centimeters DBH and the greater the dominance and importance value of açaí. Following changes in tree composition, there is a decrease in the average canopy height from 19.0 meters to 16.5 meters and a change in first stem height from 12.4 meters to 10.0 meters. Considerably taller trees still occur on managed forests. The vigor of biomass, represented by relative dominance (basal area), also confirms the variation between both stands. An important parameter here is the increase in percentage of açaí basal area (7.2 percent to 51.4 percent) in relation to the total basal area of the stand. Management does not radically change stand biomass, but rather which species contribute to it, showing that it is possible to achieve intensification in management and production without disrupting structural-functional characteristics of the forest. The reduced canopy height and the virtual absence of understory vegetation in the managed areas made it feasible to achieve spectral separation and consequently classification of these areas on the satellite images. More detailed description about the spectral difference and mapping between managed and unmanaged floodplain forest can be found in Brondizio et al. (1996) and Brondizio (2007).

Açaí production at the regional level was estimated, based on the land use maps developed for the areas occupied by three populations (for more information see Brondizio et al. 1994 and 1996; and Brondizio 2007). This example illustrates a way to use extended anthropological fieldwork to combine ethnographic with experimental and spatial methods. These, in turn, can be combined with historical, demographic, and spectral analysis to address the multiple ways in which populations cope with the environment.

SPATIAL ANALYSIS AND THE STUDY OF INSTITUTIONS

Important literature coming primarily from political science and economics and also from anthropology, geography, sociology, ecology, and other disciplines focuses on institutions that manage common property resources. The application of spatial analytical approaches to the study of institutions is a notable advance in the field of environmental social science (Schweik 1998; Schweik et al. 2003). Common pool resources are systems in which a finite quantity of resource units is produced so that one person's use subtracts from the quantity available to others (Ostrom et al. 1994). The theory of common pool resource exploitation, developed from the 1960s to the 1980s, presumed that homogeneous, self-seeking individuals are trapped in settings where they cannot communicate and cannot make binding commitments. Consequently they make independent decisions that severely overuse, and even destroy, the resource base on which their livelihood depends (G. Hardin 1968). A tragedy of the commons occurs when those involved in an open-access commons fail to establish an effective governance system.

In the 1990s, a substantial body of empirical research challenged the theory's universal applicability by reporting on settings where the tragedy of the commons has not occurred (McCay and Acheson 1987; Berkes 1989; Ostrom 1990). A self-governed common pool resource is one in which the resource users, who are the major appropriators of the resources, are involved over time in making and adapting rules within collective-choice situations, with regard to including and excluding users; defining strategies of appropriation, obligations of participants, modes of conflict resolution; and monitoring and sanctioning access to the resources. Ostrom (1998) identified four variables associated with the attributes of a resource system (feasible improvement, availability of reliable indicators, predictability of the resource, and accurate knowledge of the resource due to limited spatial extent) and seven variables associated with the attributes of users (salient resource, common understanding, low discount rate, similar effect on participants, trust and reciprocity, relative autonomy in setting rules, and skills in organizing associations) which create a greater likelihood that participants will overcome problems of collective action and achieve patterns of sustainable resource use. She also provides a theoretical explanation for how these eleven variables affect participants' relevant benefit-cost calculus. It is not the case that resource users either destroy or sustainably manage their resources. Higher-level governments can directly affect the values of many of the variables so that community-level decisions and higher-level government decisions are closely intertwined and far from obvious. Two sets of variables—group size and heterogeneity—are particularly contested. It is insufficient to assume that changes in either size or heterogeneity will always have a similar effect on the capacity of a group to manage resource systems. In our ongoing research, we have found that neither size nor heterogeneity and neither private nor communal land tenure rights are predictably associated with improved resource management.

What is needed, according to Ostrom (1998), is a second-generation theory of rational choice. She argues that evolution has produced in humans an acutely developed capacity to seek out rules of language and social exchange around which to build institutions. Children learn these rules rapidly and apply them for the rest of their lives. Reciprocity of various types appears to be a universal form of moral relationship that is taught cross-culturally and reinforced throughout life. At the core of this second-generation theory are concepts such as reciprocity, trust, and the reputation that individuals gain for being trustworthy (Moran 2006).

In this view, whether fallible learners make good choices for themselves and for others depends not only on their values, but also on the information they possess and the learning and choice processes they have developed. Education and experience affect the level and type of information used in making decisions. Knowing who to trust, who is a group member, and who has shown group solidarity affects the strategies that individuals adopt. Rules related to information flow (for example, who must be informed about actions taken), as well as the payoffs received by participants, also affect what individuals learn about the situations they face.

In laboratory experiments, participants overused the resource and/or overinvested when they were prevented from communicating with one another, but when they had opportunities to organize, they gradually moved in the direction of more sustainable resource use that allowed all of them to obtain an acceptable rate of return for their investment (Ostrom et al. 1994). Defectors from agreed on levels of investment were treated with verbal punishment and indignation, commonly sufficient to change their behavior on the next round of the experiments.

Situations where everyone benefits by selecting some strategies rather than others are not problematic. Often, however, human use of resources is not that benign or simple. Many situations have the characteristics of social dilemmas and collective action problems. Collective action problems exist whenever there are substantial gains to be achieved—when a group of individuals coordinate their strategies, while at the same time individuals find it advantageous to seek out independent strategies that leave them better off if everyone else coordinates. These are referred to as social dilemmas (Ostrom 1998; Tucker and Ostrom 2005; Moran et al. 2002b).

Integrating remotely sensed data, GIS, and fragmentation analysis of forest cover with the study of the institutions has made considerable progress (Tucker and Ostrom 2005; Schweik 1998; Schweik et al. 2003; Nagendra 2002). Weak institutions may result in degradation of forest understory or changes in species composition that result in forest impoverishment. Robust institutions, on the other hand, may produce increases in forest biomass and economic value of forests to the community. An optimal means of evaluating forest conditions is to compare a study site with a reference forest that has undergone little human modification in a given habitat (Tucker and Ostrom 2005:93). Policymakers have tended to view property rights as a way to reduce environmental degradation and presume, incorrectly, that private tenure is the universal remedy. The evidence is that no formal tenure arrangement—whether private, common property or public ownership—guarantees stewardship of forest resources (Tucker 1999; Southworth and Tucker 2001). Enforcement of penalties for violations, regardless of tenure regime, tends to be more closely associated with healthy forest conditions for human communities.

These human-environment situations are affected by physical and biological variables, by the structure of the surrounding community and economy, and by the specific rules in use by the population. The expected benefits of planting tree crops, for example, depend on the soil, the climate, the location of the decisionmaker, the characteristics of the crops, the shared values held by those considered to be part of the decisionmaker's community, and the rules of use specifying what may or many not be planted. All these variables are scale-dependent, as one goes from local to global scales, and they change the relevant physical and biological world, the human community, and the relevant rules that are implemented. Therefore the study of common property resources and institutions is closely tied to concerns with how to design research and policies that take into account spatial, temporal, and scale differences in the study of decisions about resources (cf. Ostrom 2005).

SUGGESTED READINGS AND USEFUL WEBSITES

Many books, journals, and websites offer detailed information and social and biophysical data of land use and land cover change. Several edited volumes, including *Population, Land Use, and Environment: Research Directions* from the NRC (2005a); *Seeing the Forest and the Trees: Human-Environment Interactions in Forest Ecosystems* edited by Moran and Ostrom (2005); *Land Change Science: Observing, Monitoring, and Understanding Trajectories of Change on Earth's Surface* edited by Gutman et al. (2004); *People and the Environment: Approaches for Linking Household and Community Surveys to Remote Sensing and GIS* edited by Fox et al. (2003); *Linking People, Place, and Policy: A GIScience Approach* edited by Walsh and Crews-Meyer (2002); and *People and Pixels: Linking Remote Sensing and Social Science* from the NRC (1998) describe the integration of social and environmental data in spatial analyses.

The journals *Photogrammetric Engineering and Remote Sensing*, from the American Society for Photogrammetry and Remote Sensing (www.asprs.org), the *ISPRS Journal of Photogrammetry and Remote Sensing*, from the International Society for Photogrammetry and Remote Sensing (www.isprs.org), the *International Journal of Remote Sensing* (www.tandf.co.uk/journals/titles/01431161.asp), and *Remote Sensing of Environment* (www.elsevier.com/locate/rse) regularly publish articles incorporating remote sensing and GIS analyses.

Excellent journals covering economic and ecological modeling include *Experimental Economics*, from the Economic Science Association (www.economicscience .org), *Ecological Economics*, from the International Society for Ecological Economics (www.ecoeco.org), *Ecological Modeling* (www.elsevier.com/wps/find/journal description.cws_home/503306/description#description). The International Society for Ecological Modeling (www.isemna.org) links researchers in this field. The WWW Server for Ecological Modeling provides a searchable database of different mathematical models (www.wiz.uni-kassel.de/ecobas.html) and includes links to other modeling resources here: www.wiz.uni-kassel.de/mod-info/all.html. The National Center for Environmental Economics of the U.S. EPA (http://yosemite .epa.gov/ee/epa/eed.nsf/pages/homepage) also provides research and data on economy, environmental health, and environmental pollution. The National Bureau of Economic Research maintains a program (www.nber.org/programs/eee/eee.html) and working group (www.nber.org/workinggroups/ee/ee.html) dedicated to environment and energy economics. Additional environmental economic resources can be found at the Association of Environmental and Resource Economists (www.aere.org), particularly the *Journal of Environmental and Economics Management* (www.aere.org/journal/index.html). The book *Environmental Economics: An Elementary Introduction* by Turner et al. (1993) describes the relationship between economics and environmental policy. The International Association for the Study of the Commons (www.iascp.org) unites researchers studying resources that are collectively held or used. Also see the new journal *Review of Environmental Economics and Policy* (reep.oxfordjournals.org) and the new book *Ecological Modeling: A Commonsense Approach to Theory and Practice* by Grant and Swannack (in press), as well as *The Commons in the New Millennium: Challenges and Adaptation* edited by Dolsak and Ostrom (2003).

Several books and websites provide background on GIS and remote sensing technology, including detailed descriptions of the various satellite sensors currently in use. Excellent textbooks on GIS and remote sensing include *Getting Started with Geographic Information Systems* by Clarke (2001), *Remote Sensing and Image Interpretation* by Lillesand et al. (2004), and *Fundamentals of Remote Sensing and Airphoto Interpretation* by Avery and Berlin (1992). The U.S. government provides a detailed description of GPS technology (www.gps.gov), while both ESRI and the U.S. Geological Survey (USGS) describe the functions and uses of a GIS (www.gis.com, http://erg.usgs.gov/isb/pubs/gis_poster, respectively). A detailed online tutorial about remote sensing is available from NASA (http://rst.gsfc.nasa.gov). The European Space Agency (ESA) maintains a detailed overview of several satellite platforms and missions (http://earth.esa.int/missions), while more information on other satellite platforms and missions can be found at the following websites on the Landsat (http://landsat.gsfc.nasa.gov/), AVHRR (http://noaasis.noaa.gov/NOAASIS/ml/ avhrr.html), SPOT (www.spot.com), and MODIS (http://modis.gsfc.nasa.gov) platforms, higher-resolution satellite sensors, including the IKONOS (www.geoeye.com)

and Quickbird (www.digitalglobe.com) satellite systems, and the hyperspectral Airborne Visible/Infrared Imaging Spectrometer (AVIRIS) (http://aviris.jpl.nasa.gov/). Other remote sensing systems include radar (http://srtm.usgs.gov, http://southport.jpl.nasa.gov/) and lidar (http://lidar.cr.usgs.gov, www.ghcc.msfc.nasa.gov/sparcle/sparcle_tutorial.html) imaging for topography and other remote sensing measures.

Many governmental and nongovernmental websites provide GIS and remote sensing data to the public that cover a diverse range of subject matter, including websites from the U.S. Fish and Wildlife Service (www.fws.gov/data), the USGS (http://gisdata.usgs.gov/, www.usgs.gov/ngpo, http://waterdata.usgs.gov/nwis, www.usgs.gov/pubprod, http://library.usgs.gov), the U.S. Department of Agriculture (http://datagateway.nrcs.usda.gov), and the U.S. Census Bureau (www.census.gov/geo/www/cob/index.html). The GIS Data Depot provides GIS data sets for a small fee (http://data.geocomm.com). The U.S. Federal Geographic Data Committee Clearinghouse (www.fgdc.gov) coordinates data sharing and provides comprehensive standardization of GIS data for U.S. government GIS data (available at http://geodata.gov). The NASA Earth Observing System (EOS) Data Gateway (http://redhook.gsfc.nasa.gov/~imswww/pub/imswelcome) provides remote sensing data from a variety of satellite sensors, including MODIS and AVHRR. Landsat data can be searched and purchased through the USGS global visualization viewer (http://glovis.usgs.gov) and shared and acquired from the Global Observatory for Ecosystem Services at Michigan State University (www.landsat.org). The USGS Earth Resources Observation and Science (EROS) (http://edc.usgs.gov/index.html) also is an excellent resource for spatial data. Additionally, ESRI provides web-based geographic information at the Geography Network (www.geographynetwork.com). Spatial social data is available at the Socioeconomic Data and Applications Center at Columbia University (http://sedac.ciesin.org). Detailed GIS and spatial information is also available from many state and local government agencies. Data on climate change scenarios is available from the Intergovernmental Panel on Climate Change (IPCC) Data Distribution Center (www.ipcc-data.org) and the National Center for Atmospheric Research–Geographic Information Systems Initiative–GIS Climate Change Scenarios (www.gisclimatechange.org).

Popular GIS and remote sensing software include IDRISI from Clark Labs (www.clarklabs.org), ArcGIS from ESRI (www.esri.com), GRASS from the Geographic Resources Analysis Support System (http://grass.itc.it), ERDAS Imagine from Leica Geosystems (http://gis.leica-geosystems.com), Manifold Systems (www.manifold.net), MapInfo (www.mapinfo.com), and the Environment for Visualizing Images (ENVI) from ITT Visual Information Systems (www.ittvis.com).

Several centers and institutes utilize socioeconomic and demographic, institutional, and environmental spatial data in their research and analyses, including the Center for the Study of Institutions, Populations, and Environmental Change at Indiana University (www.cipec.org), the Anthropological Center for Training and Research on Global Environmental Change at Indiana University (www.indiana

.edu/~act), the Center for Spatially Integrated Social Science at the University of California-Santa Barbara (www.csiss.org), and the National Center for Geographic Information and Analysis (www.ncgia.ucsb.edu).

Various national and international programs have provided funding and research on land use/land cover and climate change, including the U.S. Climate Change Science Program (www.climatescience.gov), the IPCC (www.ipcc.ch), NASA's Land-Cover and Land-Use Change Program (http://lcluc.umd.ed/), the U.S. Global Change Research Program–Land Use/Land Cover Change Program (www.usgcrp .gov/usgcrp/ProgramElements/land.htm), the National Science Foundation (NSF) Directorate for Social, Behavioral, and Economic Science (SBE) (www.nsf.gov/ dir/index.jsp?org=SBE), the NSF funding competition for Biocomplexity in the Environment (www.nsf.gov/geo/ere/ereweb/fund-biocomplex.cfm), and the NSF program on Human and Social Dynamics (HSD) (www.nsf.gov/news/priority_areas/ humansocial/index.jsp). The Forum of Science and Innovation for Sustainable Development also lists various research opportunities and results from environmental change and spatial analyses (www.sustainabilityscience.org).

NOTES

1. A center for advancing the development of spatially explicit social science was funded in 1999 by the National Science Foundation and is located at the University of California located at Santa Barbara (www.ncgia@ncgia.ucsb.edu/CISS).

2. I am grateful to Eduardo Brondizio for his substantial contribution to this discussion, based on two joint papers (Moran and Brondizio 1998, 2001).

PART

TWO

STUDIES OF
HUMAN ADAPTABILITY

Photo by Kenny Viese
Source: iStockphoto

5

HUMAN ADAPTABILITY
TO ARCTIC ZONES

The study of human adaptation to arctic conditions has engaged scholars in many fields since the late nineteenth century, but it is only since the 1950s that we can speak of a distinct field of arctic human ecology (Krupnick 1993:12). The field has advanced since then through important syntheses (Nuttall and Callaghan 2000; Hessen 2002; Hassol 2004; Stern and Stevenson 2006) and growing research support at places like the National Science Foundation Organization of Arctic Sciences and the NSF Office of Polar Programs (OPP). In this chapter we will focus on the problems posed by the arctic environment of northern Alaska and on the adaptation strategies used by the Inuit population. (The term Inuit, "the people," is preferred by the native peoples over "Eskimo" and will be used throughout this discussion.) Their adaptative strategies have changed as a result of the exploitation of petroleum, contact with American society, and biophysical changes taking place in the arctic as a product of global warming and other global climate changes, which appear to affect the arctic earlier and harder than elsewhere (Overpeck et al. 1997).

Contemporary climate changes are making a dramatic impact on arctic ecosystems (Chapin et al. 2000), particularly a warming trend that is expected to change the freshwater balance in the Arctic Ocean—with all the dangers this carries for launching the planet into another glacial period (McGuire et al. 2006; Berner et al. 2005). The signature species for the new challenge of climate change is the polar bear, which lives throughout the ice-covered waters of the circumpolar arctic—the area most likely to be altered by global warming. Given the rapid pace of these changes, polar bears will be threatened as a species if sea ice disappears (Derocher et al. 2004). Marine birds are also diagnostic of these changes (Mallory et al. 2006) because they feed at the top of the arctic food chain. While the discussion in the chapter focuses on the Inuit, it will refer to other arctic populations for the sake of comparison and to enrich the perspective of human adaptability to cold environments.

Human populations inhabiting these regions must cope with extreme cold, low biological productivity of the terrestrial ecosystem, periods of prolonged light and darkness, and the dangers of working on snow and ice. Housing and shelter provide regulatory adjustments to cold stress, while acclimatory and developmental adjustments protect human extremities from damage during hunting activities. Particularly significant in such protection are a high rate of peripheral blood flow to the extremities, rapid warming of the body, and nonshivering forms of heat production. Their chief adaptive strategy, however, has always been a dynamic and flexible use of the environment. Climate change today makes this flexibility more important than ever, and the capacity for learning and self-organization of local populations is required to survive (Berkes and Jolly 2002; Ford et al. 2006).

The low biological productivity of the tundra made the Inuit turn to ocean resources, enriched by **upwelling,** and to animals that migrate between the arctic tundra and the subarctic taiga. Flexible forms of social organization extended the network of individual households through noncousin marriage, adoption, spouse exchange, and meat-sharing partnerships. Hunters were taught animal **ethology** that gave them skills in observing, stalking, and killing game. Inuit animistic religion helped reduce anxiety during winter, and the feasts that accompanied religious rituals served to reduce hostilities and provide an artificial schedule during the perpetual darkness of winter, as well as socialization opportunities. The following section will describe some of the characteristics of the environment in which the Inuit must cope.

THE ARCTIC ECOSYSTEM

Arctic ecosystems probably go back to mid- to late Pleistocene times. The flora and fauna of the arctic probably evolved in highland areas of central Asia and the Rocky Mountains and then colonized the tundra (Bliss et al. 1973:360). Throughout the many climatic fluctuations of the past 150,000 years, arctic ecosystems and biota in the most recent 10,000 years (Callaghan et al. 2004) have suffered repeated losses of diversity as a result of extinctions during the rapid global warming at the end of the last glacial stage (Callaghan et al. 2004). Thus they are particularly vulnerable to contemporary rapid global warming. Terrestrial ecosystem models and satellite records yield a strong trend toward thawing earlier by five to eight days between 1988 and 2000, reduction in soil carbon, increases in vegetation, and loss of permafrost (Euskirchen et al. 2006).

The tundra is the northernmost frontier of vegetation. The landscape is treeless and the temperatures bitterly cold. Summers are cool and short, but summer days are long. The vegetation resembles that of the high mountain Alps, the area between the tree line and permanent snow. The situation is even harsher in the antarctic. The continent covers 14.24 million square kilometers of which only 10,350 square kilometers are estimated to be suitable for sustaining life. The largest permanent inhabi-

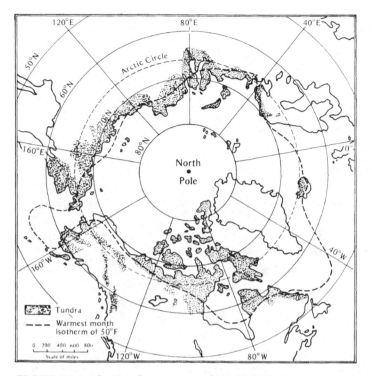

FIGURE 5.1 The Tundra Areas and the 50°F Isotherm

tant is a tiny fly. There are no land vertebrates, no birds, no amphibians, no reptiles, no freshwater fish, no mollusks, and no earthworms; only lichens, mosses, and fungi in protected coastal areas (Natani and Shurley 1974:90–91). This discussion will therefore focus on the arctic. The boundary of the arctic varies with the discipline studying it. Botanists use the forest boundary, whereas climatologists use the annual mean temperature of the warmest month, soil scientists use the area in permafrost, and so on (Remmert 1980; Virtanen et al. 2004). With arctic warming of 3°C expected no later than the end of the twenty-first century, temperature will not limit the advance of forests into the tundra; the greatest limiting factor has been permafrost, which is rapidly disappearing.

Despite these differences, and because the most severe constraint in this ecosystem is extreme cold, summer temperatures are used to define tundra ecosystems. The definition most commonly used is Koppen's boundary line of the 50°F (10°C) isotherm for the warmest month of the year (see Figure 5.1). However, other factors besides actual temperature are involved in the formation of tundra. Throughout the arctic, tundra vegetation can be found south of the 50°F July isotherm (J. R. Mackay 1969:327). Wind is an important factor because of the absence of trees, but topographic gradients can be important (Ostendorf and Reynolds 1998). At ground level the wind can rapidly produce dehydration and frostbite.

The tundra-taiga ecotone is the world's largest, stretching over 13,400 kilometers (Ranson et al. 2004), and changes can be studied by use of multisensor satellite data. Like other biomes, the tundra is not wholly undifferentiated. From the margins of the subarctic boreal coniferous forest, or **taiga,** to the polar desert at least four types of tundra vegetation can be noted. Forest tundra characterized by dwarf trees, low- and tall-shrub tundra grades off into the broader expanse of grass tundra (both cottongrass-tussock and sedge-moss meadow tundra) composed of a nearly continuous mat of mosses, lichens, and bushes that tend to lie prone on the ground. The vegetation rarely exceeds knee height (Bliss et al. 1980). Areas of little or no vegetation are referred to as polar deserts (Bliss et al. 1994; Tedrow 2004). When the soil surface thaws out in summer, the water does not drain but is absorbed by the spongy vegetation. The depth of thawing may vary from a few inches to about two feet. Below this, the ground remains frozen and impermeable to both water and plant roots (R. L. Smith 1974:578). Most of our knowledge of how the arctic will respond to global warming comes from experiments conducted during the arctic summer. This limits predictions on the impact of global change, since recent studies show that arctic ecosystems are not dormant during the winter (Phoenix and Lee 2004).

Tundra soils may contain high accumulations of peaty organic matter caused by the slow decomposition of plant material (Tedrow 1977). Boreal peatlands, impressive accumulators of carbon over millennia, are now under threat from wildfires, climate change, and other sources (Wieder and Vitt 2006). Tundra gley soils developed under strongly hydromorphic conditions and occupy considerable areas of the Russian arctic (Fominykh and Zolotareva 2004). Contemporary ecological analysis is trying to assess the implications of global warming on the arctic and the biosphere. Longer thaw periods are likely to release the sequestered carbon in peat to the atmosphere, exacerbating carbon dioxide accumulation. However, this warming may lead to longer growing periods in which vegetation sequesters atmospheric carbon (Jones et al. 1998). Recent manipulation of nonacidic tundra with nitrogen and phosphorus did not increase, but in acid tundra biomass did increase (Gough and Hobbie 2003). The net outcome of these processes remains uncertain despite a growing number of studies (Callaghan and Maxwell 1995; Wadhams et al. 1996; Rath 1998; Chapin 1992; NRC 1997b, 1989; NSF 1997; Henry and Molau 1997; Smedberg et al. 2006).

Tundra occupies about 8 million square kilometers of land or one-twentieth of the earth's land surface (Webber 1974). It is sparsely populated, between .02 and .08 persons per square kilometer, except near petroleum exploitation areas and developed cities. The largest groups of Eurasian people who inhabit the arctic include the Lapps, Samoyeds, Yakuty, and Chukchi (Irving 1972:23; Krupnick 1993). Studies of Inuit groups by R. F. Spencer (1959) and Oswalt (1967) emphasized cultural distinctions in Inuit lifestyles that result from ecological adjustments to either coastal or inland resources. The synthesis by Krupnick (1993) provides a nuanced interpretation that privileges the Eurasian materials but also includes insightful comparisons between North American and Eurasian populations. This analysis provides a more nuanced picture of the tremendous flexibility in adaptive strategies evident in arctic populations, from nomadic to sedentary, from coastal to inland, from herding to hunting.

R. F. Spencer (1959) divided the Inuit populations into *nuunamiut* (people of the land) and *tareumiut* (people of the sea) in accordance with the predominant subsistence strategy. Each group practiced a well-defined strategy consonant with the resources available in their respective environments. These groupings are paralleled in the contrast between the maritime and reindeer Chukchi (Spencer 1959:126). The *nuunamiut* and *tareumiut* were economically interdependent, but they avoided intermarriage and quasi-kin ties. The distinctiveness of the two groups was reinforced by differing skills that made marriage between them impractical. Other ethnographers have noted this tendency toward endogamy (Campbell 1968) resulting from the specialization required to exploit their respective resources (Burch and Correll 1972:24). Among the coastal population the village was a stable unit because of the resident whaling crews. The caribou hunts of the inland Inuit never played this sort of stabilizing role.

The inland adaptation, based on caribou hunting, ended once in the 1920s and again in the 1950s. In the 1920s the outmigration was caused by shifts in caribou migratory routes, whereas in the 1950s new weapons and overhunting reduced the size of the herds so that they could no longer sustain the human population (Spencer 1959:28; Gubser 1965; Shelford 1963). Since then, inland Inuit have joined the maritime Inuit in a few large coastal villages (Jamison 1978; Arima 1975:175). In some areas, caribou populations have rebounded and provide new opportunities to appreciate the superb environmental knowledge of the Inuit, who recognize the cyclical nature of caribou population fluctuations (Ferguson et al. 1998) and distinguish between resident caribou populations and migratory herds, each of which has distinct seasonal patterns of availability.

Paleoindians occupied areas of the arctic foothills as far back as 10,300 BP (before the present). Mann and colleagues (2001) suggest that Paleoindians moved into arctic Alaska to exploit large ungulates. Environmental changes, particularly rising sea levels during the Early Holocene, caused summer temperatures to fall and precipitation to increase, resulting in a more stable climate and the spread of tussock-tundra vegetation; both the ungulates and Paleoindians left the region (Mann et al. 2001). The rate of contemporary environmental change, however, dwarfs the experience of that period (S. E. Lee et al. 2000; Kister 2005).

Tundra ecosystems are heat limited (Bliss et al. 1973), which results in low species diversity, low productivity, and a largely insignificant plant **succession.** The short growing season in the arctic inhibits levels of production capable of supporting a large herbivorous population. Mosses yield the highest proportion of total phytomass, followed by phanerogams and lichens (Matveyeva et al. 1975:67). Tundra and desert ecosystems share similar problems; the crucial difference is that one ecosystem is limited by water availability, the other by extreme cold.

Plants have numerous physiological adaptations to cope with arctic conditions: prolonged seed dormancy and rapid germination, vegetative reproduction and metabolic systems able to capture, store, and use energy in a short time (Billings 1974:417). Nitrogen uptake, among others, is limited by temperature, with little limitation in uptake at 15°C, whereas at 6°C net nitrogen uptake is severely reduced (Volder et al. 2000). A large proportion of the plant biomass is below ground, protected from arctic wind, cold, and herbivore pressure (Webber 1974:457).

The environment has been described as fragile because it is biologically simple and because of the long time lapse required for its return to steady state. Damage to tundra vegetation by tracked vehicles alters plant cover and reduces both surface insulation and **albedo.** As a result, more heat is absorbed, which leads to deeper thawing and greater erosion (Webber 1974:465). Erosion is difficult to control because of the slowness of plant succession. Once an eroded niche becomes empty, there are few species than can occupy it. This is a result of the low species diversity (Bliss et al. 1973:360–361). Arctic soils are of recent origin and tend to be **hydromorphic.** Most of the soil nutrients are not available to plants because of permafrost. To survive, therefore, plants use complex internal cycles that retain and reincorporate nutrients rather than relinquishing them to the decomposers. Phosphorus appears to be a limiting factor to arctic plants' productivity (Bunnell et al. 1975:117), as is nitrogen and potassium (J. Brown et al. 1980:165–168). Moist acidic tundra is primarily nitrogen limited, whereas wet sedge tundra is primarily phosphorus limited (Gough and Hobbie 2003).

Many of the land animals, such as reindeer in Eurasia and caribou in North America, migrate over vast expanses of tundra territory in summer and exploit the richer boreal forests to the south (that is, the taiga). Caribou and reindeer are essential resources to the inland arctic populations, as documented by Gubser (1965), Balikci (1970), and Arima (1975). The musk ox was once important but has been brought to near extinction. Reindeer herding is the only other effective way of supporting human populations in the inland tundra areas (Kallio 1975:219; Pelto 1973; Ingold 1974; Müller-Wille 1974).

Smaller fauna are found in greater densities.[1] Insects are restricted to a few genera but are abundant in midsummer. Black flies, deerflies, and mosquitoes are so numerous that many Inuit must keep their bodies covered, despite the pleasant temperatures. Arctic birds have a short life cycle, similar to that of rodents. The ptarmigan and the redpoll have thick fat layers and dense feathers for protection against cold. Ducks and geese are also important resources to the Inuit. Most bird and insect species, however, leave the tundra for more southern regions as winter approaches (R. L. Smith 1974:587).

FIGURE 5.2 Umiak Whale Hunting
Photo by R. Meier

The Arctic Ocean on a volume basis has the highest terrestrial input in terms of freshwater and organic matter, and the arctic drainage areas contain more than half of the organic carbon stored globally in soils (Dittmar and Kattner 2003). The total amount of dissolved organic carbon discharged by rivers into the Arctic Ocean is similar to that of the Amazon (18–26x10 to the 12th g C per year). Moreover, research shows that the Arctic Ocean has active carbon cycling and plays an important part in the global carbon cycle (Chen et al. 2002). This makes the Arctic Ocean an important sink for soil carbon, and explains why the ocean fauna is so rich and productive (compare Royer and Grosch 2006 for a discussion of impacts in the northern Pacific, Bering Sea, and other high latitude oceans).

Ocean fauna has always been more important to the arctic human population than land fauna. Ringed seals (*Phoca foerida*), barbed seals *(Erignathus barbatus),* walruses *(Odobenus),* whales (especially beluga, bowhead, white, and fin types; Huntington 1999; Mymrin and Huntington 1999; Furgal et al. 2002 and Figure 5.2), and fish and shellfish varieties are among the most important maritime resources exploited. Other seals, such as the spotted seal *(Phoca vitulina),* the bladdernose

(Cystophora cristata), saddleback *(Phoca groenlandica),* fur seal *(Arctocephalus ursinus),* sea lion *(Eumetopias jubatus),* and ribbon seal *(Histriophoca fasciata),* avoid firm ice and are less available in winter to Inuit hunters. Seals provide many raw materials that make Inuit cold adaptation possible, such as mittens, boots, summer coats, trousers, and sinew thread. Breaking through the roof of a lair of ringed seals was observed to be the most common hunting technique used by Inuit in Nunavut (Furgal et al. 2002). They are the most important animal used by Arctic Bay Inuit. The hunt for seals is surrounded by myths, legends, rituals, and traditions that reflect their importance (Pelly 2001).

Smaller animals also play an important ecosystemic role. For example, the brown lemming *(Lemmus sibericus)* is the dominant herbivore of the arctic. Unlike animals that leave the tundra seasonally, the lemming is active year-round. Researchers have noted that lemming densities vary in cycles of three to five years. Its boom-and-bust population cycles mark significant cycles in standing crops, soil temperatures, depth of thaw, and rates of organic decomposition (Bunnell et al. 1975:95). Numbers decline in summer as a result of predation but steadily increase over time until overgrazing and natural increases in the predator population bring on a sudden decline (Angerbjoern et al. 1999). Following a population crash, lemmings and their predators remain at low densities, thus permitting a recovery in tundra vegetation.

The spatial distribution of nutrients can be altered by the grazing habits and consequent fecal deposition of lemmings. During the yearly melt-off, they facilitate a flush of nutrients that tends to collect in crevices and ponds. The feedback of nutrients from the lemming population to the soil and to plant components is crucial to the system's productivity. Even though this flow is determined by the timing of the thaw, coastal Inuit rely for up to 83 percent of subsistence on marine and freshwater aquatic resources, rather than on terrestrial production. The inland Inuit population relies on a more evenly balanced seasonal exploitation of both aquatic and terrestrial animals.

ADAPTATION TO COLD STRESS

Inuit adaptive strategies for coping with cold stress involve both physiological and cultural adjustments. For a while the Inuit were thought to have unique genetic adaptations that facilitated cold adaptation. One common misconception was that they had a great deal of body fat when in reality they were relatively lean in the past (Laughlin 1966). Other factors often cited as morphological adaptations to cold stress were eyefold characteristics and facial flatness. But these morphological characteristics were shown to offer little protection (Steegman 1967, 1970). Laughlin noted that the frequent use of slit goggles and visors during travel demonstrates the inadequacy of Inuit morphological characteristics (Laughlin 1966:476).

Inadequate protection from cold stress can result in cold injury, frostbite, **hypothermia,** and eventually death (Carlson and Hsieh 1965:16). (The thermoregulatory system fails when body core temperature is near 33°C, and death occurs at 25°C.) Among the cultural practices that facilitate Inuit adaptation to cold are clothes, shelter, seal oil lamps, and the sharing of body heat and diet. Recent writings have described the exposure of the Inuit to the arctic cold as chronic but moderate. In fact, the **microclimate** of men in arctic clothing was found to be the same as that of men working in temperate zones with light clothing.

Cultural Regulatory Adjustments

Insulation is an important way of preventing cold stress. The insulation problem is dual: how to provide for continued warmth and how to prevent overheating during periods of strenuous work. Sweat-soaked or frozen clothing loses its cold protection effectiveness. Irving (1972:181) described how the Inuit hang their clothes so the moisture will freeze and then beat out the frost with a stick. Eventually they must scrape the leather to restore its pliability.

Two methods are commonly used to prevent overheating. In summer when the Inuit do heavy work, they remove their impermeable outer parkas and remain relatively cool in the outside temperature. The more important method, however, is the design of Inuit clothing. The traditional clothing of the arctic has many vented openings through which air constantly flows in and out. Figure 5.3 illustrates some of the venting areas of arctic fur clothing, which can be released or closed by drawstrings (Folk 1966:123). This is one way the traditional Inuit adapted their clothing to ambient conditions. The other is that the clothing has numerous layers that trap and warm the air and act as an insulator. Because the outside layer is windproof and impermeable, the clothing holds the heat in and keeps cold and moisture out (Edholm and Lewis 1964:436). Because of the difficulty of matching activity and weather to clothing while on the move, they commonly tolerated moderate degrees of thermal discomfort (Budd 1974:33–34). They dressed too warmly and consequently tolerated sweating during work periods and shivering during rest periods. Some of these adaptations have gradually eroded among Inuit populations, as many now purchase commercial parkas made from nylon and other fabrics. This has gone along with greater dependence on overheated housing and reduced exposure to the elements through reduced subsistence hunting and long-distance migrations.

Traditional seal boots *(kimik)* called for special attention, since the sharp ice at subzero temperatures can cut the best footgear. Traditionally the soles were made of carefully prepared bearded sealskin, while the uppers were made from split ringed sealskin. They were sewn with sinew, but taking care that needle holes did not go all the way through the skin layers to ensure waterproofness. Stockings were made from the fragile fur of the arctic hare and were kept dry by inserting a pad of dry grass between the sole of the boot and the sole of the stocking. This pad absorbed moisture from outside or from foot perspiration (Ekblaw 1927:181–182). Similarly, sealskin mittens were filled with grass pads to protect the hands on long trips. Traditional

FIGURE 5.3 The Chimney Effect in Inuit Fur Clothing

Vents in clothing can be opened by releasing drawstrings during exercise to allow sweat to evaporate.

boots have given way to commercial rubber and leather boots in recent years among the majority of Inuit.

Like clothing, Inuit shelters must hold in heat and keep out wind. Cold-adapted housing includes compact design, minimal exposure to external surface areas, use of insulating materials, and reflecting heat from internal heat sources (for example, lamps, stoves, and body heat) (Rapoport 1969:95). While pursuing a nomadic subsistence, Inuit traditionally built snow shelters (igloos). They have been described as excellent insulators by virtue of myriad small air cells in the ice. The igloo offers minimal wind resistance, provides maximum volume with the least surface area, and is effectively heated by a seal oil lamp, which also provides interior light. The heat of the lamp causes minor melting of the inside snow surfaces, which refreeze during the night and form a smooth reflecting surface that conserves radiant heat. The outside surface becomes encrusted with snow and forms an airtight seal.

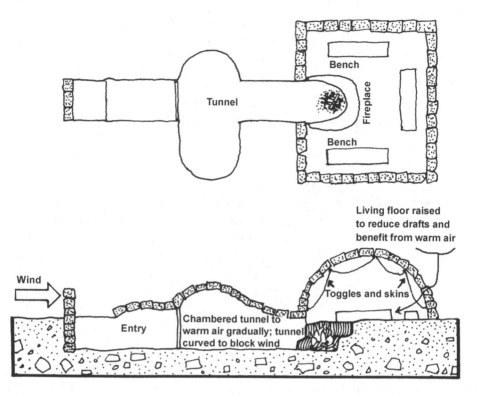

FIGURE 5.4 Features of Inuit Housing

Three architectural features are particularly significant: the presence or absence of a fireplace, the positioning of benches, and the depth of the tunnel doorway. Fireplaces were associated with availability of wood in winter. If the tunnels were not subterranean, floor temperatures could drop below freezing. *Source*: A. Rapoport, *House Form and Culture* (Englewood Cliffs, NJ: Prentice-Hall).

In summer people lived in sealskin tents. Made of dark-colored skins to absorb solar energy, they are double-layered and provide a comfortable temperature during warmer periods (Edholm and Lewis 1964:436). The sealskin tent is made of many skins sewn into a continuous cover. Large tents require more than sixty skins. An inner tent and outer tent create an area of dead air that facilitates warming during cold periods but can be opened during the summer months (Ekblaw 1927:161).

Northern Alaska Inuit also built houses from semisubterranean stone or driftwood, covered with turf and snow for insulation. They were frequently located in protected hillside spots. These houses consisted of walls five feet in height, with narrow underground entrances and with the living area at a higher level than the entry (see Figure 5.4). Like Inuit clothing, these houses had ventilation holes to allow circulation and prevent overheating. The interiors were covered in sealskins. Thus constructed, the subterranean winter home kept temperatures between 15.5°C and 21°C (Ekblaw 1927:169). (The Yakuty of Siberia used a timber frame covered with wood and a heavy layer of sod [Rapoport 1969:96].)

The traditional Inuit diet was high in fat, protein, and calories. To keep warm and to carry out strenuous activities, such as sledding, a man required approximately 5,000 calories daily (Edholm and Lewis 1964:44). Body weight and subcutaneous fat rise in winter and decrease in spring and summer. This may be a biological rhythm that enhances adaptability to cold, as well as the result of the relative inactivity of winter (Edholm and Lewis 1964:441).

A study of the diet of Inuit women noted that older Inuit rely more heavily on a traditional diet than younger women do, and that market food contributes more calories. But a large percentage of protein and important nutrients such as vitamin D, iron, phosphorus, and zinc come from the traditional diet (Blanchet et al. 2000). The traditional diet was low in calcium and vitamin A, and the market diet seems to have increased this deficiency among younger women. With the westernization of diet, the number of overweight Inuit, particularly males, has increased. Interestingly, the number of slim women doubled between 1963 and 1998, as did the number of overweight women, according to a comprehensive study of Inuit in Greenland (Andersen et al. 2004). Traditional food is consumed with greater frequency among older Inuit, most frequently seal meat (Pars et al. 2001), but the declining consumption among younger Inuit results raises concerns with the future nutritional status of the Inuit (Pars et al. 2001). A deficiency in vitamin D (Rejnmark et al. 2004) and increased lipid levels (Bjerregaard et al. 2004; Deutch et al. 2004) are potential hazards.

Physiological Adjustments

Although clothing and shelter can provide warm microclimates, the Inuit are exposed to extreme cold during winter seal hunting and ice fishing. To maintain body core temperatures within a permissible range, a number of physiological responses may come into play (see Figure 5.5), including shivering, vasoconstriction, increase of basal metabolic rates (BMR) and oxygen consumption, acclimatizational changes, and behavioral responses (Van Wie 1974:815). In addition, exposure to cold increases blood pressure (Leppaeluoto and Hassi 1991) but may have the secondary effect of contributing to greater mortality due to cardiovascular diseases and stroke observed during the prolonged winter season.

The most rapid and effective way to increase heat production is by vigorous exercise, but this response cannot be maintained for long periods of time (Hanna 1968:216–217). Shivering is a frequent response, which can increase heat production threefold, but it does not increase the total heat content of the body to any significant degree (Folk 1966:102). More useful and effective is the activation of

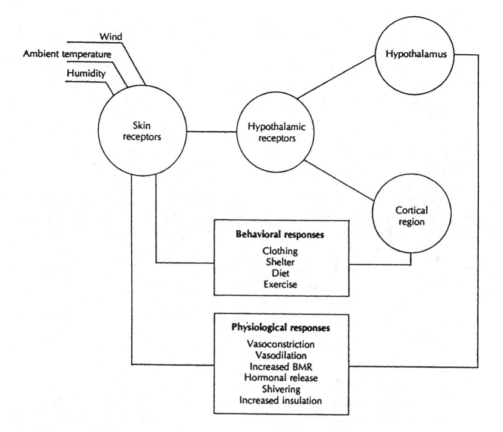

FIGURE 5.5 Cold Thermoregulation in Human Beings

Both behavioral and physiological responses are implicated in adaptation to cold and involve the hypothalamus and cortical parts of the brain responding to the skin receptors.

nonshivering thermogenesis. This chemical response refers to increases in cellular metabolism without any accompanying muscular movement. Adults are able to elevate metabolism 25 percent over basal levels, while infants are able to increase it by 170 percent over BMR (Little and Hochner 1973:6). Nonshivering thermogenesis is more effective than shivering since it is located in the body core rather than the skin surface. It is associated with the presence of brown adipose tissue in all human infants, and this response is apparently maintained in adults native to cold areas (Little and Hochner 1973:6–7). The nonshivering metabolism of all Inuit is 30–40 percent greater than in control groups (Folk 1966:110).

There is some evidence that Inuit exhibit a kind of metabolic acclimatization (Hammel 1964:425). Their 20 to 40 percent higher BMR reduces the risk of hypothermia, cold discomfort, and pain. It is still not clear whether this is a physiological response to cold or a result of their protein-rich diet (Hammel 1964:430–433); Edholm and Lewis (1964:444). In either case, the result is a slightly warmer core temperature. Recent studies of indigenous Siberians show a significant elevation in basal metabolism compared with reference values (Leonard et al. 2005). Thyroid hormones appear to play an important role in shaping metabolic processes among Siberians. Their adaptation is a combination of short-term acclimatization and genetic adaptations, not unlike that of the Inuit of Alaska and Greenland (Leonard et al. 2005).

Inuit have also been noted to have a high rate of peripheral blood flow to the extremities when exposed to cold. This has been demonstrated by high finger temperatures in cold water immersion tests (Hanna 1968:230). Warmer finger temperatures occur in persons habitually exposed to cold at the extremities, thereby preventing injury and allowing greater hand dexterity in cold environments (Hanna 1968:220). Harrison and colleagues (1977:429) have noted that this localized response is cyclical: intense vasoconstriction is followed five minutes later by vasodilation and then a return to vasoconstriction and so on. This response at the extremities prevents tissue temperature from dropping to frostbite levels.

The higher BMR of the Inuit is complemented by their ability to respond quickly to cold exposure, both in the extremities and throughout the body. This ability is the result of high core-to-shell conductance, or rapid response when exposure to cold occurs. This response is as much as 60 percent faster among Inuit than among white controls. The mechanism is commonly associated with a high rate of blood flow to the extremities. High heat conductivity, combined with high heat production, enables Inuit to temporarily expose body parts without experiencing frostbite (Hanna 1968:229–230). Although this type of response consumes a great deal of energy, this has not normally been a problem among the Inuit as their diet provides them with adequate calories.

In summary, then, although localized acclimatory adjustments to cold are noted in the extremities, the evidence does not suggest a general adaptation to cold by Inuit and other arctic natives.

COPING WITH SNOW AND SEA ICE

A great deal of Inuit ecological knowledge centers on identifying minute differences in ice and snow characteristics. Such knowledge is essential to survive in an environment where death from cold exposure can occur rapidly. Inuit children learn experimentally to identify these differences because of their survival value. Collier has described traditional Inuit education as nonverbal and ecological, facilitating weather prediction as well as recognition of blizzard warnings and migratory patterns of game (1973:39). Boas related sea ice conditions and the habits of ringed seals to the demographic distribution of central Inuit (1964:417).

Laughlin (1968a) viewed the training of a hunter as a biobehavioral system. Adult hunters program the child into habits of observation, systematic knowledge of animal behavior, and multiple uses of game. Because hunting cultures often endow animals with spirits or souls, the hunt may be regarded as hazardous. Thus the child is taught to have respect for hunting and for the prey, to scan, stalk, immobilize, retrieve, and share his fortune with others. Traditional Inuit hunters had to get close to their prey, and learning how to do this required a lengthy investment in childhood and young adult education. Adults would sometimes capture animals to use during instruction in animal habits and anatomy. Playacting and sportlike events included content valuable in the hunt (Chance 1966:74). Perseverance, toughness, and generosity were desirable traits (Nelson 1969:375–576). Generosity, particularly toward kin and meat-sharing nonrelatives, plays an important adaptive role in regions such as inland Alaska where resources are irregular in both quantity and quality. This has been noted to have evolutionary value among foragers (Winterhalder 1986).

Inuit on land must know the behavior of game, and on sea ice they must also know the behavior of the ice (Nelson 1969:9). Such knowledge comes slowly, mainly through the childhood **socialization** process described above. Inuit, for example, know that young salt ice (that is, the state of the ice in the autumn) is flexible rather than brittle. When sleds begin to sink, they know that it is best to keep the sled moving and "ride out" the thin ice spots. The Inuit use color as a distinguishing feature between different types of ocean ice. Unsafe thin ice tends to be dark. As it thickens it becomes gray, and from this point to darker color gradations, it is safe enough to support a man and a loaded dogsled (Nelson 1969:16). Color distinctions allow an Inuit to determine conditions ahead of time and lead his dogs appropriately. This method is said to be nearly 100 percent effective, although not infallible. For example, color of inland lagoons is deceptive as a result of suspended sediment.

The Inuit avoidance of risky situations and knowledge of ice serve them well, but accidents still occur. In the past, the Inuit were prepared for many types of emergencies on ice. Hunting partnerships helped provide protection and assistance in mishaps. The *unaok,* or ice probe, a long stick used to probe the ice thickness is used to avoid being swept by the current underneath the ice. Someone who did fall through the ice and got soaked would run back to the village. If the settlement was too far away, the hunting partners would lend the person items of clothing to wear until his soaked garments dried. Clothing made from fur and skins is relatively waterproof, and powdery snow can be used to blot the moisture before it soaks in and freezes (Nelson 1969:24–28). Today hunters on snowmobiles go farther out from settlements, travel at greater speeds, and have less ability to judge ice conditions. If hunting had continued at the same levels, dramatic increases in death by hypothermia from snowmobile accidents would have been expected. However, the decline of hunting for subsistence (and greater sedentarization) has prevented higher mortality rates from cold exposure.

Weather prediction is important and, at least in northwestern Alaska, relatively easy once the indicators are known. Changes in barometric pressure are reliable indicators in predicting winter storms. Strong winds are forecast by elongated clouds and by ice mirages resembling low clouds. Wind conditions may forecast the continuation or end of a storm. Subsiding winds indicate the storm is ending, while strong gusts followed by normal wind speeds suggest continuation. Dogs traditionally provided excellent weather forecasting. They howled more frequently right before winter storms and again before the storm ended. Today Inuit increasingly rely on radio broadcasts for weather forecasting (Nelson 1969:29–47).

In addition to possessing extensive knowledge of the environment, traditional Inuit were in good physical condition. When Shepard (1974) reviewed work performance among Inuit and Ainu populations, there appeared to be no appreciable differences between mean values for Inuit VO_2 max and those for other populations. However, Inuit performance, patience, experience, and skill in interpreting small signs were more important than a superior oxygen transport system (Rennie 1978). In recent years changes in lifestyle have resulted in a steady deconditioning in physical capacity. Young Inuit are less willing to face up to the rigors of the hunting way of life (Nelson 1969). Among the Canadian Inuit, there is a strong movement to incorporate Inuit *qaujimajatuqangit*—information on how Inuit conceptualize human-animal relations, how they use wildlife, and how they manage these resources (Wenzel 2004).

To cope with snow and ice cover, Inuit rely greatly on observation both to avoid unnecessary energy expenditures and to circumvent unnecessary dangers. Foresight is crucial to the Inuit and is evidenced by their unwillingness to travel onto sea ice in winter unless they have carefully excluded all potential signs that they might be set adrift on a loose floe. Nelson has noted that Inuit seldom act in the Western manner of doing something for the excitement of taking a chance (Nelson 1969:377). Instead, the Inuit carefully avoid percentage risks, even when the risk may be as low as 20 percent. Alertness is also valued. Seldom do they give their full attention to a single activity, but instead commonly glance around to survey their surroundings. Such alertness minimizes the danger of being carried away by floating ice, presents opportunities for hunting animals other than the one being stalked, and familiarizes each person with his surroundings. When crises arise, Inuit hunters exercise unusual experimentation. In one case noted by Nelson they constructed an emergency sled from pieces of frozen meat (Nelson 1969:378).

Cooperativeness in hunting also enhances the survival chances of the individual through pooling of physical effort and environmental knowledge. The Nelson Island Inuit continue to distribute meat during seal-hunting parties, despite its demise at other locations (Fienup-Riordan 1983). Laughter rather than anger was the typical reaction to a mistake, and this helped to alleviate the frustrations that occur frequently in an environment where so much can go wrong. Many of these traits have begun to disappear with the steady acculturation of the Inuit to Western culture.

ADAPTATION TO PROLONGED
LIGHT AND DARKNESS

Arctic populations are subject to fluctuating cycles of light and darkness in the spring and fall and to no cycling at all in midsummer and midwinter (Foulks 1972:83). Above the Arctic Circle daylight changes dramatically with the seasons. In late June the sun hovers around the horizon and does not set. By contrast, in late December the sun never comes above the horizon. This pattern is believed to have a negative effect on the well-being of populations. Human physiological functioning is, to an extent, regulated by the pattern of light and darkness in a twenty-four-hour period. Numerous physiological functions in human beings are known to vary according to a circadian rhythm synchronized to a twenty-four-hour scheme. Body temperature, blood pressure, pulse, respiration, blood sugar, hemoglobin levels, amino acid levels, levels of adrenal hormones, and levels of minerals excreted in the urine all follow a daily rhythm. The development of this pattern may be associated with human phylogenetic development in equatorial regions. When people move to arctic zones, which are subject to twenty-four hours of light in summer and twenty-four hours of darkness in winter, adjustments must be made. Antarctic psychological researchers have noted that insomnia, disrupted sleep, anxiety, depression, and irritability are common during winter. The problem, however, is believed to be largely social and related to prolonged confinement (Natani and Shurley 1974:92).

Physiological Disturbances

Bohlen and colleagues (1970) have shown that the extreme seasonal changes in light and dark seriously disturb Inuit physiological functioning. They found that body temperature and urinary potassium excretion maintain twenty-four-hour rhythms, but that urinary excretion of calcium leads to mild anxiety and depression. In individuals who are predisposed to anxiety, this phenomenon can precipitate behavior characteristic of arctic hysteria, or *pibloktok*. Arctic hysteria is a temporary mental disorder characterized by alterations in consciousness, memory loss, psychomotor seizures, and other symptoms typical of epilepsy. Arctic hysteria encompasses two general types of behavior: imitative mania and frenzied disassociated states. The former is confined to Siberia, while the latter is found throughout the arctic. A role model for the frenzied behavior manifested in arctic hysteria is said to be shamanistic spirit possession (Foulks 1972).

Cases of arctic hysteria have been noted for as long as outsiders have had contact with Inuit populations. They were said to be more frequent among women than men, but no one ever gave the matter sufficient attention to permit any assertions on the subject (Foulks 1972:17). Nachman suggests that such attacks may have served as social expressions of role demands (1969:7–11). He explains that for women the attacks might provide an opportunity to acknowledge sexual threats and temptations normally not permitted. By the same token, men might be able to express fears about their inability to fulfill the responsibilities of married life. Gussow (1960) argues that arctic hysteria was a basic way in which the Inuit reacted to intense stress. Such stress may have been associated with dwindling winter food supplies. Wallace (1956) has suggested that numerous factors were probably implicated: shamanistic outlets for hostility, hypocalcemic levels resulting from low calcium levels and low vitamin D synthesis during winter darkness, and anxiety over subsistence. Landy (1985) implicates vitamin A, which can reach toxic levels in cases of arctic hysteria. A study of seasonal affective disorder among Inuit found that older people were more affected by this but found no significant differences in gender (Haggarty et al. 2002).

Religion as a Regulatory Adjustment

The stress that is implicated in arctic hysteria was relieved through religious practices. Inuit religion was essentially animistic, with animals, the moon, and other environmental features being imbued with supernatural will and power. Religion sought to create a meaningful and peaceful relationship between Inuit and game animals through taboos, ceremonies, and practices that prevented excess slaughter of animals, provided release from tensions, and defined human roles and actions (Martin 1976:18).

Inuit groups regulated the use of animals and the distribution of game and defined hunters' obligations through religious taboos. Rituals centered on economically important animals and their spirits. The corpses of animals and human beings received similar treatment (Weyer 1932:336), and animals, like people, were divided along inland/maritime lines. Sea and land animals were said to be displeased at contact with each other. Rituals helped ensure that the spirits of the animals killed would return in new bodies to offer themselves again to the hunter. However, the Inuit believed that if a hunter killed too many animals, the animal spirits would withdraw.

Religion also helped the Inuit explain bad weather or reduced game supply (Chance 1966:35). Personal guilt and misfortune could be attributed to the machinations of angry spirits, thus reducing personal anxiety (Weyer 1932:231). Taboos helped regulate the time for making new clothes and establishing social priorities. They may also have helped to establish a **circannual rhythm** that could have alleviated the disturbances caused by the light-dark arctic pattern.

The shaman played a crucial role in regulating social activity. A shaman who could forecast the weather, help cure the ill, bring good luck to hunters, and make game receptive to hunters could achieve respect and wealth. However, if his powers failed to improve the group's life chances, he might be deposed or killed (Weyer 1932:451–452). The group, then, selected individuals who manifested skills in forecasting crucial factors involved in survival and could educate the population into the behavior required for well-being.

One means of coping with winter stress is to hold ceremonial feasts where foods and other goods are distributed to the less fortunate in the group. The bladder festival held in west central and southwestern Alaska ensured that the bladders of the animals caught in the past year would return to the animals and enhance future hunting chances. Shamanistic seances, the mimicking of hunting dramas, and purifications were also a part of the ceremonies. The poor and the elderly received special treatment, as well as a substantial portion of the food and goods distributed (Lantis 1947:60–62).

Ceremonies that provided relief from sexual tension were also common. The Inglalik feast for the dead and the western Alaskan asking feast included exchange of favors and sex and ritual exchanges of male and female roles and dress (Lantis 1947:74). Although their purpose was to stimulate animal reproduction and enhance hunters' chances in the next season, they probably also helped to relieve social and psychological tension (Martin 1976:36). The messenger feast was a high point of winter and served to facilitate social and economic exchange (Spencer 1959:216–228). It manifested numerous similarities to the potlatches of the Northwest Coast.

Changes in Regimentation and Diet

Western regimentation and diet have facilitated Inuit adaptation to patterns of light and dark. The Inuit have acquired watches, and schools have adopted scheduling that socializes children into a twenty-four-hour rhythm. The introduction of milk products into their diet has enhanced the calcium levels of the Inuit and facilitated calcium homeostasis (compare Andersen et al. 2004 for a discussion of Inuit in Greenland and the impact of westernization on their weight and nutrient intake). The adoption of wage labor requires being at work at set times, often according to a schedule more appropriate to New York than the arctic. These socially prescribed schedules have improved some aspects of Inuit physiological performance. One notable change has been a transformation from strong seasonality in births to the current lack of seasonality, which has been interpreted as a result of social change processes such as the end of subsistence-based hunting economy, wage employment, and sedentarization (Condon 1991). However, not all the changes have been for the better. Concentration in villages has led to abandonment of traditional housing and adoption of less healthy shelters. Instead of the sod and snow igloos, Inuit now live in plywood shacks or government-built prefabricated homes heated by coal stoves where air is not properly humidified. As a result, the population is more susceptible to respiratory infections (Koch et al. 2003; Krause et al. 2005). Chronic respiratory ailments surely affect the emotional profile of the Inuit and foster susceptibility to nervous disorders similar to arctic hysteria. Such impairment may also be implicated in problems associated with foreign language learning and school performance (Foulks 1972).

COPING WITH LOW BIOLOGICAL PRODUCTIVITY

The low net productivity of the tundra imposes constraints on the human population that they cope with by using flexible forms of social organization, exploiting coastal and more southerly taiga resources, and receiving subsidies provided by government agencies, tourism, and other outsiders. Interdependence between coastal and inland groups was created by the need of each to trade for the resources of the other (Spencer 1959:76). The coastal Inuit lived in small, relatively permanent settlements oriented to the seasonal appearance of sea mammals that were used for food, clothing, and fuel. Inland Inuit, on the other hand, followed the herds of caribou and exploited river fish and, in their excursions to the coast, sea mammals. The inland population depended on the coast for supplies of seal oil and other fuels, while the coastal population depended on the interior for caribou skins and plant products, particularly vitamin-rich berries. Not much has been made of the Inuit use of plant foods, but it is known that when berries were available they stored them in seal oil or in the permafrost (Nickerson et al. 1973).

Social Adjustments

The Inuit maintained flexible alliance systems. They recognized bilateral or bilineal descent, and consequently individuals could count on many kinsmen. Kinship bonds assured cooperation, mutual aid, and responsibility for each other's actions. Essentially, the basic principle of Inuit social organization was to extend, by kin and quasi-kin ties, the sphere of social obligations. Although intermarriage across the inland-coastal boundary was rare, an elaborate quasi-kin system evolved that allowed the extension of hospitality and protection, and encouraged trade (Spencer 1959:95). The flexible Inuit kinship system also permitted inclusion of new members into the network whenever appropriate (see the review of alliance practices in Guemple 1972).

The flexibility of Inuit settlements was a response to scattered resources, aimed at an increasingly secure subsistence. Policies that encouraged relocation to larger settlements, started in the 1950s and 1960s, were largely voluntary and resulted in a major shift in health, nutrition, and employment (Damas 2002). The single **nuclear family** unit was maintained year-round, but other **affinal** and **consanguineal** ties may have been present as well. Aggregation, when such groupings maximized hunting chances and provided greater security at uncertain periods (winter), also occurred and was facilitated by the yearly cycle of religious feasts. Winter sealing fostered the formation of relatively large winter villages made up of several **extended families,** whereas summer fishing was a time for the efforts of small families. Patterns of sharing seal meat reflected precise rules of cooperation:

> The seal-meat sharing system functioned as follows: every hunter had a number of sharing partners for each part of seal meat and blubber. . . . Ideally, there were twelve and they were chosen by the hunter's mother either shortly after birth or during his childhood. Whenever the hunter killed a seal his wife cut up the animal and gave the appropriate parts to each one of his partners' wives. (Balikci 1970:135)

Partners named each other after the part of the seal exchanged, and this reinforced the sense of cooperation required during the long, dark winter months. What is of great ecological and social interest is that close relatives and members of the same commensal unit could not become partners. Only distant kin or nonkin were eligible, thereby extending the network of subsistence and overcoming the hostility that was often directed at those outside the extended family (Balikci 1970:138). Yengoyan (1976:129) points out that any society inhabiting an environment with marked fluctuations in resources requires structural devices, such as meat-sharing partnerships, that allow local populations to expand and contract in response to resource availability. A broad network of partnerships allowed individual households to move without losing the security of having help in new areas (compare Winterhalder 1986).

Scarce and sometimes fluctuating resources necessitated that the Inuit adjust the size of families to the capacity of the provider and to enhance the survival of the living and productive members of the group (Balikci 1968:81). The most common population control practice was female infanticide. During times of stress, general infanticide—regardless of the sex of the infant—took place. Consequently the mother and the group were relieved of the emotional and physical costs of a dependent child. The long-term effect of this practice may have been to increase the proportion of older individuals in the population, thereby bringing about a more stable population structure (Freeman 1971).

Female infanticide was based on a cultural preference for boys and on the fact that girls were considered less productive than their male siblings, who became hunters. Thus families tried to maximize the number of boys. Female infanticide may have taken into account the higher death rate of males, who froze to death while hunting or were killed in disputes. Juvenile males numerically predominated over females, but adult females were more numerous than males. Schrire and Steiger (1974) gleaned ethnographic accounts of female infanticide and tried to test the effects of such a practice on the population. The evidence suggests that the rate of female infanticide had to be below 8 percent to maintain group survival. Infanticide was likely an opportunistic response to crisis and stress rather than a normal cultural practice.

Suicide, senilicide, and invalicide eliminated unproductive members of society—a task that they often allocated to themselves through voluntary abandonment of the band or group (Spencer 1959:92). There is no reason to assume that female infanticide and other population controls were evenly practiced throughout the arctic. In areas where winter ice prevents access to intertidal areas, the old, the infirm, and the young became potential candidates for abandonment and exposure to the elements. These practices were less frequent in areas where the nonproductive subgroups could obtain a sizable portion of their own food supply, in particular shellfish (Laughlin 1968b:242). When such intertidal areas or coastal resources were not available, a feedback process may have been effected by which the population adjusted to the leanest months of the year and to the areas with the fewest resources. The population may also have used prolonged nursing, abortion, and sexual abstention, as well as infanticide, to limit its numbers.

Four social features appear to enhance the adjustment of the arctic population, particularly to the inland areas: marriage practices, adoption, child betrothal, and spouse exchange (Damas 1969:32). The goal of Inuit marriage appears to have been to extend, as far as possible, the bonds of mutual aid and cooperation. Marriage between cousins was discouraged, and no **levirate or sororate** was practiced. Even marriage between quasi-kin (for example, trading partners) was viewed as undesirable. Through adoption, the population could be redistributed according to sex, as well as number, into viable units adjusted to current environmental conditions. The value of child betrothal is tied to the practice of female infanticide. A male could assure himself of a spouse by arranging to marry a female infant. Such an arrangement would free him from devoting time to searching for eligible females and allow him to give full attention to hunting. Child betrothal may have reduced the incidence of female infanticide. Spouse exchange is cited as a means of extending one's quasi-kin network and of expressing mutual aid and cooperation (R. F. Spencer 1959). Damas (1969) suggests that it might have alleviated the tensions of monogamous sexual life. All four of these social features helped regulate group size, reproduction, and distribution, as well as affirming bonds of cooperation.

The practice of senilicide was once connected to a pathological condition in aging Inuit known as bone resorption. Aging Inuit appeared to lose bone mineral content at an accelerated rate, possibly as a result of high-protein, high-phosphorus, low-calcium diets and marginal vitamin D intake (Mazess and Mather 1978; Zegura and Jamison 1978). This condition is known to lead to increased frequency of vertebral fractures. It is a general problem associated with aging, particularly among individuals who have not developed substantial bone mass during the first thirty years of life through calcium-rich products like milk and cheese. Bone loss among the aged was a major impairment that drained seminomadic Inuit communities. Coastal populations were able to store food for lean times, which permitted the old and infirm to continue contributing to group subsistence instead of becoming burdens (Spencer 1959:92–95), as has the greater sedentariness of contemporary Inuit. Laughlin has pointed out that the richness of the Aleut intertidal ecosystem permitted greater longevity than elsewhere in the arctic and that older Aleuts played an important role as "consultants and cultural librarians" (1972:386).

Diet

Despite the absence of plants in their barren tundra surroundings, the northern Alaskan Inuit practicing a traditional subsistence pattern had a nutritionally adequate diet. The major portion of the native diet consisted of seal, walrus, caribou, and fish. It was a diet high in protein and fat but low in carbohydrates. This native diet, when prepared in a traditional manner, furnished all essential nutrients (Draper 1977). From meat, Inuit obtained protein and an adequate supply of vitamin K and the B-complex vitamins—the latter usually associated with enzyme proteins. The oils of fish and marine mammals supplied vitamins A and D. For a long while it was thought that Inuit diets were deficient in vitamin C, but, surprisingly, no symptoms of such a deficiency were noted. Some have suggested that the Inuit must have obtained vitamin C by consuming caribou rumen filled with undigested plant materials (Nickerson et al. 1973). Studies of cattle, however, have shown that vitamin C is rapidly destroyed in the rumen. It is now believed that the ascorbic acid was derived chiefly from fresh meat consumed raw or only slightly cooked (Draper 1977). The biggest source of vitamin C in a recent study of Inuit women was found to be fortified Western foods (Fediuk et al. 2002). For this population of women, between twenty and forty years old, eating traditional foods supplied only 20 percent of total vitamin C intake.

The traditional Inuit diet was high in phosphorus and low in calcium. This high phosphorus intake is not only associated with bone loss but also implicated in the abnormal calcium homeostasis discussed earlier. High protein consumption raises a potential problem in glucose homeostasis. A diet that includes only minimal amounts of carbohydrates (about 2 percent) would seem to impair glucose homeostasis. An all-meat diet provides about 10 grams of glucose per day in the form of glycogen, but the adult brain consumes well over 100 grams of glucose per day. The body obtains the glucose it needs by protein digestion and release of amino acids for conversion to glucose (Draper 1977:311). The high fat content of the Inuit diet was thought to be associated with saturated fat. However, native animals contribute mainly polyunsaturated fats to the diet, and this is implicated in the typical health profile of the traditional Inuit population, characterized by low blood pressure, low blood cholesterol, and lean body mass.

The well-being that the traditional diet supported is dramatically illustrated by recent changes in Inuit health status. In the past forty years, the Inuit diet has changed to resemble that of Western industrial nations. A greater proportion of calories are now derived from carbohydrates—especially breads, cereals, rice, and sugar. Over half of the fat currently used is imported, primarily in the form of hydrogenated shortenings and margarine. **Anemia** is now a common problem. Obesity, especially among females, is found with greater frequency (Blanchet et al. 2000; Andersen et al. 2004). Diabetes and impaired glucose tolerance are increasing among the Inuit, with heredity, obesity, and diet being important factors (Jorgensen et al. 2002). Hypertension is no longer rare in Alaskan natives and is associated with obesity, nonindigenous diet preferences, sedentary lifestyles, and glucose intolerance (Murphy et al. 1997; Johnson and Taylor 1991). Blood pressure is lower among Inuit compared with most European populations, but higher than in several Asian populations and Amazonian Indians (Bjerregaard et al. 2003). Hypercholesterolemia is increasing throughout the population, particularly among the aged (Bell and Heller 1978; Way 1978; Zegura and Jamison 1978). Increased consumption of sweets and less frequent use of the teeth as tools have led to a rapid increase in periodontal disease and dental caries. On the other hand, the new diet contributes to the accelerated growth trend noted by Jamison (Jamison 1978).

CHANGE IN THE ARCTIC

Arctic regions have gained prominence in contemporary studies of global climate change because climatic changes are expected to be more deeply felt and may be measurable there sooner than in midlatitudes (Garfinkel and Brubaker 1980; Lachenbruch and Marshall 1986). Arctic regions are, in a sense, early warning systems for processes occurring more slowly elsewhere. (Compare the special polar science section in the March 16, 2007, issue of *Science*, reporting on a two-year research initiative called the International Polar Year [2007–2009].) Global warming due to greenhouse gases might be expected to increase both primary production and soil respiration. If the former increases faster than the latter, carbon will be removed from the atmosphere; if the reverse occurs, carbon will be released to the atmosphere, exacerbating global warming (Shaver et al. 1992). Research has focused on the wet and moist tundras of the low arctic, but most of the carbon and nutrients in arctic ecosystems reside in soil organic matter pools that turn over very slowly. In many areas, large amounts of organic matter are held in the permafrost below the currently thawed layer. But these large pools could become a part of the carbon cycle if permafrost warming is followed by deeper thawing (Shaver et al. 1992).

Global climate change appears to be amplified in the arctic by a number of positive feedbacks, including ice and snow melting that, in turn, decrease albedo (Overpeck et al. 1997). From 1840 to the middle of the twentieth century, the arctic recorded the highest temperatures in 400 years. This warming marked the end of the Little Ice Age in the arctic and brought about retreating glaciers, melting permafrost, and alterations in the arctic ecosystems (Overpeck et al. 1997; compare Serreze et al. 2007 for a state-of-the-art discussion of the shrinking arctic ice cover; and Shepherd and Wingham 2007 for the contributions of the antarctic and Greenland ice sheets to sea level rise). Arctic people have had to cope with these changes, as well as with the arrival of Europeans and the growing impact of their presence on the availability of resources.

In the past, arctic peoples were portrayed as existing in harmony with their environment, experiencing long periods of stability, and having a conservation ethic. But ongoing research yields a very different picture. Human occupation of the arctic is characterized by disruptions, crises, shifting cultural traditions, and profound demographic and ecological shocks (Krupnick 1993:221). A careful reading of arctic ethnohistory in the seventeenth and eighteenth centuries yields a story of epidemics, famines, internecine conflicts, ecological disasters, enslavement, assimilation, and massacres. Yet despite all these shocks, the total native population of the arctic actually increased during European contact, particularly in Siberia and Greenland. Natives of the North American arctic seem to have experienced greater demographic losses than those of Eurasia. Krupnick (1990) did not find any evidence for a universal pattern of demographic decline resulting from contact. Unlike other hunter-gatherer populations, arctic peoples show greater stamina, resilience, and demographic bounce-back than most other foragers. This ability to surpass previous populations is a quintessential arctic adaptation that has led to questioning earlier literature that overemphasized the role of infanticide in arctic adaptations.

Inuit sexual norms always expressed a desire to maintain as high a birthrate as possible (Weyer 1932), and childlessness was seen as a great misfortune. While infanticide was practiced in the arctic, as elsewhere, it is now seen as a rare and locally emergent solution under very stressful circumstances, not a routine method of population regulation (Krupnick 1985). Rather, traditional arctic community dynamics give clear evidence of tendencies toward territorial expansion, maximum resource utilization, and high birthrates that provided communities with a capacity to replenish their population rapidly in face of the short life expectancies, high death rates, game shortages, and the ubiquitous dangers of life in the arctic (Krupnick 1993:226). The archeology of the arctic shows rapid population increases and declines, with whole villages replaced in a matter of generations.

Ever since the first Inuit came in contact with whaling ships in the 1870s, Inuit adaptive practices have steadily eroded. The acquisition of rifles meant that subsistence could be secured at a faster rate. Because they desire Western goods and need money to pay for them, the Inuit now work for wages. Although boom conditions exist in Alaska, most jobs have gone to skilled outsiders. The result has been high unemployment rates for Inuit (Bureau of Indian Affairs 1971:60).

Several factors have contributed to the process of change, but the most significant are Western education and technology. Instead of the experiential environmental education of yesteryear, modern Inuit attend schools where education focuses on literacy gained by reading the wisdom of non-Inuit. Especially influential are boarding schools that separate children from parents at a crucial time in their education as hunters. To a large extent, the influx of outsiders to the arctic and the presence of nonnative teachers have caused children to lose respect for their traditional social and cultural values and practices. Rather than a guarded disapproval of change, they have learned an appreciation of technological innovations and Western ways of achieving success. Recent research shows that natives use newspapers, radio, and television programming for resistance to the economic and cultural agendas of nonnatives, and telling their own stories to ensure their self-determination—using the Internet and cyberspace to define their identities (Daley and James 2004; Christensen 2003). More promising still are findings which suggest that younger Inuit continue to define life stages and the life course in a manner consistent with that of their elders—valuing the development of *ihuma,* knowledge or wisdom, as defining adulthood (Collings 2000). A mix of traditional and modern activities and developing innovative markets of arctic products such as fur, leather, fish, clothing, crafts, and tourism can lead the new generation to combine traditional knowledge with the need to be part of the global economy (Myers 2000).

Technological Adjustments

The Inuit, like the Laplanders, readily adopted the snowmobile. Since the snowmobile was first developed in 1962, sales in North America have grown continuously (Ives 1974:908). Osburn (1974) studied the adoption of snowmobiles among the Nunamiut Inuit of Anaktuvuk Pass, Alaska. Before the 1960s, the population had been seminomadic caribou hunters. The snowmobile was advantageous for caribou hunters because the caribou appeared to be less afraid of its noise than of the dog teams. By 1969 the switch from dogsledding to snowmobiles was complete. Inuit stopped walking and drove everywhere on their machines, even if their destination was only one block away in the village. Such overuse eventually took its toll, and the machines began to fall in disrepair. Lacking the capital to replace them or the expertise to fix them, the Inuit increasingly depended on handouts and wages.

The transition to snowmobiles was just as rapid among the Finnish Lapps (Müller-Wille 1974; Pelto 1973; Linkola 1973). They abandoned reindeer sledding within a couple of years, and the snowmobile became universal. But the Lapps continued to herd reindeer and felt they could do so more effectively with their snowmobiles. Before the arrival of the snowmobile, Lapps had year-round contact with herds and could easily make herd management decisions. With the adoption of the snowmobile, there has been increasing pressure to hold several roundups during the year, instead of only one. This represents a response to market demand for their product and to their need to meet payments on their snowmobile equipment. Linkola (1973:130) estimates that the profits from one-third of the reindeer sold yearly go toward the purchase of and maintenance of snowmobiles. The result has been a steady depletion in the size of the herd. The snowmobile has enhanced class distinctions and economic differences among arctic peoples, with the small herder having to abandon his occupation and become a full-time wage earner to sustain his family and machinery. In addition, the snowmobile scars the arctic. Ecologists have noted that plant recovery is slow and damage still evident even when ten years have elapsed since snowmobile tracks were first cut (Bliss 1975:57).

Future development in the arctic will follow an **extractive** path, and it can only be hoped that its effect will not resemble the results of the Amazon basin rubber boom of the late nineteenth century. When it ended, the region was still undeveloped, and economic development schemes have not produced any marked increase in regional wealth (R. Walker et al. in press). An evaluation by the Bureau of Indian Affairs on the impact of the proposed trans-Alaska pipeline concluded that, although the pipeline did not cut across a sizable number of Inuit villages, it would increase the pace of acculturation and absorption of Inuit into Western culture (Bureau of Indian Affairs 1971:39). There have been regular reports of oil leaks along the pipeline and scandals connected with the monitoring and maintenance of the pipeline. Like any nonrenewable resource, the oil will cease to flow eventually, and the sustainability of current patterns of energy use and renewable resource use will be challenged by the kind of economy and ecology that emerge. Changes in the arctic have led to the rise of an Alaskan native bourgeoisie, and what role it will play in the future of the native population's adaptation to a changing arctic society remains to be seen (Mason 2002).

Tradition, Modernization, and
Changing Gender Roles and Participation

One of the best hopes for the future of the Inuit and other arctic peoples is to maintain indigenous environmental knowledge and environmentally relevant behaviors. Although Inuit interpersonal relationships have changed a great deal, recent events have sparked a renewal of Inuit traditions. Modern communications equipment that is available to the mass consumer has facilitated a return to wider kin networks. Most Inuit in northwestern Alaska have tape recorders and use them to communicate with relatives in distant villages. Even relatives who have never met are included in these tape networks, which serve to integrate the population. Another crucial change has been the construction in most villages of landing strips that allow residents to fly to cultural events in other villages.

The Internet has been used to strengthen native identity, and global positioning systems (GPS) have been integrated with Inuit systems of finding their way on the land (Aporta and Higgs 2005). Concerns expressed in the mid-1990s that these tools could displace the more complex traditional ways of finding one's way (snowdrift patterns, animal behavior, tidal cycles, currents, and astronomical features) among the younger generation seem to have been put to rest as the new tools are being integrated with traditional knowledge. However, there is some evidence of a growing number of episodes of geographical disorientation and spatial conflicts during group travel resulting from a growing divergence in cultural knowledge and navigating through the landscape (Sonnenfeld 2002).

Although Inuit economic behavior is increasingly Western, many of the kinship obligations still function and appear to be in a state of revival. Average household size has decreased in recent years with nuclear families dominating village settlements (Jorgensen 1990:209). In some areas family size has increased due to bottle-feeding of infants, improved medical care, sedentarization, and increased economic security and wealth (Condon 1987). Infanticide has virtually disappeared (Condon 1987:36). Despite these changes, however, hunting is still organized by kinship and it is the organization of skills, production, distribution, and consumption that connects the villagers of today with those of the past (Condon 1987:216). The introduction of permanent household structures, in contrast to the tents and igloos of the past, has led to a loss of autonomy since families are assigned houses based on need and family size rather than on proximity to social or kin relations (Condon 1987:47; see Stern 2005 for a discussion of the impact of nucleation on Inuit households in Canada; see also Damas 2002).

Arctic women make up the vast majority of activists and organizers of grassroots organizations (see Stein 2004, which includes a chapter on Inuit women's roles in NGOs), but they remain underrepresented in the political sphere (Minor 2002). Circumpolar peoples, both men and women, have a remarkably high degree of complementarity in seeking their livelihoods, perhaps a heritage of their foraging lives in the past, which still affects the contemporary division of labor (Jarvenpa and Brumbach 2006). This cooperation is manifested also in the creation of the Arctic Council that takes account of traditional knowledge provided by indigenous peoples who participate in it (Stenlund 2002).

Arctic peoples have shown that they can act to preserve their cultural heritage, gain a voice in how their environment is exploited, and establish conservation measures that will allow them to sustain a hunting way of life in the modern world (Morgan 1977). A study of Inuit at Nunavik showed that money and commodities represent an increasing portion of the economic resources of households (Wenzel 2000) but that tradition and customary obligations continue to play an important role in economic decisions. Despite initial difficulties in communication, the Inuit have arrived at unified resolutions. Whether this growing unity is translated into growing control over their destiny remains to be seen, but the goal of a renewed Inuit lifestyle more closely attuned to the opportunities and limitations of the arctic environment is a hopeful one. The influence of outsiders has thus far meant a replacement of adaptive behavior by technological subsidy. Such a subsidy can be expected to continue only as long as the area yields high-value, nonrenewable resources. Once they have been extracted, the arctic will once again need the ancient strategies of the Inuit population. We can only hope that the adaptive value of such a lifestyle is recognized and nurtured by both Inuit and outsiders (Chance 1990). Maintaining flexible adaptive systems will be crucial to the survival of people in the arctic. The current emphasis on oil exploration, a nonrenewable resource, could leave the arctic a barren urban desert. Ways to accommodate the indigenous knowledge of arctic resources, with commercial activities (whether ecological tourism or electronics) will be crucial to the survival of people in the cities they have created. These accommodations will require the same sort of flexibility that has been the hallmark of arctic adaptations for centuries (Krupnick 1993:268; Couzin 2007:1518–1519).

SUGGESTED READINGS AND USEFUL WEBSITES

The two-year period 2007–2009 has been named the International Polar Year, sponsored by the World Meteorological Organization (WMO) and the International Council for Science (ICSU), with the support of dozens of nations. The website devoted to this celebration provides information for the public, media, educators, scientists, tourists, and others about arctic and polar issues (http://classic.ipy.org).

The American Association for the Advancement of Science has an Arctic Division (Arctic AAAS) specifically related to arctic and polar research (http://arctic.aaas .org/index.html). The website of the University of the Arctic (www.uarctic.org) serves as a network of higher education and research institutions in, near, and related to arctic and polar regions. They provide a web page of additional website links that gives further information about these cooperating institutions (www.uarctic.org/ compactArticles.aspx?m=197).

Several journals and research societies are dedicated to arctic and polar scientific research issues, including the journal *Arctic, Antarctic, and Alpine Research: An Interdisciplinary Journal (AAAR)* (http://instaar.colorado.edu/AAAR/about_aaar/index .php), the journal *Arctic* (www.arctic.ucalgary.ca/sections.php?sid=publications&cid =arctic_journal) of the Arctic Institute of North America (www.arctic.ucalgary.ca), and the journal *Arctic, Antarctic, and Alpine Research* (http://instaar.colorado.edu/ AAAR/about_aaar/index.php) from the Institute of Arctic and Alpine Research (http://instaar.colorado.edu). Other journals discussing arctic research include *Polar Biology* (www.springerlink.com/content/100450), *Polar Bioscience* (http://polaris .nipr.ac.jp/~penguin/polarbiosci), *Polar Research* (www.blackwellpublishing.com/ POR), *Polish Polar Research* (www.polish.polar.pan.pl), and *Polar Record* (http:// journals.cambridge.org/jid_POL).

Many recent books and textbooks offer detailed data and information about arctic and polar ecology, particularly the climate, vegetation, and fauna of these areas. They include *The Climate of the Arctic* by Przybylak (2003); *The Biology of Polar Habitats* by Fogg (1998); *Ecosystems of the World: Polar and Alpine Systems* by Wielgolaski (1997); *Ecology of Arctic Environments* by Woodin and Marquiss (1997); *Plant Ecology in the Sub-Arctic Swedish Lapland* edited by Karlsson and Callaghan (1996); *Landscape Function and Disturbance in Arctic Tundra* by Reynolds and Tenhunen (1996); *Arctic and Alpine Biodiversity: Patterns, Causes, and Ecosystem Consequences* by Chapin (1995); *Toolik Lake: Ecology of an Aquatic Ecosystem in Arctic*

Alaska edited by O'Brien (1992); *Polar Ecology* by Stonehouse (1989); *To the Arctic: An Introduction to the Far Northern World* by Young (1989); *The Living Tundra* by Chernov (1985); and *Tundra Ecosystems: A Comparative Analysis* edited by Bliss et al. (1981).

As the arctic environment is increasingly threatened by global climate change, many research efforts have been devoted to documenting and modeling changes within the arctic, particularly for nutrient cycling (Shaver et al. 1992; Bonan et al. 1990; Garfinkel and Brubaker 1980). Several books also provide results of research on climate change in arctic polar environments, including *Arctic Alpine Ecosystems and People in a Changing Environment* edited by Orbaek et al. (2006); *Arctic Environment Variability in the Context of Global Change* by Bobylev et al. (2003); *Global Changes and Arctic Terrestrial Ecosystems* edited by Oechel et al. (1996); and *Arctic Ecosystems in a Changing Climate: An Ecophysiological Perspective* edited by Chapin et al. (1991).

Institutions from many different countries are conducting long-term ecological research and experiments to better understand arctic and polar environments. Within the United States, much arctic research has been conducted within the Long-Term Ecological Research network (Arctic LTER) (http://ecosystems.mbl.edu/ARC), operated through the Marine Biological Laboratory (www.mbl.edu/index.html) and the University of Alaska-Fairbanks Toolik Lake Field Station (www.uaf.edu/toolik). The Institute of Arctic Biology at the University of Alaska-Fairbanks (UAF) also supports faculty research and education in arctic ecology (www.iab.uaf.edu/about.php), while the Arctic Geobotanical Atlas (www.arcticatlas.org/index.shtml) provides maps and other material about topography and landforms near Toolik Lake, Alaska.

The U.S. Arctic Research Commission (www.arctic.gov) oversees many of these research efforts and guides federal policy in the arctic. Other agencies of the U.S. government have dedicated programs related to arctic affairs, including the NOAA Arctic Research Office (www.arctic.noaa.gov/aro), the NSF Office of Polar Programs (OPP) (www.nsf.gov/dir/index.jsp?org=OPP), and the NSF Organization of Arctic Sciences (www.nsf.gov/div/index.jsp?org=ARC). The Polar Research Board of the National Academies serves as an independent body to guide federal research efforts in the arctic (http://dels.nas.edu/prb/index.shtml). The Arctic Research Consortium of the U.S. (www.arcus.org) is a nonprofit organization of researchers and research organizations that complements other advisory organizations concerning arctic research. Their page links to additional websites (www.arcus.org/ARCUS/links/index.html) and provides an exhaustive list of arctic and polar-related websites.

The National Research Council of the National Academy of Sciences has published several books that discuss research in the arctic and polar areas, highlight the contributions of this research to the overall research community, develop new policy concerning protection and use of these areas, and indicate future research directions and needs. Among these books are: *Toward an Integrated Arctic Observing Network*

(2006); *Arctic Contributions to Social Science and Public Policy* (1993); and *NOAA's Arctic Research Initiative: Proceedings of a Workshop* (1997).

Additional research institutions and bodies dedicated to arctic biology and ecology with useful websites include the Byrd Polar Research Center located at Ohio State University (www-bprc.mps.ohio-state.edu), the Roald Amundsen Centre for Arctic Research located at the University of Tromsø, Norway (www.arctic.uit.no/English/index.html), the Norwegian Polar Institute (http://npiweb.npolar.no), the North Atlantic Regional Studies at Roskilde University, Denmark (www.geo.ruc.dk/nors), the Scott Polar Research Institute at Cambridge University (www.spri.cam.ac.uk), the Swiss Committee on Polar Research (www.polar-research.ch), the Belgian Polar Platform (www.belspo.be/belspo/BePoles/index_en.stm), the Polar Research Institute of China (www.coi.gov.cn/eoverview/ejd), and the Alfred Wegener Institute for Polar and Marine Research (AWI) in Germany (www.awi.de/en/home). The Canadian Circumpolar Institute at the University of Alberta (www.uofaweb.ualberta.ca/polar) also supports interdisciplinary research in the arctic, while the Canadian Polar Commission oversees Canadian research efforts in the arctic and polar regions (www.polarcom.gc.ca). The Scott Polar Research Institute website provides a detailed list and directory of companies and organizations dedicated to arctic and polar affairs, separated by country of affiliation (www.spri.cam.ac.uk/resources/organisations).

The website of the International Tundra Experiment (ITEX) (www.geog.ubc.ca/itex) provides data and information based on a network of researchers studying the impact of climate change on tundra and alpine vegetation. Many other international polar research efforts are coordinated through the United Nations Environment Programme (UNEP)'s Key Polar Center (http://polar.grida.no), which oversees programs specifically related to the UNEP. Also see the website of the International Arctic Science Committee (www.iasc.se), which provides a guide to research funding in arctic affairs (www.arcticsciencefunding.org/index.html). The International Arctic Research Center at UAF (www.iarc.uaf.edu) works to integrate U.S.–based climate change research in the arctic with other research efforts worldwide.

Many organizations dedicated to indigenous arctic residents provide websites with information about their research and services; the Alaska Native Knowledge Network, based at the University of Alaska-Fairbanks (http://ankn.uaf.edu/index.html) makes available information about indigenous knowledge and resource use. Also, the website Human Role in Reindeer/Caribou Systems from UAF (www.rangifer.net/rangifer/index.cfm) discusses human use of and interaction with caribou populations in the arctic. The Arctic Council (www.arctic-council.org) coordinates arctic states, communities, and residents (additional information can be found at the website Arctic Peoples, www.arcticpeoples.org). The Arctic Portal website (http://arcticportal.org) provides a forum to address concerns by arctic peoples and governments. The Indian and North Affairs Canada (www.ainc-inac.gc.ca) coordinates Canadian government programs related to indigenous arctic affairs. Many arctic indigenous groups have websites devoted to cultural and social development; examples include the Gwich'in Tribal Council (www.gwichin.nt.ca) and the Inuit Circumpolar Council (www.inuit.org). The journal *Etudes Inuit Studies* (www.fss .ulaval.ca/etudes-inuit-studies) also discusses traditional and contemporary issues related to Inuit societies.

Social science research and data within the arctic is available online; the website of the Arctic Social Sciences Program at NSF (www.mnh.si.edu/arctic/html/ nsf.html) provides information about arctic research funding and results. Additional social science research can be found in the journal *Arctic Anthropology* (www.wisc .edu/wisconsinpress/journals/journals/aa.html) and at the International Arctic Social Sciences Association (www.iassa.gl/index.htm). UAF publishes an annual volume dedicated to anthropological research in the arctic (Anthropological Papers of the University of Alaska, www.uaf.edu/anthro/apua.html). Additionally, UAF offers researchers principles and guidelines for conducting research in the arctic (http:// ankn.uaf.edu/IKS/conduct.html).

The Arctic Health website (www.arctichealth.org) provides health information related to arctic residents. Additional health information can be found through the International Union for Circumpolar Health (www.iuch.org) and their journal *International Journal of Circumpolar Health* (http://ijch.oulu.fi). The Centre for Indigenous People's Nutrition and Environment (CINE) at McGill University, Canada (www.mcgill.ca/cine) also provides research and resources about indigenous health issues. Specifically, the website Survey of Living Conditions in the Arctic: Inuit, Saami, and the Indigenous Peoples of Chukotka (www.arcticlivingconditions.org) discusses research results of the international effort to document arctic living conditions.

Further detail on specific indigenous groups of the arctic and polar regions can be found in the books *Critical Inuit Studies: An Anthology of Contemporary Arctic Ethnography* edited by Stern and Stevenson (2006); *Caribou Rising: Defending the Porcupine Herd, Gwich'in Culture, and the Arctic National Wildlife Refuge* by Bass (2005); *A Yupiaq Worldview* by Kawagley (2005); *Identity and Ecology in Arctic Siberia* by Anderson (2002); *Peoples of the Tundra* by Ziker (2002); *Northern Passage: Ethnography and Apprenticeship Among the Subarctic Dene* by Jarvenpa (1998); *Contested Arctic: Indigenous Peoples, Industrial States, and the Circumpolar Environment* by Smith and McCarter (1997); *Shamanism and Northern Ecology* edited by Pentikainen (1996); *Inujjuamiut Foraging Strategies: Evolutionary Ecology of an Arctic Hunting Economy* by E. A. Smith (1991); *The Inupiat and Arctic Alaska* by Chance (1990); and *The Arctic: Environment, People, Policy* edited by Nuttall and Callaghan (2000).

More historical information about indigenous arctic residents can be found at the Arctic Studies Center at the National Museum of Natural History of the Smithsonian Institution (www.mnh.si.edu/ARCTIC/index.html) and the Archaeological Survey of Canada at the Canadian Museum of Civilization (www.civilization.ca/ cmc/archeo/homee.html). Further reading on arctic archeology can also be found in

A Prehistory of the North: Human Settlement of the Higher Latitudes by Hoffecker (2004); *Ancient People of the Arctic* by McGhee (2002); and *Arctic Archaeology: Issue 3* by Rowley-Conwy (2001).

NOTE

1. Studies of reindeer herding and its modernization include Pelto 1973; Ingold 1974; Müller-Wille 1974; Anderson 2002; Schneider 2002; Schneider et al. 2005; Reinert 2006; Kofinas et al. 2000; VanStone 2000.

Photo by Bryan Busovicki

Source: iStockphoto

6

HUMAN ADAPTABILITY
TO HIGH ALTITUDES

Research on human adaptability to high altitudes is among the most advanced
and well-integrated work in biocultural and environmental anthropology (Boetsch
and Rabino-Massa 2005). Extreme environments such as high altitudes provide natural experimental settings for the working of evolution and adaptation because of
the immediate and persistent need to cope with low oxygen pressure (Beall 2000).
These regions are important as windows into past and future global environmental
change (Parish 2002). Ice cores from the Andes, the Himalayas, and other high
mountains provide windows into carbon dioxide levels in the ancient past, and
glacial melting on many high peaks is taken as solid evidence for global warming
(Bowen 2005; Thompson et al. 1993, 1994; Lachenbruch and Marshall 1986; Ives
and Messerli 1989). Mountain regions occupy nearly a quarter of the global terrestrial land surface and provide goods and services to a large proportion of the total
population of the planet (Huber et al. 2005).

This chapter will introduce the crucial problem faced by populations inhabiting
high altitude zones: **hypoxia,** or low oxygen pressure. Other problems associated
with high altitude adaptation are cold stress, aridity, shallow soils, steep slopes, low
biological productivity, and pulmonary disease. These physical stressors are compounded by poverty (R. B. Thomas 1998) and poor infrastructure (roads, schools,
health services; Leatherman 1998). Andean scholars have been leading the way in a
new biocultural synthesis that links political economy to biocultural anthropology
(Goodman and Leatherman 1998), which is influencing research in other areas of
the planet. Archeologists have shown that preindustrial societies implemented antic-
ipatory forms of adaptive responses to transient phenomena such as El Niño and
protacted events such as desertification (Dillehay and Kolata 2004).

As in the arctic, researchers in high altitude zones have found little evidence of
definite genetic (evolutionary) adaptation. However, Beall (2000) has been systematically showing the interaction of evolution and adaptation at high altitudes by

revealing the significant differences between Tibetan and Andean patterns and has reported detecting a gene for oxygen saturation among Tibetans, indirectly suggesting population-level genetic differences. In short, microevolutionary processes may have operated differently in Tibet and the Andes despite exposure to the same environmental stress and consequently resulted in different phenotypical outcomes (Beall 2001). For example, women with the high oxygen saturation genotype have more surviving children, but this occurs only in Tibet (Beall 2006). In contrast, both Tibetan and Andean populations developed hemoglobin concentration capacity as a heritable factor. The high oxygen saturation allele may be increasing through natural selection among high altitude Tibetan populations (Beall 2006). While most of the mechanisms for coping with the biological stress of low oxygen pressure are physiological, the above evidence suggests that more comparative work is needed. This is further supported by a third pattern of adaptation to high altitude hypoxia documented for populations in Ethiopia, where highlanders maintain venous hemoglobin concentrations and arterial oxygen saturation similar to those of sea level populations, despite the decrease in ambient oxygen tension (Beall et al. 2002). Obviously more work is needed to disentangle the complex ways in which human populations have adapted and developed genetic and physiological responses to the challenge of hypoxia. Some mechanisms are regulatory, such as increased rates of pulmonary ventilation. Others are acclimatory and developmental: increases in red blood cells and total hemoglobin, enlargement of the capillary network, and chemical-enzymatic changes related to internal respiration that enhance oxygen utilization at the tissue level (Greksa 1990; Frisancho 1993).

Cold stress is handled by regulatory adjustments, such as warm clothing and shelter, and by scheduling activities to allow maximum time in the sun. Developmental adjustments also improve the degree of adaptation of native populations to the cold at high altitude. Chief among these are nonshivering thermogenesis and increased blood flow to exposed extremities (Little 1976).

High altitude populations cope with low productivity by seasonal migration, by marriage prescriptions that serve to distribute the population, tight integration of agricultural and pastoral production, use of a large number of crop varieties, relatively little sexual division of labor, a mixture of household and community control of land, and interzonal trade (Farooque et al. 2004). Maintenance of crop diversity, diversification of activities, and self-organization into multiple groupings provide additional protection from the patchiness inherent in mountain ecosystems (Sinclair and Ham 2000). To minimize energy costs at the population level, children are assigned the tasks of herding, thereby reducing the caloric requirements of households. Preservation techniques play an important role in providing food stores for lean times. This chapter will focus on adjustments made by Andean populations coping with high altitude stresses.

A synthesis of the human ecology of the Andean and Tibetan regions found different intellectual trajectories that throw doubt on whether the differences result from environmental, historical, or intellectual emphases (Orlove and Guillet 1985:16).

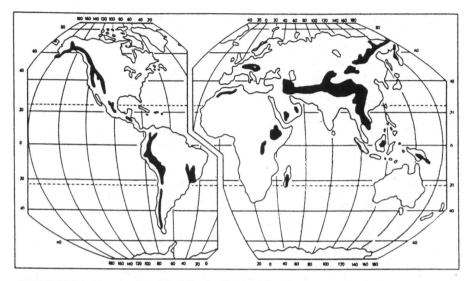

FIGURE 6.1 Tropical and Midlatitude Highlands of the World

MOUNTAIN ECOSYSTEMS

Since prehistoric times, human populations have occupied high altitude zones despite the numerous problems initially encountered by persons entering such areas. Anyone who has grown up at sea level, when first exposed to high altitudes, will experience symptomatic discomfort, reduced work capacity, accelerated breathing, higher hemoglobin levels, and higher arterial pressure. It is not surprising that relatively few people live at high altitude. The majority of the areas occupied are within 40 degrees of the equator where solar insolation is greater and, all things being equal, biotic productivity is higher. These areas include the South American Andes, the mountains of Ethiopia, the Caucasus of southern Russia, the Asian Himalayas, and the Rocky Mountains of the United States (see Figure 6.1). In the 1970s and 1980s many scholars and agencies predicted a dire future for mountain peoples and environmental disaster. This perception was challenged by Ives and Messerli (1989) and more recently by Ives (2004), showing that it was based on external perceptions rather than inherent weaknesses of the people or the ecosystem.

High altitudes have been the subject of intensive research in human biology and ecology. In most other biomes, cultural practices can play a major buffering action. But in the high altitude biome, hypoxia means that acclimatory and developmental adjustments take precedence over behavioral regulatory adjustments (Baker 1976a:2). These regions provide human biologists an ideal setting to study potential genetic and physiological adaptations. These studies were stimulated by the writings of Carlos Monge (1948), who postulated that Andean natives are biologically different from lowlanders and possess unique adaptive characteristics. Since then numerous workers have sought to test the validity of Monge's hypotheses.[1]

Mountainous regions have complex distributions of **biotic communities.** Three major ecological features are relevant to human habitation: vertical biotic zonation, irregular biotic distribution, and geologic features such as slope and rugged terrain (Denevan 1986; Winterhalder et al. 1978; Rhoades and Thompson 1975). With increased elevation rapid changes take place in vegetation and animal life, commonly distributed in distinctive life zones or biomes. On a given mountain it is possible to have four or five major biomes and numerous **ecotones,** or transitional zones (see Figure 6.2).

Vertical Zonation

Figure 6.2 illustrates general conditions possible in a variety of mountain ecosystems. Note that latitude plays an important role in defining the biotic characteristics at the bottom zone. Natural vegetation may go from tropical forest to tundra in the tropical highlands, but in temperate latitudes it may begin with coniferous forest. Climatic factors such as temperature and moisture play dominant roles in species composition, as do highland features such as slope, contour, and differential exposure to wind and light (Dettwyler 1977; James 1966:379–420). Winterhalder and colleagues (1978:77) note growing evidence of substantial environmental modification by prehistoric Andean populations, especially through overgrazing and utilization of ancient forests for construction materials and fuelwood (see Thompson et al. 1994; also Browman 1974, 1987).

Although there is a greater chance of biota interchange in mountain ecosystems than in other types of ecosystems, the narrowness of each mountain life zone and the isolation created by the rough topography make the species of each area unique in the whole world (E. Odum 1971:402). Native fauna is distributed in accordance with zonal characteristics. Animals inhabiting lower levels move one or two zones up, but usually no farther. Some of the animals have characteristic adaptations, such as rock-dwelling rodents *(Andean vizcacha)* and the furry yak of the Himalayas, the vicuña, llama, and guanaco *(Andean camelids;* Tomka 1992). Agriculture is zonally distributed according to changes in altitude (see Figure 6.2), and there seem to be broad world patterns in the nature of the agropastoral economy. Rhoades and Thompson (1975) note that parallels in subsistence are based on the success of the vertical oscillation of cultivators, herders, and beasts that follow the zonally available productive areas.

Geoclimatic Characteristics

Rarely are vertical zones the neat layers shown in Figure 6.2. A variety of geological features, such as angle of sunlight in valleys, lead to the creation of microhabitats.

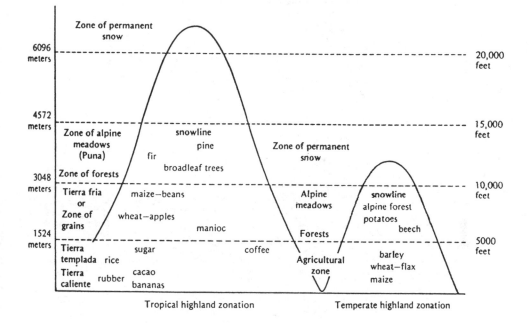

FIGURE 6.2   Zonation in Tropical and Temperate Highlands
Mountains have narrow zonation and growing zones with a lower snowline in temperate highlands.

The amount of rainfall depends on both altitude and exposure to air currents. Exposed slopes receive greater rainfall than areas shielded by some geologic feature. Ruggedness and slope can make some mountain areas useless for agriculture or herding.

Human adaptability was intensively studied in Nuñoa district, Peru, as part of the International Biological Program's human adaptability studies (Baker and Little 1976). The Nuñoa area ranges from 4,000 to 4,800 meters above sea level in the altiplano—the treeless portion of the central Andes above 3,600 meters altitude surrounding Lake Titicaca and Lake Poopo. (The terms "altiplano" and "puna" are used interchangeably in the literature; Thomas and Winterhalder 1976:22.) Strictly speaking, however, "puna" refers only to grassland. Figure 6.3 shows the location of the altiplano in South America.

At the time the International Biological Program (IBP, 1964–74) study began, over 8,000 Quechuas were living in Nuñoa and pursuing a traditional pattern that combined pastoralism based on camelids and sheep with seasonal agriculture in lower altitudes. As is typical of tropical highlands, mean annual temperatures are

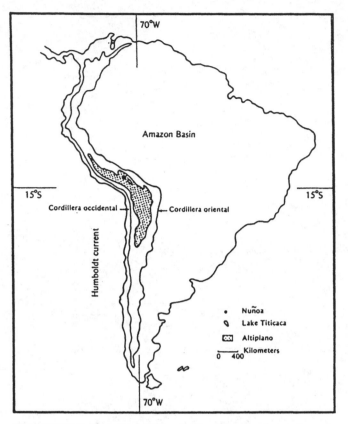

FIGURE 6.3 Location of the Andes (Approximately 2,000 Meter Isography) and the Altiplano (Shaded Area)

relatively constant, but there is a considerable range between maximum and minimum temperatures. Mean annual temperature is about 8°C, but maximum and minimum can vary by 20°C. Frosts occur frequently and can result either from rapid loss of lower air and ground heat at night or from movement by cold air masses (Thomas and Winterhalder 1976:31). Precipitation is seasonal and averages 830 millimeters. Little or no precipitation falls four to five months out of the year, and droughts lasting a year or longer occur randomly. Productivity is low and highland populations must trade with lowland areas to cope successfully with the scarcity of energy on the altiplano.

Plant Productivity

The frost zone in the Andes begins at about 2,500 meters and marks a significant change in plant cover. Below this zone lie tropical montane forest and patches of tropical savannas (see Figure 6.2). Above 2,500 meters, the tropical trees grow shorter and are replaced at about 4,000 meters by scrub and grass steppes. The steppe thins out and becomes a frost desert between 4,500 and 4,900 meters. Higher still are permanently frozen areas. The human population is concentrated on the altiplano. Three major vegetation zones (moist, dry, and desert puna) are distinguished according to the moisture they receive. The moist puna is characterized by bunch grasses and some shrubs, and the dry puna by **xerophytic vegetation.** The desert puna is an area without vegetation except where scant precipitation collects (Thomas and Winterhalder 1976:39). Deserts are created on the **lee side** of mountains due to the blocking effect of clouds, while bounteous precipitation falls on the windward slopes (Heintzelman and Highsmith 1973:368). A disproportionate number of altiplano plants are low and compact, with growth organs below or only slightly above the ground. These features provide protection against cold, drought, and frost. **Cushion plants** are able to minimize exposure to the elements, keep a relatively warm interior, and absorb and retain moisture. Spines provide protection against herbivores (Thomas and Winterhalder 1976:43).

The plant productivity in the Andean altiplano is low because of soil aridity, cold temperatures, and low levels of soil organic matter. High levels of solar radiation, however, permit surprising levels of **net primary production,** aided by reduction of the costs of respiration during cold nights. Harvestable biomass in one estimate was only eighty kilograms per **hectare** per year in moist puna (Thomas and Winterhalder 1976:43). Much of the productivity of plants is stored below the ground, away from the elements and the grazing population. Animal biomass is therefore also low (Fittkau 1968:641). Both the animal and the human population must adapt to the constraints of a high altitude zone, particularly hypoxia.

ADAPTATION TO HYPOXIA

Physiological Adjustments

Hypoxia, or low oxygen pressure, is the most important biological stress facing populations living at high altitude (cf. Houston et al. 2005). Cultural practices cannot increase the amount of oxygen available to people, but some of its associated problems (for example, reduced ability to carry a fetus to full term and high rates of neonate mortality) have been minimized through diet, work patterns, and cultural attitudes toward reproduction. Populations native to high altitude were once thought to have genetic adaptations that permitted them to reproduce and live with no apparent difficulty where outsiders experienced serious malfunctioning (Monge 1948). It now appears that there is no direct evidence of population-level adaptation to hypoxia in humans, but only indirect evidence, based on inferences from individual and infra-individual adaptations (Mazess 1975:193; compare earlier discussion of recent findings for microevolutionary processes in native Tibetan populations, Beall 2000, 2001, 2006; Beall et al. 2002). Human adaptations to hypoxia appear to reflect the general genetic plasticity common to all. However, recent studies point to the role of specific genes that influence control of hypoxic ventilatory responses (HVR), but separating the genetic component from metabolic and thermoregulatory processes prevents a conclusive result as to whether there is a genetic basis for variation in acute and chronic HVR (Soutiere and Tankersley 2001).

The most common research design contrasted indigenous populations with outsiders (Baker 1978). The one designed by Haas (1976) contained multiple comparisons along the lines of social class, urban versus rural residence, and ethnic differences by altitude. He demonstrated that in southern Peru altitude is the major factor affecting infant growth rates. The partial pressure of oxygen decreases with increasing altitude. Hypoxia results whenever physiological, pathological, or environmental conditions cannot deliver an adequate supply of oxygen to the tissues. Since air is compressible, at high altitudes it is less concentrated and under less pressure (see Figure 6.4). At 4,500 meters the partial pressure of oxygen is decreased by as much as 40 percent, in comparison to pressure at sea level. This reduces the amount of oxygen available to the tissues (Frisancho 1975). A more recent comparison sought to find out if Tibetans lost their adaptation after residence at sea level. The study found that Tibetans maintained a lower heart rate and greater heart rate variability than a Han control population (Zhuang et al. 2002) and thus maintained their native adaptability to high altitude, at least for one generation.

Adaptation to high altitude hypoxia results in a series of modifications in body functioning that are oriented toward increasing the supply of oxygen. Because some of the adjustments are developmental, it is not surprising to find different adaptive mechanisms in sea level and highland populations. Figure 6.5 is a schematic representation of these two patterns of adaptation. Sea level or lowland populations utilize the less efficient response of increased pulmonary ventilation, in contrast to the developmentally acquired advantage of increased lung volume, to achieve the same adaptive result. A study found that Tibetans of both sexes possess significantly larger chest circumferences than Han males and females, which also grew at high altitude. The Tibetan advantage may be due to genetic differences in the response to hypoxia during growth and development (Weitz et al. 2004). Moreover, this difference is exacerbated with altitude. A study of Qinghai Tibetans living at three levels of altitude (3,200, 3,800, and 4,300 meters) found that only minor differences existed in thorax dimensions in either males or females at 3,200 and 3,800 meters, but that at 4,300 meters Tibetan males possessed narrower and deeper chests suggesting the effect of hypoxia on development (Weitz et al. 2000). Weitz and colleagues (2002) report a similar result among Han Chinese living at high altitudes. The positive role of hypoxia training on athletic performance is increasingly recognized, and some heart specialists believe it can have a positive effect on cardiovascular diseases if managed with care (Hoppeler and Vogt 2001).

The adaptive responses to hypoxia include increasing the availability of oxygen and the pressure of oxygen at the tissue level. Some of the physiological mechanisms

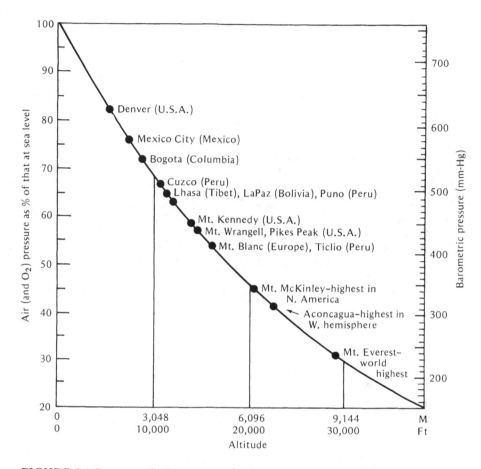

FIGURE 6.4 Barometric Pressure and Oxygen Pressure at High Altitudes

With increasing altitude, there is a marked percentage decrease in both air and oxygen pressure. *Source:* R. Frisancho, "Functional Adaptation to High Altitude Hypoxia," *Science* 187 (1975): 313–319. Copyright 1975 by the American Association for the Advancement of Science.

that facilitate adaptation to hypoxia operate along the oxygen pressure gradient in the body and permit oxygen to reach tissues despite the low atmospheric pressure. Other mechanisms operate at the level of the tissues and include enlargement of the **capillary** bed and chemical-enzymatic changes related to internal respiration (Hurtado 1964:844; compare Moore 2000).

At high altitude, oxygen pressure can be 40 percent or more below sea level pressure (Baker 1968:9). Without adaptive mechanisms, the tissues of a man living at

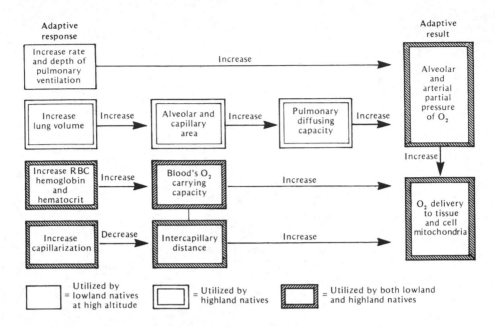

FIGURE 6.5 Schematic Summary of the Adaptive Responses (Physiological) to Hypoxia

Source: R. Frisancho, "Functional Adaptation to High Altitude Hypoxia," *Science* 187 (1975): 313–319. Copyright 1975 by the American Association for the Advancement of Science.

4,540 meters would have an oxygen tension inadequate to diffuse oxygen and make it available for cell metabolism. Figure 6.6 illustrates the remarkable economy of the oxygen pressure gradient among natives of high altitudes as compared with that of people at sea level. This economy is possible mainly because of increased lung ventilation, decreased alveolar-arterial oxygen gradient, and polycythemia (Hurtado 1964:845). Because oxygen is consumed as it goes through successive tissue layers, partial oxygen pressure tends to drop. At high altitude, where pressure is low to start with, the organism adjusts by shortening the distance the oxygen must travel. This is accomplished by an increased number of capillaries.

A common response to high altitude is an *increase in pulmonary ventilation*. Natives have a 20–40 percent faster breathing rate than sea level populations, and newcomers to high altitudes begin to **hyperventilate** (breathe rapidly) upon arrival. Surprisingly, the higher breathing rate of the native population is accomplished without an increase in metabolic rates. Why this happens is not clearly understood, but in experimental situations it appears to be related to chemical stimulation by the blood carbon dioxide level (Hurtado 1964:848). The high altitude resident is in a

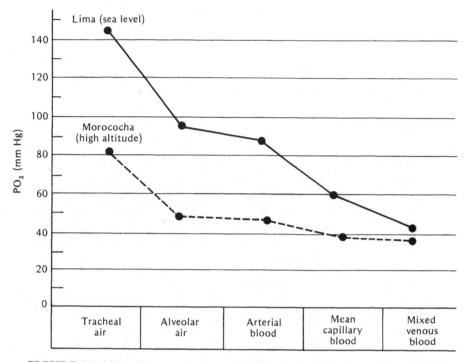

FIGURE 6.6 Mean Oxygen Pressure Gradients from Tracheal Air to Mixed Venous Blood

Values are derived from a sample of sixteen healthy adult subjects, eight of whom reside at sea level and eight at an altitude of 4,540 meters. *Source*: A. Hurtado, "Animals in High Altitudes: Resident Man," in *Handbook of Physiology: Adaptation to the Environment*, edited by D. B. Dill (Washington, DC: American Physiological Society, 1964). Used with permission from American Physiological Society.

state of hypocapnia (low carbon dioxide), and adaptation to this condition is achieved by avoiding excessive hyperventilation because of the low pH of the cerebrospinal fluids resulting from increased anaerobic glycolisis in the brain (Ward 1975:147–148). Newcomers to high altitude sometimes suffer from hypocapnia, if they arrive too abruptly and do not reduce their activity level during a brief adjustment period. People exposed to high altitude experience somatic symptoms such as breathlessness, palpitations, dizziness, headache, and insomnia—and even cognitive misinterpretations (Roth et al. 2002). Other disturbances felt by newcomers to high altitudes include acute mountain sickness, high altitude cerebral edema, and high altitude pulmonary edema (Rodway et al. 2003). The best way to prevent these disturbances is to ascend slowly to altitude and gradually acclimatize, and the best cure is to descend to lower altitudes. Chronic mountain sickness (CMS) is a product of low oxygen pressure. A lower incidence of CMS occurs in Tibetans as compared to Andean populations, and the difference has been proposed to lie in genetic adaptations to hypoxia among Tibetans (Wu 2001; see Rupert and Hochachka 2001 for a detailed discussion of genetic versus developmental adaptations to hypoxia; and Maloney and Broeckel 2005 for risk factors when low altitude populations move to high altitudes).

The decreased alveolar-arterial oxygen gradient results from greater residual volume in the dilated alveoli of the lungs and from the permanent dilation of the capillary bed in the lungs of natives (Hurtado 1964:849). Highland natives have a larger lung volume and greater residual lung volume (the volume of air that remains in the lungs after maximum expiration). This increased volume is a developmental adjustment accomplished by the proliferation of alveolar units and an increase in alveolar surface area during childhood (Frisancho 1975). The effects of high altitude, however, can vary. Beall and Goldstein (1982) note that Tibetans living at very high elevations in Nepal have smaller chests than Andean natives. Later Beall (2001, 2006) found that the difference may be due to microevolutionary adaptation resulting from a gene for oxygen saturation detected among Tibetans, indirectly suggesting population-level genetic adaptation. The width of the chest starts smaller in Andean populations but when growth is completed, they have wider chests. Nepalese Sherpas, well-known mountain trekkers, have significantly smaller chest circumferences than Tibetan neighbors or Andean natives. Whether this is a product of genetic differences or nutritional and health status remains under investigation (Weiss and Mann 1991).

Polycythemia refers to an increase in the number of red blood cells and in the amounts of hemoglobin in persons acclimatized to high altitude. It does not appear to be present in uterine life but develops within a few days after birth (Hurtado 1964:850). Prolonged exposure to hypoxia has a stimulating effect on bone marrow growth. As a result, more red blood cells are produced and the total volume of red blood cells in the body increases (that is, the blood thickens) (Grover 1974:823). However, Beall and Goldstein (1987) found much lower hemoglobin levels among Tibetan pastoral nomads than among Andean Quechua natives, suggesting interpopulation variability in developmental responses to hypoxia. Along with the increased production of red blood cells, the volume of blood plasma decreases. Consequently the blood contains a larger volume of red blood cells and hemoglobin and can carry a greater quantity of oxygen, which helps reduce the oxygen gradient between arterial and venous blood and aids the buffer capacity of blood for carbon dioxide (Grover 1974:823; Hurtado 1964:851).

Other stressors associated with living at high altitude are a greater concentration of ultraviolet radiation, since the air is thinner and offers less protection; rapid heat loss to the atmosphere resulting in cold stress; and dry conditions produced by high winds and low humidity (Relethford 1999:155). Frisancho (1993) has suggested the need to think in terms of multiple stresses to fully understand the human adaptability of high altitude populations.

Work Capacity and Diet

Accounts of the great physical capacity of natives at high altitudes are exaggerated. Although natives perform better than newcomers at high altitudes, carefully designed experiments have not shown any significant superiority in natives when they move to lowland areas. Baker (1968:16) notes that good physical training and lifelong exposure to high altitude act to increase maximal oxygen consumption. Grover (1974:826) finds Andean natives physiologically similar to athletes: both share a high aerobic or maximal work capacity. The native accomplishes this by exposure to atmospheric hypoxia and an active life, and athletes by subjecting themselves to strenuous exercise that produces tissue hypoxia in muscles.

Hurtado (1964:854) noted that at sea level natives have a higher ventilation rate, lower pulse rate, and smaller increases in blood pressure than athletes.[2] This is related to the high altitude native's efficient oxygen diffusion and the marked economy of the oxygen disassociation curve (see Figure 6.6). Childhood development at high altitude, on the other hand, enhances adult work capacity and when combined with high activity levels results in a superior work performance capacity (Frisancho and Greksa 1989; Greksa et al. 1985). Figure 6.7 illustrates the relationship between age at the time of migration from sea level to altitude and VO_2 achieved. The data in Figure 6.7 are based on a small sample, but suggest a critical age at which migration must occur if the individual is to achieve a high VO_2 max as an adult (Greksa et al. 1985:310–311). Whether a genetic factor is involved remains unresolved (Brutsaert et al. 2004). Mazess attributes the higher work capacity of natives to their lower body weight, vigorous work in the pursuit of subsistence, and characteristic high carbohydrate diet. A high carbohydrate diet has been shown to enhance endurance through increased muscle glycogen (Mazess 1975:177), a finding utilized by athletes. There is clear evidence of a developmental gradient along an altitudinal gradient, with high altitude prehistoric populations in the Andes having shorter limbs than neighboring groups at low altitudes (Weinstein 2005).

Natives claim that chewing coca leaves enhances their work capacity, and in the past many refused to work unless coca (*Erythroxylon coca*) was provided. Hanna (1976:370) found a slight elevation in heart rate during work when coca leaves were chewed, but he also determined that the effect was no different from that produced by ingestion of caffeine or other psychostimulants. Coca is also implicated in a mild vasoconstriction of blood vessels in the extremities. This results in reduced heat loss and slightly higher core temperatures and is advantageous when outside work must be performed and there is potential cold stress. The use of coca goes back to ancient times, as archeologists have found mummies in the south central Andes bearing evidence of long-term coca chewing (Rivera et al. 2005; Indriati and Buikstra 2001).

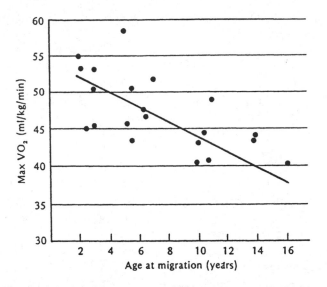

FIGURE 6.7 Relationship Between Adult VO₂ Max at 3,400 Meters and the Age at Migration from Low to High Altitude

Source: Adapted and reprinted, with permission, from P. Baker, "Work Performed of Highland Natives," in *Man in the Andes: A Multidisciplinary Study of High-Altitude Quecha*, edited by P. Baker and M. Little (Stroudsburg, PA: Dowden, Hutchinson & Ross, 1976).

Picón-Reátegui (1976:234–235) found no major nutritional deficiencies in the Andean population and no advantage in coca chewing from a nutritional point of view. Burchard, on the other hand, suggested that coca chewing, in combination with a high-carbohydrate, low-protein, and low-fat diet, is an important strategy for managing hypoglycemia (low blood glucose) and carbohydrate malabsorption (1976:27).

Body tissues require a constant supply of carbohydrates to provide energy. Absorption of ingested carbohydrate in the intestine depends on the time the carbohydrate is in contact with the absorbing surface and on the supply of enzymes for the oxidation of carbohydrate. Once oxidized, carbohydrate is absorbed into the bloodstream as glucose, galactose, and fructose. The last two are later transformed to glucose in the liver. Glucose is stored as glycogen and reconverted to glucose as needed. Bolton found that "coca chewing has immediate effects in raising glucose levels, probably by stimulating the transformation of glycogen stores" (1973:253). Figure 6.8 illustrates the change in blood glucose after coca leaves are chewed. Even after four hours, glucose levels are moderately higher than the levels of those who do not use the leaves. Low levels of glucose and carbohydrate malabsorption are apparently widespread health problems in highland Peru and are related to undernutrition, especially inadequate protein due to poverty (Gray 1973:70–71). On the positive side, there is now evidence that Andean (Aymara) natives have low prevalence of type 2 diabetes, despite a high average body mass index (Santos et al. 2001). High levels of physical activity and low concentrations of plasma insulin may be responsible for this lower prevalence. It is not clear, however, to what extent the general reduction in food utilization is a result of hypoxia or of anorexia and hypohydration (Mazess 1975:182). Gray points out that atropine, an amino alcohol found in coca, increases contact time between carbohydrates and the intestinal mucosa (1973:122–123). Burchard notes that coca is chewed often before and after meals, which relaxes the small intestines and facilitates adsorption (1976:266–267). If this is the case, it may explain natives' ability to perform well at work, despite diets that only meet minimum recommended dietary requirements. Coca-induced intestinal absorption of food may help individuals meet the increased costs of keeping warm in a cold environment, of heavy work schedules, and the needs of pregnancy, lactation, and growth (Picón-Reategui 1976:235).

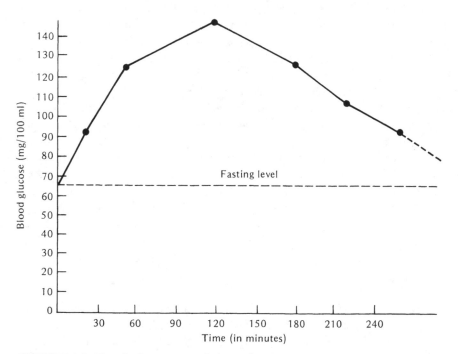

FIGURE 6.8 Blood Glucose Levels in Coca Chewers After Chewing 1–1.5 Ounces of Leaves

Source: Based on Roderick Burchard, "Myths of the Sacred Leaf: Ecological Perspectives on Coca and Peasant Biocultural Adaptation in Peru" (Ph.D. diss., Indiana University, 1976).

It has long been observed that populations at high altitude are characterized by iodine deficiency and a high prevalence of goiter (Kvitkova et al. 2005). Another study found that children at high altitudes were 2.5 times more likely to develop goiter when compared to their counterparts at sea level, but there were also important differences in rates within mountain populations, suggesting that not only altitude but the source of water and other environmental factors may be implicated in the high rates (Abu-Eshy et al. 2001).

Reproduction and Maturation

Hypoxia appears to affect reproduction. Monge (1948) found Spanish documents from the early colonial period that explained, and probably exaggerated, that no European woman could carry a child through term at high altitude. They attributed the problem to the "thin air" and justified moving the capital from the highlands (Cuzco) to sea level Lima on those grounds (Baker 1968:2). Newcomers to high altitude do experience a reduction in fertility, reduced ability to carry a fetus to full term, and high neonatal mortality. Mazess (1975), however, found that the moderately high altitudes where most Andean populations live have only a mild effect on fecundity and reproductive performance. A more dramatic effect on reproduction is reflected in lower birth weights and increased postnatal mortality (Mazess 1975:185; see Wiley 2004 for a biocultural discussion of these processes in the western Himalayas of India). Although short-term difficulties in spermatogenesis and menstruation are experienced by those who move to high altitudes, men and women native to the area appear normal in these respects. There appears to be no hypoxic stress on the fetus during pregnancy, possibly as a result of an increase in the size of the placenta (Hoff and Abelson 1976). There is also a decrease in the birth weight relative to the placenta, which facilitates delivery of oxygen to the fetus without unduly increasing the demands on the mother. Infant mortality is most often a result of low birth weight. The stress of altitude is further exacerbated by poverty and poor health services (Thomas 1998). A recent study shows that birth weights are lower at higher altitude for infants born between thirty-six and forty-two weeks, suggesting inadequate maternal oxygenation later in pregnancy at high altitude (Hartinger et al. 2006). When controlling for socioeconomic factors, birth weight reduction occurs only in births at term and is less severe when the mother is a long-term resident at high altitude (Hartinger et al. 2006).

Although the explanation for this phenomenon has not been clearly demonstrated, the relationship between higher altitude and reduced fertility may be attributed more to differences in infant and child mortality than to lower fecundity (Dutt 1976). To overcome this threat to the population, the Quechua share an ideology that aims at maximizing births. As a result, despite high rates of abortion and neonatal mortality, Quechua females at Nuñoa have a high rate of complete fertility (6.7 births per woman). This is accomplished by incorporating almost all women into the breeding population, by cultural preference for large families, and by the enlarged placenta, which provides a more favorable uterine environment by minimizing hypoxic stress on the fetus. Recent studies suggest that Andean women at high altitude have higher uteroplacental oxygen delivery than European high altitude residents due to more complete growth and remodeling of maternal uterine vessels (Rockwell et al. 2003). While more data are needed, several studies suggest that in some parts of the Andes and Himalayas the numbers of males born relative to females is higher than expected but that mortality of male children is much higher than elsewhere, leaving an adult population with an excess of females. However, this ratio may be confounded by high male outmigration (Baker 1978:321–322; Goldstein and Beall 1991). Demographic strategies can vary from region to region, and in the Himalayas celibacy (for example, lamas and female nuns), late marriage, and outmigration to relieve local demographic pressure (Childs 1998) are more common.

At high altitude growth and development are slow. This may be related to the demands of chest and bone marrow development (Frisancho 1976:199). During childhood important changes occur in alveolar area and diffusion capacity that facilitate the diffusion of oxygen. Maturation is delayed at high altitude, and sexual dimorphism (differences between males and females as manifested in body size and muscle size) appears to occur only after the sixteenth year. Hypoxia alone is not sufficient to explain the morphological differences among inhabitants of different altitudes. Cold and hypoxia may be jointly implicated in the slower development of children at high altitude. The diversion of calories to heat production, instead of to storage or growth, appears to be involved in the slower development of Quechuas (Little and Hochner 1973:17). Hypocaloric stress and possibly genetic factors are also involved in the slow growth and development of the Andean population. Increasingly, studies suggest that the role of malnutrition and undernutrition plays a larger role than was recognized in the past (Harris et al. 2001; Leatherman 1998). The same seems to be true for Tibetan children living at high altitudes, with 39 percent stunted, 23 percent underweight, and 5.6 percent wasted (Dang et al. 2004). Anemia and early childhood mortality have been found in pre-Columbian Peru to follow an altitudinal gradient, with higher rates of both anemia and child mortality at higher altitudes than at lower altitudes, where marine resources may have provided nutritional relief (Blom et al. 2005).

Maladaptations

Not all individuals native to high altitude adapt to hypoxia, and some lose their adaptation. This is known as chronic mountain sickness (CMS) and involves loss of normal breathing stimulation, which leads to low oxygen pressure in the lung alveoli and the arterial blood. To compensate, the body experiences excessive polycythemia (blood thickening). This is treated by reducing the amount of blood cells every two or three weeks, but the best solution is to leave the high altitude zone (Grover 1974).

Since high altitude natives sometimes make seasonal migrations to the lowlands, they may also experience pulmonary edema on returning to altitude (that is, buildup of fluid in the lungs, which interferes with the transfer of oxygen from the air to the bloodstream). Following several weeks at sea level, even natives may experience this temporary illness when they return to high altitude (Grover 1974:827). Hypoxia seems to increase the seriousness of pulmonary disease as well as the frequency of patent ductus arteriosus (Baker 1978:329). Inherited or acquired anemia has more serious consequences at high altitude than at sea level (Baker 1978:330). The high tuberculosis and echinococcus rates (the latter associated with sheep pastoralism) further aggravate pulmonary stress. On the positive side, malaria and yellow fever are largely absent at high altitudes, as are arboviruses. The low prevalence of diarrhea and other gastrointestinal problems common to lowland areas reduces the impact of this important cause of child mortality.

ADAPTABILITY TO COLD STRESS IN THE ANDES

Next to hypoxia, cold is the most significant stress felt by high altitude populations. However, it is more amenable than hypoxia to management by appropriate cultural practices. The cold stress felt by the Andean population is unique: it is nonstressful during the day because of high solar radiation and relative dryness, but by night, because heat escapes rapidly from the ground, the population may experience significant cold stress (Baker 1966:276).

Physiological Adjustments

Long-term exposure to cold stress may lead to acclimatization. Those habituated demonstrate increased peripheral blood flow to the extremities (Hanna 1968:220) that prevents cold injury, limits heat loss through the hand, and permits easier hand functioning in cold conditions. This difference in response appears to be developmental. Studies of foot exposure to cold air at 0°C in the Andean highlands showed that both native adults and children maintain warmer skin temperatures than whites, but differences between the juvenile and adult Quechua studied suggest that this ability increases through the developmental period. If so, the neonate may experience severe cold stress. Brown adipose tissue (BAT) is present in human infants and helps maintain high core temperatures and promotes nonshivering thermogenesis. Normal fat as a percentage of body weight is lowest at birth. Between birth and age one, however, it increases sixfold, while the stores of brown adipose tissue are slowly depleted (Little and Hochner 1973:6).

Cultural Adjustments

Housing and shelter are the most evident means by which Andean populations deal with potential cold stress. Two types of houses are seen in this region: one made of piled stones with a grass roof, the other made of **adobe** with a roof of grass, straw, or metal. The stone houses are chiefly found at higher altitudes and are used by the pastoralist population when they graze their animals at higher levels. Although easily constructed, they offer less protection from cold; the temperature inside is only 2–3°C higher than the temperature outside at night (Baker 1968:18). The adobe houses, by contrast, are 7–10°C warmer than outside ambient temperatures, but construction of the foot-wide adobe walls is time-consuming.

Clothing increases body temperature (Hanna 1976:329). Outer garments are made of wool and tend to be of dark colors that provide maximum daytime heat gain (Hanna 1968:309). Wool is an ideal material for clothing insulation since it resists crushing and tends to maintain its original volume of trapped air. The trapped air is only insulative if it can be kept from escaping, and this is achieved by wearing outer garments of such a tight weave that they are almost waterproof (Hanna 1976:328). Open weave clothes are worn in layers to provide added dead air spaces for insulation. During heavy physical work, natives remove some of the layers that normally prevent cooling, and perspiration can escape (see Figure 6.9). Finally the layers are replaced. Men often wear trousers, a shirt, a sweater, a vest, a short jacket, and a poncho, in addition to a cap or hat. Women wear from two to seven skirts, a blouse, a vest, a shawl, and a derby hat (Little 1968:376). Despite their lack of footwear and gloves, the Andean natives are well protected from the cold.[3]

FIGURE 6.9 Andean Natives Working in a Field

At midday, several layers of clothing may be shed, to be replaced as the sun sets or the activity comes to an end. Photo by E. Moran.

As already noted, blood flow to the extremities affords some physiological protection from exposure to cold. Hanna (1976:329; 1968:308) explains that although the Quechuas could manufacture footgear made of hides, it would be detrimental during the rainy season. The whole region becomes mired, and sodden footgear would increase heat loss and cooling of the extremities. Because of their impermeability, shoes or boots would also hold in sweat during periods of hard work and promote a harmful cooling of the extremities. Bare feet and open sandals, on the other hand, do not become water-soaked and dry rapidly. The protection provided by greater blood flow to the extremities is sufficient to protect them from injury.

Scheduling of work activities also helps protect Andean populations from cold. People rise after dawn and go to bed at sunset (Baker 1966). They spend most of the day outside, taking advantage of the solar radiation. Women and children do most of the herding, which primarily involves walking. Men do agricultural work or labor for wages in copper and tin mines. (Mountain areas have long been exploited for their minerals. Copper and tin have been particularly important in the Andes.) At night, natives sleep in their clothing with added layers of hides on sleeping platforms. Native bedding is adequate to meet minimum temperature levels that prevent shivering and cold stress. Although children have higher rectal temperatures than adults during the day (probably as a result of higher physical activity), at night their temperatures are lower than those of the adults (Little and Hochner 1973:15).

Because children are more subject to cold stress, child care practices of Quechuas center on efforts to reduce cold stress (T. Baker 1976:90). Children are placed in the sun to absorb maximum solar heat during the day or next to a fire, and at night they are bedded with siblings. Young infants are kept completely wrapped, with infrequent diaper changes, helping maintain a warm, humid microenvironment that protects the infant against both cold and dry air. Demand feeding provides a constant supply of nutrition to the child (T. Baker 1976:91).

ARIDITY AND LOW PRODUCTIVITY

As already noted, increasing altitude limits plant productivity, which at the highest altitudes includes high winds, high levels of solar radiation, a largely treeless landscape, and low moisture conditions. Droughts have a major impact on agriculture in the Andes. Vulnerability to drought played a role in the collapse of the Wari and Tiwanaku states, as management of water was disrupted by political instability (P. R. Williams 2002). Orlove and colleagues (2000) have noted that in the central Andes poor visibility of the Pleiades in June and reduced rainfall during the growing season are associated with El Niño events. This indigenous system of forecasting permitted farmers to alter their cropping strategies. The system of indigenous El Niño forecasting is the first one shown to be consistent with scientific data to date. Human occupation of highlands has involved a sensitively coordinated ecological verticality (biotic zonation) (Brush 1976; Troll 1958). Pre-Incan populations sought access to

TABLE 6.1 Production Zones in Three Mountain Areas

	S. Switzerland		Andes		Nepalese Himalayas	
	Altitude	Products	Altitude	Products	Altitude	Products
Low altitude	less than 1,000 m.	vineyards	less than 1,500 m.	sugar cane, coca, fruits, rice	less than 1,500 m.	rice, fruit
Mid-altitude	1,000–2,000 m.	cereals, hay, gardens	1,500–3,000 m.	cereals	2,000–3,000 m.	cereals, tubers
Mid-/high altitude	2,000–3,000 m.	forest	3,000–4,000 m.	tubers	3,000–4,000 m.	forest
High altitude	2,300–3,000 m.	pasture	4,000–5,000 m.	pasture	4,000–5,000 m.	pasture

Source: Adapted from Stephen Brush, "Man's Use of an Andean Ecosystem," *Human Ecology* 4, no. 2 (1976): 128–132, 147–166.

islands of resources by sending people to colonize the various zones up and down the mountain and then trading with people of their own ethnic group (Murra 1972:431). Ecological verticality allowed groups to exploit resources from a variety of ecological zones located at different altitudes (Burchard 1976:37). Moreover, there is mounting evidence that coastal civilizations flourished during periods of aridity at high altitudes in the Andes (Thompson et al. 1994).

Types of Subsistence Strategies

Human societies overcome low productivity through trade, **exchange networks,** and seasonal migration to more productive zones. These responses can be severely limited by poverty and inequitable land tenure systems. Though high altitude may play a role in nutritional stress, income and access to land play a no less important role. A study in Peru has shown that nutrition is a major influence on stature (Leonard et al. 1990). In other high altitude areas such as Ethiopia, there are fewer growth deficits than those recorded for Peru due to higher standards of living. Trade, for example, is important in Tibet, where even the religious system is partially supportive of its demands (Downs and Ekvall 1965:173). In summer people take their herds to higher slopes where excellent alpine meadow pasture is still common (James 1966:401).

Brush (1976) distinguished four zones in the Swiss Alps, the Andes, and the Nepalese Himalayas on the basis of products and production regimes (see Table 6.1). Subsistence strategies in each area were designed to provide access to the products of the differing zones (Dutta et al. 2004). Among the notable cross-cultural and cross-ecological similarities were reliance on an agropastoral economy, the use of trade to maintain linkages between zones, and the utilization of similar crops and animals. Netting (1976:137) has suggested that the corporate forms of land tenure commonly encountered at higher altitudes may be related to harsh environmental conditions and subsistence requirements that are more effectively controlled by group consensus than by individual effort (Netting 1981).

Animals and Exchange

The utilization of domestic animals is regulated by altitude. In the central Andes, alpaca and llama are concentrated at very high altitudes, sheep occupy an intermediate zone, and cows and horses the lower elevations. Natives cite the lower fertility of the cattle and the low viability of the young as reasons for their absence at high altitudes. Cattle also lack the thick insulative fur of the sheep and camelids.

In the Tibetan Himalayas the yak *(Poephagus gruniens)* provides meat, milk, blood, butter, cheese, hides, fur, horns, and transport to the Tibetan population (Downs and Ekvall 1965:173). Horses and cows are found at middle altitudes, and the donkey at lower levels. To overcome potential problems in trade and mobility, Tibetan populations have produced intermediate hybrids capable of moving up and down the Himalayas with less stress and with a greater capacity for useful work. The *dzo,* a cross between the yak and the cow, can carry one-third more weight than a yak and is faster and more tractable and capable of moving into lower altitudes than the yak (Downs and Ekvall 1965:176–177).

In the Andes, neither wild plants nor wild fauna provide much food. Fishing provides an important food supplement for certain periods. Human occupation has depleted the native population of vicuña, guanaco, and deer, and domesticants have been introduced to replace them. Alpacas, llamas, sheep, cows, horses, and guinea pigs supply a variety of resources that are essential for life as it presently exists in the Andes.

The llama has long been a necessity of life in this region (see Figure 6.10). In pre-Incan times, it was a basic right of the peasant household and a keystone of the economy (Murra 1965:211). The reason for its importance lies in the variety of resources it provides the highlander: transportation, hides, wool, dung, and food. The mobility required in a zonal environment like that of the Andes makes the use of llamas for transporting loads essential. The animal is well adapted to the bunch grasses that predominate in the moist puna and to the high altitude and cold. The camelids are better able to tolerate highland climate stresses than other herding animals. In the 1982–1983 drought associated with El Niño, for example, typical sheep losses were as high as 40–50 percent, whereas alpaca losses were only 10–20 percent (Browman 1984, 1987:126). Alpacas and llamas transform high cellulose grasses into biomass, and their relatively soft hooves reduce trampling damage (Ellenberg 1979). Llamas and alpacas concentrate the dispersed energy of pasture grasses in the form of dung, which is preferred as cooking fuel. The dung is easy to collect because camelids have special sites for defecating (Orlove 1977:93). It appears to have 10 percent more potential energy than that of sheep (Thomas 1976:394). A lot of the weight that llamas must carry across zones is dung; sheep dung tends to be carried the greatest distances because of its importance as fertilizer.

One important exchange that occurs in the Andes and has important implications for human ecology is the transfer of dung to lower altitudes and the reciprocal transfer of coca to higher altitudes. This seasonal exchange of dung for coca is an important economic activity of the southern highland population of Peru. Coca has been mentioned already as a possible factor in improved carbohydrate absorption and temporary relief of hypoglycemia. It also has a stimulating effect comparable to that of caffeine. Dung is an important resource of the highland pastoral areas and is absolutely essential to agricultural productivity.

Winterhalder and colleagues (1974) have shown that the soils of Nuñoa are deficient in nitrogen, phosphorus, and organic matter, in addition to having drainage and erosion problems. The addition of dung to the fields increases organic matter by 31 percent. Organic matter also improves the physical aspects of the soil: aeration, soil moisture relationships, and water-holding capacity. In a generally arid environment this is an important consideration. In the area studied, camelid dung is primarily used

FIGURE 6.10 Llamas and Other Andean Camelids

They are the sine qua non of Andean pastoralism and subsistence at high altitudes. Women and children commonly herd these animals. Photo by E. Moran.

as fuel in household cooking and sheep manure is used for fertilizing fields. This is an appropriate choice, since sheep manure is higher in nitrogen, magnesium, calcium, and potassium.

The vertical ecological zones in the Andes provide an abundance of products for trade or exchange (Knapp 1991). Coca is the major facilitator of interzonal exchange. It is the universal social lubricant and is necessary for most social transactions: getting married, borrowing, buying, and selling. Coca only grows at lower altitudes, but its use increases with altitude (see Table 6.2). High altitude dwellers, therefore, must obtain access to coca leaves through direct cultivation (seasonal migration to the lowlands and getting paid in coca) or purchase and exchange. Exchange is facilitated by kinship, *compadrazgo* (fictive kinship), and friendship ties (Burchard 1976:40). Direct access to multiple zones continues today, even in unexpected areas such as the narrow valleys of the northern Chilean desert following the archipelago pattern discussed earlier as a traditional pattern of the region (O. Harris 1981).

Agricultural Practices

The Andean population has overcome the limitations of the poor productivity of wild plants by using productive domesticates. Domesticated plants do not grow

TABLE 6.2 Relationship Between Incidence of Coca Chewing and Altitude

Village	Altitude (in feet)	% Males	% Females	Mean
1	377	2.8	2.5	2.7
2	2,130	35.7	21.8	28.7
3	6,150	45.4	10.4	27.9
4	11,500	68.7	74.4	71.5

Source: Based on Roderick Burchard, "Myths of the Sacred Leaf: Ecological Perspectives on Coca Peasant Biocultural Adaptation in Peru" (Ph.D. diss., Indiana University, 1976).

above 4,500 meters. Those grown near human habitations of 4,000 meters are of ancient use: the grains quinoa *(Chenopodium quinoa)* and cañihua *(Chenopodium pallidicuale)* and tubers, which include oca *(Oxalis crenata)*, olluco *(Ollucus tuberosa)*, isano, and three types of potatoes *(Solanum tuberosum, S. juzepozukii, and S. curtilobum)*. The last two types of potatoes are frost-resistant varieties grown at the highest elevations where agriculture is practiced.

The population practices a precise form of cultivation using the numerous microenvironments found in close proximity to a large variety of plants that are capable of making full use of each area. Wet slopes are commonly planted while dry slopes usually remain uncultivated. Less than 2 percent of the total land area is suitable for agriculture, which at these heights is both uncertain and of low productivity (Thomas and Winterhalder 1976:55–56).

Terracing and irrigation have been widely used in both the Andes and the Himalayas. These techniques extend agriculture to marginal areas and help overcome the environmental constraints of thin soils and inadequate soil moisture. The expansion and contraction of terrace agriculture in the Andes is associated with availability of mountain springs, population density, and the political economy (Guillet 1987).The cost of maintaining terraces is very high, and thus they tend to be abandoned when population density declines (as it did after contact with European diseases) or the political economy does not provide prices or subsidies to ensure their maintenance. Crops are planted on protected slopes where there is the least danger of frost (Orlove 1977:93).

In addition to frost, dryness can also prevent food production. A number of practices have been noted that enhance retention of soil moisture and increase solar insolation (Evans and Winterhalder 2000). Guillet (1987) has pointed out that agricultural intensification and declining intensification, particularly of agriculture in terraces, is closely related to water availability. Households abandon terraces when they lack adequate access to water, whether human- or climate-induced, but they rebuild them during periods of relative water abundance and access. Manuring has a beneficial effect (Winterhalder et al. 1974). Making furrows in fields, as well as digging shallow depressions *(qochavina)* that retain water longer and make it available for crops, facilitates water retention while preventing waterlogging (Orlove 1977:95–96). There are good years, as well as bad ones, and during the good years the Quechua utilize preservation techniques that allow them to store products for several years. One technique of special significance is the freeze-drying of bitter potatoes to make *chuño*, which is said to keep for several years without spoilage (Orlove 1977:94).

Four major stages occur in the yearly cycle of subsistence: the planting and shearing period; the growing period; the harvest period; and the postharvest and slaughter period (Thomas 1976:383). During the planting period, work input and food intake are high, but stored food is sufficient to sustain such demand. Food stores are at their lowest during the growing period, but it is also a period when work is not intensive or arduous. Some food can be bought during this period from the proceeds of wool sales, and the meat of young herd animals that die is also consumed. During the harvest, work is hard, but food is abundant and a portion of the herd (10–20 percent) is slaughtered. In the postharvest period, food consumption is at its highest, although work is relatively light.

CLIMATE CHANGE AND
HIGH ALTITUDE ECOSYSTEMS

High altitude mountains are the focus of research on climate change (Broll and Keplin 2005) because of the availability of ancient ice cores that trapped particles that can be used to reconstruct past climates. Two major dust events around AD 920 and AD 600 suggest major anthropogenic impacts on the altiplano of Peru. Recent studies (Thompson et al. 1993) suggest that the ice cores collected just a few years ago at Quelccaya ice cap are not being preserved, as melting is now taking place at the summit and water is moving vertically through the ice cap, destroying the integrity of the ice core records (Thompson et al. 1994). Brecher and Thompson (1993) add that the whole ice cap is experiencing a rapid retreat due to global warming. While complete loss of these high altitude glaciers may still take a few decades, their gradual meltdown is already destroying the value of the ice caps as accurate summaries of the paleorecord. As with the arctic and antarctic regions, global warming has accelerated the melting of glaciers and their demise in some places is already complete, as on Mount Kilimanjaro (Thompson et al. 1994).

Research on the emergence of agriculture (c. 1500 BC) and the collapse of the Tiwanaku civilization (c. AD 1100) coincides with periods of abrupt climate change. Prior to 1500 BC aridity in the altiplano precluded the development of intensive agriculture. During the wetter years of 1500 BC to AD 1100, the Tiwanaku and their predecessors developed a successful agricultural system that sustained a growing population. The arrival of another prolonged arid period that lasted from AD 1100 to

1400 led to the collapse of agricultural production and the Tiwanaku civilization (Binford et al. 1997; Kolata 1993). Janusek (2006) suggests that Tiwanaku religion and ritual practice shaped the rise of the Tiwanaku state by integrating the symbolism of prominent generative forces such as mountains and vital elements such as water and recurring celestial cycles. This set of complex knowledge may have been important in effective coordination of fishing, herding, and farming that teetered between success and collapse (Janusek 2006).

The stable system that Paul Baker and his associates described and analyzed in Nuñoa during the IBP has been changed by modernization and revolution. The area became a hotbed of the Sendero Luminoso guerrillas and for years experienced high levels of violence. This situation has now changed, and researchers are renewing their work in the region and the population is free to move about without fear. Elsewhere in the Andes, modernization, especially the development of roads to remote villages, has forever changed intervillage patterns of trade and exchange. However, the resiliency of the Andean population through the centuries and the adaptive value of their practices suggest that newcomers have more to learn from the Quechua than the Quechua from the newcomers.

Mountain ecosystems present particularly difficult challenges to the application of remote sensing techniques to monitor environmental changes (Casimir and Rao 1998; Gautam et al. 2004; Bishop and Shroder 2004). It is essential that detailed field studies be carried out to georeference the spectral information. The SPOT satellite sensor, operating at 832 kilometers with a panchromatic resolution of 10 meters by 10 meters, can provide adequate detail in mountain regions. By digitizing contour lines from topographical maps of the study area, a digital elevation model (DEM) can be created and subsequently a digital terrain model of relief (DTM) to facilitate the assignment of classes to land cover. Significant advances in the past decade make these tasks more precise and productive (Bishop and Shroder 2004).

The integration of many mountain regions to the national and global economy has helped residents abandon high altitude regions and has increased participation in the economy through improved roads and infrastructure (Mishra et al. 2003). The fragility of mountains to degradation through erosion remains one of the great challenges to human populations (Körner 2003). Pasture and crop conservation practices can reduce this vulnerability, but evidence is that in many regions degradation is increasing (Loffler 2000). Particularly vulnerable, since prehistoric accounts, are the human populations who persist in poverty, malnutrition, and poor health in many areas (Leatherman 2005). Mountain regions continue to be areas of interest as early warning systems for the processes of climate change (Diaz 2003).

SUGGESTED READINGS AND USEFUL WEBSITES

In 2002 the United Nations declared that year to be the International Year of Mountains, hoping to foster discussion and further research on mountain and alpine environments and their resident populations. The United Nations University hosts a website discussing this celebration: www.unu.edu/mountains2002/index.htm. The Global Mountain Biodiversity Assessment (http://gmba.unibas.ch/index/index.htm; www.diversitas-international.org/cross_mountain.html) provides research and detail related to biodiversity and sustainable use of mountains. The International Biological Program (IBP) (www7.nationalacademies.org/archives/International_Biological_Program.html) also spearheaded research into mountain and high alpine terrestrial environments. The report by Becker and Bugmann (1999) entitled *Global Change and Mountain Regions: Initiative for Collaborative Research* discusses the role of mountain and alpine research within the framework of global change studies, as part of the IGBP (Messerli and Ives 1997; Allan et al. 1988).

The journal *Mountain Research and Development* (www.mrd-journal.org) from the International Mountain Society (www.mrd-journal.org/about_mrd.htm#ims) is an interdisciplinary journal discussing mountain-related research. Several policy and development institutions related to mountain and alpine environments are also affiliated with the International Mountain Society, including the Mountain Research Initiative (http://mri.scnatweb.ch) from the IHDP (www.ihdp.uni-bonn.de/html/initiatives/i-mir.html), the International Centre for Integrated Mountain Development (www.icimod.org/home), the Swiss Agency for Development and Cooperation (www.sdc.admin.ch), the United Nations University (www.unu.edu), the Food and Agriculture Organization (www.fao.org), the Centre for Development and Environment (www.cde.unibe.ch), and the World Wildlife Fund International (www.wwf.org). Additional mountain resources can be found at the Mountain Forum (www.mtnforum.org), a network of individuals and organizations designed to promote sustainable development in mountain regions, and the International Mountain Partnership (www.mountainpartnership.org), a network of individuals, nongovernmental organizations, and countries dedicated to mountain environments and the people who live in these places. The National Biological Information Infrastructure (http://international.nbii.gov/portal/server.pt) serves as a data and information portal for a variety of habitat types, including mountain areas.

Additional useful readings and books on alpine and high altitude environment and ecology, especially human impacts and climate change, include *Land Use Change and Mountain Biodiversity* edited by Spehn et al. (2006); *Mountain Ecosystems: Studies in Treeline Ecology* edited by Broll and Keplin (2005); *Alpine Plant Life: Functional Plant Ecology of High Mountain Ecosystems* by Körner (2003); *Rocky Mountain Futures: An Ecological Perspective* edited by Baron (2002); *Mountain Environments* by Parish (2002); *Global Environmental Change in Alpine Regions: Recognition, Impact, Adaptation, and Mitigation* edited by Steininger and Weck-Hannemann (2002); *Environmental Change in Mountains and Uplands* by Beniston (2000); *Land-Use Changes in European Mountain Ecosystems* by Cernusca et al. (2000); *Arctic and Alpine Biodiversity: Patterns, Causes, and Ecosystem Consequences* by Chapin (1995); *Biodiversity and Conservation of Neotropical Montane Forests* by Churchill (1995);

Mountain Environments in Changing Climates by Beniston (1994); and *Human Impact on Mountains* by Allan et al. (1988).

Several research stations provide data, facilities, and resources for conducting ecological research in mountains and high altitude environments. At the Niwot Ridge Long-Term Ecological Research (LTER) (http://culter.colorado.edu/NWT), part of the LTER network of research sites, researchers collect a variety of climatological, vegetation, and faunal data. The University of Colorado also has its own Mountain Research Station and website affiliated with the Niwot LTER research site (www .colorado.edu/mrs). The Mountain Research group of the Institute of British Geographers (www.cms.uhi.ac.uk/rgsmrg) links mountain and alpine researchers with a distinct spatial focus. The Global Observation Research Initiative in Alpine Environments (www.gloria.ac.at) works to unite worldwide observation sites for alpine research, particularly changes in temperature and species biodiversity.

Because mountain environments present challenging environmental conditions for living and survival, much research has been conducted concerning the health, adaptation, and well-being of residents living in these areas. The journal *High Altitude Medicine and Biology* (www.liebertpub.com/publication.aspx?pub_id=65) publishes many articles about high altitude life sciences, including physiology, pharmacology, pathology, anthropology, and human ecology. The paper "Human Adaptation to High Altitude: Regional and Life-Cycle Perspectives" by Moore et al. (1998) summarizes studies about adaptation to high altitude conditions in the Himalayas of Asia, the Andes of South America, and the Rocky Mountains of North America. Additional resources can be found at the Altitude Research Center of University of Colorado (www.uchsc.edu/arc), High Altitude Adaptation at the Center for Research on Tibet (www.case.edu/affil/tibet/moreTibetInfo/hypoxia.htm), and through the International Society for Mountain Medicine (www.ismmed.org).

Additional readings on health and adaptation to high altitude environments include *Problems of High Altitude Medicine and Biology* edited by Aldashey and Naeije (2007); *An Ecology of High-Altitude Infancy: A Biocultural Perspective* by Wiley (2004); *High Altitude: An Exploration of Human Adaptation* by Hornbein and Schoene (2001); *High Life: A History of High-Altitude Physiology and Medicine* by West (1998); and *High Altitude Medicine and Physiology* by Ward et al. (1995).

Cultural adaptations to life in high altitude and montane environments have been a focal point of study by researchers in the social and natural sciences. Specifically related to agriculture in high altitude environments, the Program of Sustainable Agriculture and Natural Resources in the Andes (www.lanra.uga.edu/sanrem) promotes sustainable development in high altitude watersheds of Ecuador, Peru, and Colombia. The Consortium for the Sustainable Development of the Andean Ecoregion (CONDESAN) works to unite public and private sectors to develop sustainable policy in the Andes (www.condesan.org); within CONDESAN, the International Potato Center (www.cipotato.org) focuses specifically on potato research in the Andes in order to increase food security and reduce food scarcity.

Additional readings on cultural adaptations and land use in high altitude environments include *The Aymará: Strategies in Human Adaptation to a Rigorous Environment* edited by Schull and Rothhammer (2006); *Political Ecology, Mountain Agriculture, and Knowledge in Honduras* by Jansen (1998); and *Cultural Adaptation to Mountain Environments* edited by Beaver and Purrington (1984). Robert Netting (1981) described cultural adaptations and land use changes related to altitudinal gradients within a Swiss village in the Alps. Robert Rhoades (and others) have studied mountain cultures and adaptations to high altitude environments, particularly related to sustainable use and development of these areas (Rhoades and Thompson 1975; R. Rhoades 1986, 1992, 1997, 1999, 2000, 2001; Vedwan and Rhoades 2001).

The literature on the Himalayas has been rapidly expanding (Beckwith 1987). A special issue of the journal *Human Ecology* (17 no. 2 [1989]) included articles on subsistence production, animal husbandry, settlement ecology, and demography (Fricke 1989). Transitions from a subsistence to a monetized economy in Nepal are discussed by Fricke and colleagues (1990). As in the Andes, a growing concern with political ecology emphasizes the dialectical relationship between local level human adaptation and the wider political economy (English 1985:76). The Himalayan region is less unified than the Andes—a refuge for a variety of cultures. Trade is more international, rather than simply intramontane. The impact of colonialism is more recent, as is the political development of states in the region. Particularly important in this regard have been the Chinese occupation of Tibet and the increase of trade between India and Nepal with improvement in road infrastructure (Fisher 1986). Mountain villages high in the Himalayas may be unable to produce adequate food supplies and must rely on trade to make up the difference (Childs 1998). Political instability has sometimes disrupted patterns of trade, and innovative demographic responses have resulted, such as lamas that marry, have children, and own land, and significant proportions of celibate nuns in villages that dampen total fertility (Havnevik 1989; Childs 1998).

NOTES

1. Other useful works are Hatcher and Jennings 1966; Pan American Health Organization 1966; Porter and Knight 1971; Van Liere and Stickney 1963; and Weihe 1963. Among the major synthesis articles are those of Hurtado (1964) and Mazess (1975). Much of the following material is drawn from the studies of high altitude Quechua from southern highland Peru. This is the region best known from a multidisciplinary human ecological perspective. Some of the adaptations found in the southern highlands are not present in the northern highlands; for example, llamas are not found and *chuño* is not widely made (Baker 1976b; Baker and Dutt 1972; Buskirk 1976; Flannery et al. 1989).

2. Baker (1976b:302) notes that the technique for determining output versus oxygen consumption may explain the different results. Some of the studies used a bicycle

ergometer. Natives were unfamiliar with bicycle riding and may have experienced unusual muscle reactions.

3. Comparable protection is experienced by the Sherpas of the Himalayas, who use sheepskins and wool as clothing. Their houses are partially heated by the body warmth of the animals. The people live on the upper story, while the animals are corralled at night on the lower story. Hearth fires also help keep the house warm (Pugh 1966).

Photo by Alain Couillaud
Source: iStockphoto

7

HUMAN ADAPTABILITY
TO ARID LANDS

Arid lands would have great potential productivity for human populations if water were in more abundant supply. When water can be secured and managed, the desert can have high biomass productivity and can support substantial human populations. How populations have adjusted to a scarce water supply is the central focus of this chapter. Arid lands, or deserts, are characterized by low and random distribution of rainfall, high levels of solar radiation, high daytime temperatures, high levels of **evapotranspiration,** and a consequent scarcity of plant cover during most of the year. Human populations have lived for a long time in desert regions and developed sophisticated solutions to the inherent water scarcity (Veth et al. 2005).

Human populations appear to have neither genetic nor developmental adaptations for living in dry heat areas. They depend instead on acclimatory and behavioral adjustments that facilitate their occupation of these regions. Acclimatization to desert conditions actually occurs within a week or two. However, it is the problem of locating water, storing and distributing it, managing its consumption, and minimizing its loss in transit that is central to human adaptation to arid conditions. There is a growing consensus that the next environmental crisis will be over global water supplies. Micklin (2000) notes that these conflicts have already begun in Central Asia (Kazakhstan, Uzbekistan, Turkmenistan, Kyrgyzstan, and Tajikistan). Transboundary, interstate, and global movement of water is expected to become more common in the future, but also more politically and economically constrained by diminishing supplies and growing demand (Herrick et al. 2006; Griffith 2001).

In ancient times arid lands served as cradles of civilization. Today they include both the richest and the poorest regions of the earth, for example, the productive Imperial Valley of California and the impoverished interior of northeastern Brazil and Mali (Aw and Diemer 2005). Of the earth's surface, 20–30 percent is classified as arid lands (D. H. K. Lee 1964:552), and some areas that were once fertile have turned to desert in our own time (Glantz 1977, 1996; Hoeckstra and Shachak 1999; Reynolds and Stafford Smith 2002; Amin 2004; Singh 2005). Under some scenarios of climate change, desert areas are predicted to increase by more than 15 percent (Hoeckstra and Shachak 1999:6). Desert expansion is closely tied to how human populations interact with climate and environmental change in the coming decades. The costs of desertification have been increasing: in 1980 it was estimated that the annual income lost to desertification, including the expenditures required to rehabilitate desertified land, was US$26 billion; by 1991 that cost had risen to US$42 billion (Safriel 1999:135). Advanced techniques of remote sensing (imaging spectroscopy and shortwave-infrared spectral mixture analysis) have been used to complement biological methods for monitoring and assessing the impacts of desertification on regional climate-ecosystem interactions (Asner and Heidenbrecht 2005).

In the past twenty years there has been growing interest in issues such as desertification (Borowiec 2003; Gaur and Gaur 2004), water-saving approaches to irrigation (drip irrigation), and notable advances in management of arid lands (Mainguet 1999; Hao et al. 2005). In the 1970s attention was focused on patterns of primary production, relationships of plant and animal communities, and biogeochemical cycling within an ecosystem framework (Likens and Bormann 1975). In the 1980s ecosystem research was extended to multiple spatial scales, particularly landscape units of analysis with an explicit human component (Risser 1992). In the 1990s the latter has gained prominence, as we appreciate better how drought contributes to desertification but also how human populations affect the magnitude and outcome of droughts (Allen 1988; Graetz 1991; Boecken and Schachak 1994). Holmgren and Scheffer (2001) suggest, for example, that El Niño events (very wet years in areas like the southwestern United States), together with control of grazing animals, can provide opportunities to restore degraded areas. Scanlon and colleagues (2005), on the other hand, point out that the rapid increase in vegetation as a response to higher precipitation during El Niño events can prevent the predicted soil water storage increases in the Mojave desert from taking place, thereby nullifying the potential of this additional moisture to recharge the water table.

This chapter begins with a brief discussion of the characteristics of desert ecosystems and the special adaptations of desert plants and animals, followed by a discussion of the physiological and cultural adjustments of human populations to the problem of dry heat. Our discussion will focus on the exploitation of surface resources by the hunter-gatherer !Kung populations of the Kalahari desert. We will then examine the exploitation of the Nile River over time by farming populations. One interesting and exciting new direction in research on these issues is the study of common pool resources (CPR) to understand the way communities regulate access to and use of irrigation water (Ostrom 1990).

DESERT ECOSYSTEMS

Deserts vary considerably in characteristics (see Figure 7.1 for the geographical distribution of deserts). Detailed accounts of particular deserts can be found (Phillips

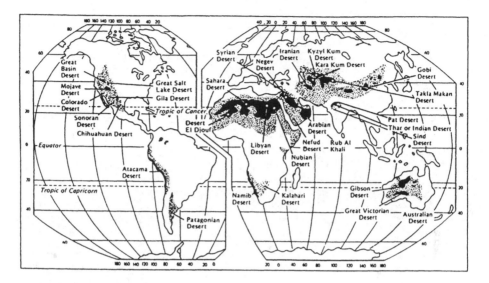

FIGURE 7.1 Deserts of the World

et al. 2000 for the Sonoran desert; Edgell 2006 on Arabian deserts, among others). Generally speaking, deserts are areas of low rainfall and high evaporation where vegetation is scanty. The precipitation is infrequent and erratic as well. True, or extreme, deserts are said to be those with less than 100 millimeters of annual rainfall. Deserts are also characterized by severe moisture deficits, local rainfall events of short duration but high intensity, high evapotranspiration, relatively strong, turbulent winds, and thermal extremes (Nicholson 1999:33). Table 7.1 outlines some of the major types of arid ecosystems and their respective levels of primary production (Whitford 1986). Walter shows that the annual production of dry matter in the desert is a linear function of rainfall (1973:87). Moisture levels control the system (Evans and Thames 1980), but climate-ecosystem interactions can be complex (Asner and Heidenbrecht 2005).

Deserts can be areas of surprising contrasts. Daytime temperatures may rise to over 50°C (58°C has been recorded in the Sahara desert and Death Valley, California), while at night they may drop as low as -58°C (in Asian deserts at high altitude), although 0°C may be more common in tropical deserts (Nicholson 1999). Surface heating is rapid, but cooling is just as rapid when the sun sets because of high albedo (surface reflectivity) and clear skies—with differences of 40°C to 50°C recorded at numerous stations (Nicholson 1999:34). The topography is reminiscent of a region in formation. Weathering is slow and the absence of vegetative cover and minimal cloud cover makes every detail visible. This makes deserts ideal areas for environmental monitoring by satellite imagery. Large and small closed basins dramatically cut by

TABLE 7.1 Classification of Arid Ecosystems

Type	Mean Annual Precipitation	Above Ground Primary Production	Below Ground Production
Extremely arid or "true desert"[a]	less than 60–100 mm.	less than 30 g/m^2	less than 100 g/m^2
Arid[b]	from 60–100 mm. to 150–200 mm.	30–200 g/m^2	100–400 g/m^2
Semiarid[c]	from 150–250 mm. to 250–500 mm.	100–600 g/m^2	250–1000 g/m^2

[a]In true deserts, vegetation is restricted to favorable areas only.
[b]In arid areas, one finds diffuse natural vegetation.
[c]In semiarid areas, it is possible to carry out diffuse dryland farming, but its success is highly unreliable.

Source: Adapted from Imanuel Noy-Meir, "Desert Ecosystems: Environment and Producers," *Annual Review of Ecology and Systematics* 4 (1973): 25–31, 44–45. Reproduced with permission from the *Annual Review of Ecology and Systematics*, vol. 4 © 1973 by Annual Reviews, Inc.

surface runoff and erosion are common (Harvey et al. 2005). During rare episodes of rainfall, water may be carried to the center of a basin, forming a temporary lake called a playa. The continuously changing streambeds, or **wadis,** along which the rushing waters run are characteristic of deserts. During a sudden rainfall, the water runs downslope seeking old gullies or etching new ones, until it reaches the wadis where the now raging flash flood forms **alluvial fans** rich in sediment. Gently inclined slopes have greater water-capturing capacity, and the runoff there is more likely to create conditions favorable for human populations (Steward 1938:12).

Lack of rain is not the only factor in the creation of desert conditions. Low air humidity also affects the distribution and behavior of plants and animals. Because the rate of evaporation is high, an organism can quickly become stressed by aridity. Although measuring actual evapotranspiration is difficult, potential evapotranspiration is commonly used to determine the water balance of a region and estimate which plants may be able to grow in the area (Polis 1991; Goodall and Perry 1979; compare Mata-Gonzalez et al. 2005 about inappropriate use of transpiration coefficients in determining plant evapotranspiration in arid environments; this simple traditional method does not take into account stomatal regulation and plant adaptations to drought). The relationship between ecosystem productivity and species richness has been well established in arid ecosystems, as compared to more moist regions. Cox and colleagues (2006) suggest that annual primary productivity is a weak predictor of mean species richness in arid communities (based on a study in the Chihuahuan desert in New Mexico).

Desert Plants

Desert plants cope with moisture deficits by avoiding or resisting drought, or both (for a comprehensive treatise on plant adaptations to extreme desert conditions, see Gutterman 2002). Drought avoidance refers to adaptational features by which plants remain **dormant** during the dry season but rapidly respond to seasonal rains. It also refers to plants with compressed life cycles that permit them to reproduce during brief rainy periods and plants that drop their leaves during the dry season in order to conserve water. Drought resistance, on the other hand, refers to numerous physiological features that enable plants to collect, store, and retain water. Some of these plants exhibit extensive subsurface root growth or deep taproots that reach the water table. Drought-resistant plants reduce water loss from leaves through waxy coverings, hairiness, or leaf angle; some are able to utilize water more efficiently (Cheng et al. 2006; Arndt et al. 2004). Deep rooting is another adaptive mechanism. Once it was understood as a response to lack of surface water and a way to tap deep soil water. However, recent studies suggest that deep rooting is also a way to access deep soil nutrients and make them accessible to plants (McCulley et al. 2004). Relative rooting depth tends to increase with aridity, but absolute rooting depth decreases with aridity (Schenk and Jackson 2002).

Figure 7.2 lists most of the features of desert plants. Succulents store considerable water in their fleshy leaves and stems. Waxy leaves are able to reflect heat and keep the leaves cooler. Hairiness helps the leaves break up the flow of drying air near the tiny leaf openings **(stoma)** through which carbon dioxide and oxygen are exchanged during **photosynthesis** and thus helps prevent excessive drying. Some desert plants orient their leaves to minimize the leaf area exposed during the hot hours of the day by changing the angle of exposure. Results of International Biological Program (IBP) research in desert ecosystems is synthesized in Evans and Thames (1980). Soil moisture, texture, and available nutrients are highly correlated with the structure and pattern of vegetation in a study of the southeastern Tengger desert in China (X. Li et al. 2004). Many plant adaptations to arid ecosystems address in some fashion the pulsed events (surges in precipitation) that characterize these areas; these pulses shape population dynamics, species interactions, and ecosystem processes (Schwinning and Sala 2004).

Desert Animals

Desert animals possess biological rhythms that lower their potential water loss. Special physiological adaptations (such as size) or behavioral adjustments (such as inactivity and migratory habits) improve their life chances in the desert (Plummer 2004). Most

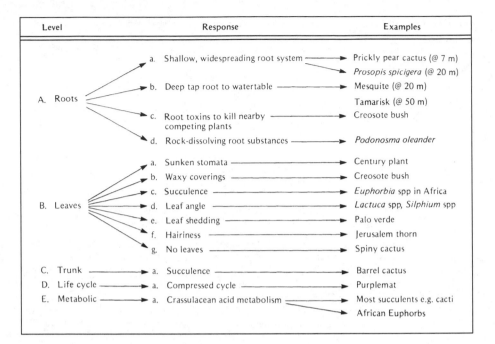

FIGURE 7.2 Levels of Adaptation of Desert Plants

Desert plants use more than one adaptation to cope with water scarcity.

species are nocturnal in habit and spend the day burrowed in holes, rock shelters, or other retreats. Those that are active during the day retreat once the temperature reaches 50°C. Most of these daytime animals are birds (Dean 2004) and large mammals such as the puma (Logan and Sweanor 2001). Birds rely on seasonal migration and a no-madic lifestyle to find patches of resources in deserts (Dean 2004). Other animals rely on estivation for survival in the desert. **Estivation** refers to dormancy during the hot, dry summer and is often related to **diapause**—a state of suspended development accompanied by greatly decreased metabolism (Cloudsley-Thompson 1977:74). One study noted that after two weeks of reduced food availability the desert mouse re-sponded by "switching down" its resting metabolism and was able to maintain its weight, temperature, and activity level on a very limited food supply (Merkt and Tay-lor 1994). When food returned to normal levels, it was able to "switch up" its resting metabolism within one day. This metabolic switch may be an amplification of a more general metabolic response for coping with food scarcity common to all mammals, including humans (Merkt and Taylor 1994). Estivation includes a strong reduction in metabolic rate, primary reliance on lipid oxidation to fuel metabolism, and water retention (Storey 2002). The mechanisms that go into play in estivation are similar to those seen in hibernation (Storey 2002, 2001). Animal fertility is carefully timed to the arrival of the rains. During the dry season, reproduction may be interrupted, but rapid population bursts occur within weeks after the winter rains arrive. A common physiological adaptation of many desert species, particularly rodents, is their ability to survive on moisture obtained from solid food.

Burrowing animals form an important food source for hunter-gatherer populations because burrowing minimizes the effort required to catch them and because their high rates of reproduction guarantee a secure food source. The larger desert animals, such as antelopes, camels, and gazelles, are too big to avoid daytime conditions and rely on adaptations that reduce water loss and thermal stress. Camels have very concentrated urine and nearly dry feces. Their coarse hair insulates them from solar radiation, and they can tolerate greater dehydration than most mammals. The camel can recoup its liquid losses very rapidly when it encounters water. While small desert animals avoid extreme conditions, larger ones resist them by reduced surface and/or volume ratios and by physiological adjustments that reduce water loss, improve insulation, and permit rapid gain of body fluid losses (Schmidt-Nielsen 1984, 1990; see Logan and Sweanor 2001 for an excellent synthesis of the desert puma).

Soil Conditions

The limited amount of rain in deserts falls during ten to fifty rainy days. On only five or six of these days is the amount of rainwater sufficient to affect the biotic parts of the system (Noy-Meir 1973:28). These pulses in precipitation affect the various component of the ecosystem, as organisms transition from lower to higher levels of physiological activity. Brief, shallow pulses only affect surface-dwelling organisms with fast response times and high tolerance for low levels of resources. On the other hand, higher plants are more affected by larger precipitation events or pulses, and require deeper infiltration of moisture (Schwinning and Sala 2004; Schwinning and Ehleringer 2001). However, most of the rainy days affect soil formation. Despite the common denominator of low rainfall and high potential evapotranspiration, desert soils are quite variable in physical, chemical, and biological characteristics. Exposed rock experiences rapid daily temperature variations. When moisture is present to expand or contract in small fissures, rocks may be broken up. Wind also exercises a powerful and abrasive force—as do torrential flash floods in wadis, with their lack of protective ground cover.

The rapid flow of water over the surface prevents the formation of soils of much thickness in any given area—except in alluvial basins at the end of wadis (Cloudsley-Thompson 1977:15; Al-Farraj and Harvey 2000). Over time, such basins may become filled with alluvial deposits and form salt flats with saline crusts. (When the water stands in a basin and forms shallow lakes, slow evaporation removes the water but leaves behind the mineral salts carried from the surrounding hills. The end result is a saline crust.) Biological soil crusts, made up of communities of cyanobacteria, lichens, and mosses that live on the soil surface, occur throughout the world in desert regions (Belnap et al. 2004; X. Li et al. 2003). They provide soil stability, and when wet the biological organisms become metabolically active and contribute to soil fertility. If climate change leads to declining summer rainfall events, soil lichen cover and richness may decline and make desert soils less productive and less stable (Belnap et al. 2004). Precipitation events are closely connected to vegetation biomass and to fundamental processes such as nitrogen cycling (Aranibar et al. 2004). While deserts have low nitrogen globally, there can be a great deal of variability with soil types and in different regions. For example, peat soils in southeastern Tibet and southwestern China have very high nitrogen values (Tian et al. 2006).

Saline soils present special problems for agriculture since they can only become agriculturally productive if the salts are flushed out. This requires an intensive use of water, which may not be easy to obtain in the necessary quantities. Nonsaline alluvial basins, when irrigated, can be very fertile because of the deposition of nutrient-rich sediment. Youthful soil forms also exist. Rock desert soils, known as *hammada* in the Sahara, exhibit denuded solid rock, smoothed and polished by the wind. Stony desert soils (regs) are formed when wind erodes smaller particulate matter, leaving only larger particles behind. Finally, sandy desert soils (ergs) consist of windblown dunes. The largest erg in the world is located in the southern Arabian desert. A lot of progress has been made in recent years in ways to stabilize desert sands. *Tamarx aphylla* has been a good pioneer species, while *Acacia*, *Casuarina*, and *Eucalyptus prosopis* have been also successful (Achtnich and Homeyer 1980). Global climate change is likely to have a dramatic impact on desert ecosystems. Deserts are naturally low in soil nitrogen. However, with growing atmospheric nitrogen deposition this may change and facilitate the colonization of desert systems by alien species and decrease the diversity of native annual plants (Brooks 2003).

ADJUSTMENTS TO DRY HEAT

Before a human population can exploit the resources of a desert, its individual members must be able to cope with the hot, dry conditions of the ecosystem (D. H. K. Lee 1968). The desert constantly threatens people with dehydration and physiologically dangerous heat loads (see Wilson et al. 2006 for a recent assessment of the impact of heat stress). While there is no single index of heat stress that can accurately predict physiological responses over a wide range of ambient conditions, a deep body temperature of 38°C has been suggested as an upper limit for work (Khogali and Awad El-Karim 1987). At temperatures of 42–44°C thermoregulatory failure will occur (Kenney et al. 2004). Populations familiar with desert heat reduce stress by replacing water and salt and by staying lean (Khogali and Awad El-Karim 1987). Thermal sweating helps reduce heat gain through evaporation of moisture at the skin surface. When air and ground temperature are below 92°F (33.3°C), human beings can lose heat by radiation to cooler ground or by convection to cooler air. In the desert, however, daytime temperatures are often higher and sweating is the only

effective mechanism (Poulton 1970:133). To cool off, we pay with loss of body water (Adolph 1947:3). The human body seems dry in the desert because evaporation
is so rapid that sweat disappears as it nears the surface (insensible evaporation). No
changes in metabolism are needed to maintain this cooling system, but an equal
amount of liquid must be consumed to replace what is lost.

Water requirements are a function of ambient temperature, air humidity (or vapor pressure), diet, and level of activity. A body at rest (basic metabolic rate, or
BMR) that is protected from the sun requires at least five ounces of water per hour
to remain in body fluid equilibrium. Lower water intake means the body utilizes liquid stored in tissues, eventually resulting in dehydration and thermostatic deregula-
tion. Exposure to solar radiation adds an extra sixteen ounces per hour to this
equilibrium requirement, and walking an additional twelve ounces per hour
(Adolph 1947:8). Water requirements increase proportionately according to increase
in activity level and temperatures. Reducing activity and adopting a relaxed posture
that increases surface area help compensate for increases in heat load in the human
body. Figure 7.3 plots daily water requirements at three levels of activity and at various temperatures.

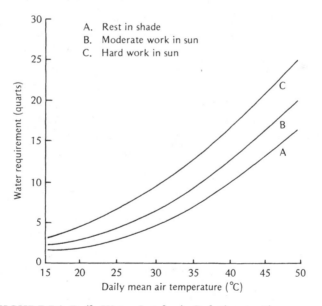

**FIGURE 7.3 Daily Water Intake in Relation to Air
Temperature and Level of Activity**

The amount of activity or work affects the daily water intake requirement.
Regulating the pace of work and the time of day it is undertaken is a fun-
damental adaptation. *Source:* D. H. K. Lee, "Men in the Desert," in
Desert Biology, edited by G. W. Brown (New York: Academic, 1968).
Note: One quart = 0.95 liter.

Physiological Adjustments

To date, physiological studies tend to agree that human populations acclimatize to desert conditions within a week or two (Cane 1987; D. H. K. Lee 1964, 1969; Adolph 1947; Yamazaki and Hamazaki 2003). Little difference in heat adaptation has been noted between desert natives and nonnatives. Diminished pulse rate, lower rectal temperature, increased sweating, and ability to work in the heat are remarkably similar among human populations (Wyndham 1966:237). Acclimatized individuals show a reduction in the salt concentration of sweat, which prevents cardiovascular inadequacy and violent muscular cramps. Urine volume is also reduced as a homeostatic compensation for increased dehydration (D. H. K. Lee 1969:239; Newman 1975:87). These few factors represent the bulk of physiological changes that occur. Adolph (1947:34) raised questions about limitations on the amount of physical work that can be achieved in a desert ecosystem, but concluded that the limitations are not significant as long as people have enough water. A recent study noted that drinking water at a colder temperature reduced the effects of heat stress by acting as a heat sink and making it easier to consume a larger volume of liquid (Mundel et al. 2006).

Body size, shape, and composition can also influence the heat exchange process. The ideal body type for desert conditions is tall, with long, lean extremities and low subcutaneous fat. Tallness maximizes the surface area-to-weight ratio for enhanced cooling, while lean body composition minimizes the presence of insulating fat that may limit heat flow from core to shell to cool the body. The Nilotic peoples of the Sudan are often cited as an example of optimal human form for desert environments. However, it could also be argued that greater surface area would maximize evaporation of sweat and expose those individuals to dehydration unless other factors intervened to ameliorate that possibility. In fact, social and cultural patterns provide exactly such protection.

While there is some positive correlation between ideal body type and body temperature (Harrison et al. 1977:435), factors such as migration, nutrition, and disease preclude a perfect association between body shape and environment (D. H. K. Lee 1964:563). In desert areas today, we find people of all shapes and sizes. The major adjustments of humans are not small size and nocturnal habits, nor complex physiological adjustments (as among camels); rather, they are cultural and behavioral in nature. The problem of how to cope with aridity may be overcome by activity patterns, clothing, shelter, diet, and similar adjustments.

Cultural Adjustments

While human beings must find and manage water in the desert, they must also conserve it once it enters their bodies. In this process, the cultural adjustments of clothing and shelter play a crucial role. Clothing helps cut direct solar radiation. The same may be said of shelter. The ideal clothing style depends on prevailing environmental conditions and the load of physical work. At rest and at moderate levels of activity, loose-fitting, loosely woven clothes are best, while during hard physical work, little or no clothing is best (Ingram 1977:100). Loose-fitting clothing allows free passage of evaporation from skin to atmosphere and also ensures that a layer of insulating air is maintained between cloth and skin. This explains why black Bedouin robes are no hotter than white clothing in the desert. The heat absorbed by the black robes is lost before it reaches the skin by its looseness and air convection (Scholnick et al. 1980).

Clothing is important in coping with hot desert winds. This is one of the most serious stresses faced by desert populations (Leithard and Lind 1964). A hot wind lowers the threshold of resistance to dry heat by accelerating the dehydration process. If this occurs quickly enough, the victim collapses, loses consciousness, and dies. Heatstroke results from a breakdown in the thermoregulatory system and consequent hyperpyrexis (high fever) when sweating fails. The sudden deaths that have occurred in deserts appear to result from sandstorms and subsequent rapid dehydration (Briggs 1975:97). In addition, driving rapidly across the desert without adequate protective clothing can cause heatstroke and dehydration equivalent to a hot desert wind.

Briggs points out that Saharan peoples conform to the established rules governing adaptive clothing (see Table 7.2). Ordinary clothing, including turbans, is loose fitting and made of lightweight material. Trousers are long and baggy, with a narrow opening at the ankle barely wide enough for one's foot to go through—which acts as an excellent dead space insulator. Sandals with soles that project an inch in all directions are the usual footwear (Briggs 1975:122–127). The projections protect the feet from the heat reflecting from the ground.

Housing in hot, dry areas delays the entry of heat into the living quarters as long as possible (Cooke 1982). This is best achieved by use of high heat-capacity materials, compact geometry, closely spaced units, subterranean construction and high-reflectivity colors, and by removal of heat-generating sources (cooking fires). High heat-capacity materials, such as adobe, mud, and stone, absorb heat during the day and reradiate it at night (Keiser 1978). Compact design minimizes surface area exposed to the outside. This may also be achieved by building houses close together, which both reduces ventilation and increases the time heat takes to build up. Reduction of ventilation is effective only if the walls and roof are thick enough to delay heat penetration. The pueblos of the Southwest are an excellent example of this kind of housing (see Figure 7.4). Arab tents cannot provide this type of insulation and must therefore promote ventilation. Subterranean and semisubterranean dwellings are built in extreme deserts to take advantage of the heat capacity of the earth itself. Rooms in Matmata houses in the Sahara are under thirty feet of earth and are comfortably cool (Rapoport 1969:89–93). Contemporary urban desert housing violates most of these rules, and these homes are habitable only in the presence of air-conditioning. Adobe homes in the Southwest are

TABLE 7.2 Principles of Clothing and Shelter in Hot, Dry Conditions

Objective	Clothing	Shelter
Reduce heat production	Lightweight, absence of constriction; functionally convenient	Use of semisubterranean shelters; cooking devices that do not concentrate heat
Reduce radiation gain	Provide shade; reflect shorter wavelengths; insulate by use of multiple layers	Cubical design; trees and bushes conveniently located to shade; light-colored exteriors; heat insulation
Reduce conduction gain	Insulate by use of multiple layers; wind-excluding	Controlled ventilation; free flow of air
Promote evaporation	Sufficient perflation	Openings closable on hot days and capable of opening on cool nights; use of evaporative cooling devices

Source: D. H. K. Lee, "Terrestrial Animals in Dry Heat: Man in the Desert," in *Handbook of Physiology: Adaptation to the Environment*, edited by D. B. Dill (Washington, DC: American Physiological Society, 1964). Used with permission from American Physiological Society.

inhabited by people at both the top and the bottom ends of the economic scale, but not by the majority of the population. Evaporative coolers provide relief seasonally but not during the rainy season. The habitability of most homes depends on the price of energy and the income level of the population.

Deserts cool rapidly at night. Populations inhabiting thick-walled dwellings maintain a comfortably warm microenvironment in the evening. Hunter-gatherers, on the other hand, do not build complex dwellings and are exposed to extreme body cooling at night. Central Australian aborigines sleep naked with no apparent discomfort at air temperatures of about 0°C. They appear to endure a greater drop in skin temperature without shivering (Harrison et al. 1977:430). Kalahari hunter-gatherers build fires and sleep with their feet toward the flames, huddled under their cloaks and close enough to one another to share body warmth. Researchers have noted that in this manner they create a microclimate close to the **thermo-neutral temperature** of 25°C (Wyndham 1966:206–207). Steegman suggests that tropical hunters may be employing ancient cold adaptation mechanisms not found among the more recently adapted temperate and arctic populations (1975:157). In northern cold, peripheral adaptations were selected since the core was well protected by clothing and shelter appropriate to the environment.

FIGURE 7.4 The Pueblos: An Example of Adaptive Desert Housing

The deep adobe walls of the pueblos provide little heat transfer and keep the inside reasonably comfortable in the very hot temperatures of the desert Southwest. Photograph by Arthur Rothstein from the Library of Congress collection.

UTILIZATION OF RESOURCES

The most important exploitable resource in a desert is surface water. It is also the one that requires the least technological sophistication to exploit. Hunter-gatherers, with relatively simple tool kits, have relied on surface water for their subsistence. The Kalahari desert is the habitat of the !Kung San. ("San" is the term preferred by the population over the older term "Bushmen.") Numerous human ecological studies of the !Kung are available and from them a comprehensive view of !Kung use of resources is possible. The !Kung inhabit an area where resources are scattered, water is available in varying amounts throughout the year, and vegetation varies from shrub savanna to arid desert. This discussion of !Kung adaptations to the Kalahari will refer to the Dobe !Kung and to the Kade San to the south (see Figure 7.5).

Utilization of Surface Water

The Dobe area of the Kalahari lies on the northern fringe of the desert and is part of a transitional zone between the drier shrub savanna to the south and the lush region of the Okavongo River to the north. The Dobe area is a **semiarid area** with a hot summer from October to March, when temperatures can reach 35°C to 45°C and sweat losses are severe. On the other hand, between June and August the temperature falls

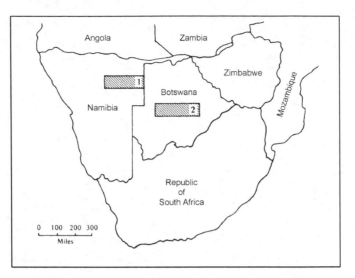

FIGURE 7.5 Location of the Dobe !Kung (1) and the Kade San (2)

below 5°C. Fortunately, all the rainfall is concentrated in a four- to six-month rainy season during the hot summer months, but, as in other deserts, rainfall is erratic. Ranges of 239 to 597 millimeters per year have been noted; in addition, temporal and spatial variability further increases the uncertainty of precipitation. Drought conditions characterize about half the recorded years (R. B. Lee 1972:132).

The !Kung rely on three types of standing water sources: large collecting **hardpans** in dry river channels, smaller depressions between dunes (molapo pans), and holes in large trees. Hardpan sources are the most important since some hold water year-round. The molapos offer a varying water source that depends on the size of the catchment and the length of the rains. Water from the tree trunks is important not so much for its quantity, but because it is usually the only water source in food-rich dune crests. Water from roots is also used, but it is costly to obtain. The root must be dug from depths of up to 40 centimeters (15 inches), and over twenty roots are necessary to provide the fluid needs of one person per day (R. B. Lee 1972:134). In choosing which water resources to use, the !Kung must sort out the costs from the benefits of gaining access to food and water in a given location at a given point in the yearly cycle.

The Dobe territory has only nine "permanent" water holes, and this limits the area that the Dobe !Kung can exploit. During the rainy season, groups move away from the permanent water holes and disperse over the territory. With the approach of the dry season, however, bands congregate first at the larger seasonal pans, and, with increased aridity, at the nine permanent water holes. Life is difficult, but—unlike the southern Kade San—they do have permanent water holes to assure their basic needs.

Access to water holes is maintained by widespread sharing among groups. While a group is normally associated with an area of land and a specific water hole, rarely does a group's association with a given water hole exceed fifty years (R. B. Lee 1972:129). Moreover, rules of reciprocity ensure that any relative or visitor can share equitably in the camp's resources. Such reciprocity and hospitality have often been observed among hunter-gatherers and pastoralists inhabiting desert areas. Cole (1975:68) notes that hospitality is adaptive in areas where resources are widely spaced and of uncertain reliability.

In the rainy period, camps are evenly spaced over the Dobe region, but as the summer heat evaporates the standing water, groups begin to converge at the few permanent water holes (see Figure 7.6). The settlement pattern of the !Kung reflects the ecological principle that settlements reflect people's decisions, both conscious and unconscious, about how they relate to their environment and to one another (Yellen 1976:48).

Unlike the San of the Dobe area, the Kade San have no standing water sources and must obtain most of their water from plants. The environment is rich in a variety of vegetable foods. For the Kade San the primary concern in migrating is not the location of water per se, but the location of the plants that supply them with their water requirements. The amount of work they devote to subsistence is relatively small, even though it is nearly twice that of the neighboring Dobe San. Unlike the Dobe San, the Kade San cannot rely on a major nutritious food source such as the mongongo nut that is available to the Dobe San, but must diversify with a variety of foods throughout the year (Tanaka 1976).

After rainfall events, some water collects in pans and molapos, creating shallow water holes. The Kade San move their camps to take advantage of this water, which is available thirty to sixty days out of the year. On the other 300 days, they are obliged to look for water in plants, particularly two species of melons (*Citrullus lanatus* and *C. naudinianus*), two species of tubers (*Raphioonacme burkei* and *Coccinia rehmanii*), and an aloe (*Aloe zebrina*). Blood from animals is not a useful water source because of the water required to process the ingested protein. The major and most dependable water source is *Citrullus lanatus* (bitter melon), since it keeps for most of the year and is comparable to the watermelon in water content. Tanaka (1976:104) estimates that the Kade San obtain 3,500 milliliters of water per person per day from melons.

Utilization of Groundwater

Groundwater occurs below the surface in a zone of saturation, where permeable rocks become saturated under hydrostatic pressure (the pressure of a liquid at rest)

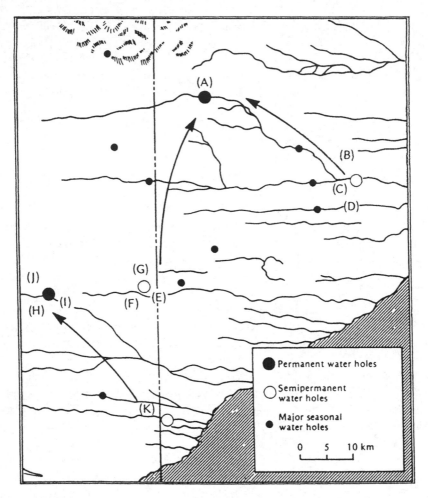

FIGURE 7.6 Movements of San Bands in Times of Drought

Bands (A)–(K) each have their traditional water holes, but (as shown in the figure) they may regroup in different patterns when some water holes become dry. *Source:* Adapted from p. 141 of R. B. Lee, "Kung Spatial Organization: An Ecological and Historical Perspective," *Human Ecology* 1, no. 2 (1972): 125–147.

with water that flows between impermeable layers of soil or rock (Cantor 1970:5). Groundwater acts as a replenishable reservoir that can raise the water table during wet periods. It can also sustain considerable exploitation.

Groundwater can be a product of both local rainfall and extra-regional sources. Water can originate in areas far beyond the desert and arrive there by flowing underground for great distances. Oases form as a result of folds in the underground strata

(Evenari et al. 1971:151). They are important water sources but are usually too far apart to enable nomadic human groups to depend on them solely. Local sources for underground water include rain that seeps through the gravel beds in the wadis during or immediately after local flash floods. Since the wadi beds usually overlie a less permeable limestone formation, the water that infiltrates remains trapped underground and becomes a perched water table with the gravel bed acting as the **aquifer.** Flash floods sweep down the wadis, leaving the bed puddled and muddy, and animals can be seen drinking there. After the surface of the bed dries, animals may dig to a depth of 20 centimeters to reach the underground water. Human groups have also learned this lesson.

Wells are probably next in the evolution of groundwater use. Bedouins still use a type of primitive well characterized by shallowness (3–6 meters deep) and a narrow throat (50–60 centimeters in diameter) that is usually capped by a rock. A refinement of this form consists of a chain of wells across the face of a slope. In this system, a number of wells are dug into the aquifer and from there the water is led gradually away through underground tunnels until the lower-level surface is reached.

A larger version of the chain well, which uses the same principle, is the kanat, or drainage tunnel (see Figure 7.7). A kanat may be a few hundred meters to many kilometers in length and may yield 500 gallons per minute. Excavation begins with vertical shafts, which have to be driven to a depth of 20–100 meters on alluvial fans. Kanats are found from western China through Afghanistan. They were introduced into the Atacama desert of South America as well. Although construction costs are high, the kanat provides a secure water source in areas where surface water is scarce. Since it uses the force of gravity, the system is not energy intensive and has low capital and maintenance costs.

A final refinement in the use of groundwater is the deep well, which requires an understanding of the relationship between the water-bearing layer and the impermeable stratum. It also requires heavy labor and technological capacity. The !Kung, for example, are unable to excavate wells to tap deep sources of underground water because their digging sticks cannot pierce the underlying hardpan. The labor required in constructing deep wells is only justified when large populations must be supported.

Utilization of Plants and Animals

Even in the Kalahari, life depends on more than water supplies. As they look for water, both San groups exploit a variety of other resources. The management of wild plants and animals, as practiced by hunter-gatherers, appears simple, but the body of knowledge brought to bear is extensive. The !Kung name and recognize almost 500 species of plants and animals in the Kalahari. Out of these, they use 150 species of plants and 100 species of animals. Like nearby pastoralists, they have an accurate knowledge of animal behavior that amazed the ethologists who interviewed them (Blurton-Jones and Konner 1976).

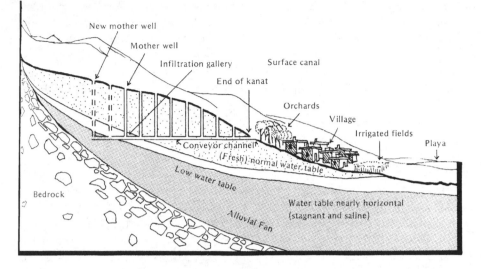

FIGURE 7.7 Diagrammatic Cross Section of a Kanat

This ancient, laboriously hand-constructed water supply system brings life to the dry lands of North Africa and Asia. It is found to a lesser extent in South America. In construction, the water supply is located by first digging the horizontal tunnel on a gentle grade from where water is desired to the source. Vertical shafts are spaced along the line to bring the excavated material to the surface. *Source*: O. H. Heintzelman and R. M. Highsmith, *World Regional Regional Geography*, 4th ed. (Englewood Cliffs, NJ: Prentice-Hall, 1973), as adapted from p. 28 of George B. Cressy, "Qanats, Karez, and Foggeras," *Geographical Review* 48, no. 1 (1958): 27–44. Adapted, with permission, from the American Geographical Society.

The diet of both San groups is rich and varied. In the Dobe area, however, the people concentrate on collecting the abundant mongongo nuts *(Ricinodendron rautanenii).* Although this choice may be based primarily on their relative abundance, nutritionally the mongongo nut is an excellent choice as well. It has a 27 percent protein content and 600 calories per 100 grams of edible portion. The baobab fruit *(Adansoma digitata),* which is rich in vitamin C, calcium, and magnesium, is also used. *Bauhinia esculenta,* a bean, is also a rich food and is available in the drier areas of the Kalahari where the Kade San live.

In their drier environment, the Kade San follow a varied subsistence strategy that includes thirteen major vegetable foods. During the rainy season, *Bauhinia macrantha* is an important food source. This species of bean constitutes the main element in the diet when standing water is available. *Bauhinia macrantha* is rich in protein and fat and displaces all other foods for a period of four months. In May, the Kade San turn to water-storing melons. As the dry season lengthens, these water sources become scarce and the San turn increasingly to underground tubers that are dug up approximately 70 centimeters from the surface.

Game meat is important and provides 20–50 percent of the diet by weight, depending on the season and the number of hunters. Techniques for stalking are varied and effective: bow and poisoned arrow, hunting dogs, snares, and probing in underground burrows are all used. Probing in underground burrows is particularly rewarding since it requires less pursuit and the animals tend to be fatter. Animal fat, a concentrated caloric source, is a scarce element in the San diet and is highly prized. Small burrowing animals are the main prey, but larger ungulates are also captured, less frequently. This is generally true of desert areas. The inhabitants of the Great Basin hunted jackrabbits (*Lepus spp.*) in seasonal communal hunts (Steward 1938:33–35). Small game animals do not require the long chases that larger animals do, and they reproduce faster, thereby providing a more secure source of protein. Small animals may also be hunted to prevent excessive competition for plant food sources.

The !Kung prefer to make camp where a mix of resources is readily available, but if news of game arrives, they may be willing to risk a longer excursion away from their water hole. The !Kung usually locate their camp near a mongongo nut grove and an accessible water source so that they may rest, regain their water losses, and have abundant food. They also tend to select newer sites in the same general area but in previously uninhabited locations, which are freer of insects. In addition, resources closest to the camp are not as likely to be overexploited. Such a pattern facilitates the productivity of the groves over time.

Effects of Social and Cultural Practices

The availability of plants, animals, and surface water would be rapidly depleted in the absence of controls on the density of the human population. Nomadic hunter-gatherers such as the !Kung must keep their numbers low if the resources on which they rely are to be naturally renewed. Research by Knodel (1977) suggests that prolonged nursing, under certain conditions, may reduce women's fertility. Lactation seems to prolong the period of postpartum amenorrhea (the time before menstruation begins after pregnancy). In addition, fertility may be reduced by cultural taboos on intercourse during lactation. Frisch and McArthur (1974) believe that the crucial factor may be nutritional. They assume that a minimum level of stored energy is required for the maintenance of regular ovulation. The newborn can draw about 1,000 calories per day from its mother, and so prevent her from regaining the body fat required to accommodate a growing fetus. Thus by prolonging lactation, !Kung women not only ensure that their children are adequately nourished but also delay pregnancy for up to four years. Bentley (1985) suggested that their high activity patterns and endocrine functions are also implicated in the low number of births among the nomadic !Kung San (see below).

The diet of the !Kung appears to be rich in animal and plant proteins but low in fat and carbohydrates. This diet tends to reduce the ratio of body fat to body weight, delay menarche (the onset of menstruation), and delay resumption of ovulation after childbirth (postpartum amenorrhea). Howell notes that the maximum number of live births per woman among the Dobe !Kung was seven and that the mean was five (1976). The effectiveness of delayed menarche and postpartum amenorrhea is evidenced by the slow rate of population growth among the !Kung—0.5 percent per year. The rate is all the more remarkable in the absence of infanticide, famine, and war. With greater sedentarization, their rates of population growth now resemble those of farming populations in the same region.

!Kung camps are noncorporate, bilateral groupings of people with a flexible social structure. This social strategy provides a sensible adjustment to the drier periods in the Kalahari. Central to this social adaptation is a seasonal pattern of concentration and dispersion and a set of rules and practices for allowing reciprocal access to, and joint exploitation of, key resources (R. B. Lee 1976:91). The seasonal pattern provides flexibility in adjusting **population pressure** on resources in both the short and the long term.

Similar patterns of organizational flexibility have been observed among desert pastoral nomads. The al-Murrah congregate during dry periods in large groupings in maximal lineages around a well, whereas they disperse into smaller segments of the lineage during the wet season to better exploit grazing land (Cole 1975:41). The set of rules and practices provides the mechanism for maintaining relations that may be crucial to the survival of the group over the long run, but the mechanism must also be used in the short run to be readily available in the social system. Dietary practices, cultural patterns associated with lactation, and the energy costs of nomadic movement effectively limit population growth (Bentley 1985). !Kung who have become sedentary farmers have a faster population growth rate than their nomadic counterparts. They show signs of malnutrition and thiamine deficiency, particularly those with the least economic means (van der Westhuyzen et al. 1987). Their adjustment to dryland farming was the subject of a study (Ikeya 1996). The challenges of dryland farming persist, particularly in the face of increasing uncertainties posed by global climate change (Mortimore 1998). Irrigation has been the chief means to reduce the risks associated with dryland farming.

IRRIGATION

Where water is a limiting factor, societies have sought to divert surface water and groundwater to crops. In the simplest and most productive forms of irrigation, water is diverted from major rivers (for example, the Nile; Waterbury 2002; Wahaab and Badawy 2004; Svendsen 2005). Although the development of irrigation is associated with the development of agriculture and complex social systems, it is still unclear whether irrigation preceded or followed urbanization (Adams 1966; Steward 1955b;

Downing and Gibson 1974). However, whether large-scale irrigation created the state or was created by an already developed state is academic; as Steward notes, "neither could exist without the other in extremely arid areas" (1977:91). In some cases underground aqueducts were constructed, such as the *puquios* at Nasca in the Peruvian desert (Schreiber and Lancho Rojas 2003).

Irrigation provided the agrarian basis for several great civilizations of the past. And by the same token, several collapsed when water supplies failed or were improperly managed (for example, the Sumerian civilization in Mesopotamia and Roman North Africa) (El-Ashry 1995). Three important aspects of any irrigation or runoff control scheme are worthy of attention: the distribution of water, the relative accessibility to water by the individual user, and the scale of technology employed (Spooner 1974). After a brief consideration of these factors, we will proceed to a diachronic examination of Nile River irrigation.

Water Distribution

There are many irrigation methods that can move water from its source to the fields. Human and animal power has been used in the past, and powerful pumps facilitate such work in our time. Water wheels and well sweeps are still common in many regions of the world (a well sweep is a counterpoised lever enabling a man to lift water from a lower-lying source and tip it into an irrigation canal). Canals and dams increase the ability to harness water, enlarge the area that can benefit from irrigation, and provide access to water on a year-round basis. The labor required to establish an irrigation system is justified by the scarcity of water and by the potential for relatively permanent agriculture. River alluvium supplies of soluble minerals needed by plants are renewed annually by flood deposition. Reliable yields are thereby possible—if water can be ensured (Aschmann 1962:8).

Since water is the fundamental factor limiting production in arid areas, control over its distribution is a form of wealth and power. The greater the dependence on water to achieve production, the greater the role of water in the society. Wittfogel (1957) believes that large-scale irrigation led to centralization of political power and to despotic centralized states (opposite views have been presented by other authors, among them Steward 1955b; Wheatley 1971; Adams 1966; Butzer 1976; Wolf and Palerm 1955).

Much of the irrigation literature since Wittfogel has focused on how irrigation systems did not automatically lead to complex, centralized, and highly bureaucratized political systems. On the contrary, many of the best-known irrigation schemes began as small, locally controlled systems characterized by ease of maintenance and inherent conflict over water distribution (Millon 1962; Lees 1976; Guillet 1987). Fernea (1970) suggests that less centralized political organization may serve a population better, citing the way populations in southern Iraq coped with the threat of salinization. These people shifted fields often, and consequently tribal controls were more likely to function effectively than rigid state administration. Most irrigation systems in prehistoric times were on a scale too small to demand complex coercive institutions (Geertz 1972; Leach 1961; Netting 1974b). However, centralized control may be required when the scope of the project is too great to be dealt with by local associations or when water scarcity threatens the social order.

Access to Water

Access to water is not purely a function of distribution. It also depends on the distribution of other forms of wealth (for example, land and animals) or on periodic changes in land productivity. Wittfogel (1956) argues that precise water control for specific crops grown in arid conditions was a crucial requirement of political systems. Central authorities were required to ensure accurate timing in irrigation and provide accumulated knowledge about astronomy, agriculture, and climate. However, such centralized political units, while possessing greater knowledge, may have lacked insight into local crop needs and local hydrologic conditions.

All irrigation systems require cooperative construction and maintenance. Specific engineering problems, existing political structures, domesticants used, and technological limitations are but a few of the factors that may cause social and environmental variations (Steward 1977:95). Although overall production may serve the needs of a state, local irrigation water use is often determined by local decisions in regard to spatially extensive systems.

Leach has argued that small-scale irrigation systems present the advantages of reduced planning and resource costs, and they may be more stable as well (1961:165). Such systems may utilize a minimum of formal cooperation and function through intricate, informal water-sharing agreements based on crop requirements. Normal maintenance work and access to water are mutually agreed on by local farmers, and self-regulation is assured by the personal interest of the individuals involved (Netting 1974b). When the water source is outside the territorial control of the local group, it may be necessary to have a military force that can ensure access to the source of water.

As small irrigation systems attempt to expand in size, they appear to become increasingly inefficient. Conflict over water and land rights increases, and the need for centralized control grows. Under conditions of population pressure, water shortages require central policing to resolve the conflicts arising over competition for scarce resources. The complex design of irrigation canals, therefore, may make local skills inadequate to the tasks of maintenance, and a centrally organized workforce may be necessary to keep the system in operation (Hunt and Hunt 1974). Moreover, numerous cases suggest that increased centralized control over the water supply is accompanied by increased instability and possible breakdown in agricultural production.

The most common causes of irrigation failure are waterlogging, salinization, and alkalization of the irrigated soil as a result of seepage from canals or overirrigation.

The effects may not be visible for years and correction may be too costly by the time the problem is diagnosed. Waterlogging occurs when the water table rises as a result of deep percolation losses and the crop root zone becomes waterlogged. To prevent this, a network of wells is used to monitor the location of the water table. Effective drainage, which helps prevent waterlogging, is a sine qua non of a successful irrigation system. Salt becomes concentrated in the soil as water is removed by evaporation. To prevent salinity and alkalinity from reaching a level damaging to plants, frequent irrigation is necessary. In extreme cases, flushing the area to leach out the salts has been successful (see Figure 7.8).

The first irrigated areas were probably river valleys and deltas that possessed alluvial and nonsaline soils. Only later did populations attempt to put the salt deserts into production. These areas are the primary focus of much of the current technical work on irrigation. When too much water is withdrawn, the environmental consequences are horrific (for example, the Aral Sea). A comprehensive assessment of dead, dying, and endangered lakes and seas from all over the world is now available (Nihoul et al. 2004), examining both the climatic and anthropic causes of their demise.

Investments in Irrigation

Investments in irrigation vary from place to place and in levels of complexity. Size alone may not explain the costs of the system. Irrigating a small surface area may be costlier than irrigating a large one because of the intensive forms of channel

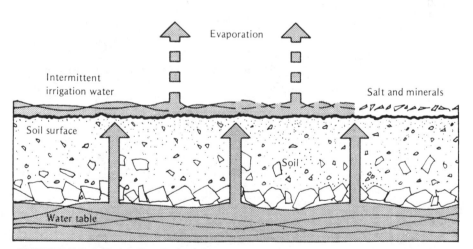

FIGURE 7.8 Salinization Process

This process results from capillary ascent (continuous arrows) by the groundwater (horizontal dashes) and evaporation of water from the soil surface.

construction that may be needed. These costs are reckoned in terms of time, labor, capital, and the social organization required. On the other hand, a more extensive system, controlled by small local units, may require a smaller investment of labor per capita and less centralization for its functional operation (Downing and Gibson 1974:ix–x). Such costs may be even smaller if the system develops slowly over time in piecemeal fashion.

Once labor has been invested in establishing irrigation works, it acts as productive capital to subsequent generations. Although later generations may choose to invest more labor to expand the system, they may also choose to carry out only routine maintenance and thereby reduce the costs of the system over time (Aschmann 1962:9). Like all large-scale public works, an irrigation system may represent huge initial costs, but over the lifetime of the system, it represents only a small cost per user and per unit of output. A major difference exists between humid tropical irrigation (where water serves mainly as a nutrient carrier) and irrigation in arid lands (where water is the chief constraint, not nutrients). Irrigation probably has a more significant impact on the latter than on the former.

Nile River Irrigation

One of the best-known irrigation systems existed in ancient Egypt. Agriculture was brought to Egypt by Asian invaders in 6000 BC, but it did not replace the existing hunter-gatherer economy for another millennium (Butzer 1976:7). Explanations for this conservative behavior vary, but the effectiveness of hunting and gathering in the Nile Valley probably slowed the adoption of agriculture by the pre-Neolithic occupants of this region. Hassan (1972) has suggested that some exceptionally wet years or high floods may have discouraged the trend toward sedentariness and agriculture near river banks. The earliest evidence of Neolithic adaptations suggests that subsistence patterns continued to emphasize riverine, lacustrine, and oases' faunal-rich resources (Butzer 1976:11). Hunting and gathering and fishing continued as important subsidiary activities to farming.

The Nile Valley is seasonally inundated and accumulates silts and clays primarily through bank overflow (Butzer 1976:15). This seasonal inundation represented the dominant factor in promoting plant growth. Early farmers continued to live on the upper reaches of levees while they planted crops in the alluvial basin. This phase has been called natural irrigation—no drainage was practiced and low population densities were supported.

By 3100 BC, Egyptian water management had moved from natural to artificial irrigation forms in which natural features of the drainage system were extended and maintained by human action. Artificial irrigation included annual dredging of natural overflow channels in the levee, digging short ditches at low points in natural levees, blocking off streams by earthen dams, and using levered buckets to raise water from residual ponds or natural channels to fields (Butzer 1976:20). These improvements increased the area that could benefit from the annual floods, kept water in the basin longer during brief floods, and permitted two or three harvests yearly rather than just one.

Shifts in climate, particularly rainfall patterns, have influenced changes in this irrigation system. After 2900 BC rainfall became increasingly rare throughout most of Egypt, and the impact of low floods was deeply felt throughout the region. The trend toward lower floods led to channels, levees, and flood basins. Technological changes were geared primarily toward using dams to subdivide flood basins into manageable special purpose units (Butzer 1976:47). The major limiting factor was the lack of suitable mechanical water-lifting devices. Manual lifting was only practical for small-scale horticultural activities and could not effectively reach the lower water levels during drier years. During the Dynastic period, irrigation efforts were geared to coping with the high floods that caused crop loss and disaster rather than low floods. However, local efforts to improve the efficiency of artificial irrigation threatened the efficiency of the total irrigation system during cyclical reversals to lower floods (Butzer 1976:41).

Subsistence at this time was based on cereal grains, especially wheat and barley; vegetables such as beans and chickpeas; and flax, which was planted as a textile material. If irrigation was adequate to permit a second crop sequence, onions, lentils, and fodder crops were planted. Near the natural levees, date palms, sugar cane, cotton, and sorghum were cultivated. Thus land use in Egypt during the Dynastic period (2700–332 BC) consisted of flood basin agriculture that was locally controlled by headmen rather than directed by royal or central authorities. In time, repeated technological failure to adjust irrigation to varying flood levels introduced the social and political unrest that characterized the later sequences of Egyptian dynastic history (Butzer 1976:56).

Population expansion after 1800 BC was associated with modest increases in cultivated land and the introduction of devices that permitted irrigation agriculture even during low floods. Figure 7.9 shows the progressive intensification of irrigation and associated population changes. The progressive expansion of population also reflects the gradual abandonment of hunter-gatherer and pastoralist activities on the floodplain. The population seems to have peaked during the first century AD, possibly in response to Roman colonial domination and Roman demands for food. Civil and religious wars, mismanagement of waterworks, and disease were responsible for declines in population over the following six centuries (Butzer 1976:85–92).

Foreign domination of Egypt did not have much effect on the traditional irrigation system until the late nineteenth century. The construction of the Suez Canal, completed in 1869, made Egypt an important connecting link between Britain and the rest of her empire. British interest in Egypt was reflected in efforts to improve health conditions, change subsistence agriculture into commercial production, and improve control of the Nile floods (James 1966:67). After the first Aswan dam was completed in 1902, annual basin flood irrigation was abandoned in favor of perpetual irrigation. Under this system, water is directed to fields at any time of the year, and three harvests a year became common.

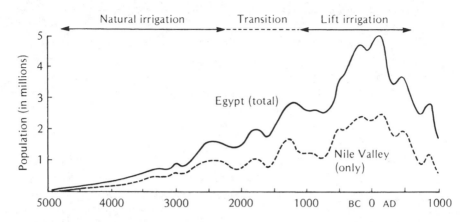

FIGURE 7.9 Hypothetical Demographic Development of Egypt and Types of Irrigation Used Between 5000 BC and AD 1000

Source: Adapted from Karl Butzer, *Early Hydraulic Civilization in Egypt: A Study in Cultural Ecology* (Chicago: University of Chicago Press, 1976).

The changes introduced by the British reoriented traditional land-people relationships. The power of the Egyptian elite increased, while the role of local groups to make irrigation innovations was restricted. New commercial and subsistence crops were introduced, soil conditions deteriorated, and population density began to increase rapidly. Today the Nile has population averages 1,800 to 3,000 people per square mile—a figure exceeded only by a few rural areas of China (James 1966:69).

The Aswan dam prevents the annual floods from depositing their renewing sediments of nutrient-rich alluvium in the lower river. Since 1902 Egyptian agriculture has depended on imported fertilizer. Increases in food production have not matched population growth: per capita food supplies have steadily lagged behind. The construction of a new high dam by independent Egypt in the 1960s again altered the system of irrigation but did not ameliorate the problem of supplying enough food for a rapidly growing population. The loss of nutrient-rich sediments has harmed not only agriculture but fishing as well. The Nile delta fisheries have been all but ruined. Catches of sardines in the delta declined from 18,000 tons in 1964 to 500 tons in 1969 (Cloudsley-Thompson 1977:163).

The potential of irrigation for solving the problems of arid lands is limited by the total areas that can be adequately irrigated. Only 2.5 percent of the total land area of Egypt is irrigated. Even when multiple cropping is used, there are limits to the size of the population that can be supported. Famine and widespread rural destitution suggest that the current densities are inappropriate to an arid region. Moreover, a substantial portion of the land is in the hands of landlords who do not make improvements in their properties to increase productivity but extract rent from farmers (Heintzelman and Highsmith 1973:168). Despite the many changes in Egyptian agriculture over the centuries, production still depends on the farmer cultivating crops on a one hectare plot with the help of water buffalo, pole-and-bucket lift irrigation, hoe, and wooden plow. In Egypt, as well as in other arid lands, the race is a close one between rising population and the food-producing capacity of irrigation intensification.

Harnessing Runoff for Agriculture

In arid regions without large rivers, agriculture requires collecting surface water runoff or exploiting underground water sources. Runoff agriculture is possible under special conditions. Rainfall must come in relatively light showers, wet soils must form an impermeable crust on a sloping terrain, and the terrain must have gentle inclines feeding into small catchment areas, or wadis. Utilization of runoff for cultivation of streambed alluvial fans has been observed among the North American Hopi and the Negev dwellers of the Middle East. Runoff control was noted to be particularly sophisticated in the Negev desert.

The Negev is a desert that receives 60–100 millimeters of rain; it has a relative humidity of 40–60 percent and high potential evapotranspiration (1,700–2,700 millimeters per year). There is an average of sixteen rainy days per year with over 80 percent falling in light showers of less than 10 millimeters. The showers do not penetrate the ground but rush down the hillsides into gullies and wadis in the form of short-lived flash floods. Ancient desert dwellers observed the floods created by runoff and learned how to harness the water for their own benefit. Figure 7.10 illustrates what happens to rainfall in the Negev. Water retention depends on soil type. What does not evaporate from the surface or is retained in the wadis quickly disappears to replenish the groundwater.

Various populations in different historical periods have settled in the Negev. The golden period seems to have started near the end of the third century BC with the rule of the Nabateans, a tribe from southern Arabia that specialized in trade, transporting luxury goods such as Indian and Arabian spices and Chinese silk. For a long time they enjoyed a thriving trading monopoly. Such profitable trade had to be protected, and the Nabateans built towns and fortresses along their trade routes. At its peak, the kingdom covered most of the Negev area. The rise of Rome led to the decline of the Nabatean kingdom, which it conquered in AD 106, but the settlements continued, now serving as frontier outposts for the Roman Empire. When the Roman Empire was divided between east and west in AD 392, the Negev fell under the jurisdiction of Constantinople, and a flourishing period of trade ensued. Pilgrimages to Palestine helped support the Negev communities during the Christian period. After the Islamic victory over Byzantium, the area was abandoned. The new rulers had neither religious nor military motives for maintaining the costly outposts of the

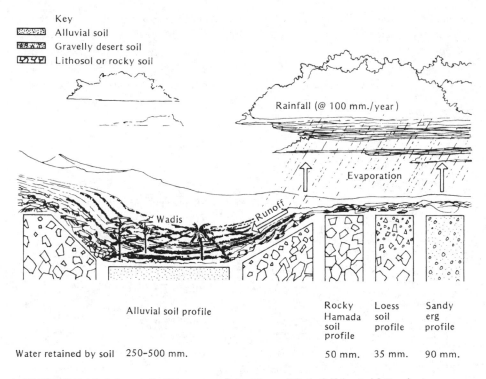

FIGURE 7.10 Schematic Diagram of the Fate of Rainfall in Arid Regions

Slope and soil type are major variables in determining how much water is retained by soils before evaporation. Valley bottoms benefit from the precipitation as well as watershed runoff.

Negev (Evenari et al. 1971:18–27). In the past four decades Israeli settlers have moved into the area and have begun applying principles of runoff management to sustain their communities.

Since the time of the Nabateans, Negev populations have sought to control flash floods by constructing terrace walls running across the course of the floodwaters. Three agricultural mechanisms have been used: individual terraced wadis, groups of terraced fields with farmsteads, and extensive terracing on the floodplain adjacent to the largest wadis of the area. Openings in the walls direct the slowed waters down a series of steps that further control the speed of the water. The wadis at the bottom are already prepared for planting, and water is channeled to flood and slowly soak the fields so that crops can receive adequate moisture.

The individual terraced wadis are the simplest and possibly the oldest Negev floodwater containment systems, and they have been employed by all the people who have cultivated the Negev. From the air, the wadis look like rows of steps, but field inspection reveals a terrace with a wall of stones built at right angles to the wadi. Behind the wall, the wadi is filled with silted loess soil. Spacing between walls is 12–15 meters, and the length across terraces is 6–20 meters, depending on the slope of the wadi bed. Walls are 60–80 centimeters in height and built of five to seven layers of stones. Low inedible shrubs grow on the periphery and aid in stabilization of the area. In these terraced wadis, floodwater cascades gently from terrace to terrace slowly penetrating into the soil. (Figure 7.11 illustrates one such system of flash flood control.) In addition to controlling erosion and floods, the terracing wets the soil thoroughly to prepare it for agricultural use.

Groups of terraced fields surrounded by stone fences adjoining a farmhouse are common. Such farm units are always located in small tributary wadis surrounded by barren hillsides that are essential to the system. Channels for collecting runoff were designed to cross these hillsides and lead the runoff to a catchment area below and eventually to the terraced fields. Evenari and colleagues (1971) described a field in which the water channels drained an area of about 17.5 hectares (about 43.5 acres) and channeled a remarkable amount of water across a special opening in a fence with well-built gates or drop structures (stone steps). These steps broke the impact of the rushing waters and allowed easier control of runoff irrigation.

Since the amount of runoff is a function of the size of the hillside catchment area, each farm unit extends its water resources by building special water conduits to storage areas adjacent to farms. Every hectare of catchment supplies an average of 100–200 cubic meters of runoff water (1 millimeter of rainfall equals 10 cubic meters of water per hectare). Since the ratio of catchment area to cultivated area in the Negev was 20 to 1, each hectare of cultivated land received runoff from 20 hectares of slopes, or 1,000–4,000 cubic meters of water. Thus the cultivated area received the equivalent of 300–500 millimeters of rainfall, although total annual precipitation is only 100 millimeters in the area. The conduits drained relatively small areas (one-tenth to three-tenths of a hectare) and divided runoff into small streams of water, thus venting flash floods. The drop structures, ditches, and spillways gave farmers control over moving water and minimized wasted water. The overall design permitted allocation of water in accordance with plant requirements.

This type of runoff agriculture is an ideal adaptation to the Negev desert. The loess soils that characterize the region form an impermeable crust when wet, which makes even light rains run off and turn into flash floods. It is this same impermeable crust, however, that allows for technological control and runoff farming (Evenari et al. 1971).

The third type of mechanism for water control is the most complex, as it requires large, intricate structures. It is also the least common since it requires diverting large flash floods from the larger wadis. The fields supplied are large, often extending for hundreds of hectares. Despite the added complexity, however, the total water yield per unit area was low when compared with that of small watersheds. Less than 2 percent of the annual rainfall made its way to the farms studied, as compared with

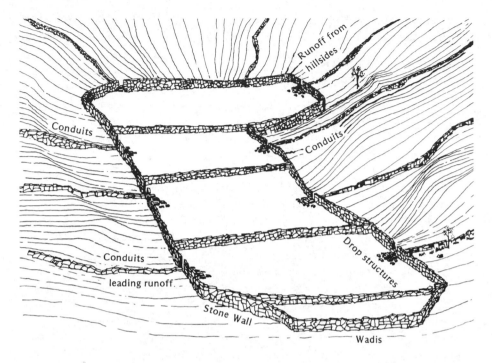

FIGURE 7.11 Aerial View of a Runoff Agricultural Structure with Individually Terraced Wadis

Source: Based on M. Evenari et al., *The Negev* (Cambridge, MA: Harvard University Press, 1971).

10–20 percent net yield from small watersheds. This runoff system did not develop suddenly but appears to have evolved through three stages of experimentation and continuing difficulties in mastering the flash floods in the large wadis. The most marked characteristic of this system is the height of the restraining wall. Walls often reached 6 meters in height along the wadis, suggesting that silt deposition was a continuing problem.

The Negev systems of narrow terraced wadis and farm units with small watersheds are rational uses of technology in the desert. They prevent erosion and involve controlling and slowing down flash floods, and they create no threat of salinization. The danger of overirrigation, so common in irrigation situations, did not occur because of the limited water resources available. Most desert plants live on runoff, and irrigation, in its imitation of nature, has been both profitable and enduring. Israel is now employing the same imitative devices in efforts to make its desert areas productive.

Despite their success, the ancient Negev dwellers made mistakes; for example, they harnessed the flash floods in large wadis. The temporary success of this venture ultimately proved costly in terms of erosion, silting of wells, and even destruction of fields. Having overextended their exploitation of natural forces, they abandoned this costly and unprofitable system to resume their exploitation of the area in smaller watersheds, using the two alternative systems. The overcontrol of natural forces seldom benefits human populations in the long run.

Runoff agriculture, as practiced in the Negev, is an important water-use strategy. It is also a costly one. In the absence of major rivers, a population will maintain an extensive network of towns in a desert only under certain conditions: to protect border areas, to exploit valuable resources, to preserve important cultural purposes, or to seek relief from persistent population pressures, once all cultivable land has been occupied. For each sedentary Negev settlement, one or more of these conditions existed.

Border protection has often been invoked in the occupation of marginal lands, and the force of such geopolitical arguments cannot be ignored. Resources change over time, and contemporary resource depletion in prime areas is likely to lead modern populations to exploit desert resources with increased frequency. The Middle East oil boom of the 1970s is an example of such exploitation. The desert, because of its starkness, has had important religious value on most continents. Its usefulness for spiritual revitalization is not likely to end in our secular age. The last condition for maintaining a network of towns in the desert is, for some nations at least, the most important. Israel, for one, has 60 percent of its territory in the Negev, and it must find ways to extract food, fiber, and drink from it. Egypt and numerous Middle Eastern and African nations also face the need to exploit desert resources.

Negev populations continue to innovate. In the Arava region of the Negev they cultivate the sands using drip irrigation technology. Yields have steadily increased as they learn how much water to use. There is virtually no salinization and little loss of moisture by evaporation. It is costly initially to install (like any other irrigation technology) but it becomes cheaper over time in terms of increasing production and saving water (Huchman et al. 1985). The use of solar-powered drip irrigation makes these systems sustainable in desert areas and environmentally appropriate (Norum and Zoldoske 1985). In the Jordan valley, drip irrigation has increased yields by 100 to 530 percent, without increasing the total amount of water used (Or et al. 1985).

At other locations irrigation has brought about potentially irreversible damage. Use of water from the rivers feeding the Aral Sea, the world's fourth largest lake, covering 25,476 square miles, in south central Asia have led to alarming shrinkage of the lake in the past thirty years. The water level has dropped between 40 and 50 feet, and 60 percent of its total volume is gone (Wolf and Mahmood 1997). In places the shoreline has receded by sixty-two miles. Kotlyakov (1991) calls this "anthropogenic desertification" because it is the product of diverting the water to irrigated agriculture. Fertilizers, pesticides, and defoliants have polluted the water and resulted in high infant mortality due in large part to waterborne pollutants (Wolf and Mahmood 1997). In addition to the environmental costs, there have been other consequences as well: deteriorating human health, increasing unemployment as the area becomes less sustainable, and declining yields of agricultural commodities. Similar processes have been noted in the basin of Lake Baikal and elsewhere.

CHANGE IN DESERT ECOSYSTEMS

Drylands have become increasingly attractive areas for urban development and for retired communities since the widespread use of air-conditioning, cheap energy, and rising incomes of some groups in developed societies (a discussion of urban sustainability in desert regions will be found in Chapter 10 of this book). Up to 90 percent of the water consumed in the southwestern United States goes to irrigated agriculture (El-Ashry and Gibbons 1988; see Lewis et al. 2006 for a discussion of how past agriculture affects urbanizing arid areas). Cities like Tucson and Phoenix in Arizona, Palm Beach and San Diego in southern California, and several desert Nevada cities are among the fastest growing US metropolitan areas, with annual rates of population growth in excess of 10 percent sustained now for decades. This presents new challenges to environmental management (Beamont 1989). One solution is to bring water from distant sources, like the Colorado River, as the Central Arizona Project (CAP) has done. However, if populations continue to increase and irrigation efficiency does not increase, and if water consumption by households does not decrease, we are poised at the brink of a crisis of major proportions. The elderly have invested a substantial portion of their life savings in housing in the desert, with property values inflated by the explosive rates of growth and the promise of perfect weather and year-round recreation. In 2007, the Southwest is deep into a multiyear drought with water levels in lakes at half of normal, with no end in sight, with some scientists doubtful whether the vegetation can recover, and with fires raging in areas that have pine and other flammable vegetation.

Irrigation efficiencies in agriculture have not substantially increased (Thompson 1988) for decades, nor has its application on golf courses in the desert improved the situation. New approaches must be tried. Oron and DeMalach (1987) report that in Beersheva, Israel, domestic sewage is treated in a set of ponds and then used for agricultural irrigation. Due to the nutrient content of the sewage, no fertilizers are required to reach impressive yields of cotton (5,500 kg/ha) and wheat (7,500 kg/ha). Wilson and Coupal (1990) developed an econometric model which reveals that urban wastewater could be used in place of groundwater for agriculture in the periphery of Tucson, Arizona, thereby reducing water demand and benefiting both rural and urban areas. This model remains unapplied, and drip irrigation is largely used by homeowners rather than by the farmers. A transition in water use from irrigation farming to urban use, with emphasis on water conservation, is necessary to reduce the potential for conflict and vast losses in ecosystem and socioeconomic terms. Irrigation in the southwestern United States is influenced by laws and customs of native American, Spanish, Mexican, and US cultures (Esslinger 1998), different systems of use that have led to conflict over the years (Sheridan 1988) and can only grow worse as supply diminishes and demand increases. Similar challenges face other countries with vast deserts, such as Sudan (El Gamri 2004). Political control of water, to the detriment of local communities, can result in explosive revolution, as was witnessed in Peru during the Shining Path guerrilla days (Trawick 2003). Local populations know the importance of traditional systems of water control and management, built on traditions of self-organization (see Kreutzmann 2000 for a detailed discussion of this knowledge in South and Central Asia).

A major research focus in arid lands is on strategies for fighting desertification (Pasternak and Schlissel 2001). Hundreds of millions are affected by the declining productivity of their land, and combating it must involve institutional, social, and technical approaches (Simmers 2003). The use of GIS and remote sensing, as noted earlier, is particularly useful over deserts, since the low cloud cover allows features to be visible over time and space (Dawoud et al. 2005; Yagoub 2004). Desertification processes are also taking place in southern Europe, particularly Portugal, Spain, Italy, and Greece (Wilson and Juntti 2005; Kepner 2006) and in the former Soviet republics of Central Asia (Gintzburger et al 2005). In the past decade the Eastern Province of Saudi Arabia has witnessed a growing threat in sand movement and declining production (H. J. Barth 1999). Grazing and recreational use of rangeland seem to be the primary causes of growing desertification in this region. One solution is to plant trees in areas experiencing degradation, but recent research suggests that this must be done in combination with other strategies that produce multiple benefits to local people to be successful (Ma 2004).

Climate change is having an impact on deserts. A study of the hottest desert of North America, the Sonoran desert, finds evidence for widespread warming trends in winter and spring, decreased frequency of freezing temperatures, a lengthening freeze-free season, and increased minimum temperatures in winter (Weiss and Overpeck 2005). Consequences may include a contraction of the overall boundary of the Sonoran desert in the southeast, and its expansion north, east, and into higher elevations—as well as changes in plant species characteristic of the Sonoran desert (Ma 2004).

Oases form an important research frontier in arid land studies (Achtnich and Homeyer 1980; Yagoub 2004). There is evidence that many millenarian oases have been drying up (Meckelein 1980). Some cases appear to result from state policies (Ehlers 1980), others, from overuse of the oasis vegetation resulting from population increase by migrants unfamiliar with the fragility of oases, or from secular climate trends. The sedentarization of nomads, for example, in the Tunisian Sahara has provoked two phenomena: population concentration around oases and depopulation of remote areas, creating a demographic disequilibrium that threatens the capacity of oases to support human and animal populations at all (Sghaier and Seiwert 1993).

This pressure on oases is evident in the enlargement of the circles of degradation around them. Meckelein (1980) convincingly argues that most of the oasis loss is a result of human impact. The same can be said about the debate over the spread of deserts (Grainger 1982; Mortimore 1989). While some blame pastoralists for overgrazing marginal areas, there is as much evidence to suggest that most pastoralists who can move their herds freely do not overgraze sufficiently to damage the return of vegetation. Restrictions on pastoral movement dictated by state policies, privatization of grasslands, and population migration to empty areas are the factors that have led to overgrazing and desertification.

Further research is needed on both prehistoric and contemporary forms of coping with the limitations of water availability. In the past, poor irrigation management turned arid lands with great agricultural potential into biological deserts. Improved ways must be found to exploit and above all protect the resources of arid lands on a long-term basis. This requires a solid understanding of both short-term and long-term fluctuations in water availability, of physiologically adapted plants with economic potential, and of the value and limitations of pastoral nomadism in areas of unpredictable rainfall. We must learn which population distributions will outrun a region's resources and fail to provide adequately for their well-being and survival. Extended droughts in the Sahel, prehistoric decades-long droughts in the Great Plains, and the scientific study of desertification and climate change present important challenges to environmental scientists in the social and biogeochemical sciences. Half the nations in the world have part of their territory in arid zones, a third of which are threatened with total loss of productive capacity. The impact of global climate change on these regions will be variable: they may become uninhabitable due to further drying, or they may become attractive if precipitation increases and temperatures drop.

SUGGESTED READINGS AND USEFUL WEBSITES

The *Journal of Arid Environments* (www.elsevier.com/locate/jaridenv) provides research articles on the biological and anthropological features of arid, semiarid, and desert environments. *Arid Land Research and Management*, formerly *Arid Soil Research and Rehabilitation* (www.tandf.co.uk/journals/titles/15324982.asp), highlights the flora and fauna of arid soils, especially recovery of degraded areas.

The International Arid Lands Consortium (http://cals.arizona.edu/OALS/IALC/Home.html) is a consortium of academic and research institutions from different countries for identifying and studying issues related to arid and semiarid environments, especially for establishing sustainable agricultural practices in these areas. The International Center for Agricultural Research in the Dry Areas (ICARDA) (www.icarda.cgiar.org), part of the network of research institutions of the Consultative Group on International Research (CGIAR) (www.cgiar.org), works to develop sustainable agricultural practices in dry areas in the developing world, with particular regard to free exchange of germ plasm and protection of indigenous knowledge and property rights.

Some useful books and introductory textbooks about various aspects of the ecology of desert and arid systems include *Ecology of Desert Systems* by Whitford (2002); *Desert Ecology* by Sowell (2001) (a good textbook for beginning undergraduate students); *Riparian Ecosystem Recovery in Arid Lands: Strategies and References* by Briggs (1996); and *Seed Germination in Desert Plants* by Gutterman (1993).

Many universities worldwide maintain dedicated research centers for understanding the ecology of desert systems, for developing improved agricultural practices in arid environments, and for studying the role of human activity and interaction with the environment in these areas. The Nevada Desert Research Center at the University of Nevada-Las Vegas (www.unlv.edu/Climate_Change_Research) specifically studies the ecological structure and function of the Mojave desert, particularly in regard to climate change. The Desert Research Institute (www.dri.edu), including its Center for Arid Lands Environmental Management (www.calem.dri.edu/calem_web), also part of the Nevada System of Higher Education, integrates terrestrial, hydrologic, atmospheric, and anthropologic research to advance understanding of sustainable natural resource use.

The ANR Desert Research and Extension Center of the University of California Agriculture and Natural Resources (http://groups.ucanr.org/desertrec) focuses on the development of crops and agricultural practices suitable for desert environments. Additionally, the Semi-Arid Land-Surface-Atmosphere (SALSA) program involves several government agencies, universities, and organizations in the study of the Upper San Pedro River basin in southeastern Arizona and northeastern Sonora, Mexico (www.tucson.ars.ag.gov/salsa/salsahome.html).

The Office of Arid Lands Studies at the University of Arizona (www.arid.arizona.edu/index.asp) addresses issues related to the sustainable use of dry lands, and operates four divisions within this office: the Arid Lands Information Center (www.arid.arizona.edu/Divisions/division.asp?div=ALIC), the Arizona Remote Sensing Center (www.arid.arizona.edu/Divisions/division.asp?div=ARSC), the Desert Research Unit (www.arid.arizona.edu/Divisions/division.asp?div=DRU), and the Southwest Center for Natural Products Research and Commercialization (www.arid.arizona.edu/Divisions/division.asp?div=DRU). The Office also publishes the *Arid Lands Newsletter* (http://ag.arizona.edu/OALS/ALN/ALNHome.html), which discusses issues related to arid lands research, resource use, and policy.

The Sonoran Desert Research Station of the U.S. Geological Survey (USGS) (www.srnr.arizona.edu/nbs), affiliated with the University of Arizona, collects and manages data on the ecology and management of desert and arid environments. The USGS also maintains a detailed online publication of deserts and arid environments (http://pubs.usgs.gov/gip/deserts). Remotely sensed data for desert and arid environments is available from the USGS Terra Web–Remote Sensing in Arid and Semi-Arid Environments website (http://terraweb.wr.usgs.gov/arid.html).

The Jacob Baustein Institutes for Desert Research at the Ben-Gurion University of the Negev (http://bidr.bgu.ac.il/bidr) focuses on ecological and climate research in desert environments, with particular attention paid to water resource management, conservation biology, and plant and animal physiology. Similarly, the Desert Research Center in Egypt (www.drc-egypt.org) assesses groundwater and agricultural issues within Egypt. At Oxford University, the Arid Environmental Systems research cluster at the Centre for Environment (www.ouce.ox.ac.uk/research/arid-environments) analyzes terrestrial and atmospheric dynamics, particularly the geology and geomorphology of desert and arid environments.

The International Geographical Union's Commission on Arid Lands, Humankind, and Environment (http://ahe.uni-koeln.de/index.html) promotes the study of geographical research and monitoring of human-environment interactions in arid lands. Arid lands and their role in climate change scenarios also have been a focus of research for the Global Carbon Project (www.globalcarbonproject.org). Additionally, the International Geoscience Program (IGCP), in cooperation with several other international research programs, maintains the IGCP 500 program Dryland Change: Past, Present, and Future, a successor to the IGCP 413 (Understanding Future Dryland Changes from Past Dynamics), to increase understanding of dryland landscapes, especially in developing countries. Specifically concerning Africa, the Arid Climate, Adaptation, and Cultural Innovation in Africa (ACACIA) (www.uni-koeln.de/sfb389/index.htm), based at the University of Cologne, Germany, looks at historical and current land use and cultural change in light of climate and landscape change.

An outstanding book reviewing drylands, drought, soils, vegetation, water scarcity, and erosion is available (Mainguet 1999). It views the neglect of the land as more serious than the lack of water and erosion of soils as a greater threat than aridity. Cloudsley-Thompson (1984) has a fine book that covers the climate, geology, flora, and fauna of the Sahara desert. It also describes the biology and physiology of desert organisms and the prehistory of the human inhabitants. It even covers issues of current debate such as desertification (see also Graetz 1991) and oasis degradation. Allen (1988) surveys efforts to restore desertified areas.

Publications are produced on a continual basis by the UNESCO Arid Zone Research series. The data included in these publications are numerous and of high quality. The U.S. IBP Desert Biome Program has carried out extensive research and much of their data complements the scheme presented in this book. Evans and Thames (1980) are editors of one of the several IBP synthesis volumes. A related synthesis of desert ecosystems is that of Evenari et al. (1985). The consequences of El Niño are explored in a volume by Glantz (1996), which is apropos of arid lands.

Ecological anthropological studies of desert populations are dominated by the contributions of archaeologists (Butzer 1976; Fish and Fish 1990) and the collections by Downing and Gibson (1974) and by Steward (1955b). Horowitz (1990) has produced a thoughtful discussion on the consequences of multilateral loans on pastoralist societies and desert regions, with a political ecology perspective. A special issue of the *Journal of Arid Environments,* "Combatting Desertification: Connecting Science with Community Action," offers a participatory set of studies on solving these community problems. A touching account of the consequences of nutritional inadequacy in Mali is the account by Dettwyler (1994), which won the Margaret Mead Prize.

Photo by Siew Yee Lee
Source: iStockphoto

8

HUMAN ADAPTABILITY
TO GRASSLANDS

Grasslands constitute important and sizable areas of land that have long provided human populations with subsistence (Reynolds and Frame 2005). Grasslands, or savannas, cover a third of the world's land surface and support a fifth of the world's population (Mistry 2000; Suttie et al. 2005). Some grasslands are natural to a biogeographic region (for example, the North American plains and the Russian steppes), while others are the result of human management (for example, the grasslands of Japan). Figure 8.1 illustrates the extent of grasslands today. Human adaptation to these areas has emphasized hunting of wild game, herding of domesticated livestock, or a mixed pastoral and agricultural strategy (Driel 2001). Managed grasslands cover more than 25 percent of the global land surface and have a larger spatial extent than any other form of land use (Asner et al. 2004). Because grassland ecosystems have an inadequate supply of rainfall to sustain agriculture on a regular basis and severe droughts are not uncommon, herding has been the most common subsistence mode in the past, although irrigation in these regions has shifted some of them toward permanent intensive cultivation. In temperate grasslands, agriculture did not begin until steel plows to break the sod became available, as well as special crops and management techniques. However, in tropical grasslands agriculture has been practiced in restricted areas since Neolithic times. Pennington and colleagues (2006) provide a useful compilation of patterns of plant biodiversity and conservation in neotropical savannas (see also Watkinson and Ormerod 2001). Pastoralists practice agriculture in both temperate and tropical areas when the rains permit. Asner and colleagues (2004) note that grassland conditions result in the emergence of three syndromes inherent to grazing: desertification, woody encroachment, and deforestation. Human populations have dealt with these potential problems in various ways over the millennia.

Changes in land use in grasslands have been dramatic in the past fifty years. For example, in the South Platte basin of Colorado, Nebraska, and Wyoming one-third of the land area has been converted to cropland (Baron et al. 1998). Drought, war, famine, climate change, growing human and animal populations, environmental degradation, sedentarization, and government policies have increased the vulnerability of pastoral societies and semiarid grassland ecosystems, as well as absentee herd ownership, wage labor, and forms of sedentary pastoralism that overuse some range areas while underusing others. These processes are not explainable by purely environmental or social analysis. They require examination of political ecology (Barker 1985; Franke and Chasin 1980; Watts 1983; Horowitz 1990; P. Little 1992) to complement biocultural and bioecological studies.

In this chapter we will briefly examine the characteristics of both temperate and tropical grasslands and the various adaptability strategies found in both types of areas. The chief problems presented by grassland ecosystems center around water and pasturage, herds, relationships between pastoralists and agriculturalists, and the balance between the human and the animal population under conditions of climatic uncertainty and frequent lean times (Suttie et al. 2005). These topics form the major sections of this chapter. Because of the patchy characteristics of the environment, **nomadism** has commonly been used to secure an adequate supply of pasture and water. This pathway of adaptation is increasingly restricted by states wishing to sedentarize pastoral populations under the charge that pastoralists degrade their grassland ecosystem (see Lamprey 1983; and critique by McCabe 1990).

The size and composition of herds reflect both the diet required to sustain the group and the social exchanges that occur among neighbors. Relations between pastoralists and neighboring cultivators may be tense but are usually **mutualistic,** since neither can manage well without the other's resources. Pastoralists inhabiting arid tropical grasslands have the same acclimatory adjustments to dry heat as populations inhabiting arid lands and do not require repeating here.

The social and cultural adjustments that characterize the occupation of temperate grasslands in North America result from various economic and ecological considerations. Subsistence on the plains evolved from hunting and gathering through specialized cattle herding to a combination of restricted herding and seasonal agriculture. There has been great concern in recent years over the problem of desertification in both temperate and tropical grasslands (Reynolds and Stafford Smith 2002). Areas where wild and later domesticated ungulates once grazed have become permanently degraded into deserts. The recent documentation of past drought cycles of long duration is particularly worrisome. Clark and colleagues (2002) have shown that there were 100- and 130-year drought cycles in the northern Great Plains of the United States during the arid Middle Holocene (8,000 BP). During these droughts grass productivity declined, erosion and forbs increased, and fire declined due to lack of fuel and dead vegetation. A repeat of these drought cycles of long duration is conceivable under scenarios of future climate change, but next time the economic and environmental impact will be far more severe due to the larger human and animal populations in the region, and the vast economic investments in these areas (Clark et al. 2002).

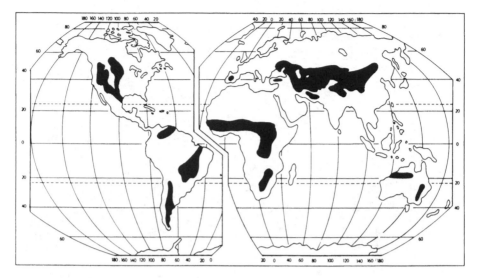

FIGURE 8.1 World Distribution of Grasslands

GRASSLANDS ECOSYSTEMS

Natural grasslands occur where rainfall levels are generally too low to support forests but higher than the levels commonly associated with desert ecosystems. The grassland is a transitional biome characterized by a gradient by which temperature, rainfall, and humidity determine many of the characteristics of vegetation and other dependent life forms. In addition, grasslands are characterized by high rates of evapotranspiration in summer, periodic severe droughts, and rolling to flat terrain (R. L. Smith 1974:552). Grasslands are also found in areas with a high water table or are maintained by human intervention. The significance of precipitation in defining the characteristics of a natural grassland is best illustrated by a cross-sectional view of the North American Great Plains (see Figure 8.2). Seasonal moisture is the crucial factor in determining ecosystem structure and function, as well as the crucial constraint in the utilization of grassland areas (recent assessments confirm the importance of the precipitation and temperature gradient in the plains in shaping people and environment interactions; Gutmann 2000; Cunfer 2005).

Climatic and Vegetation Features

The grasslands climate is characterized by extremes. Rainfall is seasonal and fluctuates widely. The average rainfall indicates very little about actual conditions faced by plants and animals in the region. Dry and wet years appear to follow each other in cycles, but until recently the climatological data have been too restricted to permit any useful quantitative manipulation that might suggest the patterns that are taking

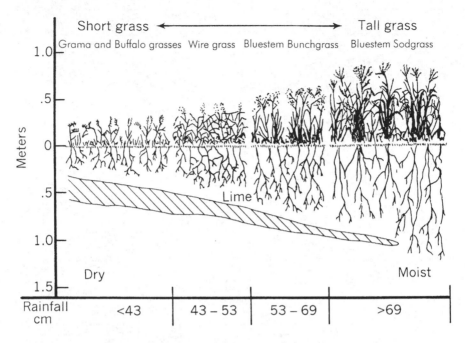

FIGURE 8.2 A West-East Transect of the Great Plains

There is a clear rainfall-dependent gradient across the plains, with tallgrass prairie in the wetter area to the east, and declining above- and belowground biomass as we move west into the shortgrass prairie. *Source:* Adapted from Lynn Porter, "Nitrogen in Grassland Ecosystems," in *The Grassland Ecosystem*, edited by R. L. Dix and R. G. Beidleman (Fort Collins: Colorado State University, Range Science Department, 1969).

place—if any are. The major management problem presented by semiarid grasslands is that moist cycles tend to create the illusion that those conditions will last and when drought comes, as it always does, the population is caught unprepared and far too numerous for the capacity of the now desiccated environment to feed. There is growing evidence that drought conditions which led to the American Dust Bowl in the 1930s were *mild* in comparison to ancient multidecadal droughts recently documented by paleoclimatologists for the Great Plains (Clark et al. 2002).

In the Great Plains the 500 millimeter rainfall line (the area between the 98 and 100 degree meridians) marks the difference between the shortgrass and highgrass plains (see Figure 8.3). The rainfall pattern in this transitional zone (Ottoson et al. 1966:4) can shift by as much as two hundred miles to the east or west (Wedel 1961:453). When drought occurs, the temperatures can go to 37.8°C or higher, causing damage to both wild and domesticated crops. At either end of the humidity spectrum are different species of grasses, but in this transitional area a combination of species adjusts phenotypically to aridity.

Tropical grasslands, or savannas, are found in tropical regions with 500 to 1,250 millimeters of rainfall, but with higher rates of evapotranspiration than temperate grasslands. In east Africa the distribution of rainfall is bimodal—distributed in two short wet seasons. Each season by itself is inadequate to support agriculture, but bimodal rainfall distribution is helpful in the maintenance of a quality rangeland (Pratt and Gwynne 1977:16).

The savanna, as a transitional ecosystem between desert and forest, manifests a steady gradation and a rich variety of climatic and vegetation characteristics. The humid savanna supports a sizable tree population, while the arid portions of savannas resemble desert ecosystems. Although a clear delineation of the worldwide characteristics of tropical savannas is difficult, a number of features seem to be always present (see the synthesis in Bourliére 1983 and Sarmiento 1984, as well as the synthesis of the Brazilian savannas, or cerrados, by Oliveira and Marquis 2002). Savannas are dominated by xerophytic vegetation, with grasses as the chief components. They

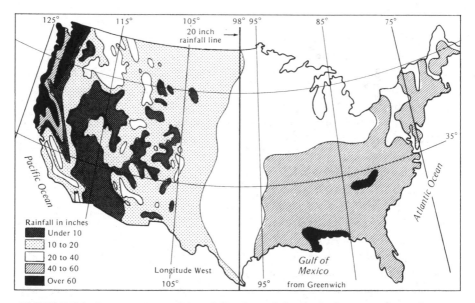

FIGURE 8.3 Average Annual Precipitation of the United States Along the 98°–100° Meridian, the Dividing Line Between the Short- and Tallgrass Prairies

As noted in Figure 8.2, there is no sudden change from tall- to shortgrass prairies. What we have is a gradient from one to the other associated with declining rainfall from east to west.

occur at elevations between sea level and 2,000 meters on low-nutrient soils. The water cycle follows a wet-dry rhythm both annually and in the long term. Most scientists agree that the savanna is a fire-managed ecosystem where vegetation has been burned as often as once a year since time immemorial (see Kull 2004 on the political ecology of fire in Madagascar). A great deal of the vegetation is fire adapted (Hills and Randall 1968). The morphology of many grasses is adapted to withstand fires and even thrive on them. At issue is the management of this ecosystem by fire (Brown and Smith 2000; see also Andersen et al. 2003 on fire in tropical savannas, particularly results from experiments in Australia).

Explanations for the origins of savannas differ a great deal. Some postulate the importance of alternating wet and dry seasons; others focus on the lack of soil fertility and the soils' deficient drainage; and still others stress the importance of fire in maintaining the grass **climax community.** It is most likely that different savannas arose as a result of one or more of these factors, but it is unlikely that any one factor could explain the existence of all savannas. Climatic and topographic gradients are considered the primary controls on soil processes, with a not insignificant role played (especially for nitrogen cycling) by migratory ungulates (Frank and Groffman 1998).

Soil Conditions

Although they can occur on a wide range of soils (Duffey et al. 1974:82), temperate grasslands have been in existence long enough to have developed a distinctive soil type (James 1966:282). Temperate grasslands have given rise to chernozem or mollisol soils. A map of the mollisols (see Figure 8.4) clearly shows how closely they are associated with the major temperate grassland areas of the world: the North American prairies, the Argentinian pampas, and the Eurasian steppes.

Mollisol soils have a surface horizon that retains its soft character even during dry periods and has high base saturation. The soil humus tends to be distributed throughout the profile. In contrast to humus formation in forests, which occurs primarily by leaf fall and soil surface decomposition of soil fauna, humus in grasslands is formed primarily by the decomposition of the root network of the plants. Grasses produce both an organic mat at the surface and a dense underground root system that decomposes steadily through time (Steila 1976:113). Since grasses require greater amounts of mineral nutrients than do trees, the organic materials decomposed in grass areas are richer in bases, particularly calcium (Steila 1976:114). Mollisols do not generally derive from hard rocks like granite but from calcareous sediments rich in bases. Mollisols are considered prime agricultural soils because of the ease with which they can be tilled, the flatness of the grassland terrain, and the deep humus layer.

This deep humus layer is rich in accumulated carbon, making it important in current concerns over carbon emission and sequestration. Management techniques

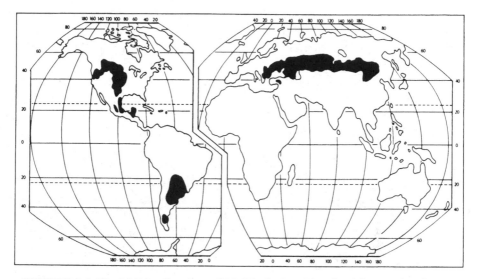

FIGURE 8.4 World Distribution of Mollisols Associated with Grasslands

aiming to increase forage production may potentially increase soil organic matter, thus sequestering atmospheric carbon (Conant et al. 2001). Among the improvements one finds fertilization, grazing management, conversion from cultivation or native vegetation to grassland, and sowing of legumes and grasses. Cultivation, the introduction of earthworms, and irrigation resulted in the largest increases in soil organic matter and carbon in 115 studies (Conant et al. 2001). Some believe that grasslands can make a particularly important contribution because of the extensive rooting network that transfers at least 50 percent of carbon sequestered below ground (Rees et al. 2005).

Phosphorus is often a limiting factor in grasslands where animals graze. There is a continual loss of phosphorus from range soils because a major portion of the phosphorus in the forage is deposited in the animal's bones, hair, wool, and horns. Thus when animals are marketed outside the area, the rangeland experiences a permanent loss of phosphorus (Humphrey 1962). This situation may be even more severe in tropical grasslands, since tropical ecosystems are phosphorus limited as compared to temperate ecosystems, which are largely nitrogen limited.

Soils in tropical savannas are generally low in fertility, except those of volcanic origin or those that are enriched by alluvial deposits (Pratt and Gwynne 1977:11). Their year-round exposure to the elements has made the soils low in organic and mineral content. The high aluminum content of the dominant oxisols in tropical savannas prevents root penetration to any great depth, and thus we do not find the deep soil organic matter accumulation in tropical savannas that we find in temperate grasslands. Methods have been developed using no-till and minimum tillage and mulches and rotations that improve soil conditions, particularly organic matter and phosphorus, which are traditionally most limiting (Basamba et al. 2006). Because of a lack of colloids, they respond poorly to inorganic fertilizers. In savanna areas nearest the boundary between grassland and forest, water is more abundant and plant and animal productivity are greater. These areas can be made agriculturally productive. In savanna areas that are near deserts, aridity prevents the regular cultivation of soils. Grazing is the only effective way to utilize the area without irrigation. Specialists have observed that in these areas wild ungulates outproduce domestic livestock and have suggested that these regions could be more effectively utilized by harvesting the wild species. Eland, oryx, and addax are three African savanna species able to occupy and exploit areas far from permanent water sources where domestic livestock cannot survive.

Formation and Development of Grasslands

Most grassland biomes developed from previously existing ecosystems as a result of changing climatic, geological, and anthropogenic factors interacting through time (Lewis 1970:1). It is now generally agreed that grasslands are not exclusively a climatic formation but require periodic burning or steady grazing pressure for growth and maintenance. Although fires are occasionally caused when lightning ignites the dry grassland, some grasslands are believed to have been consciously created by hunters seeking to drive herds toward a narrow point where fellow hunters were concentrated, or by pastoralists seeking to encourage the growth of nutritious young shoots for their herds. As frequently noted, in the absence of fire, many grasslands turn to shrub or tree communities (Moore 1966:201). Grasslands have expanded and contracted over millennia as a result of climate change (Bradley 1989).

The growing importance of grasslands is associated with the rise of two great ungulate orders of herbivorous mammals in early Tertiary times: periosodactyls (for example, horses, rhinos, tapirs) and artiodactyls. The latter order includes both nonruminant (for example, pigs, camels, hippos, peccaries) and ruminant types (for example, cattle, buffalo, sheep, goats, deer, and antelope). The biomass of wild ungulates in East Africa has been as high as 35,000 kilograms per square kilometer (Pratt and Gwynne 1977:30). A more average figure is 12,000 to 17,000 kilograms per square kilometer for the biomass of wild ungulates. When domestic livestock graze in conjunction with the wild species, the biomass can decline to about 6,000 kilograms (Little and Morren 1976:55).

The great diversity of animal species exercises an important selective role on the natural vegetation that encourages grasses at the expense of trees (Little and Morren 1976:33). A grazing herd has three main effects on grassland: grass defoliation, nutrient redistribution, and plant trampling. Studies put cattle consumption of net primary production between 10 and 17 percent, depending on the cattle variety. Cattle are among the least efficient herbivores and convert only one-twentieth of the grass ingested into meat (Strickon 1965:233). Two-thirds of the herbage is rejected as feces. Such rejection plays an important role in nutrient redistribution. Cattle and other herd animals have favorite dunging sites within a restricted pasture. Such areas contain concentrations of phosphorous and potassium. Environmental degradation is not thought to occur unless more than 50 percent of aboveground net primary production is consumed by animals (Coughenour et al. 1985), and most pastoral populations where measurements have been taken are said to be well below 25 percent (Coppock 1985). Long-term ecological studies among the Turkana have noted that even in years of severe drought, and with severe losses of cattle herds, there was no incidence of ecosystem degradation (desertification). Rather, ecosystem aggradation was found to be taking place, and herds rebounded rapidly following devastating losses (McCabe 1984).

Grazing animals have a systematic relationship to grasslands. Differences in animal growth patterns, biomass production, and behavior reflect environmental constraints, rather than mere species differences. In areas where cattle ranching is market-oriented, biomass production per unit of consumption exceeds, by up to eight times, the ratio in areas where systems are geared at biomass stability or subsistence. In the latter areas, forage is often of lower quality. In addition, acquiring it may mean traveling great distances at great energy cost. Indian cattle appear highly efficient, probably because of the intensive demands of the human population and conscious selection. Animal biomass production in India is 3.6 percent of net primary production. North American Pawnee and East African Karamojong conversion rates are 0.47 percent and 0.043 respectively. These efficiencies reflect efforts by cattle managers to fit their animals to the requirements of their respective systems (Ellis and Jennings 1975).

Fire Management

The need for fire management of grasslands is illustrated by two major types of temperate grasses: sod grass and bunch grass. Sod grasses form a solid mat over the ground, while bunch grasses grow, as their name suggests, in clumps. Some grasses exhibit both growth patterns, depending on the local environment (R. L. Smith 1974:552). Unless mowed, burned, or grazed, grasslands accumulate a thick layer of **mulch** at ground level that may take three years or more to decompose completely. The thicker the accumulation, the longer decomposition may take. The costs and benefits of this mulch accumulation are debated by scholars. Some argue that mulch accumulation increases soil moisture available to the live vegetation, decreases runoff, stabilizes soil temperatures, and improves soil conditions (R. L. Smith 1974:554). Others maintain that accumulation of mulch from one species can have a toxic effect on the germination and development of other species. Still others maintain that it can facilitate the invasion of a grassland by a woody species. Some range ecologists believe that heavy mulch accumulations lead to decreased forage production, smaller root biomass, and a lower caloric value to the living shoots (R. L. Smith 1974:555). From the point of view of the hunter or pastoralist, food value, elimination of woody growth, and prevention of toxic conditions were probably the most important considerations. Fire is an obvious way to reduce the natural accumulation of mulch. Less **litter** accumulation has been noted in semiarid savannas, but fire's beneficial effects in releasing nutrients, encouraging the growth of young shoots, and suppressing insects are equally important in temperate and tropical grasslands.

The literature on man's use of fire to modify the earth's vegetation is vast (Heizer 1955; Hills and Randall 1968; Iizumi and Iwanami 1975; Stewart 1956; Sauer 1958). Fire can be a useful means of controlling undesirable species, eliminating excess litter, suppressing insects, preparing the seedbed, facilitating livestock movement, and fertilizing the soil. By eliminating excess litter, periodic firing prevents the occurrence of devastating natural fires (E. Odum 1971:150). These recurrent fires maintain woody species in a juvenile, nonfruiting stage and at the same time permit perennial grasses to put out new growth. Grasses are morphologically better adapted than shrubs to withstand fires because a large proportion of grass biomass is protected below ground. In addition, because their seedheads are designed to easily broadcast their contents, grasses are effective colonizers of terrestrial ecosystems (Tivy 1971:298). Fire increases the supply of nutrients available at the soil surface, raises soil pH, and significantly expands the supply of phosphorus and potassium (Vallentine 1975:164; see Bowman and Prior 2004 for a discussion of the impact of Australian Aborigines' use of fire in managing vegetation in Arnhem Land). Some authors point out a few undesirable effects of burning grassland areas: substantial amounts of nitrogen are lost during the fire; fire can spread to nearby forested areas; and if too hot or improperly timed, burning can harm desirable species of grass and legumes (the latter lacking the same fire resilience as grasses). Even in humid tropical environments, fire spread is replacing intentional burning as it becomes responsible for a larger proportion of total areas experiencing fire (Nepstad et al. 1999).

HERD MANAGEMENT

A major difference between herders in East Africa and herders in many temperate grasslands lies in the objectives of their economic activities. Cattle raising on the North American plains is clearly market oriented, although the ranching lifestyle has romantic overtones and elicits a sentimental attachment from the population (Bennett 1969:172). A market orientation leads to a different set of management strategies (Bennett 1992). If the goal is to maximize milk or meat production for sale, the objective is to have a herding operation that will give the best returns with a minimum investment of labor. When cattle are raised for subsistence and constitute the essential life support of a population in a semiarid environment, the results are quite different (Dyson-Hudson and Dyson-Hudson 1969:2). For example, Turkana pastoralists subsist primarily on milk and blood tapped from nonmilking animals, and they accumulate the animal biomass in the form of living animals (Dyson-Hudson and McCabe 1985:5–6). Herds provide subsistence as well as a measure of status and influence through their role in wife acquisition and as old-age insurance. All the potential satisfactions of social life depend on the acquisition or availability of an adequate number of animals (Evangelou 1984). A. B. Smith (2005) provides a broad discussion of modern African pastoral peoples and their antecedents, and their ancient relationships to the Middle East.

Gaining Access to Water and Pasture

East African pastoralists resort to seasonal nomadism to gain access to both water and savanna pastures. Each occasion for nomadic movement involves obtaining information, assessing its reliability, forming a personal opinion, and making a decision. McCabe (1983:125) notes that Turkana herd owners acted as independent decisionmakers and that they adjusted their herd movement and management in response to environmental change, social conditions, fluctuations in productivity, and seasonality. They share common access to grasslands but water rights, especially to dug wells, may be privately vested in the families who dug the well. In pastoral decision-making, no single or best choice is likely to exist. Pastoralists must instead deal with a set of better or worse options. Pastoral economics in semiarid tropical grasslands involves a no-win situation: if the population adapts to the normal bad years, it will leave large areas of territory unexploited; if it adjusts to good years, it will find itself overextended and facing famine and death. Information is seldom complete and is usually of doubtful reliability. Yet the population must act. Edgerton describes the decisionmaking process in this manner:

> The care of livestock involves the husbandman in a constant pattern of decision-making. His seasonal round of activities is not routinized; he must decide each day where to take his animals, and he may have to include many diverse factors in his computation—the potential quality of the grass, the availability of water, the probability of predators, the competitive action of other herders, and so on. The cumulative quality of such decisions will determine whether the herd prospers or not. The pastoralist must be constantly aware of the condition of each animal and meet its needs. While African pastoralists do not maintain genetic records, the good husbandman does recognize that some animals should be culled, and when the opportunity arises, it is these animals that are slaughtered, exchanged, or, nowadays, sold. This matter of exchanging and selling animals is of particular importance; the herdsman is engaged in recurrent economic transactions with his neighbors, and the cogency of his decisions and the capacity to arrive at satisfactory bargains are vital to the furtherance of his welfare. (1971:281)

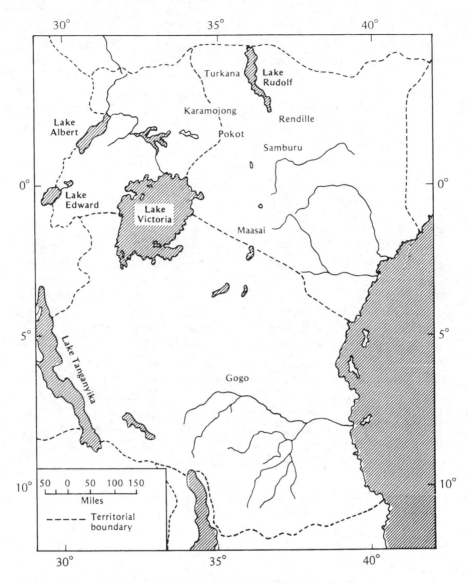

FIGURE 8.5 Tribal Groups of East Africa Discussed in Chapter 8

Most of the time, the East African pastoralist has a range of choices. Only at the end of the dry season, when few places are left with water and pasture, is choice so narrowly constrained that the direction of nomadic movement is clear and unambiguous. Figure 8.5 shows the location of the various tribes that will be discussed in the rest of the chapter.

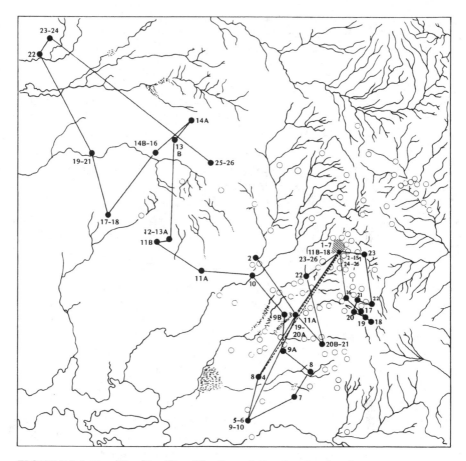

FIGURE 8.6 Two Herding Families Search for Grazing Land

Source: From V. R. Dyson-Hudson and N. Dyson-Hudson, "Subsistence Herding in Uganda," *Scientific American* 220 (1969): 76–89. Copyright © 1969 by Scientific American, Inc. All rights reserved.

The Karamojong of Uganda provide a good example of East African pastoralist strategies. Figure 8.6 illustrates the wanderings of two cattle herds in this area. In this case, the size of the herding family played a major role in how the cattle were moved. The family with the larger number of herders could afford to send its animals to areas as far as fifty-five miles from camp for the best pastures without fear of losing the animals to raiders. The second family, constrained by limited numbers of males, moved its cattle only twelve miles. In bad years such a strategy can have serious consequences, with the family losing all its animals because of inadequate forage and water. The size of herding families is directly related to management strategy: the more people, the greater the dispersion, the more abundant the forage and water, and the larger the herd (Dyson-Hudson and Dyson-Hudson 1969:9). East African pastoralists herd cattle great distances at little more cost in food and water required than if the animals were moved lesser distances (Western and Finch 1986).

Social considerations, as well as information about the location of water and pasture, influence decisions on moving the herds. According to Gulliver (1975), herders do not necessarily follow kinship lines in choosing partners for their treks. A herder may be aware of several watering places within a reasonable distance. One place may be richer in certain grasses but poorer in water sources. Another may be near good watering holes but involve crossing rough terrain that can exhaust the cattle and herder. Good spots may be known to other herdsmen, leading the herder to anticipate resource depletion and avoid them. The herder may also avoid favor grazing areas because of possible confrontations with other herders who have a claim on his property (McCabe 2004). Memory of past raids and homicides has a persistent influence on decisions of where to move cattle.

Herd movement may be constrained by other activities of the population, such as the seasonal practice of agriculture. During the wet periods, women engage in agriculture and the herd must be kept within a reasonable distance of the camp to provide the female cultivators with the milk and blood that are a crucial part of the diet (Dyson-Hudson and Dyson-Hudson 1969:10). During the dry season when pasture land is reduced, the whole camp may travel together.

The limited possibilities of the East Africa savanna environment were convincingly outlined in 1940 by Evans-Pritchard. He described an environment intimately known by the Nuer whose subsistence activities and social life are conditioned by the environment. As is the case for so many pastoralist populations, agriculture is uncertain and the growing season short before the dry season returns. The Nuer, therefore, place a high cultural value on cattle herding. Cattle can be moved to where resources are available. Furthermore, the species the Nuer use have proved their hardiness and adaptability and are able to switch from grazing to browsing when grass is unavailable. Browsing animals eat twigs and shoots from trees, shrubs, and vines. Movement follows a rhythm between social aggregation (in the moist winter) and far-flung migrations by small groups (in the dry season). In turn, as the dry season progresses, the groups congregate around the limited number of permanent water sources.

Gulliver's comparison of the Jie and the Turkana further confirms the notion that pastoralist movements in East Africa reflect adjustments to microenvironmental conditions (1955). The Jie mix farming and transhumant cattle pastoralism; the Turkana are nomadic herders who rarely practice agriculture. Jieland is richer in grasslands, and the moisture is adequate for the cultivation of sorghum. The population is sedentary but engages in seasonal movement (**transhumance**). The Turkana inhabit poorer grasslands and cannot rely on farming, depending almost totally on their herds for their needs. The need to move eliminates the possibility of stable residence (Dyson-Hudson and Dyson-Hudson 1969:44). Despite the uncertain agricultural conditions, the past three decades have seen agriculturalists expand into pastoralists' traditional grazing lands. Even the Maasai have seen some of their best grazing areas occupied by farmers (Grandin 1988; Raikes 1981). The greatest threat to rangeland in Africa comes not so much from pastoralists but from various forms of sedentary land use in unsuitable regions (Horowitz and Salem-Murdock 1987) and from the civil wars that have plagued that region in recent years (Yang 2002), in some cases leading hundred of thousands of war refugees into tribal lands. East African pastoral peoples respond differently to external crises and assess risk differently as well (K. Smith et al. 2001).

In other grassland regions of the tropics, these complex interrelationships also occur. Driel (2001) discusses changing relations between agriculturalists and pastoralists in the Niger valley as a result of drought, technological innovation, and changing government policy.

Herd Size and Composition

East African pastoralists understand that herds must maintain a certain minimum size for efficient management. The Pokot consider a man with a hundred cows rich, one with ten poor, and one with none to be dead (Schneider 1957). As the herd grows, so do management problems. A man with too many animals will be sought after by those less fortunate and be required to lend a portion of his herd. A herd of three hundred cattle cannot be effectively managed by a single homestead: watering takes too long, and fodder per locality may be too quickly depleted. In addition, a herd of this size requires constant movement because it rapidly defoliates a given area.

The Samburu deal with the problem of maximum herd size by dividing the herd among the wives of the male headman (Spencer 1965). Another strategy for reducing herd size is trusteeship. Among the Gogo when a herd gets too large for the owner to handle, he divides it among associates, or trustees, who are permitted to use the milk from the cows but promise to give the rightful owner all the offspring produced (Rigby 1969). In this manner the pastoralist achieves a modicum of wealth during good times and, by dividing his herd among a variety of managers, enhances his cows' likelihood of surviving drought periods. Among the Turkana, a herder may pool his animals and labor resources with agnates, affines, and friends to ensure a good match between labor and herd size (Dyson-Hudson and McCabe 1985:73). In the case of large-scale losses in his region, this strategy permits the herder to collect his scattered animals and resume pastoral activities instead of being forced out of business. De Vries and colleagues (2006) show that bride wealth, exchanges, gifts, payments, and requests play a key role among the Turkana in coping with the challenges of herd management dynamics.

Pastoralists may also distribute their herds over a vast territory through complex forms of lending and borrowing (Galaty and Johnson 1990; Gulliver 1955). An individual pastoralist may give some of his animals to another pastoralist who temporarily needs more animals; the owner will be paid back with an equivalent number at a later date.

Pastoralists recognize that their most important resource supplies them with renewable fluid resources in a semiarid environment. Milk is the major item in the diet of many East African pastoralists (for example, the Samburu, Ariaal Rendille, and Turkana). Grandin (1988:6–7) notes that milk and its products contribute over 60 percent of total calories for every stratum of pastoral society in East Africa (Awogbade 1983:69 suggests even greater milk dependence among pastoralist Fulani; see Wagenaar et al. 1986). During the wet period it is drunk whole, and during the dry period it is mixed with animal blood. East African pastoralists take blood from their animals by piercing the jugular vein and collecting four to eight pints of blood from each at intervals of three to five months (Dyson-Hudson and Dyson-Hudson 1969:5–6). Blood mixed with milk is most important for pastoralists in arid grasslands, as compared with agropastoralists for whom milk may be only 25 percent of their diet (Loutan 1985).

By providing milk and blood, the animal can sustain the population without signifying a loss of productive capital. If East African pastoralists began to rely on beef cattle for their calories, instead of on grain obtained by sale of cattle, they could not sustain the current population density. In other words, they would move to the top of the food pyramid and experience a reduction in total calories available.

The pastoralists' strategy of trying to maximize herd size is related to their dietary requirements and to the cyclical droughts that decimate the herds. Among the Ariaal Rendille, milk constitutes up to 70 percent of the calories consumed by the population for a substantial portion of the year (Fratkin 1991). This proportion declines during the dry season. Among the Turkana, milk constitutes the main goal of cattle production. When the milk supply goes down in the dry season, the frequency of bleeding the animals increases. The frequency of such bleeding varies with the type of stock and the relative wealth of the owner. Poorer herders with less stock bleed their animals more often than wealthier herders (Galvin 1988). Pastoralist diets tend to have abundant protein but may be marginal in terms of calories (Grandin 1988; Galvin 1988). This pattern of shifting from a milk-based diet to one that mixes milk and blood during the dry season has also been noted among the Maasai.

Small stock, primarily sheep and goats, provide most of the meat consumed by pastoralists. Small stock has turnover rates five times higher than those of cattle and are less a part of the social obligations of meat sharing. Where meat is preserved by sun drying, small stock have the advantage of providing a smaller amount of meat to be preserved and consumed at one time. A family of eight would have to kill six steers per year to meet its subsistence needs. However, preservation would be difficult, most of the meat would have to be redistributed, and productive capital would be reduced. Moreover, the value of cattle as an item of trade is greater than its value as meat. The steers sold in one year supply a family of eight with all its grain needs (Pratt and Gwynne 1977:36–39).

Large herds are required to produce the milk and blood necessary for subsistence and long-term herd maintenance. East African cattle are hardy, but environmental limitations delay their maturation (up to seven years) and lower their calving rate. According to a recent study, a pastoralist family of eight must keep a minimum of twenty animals averaging 450 kilograms each to subsist in the savanna. An equivalent weight of small animals can be equally satisfactory. These animals require approximately one hundred hectares of usable pasture at density of one stock unit per five hectares (Pratt and Gwynne 1977:37–38). These conditions are seldom present. Most pastoralist households have fewer than this ideal number of animals, and human population density is more than the eight persons per square kilometer suggested by Pratt and Gwynne. This implies greater demand on resources and less available supply.

The pastoral economy of East Africa values female animals. Most studies suggest that the reason for this preference is the reliance of the population on milk (Pratt and Gwynne 1977:36; Brown 1971). It is not uncommon to find as much as 50–60 percent of a herd made up of breeding females, as opposed to only 20–25 percent in temperate grassland ranches. Although such a strategy promotes nutrition, it also allows herd numbers to recover following epidemics, drought, and other devastations. Maximization of females increases the recuperative powers of the herd. McCabe (1990) reports that the Ngisonyoka Turkana lost 60–90 percent of their herds during the 1979–1981 drought. Dahl and Hjort (1976) report losses of 88 percent for cattle and 69 percent for camels from the 1970–1973 drought. Other studies report 60 percent mortality (Homewood and Lewis 1987; Campbell 1984).

Disease

The human and livestock populations of East Africa periodically suffer devastating losses. Between 1901 and 1908 sleeping sickness killed 200,000 to 300,000 animals in Uganda. A rinderpest epidemic destroyed 95 percent of the herds between 1890 and 1910, and it took over forty years for herd size to return to 1890 levels (Ford 1977:148). East Coast fever, blackleg, and trypanosomiasis (sleeping sickness) are serious threats to cattle herds (Schneider 1970:32).

Trypanosomiasis is still a threat. Tsetse flies *(Glossina spp.)* transmit sleeping sickness, which affects both humans and cattle (see Bourn 2001 about efforts to control tsetse and trypanosomiasis in sub-Saharan Africa; also Kwaku 2005; Kamuanga 2003). Although sleeping sickness is responsible for fewer deaths than other diseases, it has a huge economic impact since it precludes large areas from livestock herding and human settlement (Raikes 1981:65). The interactions between tsetse, wild fauna, and domesticated livestock are complex. Reid and colleagues (1997) discuss the impact of tsetstse control on vegetation structure and tree species composition. The rinderpest epidemic of 1890 stopped the spread of tsetse because of the reduced population of host animals (cattle), but it resumed in the 1940s. A major reason for this spread is reduced numbers of elephants due to big game hunting (Ford 1977:159). Elephants modify the environment by trampling it and thus limit the tsetse habitat. The areas most free of tsetse flies are those with substantial elephant populations or those where elephants and domesticated stock coexist. This important ecological relationship has suffered from big game hunting.

In areas where the environment does not provide adequate pasture and water for their animals, herders may take their chances and enter tsetse-infested regions. Thus the Fulani of West Africa take their cattle into the tsetse-infested areas of Guinea. Wagenaar and colleagues (1986:1) note that Jafaraji pastoralists leave the delta during the wet season to avoid floods and biting insects and to prevent damage to their rice fields from cattle trampling. They migrate northwest toward the Mauritanian border where they graze their animals on high-quality pastures. Although there are losses from trypanosomiasis, the cattle seem to have acquired some tolerance for the disease and appear to be better off than if they remained in the drought areas (Wagenaar et al. 1986:160). In addition to being potentially lethal, trypanosomiasis also reduces calving. Nevertheless, the evidence in this century points to steadily increasing human and cattle populations, despite exposure to disease agents. The increases have been explosive in some areas, making migration difficult and putting unusual grazing pressure on the grasses. Although the cattle population of Rhodesia was reduced between 1890 and 1910 from 500,000 animals to a mere 25,000, the trends since that time have been clearly exponential. Many of the mechanisms that once controlled the growth of people and herds have lost effectiveness. Drought has been overcome to some degree by boring deep wells; warfare has been reduced; diseases have been controlled by public health and modern veterinary and medical sciences (West 1972:715).

Although demographic data on African nomadic pastoralists is inadequate, Swift suggests that their rate of natural increase is lower than the rates of nearby cultivators (1977). The low rate of increase may result from a combination of low birth rates, high rates of female sterility, and high ratios of men to women, at least in the Sahelian region. This suggests that pastoralist populations have a slower reproductive rate than previously thought (Meir 1987:105). In Kenya, the annual rate of human population growth is twice as high for cultivators than for pastoralists (Sindiga 1987). In southwest Masailand, a rapid increase in herds and human populations is associated with the transformation of pastoralist into agropastoral societies (Mwalyosi 1991). Resource degradation in pastures and uncertain agricultural production have resulted and may require transformations in systems of land tenure, reductions in both human and herd populations, and improved productivity. Otherwise a return to mobile pastoralism is unlikely in the current scenario of state control and rising population.

Sato (1977) presents evidence that Rendille camel herders adjust their own growth rate to that of their herds, which results in very slow population growth. Cultural preferences encourage late marriages, and bride wealth may operate as a demographic regulator. High bride prices could keep population growth down by excluding poor men from marriage and by delaying marriages (Swift 1977:470).

Sedentarization appears to result in a greater number of health complaints. Barkey and colleagues (2001) note that among Ngisonyoka Turkana, settled men had more health complaints (respiratory tract infections, eye infections, colds with cough) than nomadic men. This was thought to result from changes in diet, exposure to pathogens due to the higher population density in settlements, changes in physical activity patterns, and psychosocial stress. The settled men were also noted to have a slightly higher body mass index and other measures of body fat than the nomadic group, but this was not predictive of the specific health complaints noted. In a study of Rendille pastoral and sedentary groups, researchers found the nomadic children to be taller and heavier than those in sedentary villages (Fratkin et al. 2004). The amount of milk consumed was identified as a major factor, as well as morbidity and poverty, which were a factor in the smaller size of the sedentary children. Other studies support the negative outcome of sedentarization for children during the transition from pastoral to sedentary living (Shell-Duncan and Obiero 2000). These differences also persist among women. In a study comparing maternal nutritional status of Pokot pastoral and sedentary women, Keverenge-Ettyang and colleagues (2006) found that women in the farming community had significantly lower hemoglobin concentrations than pastoral women during the third trimester of pregnancy; that pastoral women had significantly higher serum ferritin (iron) concentrations than farming women during the third trimester of pregnancy and at four months postpartum. Moreover, mean infant birth weight of farming women was significantly lower than in the pastoral community, and the farming women had a much higher number of children born weighing less than 2.5 kilograms (Keverenge-Ettyang et al. 2006).

Diversification and Specialization

One strategy pursued by East African pastoralists that improves their long-term chances of subsistence in their savanna environment is **diversification.** Most pastoralists keep a variety of animals, some primarily for meat, others for milk and blood, and still others for transportation and special products (Spencer 1988; Fratkin 1991). Small stock offers pastoralists a way back to self-sufficiency and the possibility of building up herds that perish due to disease or predation (Spencer 1988; Fratkin 1991). Small animals are also more likely to be killed for food or cash than larger animals (Dyson-Hudson and McCabe 1985). Among the Turkana, for example, sheep are raised primarily for their meat and fatty tails. The fat is used in dressing animal skins, as a lubricant for hides and wooden vessels, and as an ointment for humans (Gwynne 1977).

A variety of livestock ensures that, as conditions change from wet to dry, the animals will differentially adjust to the poorer forage available. Table 8.1 illustrates the seasonal differences in diet of the livestock raised by the Turkana. Goats and donkeys rapidly adjust to browsing as grasses become scarce. Sheep, on the other hand, continue to rely on grasses and are more susceptible to drought than the other animals. Camels require water less often and can obtain fluid from browsing (Sanford 1983).

TABLE 8.1 Seasonal Differences in the Diet of Turkana Livestock[a]

	Wet Season		Dry Season	
	% Graze	% Browse	% Graze	% Browse
Cattle	71	19	43	57
Camel	16	84	–	100
Sheep	98	2	81	19
Goat	93	7	8	92
Donkey	94	6	10	90

[a] Based on stomach analyses uncorrected for differential digestion effects and retention times.

Source: M. D. Gwynne, "Land Use by the Southern Turkana" (paper presented at Seminar on Pastoral Societies of Kenya, Ethnographic Museum of Japan, 1977).

In the drier portions of the semiarid savanna, camel pastoralism is practiced because of the animal's special adaptation to arid conditions. Although no particular trait that is not shared by other mammals has been identified in the camel, it does have a few quantitatively different developed characteristics that enhance its adaptation to the desert. No water storage has been detected in the camel's body; when deprived of water, the camel loses weight. But, unlike other mammals, it can sustain dehydration of 27 percent of its body water without damage. It can regain this loss in a matter of minutes, thanks to an incredible drinking capacity. The camel also has a specialized kidney mechanism that concentrates urine. In addition, it is able to excrete dry feces. These and other characteristics, including its ability to go long distances between waterings, make it a remarkable desert dweller (Schmidt-Nielsen 1964).

For a population to utilize camels effectively, it needs to synchronize its social life with the needs of its herds. The Rendille of North Kenya reflect a remarkable social adjustment to their camels. Age sets are formed every fourteen years in Rendille society, approximating the generational span of a camel (13.87 years). These age sets create a close generational association between the Rendille and their camels. Increases in human population match almost exactly the increases in camel herd size. Because camels have slow reproductive rates, the population institutes a variety of social mechanisms to slow down human population increases. Celibacy for males between twelve and thirty-one is required and only 50 percent of these males will be able to afford the brideprice that must be paid in the form of camels (Sato 1977). The enforced celibacy is probably the most important population control mechanism among the Rendille.

Resource Partitioning

In some fascinating cases, resource partitioning between populations is a factor in the management of herd size and composition. The Samburu and the Rendille inhabit adjacent, though different environments (Spencer 1973). The Rendille rely primarily on camel herds as they exploit the dry lowland shrub vegetation. The Samburu herd mainly cattle in the more humid highlands and plateau zones of the district. Over the years they have acted as allies, fought common enemies, and intermarried despite differences in language and culture. A third group, the Ariaal Rendille, inhabit the transitional region between the Rendille lowland and the Samburu highlands. The Ariaal keep both camels and cattle in high numbers, in addition to sizable herds of small stock (Fratkin 1991). They have succeeded in establishing alliances with both the Samburu and the Rendille through intermarriage, descent, and friendship. Thus Ariaal have gained access to both territories. The Ariaal are almost fully bilingual. Ties to the Rendille are primarily by marriage—fully 50 percent of Ariaal wives are recruited from the Rendille. Cooperation is enforced through shared myths that foretell misfortune if "brother" does violence to "brother" (Fratkin 1977). Through this system of alliances the Ariaal have overcome environmental limitations to thrive as a herding population. The narrow strip that is their territory proper could sustain only a tiny fraction of their present herds. As it is, their share of animals is high at 3.5 cattle and 1.85 camels per capita.

The alliances between the Samburu, the Ariaal, and the Rendille were probably not typical in the distant past. Raiding was a common way of rebuilding and redistributing both cattle and camel herds (Sweet 1965; Dyson-Hudson and Dyson-Hudson 1969; Stenning 1957). Among the Jie and the Turkana, raiding was an established way of increasing herd size until the British colonial government put an end to this practice (Gulliver 1955). The success of the British was, however, highly variable. Dyson-Hudson (1966:247–249) recorded numerous raids by the Karamojong. Raiding is a response to herd depletion resulting from drought and disease, as well as an integral part of the patoralist social and political organization. Through raiding young men acquire wealth for marriage, form political alliances, and establish new sections (see also Evans-Pritchard 1940). The Karamojong have formed herds of up to a thousand animals, partly through raiding. The motivation for the raiding may have been the potential danger posed by declining herd size.

When the size of a herd drops below a certain point, the herder must seek another subsistence style. A herder with declining animal population may seek to borrow animals from a wealthier individual; if he has daughters, he may try to marry them off in exchange for cattle. A man with few cattle and many sons will see to it that they become herdsmen for others, but eventually the sons will find themselves leading a celibate existence. Thus success in cattle herding is linked with large families, which are able to enrich the family through bridal price and through improved control over the herd, wider distribution of animals, and decreased susceptibility to environmental fluctuations. Bride payment can offset the risk associated with a highly fluctuating environment, as shown in a fifty-year computer simulation (Dombrowski 1993).

In summary, the size and composition of herds is dictated by a management strategy that aims at maximizing the number of animals, especially females, and at diversifying the livestock population so that it can effectively exploit the environment and provide useful products. Because cattle and camels reproduce slowly, because environmental conditions have in the past brought about rapid herd depopulation, and because cattle and camels constitute an important means of exchange, the strategy of maximization is sensible. The major question before ecological scientists is the extent to which a radical change has taken place in East Africa. This change—cessation of raiding, development of cities in what were previously water holes, and control over drought and epidemics by foreign assistance—has led to population growth in animals and humans that threaten a way of life that has been finely tuned to local conditions. Pressures to settle include the loss of open access rangeland to private ranchers, farmers, and game parks; increased market orientation of herding; massive distribution of famine relief foods that encourages settling in towns; and dislocation by war and famine (Fratkin et al. 1997). Eicher (1985) notes that in the period between 1965 to 1980 no less than US$600 million came to Africa in order to transform the livestock sector. These massive interventions often involved new water holes, increased offtake and destocking, supplemental feeding, improved stock, and prohibition of fires (Horowitz 1990). Except for veterinary intervention, which was appreciated by herders, the rest of the foreign assistance failed to enhance producers' income, retard environmental degradation, or improve economic returns (Horowitz 1990:192). Herd redistribution mechanisms still operate in some places and may prove to be the most important factor in averting desertification. But these are only effective at low stocking rates and low human population densities. A study in the Maasai Ngorongoro region found no signs of pastoralist-induced environmental degradation (Homewood and Rodgers 1984).

Relations with Cultivators

The strategy of nomadic pastoralists is a complex mixture of productive specialization and dependence on the nearby farming population. The development of this interdependence appears to be associated with highly restricted areas where agriculture is possible and vast expanses where only grazing animals can be productive. It may also be a result of social and technological structural commitments (for example, social organization required by irrigation) that preempt the possibility of effectively moving herds over grasslands (Lees and Bates 1977:826).

Pastoralists manifest a wide diversity of specialization. As already noted, some herd a single kind of animal while others own diverse stock. The factors that prompt such varied forms of specialization are both environmental and economic. The location of the territory, the size of the herding family, and access to water and pasture play major roles in deciding which herding strategy is chosen. Rates of exchange are no less important in development of social relations between cultivators and herders.

Pastoralists can obtain grain in a variety of ways. They may diversify production within their own household or tribal group, engage in trade with other pastoral tribes, resort to raiding and other forms of appropriation, or provide services in exchange for agricultural products (Lees and Bates 1977:827). Pastoralists with access to patches of land where agriculture is seasonally possible may establish an internal division of labor by which women cultivate crops and men tend the herds. This strategy provided a reliable solution for many pastoral populations, including the East African Karamojong and Jie.

A further refinement of this labor division strategy involves specialization of subgroups within a tribe. The East African Pokot gain access to resources through the idiom of kinship relations. Certain members of the tribe carry out agriculture and transhumant pastoralism, while others are more nomadic (Schneider 1957). A similar division of labor aimed at securing resources may occur among groups that differ in language, culture, and territory. The intimate trade and alliance relations of the Samburu, Ariaal, and Rendille involve the creation of exchange partnerships guaranteed through friendship, marriage, and favorable rates of exchange.

Changes in agricultural productivity have a direct effect on the management strategies chosen by pastoralists. The growth of cities may funnel farm production away from the rural sector and restrict access to grain by pastoralists—or make it available at prices unfavorable to herders. Poorer households near cities have the highest rates of milk offtake per cow that they sell to obtain grain for their subsistence (Holden et al. 1991). However, high rates of milk offtake can affect the health of calves, and the sale of most of the milk for grain leads to malnutrition in the human population. New technological input in both farm and herd sectors probably raises costs and produces changes in exchange. Politically enforced limitations on the migration routes open to herders bring about changes in the management of herds and affect their productivity (Lees and Bates 1977:829).

Relations between pastoralists and cultivators are characterized by cyclical oscillations. These oscillations reflect adjustments to changing ecological, social, and economic conditions. Such adjustments tend to take the form of negative feedback whereby an effort is made to return the system to its perceived level of what is normal (for example, the system tries to return to a level of flour, grain, and other products comparable to previous levels). If the adjustment fails, new forms of subsistence may be sought through established channels (for example, a shift from pastoralism to wage labor on farms). When and if conditions return to a state that permits resumption of the old form of subsistence, the individual or population will abandon its farm strategy or seek a more stable mixed strategy either within the household or the tribe (Lees and Bates 1977:839).

ADAPTIVE STRATEGIES IN THE NORTHERN PLAINS

The constraints under which East Africans and Canadian ranchers operate are similar: uncertain rainfall, seasonally impoverished range, and livestock behavior that at desired densities can overgraze and destroy grassland. Both populations must adjust to these potential problems, and their respective adjustments are significantly affected by the relationship of the herder to the market and by the presence of farmers in ever increasing numbers. The data on the human ecology of the temperate grasslands is far more limited than that available on tropical grasslands. In this section we will briefly survey the historical development of subsistence strategies in the North American plains and then focus on a region of the Canadian plains that has been the subject of cultural ecological study (Bennett 1969). There are very recent efforts to study the human dimensions of global environmental change as they affect the Great Plains, and one can expect a sizable literature to emerge from studies in this region over the next few years (Gutmann 2000; cf. also Johnson and Bouzaher 2006).

Exploitation of Wild Flora and Fauna

Hunter-gatherer populations occupied the high plains between 5,000 and 10,000 years ago (Wedel 1961:458). Before the horse was introduced into North America in the 1500s, the hunter-gatherers of the plains relied on a wide variety of wild food sources. The Missouri valley populations utilized over two hundred species of plants, one-third as food and the rest as medicine, decoration, and raw material for other uses (Clements and Chaney 1936:32).

At the time of contact with Europeans, the inhabitants of the shortgrass prairies were dog-using, herd-following bison hunters (Wedel 1975:16; see the account in Binnema 2001 showing sophisticated shifts in technology on the northwestern plains). They followed the buffalo from spring to fall, drying meat for winter consumption. They overwintered in sheltered spots near water, wood, and forage (Wedel 1961:453). Buffalo hunting did not require migrations across the whole plains region. It is estimated that the buffalo of the North American prairies migrated within a relatively small territory and occurred at normal densities of one buffalo per twenty acres (eight hectares).

Buffalo, the wild ungulate of the plains, was the central resource of the hunter-gatherers. It provided skin for shelters and fur for blankets, food, clothing, and footwear. The buffalo constituted the symbolic core of the religious life of the human population (Kraenzel 1955:75). The relationship can only be described as symbiotic—human movements were governed by the movements of the buffalo between spring and fall. Hunter-gatherers engaged in trade relations with the cultivators of the wetter parts of the plains. Wild fruits, nuts, berries, roots, and meat were probably traded for corn and other agricultural products.

The human population of the short- and tallgrass plains grew more homogeneous after Spaniards introduced the horse. Plains Indian culture, as described by ethnographers, was a comparatively recent response to various stimuli, among which the horse was the most important innovation (Levy 1961). Among hunter-gatherers, the horse replaced the dog as the beast of burden and expanded the areas that bison hunters could effectively exploit (Wedel 1975:17). Farmers living in sizable villages (such as the Crow and the Cheyenne) became nomadic hunters in response to the economic advantages of hunting bison from horses (Netting, personal communication). The introduction of the horse led to a change in the social structure of the Plains Indians. From a relatively classless society, the tribes developed into societies with three distinct classes, with membership in the two upper classes determined largely by degree of horse ownership (Oliver 1962:12).

Although the Plains Indians continued the specialized exploitation of the buffalo and adjusted their movements to the buffalo migratory cycle as had earlier hunter-gatherers, the horse led to increased sedentariness among the Plains population. Since the buffalo had a migratory cycle of two hundred to four hundred miles, the distances that could be traveled on horse no longer required that the whole tribe move, but only the mounted horsemen. Women, children, and the elderly stayed behind and cultivated crops in areas where this was possible (Secoy 1953:88). The large-scale exploitation of bison by horsemen demanded a large number of hunters and encouraged concentration of larger populations in relatively permanent camps (Secoy 1953:44). Oliver (1962) notes major oscillations in the size of groups. Thus the typical profile of Plains Indian culture grew out of the annual cycle of environmental exploitation that combined nomadic bison hunting with sedentary agriculture and divided labor along sexual and/or class lines (Oliver 1962:89).

Farming Versus Ranching

As the Euro-American population moved west from its more humid eastern settlement area, it encountered the now mounted Indian population, and a lengthy struggle ensued. By the time it ended, the population of nomadic mounted hunters had been overrun by a humid zone agricultural population, and farming strategies unadapted to the plains had been introduced (Kraenzel 1955:vii). Corn, oats, barley, rye, and soft wheat were brought by the homesteaders. Humid zone strategies managed to exist only by the constant provision of subsidies from outside the region—a similar process to what we see today in the urbanizing regions of the arid southwestern United States.

The earliest homesteaders came to the Great Plains with their own ideas about farming, and they required many years and repeated crop failures to adjust to their new habitat. Properties evolved from the small, largely self-sufficient farms of the Homestead Act era (c. 1862) to increasingly larger landholdings. Management practices were conservative during the transitional period, and farmers survived by virtue of a frugal lifestyle, patience in deciding whether to increase acreage planted or herd size, and large families who could respond rapidly when opportunities arose to farm an area of their property. However, drought conditions in the 1930s and a world economic crisis resulted in the now legendary Dust Bowl and the destitution of a large population of small farmers on the plains. Hansen and Libecap (2003) show that the decade-long drought of the 1930s was due in part to the prevalence of small farms and the lack of strategies for addressing wind erosion. The soil conservation strategies implemented after 1937 helped coordinate erosion control, which explains why there has not been a repeat of the Dust Bowl, despite similar droughts in the 1950s and 1970s.

Farmers were slow to appreciate the great variability of soils on the plains. Continued cultivation of even the rich mollisols leads to declines in fertility, and not all farming has the same effect on soil fertility. Figure 8.7 illustrates the effects of various farming strategies. Corn cultivation depletes the soil most rapidly, while crop rotations combined with mulching tend to slow the rate of nutrient loss. Bennett notes that northern plains farmers in Saskatchewan resisted adopting artificial fertilization and the rotational sowing of legumes to replenish the soil (1969:236). In the more commercial operations of the central plains, the highly mechanized agricultural operations rely heavily on fertilization to maintain the high yields that characterize the so-called corn and wheat belts of the United States.

For a while, the plains were on the verge of adopting a strategy derived from Mexico, known as the Texas model of land use. In this system, part of the land sold to homesteaders bordered a stream and part of it was grazing land away from the stream. The land units were relatively large—as indeed they should be in semiarid areas such as the plains, where farmers depend on the accumulation of moisture reserves during good years to weather the adverse years. However, the humid zone pattern of small landholdings, encouraged by the Homestead Act, led to the establishment of production units that were too small to be economical and sometimes lacked access to a water source (Webb 1931:227–235). Farmers competed for the well-watered lands and reduced open ranges by fencing their farms. Conflict between homesteaders and ranchers became commonplace as the homesteaders pushed cattle herders to the more arid shortgrass plains. The use of barbed wire fencing after 1874 put an end to open range cattle. Webb (1931:239) quotes an old herder's feelings about the fencing of the plains:

> In those days (1874) there was no fencing along the trails to the North, and we had lots of range to graze on. Now there is so much land taken up and fenced that the trail for most of the way is little better than a crooked lane, and we have a hard time to find enough range to feed on. These fellows from Ohio, Indiana and other northern and western states—"the bone and sinew of the country" as politicians call them—have made farms, enclosed pastures, and fenced in water holes until you can't rest; and I say, d—n such bone and sinew! They are the ruin of the country, and have everlastingly, eternally, now and forever, destroyed the best grazing land in the world.

Farming was not seriously considered during the early stages of occupation of the shortgrass prairies. Surface runoff is inadequate for irrigating the plains, and the few underground artesian sources supply only limited amounts of water. Cattle ranching

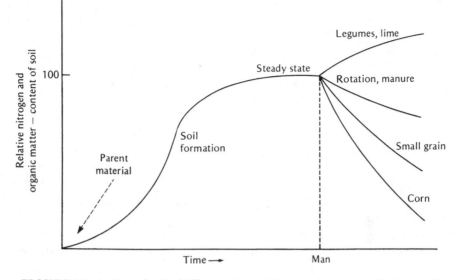

FIGURE 8.7 A Hypothetical Illustration of Nature's Buildup of Soil Fertility and Its Subsequent Modification by Humans

Source: L. Porter, "Nitrogen in Grassland Ecosystems," in *The Grassland Ecosystem*, edited by R. L. Dix and R. G. Beidleman (Fort Collins: Colorado State University, Rangeland Ecosystem Science Department, 1969).

replaced bison hunting in the 1870s and rapidly expanded. However, this specialized system of land use was short-lived. A combination of overgrazing and drought years between 1885 and 1887 decimated the cattle population and led to the collapse of the cattle industry. Since then the pattern of land exploitation has been one of large properties that combine cattle ranching with grain agriculture (Ottoson et al. 1966:42–43). The development of this strategy had to await the introduction of drill wells and windmills. This combination of mechanical devices delivered a small amount of water day and night as long as winds were blowing. The water supplied by the windmill permitted the fencing of the land and the reduction of pasture areas (Webb 1931:336). Indian tools could not break the turf of the plains, and as a result their agriculture was confined to the alluvial river valleys. The use of the steel plow and the development of mechanized farm tools made exploitation of the flat prairies practical, while requiring large capital outlays.

Besides these purely mechanical improvements, successful farming on the plains required managerial changes as well, including improvements in choice of crops grown and in tillage, fallow, and mulching practices. Drought-resistant hard wheat and other cereal varieties, which were brought to North America by Russian Mennonite immigrants, lessened the susceptibility of crops to drought. Red Fife hard spring wheat came from Russia, winter wheat from the Crimean region of Eurasia, and sorghums from Africa. These plants from dry regions have made agriculture possible where rainfall is inadequate and irrigation impossible (Bennett 1992).

The development of the management system known as dry farming was also instrumental in extending the cultivation of the plains. In dry farming, the land is allowed to go fallow every other year, and mulching is accomplished by leaving the chaff of harvested crops on the ground to facilitate the accumulation and retention of moisture and to keep soil from blowing. The field can then be replanted with adapted wheat varieties (Steila 1976:118). Tillage of the prairies should consist of loosening the soil rather than plowing deeply. This helps conserve moisture and provides better weed control. These four practices, in combination, were major breakthroughs (Kraenzel 1955:308–316).

Understanding the nature of grazing requires looking at the relationship between cattle and pasture. Usually this relationship is expressed in terms of the number of acres of land necessary to support one head of livestock per year. In the northern plains this is said to be about twenty acres (eight hectares) per head (Strickon 1965:234). However, how a pasture is grazed is primarily a function, in North American society, of the prices in the livestock market, given that cattle ranching is market-oriented. When prices decline, ranchers tend to keep their cattle longer, and this, if sufficiently prolonged, may lead to serious overgrazing problems no matter what the ratio may be. Overgrazing is not purely a matter of management but is also a result of market conditions and other factors. The 1917–1925 drought caused a mass exodus that led to plummeting human populations. As a result, cattle raising became more popular in the northern Great Plains as land once closed to ranchers by farmers became available. Sheep and cattle in combination were developed as adaptive strategies to the rigors of the area. Diversification here, as in East Africa, grew following failures of less flexible land use approaches (Thomas 1986:165). Farming too became more diversified after the early homesteading failures. Stubble mulching as a strategy for water conservation and soil moisture retention (Allen and Fenster 1986) and the use of tilling to reduce weed competition resulted in improved yields (Deiber et al. 1986).

Ranching emerged on the plains in response to the high prices offered in the growing industrial centers of the eastern seaboard (Deiber et al. 1986:236). A similar phenomenon took place in Australia and in Argentina's grasslands, but full-scale development there had to await the development of canning and refrigeration because of the distances between grazing land and markets.

Farming with Ranching

The routines followed by the Canadian plains ranchers of Jasper, as studied by Bennett, reflect the needs of livestock and the seasonality of the area (1969). All ranchers spend winter in similar ways: inspecting and feeding the herd with stored hay, keeping water sources open and running, and sheltering the herd during inclement weather. Spring is calving season, and summer is the time to wean, brand, and fatten the cattle with summer grass. In the fall, ranchers sell spring calves, culled cows, and other animals. Hay must be stored for winter, and social life becomes busy before the relative isolation brought on by winter (Deiber et al. 1986:185). Because one herdsman can handle a hundred head of cattle over a territory of more than 2,000 acres (one head per eight hectares), there is no pressure for constant innovation. Once a productive operation is established, ranchers tend to operate with minimum experimentation (Deiber et al. 1986:181).

Pastures become specific units of resources, and individuals operate through a combination of accumulated experience and adjustment to new market conditions (Deiber et al. 1986:194). Ranchers note that cattle tend to concentrate their grazing in areas near water sources and salt and that such areas tend to become overgrazed. Thus several of their management practices center around preventing the herd from following its own tendencies: (1) cattle are concentrated on high fields in summer because of the high protein values of such grasses; (2) salt is placed away from immediate watering places; (3) fences are built at higher altitudes if cattle use the grasses there during the summer; and (4) either cattle are allowed to graze one area intensively, which is then rested for a year, or they are allowed to graze all fields evenly.

These management practices affect ranchers' land tenure preferences since they require possession of both high and low fields (Deiber et al. 1986:185). Unlike the open range herding of earlier years or the contemporary herding of East African pastoralists, ranching on the Canadian High Plains involves a fixed range. This means that water must be provided by special devices (windmills); grass must be nurtured and special varieties encouraged for various livestock goals; and hay or alfalfa must be grown to feed the animals during the long winters (Deiber et al. 1986:197).

The yearly cycle of a plains farmer resembles or differs from that of a rancher depending on the farmer's degree of reliance on grain crops (Deiber et al. 1986:226). Grain planting occurs in April and May in the Canadian High Plains, and work extends through the summer and ends in September with the harvest. Late fall and winter are spent repairing tools and buildings. An increasing number of farmers have learned that total reliance on crops may result in economic instability. They have, therefore, undertaken cattle raising on portions of their land. During dry years when crops are unsuccessful, the cattle can contribute income. Such a mixed operation changes the lifestyle of the farmer so that it begins to resemble that of the rancher; animals require year-round attention.

There are probably no better examples of the adaptiveness of such a mixed strategy for the exploitation of the plains than the the Hutterites and the Amish. The Hutterites of Jasper have a communal organization, live frugally, control large expanses of land, and have adopted modern technology to increase their yields. Among the Hutterites, diversification is a cultural ideal. It is also an ideal that enabled the group to succeed on the plains. Capital expenditures that normally drain the individual farming household, such as a vehicle, are shared by up to thirteen nuclear Hutterite families—at a substantial saving to all of them. The Hutterites invest the capital thus saved in productive or innovative activities. A life of austerity and prayer means that capital is not spent on recreation. Whereas one Jasper farming family in one year spent $2,500 on recreation, a colony of seventy-four Hutterites spent a mere $1,500. For recreation they turn to crafts and the manufacture of useful items and simple tools. Hutterites make most of their own clothes, shoes, furniture, houses, buildings, and other necessities. Their farming practices are also more conservation-minded than those of other Jasper farmers. Because of the large scale of their operations, they can take poor land out of operation, improve water resources, and improve forage crop production (Deiber et al. 1986:267–268). There is evidence of growing emphasis on private property among some Hutterite communities, and even a move away from mixed farming toward just one or two crops (Peter 1987). But because they have migrated to many developing countries in their constant search for more land to support their rapidly growing population, they tend to maintain a more diversified production system where they depend on their own production for subsistence.

The Amish are more conservative and less dependent on technology than the Hutterites. The Amish view farming as the optimal setting for the good life and see nature as God's work and their role as that of stewards. Their technology is simple; their homes lack electricity, and they use horses for plowing and buggies for transportation. Their technology must constantly adjust to provide jobs for their families and sufficient profits to make the purchase of land possible for succeeding generations of Amish young people. They increasingly rent cars and other production equipment but limit their use of these mechanical artifacts depending on community-level decisions.

In every generation the Amish lose a substantial portion of their population—possibly as much as a third. The Amish who leave their settlements join neighboring Mennonite communities that use modern technology or blend into American culture. Amish technology probably could not sustain the population without this steady out-migration. Although the Amish will consult with agricultural advisers, they will not accept subsidies from agricultural support agencies. However, many groups have adopted a degree of mechanization. Despite this, their productive system is basically unsuited to economic exploitation of the Great Plains, and consequently most Amish have chosen not to move there. Characteristically, the Amish engage in small, labor-intensive farming operations that rely on the proximity of markets to sell the high-quality products of their gardens, barnyards, and farmhouses (Johnson et al. 1977:374). Thus the economic exploitation of the plains region would almost surely mean an abandonment of their cultural traditions—a task that the communal Hutterites have dealt with effectively. The Amish style of agriculture would have to become like the Hutterites' to effectively exploit the plains, just as the Hutterites would have to rely less on heavy machinery in the rolling country of Pennsylvania and southwestern Wisconsin where the Amish thrive (Johnson et al. 1977:378).

GLOBAL CHANGE AND THE FUTURE OF
GRASSLANDS AND PASTORALISM

Despite massive efforts in the past forty years to sedentarize pastoral nomads in Africa (Salih et al. 2001), many of these populations persist in using an adaptive strategy finely honed for the characteristics of the ecosystem. Agriculture is uncertain in these regions without massive irrigation, and this has made these areas more susceptible to degradation. An interesting twist to the story in Africa and North America is what is happening in China, Mongolia, and other parts of Central Asia. In these areas, pastoral systems are experiencing renewed vigor and expansion in the wake of decollectivization following the breakup of the former Soviet Union (Fratkin 1997).

In the former socialist economies of Asia, particularly Mongolia and China, the process currently under way is the reverse of that taking place in Africa. People are leaving their collective towns and setting out to freely range over their grasslands and restore their ancient pastoralist systems. In Mongolia the presocialism herding groups, or *khot ails*, have been reconstituted on the traditional basis of kinship ties (Potkanski 1993). Similar processes are under way in China and Tibet (Cincotta et al. 1992; Goldstein and Beall 1991; Li et al. 1993). Summer herds have increased significantly in a few years, and income from pastoralist activity is up. Negotiation of rights to water and pasture will permit effective pastoralism in these regions, as elsewhere. The world will need to watch the rebuilding of these societies to see if they develop a new model for pastoralist use of grasslands, or whether they fall prey to unrealistic management ideas that persist among those who view these areas as stable agricultural regions.

Agricultural expansion into grasslands continues unabated (Heady 1994). Population growth among farmers, and the perception by farmers and the state that the open access grasslands used by pastoralists are "empty" of people and need to be brought into production have led to systematic efforts to occupy these areas with farming populations (Van den Brink et al. 1995; Unruh 1991). The loss of land to cultivation and urban areas has increased the number of failed pastoralists who settle in towns (Mohamed-Salih et al. 1995). Every study noted that the health of sedentarized pastoralists (especially children) was worse than that of their nomadic relatives (Galvin et al. 1994; Hill 1985; Nathan et al. 1996; Shell-Duncan and Obiero 2000; Barkey et al. 2001; Fratkin et al. 2004; Keverenge-Ettyang et al. 2006). AIDS has grown as a grave scourge among sedentary pastoralists (Klepp et al. 1994).

A decade of intensive research among the Turkana has shown that interactions between vegetation and livestock are nonequilibrium in nature (Little and Leslie 1999). Figure 8.8 illustrates the relationship between plants and livestock and how both are influenced by drought. It shows that the density and quality of vegetation is a function of rainfall, that during wet years herds grow (A), that seasonal and single-year droughts reduce plant biomass but have little effect on livestock biomass (B and C), but that multiyear droughts can be devastating to livestock (D). The vegetation is capable of quick recovery, but livestock herds take several years to recover (E).

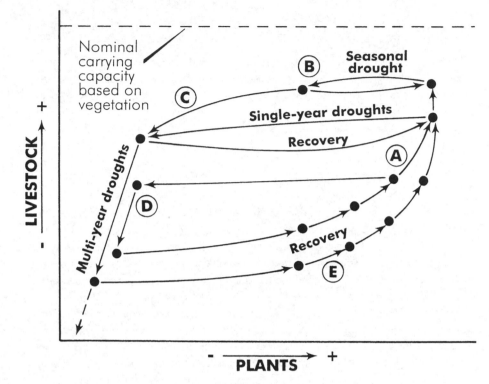

FIGURE 8.8 Interactions Between Vegetation and Livestock

Source: Adapted from M. A. Little and P. W. Leslie, *Turkana Herders of the Dry Savanna* (Oxford: Oxford University Press, 1999).

Human adaptability to grasslands primarily takes the form of social and cultural regulatory adjustments. These adjustments facilitate access to pasture and water, help adjust the size and composition of herds to prevalent socioeconomic and ecological conditions, and provide a workable idiom between cultivators and herders. Specialization in herding, to the neglect of agriculture, occurs where cultivation is highly uncertain or where relatively permanent economic cooperation has been ensured through the idiom of kinship. Research on adaptation to grasslands has not adequately dealt with the systemic interactions between short-term and long-term strategies. The trend has clearly been in the direction of converting grasslands to farmland. The energetic efficiency, the long-term stability, and the short-term profits of the farming system present conflicting goals and solutions. Under conditions of global climatic change, these conflicts are likely to become exacerbated.

SUGGESTED READINGS AND USEFUL WEBSITES

Several research societies are devoted to the study of grasslands and rangelands and maintain peer-reviewed journals focused on the ecology and management of these areas, particularly for agriculture. Among these societies are the International Grassland Society (www.internationalgrasslands.org), which covers natural and cultivated grasslands, the Japanese Society of Grassland Science (www.affrc.go.jp:8001/ grass/index-e.html), which publishes the journal *Grassland Science* (www.blackwell publishing.com/journal.asp?ref=1744–6961), the British Grassland Society (www .britishgrassland.com/bgs), which publishes the journal *Grass and Forage Science* (www.blackwellpublishing.com/journals/gfs) together with the European Grassland Federation (www.europeangrassland.org), and the Grassland Society of Southern Africa (www.gssa.co.za), which publishes the *African Journal of Range and Forage Science* (www.gssa.co.za/main.asp?nav=Publications).

The Society for Range Management (www.rangelands.org) and its journals *Rangelands* and *Rangeland Ecology and Management* (www.srmjournals.org) and the Australian Rangeland Society (www.austrangesoc.com.au) and its journal *The Rangeland Journal* (www.austrangesoc.com.au/joverview.asp) are devoted to ecosystems that have grazing resources and/or managed like rangeland. The Ecological Society of America also maintains a Rangeland Ecology section (www.cabnr.unr .edu/ESA) devoted to rangeland ecological research; its webpage of other links (www.cabnr.unr.edu/ESA/Links.htm) provides additional resources for those interested in rangeland-related topics.

Rangeland and grassland ecosystems also are an important component within the Long Term Ecological Research (LTER) network of field stations supported by the National Science Foundation (NSF); the Konza Prairie LTER Program at the Konza Prairie Biological Station, Manhattan, KS (http://climate.konza.ksu.edu) offers resources and data about tallgrass prairie ecosystems; the Cedar Creek LTER at the Cedar Creek Natural History Area in Minnesota (www.lter.umn.edu) is located at the boundary between upland forests and prairie and includes areas of abandoned agricultural land; the Sevilleta LTER (http://sev.lternet.edu) located near the Sevilleta National Wildlife Refuge also lies at the boundary of several ecosystem types: grasslands (including desert grasslands), shrublands, and upland woodlands; the Shortgrass Steppe LTER located on the Central Plains Experimental Range encompasses a predominantly shortgrass temperate ecosystem (http://sgs.cnr.colostate.edu). The U.S. Forest Service also offers a detailed website on rangelands (www.fs.fed.us/rangelands), as does the Australian Commonwealth Scientific and Industrial Research Organization (CSIRO) (www.cse.csiro.au/research/ras).

At Colorado State University, the Natural Resource Ecology Laboratory (www.nrel.colostate.edu) facilitates interdisciplinary research in a variety of ecosystems around the world, including grasslands, rangelands, and other ecosystems in Africa. The Institute of Grassland and Environmental Research (www.iger.bbsrc.ac.uk/

default.asp) in the United Kingdom undertakes research on sustainable agriculture in grassland areas, with studies on the interactions between soils, plants, animals, and other organisms. The Park Grass Experiment at Rothamsted, UK, is described as "the longest running ecological experiment in the world", and is a continuously fertilized (with different treatments) area of hay meadow first established in 1856 (www.res .bbsrc.ac.uk, www.open.ac.uk/science/biosci/research/ecology/silvertown/M_Dodd/ PGEtxt.htm). Data from this research site are available at www.era.rothamsted.ac.uk.

Some useful books for additional information about the ecology of grasslands and rangelands, especially with regard to management and conservation, include *California Grasslands: Ecology and Management* edited by Stromberg et al. (2007); *Dryland Ecohydrology* edited by D'Odorico and Porporato (2006); *Conservation of Great Plains Ecosystems: Current Science, Future Options* edited by Johnson and Bouzaher (2006); *Monitoring Manual for Grassland, Shrubland, and Savanna* by Herrick et al. (2005); *Desertified Grasslands: Their Biology and Management* by Chapman (1992); *Savanna Ecology and Management: Australian Perspectives and Intercontinental Comparisons* edited by Werner (1991); and *Ecosystems of the World: Managed Grasslands* edited by Breymeyer (1990). The role of fire in grassland ecosystems is discussed in several books, including *The Ecology of Fire* by Whelan (2004) and *Fire Ecology: United States and Southern Canada* by Wright and Bailey (2004). Also useful for grassland studies is *Issues and Perspectives in Landscape Ecology* edited by Wiens and Moss (2005), especially for understanding the spatial dynamics and use and management of grassland ecosystems.

The Center for Great Plains Studies at the University of Nebraska (www.unl.edu/ plains/index.html) and its publication *Great Plains Quarterly* (www.unl.edu/plains/ publications/GPQ/gpq.html), are dedicated to the study of people, culture, and environment of the Great Plains of North America. The Bureau of Land Management of the U.S. Department of Interior maintains the program of Cultural Heritage, Paleontological Resources and Tribal Consultation on the Public Lands (www.blm .gov/heritage), which provides information about cultural resources found on public lands, including archeological sites.

Several useful books discussing historical and current land use in grasslands and rangelands include *Savannas and Dry Forests: Linking People with Nature* edited by Mistry and Berardi (2006); *Human Ecology: Following Nature's Lead* by Steiner (2002); *Ancient North America: The Archeology of a Continent* by Fagan (1995); *Rangeland Health: New Ways to Classify, Inventory, and Monitor Rangelands* from the National Research Council (NRC 1994a); *Ecology and Human Organization on the Great Plains* by Bamforth (1988); and *Human Ecology in Savanna Environments* by Harris (1980).

Studies of East African savannas are numerous and their human ecological relevance has increased in the past twenty years. A particularly useful recent volume that integrates perspectives from archeology, history, labor, demography, health and nutrition, and tenure was edited by Fratkin et al. (1994). The intimate relations of pastoral nomads with their environment have been topics of interest to many researchers and have generated useful data on their adjustments (Dahl and Hjort 1976 is probably the single best source on production considerations in African herd management). The synthesis of the decade-long Turkana Project is now available (Little and Leslie 1999; see also McCabe 2004, which expands on the social dimensions and the nonequilibrium nature of these systems).

Photo by E. Moran

9

HUMAN ADAPTABILITY
TO THE HUMID TROPICS

Tropical rain forests are one of the world's most extensive biomes and today one of the most threatened (Bermingham et al. 2005). There is growing evidence of the potential for major extinctions as a result of global climate change in the humid tropics (Williams et al. 2003; Vandermeer and Perfecto 2005). Some current modeling efforts even suggest the collapse of the Amazon rain forest (Oyama and Nobre 2003) except for small refuge areas—something that took place earlier, during the Pleistocene, according to some scholars (Haffer 1969). Tropical rain forests are not monolithic but differ a great deal from one another (Primack and Corlett 2005). Evidence suggests that it has existed continuously since the beginning of the angiosperms over 100 million years ago (Morley 2000). Human populations have long occupied these humid tropical areas, adapted to their constraints, and benefited from their opportunities.

There is evidence suggesting forager occupation of caves in Sarawak going back to 45,000 BP (Barker 2005). These Pleistocene foragers used a combination of hunting, fishing, mollusk collecting, and plant gathering—largely tuberous forest plants such as aroids, yam, taro, and sago palm which have dominated the diet ever since (Barker 2005; Barton 2005). Even with the arrival of the Neolithic, the population continued to rely heavily on forest foraging (Barker 2005; Barton 2005). Hunter-gatherers also have an ancient presence in the rain forest regions of South America, going back to 12,000 BP, and they produced ceramics by 8,000 BP (Scheinsohn 2003: Roosevelt et al. 1992; Roosevelt 1989). The earliest evidence for gathering, hunting, fishing, and banana cultivation in Central Africa has been documented for the first millennium BC in southern Cameroon (Mbida et al. 2000).

Contemporary environmental concerns have focused on the effects of deforestation on biological diversity (Wilson 1988), climate change (Dickinson 1987; Shukla et al. 1990; Aber and Melillo 1991; Oyama and Nobre 2003; Gash et al. 1996), and atmospheric trace gases (Dickinson 1987; Andreae and Schimel 1989; Crutzen and Andreae 1990; Dale et al. 1991). Attention has also been brought to tropical forests' contribution to the global carbon cycle (Detwiler and Hall 1988), although there are still notable uncertainties about the carbon budget. Moist forests of the tropics cover only about 11 percent of the earth's land surface but are estimated to contain 41 percent of the global terrestrial biomass and over 50 percent of the world's species. Some humid tropical forests are particularly important. The Brazilian Amazon contains 26.5 percent of the earth's moist forests (Whittaker and Likens 1975; Prance and Lovejoy 1985; Silver 1990). The continental size of the Amazon basin and its high evapotranspiration rates make it a notable influence on world climate (Salati 1985; Molion 1987; Gash et al. 1996). Removal of Amazonian vegetation on a large scale would bring about changes in the region's hydrological cycle and climate large enough that the forests might not be able to reestablish themselves (Shukla et al. 1990; Henderson-Sellers 1987; Lean and Warrilow 1989; Oyama and Nobre 2003) or might experience significant change in species composition, structure, and function (Bierregaard et al. 2001).

The scale of these processes has attracted the attention of researchers attempting to forecast the impact of deforestation on the climate of the earth and the tropical world. Most notable among these has been the use of global circulation models (GCM) (Gash et al. 1996; Henderson-Sellers 1987; Molion 1987; Salati and Vose 1984). According to Henderson-Sellers (1987), GCM models predict a 223–239 millimeter reduction in annual rainfall, a 1–5 millimeter reduction in daily rainfall, a 0.5–5.0 millimeter daily evaporation increase, an increase in albedo from 0.11 to 0.17, and reduced cloud cover. Lean and Warrilow (1989) conclude in the journal *Nature* that GCM experiments were highly sensitive to the formulations of the models and that their ability to make firm predictions was inhibited by a lack of observations in forested and deforested areas that could verify the models. They called for more ground-based measurements, together with more data on vegetation types derived from satellite data. GCMs sometimes assume the complete removal of tropical forest and its replacement with pasture—a scenario that is possible but unlikely (Lean and Warrilow 1989; Shukla et al. 1990; Gash et al. 1996). The rates and the types of processes of concern to social scientists are not usually considered in modeling studies, which take fixed inputs rather than the transient responses more typical of human systems. There is no adequate model at present for predicting the impact of deforestation on regional climates, nor for how climate shifts may affect the future trajectory of forests. This is currently viewed as a top priority in research on land use and land cover change at NASA and other funding agencies.

Regional rainfall in the humid tropics is highly variable, in both space and time, owing to variations in tropical ocean temperatures. This makes the hydrological component the weakest element in climate models (Dickinson 1989:343; see also Dickinson and Kennedy 1992). Henderson-Sellers (1987) has also advocated a more regional, less global approach as more appropriate to predicting climatic impacts of forest removal (see also the recent synthesis of land change science in Gutman and col-

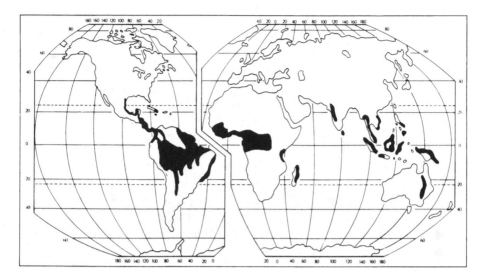

FIGURE 9.1 **Distribution of Tropical Rain Forests**

leagues (2004), which tends to support these arguments with more recent data, and synthesis volumes from the LBA project (Melillo et al. in press; Keller et al. in press).

Our discussion of human adaptations to these areas begins with the structure and function of the ecosystem, emphasizing their diversity and complexity. Ecosystem diversity and vigorous **secondary growth,** or succession, represent both constraints and opportunities. Human populations in the past managed these problems through slash-and-burn agricultural techniques, multistoried intercropping of fields (which mimics the system's complexity), and wide separation of fields. The productivity of the ecosystem hinges on preventing erosion and on soil nutrients being available after forests are cleared. The techniques applied to managing weeds and pests are also effective conservation measures, as are population controls and the practice of lengthy fallows. The variations in population density throughout rain forest regions provide an opportunity to observe the relationship of population density to subsistence strategy and labor returns. High humidity and high ambient temperatures present a problem to which human populations have responded by regulatory adjustments: thermal sweating, minimal use of clothing, locating settlements on a rise of ground, and scheduling activities appropriately to reduce the heat load.

This chapter provides examples of the tropical forest populations of South and Middle America, Melanesia, and Africa. The study of human adaptations to these areas is of more than passing interest. Tropical rain forests are the last cultivable frontiers on earth. Since fossil fuels are limited in supply, the solar energy available in these areas provides an important energy source that is rich and renewable. The humid tropics receive solar radiation year-round, and their complex flora converts this radiation into a lush, green landscape.

As other areas have felt the pressure of growing population, governments have seen fit to build roads that cut across these hitherto undeveloped regions (Moran 1981; N. Smith 1982a; Pedlowski et al. 1997; Rudel and Roper 1997; Tole 1998; Geist and Lambin 2001; Rudel 2005). Road construction has been followed in many instances by a great influx of humanity, not always knowledgeable of the ecosystem it has come to exploit. Mining, ranching, and modern agricultural populations are penetrating the rain forests, and ecologically oriented scientists have expressed concern for the impending demise of the unique evolutionary accomplishment that tropical rain forests represent (Denevan 1973; Gómez-Pompa et al. 1972; Dickinson 1972; Meggers 1971; Shukla et al. 1990; Oyama and Nobre 2003). To learn how some populations have adapted to life in this biome is a matter of scientific interest as well as immediate significance to the well-being of all. This biome is our richest source of biodiversity (Connell 1978; Mabberly 1991; Baskin 1994). Throughout this chapter, the term "rain forest" is applied to humid tropical regions.

TROPICAL RAIN FOREST ECOSYSTEMS

Areas covered by tropical rain forests form a belt around the globe, with most of the area lying north of the equator. Three major tropical rain forests have been identified: South American, African, and Indo-Malayan. The largest of these is the South American rain forest, which covers most of the Amazon basin and extends into the drainage areas of the La Plata and Orinoco Rivers (see Hammond 2005 for a comprehensive examination of the tropical forests of the Guiana shield; Lisboa 1997 on the Caxiuanã protected forest region in the Brazilian Amazon; Bierregaard et al. 2001 on the fragmented forests of central Brazil near Manaus). Isolated areas also exist in southern Mexico and Central America, primarily along the Caribbean coast. Of particular note is the well-studied rain forest at Barro Colorado Island, Panama, which has been the focus of studies by the Smithsonian Tropical Research Institute for decades (see the synthesis by E. G. Leigh Jr. 1999). The once extensive African rain forest has been significantly reduced by human activities (Bates 1960:102). Rain forests in the Congo basin and areas along the Gulf of Guinea to Liberia are disappearing quickly due to logging (see Weber et al. 2001 for a discussion of African rain forest ecology and conservation; and Martin 1991 on the rain forests of West Africa). The largely insular Indo-Malayan forests cover decreasing portions of Sumatra, Borneo, Celebes, New Guinea, and the Philippines (see Okuda 2003 for a detailed account of the Pasoh forest reserve in Malaysia; Kummer 1991 for deforestation in the Philippines; the role of loggers is particularly significant in these regions). The coast of Indochina and a portion of the Australian coast are also covered in rain forests (see Figure 9.1).

Climate and Productivity

Both plants and animals are affected by the climatic characteristics of the humid tropics. Temperature means vary little throughout the year, usually hovering near 26°C. Daily temperatures, on the other hand, can vary as much as 9°C on sunny days. Rainfall, distributed in two "seasons," commonly exceeds 2,000 millimeters annually. Months with less than 100 millimeters are considered dry. During such periods of relative dryness, plants respond in a manner similar to plant responses to cold in temperate areas: they shed leaves, become dormant, and close stomata to preserve moisture (Sanchez and Buol 1975). Humidity hovers between 75 and 100 percent year-round. On the average, the humid tropics receive two and a half times as much solar radiation as the poles (Barry and Chorley 1970:33). Atmospheric circulation, however, carries away 80 percent of the surplus energy and prevents the area from overheating (Steila 1976:152). The biggest similarity that has been noted among lowland rain forests is that annual evapotranspiration is near 1,400 millimeters per year (Leigh Jr. 1999).

Because of the high solar radiation, long growing season, and abundant moisture, tropical rain forests have a high gross productivity.[1] This means that large amounts of biomass die and form ground litter. Most rain forests drop between 6 and 8 tons dry weight of leaves per hectare per year (Leigh Jr. 1999). Such litter is quickly mineralized and nutrients are rapidly absorbed by roots. Despite the high rainfall, there is no appreciable loss of nutrients due to leaching. Research in the Brazilian Amazon has found that the feeding rootlets of trees possess, at a depth of only 2–15 centimeters, mycorrhiza (root fungi). Through these fungi, trees are directly connected with the litter layer. The trees can thus exploit the fungi to obtain their inorganic nutrients directly from the litter. Stark (1969) estimates that 5.4 grams per square meter per day are mineralized, a figure that approaches the gross primary production of 6.0 grams per square meter per day. Tree mortality is about 1–2 percent per year and is roughly the same for trees of all size classes above 10 centimeters DBH (diameter at breast height) (Leigh Jr. 1999).

Climate change impacts on biological productivity are currently being studied (Gash et al. 1996). Increases in atmospheric CO_2 do not appear likely to lead to significant increases in biome productivity, but it is too early to be sure. Preliminary data suggest that mature forests are still growing and fixing carbon at totally unexpected rates (Grace et al. 1995a,b).

Soils of the Humid Tropics

Many of the soils of the humid tropics are thought of as too poor to support sustainable agriculture. However, there is growing evidence that prehistoric populations in the humid tropics living in permanent communities created sustainably fertile soils through their intensive management. Known as "terra preta" soils, they are anthropic and often associated with pottery and charcoal remains. They have higher levels of organic matter and phosphorus than soils in adjacent areas. Glaser and colleagues (2001) show that these soils contain up to seventy times more black carbon than surrounding soils (black carbon is the residue of incomplete combustion of organic material) and that they can persist for centuries because they are chemically and microbially stable and can hold on to other nutrients (see also the recent synthesis by Lehman et al. 2003). Work is under way to learn how to create these soils as a way to increase the productivity of otherwise nutrient-poor soils.

In the past, soils of the humid tropics were mistakenly referred to as characterized by **laterite**. Soil scientists have since abandoned the term. The term "plinthite" has replaced it to refer to the iron-rich, humus-poor soil material that irreversibly hardens after repeated wetting and drying once it is exposed to air. It has been estimated that plinthite occurs in only 7 percent of the tropical world (Sanchez and Buol 1975). Plinthite can be a useful resource: in Thailand it is poured into large blocks before it has time to harden and used in construction. Some ancient Thai temples are made from this material, and it serves as the equivalent of gravel when crushed and used as a road surface in Brazil.

Tropical soils have long been characterized as old, leached, acidic, lacking in horizons, poor in nutrients, and cultivable for only a couple of years. Agronomic research, however, has shown that soils under tropical rain forests tend to resemble those in the forested areas of the nonglaciated temperate zone. For many of these soils, nutrients are the limiting factor (Herrera et al. 1978, Herrera 1985; Jordan and Herrera 1981; Sanchez et al. 1982; Sanchez and Benites 1987). Figure 9.2 is a map of the major soil types found in wet, humid regions. Where the parent materials are acidic, the soils closely correspond to those of the southeastern United States and southeastern China. Both of these areas are now under highly productive, intensive cultivation with use of inorganic fertilizers. These soils all share problems of low **cation** retention, high acidity, and high exchangeable aluminum content (Cochrane and Sanchez 1982).

Three soil types predominate in the humid tropics: oxisols, alfisols, and ultisols. The most extensive are the oxisols, characterized by an oxic horizon (that is, they consist of hydrated oxides of iron and/or aluminum). When the conditions that create the oxic horizon are accompanied by a fluctuating water table, plinthite develops. Alfisols and ultisols are soils of humid moisture areas, but they are less weathered than oxisols and commonly result from weathering of basic rocks.

In the 78 percent of the tropics where there is a pronounced dry season of at least ninety days, the lack of moisture greatly reduces organic matter accumulation. This effect is similar to the effect of low winter temperatures in temperate regions, which greatly reduce biological activity. A comparison of soils in the United States, Brazil, and Zaire led to the conclusion that differences in organic matter content are agronomically and statistically insignificant. The average organic matter in the top one meter of southeastern US soils was 1.11 percent while it was 1.05 percent for those

Distribution of oxisols

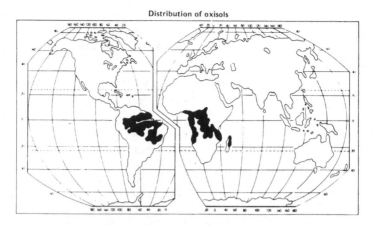

Distribution of ultisols

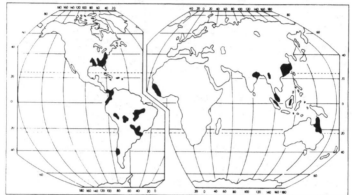

Distribution of alfisols

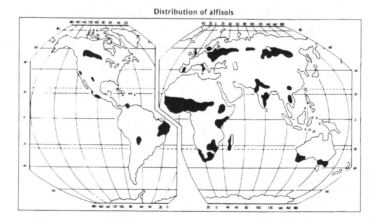

FIGURE 9.2 Soils Most Commonly Found in the Humid Tropics

Note that they are found elsewhere as well, and it is not only weather but also parent material that affects the soil types in a biome.

of Zaire and Brazil. In general, organic matter content is higher in tropical soils than in US soils with comparable temperature and rainfall regimes (Sanchez and Buol 1975). Recent studies point to a growing understanding of soil heterogeneity and vegetation in regions of the humid tropics, such as the Amazon. Studies, however, show that despite significant differences in soil texture and in soil nutrients, tree species achieve remarkably comparable gross primary productivity (Williams et al. 2002). Paoli and colleagues (2005) found that trees on phosphorus-limited soils achieved a higher than expected plant productivity due to special adaptations that conserve phosphorus and use it more efficiently than trees on phosphorus-rich soils, which grow faster but do not conserve phosphorus to the same degree.

Rain Forest Flora

The most conspicuous feature of tropical rain forests is the large number of tree species and the small number of individuals of a species in a given area. The heterogeneity of rain forests has been explained as resulting from herbivore pressure. The seeds, fruits, and seedlings of trees are major food sources for many animals. The pressure is greatest close to the parent tree, since the predator population concentrates its numbers near it. With distance the number of herbivores decreases, and thus the likelihood of a seedling surviving is greatest the farther one goes from the parent tree (Richards 1973). Cain and Castro (1959:61) note that in some stands studied by sample plots, every third tree was a new species. In a central Amazonian forest, Klinge and colleagues (1975:119) found six hundred species per hectare, of which five hundred were identified in the 0.2 hectare sample plot. There has been a virtual explosion of research in the humid tropics in the past twenty years (for example, Gentry 1990; Prance and Lovejoy 1985; Browder 1989b; Anderson 1990; Posey and Balée 1989; Goulding et al. 1988; Redford and Padoch 1992; Moran 1993b; Laurance and Bierregaard 1997; Bierregaard et al. 2001; Gash et al. 1996; Palm et al. 2005).

The rain forest biome has the largest known standing crop biomass, due to the high levels of solar radiation, generally favorable environment, and twelve-month growing season. Not only is there a greater accumulation of biomass, but it reaches a steady state in a shorter time (Farnworth and Golley 1974:76; Leigh Jr. 1999). Tropical forests approach maximum biomass value in about eight to ten years (Sanchez 1976:351), while temperate forests reach steady state in fifty to one hundred years (Farnworth and Golley 1974:76). This means that the tropical forest ecosystem has incredible recuperative powers, and that secondary succession can occur with surprising vigor. However, large variations between sample plots at a given age have been noted and reflect differences in biota and other environmental factors (Farnworth and Golley 1974:123; Gentry 1990; Moran et al. 1994a,b, 1996; Tucker et al. 1998; Moran and Brondizio 1998).

Current knowledge of the ecology of tropical tree species is limited with detailed information on only a few hundred of the thousands of species that occur. Turner

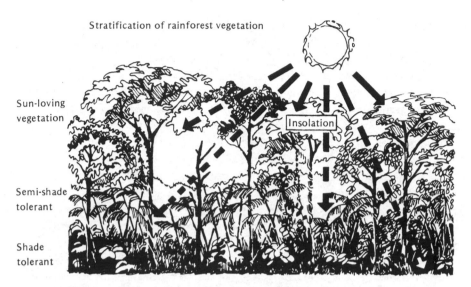

FIGURE 9.3 Structure of a Mature Tropical Rain Forest

The structure of mature tropical moist forests and rain forests is shaped by umbrella-shaped canopies that filter out much of the light, but mortality and other sources of disturbance create gaps that allow shade-tolerant species to also thrive.

(2001) provides a useful compendium with an emphasis on comparative ecology, with the goal of facilitating further comparisons across the world. Trees in the tropical forest can reach a height of 50–60 meters (emergents), but such instances are rare. More common are heights of 25–35 meters, with many individuals well below that average height (Tucker et al. 1998). Some ecologists hold that three strata are recognizable (see Figure 9.3). The highest stratum consists of solitary giants with umbrella-shaped crowns that reach far above the other trees. Observers flying over the tropical rain forest have noted that the middle stratum gives the appearance of uniformity. The lower stratum is made up of mosses, ferns, palms, and epiphytes that receive little light. The trunks of rain forest trees are usually slender and have thin bark. The crowns begin high up and are relatively small as a result of crowding. It is difficult to judge the age of the trees since annual rings are not present, but some are estimated to be 200–250 years old. Some of the vegetation lacks deep roots, and the trees achieve support by developing plank buttresses that reach as high as nine meters up the tree. Recent studies have dug deep and discovered that in regions with a strong dry season, trees have very deep roots of twelve meters and more (Nepstad et al. 1999). Because of the high evapotranspiration rates of tropical rain forests (roughly 1,400 millimeters per year), vegetation can exhaust moisture near the surface after a week of rainless days but it will draw on deep soil moisture to sustain leaf cover and photosynthesis.

Both growth and flowering are periodic but fairly independent of season, since external conditions are relatively constant. In some tree species, leaf fall occurs before the new leaves begin to form, and a tree may even be bare for a short period. Individuals of the same species may bloom at different times or the branches of the same tree species may bloom at different times. These are all manifestations of an autonomous periodicity that is not bound to a twelve-month cycle. This means that a rain forest has no definite flowering season, but some variety of trees is always in bloom. This presents a problem for tropical animals and humans, who depend on forest resources for survival. They are forced to resort to nomadism to take advantage of this continuous, but dispersed, resource base.[2] Forests in the humid tropics can produce notable amounts of fruit. Forests at Barro Colorado, Panama, and those of Manu in Amazonian Peru drop about two tons of fruit per hectare per year (Terborgh 1983; Leigh Jr. 1999:156). Despite this richness of fruit production, there is good evidence to suggest that in many (if not most) rain forests herbivore populations are limited by seasonal shortages of fruit and new leaves (Leigh Jr. 1999). Tropical rain forest trees produce mature leaves that are too tough and poor in protein for most animals or insects to eat. Thus vertebrate folivores and insects are constrained by the seasonally limited availability of young leaves and fruit (Leigh Jr. 1999).

Rain Forest Fauna

In the rain forest, plants have evolved effective ways of repelling and/or controlling the herbivore population. For example, in Barro Colorado, Panama, animal population growth is restricted by alternating seasons of fruit abundance and shortage. During a season of shortage, mass starvation can occur (Leigh Jr. 1975:82). In rain forests some trees reproduce by means of large, hard nuts. The hard endocarp protects the nuts from predators, but the mesocarp tends to be rewarding and some species of animals function as dispersal agents (N. Smith 1974). Animals play important roles in processes such as pollination, fruiting, flowering, litter decomposition, consumption of green plants, and mineral cycling (Fittkau and Klinge 1973). Animal consumption of plant tissue and consequent excretion of feces represent a shortcut in nutrient cycling.[3]

Animals represent a small fraction of the ecosystem's total biomass and are largely unobtrusive. Fittkau and Klinge (1973) calculated that the living plant biomass was nine hundred metric tons per hectare, while that of animals was only one-fifth of a ton. Leigh Jr. (1999) finds these estimates crude but notes that there have been no other systematic efforts to quantify the animal biomass in rain forests. A number of biogeographers and ecologists have indicated that the low net productivity of the rain forest biome provides little food for forest animals, and for this reason animal biomass per unit area is quite small. Although this argument is sound, it overlooks the large area utilized by most indigenous populations and the lack of adequate quantitative data. A more useful study of animal biomass is that of Eisenberg and

Thorington (1973) in Barro Colorado. They estimated 4,431 kilograms per square kilometer of nonflying terrestrial mammals, of which 72.3 percent is entirely arboreal. The hunting territory of human groups varies with population size and settlement pattern. In a quantitative study of hunting among the Siona-Secoya in lowland Ecuador, Vickers (1984, 1988) showed that the population harvested 9.8 percent of the potential 337,000 kilograms of animal biomass of interest to hunters—a not insignificant amount of meat for a population of 132 persons.

Some mammals adopt a more or less uniform distribution of individuals, each defending a home range; others pursue a continuous nomadism over a wider area in search of fruiting trees. These two strategies are not necessarily exclusive. Most nonarboreal rain forest mammals are solitary and have a dispersed form of social organization. Among arboreal rain forest mammals, two major trends are discernible: small troops scattered over the habitat range of the species and a more fluid type of social organization where the age and sex groups join and separate according to prevalent food distribution. Without their mammal components, tropical rain forests would not be self-perpetuating. Bats and marsupials contribute to the dispersal of many species, primarily through ingestion and transportation of seeds without loss of germinative potential. Through predation they help scatter numbers of individuals in a given area (Meggers et al. 1973:279).

A great deal of research has been undertaken in the past two decades on the fisheries of the humid tropics (see Dudgeon 2000 for Asian rivers and streams; Goulding et al. 1988; Goulding 1980, 1981, 1990 for Amazonian rivers). Despite the wealth of fisheries in some of these rivers, they are being fished out by commercial firms; the Amazon fishery has been said to be near collapse in its yields. Inaccessibility to many areas is the only thing keeping the fishery from being destroyed. The greatest impact is at the mouth of the Amazon and estuary, which are easily reached by large trawlers.

Our views have moved away from notions of equilibrium to disequilibrium in understanding humid tropical forests. Tree falls and other natural disturbances create a mosaic of biotic communities at different stages of succession (Uhl et al. 1989). They may be a significant component of maintaining high biodiversity (Lugo 1988; Whitmore 1989). Less well-known is how human populations use these natural gaps, or whether they create managed gaps and fallows to make their task of harvesting biodiversity easier and more productive. One example of this may be the Kayapó practice of creating resource islands (Posey 1982) along their trekking routes (Denevan and Padoch 1987).

COPING WITH ECOSYSTEM COMPLEXITY

Human adaptations to tropical rain forests suggest several strategies, each of which reflects efforts to deal with the diversity and complexity of the habitat. Hunting requires a finely tuned knowledge of animal sounds, food preferences, and migratory behavior. Such human adjustments are closely tied to complex systems of belief that clearly define the relationship of the hunter to the game. Food gathering is less clearly defined in belief systems but forms an important element in the diet of many tropical populations. Given the periodicities of tropical trees, seasonal nomadism is required for adequate exploitation of the fruits and nuts of the forest.

Fishing and animal husbandry are practiced by more sedentary populations. Because these two subsistence strategies generate a considerable amount of protein, population concentrations are greater, and warfare between groups aspiring to possess those resources is not uncommon. Such warfare may serve to redistribute populations and prevent depletion of a region's resources.

Farming requires identification of appropriate soils and location of fields in ways that both decrease labor costs and prevent pest damage. It also requires an adequate fallow to ensure the continued fertility of the system. Such a fallow is guaranteed by ritual regulation, automatic field abandonment after one or two years, or other means.

The integrity of shifting agricultural systems is predicated on a careful balance between population and resources. Infanticide, sexual abstention, and other means of population control are used to maintain such a balance. Human populations are relatively low in most of the humid tropics. Densities of 0.6 to 1.0 persons per square kilometer are still common in South America but higher in Africa (7–10 persons per square kilometer) and Asia (20-plus persons per square kilometer). Indonesia is a notable exception. It has engaged in major population transmigration to move people out of overpopulated Java (with densities in the hundreds) to the outer islands to reduce population at the current location and meet the demand for land resources. The results have been devastating in Kalimantan and other islands (Fearnside 1997). Conservation and management of tropical forests is one of the grand challenges to ecology and many fields (see Montagnini and Jordan 2005 for a multidisciplinary approach to conservation and management).

Hunting and Gathering Strategies

Human populations dependent on hunting technology exploit tropical forest resources in variable ways that reflect local habitat characteristics, periodicity, seasonality, and previous patterns of exploitation in the territory. Hunting technology in the tropical rain forest consists primarily of bows and arrows, lances, and blowguns. These weapons vary across continents, and no analysis has adequately explained the benefits of one type vis-à-vis another. Hunting has been a male-dominated occupation, and observers have noted that it is viewed as half work and half sport (Vickers 1976:96). The use of blowguns with poisoned tips is a delicate art and allows hunters to shoot repeatedly without frightening their prey, thereby increasing the chances of a multiple kill. Blowguns are used primarily against arboreal fauna, while lances are used mainly in hunting the larger land mammals, which usually involves open pursuit. Tapirs, boars, and other group animals are pursued by several hunters who foresee in a good kill a chance of several days rest from hunting work. Wherever bows and arrows are used, they usually preempt use of the blowgun.

Hunters have various goals that reflect adjustments to resources and affect the methods used. Hunters of forest vertebrates have long had an impact on the animal and plant populations they hunt. Hunters alter plant species composition by their choice of prey (which has given eating habits), by their intensity in hunting, and by whether they hunt alone or in groups (Wright 2003). Linares (1976) has noted that hunting in the vicinity of planted gardens may have partially eliminated seasonality and scheduling problems. It also increased the biomass of selected animals that live at the edge of the forest (for example, armadillos, rodents, and small deer raid gardens looking for food to eat and are caught in so doing) and served as a substitute for animal domestication.

Some hunts occur in daytime only and may involve a single hunter. If the lone hunter identifies the presence of a band of animals, a group hunting effort may emerge. Group hunts involve two or three hunters who carry out this work as part of their kinship obligations to provide for their families. Africa has seen growing populations in the rain forest regions and a booming demand in the so-called bush meat market. This boom, which has now gone on for several years, would suggest that the forest is rich in fauna for the hunter. According to Barnes (2002), however, this boom is illusory. His study shows, through simulation modeling, that large harvests can be obtained for many years but that a population collapse can happen suddenly and will inevitably occur.

Hunters must rely on not only appropriate hunting technology but also intimate knowledge of the forest and the animals. Ohtsuka and Suzuki (1990:50) found that married hunters among the Gidra of Papua New Guinea were twice as efficient as unmarried men and suggest that with age comes growing knowledge of animals and the environment, as well as skillful use of hunting technology. Tropical rain forest hunters are capable of imitating the calls and sounds of most animals they hunt, as well as recognizing their telltale footsteps. Knowledge of the animals' diet is particularly useful. As hunters move through the forest, they note the location of trees that are flowering or fruiting and use the knowledge in their next hunting expedition. Since trees of a given species do not flower simultaneously, hunters must pay constant attention to these details. They may have to cover a wide range of hunting territory in a given period to find trees that are attractive to game. Anthropologists have often noted that one of the major reasons for the lack of sedentary villages in many tropical forest areas was the necessity of relocating to maintain productive hunting (Carneiro 1970:243). This is much less the case today due to greater dependence on the outside, the creation of schools and churches in indigenous communities, and reduced territory.

Yields from hunting are variable, as Table 9.1 indicates. Gross (1975) suggests that hunting productivity limits the size and permanence of settlements in the Amazon.

Such single-factor explanations have been questioned. Vickers (1975, 1976) demonstrates that the amount of game obtained is surprisingly large in both new and old settlements. Most statements on the lack of meat among native South Americans are based not on personal observation and careful gathering of data on game hunted and eaten, but on the acceptance of the natives' point of view (that is, folk categories). Indeed, among tropical forest peoples, "hunger for meat" was a constant concern (Holmberg 1969; Siskind 1973). However, that ethnoecological concern may not be based on a real dietary lack. Ruddle (1973) has noted that the consumption of insects by native South Americans helps compensate for protein deficiencies. Dufour (1987) observed that a Tukanoan population in Colombia obtained 12–26 percent of their animal protein during part of the year from twenty different species of insects (see Ruddle 1973; Milton 1984; Smole 1976; Lizot 1977 for comparable practices among the Yukpa, the Makú, and the Yanomamo). Today, most indigenous communities keep chickens, pigs, and other domestic animals that reduce the contribution of hunted meat to the diet.

Among the Siona-Secoya, the least successful hunter managed a mean of 13.08 kilograms of butchered meat per hunt—with the average for all hunters being 21.35 kilograms. Even in an area continuously inhabited for thirty-two years, the mean kill was 5.67 kilograms per hunt per hunter. Over the whole year, the Siona-Secoya hunted the equivalent of 255 kilograms of meat for each of the 132 persons in the village. This translated into 65 grams of animal protein per person per day. However, in view of the nocturnal habits of much of the game, the high canopy habits of most of the birds and monkeys, and the aggressiveness of the peccaries, it is not surprising that a great deal of cultural attention is given to relations between hunter and prey. Religion and ritual are filled with taboos for hunters that define the behavior of one for the other and the dangers of such encounters. Of all the subsistence activities, hunting is the least secure.

In numerous aboriginal societies, symbolic systems define hunter behavior and control depletion of wild game (see Seeger 1982 for a contrasting view). These symbolic systems reflect culturally sanctioned adjustments of populations to resources. According to Reichel-Dolmatoff (1971, 1976), the Tukano of the Vaupés River in the Colombian northwest Amazon see human society and the fauna of their habitat as sharing the same pool of reproductive energy. The fertility of both men and animals has a fixed limit, rather than being an infinite or unrestricted resource. It is therefore important for the Tukano to seek an equilibrium in human sexual activity so that the animals of the forest can reproduce and, in turn, serve as nourishment for the human population. Cultural rules control the recognized tendency of people to exploit the environment to the limits of their technological capacity.

Within this system of controls, sexual repression of the hunter plays a major role. Since this repression could have undesirable psychological effects, the Tukano have filled the relationship between hunter and prey with erotic content. The hunter dreams and hallucinates about sexual contact with the animals, which he fertilizes

TABLE 9.1 Estimated Rates of Animal Protein Capture for Nine Tropical South and Central American Societies

Society	Location	Habitat Type	Firearms Present?	Principal Food Staple	Animal Protein Per Capita Per Day (g)	Length of Study (days)	Average Size of Pop. Unit
Campa	E. Peru	interfluve forest	+	manioc (72%)	15–20	3	5–15
Bayano Cuna	Panama	riverine forest	+	bananas (89%)	18	14	170
Miskito	Eastern Nicaragua	tropical forest (coastal)	+	manioc	20	365	997
Kaingáng	Southern Brazil	subtropical forest	–	pine nuts	19	38	106
Sirionó	Eastern Bolivia	interfluve forest	–	maize and manioc	44	92	60–154
Wayaná	Guyana–Brazil	riverine forest	–	manioc	31	365	16
Sharanahua	E. Peru	riverine forest	+	manioc	63	28	90
Shipibo	E. Peru	riverine forest	+	plaintains	48	365	107
Waiwai	Guyana–Brazil	riverine forest	–	manioc	54	varies	77
				mean =	35 g		

Source: Daniel Gross, "Protein Capture and Cultural Development in the Amazon Basin," *American Anthropologist* 77, no. (1975):526–549. Reproduced by permission of the American Anthropological Association from the *American Anthropologist* 77:531, 1975.

and which multiply for his benefit. At times, the animals ravish the hunter in dreams. The hunt is part courtship and part sexual act, filled with care, respect, and ritual. The verb to hunt is *vai-mera gametarari,* which means literally "to make love to the animals." Courtship behavior manifests the idea of sexually attracting the game so it can be killed, and the kill has a strong element of sexual domination. Before the hunt, as well as after, the hunter abstains from sexual contact. None of the women in the big house *(maloca)* must be menstruating, nor should the hunter allow erotic dreams before a hunt.

Such a system limits the sexual activity of the hunter as well as the frequency of hunting. A child is gradually indoctrinated into this complex set of beliefs and before puberty already knows that he should never mock a dead animal or treat animals carelessly. He also knows that not all animals can be hunted, but only some of them, and those only under stringent conditions. Noncompliance leads to fear of death, since the spirits of the animals can lure the hunters away from familiar terrain and kill them.

There is cultural hostility among the Tukano toward families with numerous children. Their lack of sexual abstinence robs the animals of their energy for reproduction. Furthermore, these families demand more meat to feed their excessive number of children. The animals are believed to grow jealous and refuse to serve as prey, an idea that reflects lower hunting yields under conditions of population growth.

Systems of belief such as those of the Tukano operate well under aboriginal conditions but are disrupted by contact with outside groups (see Dwyer 1990, on changes among the Etoro of highland Papua New Guinea). This is particularly the case if the cultural contact is associated with the spread of diseases to which the population has no immunity. In a comparison of two South American tribes, Wagley (1969) shows that the one with the stricter ideology that encouraged small families was threatened with extinction following exposure to European diseases. The other one, which actually encouraged large families, withstood depopulation more successfully.

Like hunting, the gathering of forest products is subject to the peculiar periodicities and seasonality of the tropical forest. Forest populations have traditionally engaged in concentrated gathering efforts during the dry season, not only because of product availability but also because of the greater ease of traveling during that time. Forest plant products make important contributions to the diet and are gathered by men, women, and children. Table 9.2 documents the yields by a household of Ecuadorian Siona-Secoya (Vickers 1976:117). Gathering is nutritionally significant, not so much for the total calories it provides as for its mineral, vitamin, and micro-nutrient content. In hunting, the men do not overlook the presence of plant resources and may collect or consume them on the spot. A wide variety of products is gathered, but major contributors, by volume, are few in number. For ecological analysis, however, even small amounts may provide crucial trace elements. Brazil nuts *(Bertholletia excelsa)*, for example, are crucial because they contain large amounts of the amino acid methionine, which Gross (1975:534) cites as perhaps the most limiting nutritional element in Amazonian diets. In areas of low population density and abundant land, gathering can be more productive than horticulture. Among the Gidra of Papua New Guinea sago making provided only one-half to two-thirds of the energy return per man-hour of collecting wild fruit (Ohtsuka and Suzuki 1990:58).

To date, there has been no documented systematic measurement of the consumption of Brazil nuts or other wild plant products by South American aboriginal or peasant populations. This is partly the result of a tendency by many populations to gather and eat edible products they come across on the spot.

Fishing Strategies

Populations inhabiting coastal or riverine habitats find it easier to become sedentary than seminomadic hunters do. Large rivers and coastal areas offer tremendous resources that encourage both sedentariness and increased dependence on horticulture. Examples of river-adapted populations are the Kalapalo and the Kuikuru of central Brazil (Basso 1973; Carneiro 1957). Observers have noted that these two riverine groups show little interest in wild game and even surround its exploitation with taboos—cultural prohibitions that emphasize the poor return of labor invested on hunting (vis-à-vis fishing) in a riverine environment (Ross 1978). Efforts to systematically compare hunting and fishing show that fishing is more efficient (see Table 9.3) except during the rainy season, when fishing yields decline.

The rich variety of species found in rivers cutting through tropical rain forest regions has only begun to be carefully studied. Junk notes that 1,300–2,000 fish species have been identified in the Amazon rivers and that yearly harvests of 633,000 metric tons are theoretically possible (1975:109). However, such potential has never been realized, and the intensive utilization of the larger aquatic resources has led, in our day, to the clear danger of species extinction—for example, of the giant Amazon river turtle, the cayman, and the giant manatee.

Before adopting the hook and line, tropical forest populations used a variety of harpoons, bows and arrows, traps, and poisons to capture fish. These are specific techniques used in particular times and places to catch specific species of fish (Vickers 1976:105). Spears and harpoons are used against larger prey, such as cayman and manatee. Fishing with poisons can be practiced only in small streams and requires a large group effort. The plants used as poisons are wild, but because of their importance, have become semidomesticated. A barrier must be built in the stream to keep the fish from escaping, and the plants usually have to be beaten to release the poisonous substance. The fish are stupefied, their breathing impaired by the substance, and they float to the surface where they are caught. These communal fishing efforts occur on a restricted basis during the dry season (Vickers 1976:111).

**TABLE 9.2 Annual Collecting Yields for a Siona Household of Four in
Amazonian Ecuador, 1974**

Food	kg portion	% Edible portion	Edible kg	kcal/kg Edible portion[a]	Total kcal
Flora					
Palm fruit *(Mauritia flexuosa)*	27.22	15[b]	4.08	2,070	8,452
Palm nut *(Astrocaryum tucuma)*	22.68	28	6.35	990[c]	6,286
Heart of palm (various spp.)	0.45	100	0.45	260	117
Nut *(Caryodendron orinocense)*	18.14	37	6.71	6,420	43,078
Wild sapote *(Matisia cordata)*	10.89	26	2.83	480	1,358
Yahi fruit *(Pseudolmedia laevis)*	0.60	75[b]	0.45	810[d]	364
Wild cacao *(Herrania balaensis)*	1.56	37	0.58	710[e]	412
Groundcherry *(Physalis angulata)*	0.45	90[b]	0.40	730[f]	292
Wild guaba *(Inga* spp.)	4.52	20	0.91	600	545
Pokeweed *(Phytolacca rivinoides)*	2.72	85[b]	2.31	370	855
Uvilla (Pourouma cecropiaefolia)	1.00	80[b]	0.80	290	232
Sayaro (unidentified fruit)	1.36	40[b]	0.54	480[g]	259
Dwarf banana *(Musa* sp.)[h]	500.76	78	390.59	378	378,875
Fauna					
Turtle eggs *(Podocnemis unifilis)*	7.36	83	6.11	1,150	7,026
Honey	1.36	100	1.36	4,162	4,172
Palm grubs *(Rhynchophorus* sp.)	0.40	90[b]	0.36	1,430	860
Total					453,183

[a] INCAP 1961; Dufour 1988.

[b] Estimated.

[c] Data for *Astrocaryum standleyanum* used as analogue.

[d] Data for *Prunus capuli* used as analogue.

[e] Data for *Theobroma bicolor* used as analogue.

[f] Data for *Physalis peruviana* used as analogue.

[g] Data for *Matisia cordata* used as analogue.

[h] Higher than most years due to immaturity of cultivated plantains in gardens. (This is a self-propagating variety of dwarf banana found along riverbanks.)

Source: William T. Vickers, personal communication, 2000.

TABLE 9.3 Mean Returns from Hunting and Fishing

	Fishing g/work-hour	Hunting g/work-hour	Source
Pumé	405	810	Gragson 1989
Barí	350	135	Beckerman 1980
Shipibo	1,140	1,600	Bergman 1980
Bororo	680	200	Werner et al. 1979
Xavante	400	400	Werner et al. 1979
Mekranotí Kayapó	200	690	Werner et al. 1979
Kanela	50	110	Werner et al. 1979
Siona Secoya	675–1,000	3,200	Vickers 1976

Source: Adapted from Beckerman, "Hunting and Fishing in Amazônia: Hold the Answers: What Are the Questions?" (paper presented at Wenner-Gren Conference Amazonian Synthesis, Nova Friburgo, Rio de Janeiro, June 2–10, 1989), pp. 12, 18.

Vickers (1976:124), while studying the Siona-Secoya of Ecuador, estimated the energetic efficiency of fishing at 3:1, less than that of hunting in a new village settlement (9.33:1), but more than the return for the labor of hunting in an old village (2.48:1). Among the Machiguenga of the upper Amazon in southeastern Peru, energy efficiencies differ from those just cited. The Machiguenga live in smaller groups of seven to twenty-five members in an upland habitat where game and fish are less abundant than in the lowlands. The forest offers a low rate of return on labor: the region is mountainous, trails are steep, and resources scattered. Hunting provides 0.16 calories for each calorie spent, gathering yields 0.68 calories for each calorie spent, and fishing averages 1.95 calories (Johnson 1977). Nietschmann (1971) notes that among the Miskito of Central America the return on labor from fishing green turtles was 5.5 to 1. This figure is lower than the efficiency he noted for hunting, but the protein return was higher for fishing.

Game depletion is a problem of greater immediacy than fish depletion in aboriginal situations. Game relies on the relatively low net productivity of the forest, whereas fish can draw from nutrients carried by the river from distant areas. As a result, populations probably preferred riverine to inland locations, where they would have to rely on hunting to supply the bulk of their protein. Some researchers have attributed the chronic state of warfare and raiding in tropical rain forest regions in the past to a constant struggle for control of riverine sites where subsistence efforts, particularly in terms of securing protein, were more rewarding (see review in Gross 1975).

A study by Nietschmann (1973) of a coastal Miskito population in Nicaragua is an excellent data source on fishing adaptations to coastal resources. The Miskito have

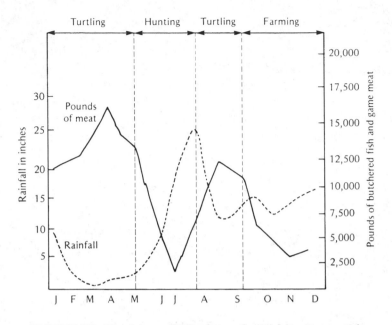

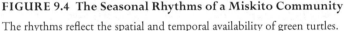

FIGURE 9.4 The Seasonal Rhythms of a Miskito Community

The rhythms reflect the spatial and temporal availability of green turtles.

long depended on the green turtle as a dietary staple and an item of trade. However, the introduction of a cash economy and the presence of two factories that process turtle meat for pet food have resulted in overfishing that threatens this way of life. The Miskito have responded to contemporary cash incentives and have abandoned the diversified subsistence economy that sustained them in the past. The young Miskito have begun to turn away from horticulture—which in the past supplied the bulk of their calories—and seasonal hunting. The net result has been a decline in the protein available to the Miskito, a steady breakdown in the system of reciprocity, and a decline in the yields of turtles per unit of effort spent on fishing them.

In exploiting the large green turtles, the Miskito adjust their subsistence technology, lifestyle, and economic patterns to the temporal and spatial occurrence of the turtles (see Figure 9.4). Relatively little attention is paid to wild game. Choices between hunting and fishing are made according to the information feedback that reflects evaluations of the dependability and productivity of each strategy. Turtlemen have a larger percentage of successful trips than hunters (73 percent and 54 percent respectively), and this is a more important consideration for the Miskito than the effort expended. Hunting provides more calories per hour invested (1,270 as compared to 962 for fishing), but calories are not in limited supply in this environment (Nietschmann 1972:59). As a result, in the past as now, the majority of the Miskito choose to specialize in turtling.

To understand human interaction with the environment, it is important to examine the processes of land use at the local level (for example, household composition, soil fertility and management, labor allocation), as well as processes at the community, regional, and national and international scale (Wood and Skole 1998; Brondizio et al.1994; Uhl et al. 1989; Mahar 1989; Moran and Brondizio 1998, 2001; Brondizio and Moran, in preparation). Deforestation is just one of many steps in a land use strategy. The farming strategies, the strategic use of fallows, and their temporal and spatial characteristics reflect the interaction of multiscale processes both biophysical and socioeconomic.

Farming Strategies

Shifting cultivation can be defined as an agricultural system in which fields are cropped for fewer years than they are allowed to remain fallow. It is a dominant land preparation technique in 30 percent of the world's cultivable soils, especially in those covered by tropical rain forest. It is a common misconception that shifting (also known as slash-and-burn or swidden) cultivation is practiced by primitive farmers on inferior soils (Kellogg 1959). Popenoe's study in Central America (1960) was among the first to refute this notion with evidence of tropical soils cultivated by slash-and-burn methods that had high levels of organic matter, low bulk densities, high cation exchange capacities, and high potassium content.

Because it is a practical and economical procedure, shifting cultivation has been practiced by over 250 million people worldwide (Spencer 1966; Sanchez 1976:346). However, Palm and colleagues (2005) have suggested that more recent data puts this data closer to 37 million working on 1 million hectares or 22 percent of the tropical land area. It is, in a sense, a pioneering system utilized today by peoples lacking capital resources and economic privilege. In this approach to cultivation, the nutrients accumulated in the forest biomass are made available to crops on a periodic basis. It is a conservative measure that, when practiced according to tradition, preserves forest complexity and provides sustained yields. With growing populations, the system is not sustainable and changes toward cultivation intensification are inevitable, including intensive agroforestry and improved fallows (Sanchez 1999; Colfer and Byron 2001; Zhang et al. 2002; Schroth 2004; Palm et al. 2005; Mutuo et al. 2005). Improved fallows and the cultivation of fast-growing species are promising pathways to sustainability, accumulation of nitrogen, and the provisioning of fuel wood in areas where this has become scarce. Another interesting alternative to traditional swidden cultivation is the combination of timber tree production with shade-tolerant species that also serve as staple food such as plantains (Norgrove and Hauser 2002).

In swidden cultivation, an area of land is cleared by cutting the standing vegetation and then burning it, after it has had time to dry. Burning brings about numerous changes in the physical properties of soils. It kills parasites, insects, fungi, nematodes, and pathogenic bacteria that interfere with crop productivity. The effect of the burn on soil physical properties depends on the soils themselves. In soils high in oxides, such as the oxisols, the structural changes are beneficial. In areas with shrinking clays, the effect may be detrimental.

With the burn, all nutrients are deposited as ash except nitrogen and sulphur, which are lost as gases. There is great variability in how many nutrients are deposited as ash. The amounts depend on the success of the burn, the humidity of the environment, and the density of the vegetation. The deposition of ashes decreases soil acidity as shown by an increase in soil pH. The effect is most marked in the top ten centimeters of soil, but studies have noted changes in pH to a depth of forty centimeters. The presence of basic cations in the ashes brings about a favorable increase in exchangeable calcium, magnesium, and potassium that improves crop growth conditions. In acid soils, burning decreases exchangeable aluminum and thereby decreases the danger of aluminum toxicity in some plants. These positive effects usually remain for only one or two years. The ash layer responsible for many of these changes is leached—washed down through the soil—or the nutrients are taken up by plants (Sanchez 1976:364–368).

Burning does not have much effect on soil organic matter. Soil temperatures during forest burns are not commonly high enough to destroy soil organic matter. Several studies have noted small increases in soil organic carbon and total nitrogen after burning (Nye and Greenland 1964). The positive effect of burning on pH and organic matter increases the cation exchange capacity (CEC) of soils and therefore overall fertility. Available phosphorus from the ash layer increases from 7 to 25 kilograms per hectare (Nye and Greenland, 1960). Many of the soils in areas where shifting cultivation is used have been noted to be deficient in phosphorus, and burning helps make such soils productive for agriculture. A growing number of methods to improve the organic content of soils under shifting cultivation have been proposed (for example, additions of manioc peel and charcoal; Topoliantz et al. 2005).

Nye and Greenland observe that when the African forest is cleared and burned, the heating of the soil leads to increased fertility, largely as a result of the change in the state of nitrogen mineralization, or **nitrification** (Nye and Greenland 1960:72). When properly timed to occur before the beginning of the rainy season, the moisture brings about a rapid increase in the amount of nitrogen available to plants. Heating the soil also has a favorable effect on the soil microbial population. Anaerobic nitrogen fixing bacteria such as *Clostridium spp.* increase their activity. Aerobic bacteria such as *Beijerinkia* are killed but appear to recolonize within a relatively short time (Baldanzi 1959).

Burning eradicates seeds and vegetative material that can lead to a large crop of weeds. It also destroys or drives out animal and insect pests. Eradication of weeds and pests is beneficial in any effort to cultivate crops. Weed invasion limits crop production not only by its natural competition for soil nutrients, but also through an accompanying increase in the rodent population. During the early stages of weed invasion, rodent populations undergo accelerated growth. Rodents can severely damage young plants (Popenoe 1960:59–62).

A series of Brazilian experiments showed that burned areas produced 30 percent more than those cleared mechanically and cultivated with a plow (Baldanzi 1959). In studies carried out in Peru, Sanchez and colleagues (1974) found that yields using traditional slash-and-burn methods were 50–60 percent higher than yields from areas cleared by bulldozer. Sanchez and his colleagues attributed the lower mechanized yields to reduced infiltration of water resulting from soil compaction, the lack of nutrients from the ash layer, and the loss of the humic horizon by bulldozer scraping (see Table 9.4).

The practice of slash-and-burn agriculture is not only economically sensible but ecologically sound. Given the vigor of secondary succession, efforts to establish simplified (monocrop) agricultural systems are likely to run into serious problems, such as pest infestation, weed invasion, and nutrient loss as a result of runoff. The intercropped fields of swidden horticulturalists imitate the natural ecosystem: generalized and diverse, multistoried, and providing good soil protection from both direct solar radiation and precipitation (Geertz 1963:16–25). Floyd (1969:181) has given an excellent description of one such field in Nigeria:

> The impression gained is one of multi-tiered systems of farming with several levels of crops being maintained on the same few square yards of soil: an ingenious technique of mixed and sequential cropping. Lowly ground creeping plants such as the cucurbits are shaded by the foliage of root crops, which in turn are found growing within the shade of the smaller "economic" trees such as banana, plantain, orange, mango, breadfruit, native pear, cashew, castor bean and kola; the ubiquitous oil palms grow taller, varying in height from some 30 to 60 feet, and are only eclipsed by scattered specimens of forest giants from the original rainforest, especially cottonwood trees. In sum, as many as a dozen foodyielding, beneficial plants may be struggling for survival and fruition in hard proximity.

Swidden horticulture thus protects the complexity natural to the ecosystem. In addition, it preserves natural controls by avoiding concentration of food sources for anthropod pests, protecting the soil from leaching and erosion, and providing intense shade that discourages the colonization of sun-loving weeds. It also reduces expenditures for fertilizers and pesticides. The new forest that it helps create provides a higher net yield for humans. Such a system requires numerous controls to assure its integrity (Conklin 1957).[4] It can break down by population increases, which lead to shortening of the fallow period; by insufficient attention to its intercropped, multistoried characteristics, which leads to erosion; and by extension of

TABLE 9.4 Effects of Land-Clearing Methods and Fertilization on Crop Production on an Ultisol from Yurimaguas, Peru (tons/ha)

Land-Clearing Method	Fertility Treatment	Continuous Upland Rice				Cassava	Soybeans	Guinea Grass (annual production)
		2nd Year	3rd Year	4th Year				
Slash-and-burn	none	1.93	1.36	0.77	22.5	0.72	9.9
	complete	3.20	3.53	2.00	34.2	2.34	24.1
Bulldozer clearing	none	1.09	0.92	0.20	10.1	0.12	8.3
	complete	2.52	3.19	1.42	32.0	1.31	18.4

Source: North Carolina State University (1973, 1974); reprinted in Pedro Sanchez, *Properties and Management of Soils in the Tropics* (New York: Wiley-Interscience, 1976).

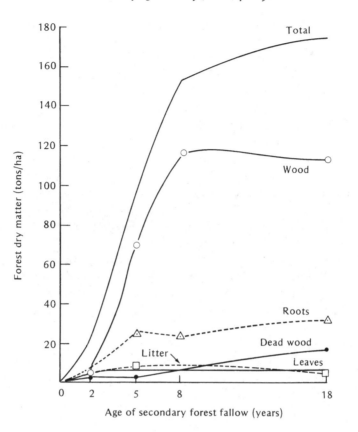

FIGURE 9.5 Increases of Biomass of Forest Components with Age of Secondary Forest Growth in Yangambi, Democratic Republic of the Congo

Note how a substantial portion of the biomass is reached by eight to ten years. *Source*: Adapted from W. Bartholomew et al., "Mineral Nutrient Immobilization Under Forest and Grass Fallow in the Yangambi (Belgian Congo) Region," *Institut National pour L'Etude Agronomique du Congo Série* 57 (1953):1–27.

the system to less humid areas where grasslands may quickly replace the primary forest vegetation.

Studies in African rain forests have indicated that 90 percent of the maximum biomass is attained within eight years after a field has been abandoned (Sanchez 1976:351). Figure 9.5 illustrates how the biomass plateau is reached on an ultisol in Zaire. Presumably regrowth may be even faster on soils with higher fertility. Seedlings and regrowth from the previous forest form a quick, low canopy that reduces soil temperatures and erosion potential. Growth is rapid, and litter is decomposed so rapidly that a nearly closed nutrient cycle is established (Nye and Greenland 1960). However, it is well established that if cropping is extended too long, forest regrowth will not occur and coarse grasses will take its place (Sanchez 1976:354).

A number of the practices of swidden cultivators assure the renewal of the forest (Denevan and Padoch 1987; Balée 1989; Ewel 1986; Hames and Vickers 1983). These planting practices mimic, in a simplified fashion, the process of secondary succession. The first crops planted tend to be those most demanding of nutrients (for example, corn, rice, millet). They are intercropped with root crops and plantains that take longer to develop, provide better shade, and are in some cases taller. By the time the grains are harvested, the other crops are well established and provide both yield and protection. Numerous cultivators seem to also plant leguminous trees and shrubs. Brookfield and Brown (1963:166) have noted such practices in southern Nigeria, Indonesia, and New Guinea. The Ibo of Nigeria plant *Acior barteri* and *Macrolobium macrophyllum* to help restore soil fertility when woody plants do not return spontaneously (Netting 1968). The practice of having small, multiple, scattered plots in the forest—instead of single, large clearings—facilitates forest succession by providing seeds that can recolonize the cultivated land when it is abandoned (Clarke 1976:250).

The productivity of swidden cultivation has been controversial. Because of research undertaken since the late 1950s, we now have an excellent database from which to judge this system's merits. Rappaport (1968) found that the Tsembaga in New Guinea obtained 15.9 calories per calorie spent on swidden cultivation. Even higher caloric returns have been obtained in Mexico, Ecuador, and Brazil under comparable technological conditions.

Animal Husbandry

Mechanisms that encourage abandonment of fields at regular intervals so that forest can take over are crucial to long-term swidden systems. In the Amazon, where land has traditionally not been in limited supply, populations shifted in response to decreased farm yields, lower returns to labor in hunting, and fear of sorcery and raids. In New Guinea, where populations have been much denser, there has been a tendency to have continuous cultivation in prime areas. This can lead to environmental degradation, and some populations have turned their montane rain forest into low-quality grassland. The Kundegai and the Fore have wrought large-scale and irreversible changes on their environment to the detriment of their own well-being (Harris 1974b:72). Another population, the Tsembaga Maring, has maintained a more stable relationship with the local environment. It has accomplished this through the workings of a complex homeostat that "effectively adjusts the size and distribution of the Tsembaga's human and animal population to conform to available resources and production opportunities."

According to Rappaport (1968, 1971), the cyclical pig festivals of the New Guinea highlands function as a logic switch that leads to the investment of the pig herd in alliance formation and at the same time eases the stress of pig population numbers. The alliances that take place at the pig festivals are a prelude to warfare. In these intertribal conflicts, people-to-land ratios are altered and prime garden lands are allowed to become fallow. Without these intertribal conflicts, overcultivation and repeated burnings would lead to soil compaction, weed invasion, and environmental degradation. The ten- to fifteen-year cycles establish a range of time in which evaluations of labor and resource use must be made. If pig husbandry succeeds to the point that pigs become "too much of a good thing," the stress is felt by the laborers, and this is translated into a cybernetic signal that is made operational by the tribal leaders.

The ritual cycle regulates the human and the pig population. In Figure 9.6 the nearly vertical portion (or A to B path) represents the drastic reduction in the pig population. This is followed by warfare, represented in path B to C, which causes a slight decrease in the human population. Both populations then increase for a number of years until a new festival initiates the cycle again (Shantzis and Behrens 1973:276). A festival is induced by an increase in labor costs of pig husbandry beyond an acceptable threshold and by growing danger of land degradation as larger areas must be cultivated. As the system moves from the safe region and enters the critical region, it must order the ritual cycle or else it enters the destructive region—where the land's productivity is threatened. The regulatory role of the pig rituals is

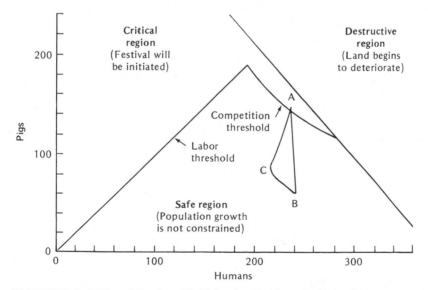

FIGURE 9.6 A Ritual Cycle with Behavior Regions Indicated

Source: Figure 9–14 reprinted by permission of MIT Press, Cambridge, MA, from S. D. Shantzis and W. W. Behrens, "Population Control Mechanisms in a Primitive Agricultural Society," in *Towards Global Equilibrium*, edited by D. L. Meadows and D. H. Meadows (Cambridge, MA: MIT Press, 1974).

predicated on the status value attached to pigs. Without this value, the pig herd would not receive the attention necessary for it to function as an information indicator or signal (Foin and Davis 1987).

Bennett (1976) views the process as a problem of livestock management, not a cybernetic signal. The cost of raising swine in unconfined environments periodically exceeds the gain, and Melanesian men make economic decisions when the cost (of fence mending, distance to fields, fear of raids, and so on) gets too high. Ritual provides an effective cultural mechanism for maintaining a sustained-yield system, but other mechanisms could work equally well (Bennett 1976).

Friedman (1974) argues that the ritual cycle's occurrence is best understood by focusing on the strain felt by women, who carry out most of the agricultural work and pig husbandry. They complain, they nag their husbands, and they snap at their children, and it is these social facts that trigger the pig festivals and warfare cycle. According to Friedman, social relations determine the composition and quantity of labor that goes into pig raising. In a reply to Friedman and other critics in the revised edition of his book *Pigs for the Ancestors*, Rappaport argues that at low densities of pig populations the crucial factor may indeed be women's labor returns, but at higher densities the depredation caused by pigs (for example, tearing of fences and invasion of fields) may be all-important in triggering a ritual cycle (1984).

These cases of farming behavior and regulation of pig herds raise the question of how can such systems operate in the absence of ritually operated cybernetic controls? Most studies have not noted equivalent structures in other tropical forest populations. Traditional populations relied on various forms of population control, the most important being warfare, infanticide, and village fissioning. By reducing the size of their populations, other groups exerted less pressure on their land, and ritualized shifting of land was not necessary (Foin and Davis 1987).

In Latin America, the most common form of land use in the tropical rain forest regions today is cattle ranching, and this activity has been held responsible for up to 90 percent of deforestation in Brazil (Brondizio and Moran, in preparation; see also R. Walker et al. 2000). In studies of land use in Altamira, Brazil, we found that homesteaders rarely had less than 50 percent of cleared land in pasture, and often as much as 80–90 percent (Moran et al. 2002a). This choice is partly cultural, partly economic. Hecht and colleagues (1988) find that even smallholders engage in cattle ranching, given how it is favored by economic policy, as compared to staple crops. Restraining the continued expansion of cattle ranching and pastures in Latin America will be necessary if rates of deforestation are to be reduced.

Village Fissioning, Infanticide, and Warfare

Adaptation to lowland rain forests under aboriginal conditions involved a broad spectrum of practices that may be related to the characteristics of a diverse ecosystem (Dufour 1990; Bailey and Headland 1992; Redford 1991). Whenever possible, low population densities were maintained by practices that included warfare, female infanticide, and village fissioning. Carneiro (1961) said that villages rarely reach carrying capacity but fission (split up) well before they reach the point of overshooting their resources. As population increases, stresses and strains increase with it, and weak chieftainship and a lack of internal political controls do nothing to discourage a village faction from splitting off from its parent community (Carneiro 1974:78). In addition, in the past there were no ecological deterrents to village fissioning. Suitable land was easily found and the vast network of streams and rivers facilitated travel to new locations. In other words, in the absence of both internal and external deterrents, tropical forest tribes followed the path of least resistance and sought avoidance of the stresses that come with increased population density.

The situation was quite different in Asia, Melanesia, and Africa. Clarke (1966) notes that with increased population in New Guinea there is a change from extensive to intensive shifting cultivation. This is manifested in shortened fallows, lower productivity per unit of land and per unit of labor, but a higher total production as a result of higher labor input and more sedentary settlement patterns. Boserup (1965) notes a similar relationship in Africa between increased population and the intensification of agriculture.

Eder (1977) has studied a typically Boserupian scenario in the Philippines. As man-to-land ratios have declined, farmers have progressively shortened fallow periods. Returns to labor have decreased, since increased weeding has been necessary. As a substitute for swidden cultivation, the farmers have turned to vegetable gardening, which gives a poor caloric return to labor but has a high economic value in nearby markets. Gardens, however, can also absorb ten times more labor input per unit of land than swiddening and provide the most intensive forms of cultivation in rain forests today.

Female infanticide, abortion, long periods of sexual abstinence after childbirth, warfare, and a strong male fear of too frequent sexual contact with women have been observed among many of the world's peoples, including rain forest dwellers. Among some populations, intercourse between husband and wife is forbidden from the onset of pregnancy until the child is weaned—often not until ages three and five. Sexual continence is commonly required prior to ceremonies, raids, and hunting. The number of prohibitions that are practiced varies a great deal and may be related to other forms of population control (Meggers 1974:104). All these practices had the net effect of controlling the size of aboriginal populations throughout the humid tropics. This has come to an end due in no small part to the conversion of indigenous peoples to evangelical and other Christian sects that discourage abortion and nearly all forms of population control.

War in itself does not significantly control population (Livingstone 1968:8). Casualties are seldom so large that a group cannot regain its previous size within a couple of generations. The practice of female infanticide aids in reducing the number of persons capable of bearing children and increases the number of persons capable of hunting (males). Thus it also ensures higher protein per capita for the group. Warfare is the cultural price that must be paid to keep these mechanisms of population control operative. As an adaptive strategy it is more effective than abortion or contraception. The latter, until the invention of the condom, was seldom effective. Abortion could be effective, but it had the undesirable effect of killing mothers only slightly less frequently than embryos when practiced in primitive conditions (Harris 1974b).

ADAPTABILITY TO HUMID HEAT

In addition to adjustments that center on human strategies for coping with ecosystem complexity, rain forest populations must manage the potential stress and discomfort of high humidity combined with high temperatures. Most of these adjustments to humid heat are cultural rather than physiological. Unlike the dry tropics, which are generally characterized by low humidity and lack of water, the humid tropics have abundant water resources. However, high humidity and high temperatures in combination impede the effective evaporation of sweat that cools the human body. Human adaptation to humid heat is still little understood. Most of the data are from Africa (Ladell 1964), and only one field study is available from South America (Baker 1966; Hanna and Baker 1974).

Cultural adaptations to humid heat are similar throughout the world, and they are relatively few in number. Settlements are located on a rise of ground near a water source. No perfect solution for housing is available. Houses are characterized either by open design (to provide maximum daytime cooling) or by designs aimed at the conservation of heat to provide warmth during the relatively chilly nights (see Figure 9.7). Minimal use of clothing minimizes the body's heat load (Ladell 1964:650–651) and provides maximum surface area for sweat evaporation. Most clothing holds moisture and under high humidity does not evaporate and can result in severe cases of micoses.

Daily tasks are adjusted to the pattern of insolation: the population bathes frequently, starts work early, remains relatively sedentary at midday, and follows a moderate pace in work. Physiologists have noted that tropical peoples "move more efficiently" and do not allow themselves to become overheated (Ladell 1964:652). After thermal midday (2:00 PM) most tropical peoples avoid heavy work and engage in relatively unstrenuous activity in shaded areas.

The main physiological adaptation of indigenous tropical peoples is the combination of cutaneous vasodilation and a ready onset of sweating (Ladell 1964:626). On the other hand, because of the high humidity, there is a fairly low limit to the cooling that is possible through evaporation. Cross-cultural comparisons of sweat rates do not indicate any conclusive adaptations by tropical peoples (Lowenstein 1973:294). This may be associated with the low salt intake of tropical populations, which are dictated by appetite, custom, and the limited availability of salt. At

a

b

FIGURE 9.7 The Two Basic Housing Approaches in the Humid Tropics

a. Open design for daytime cooling; *b.* Closed design for nighttime warmth (Xingú maloca in central Brazil). There is no perfect solution to the problem of high daytime temperatures and cool nights in traditional housing, and populations organize their lives accordingly.

TABLE 9.5 Physiological Responses of Shipibo Indians and Peruvian Mestizos to Heat Exposure

Group		Final Rectal Temp. (°C)	Pulse Rate (per min.)	Sweat Loss (g/hour)
Moderate level	Shipibos walking at 5 km/hr.	37.78	93.55	673
	Mestizos walking at 5 km/hr.	37.83	102.73	618
Increased level	Shipibos walking at 5 km/hr.	38.24	133.33	970
	Mestizos walking at 5 km/hr.	38.24	129.92	913

Source: Paul Baker, "Ecological and Physiological Adaptations in Indigenous S. Americans," in *The Biology of Human Adaptability*, edited by P. Baker and J. S. Weiner (Oxford: Clarendon, 1966).

moderate levels of activity, tropical peoples sweat less and have slightly lower body temperatures than unacclimatized people. In addition, their heart rates increase less with rises in body temperature. Nontropical people during acclimatization over-adapt to heat by uneconomical high sweat rates and steep increases in heart rate with a rise in body temperature. This leads to fatigue, dehydration, and serious salt losses.

Other biological adaptations of value to rain forest dwellers are relative reduction of mass with respect to surface area (Newman 1960; Ladell 1964:647; Baker 1966:296); highly tannable skin; insensible sweat evaporation, which ensures maximum evaporation with a minimum loss of electrolytes (Lowenstein 1968; Ladell 1964:652); and reduced heart rates at moderate levels of activity (Hanna and Baker 1974). A study comparing Shipibo Indians with acclimatized mestizo workers in South America found that, although neither group was seriously stressed by heat and radiation loads during moderate exercise, the pulse rate was significantly lower among the native population. This advantage was lost when the level of activity was increased (Hanna and Baker 1974). Table 9.5 gives the results of the tests used in this study. Lowenstein concluded that tropical indigenous populations do not show any remarkable adaptations to heat stress but enjoy comfortable lives in humid heat because of moderate levels of activity and sensible, low sodium diets (1968:394).

GLOBAL CHANGE PROCESSES AND
ALTERNATIVES TO DEFORESTATION

Tropical rain forests represent the world's most biodiverse ecosystems and play a key role in the water cycle, carbon storage and exchange, and climate stability (Malhi and Phillips 2005; Lal 2000). Global climate change and the intensification of agriculture in areas previously covered in tropical forests (Keys and McConnell 2005) is expected to have a strong impact on this biodiversity in the future, particularly at boundaries between forest classes and ecotonal communities (Hilbert et al. 2001). Some studies suggest increasing tree biomass and changes in recruitment and mortality rates in a higher carbon dioxide world—as all models predict (Lewis et al. 2004)—yet the evidence is not entirely consistent.

The use of remotely sensed digital images has become an indispensable tool in environmental assessment and resource management (Lillesand et al. 2004; Lindgren 1985; Estes and Consention 1988; Aber and Melillo 1991). The feasibility of using this technology in mapping and managing tropical forest resources has been demonstrated in a number of studies (Baltaxe 1980; Grainger 1983; Green 1983; Danjoy 1984; Eden and Parry 1986; Green and Sussman 1990). Remote sensing is particularly valuable for research in inaccessible regions such as the humid tropics where assessment of vegetation and soils is both urgent and difficult if carried out solely by means of field studies (Danjoy 1984; Nelson and Holben 1986; Woodwell et al. 1986, 1987; Helfert and Lulla 1990). When satellite image analysis of tropical forests was first proposed, great concern was expressed as to the ability of this technology, primarily designed for monitoring large homogeneous forests and agricultural areas of northern latitudes, to discriminate the heterogeneous cover classes that often exist in small patches within tropical forests (Lillesand et al. 2004). This was true until the development of digital analysis techniques, image processing technology, and better sensors (TM and SPOT). Great advances have been achieved, including the monitoring of stages of secondary succession (Moran et al. 1994a,b, 2002a; Brondizio et al. 1994, 2002; Lu et al. 2002). One persistent problem has been acquiring closely spaced images, given the high frequency of cloud cover.

Difficulties in observing through clouds has limited use of optical remote sensing in the humid tropics, but the use of radar in floodplain regions has grown in recent years, since radar can penetrate through the clouds (De Grandi et al. 2000; Saatchi et al. 2001). The use of synthetic aperture radar (SAR) sensors has broken through this barrier (Saatchi et al. 2001; Santos et al. 2002, 2003) and newer satellites such as Radarsat2 and ALOS/PALSAR promise even greater advances in the coming decade.

The impacts of climate change on tropical forests are complex, with rising levels of carbon dioxide increasing productivity, while increased temperatures and drought diminish it (Clark 2004). A study by Schuur (2003) demonstrates that net primary production of tropical forests is highly sensitive to mean annual precipitation. Whether tree biomass increases or decreases with climate change has a huge bearing on the carbon cycle at global scale. Whether tropical forests are carbon sinks or sources is still a subject of considerable debate among scholars (Clark 2004). Not all of this carbon is in trees, but there are significant portions in soil carbon that may be sensitive to land use changes (Powers and Schlesinger 2002). McClain and colleagues (2001) provide a synthesis of the biogeochemistry of the Amazon basin, one of the key areas in the humid tropic biome.

Any contemporary system of production or conservation should give serious consideration to established practices of human adjustment to the problems of diversity and complexity in the humid tropics before discarding them as unsuitable for the modern world (Moran 1993b). Today, tropical forests and their inhabitants are feeling the impact of human-induced global climate change resulting from earth-warming gases, land cover change, and disturbances in the hydrological cycle (Zimmerer 2006). El Niño climate events are making already disturbed or stressed forests more vulnerable to catching fire from nearby cleared fields (see Guhardja 2000 for discussion of fires in East Kalimantan during recent El Niño events), and river discharge and carbon emissions spike in some but not all parts of the Amazon (Foley et al. 2002). Flowering and fruiting are being affected, as is pollination and seed dispersal (Bazzaz 1998). Structure and function may change, and losses of biodiversity impoverish human adaptability for years to come. A combination of field-based research methods and use of satellite-based sensors to map and monitor the conditions of the humid tropical forests is the only feasible way to achieve adequate coverage on a region legendary for its poor infrastructure and difficult access (Foody et al. 1997; Moran et al. 1994a, 2002a, 2006; Brondizio et al. 1994, 2002).

Whether in Indonesia (Hamilton 1997), Africa (Martin 1991), or the Amazon basin (Nepstad et al. 1999), the spread of selective logging is leaving behind a forest that is drier and more flammable. Accidental fires now are causing larger losses of forests than intentional clearing (Cochrane et al. 1999; Uhl and Kaufman 1990; Skole and Tucker 1993). Another contributing factor is the growing fragmentation of forests (Laurance et al. 1998; Laurance and Bierregard 1997). When fragmentation, selective logging, and use of fire as a management tool for pastures occur in El Niño years there is growing evidence that the Amazonian forests can easily ignite over extensive areas, whereas fires used to stop at the edge of the mature forest in the past (Nepstad et al. 1999). Evidence for past mega–El Niños has begun to be assembled and they have been associated with major prehistoric migrations and reduced areal extent of tropical moist forests (Cochrane and Schulze 1998; Fearnside 1990; Nepstad et al. 1999; Meggers 1994; Sanford et al. 1985).

Of growing concern too are the large emissions of carbon from tropical deforestation. Tropical forests are vast carbon sinks according to some scholars, and even mature forests continue to store as much as one ton of carbon per hectare per year. To take just one example, since 1900 the Philippines have lost 15.7 million hectares of tropical forests. This is equivalent to 2.7 billion tons of carbon. When we consider that the Amazon basin is being deforested at the rate of 1 percent per year (50,000 km² per year), the scale of the problem becomes striking (Lasco 1998). A recent study estimated that at current levels, forests in northwestern Ecuador will disappear within thirty years (Sierra and Stallings 1998). Rudel (2005) provides a comprehensive analysis of the regional dynamics of deforestation in tropical forest areas, showing the differences between different regions of the world.

Deforestation is having vast impacts on native animals. Conservation biologists believe many mammals are at the verge of extinction as a result of habitat destruction compounded by population growth and overhunting (Bodmer et al. 1997). Species with long-lived individuals, low rates of natural increase, and long regeneration times are more vulnerable. The threat is nearly invisible, particularly where human impacts do not result in clear-cutting. Selective logging scars are invisible within three years to satellite sensors such as Landsat TM, even though the understory may be drier and more vulnerable to fire. Hunting can affect patterns of seed dispersal, favoring some species over others. Fragmentation creates favorable habitats for edge species, rather than for mature forest species. Mortality of trees may change as the microhabitats' moisture, litter, and insolation below the canopy change (Phillips 1997).

Fortunately, tropical forests are more resilient than most people give them credit for. Forest restoration varies from place to place depending on environmental endowments (for example, quality of soil, slope, moisture regime) and the intensity of human use of the land (for example, swidden, mechanized agropastoral, mineral). Lightly disturbed sites may approximate the original biomass in as little as twenty years, whereas more intensively disturbed sites may take fifty years or more (Aide et al. 1996). In steep areas, like the Andean piedmont and Madagascar's hillsides, the return of forest may be retarded or may not occur at all, due to steep slopes and erosion of seeds unable to establish a foothold (Sussman et al. 1994). Islands are particularly vulnerable given their small size and biogeographic isolation from continental areas (Gupta et al. 2004; Kummer 1991).

Alternatives to cutting tropical forest for agricultural or pastoral uses can be found worldwide. C. Smith (1996) in a survey of 136 polycultural fields in the Amazon found 108 different agroforestry configurations involving 72 different species. Small-scale operators are experimenting with a rich variety of crops, mostly on their own initiative. These represent alternatives to letting the cleared land return to secondary growth, while still maintaining species diversity and increasing the economic returns to the population. Coomes and colleagues (2004) point to efforts by Peruvian peasants in conservation of forests, including management of fallow dynamics (Coomes et al. 2000).

Another option is to manage forests to mitigate carbon emissions (S. Brown 1993, 1996; S. Brown et al. 1993). However, great uncertainties exist due to lack of knowledge about tropical forest wood densities, variability in biomass estimation techniques, and even in the assessment of what constitutes tropical forest (Fearnside 1996; Kaufmann et al. 1995).

Kahn and McDonald (1995) provide evidence that reducing a country's foreign debt can reduce deforestation pressures. Debt-for-nature swaps and other mechanisms that reduce the need of tropical countries to generate foreign exchange to pay for their debts may provide relief on tropical forests. However, without addressing other drivers of deforestation such as population growth and migration, expansion in the area in agriculture, and the lack of effective environmental protection for reservations, the forest will continue to disappear, and the people of the forest will continue to lose their livelihoods (Houghton 1994).

Increasing population densities in tropical areas and the influx of people to these areas make it increasingly difficult to maintain the integrity of shifting agriculture. More continuous cultivation of rain forest soils seems almost inevitable, but this need not spell the creation of deserts (Goodland and Irwin 1975), nor an end to hope for populations seeking new lives in the lowland tropics (see Moran 1981; N. Smith 1982a; Nelson 1973). The change from shifting to permanent cultivation invariably involves the use of either organic or inorganic fertilization; a move from communal to private land ownership; and higher labor input, particularly into weeding. The importance of combined fertilization and weeding can be seen in an example from an alfisol of Nigeria. Without fertilization and without weeding yields declined to less than 30 percent by the second year; with weeding alone, the decline was less pronounced. With fertilization but no weeding, yields declined by the third year, but with weeding included, yields actually increased substantially. The benefits of such inputs probably compensate and justify the costs involved (Sanchez 1976:398; see also Nicholaides et al. 1983, 1985).

It has been suggested that agroforestry, or tree agriculture, might be an alternative means both of protecting the soil from leaching and of providing a profitable, sustained-yield system. Planning permanent tree crops offers the advantage of establishing an ecosystem with its own nearly closed nutrient cycle. Moreover, the areas can be cultivated with food crops while the trees grow. Tropical tree crops—such as cocoa, rubber, robusta coffee, coconuts, oil palms, Brazil nuts, guarana, bananas, plantains, and a wide variety of exotic fruits—could be cultivated in mixed stands rather than in **monocultures** on plantations. (The disaster of Henry Ford's rubber plantations in Brazil is a witness to the danger of monoculture in an environment favorable to living things, including fungi, pests, and other plant pathogens.) Such mixed stands would provide both ecosystem diversity and profitable incomes. Sioli (1973) presented such a scheme in which forest or tree agriculture on poorer soils is combined with dairying, poultry, and swine husbandry—all of which yield organic fertilizer for intensively cultivated gardens.

In Asia, large leguminous trees are planted in association with other tree crops. This system involves forest clearing and the subsequent selection of successional species that yield both profit and food for the human population Some timber species can be mixed with a view both to diversity and profit. Like tree agriculture, this production system attempts to replicate succession in a given area of land (see the synthesis of alternatives to shifting cultivation in Palm et al. 2005; Sanchez 2000).

A mulching approach to tropical agriculture has been tried in both Java and southern Brazil. In this system, vigorous **tropical legumes** are planted and then plowed under before food crops are cultivated. The legumes fix nitrogen in the soil, and the green manure adds organic matter to the soil. Among these legumes are *Centrosema pubescens, Theprosia candida, Pueraria javanica, Crotalaria spp.*, and *Mimosa invisa*. The soil is continuously covered and noxious grasses such as imperata are choked and suppressed. In addition, species are selected for specific location conditions. (For example, in Brazil *Theprosia candida* gives excellent results, while in Indonesia this is nearly impossible because of the presence of the *Theprosia* beetle.) Reports of nitrogen fixation in excess of 200 kilograms of elemental nitrogen per hectare have been recorded (Mott and Popenoe 1975:30). Mulching and minimum tillage—tilling the row only and mulching the rest—can be integral parts of tropical agriculture since they decrease soil temperature, conserve moisture, prevent erosion, and add nutrients to the soil.

Intensive multiple cropping is a modern adaptation of aboriginal practices. Effective multiple cropping minimizes the number of days that land is idle. To date, much of the research on this method has taken place at the International Rice Research Institute (IRRI) in the Philippines, but other Rockefeller Foundation centers (for example, Centro Internacional de Agricultura Tropical [CIAT] in Colombia, International Institute of Tropical Agriculture [IITA] in Nigeria, and Instituto Interamericano de Agricultura Tropical [IIAT] in Costa Rica) are now following suit. The Philippines studies are designed around rice, given its importance in Asia, while those in Colombia are centered on manioc, corn, and beans. In the Philippines, rice is planted first during the wet season and is followed by sweet potatoes, soybeans, corn, and green soybeans. In experimental situations, 22,000 kilograms per hectare of food have been produced in twelve months, a feat not possible in temperate zones where plant growth is interrupted by cold weather.

Intercropping, which is a variation of multiple cropping, is also derived from traditional systems of cultivation (Gross et al. 1979; Werner et al. 1979). Intercropping usually involves planting a tall-growing crop and one or more shorter crops. Such crop combinations can increase land productivity 30–60 percent over monoculture cropping (IRRI 1973:2). Intercropping has a number of advantages: higher total light interception, better weed control, and minimal leaching. In addition, pests have a less ideal environment for major crop damage. A diverse combination of legumes, grains, and root crops presents a higher potential for both food and income productivity (IRRI 1973:15; Vandermeer and Perfecto 2005).

All these contemporary alternatives, as well as others that have not been included here, are modern approaches that do not damage the rain forest environment but increase its net yield. Researchers need to focus on an integrated approach that combines cultural ecological studies of native systems with the scientific knowledge of forestry, agronomy, terrestrial and marine biology, and other disciplines. Such research may help ensure that we do not destroy the variety and potential of ecosystems in our efforts to feed a growing population. The hope of the present and the future lies in equal emphasis on production and conservation.

SUGGESTED READINGS AND USEFUL WEBSITES

The humid tropics are a fertile area for investigators. The complex factors that are involved have just begun to be penetrated. Bermingham et al. (2005) provide a major synthesis of recent research from paleoecology, climatology, geology, biogeography, and community ecology. Laurance and Beirregaard (1997), and the update by Bierregaard et al. (2001), provide a detailed analysis of the ecology of fragmented forests. The latter provides an overview of the most ambitious project ever undertaken in tropical ecology to understand fragmentation and the minimum critical size of ecosystems in the humid tropics, the Biological Dynamics of Forest Fragments Project in central Amazônia—the brainchild of Tom Lovejoy. A whole generation of ecologists has cut their teeth as participants in this project which is still ongoing under the National Institute for Amazonian Research (INPA) in Manaus, Brazil.

Lambin and colleagues (2003) propose a framework for studying changes in land use and land cover in these regions. A special issue of the journal *Forest Ecology and Management* (vol. 38, no. 3–4, 1991) covers a broad set of issues on the effects of deforestation in Amazônia (Sioli 1991; Houghton et al. 1991; Stone et al. 1991 among others). The journal *Climate Change* (vol. 19, no. 1–2, 1991) published an excellent set of papers on deforestation and climate change (Gash and Shuttleworth 1991 on albedo and surface energy balance; Meher-Homji 1991 on hydrology; Keller et al. 1991 on atmospheric chemistry).

The Association for Tropical Biology and Conservation (www.atbio.org) and its journal *Biotropica* (www.atbio.org/biotropica.html), the Society for Conservation Biology (www.conbio.org) and its journal *Conservation Biology* (www.conbio.org/Publications/ConsBio), the International Society for Tropical Ecology (www.tropecol.com/index.htm) and its journal *Tropical Ecology* (www.tropecol.com/journal/default.htm), and the *Journal of Tropical Ecology* (http://journals.cambridge.org/action/displayJournal?jid=TRO) regularly publish research and findings about tropical ecology. The British Ecological Society maintains a tropical ecology group (www.besteg.org) to link researchers interested in tropical studies (also see their links page, www.besteg.org/links.html, for links to other research societies, organizations, and foundations devoted to tropical research and management). Particularly useful is the Database of Research Institutions in Tropical Ecology from the German Society for Tropical Ecology (www.ibiblio.org/pub/academic/biology/ecology+evolution/people/ecotrop), which provides detailed information for approximately seven hundred institutions worldwide conducting research on tropical ecology (though at the time of writing, the page was last updated in 2002).

Several tropical research institutes are dedicated to research in tropical environments, especially biodiversity and conservation of these areas, including the Smithsonian Tropical Research Institute (www.stri.org), where the Center for Tropical Forest Science (www.ctfs.si.edu/doc) is the world's largest tropical forest research program. In Australia, the CSIRO Tropical Forest Research Centre (www.tfrc.csiro.au)

serves as a research base for tropical forest research in that country. The Tropical Resources Institute (www.yale.edu/tri), while serving primarily as a resource base for students and researchers within the Yale School of Forestry and Environmental Studies at Yale University, also discusses research efforts and results in tropical environments. Similarly, the Organization for Tropical Studies based at Duke University (www.ots .duke.edu) provides environmental training in tropical environments for undergraduate and graduate students. Within the Long-Term Ecological Research (LTER) network, research in tropical ecosystems has been conducted at the Luquillo Experimental Forest in Puerto Rico (http://luq.lternet.edu) through the Institute for Tropical Ecosystem Studies at the University of Puerto Rico (www.ites.upr.edu).

Some useful additional books about the ecology of tropical environments include *Tropical Forest Community Ecology* edited by Carson and Schnitzer (in press); *Tropical Ecosystems and Ecological Concepts* by Osborne (2000); *Tropical Forest Ecology: A View from Barro Colorado Island* by Leigh Jr. (1999); *Nutrient Cycling in Tropical Forest Ecosystems* by Jordan (1985); and *The Ecology of Neotropical Savannas* by Sarmiento (1984). Several books detailing the interaction between people and tropical environments are *Emerging Threats to Tropical Forests* edited by Laurance and Peres (2006); *Tropical Forest Ecology: The Basis for Conservation and Management* by Montagnini and Jordan (2005); and *Hydrology and Water Management in the Humid Tropics* by Bonell and colleagues (1993).

One major research focus has been development of sustainable agricultural practices in tropical ecosystems, with several institutions devoted to these efforts. The Tropical Agricultural Research and Higher Education Center (CATIE) in Costa Rica (www.catie.ac.cr) provides over seventy research, education, and outreach programs in different areas, such as biodiversity conservation, agricultural and livestock management, and economic development. The Tropical Agriculture Program at the Earth Institute of Columbia University (www.earth.columbia.edu/tropag/index.php) also addresses agricultural production in tropical areas, especially for reducing poverty and increasing economic development.

Similarly, the Global Forest Resources Assessment (www.fao.org/forestry/ site/fra/en) and Forestry Department (www.fao.org/forestry/en) of the Food and Agriculture Organization of the United Nations (FAO) provide worldwide assessments of forest status, including extent and condition of tropical forests. In Europe, the Tropical Forestry Resource Group (www.tfrg.co.uk) and the European Tropical Forest Research Network (www.etfrn.org) link individuals and institutions within the United Kingdom and Europe, respectively, who are concerned with tropical forest research. Also see the website for Tropical Forest Research (www.tropicalforest research.org) for more information about tropical forest biodiversity, the website for International Society of Tropical Foresters (www.istf-bethesda.org) for more information on development and use of tropical forests, and the website of the Association for Fire Ecology of the Tropics (www.tropicalfire.org) for more information on fire-ecosystem interaction within tropical areas.

Recent efforts by research institutes and organizations have focused on the ecology, economy, and culture found in the Amazon, specifically. The Amazon Initiative (www.iamazonica.org.br) is an international consortium of research institutions and government agencies devoted to conservation and sustainable use within the Amazon, while the International Center for Tropical Agriculture (CIAT) (www.ciat .cgiar.org), the Center for International Forestry Research (CIFOR) (www.cifor.cgiar .org), and the World Agroforestry Centre (www.worldagroforestry.org), all part of CGIAR, promote research focused on tropical agriculture and forestry. The Institute of Amazonian Environmental Research (IPAM) (website in Portuguese: www.ipam.org.br) and the Institute of Man and the Environment of the Amazon (www.imazon.org.br) are nonprofit and nongovernmental organizations that facilitate projects and research on sustainable land use, especially related to biodiversity, ecological communities, and climate change. Researchers with the Amazon Ecology Program of the Woods Hole Research Center (www.whrc.org/southamerica/index .htm) and the Ecosystems Center at the Marine Biological Laboratory (http:// ecosystems.mbl.edu) have highlighted the effects of the ongoing land use changes on the biology and chemistry of the land, water, and atmosphere in the Amazon. Also, the Amazon Forest Inventory Network (RAINFOR) (www.geog.leeds.ac.uk/projects/ rainfor) is an international network of researchers studying the biomass and dynamics of Amazonian forests.

One of the largest research programs to date on tropical ecology and land use has been the Large-Scale Biosphere-Atmosphere Experiment in Amazônia (LBA) (www.lbaeco.org), a large international project led by Brazil to understand the physical, chemical, and biological processes occurring in the Amazon, particularly in the context of regional and global change. Research results from LBA have been published in numerous journals and books (searchable on the LBA website), including series of synthesis volumes focusing on both biophysical and human dimensions (Batistella et al. in preparation; Batistella and Moran 2007; Moran and Ostrom 2005) in the journals *Earth Interactions* (special theme issue, http://ams.allenpress.com/ perlserv/?request=get-collection&coll_id=2; also see http://earthinteractions.org), *Hydrologic Processes* (vol. 20, 2006); *Ecological Applications* (August 2004); *Theoretical and Applied Climatology* (June 2004); *Global Change Biology* (May 2004); *Philosophical Transactions of the Royal Society: Series B, Biological Sciences* (March 29, 2004); *Remote Sensing of Environment* (November 15, 2003); and *Journal of Geophysical Research* (vol. 107, 2002). The ecological effect of forest simplification by modern cultivators is one of the many ecological processes that merit serious and immediate attention from researchers. New evidence suggests that forest resource extractors practice intensive forms of management of forest species (Brondizio 1996, 2007; Brondizio et al. 1996; Brondizio and Siqueira 1997; Karsenty 2000; Lawes 2004; Kumar and Nair 2006).

Indigenous knowledge, ethnobotany, and land use in tropical areas have been increasingly important areas of research, especially in regard to protection of biodiversity and use of tropical forest resources (with regard to intellectual property rights of knowledge of this use). For example, the Cultural Center of Indigenous Groups of the Amazon (website in Portuguese: www.povosdamazonia.am.gov.br) provides information about the various indigenous groups living in the Brazilian Amazon, while the National Indian Foundation (FUNAI) of Brazil is the governmental organization specifically devoted to indigenous affairs within Brazil (website in Portuguese: www.funai.gov.br).

Other Brazilian institutions that maintain useful resources about the ecology and cultural groups in the Amazon include INPA (website in Portuguese: www.inpa .gov.br) and the Emilio Goeldi Museum of Pará, which is dedicated to environmental and natural history research in the Amazon (website in Portuguese: www.museu -goeldi.br). The website of Marajoara culture (www.marajoara.com), focused specifically on indigenous groups and archeology in the Amazon River estuary, maintains a detailed bibliography of Amazonian archeology and cultural research (www .marajoara.com/bibliography.html).

Useful books to consult include *The Amazon River Forest: A Natural History of Plants, Animals, and People* by N. Smith (1999); *Floods of Fortune: Ecology and Economy Along the Amazon* by Goulding et al. (1996); *The Ecology of Tropical Food Crops* by Norman et al. (1995); *Through Amazonian Eyes: The Human Ecology of Amazonian Populations* by Moran (1993b); and *Sustainable Agriculture and the Environment in the Humid Tropics* from the National Research Council (NRC 1993b). The book *Archaeology in the Lowland American Tropics: Current Analytical Methods and Recent Applications* edited by Stahl (1995) also provides useful information about archeology in the tropical Americas.

The International Plant Science Center at the New York Botanical Garden (http://sciweb.nybg.org/science2; see also the website for the Botanical Science Division: www.nybg.org/bsci) provides valuable information on the use and diversity of tropical plants. Also see the website for the Centre for Economic Botany at the Kew Royal Botanic Gardens, UK: www.rbgkew.org.uk/ceb. Further information on ethnobotany, plant use, and intellectual property rights related to plant knowledge can be found in the journal *Economic Botany* (www.econbot.org/_publications_/ index.php?sm=01) from the Society for Economic Botany (www.econbot.org) and the journal *Ethnobotany Research and Applications*, available free online (www .ethnobotanyjournal.org). Also see the website of the National Institute of Biodiversity in Costa Rica (www.inbio.ac.cr/en/default.html), a nongovernmental research center devoted to characterizing and monitoring biodiversity within Costa Rica.

Specific readings devoted to the ethnobotany of tropical environments include *Indians, Markets, and Rain Forests: Theory, Methods, Analysis* by Godoy (2001); *Ethnoecology: Situated Knowledge, Located Lives* edited by Nazarea (1999); *Native American Ethnobotany* by Moerman (1998); *Cultural Memory and Biodiversity* by Nazarea (1998); *Valuing Local Knowledge: Indigenous People and Intellectual Property Rights* by Brush and Stabinsky (1997); and *Footprints of the Forest: Ka'apor Ethnobotany, the Historical Ecology of Plant Utilization by an Amazonian People* by Balée (1994).

More information about adaptation and health in tropical environments can be found in the journals *Tropical Medicine and International Health* (www .blackwellpublishing.com/journal.asp?ref=1360–2276), *The American Journal of Tropical Medicine and Hygiene* (www.ajtmh.org), and the *Transactions of the Royal Society of Tropical Medicine and Hygiene* (www.rstmh.org/transactions.asp) from the Royal Society of Tropical Medicine and Hygiene (www.rstmh.org). Also see the websites of the American Society of Tropical Medicine and Hygiene (www.astmh.org) and the International Federation for Tropical Medicine (www.iftm.org) for more information on tropical research. Other research organizations and institutions devoted to tropical health and medicine include the Tulane University School of Public Health and Tropical Medicine (www.sph.tulane.edu), and the London School of Hygiene and Tropical Medicine (www.lshtm.ac.uk).

Demographic, epidemiological, and nutritional studies of changes experienced by native populations are coming out in steady form (Coimbra 1988, 1989; Conklin and Graham 1995; Fleming-Moran and Coimbra 1989; Santos 1991; Early and Peters 1990; Hill and Hurtado 1996; Coimbra et al. 2002). These studies are informed by biological, historical, and political economic perspectives—and point to the growing capacity of indigenous peoples to not only survive but have their voices heard at global scale (Coimbra et al. 2002). In fact, a historical perspective on environmental change is pointing to the lasting impact of human activities, sometimes several centuries before (see van Gemerden et al. 2003, on the Central African rain forest; Balée and Erickson 2006 in the neotropical lowlands).

NOTES

1. Annual total net primary productivity averages 23.9 metric tons per hectare per year. The rate for temperate forests is only 13 metric tons per hectare per year (Farnworth and Golley 1974:81–82). In a Puerto Rican rain forest, gross production equaled energetic costs of respiration, thus permitting rapid litter turnover and high levels of transpiration (Lugo and Snedacker 1971:113).

2. Nomadism is found in most environments and is not a response peculiar to the humid tropics. It is a nearly universal adjustment to scattered or seasonally available resources and, in modern times, to economic marginality.

3. Meggers et al. (1973) have data on floral and faunal aspects of tropical rain forest ecosystems of Africa and South America; numerous articles in the journal *Biotropica* treat plant and animal interactions.

4. The most common reasons for declining yields that lead to fallowing are lower soil nutrient availability, deterioration of soil structure, erosion of topsoil, increased weed density, pests and diseases, and greater labor costs (Nye and Greenland 1960). The little weeding that has been observed among traditional populations favors forest regrowth (Gómez-Pompa et al. 1972).

PART

THREE

URBAN SUSTAINABILITY

Photo by Daniel Stern
Source: iStockphoto

10

URBAN ECOLOGY AND
URBAN SUSTAINABILITY

Cities are becoming the most dominant location of people on the earth. The United Nations predicts that 5 billion people will live in cities by 2030, up from 3.3 billion in 2007 (UN Population Fund 2007), with the change being particularly dramatic in Asia and Africa (Keiner et al. 2005). Whereas there were just sixteen cities in the world with more than a million people in 1900, that number had grown to more than five hundred cities with more than a million inhabitants by 2000, with more than a dozen of them having more than 20 million people each (Harvey 1996). Scores of cities in the developing world have already surpassed 10 million inhabitants, and at the start of the twenty-first century, more than half of the world's population can be found in cities. Some regions of the world, like Latin America, are already over 75 percent urban.

Life in these megacities is filled with contradictions and huge gaps between the rich and the poor, wasteful consumerism, excessive pollution, congestion, crime, and hopelessness (Harvey 1996). A billion people today, or about a sixth of the world's population, live in slums, 90 percent of them in developing countries. In sub-Saharan Africa more than seven in ten urban dwellers live in a slum lacking basic services such as water and sanitation, or legal rights to their housing. The elites who benefit from the concentration of economic activity in cities abandon the city and make their homes in the suburbs (in contrast, in Europe, they have returned to the city core). There is hardly a city in the past forty years that has not experienced this exodus from the city by the well-to-do, and the loss of jobs through deindustrialization (Harvey 1996).

Cities concentrate power and increase the rate at which energy is consumed, as reflected in the per capita energy consumption of modern cities vis-à-vis the rates estimated for earlier stages of cultural evolution where a more direct link existed between households and production of basic needs. Cities, in other words, have not been green, have never photosynthesized much and produced net biomass. They

FIGURE 10.1 Rio de Janeiro, a Brazilian Urban Area

Rio de Janeiro, Brazil, a major city that maintains impressive green areas. Photo by Anthony Cak.

have been largely consumers of the biomass produced by photosynthesis in rural areas and surrounding landscapes. This is not likely to change overnight, but there is a need to make our cities greener, more sustainable, and more sensitive to the impacts they have on the landscapes that support urban life. Community gardens in New York's Lower East Side and in California homeless shelters reflect this search for a more sustainable future, and for ways of reconnecting to the places where we live and returning nature to the city (Bartlett 2005).

Whether urban dwellers think of it or not, cities are embedded in a natural environment—sometimes spectacular environments, such as Rio de Janeiro (see Figure 10.1 for a view). With enough care and forethought, cities, like forests, prairies, and other natural ecosystems, could be restorative of natural processes (Bennett and Teague 1999; Beatley 2000). There is considerable variability across the world in how green cities are, with many European cities showing the way (see Beatley 2000 for a review of these lessons). The discourse today has moved toward smart growth and urban sustainability (White and Whitney 1992; Thurstain-Goodwin 2001), and this new direction will require weaving together finance, tax policy, land use regulation, densification, development and transportation policy, and many other aspects of urban planning (Berke et al. 2003; Gearin 2004; Mazmanian and Kraft 1999; Wheeler 2002; Wolch et al. 2004; Shochat et al. 2006a,b; Newman 2006). It has been amply documented that our cities have a huge ecological footprint or impact on regions far and wide through their consumption, pollution, and waste (Rees 1971; Tickell 1998; Wolch 2007). American cities are particularly wasteful of land and resources with very few of them showing much sense of restraint in their sprawling growth (Beatley and Manning 1997).

Any society depends on two kinds of energy sources: somatic and extrasomatic. Somatic energy comes to human populations via the food chain. Extrasomatic energy, on the other hand, comes from harnessing the energy found in fossil fuels, wood, wind, water, tides, radioactive materials, and heat. Preindustrial cities relied primarily on somatic energy and the limited power that could be obtained from wind, water, and animals. Contemporary industrially based cities depend on enormous inputs of extrasomatic energy to subsidize their growth and complexity. One interesting feature of cities is that they seem to function under the illusion of self-sufficiency. Anyone can observe the large number of trucks that come into cities each day supplying their material needs. Urban dwellers until recently acted as if they had a special claim on the resources they need from the natural environment, without regard for protecting the productivity of those natural ecosystems. In the past this resulted in overexploitation, salinization of agricultural lands, and species loss. In more recent years, one positive outcome of the awareness of global change has been a growing awareness of the interdependence of rural and urban areas—and the loss of a clear boundary between one and the other.

The debates over sustainability have now reached discussion of our cities (Wackernagel and Rees 1996; van den Berg et al. 2007; see Wackernagel et al. 2006 for a discussion of the ecological footprint concept in promoting sustainability planning of cities; Olalla-Tarraga 2006). Historians have shown that cities not only shaped but were also shaped by nature (Mumford 1961; Cronon 1991; Gandy 2002; Colten 2005). Political ecologists have pointed to the environmental degradation and vulnerability of urban populations (Robbins et al. 2001; Keil 2003; Desfor and Keil 2004). Geographers have a growing role in the urban planning area (see Wolch 2007 for a review of the issues for geographers). Ecologists are beginning to see that cities have an ecology and that issues such as biodiversity, energy, and material cycles are just as relevant to the ecology of cities as they are for natural systems (Platt et al. 1994; Pickett et al. 1997; Fernandez-Juricic 2000; Fernandez-Juricic and Jokimani 2001; Grimm and Redman 2004). Pickett and colleagues (2004) have proposed the "cities of resilience" notion to emphasize the role of heterogeneity in both social and ecological functioning of urban areas, and the adaptability of people and human institutions to the challenges of urban living.

A sign of the growing importance of urban ecology and the human impact on ecosystems is the recent initiation of a series of urban long-term ecological research sites (LTER), www.lternet.edu, which complement a series of LTERs around the United States that were initiated more than twenty years ago to study the major natural ecosystems of the United States. In the late 1990s these expanded into a network of international sites as well. The bioecological community thereby acknowledges that the human dimensions of ecosystem structure and function are necessary to an understanding of these systems. Several traditional LTERs now include a human dimensions component. The adaptability of our species to life in an increasingly urban world should indeed be researched. Air and water pollution are no less challenging to our species than cold or low biological productivity. Crime, crowding, and traffic jams are no less important than proximity to good soils in how we choose our settlements or location. In the past the complexity of urban ecosystems discouraged ecological scientists, who preferred to measure "natural" systems to the humanly constructed urban ones. This neglect shows signs of coming to an end with the development of urban LTERs. We now recognize that even natural systems were hardly ever pristine (see Foster and Aber 2004 on the history of Harvard Forest), and that the human imprint on all of the earth's systems is far from negligible and becomes more dominant each day. We can examine urban ecology and urban sustainability by looking at the ecology of cities, their use of energy, their spatial heterogeneity, and how they structure the behavior of the inhabitants. We begin by taking a quick look at how cities have changed through history.

THE HISTORY OF CITIES

Prior to the eighteenth century, urbanization was a limited phenomenon and cities had a coupled relationship to their surrounding rural areas. Provisioning cities back then depended on a relatively proximate rural zone near the city. Cities recycled their "night soil" and other urban wastes in the nearby rural areas, making them bad smelling but ecologically virtuous (Harvey 1996; Guillermé 1988). These same processes also made cities a locus of disease, pestilence, and plagues that decimated urban populations until the implementation of drainage systems, potable water supplies, and public health services. Before 1800 the ecological footprint of cities was light because they were embedded bioregionally and their size permitted provisioning by the immediate surrounding hinterland. Even before 1800 the city already had begun to play a key role in converting and harnessing power into a unified form (often used for the purpose of war); it "turned energy into culture, dead matter into the living symbols of art, biological reproduction into social creativity" (Mumford 1961:571).

To do all this it had to turn itself from an overgrown village into a nucleated, highly organized city. Unfortunately, for much of their history, cities were less concerned with the well-being of their residents than with growing in size and power, often at the expense of their residents. Leaders could escape to their estates outside of cities, while the rank and file lived amid crowded, unhealthy conditions. A fascinating environmental history comparing Chicago and Manchester (UK) examines how these two industrial cities transformed the use of land, water, and air; how unhealthy urban

slums crowded the city center, while garden estates were created in the suburbs; and how the ruling classes managed the creation of urban spaces to ensure financial gain to the detriment of the majority population and the environment (Platt 2004). Frightening epidemics and unnatural "natural disasters" forced city dwellers in Chicago and Manchester to clean up the slums, reduce air pollution, and improve sanitation.

Beginning in the eighteenth century, technologies developed that accelerated capitalist modes of production seeking to eliminate spatial boundaries to ensure more rapid accumulation and circulation of capital (Harvey 1996). Most significant was the revolution in transport and communications: canals, bridges, turnpikes, railroads, steamboats, the telegraph, mass transit systems, jet aircraft, television, and mass media available today on one's "smart phone." Each innovation has accelerated economic activity, broken spatial barriers, and changed the structure of urban space. They broke the city's dependency on its immediate bioregion and provided it with access to the goods and services of the whole country and the world (Cronon 1991; Platt 1991 on how technology changed the metabolism of Chicago into one of the early cities harvesting the whole world despite its inland location).

The innovations continue today and speed economic processes and the role of cities. Containers move goods around the world, jet cargo systems speed goods to countless destinations, new truck designs increase the volume that can be carried in containers, and highway specifications allow trucks to carry much greater weight, reducing the cost of moving goods and the time required to provision cities. On-demand orders via computers, cell phones, and a whole array of immediate communications (Harvey 1996) enable production on demand, virtually eliminating inventories. Urban dwellers need not think about where their provisions are coming from. They stopped depending on immediate rural areas as produce from around the world became cheaper than that from area farmers. Yet this system is filled with contradictions and inequities (Badcock 1984; Harvey 1973, 1996; Gilbert and Gugler 1992). According to a growing number of scholars, urban areas must be understood as the result of class conflict (Harvey 1973; Heynen et al. 2006a,b; see also Gilbert and Guggler 1992). This process, which characterized the development of cities in what is now called the First World, is being repeated in the Third World; the same dynamics are at play as these parts of the world become part of the global economy. The increasingly crowded slums of the Third World, particularly in Asia and Africa, are likely to make urban living ever more precarious for their residents unless action is taken to avoid the experience of Latin America in the past fifty years (UN Population Fund 2007; Keiner et al. 2005).

THE ECOLOGY OF CITIES

The relationship of the physical environment and cities has been of interest from the beginning of social theory (Heynen et al. 2006b:4). For a long time the discussion emphasized the replacement of the natural environment for a "built" environment

(Bookchin 1979), whereas other scholars pointed out that urban environments "are as natural as colonies of prairie dogs or the beds of oysters" (Jacobs 1992:443, quoted in Heynen et al. 2006b:4). Indeed, contemporary scholars of the city point out that the social processes, material metabolism (Decker et al. 2000), and spatial form of the city develop from the complex, interrelated socioecological processes that occur within cities (i.e., from the political ecology of cities; Kaika 2005; Heynen et al. 2006b). This applies to biodiversity: a study of cities worldwide found that while substantial biodiversity was present in cities overall, most residents are concentrated in neighborhoods of impoverished biodiversity (W. Turner et al. 2004).

Interest in urban ecology was shaped by the Chicago school of urban ecologists and sociologists of the 1920s, led by Robert Park and Roderick McKenzie. Although there had been earlier efforts to correlate social variables and spatial distributions, the Chicago sociologists were the first to approach the topic with a systematic theory. The theory was borrowed from biology—particularly the notion of competitive cooperation. According to Park the subject of urban ecology (or human ecology as they called it) is competition for space leading to the formation of cooperative bonds or symbiotic relationships (Park et al. 1925). As these relationships changed over time and space, successional forces came into play, dominance changed, and groups invaded either unoccupied or deteriorated areas. Park saw the other aspects of society, the cultural, as superstructure resting on the biotic forces. Only the biotic level was seen as the proper object of urban ecological study (Theodorson 1961:40; Burgess and Bogue 1964: 2–14; Robson 1969; and Quinn 1940 for summaries of the work of the Chicago school). Park believed that the biological concepts of competition, dominance, invasion, and succession were applicable to the organization of cities and the behavior of urban populations.

Michelson (1976:17) notes that the Chicago urban ecologists had an incomplete conceptualization of the environment: they viewed it as a social medium rather than as a variable. Because the urban ecologists were fixed on the use of aggregate data, they treated urban dwellers as undifferentiated masses ruled by economic forces. Firey (1945), in contrast, pointed out that historical, cultural, symbolic, and sentimental aspects played a key role in explaining the evolution of Boston's Beacon Hill district.

Because the Chicago sociologists were concerned with the spatial aspects of the relationships between people and human institutions, they initially focused on rapid changes taking place in the city of Chicago (Burgess 1925). They found similarities in how Chicago grew. Park (1926) considered the social homogeneity of localities within cities that reflected language, culture, religion, and race as shaping urban residential differentiation. They highlighted competition for space as determinant, and over time observed a successional process that reflected the natural decay of areas and their replacement by new competitors. This reflected the dynamics of the time as successive waves of immigrants came from Europe between 1880 and 1920. Naturally the newest arrivals chose the cheapest housing close to the low-skill jobs they

FIGURE 10.2 Chicago's Millennium Park

Chicago's Millennium Park combines exciting architecture and contemporary art with green areas.
Photo by Anthony Cak.

aspired to (Badcock 1984:7). Wave upon wave of new immigrants displaced those
who had improved their condition and moved outward from the center, reflecting
occupational mobility and capital accumulation by each wave of immigrants. This
view was influential for decades in urban planning and city design.

However, a land economist in the 1930s began to question this concentric model
of city growth, suggesting instead that cities grow in an axial fashion (Hoyt 1939).
This pattern reflected the housing market and people's movement to better housing
as they grew more affluent, leaving the less desirable housing for those less fortunate,
all the way down the socioeconomic scale. This supply-side theory of Hoyt's was
confirmed later in a study of Edinburgh over a sixty-six-year period (Richardson et
al. 1974; Richardson 1973). A few years later scholars were able to show that the two
approaches are complementary: that socioeconomic status is a predominantly sec-
toral phenomenom, and family status predominantly zonal (Badcock 1984). Further, comparative research has shown that world regions vary in how well they

comply with the Burgess-Hoyt prediction of an outward gradient from the city center (Badcock 1984).

Urban health stresses have been the focus of some attention. Dubos (1968a:235) reminds us that human adaptation can surprise us by its shortsightedness: inhabitants of industrialized urban areas have been able to adapt, even cheerfully, to the polluted air. We know that the body adapts to pollutants by increasing mucous secretions and other inflammatory responses that protect the organism. However, constant exposure to these irritating substances leads to chronic pathological states such as emphysema, fibrosis, and other outcomes associated with aging (Dubos 1968a:236). In short, these adaptations mask the seriousness of the pollution and prevent the population from aggressively seeking to end it. Recent research suggests that surgery patients and heart attack survivors improve markedly when green surroundings are provided during recovery, and that significant physical and psychological benefits result from connections to green spaces (Bartlett 2005).

Studies of the complex biomedical interactions that affect the well-being of urban populations have taken place (MAB/UNESCO 1973), with nonconclusive results. In part, this results from the view that many of these pathologies are "normal" (see Schell and Ulijaszek 2007 for a synthesis of the health situation of urban populations in industrialized countries). We know that the sedentary urban lifestyle results in a greater incidence of diabetes, obesity, coronary heart disease, and dental caries (Durnin 1975:129), but we now see this pattern all over the world, even in rural areas due to greater reliance on machinery rather than physical strength in carrying out tasks. Greater income and an urban lifestyle tend to be associated with greater consumption of animal protein (Durnin 1975:130), which results in coronary heart disease. The impact on health seems to come mostly from work routines in which less time is spent buying, preparing, and eating food—with greater reliance going to snacks, processed food, and alcohol for calories. The fast pace of urban life results in unhealthy eating habits in which prepared foods with too much sugar, fat, and carbohydrates dominate. When these habits are combined with reliance on the automobile and sedentary habits such as watching television, the urban resident is likely to develop obesity and heart disease.

Obesity is one of the major disabilities connected with modern urban life (Lopez-Zetina et al. 2006). In America we see today a virtual epidemic of obesity and type 2 diabetes as a result of this combination of lack of exercise and overconsumption of food. Reducing the use of the automobile and creating more vibrant pedestrian-friendly cities will go a long way toward changing our current epidemic of declining health status (McGranahan et al. 2001). This conclusion was confirmed by a study of the association between vehicle miles traveled, physical inactivity, and obesity for Californians in thirty-three counties (Lopez-Zetina et al. 2006). The difference between Americans and Europeans in girth is evident to anyone traveling overseas. The difference is public transportation, "slower" food, and a greater sense of participation in building communities.

A number of issues have risen to the top of the agenda in urban ecology in recent years:

• The choice between compact but dense cities and the dispersed sprawl of so many areas, particularly in the United States
• The greening of cities, creating more forests, green spaces, and green roofs
• The need to reduce the number of cars and promote pedestrian traffic as a way to take people into the city center
• A more integrative view of cities linking the natural and the social spheres

SPATIAL ASPECTS OF THE CITY: COMPACT VERSUS SPRAWL PATTERNS

Historically, European cities have been more compact and dense than American cities. European cities have good public transit, are walkable, and are less reliant on the automobile (Beatley 2000). European cities have denser population concentration and redevelop existing urbanized areas more than their American counterparts. In Holland, with the highest population densities in the world, cities occupy only 13 percent of the land area. In less densely populated countries like Sweden, the urban area is only about 2 percent (Beatley 2000). In other words, European cities have grown in population since World War II but have maintained their compactness and density, as compared to their American counterparts (see Table 10.1).

The European Community remains committed to avoiding sprawl and recommends redeveloping existing urban areas. This compactness is accompanied by maintaining access to open spaces and natural landscapes within easy distance of the urban area. Stockholm residents can travel to the archipelago and other natural areas by public transportation in less than half an hour, and in Vienna it is but a short tram ride from the center of the city to 7,400 hectares of protected forests. One clear advantage of this compact pattern of urbanization is the much lower per capita energy use and lower carbon dioxide emissions for European cities as compared with American cities. In cities like Copenhagen, there has been a systematic effort to convert the city from dependence on the automobile to civic and pedestrian spaces in the core (Beatley 2000). One important part of this strategy has been maintaining a substantial residential population in the city center, building urban residences above commercial shops in order to maintain a vibrant city center—and not one that closes up at 5:00 PM as in many American cities, as does downtown Los Angeles. "Sprawl" was not always a bad thing. In the late nineteenth century, Americans chose to get away from densely settled urban areas as reformers encouraged the population to move out of the urban core to experience better sanitation, flowers, and green areas (Deverell and Hise 2005).

In Europe the public sector plays a much greater role in urban development. There is greater public sector financial investment, greater emphasis on redevelopment, and

TABLE 10.1 Land Use and Transportation Data for Selected Cities, 1990

	Car Use per Capita (km)	% of Total Passenger km on Transit	Urban Density (persons per ha)
Selected European Case Studies			
Amsterdam	3,977	17.7	48.8
Zürich	5,197	24.2	47.1
Stockholm	4,638	27.3	53.1
Vienna	3,964	31.6	68.3
Copenhagen	4,558	17.2	28.6
London	3,892	29.9	42.3
Selected American Cities			
Phoenix	11,608	0.8	10.5
Boston	10,280	3.5	12.0
Houston	13,016	1.1	9.5
Washington	12,013	4.6	13.7
Los Angeles	11,587	2.1	22.4
New York	8,317	10.8	19.2

Source: Adapted from Kenworthy et al., *Indicators of Transport Efficiency in 37 Global Cities: Report Prepared for the World Bank, October 1996*, in Timothy Beatley, *Green Urbanism* (Washington, DC: Island, 2000), p. 30. Copyright © 2000 by Island Press.

explicit attention to the safety of city dwellers—and much lower homicide rates than in the United States. Fear of assault plays a role in Americans' location and lifestyle choices, and without serious gun control and more effective policing of inner cities, sustainable, compact cities are not likely to develop in the United States. However, this process is taking place in a few American cities such as Seattle, which is working to provide housing for 72,000 new residents in the downtown area, more than doubling the resident population (Beatley 2000). Alongside this residential planning, there are parks, infrastructure, and pedestrian areas. Other cities are implementing smart growth initiatives that encourage future development to be more dense, and with amenities near the city center and transportation corridors—and discouraging growth toward sensitive lands and habitats.

Urban sprawl and **suburbanization** now encroach on rural areas as much as the expansion of agriculture does. Urban expansion impacts the rural hinterland surrounding it through water and air pollution, heat island effects, resource extraction, and changes in hydrology (Berry 1990; Meyer 1996). A study of Barcelona, Spain, confirmed the impact of sprawl on the environment (Muniz and Galindo 2005). The development of more compact urban areas would reduce emissions and allow more green space to be provided to urban citizens at close proximity to the city. American cities have many classic examples of urban sprawl, among them Atlanta (Bullard et al. 2000) and Los Angeles (Osri 2004; Deverell and Hise 2005). This sprawl is associated with ever more congested traffic, as illustrated in the view of Los Angeles in Figure 10.3.

REDUCING DEPENDENCE ON THE AUTOMOBILE

Cities have grown by accelerating economic activity and the circulation of capital, without giving much thought, until recently, to the costs of pollution. Although air

FIGURE 10.3 Los Angeles Traffic

American cities, like Los Angeles pictured here, have encouraged dependence on the automobile, a result of the sprawl promoted since the 1940s. *Source*: iStockphoto.

pollution is believed to contribute to lung cancer and other ills, studies suggest that this correlation may be exaggerated by the selection of extreme cases (Buck and Brown 1964). The higher lung cancer mortality rate in cities vis-à-vis rural areas may be due to higher cigarette smoking, occupational exposure, earlier diagnosis, and other factors (NRC 1981:121). However, there is little doubt that in cities where pollution cannot escape easily, such as Los Angeles, Phoenix, and Mexico City, the entrapped pollution under certain conditions brings about serious ailments. Solving the transportation conundrum is central to developing sustainable cities.

In Europe there is a concerted effort to reduce the use of automobiles in the city center. Since 2003 London has charged a substantial daily entry fee to vehicles, which has reduced the number of vehicles by 24 percent. In Stockholm, for example, 70 percent of trips during peak hours are taken in public transit. In other cities, a combination of public transit, pedestrian, and bicycle use account for up to 60 percent of traffic into downtown. In the United States, public transit accounts for as little as 2–5 percent of home-to-work traffic (Warren 1998; Safdie 1997). Only New York City and Chicago have substantial use of public transit. In Europe, public transit is viewed as a public good, an essential public service fundamental to public welfare (Bertolini and LeClercq 2003). All European cities are continuously improving and expanding the public transit system to encourage usage and facilitate the movement of people from outside the city center. The goal is to locate public transport within a few hundred meters of a person's location. Real-time reporting on when the next train, tram, or bus will arrive encourages riders.

Commercial activities are encouraged to locate along the public transit lines, and those that rely on cars are discouraged through the tax system. Alongside this positive development of trams and other public transit is the discouragement of automobiles by reducing the number of parking spaces in the city center and raising parking fees of remaining spaces—approved by public referendum in Zurich! Even the wealthiest residents of Zurich use public transporation because it is so effective and pleasant (Beatley 2000). Zurich has managed to break the vicious circle of building more roads, creating more traffic, and having to build more roads to deal with this increase. It has done so through the use of public referendums, proving that residents support public transit more strongly than government officials do and are less influenced by corporations and others who may put a lower priority on the public welfare.

In the United States there is a move toward light rail and other forms of public transit in cities like Portland, Sacramento, St. Louis, San Diego, and Dallas. There is a need to rethink our transportation ethos: stop relegating the old, the poor, and other second-class citizens to public transportation. Rather, public transit should be available to all as a preferred mode of transportation, and automobile users should be asked to pay for the real costs associated with roads and the pollution that their cars emit—to even the social costs of this form of transportation. Road users in the United States pay only 60 percent of the costs of road construction, maintenance, and law enforcement through taxes and user charges. In contrast, road user taxes in Europe exceed government expenditures, collecting nearly twice as much from road user taxes to ensure the quality of public transit and other societal needs. In fact, American road users are subsidized by the rest of society and thus have no reason to reduce their use of roads and autos (Pucher and Lefevre 1996). Many American cities make serious efforts to develop sustainable initiatives that are integrative (for example, Portland, San Francisco, Seattle), while others confine their interests to particular issues such as waste disposal and neighborhood beautification (for example, Cleveland, Boston, Orlando) and so do little to change the structure of the city (Portney 2003).

CITIES AND THE UPCOMING WATER CRISIS

An upcoming crisis for cities is access to water. For example, since 1949 Beijing's water consumption has risen 450 percent (Smil 1984:157). Beijing's water needs are expected to increase 6–7 billion cubic meters by 2000, or 50 percent above its local availability. Water could become a limiting factor to future urban growth. This demand for urban water use conflicts with water-intensive agricultural uses. In arid lands such as the American Southwest, a common solution is to take land out of agriculture to reduce consumption and increase the catchment area that recharges the aquifer. However, in many arid regions of the American Southwest, urban people try to maintain lawns and other turf grasses and numerous golf courses. A recent study noted that 75 percent of household water consumption comes from watering grassy areas (Milesi et al. 2005). This solution separates urban areas from food-producing areas, thereby increasing the energy and transportation costs of bringing vegetables and other perishable produce to urban consumers (Smil 1984:158).

Urban populations depend on freshwater from rivers, lakes, groundwater, and wetlands to maintain human activities. This includes short-term benefits such as food, flood control, purification of waste, and habitat for plants and animals (Baron et al. 2002). It is not just the amount of water, but its quality, timing, and temporal variability that matter to maintain ecological functions and ecosystem services (Baron et al. 2002). Ecological restoration of streams in cities is a high priority (Bernhardt and Palmer 2007), particularly given the ecological degradation of streams draining urban land (Walsh et al. 2005a). A particularly important approach is to redesign stormwater systems due to the imperviousness of the surface areas connected to the stream. Designs that are more distributed, that facilitate infiltration, evaporation, transpiration, and storage for later use, are seen as the way to restore streams to ecological health (Walsh et al. 2005b). Los Angeles is a classic case of the failure of engineering to contain nature. Osri (2004) showed that despite the city's 114 debris dams, 5 flood control basins, and nearly 500 miles of paved river channels, residents still experience flooding disasters with high frequency, as much or more than if they had left the system in its natural form (see also Wolch 2007).

Urban areas consume large amounts of water, second only to agriculture (Milesi et al. 2005). Efforts to green urban areas will need to avoid increasing water consumption (Mathieu et al. 2007). Jenerette and colleagues (2006) propose the use of "water footprint" methodology (as a modified form of the ecological footprint methodology) to achieve a sustainable rate of water withdrawal from the integrated system. In Europe many urban redevelopment projects include elements to increase rainwater collection and use, recycle gray water, and conserve water and increase drainage through desealing surfaces to improve natural drainage (Beatley 2000). Berlin has been removing concrete and paved surfaces to improve drainage and planting vegetation in its place. Wolch (2007) notes efforts along the Los Angeles River to change the river from a drainage canal dominated by cement to one with more natural areas. In the Netherlands, there is a strong promotion of natural drainage ditches (or wadis) to replace conventional storm sewers, and the use of permeable bricks that help water percolate into the ground and roofs that direct water to these permeable surfaces (Beatley 2000). A study of Madison, Wisconsin, found that lower density single-family residential areas were associated with larger areas of impervious surface per unit of occupancy, as compared to higher density areas (Stone 2004). This confirms the view noted earlier, that higher density urbanization can result in more land area remaining green and a higher proportion of surfaces capable of infiltrating precipitation and runoff, and maintaining higher stream quality.

Greenroofs or ecoroofs have become increasingly common in Europe, especially Germany and the Netherlands. German studies have shown that these greenroofs contain considerable biodiversity (Mann 1996; Beatley 2000). Design of greenroofs can be sensitive to their need for water, for example, sloping them so that excess water can drain to other parts of the greenroof. Another way to green the city is to build greenwalls, using Virginia creeper and wisteria. In the United States it is common to view ivy and other clinging plants as destructive of building facades, whereas these greenwalls offer many benefits: providing shading and cooling during summer and insulation in winter (as much as 30 percent, according to Johnston and Newton 1997), and protection against chemical weathering. Greenwalls also filter air pollutants, reduce noise levels, and provide humidification. The choice of climber is important depending on aspect and climatic conditions, and the building surface must be intact. In European cities they are also seen as a way to prevent graffiti, pervasively visible in urban building surfaces (Beatley 2000). (See Figure 10.4.)

Urban gardens also offer important green spaces. In a study of different cities in the United Kingdom, researchers found that domestic gardens covered from 21.8 percent to 26.8 percent of the urban area of each city (Loram et al. 2007). Moreover, they found that 99 percent of the houses sampled had gardens, which varied in size from 155 square meters to 253 square meters and offered important wildlife habitat for a variety of species (Loram et al. 2007; see also Smith et al. 2005 for another study of urban domestic gardens in the United Kingdom and their relation to the landscape).

FIGURE 10.4 Solar Panels on an Urban Home

A combination of solar panels and greenwalls and green spaces can reduce the impact of urban living on the natural environment. Photo by Andy Nowack. *Source*: iStockphoto.

AN INTEGRATIVE VIEW OF THE URBAN ECOSYSTEM

In the past three decades a more holistic view of urban environments as ecosystems has emerged (Berkowitz et al. 2003). The science of landscape ecology offers a spatially explicit perspective to urban ecosystem studies (Forman and Godron 1986). Barrett and colleagues (1997:534) have proposed a host-parasite analogy to describe the relationship between the heterotrophic urban area and the productive agricultural and natural landscape elements in which it is embedded. This view maintains a separation between rural and urban landscapes that is no longer tenable. Rural households include members who participate in urban life through schooling, banking, trading, and not infrequently through temporary, seasonal, and permanent residence. **Telecommuting** has further eroded the distance between the rural and the urban, as a growing number of people choose to leave the density of cities to live in rural settings, thereby linking the two in bonds of mutual interdependence. Even without telecommuting, a growing number of urbanites seek access to rural properties to escape growing urban disamenities like pollution, crime, and noise, and solace from the uncertainties of a global economy undergoing transformation and creating job insecurity. Households are urban in terms of their lifestyle, goals, and decisions, but they also represent dimensions of a process of **counterurbanization** already visible in several developed countries (Berry 1990:116). Relations between rural and urban components are dynamic; they take on different characteristics over time, and the city can be both a parasite and a positive force in reconstructing a degraded rural landscape (see McDonnell and Pickett 1990). This more dynamic perspective offers students of the environmental social sciences a ripe field of study. An emphasis on material cycling is also an important perspective given that millions of tons of raw materials are used each year to build or redevelop the built environment of cities (Graham 2002).

Urban areas and their surrounding rural landscapes represent a complex pattern of human-environmental systems open to continuous change. The rapidity and scale of land use change associated with urban growth presents a unique opportunity to investigate interrelationships between urban land use processes and ecosystem dynamics. Land use processes, which are driven by socioeconomic, institutional, and cultural factors, influence natural ecosystem dynamics through events and activities that can be identified, monitored, and predicted (Haughton and Hunter 2003).

Human actions are expressed through a system of urban land uses. One way to proceed in the study of urban ecology is to examine salient aspects of land use that offer potential for investigating human-ecological interactions, for example, type and density of land use, land-use succession, scale, location, and pattern of development. A study by the Baltimore LTER found that hydrological changes associated with urbanization created riparian drought by lowering water tables, which in turn altered soil, vegetation, and microbial processes (Groffman et al. 2003). Type of activity (agricultural, residential, commercial, industrial, open space) can be described by variation in density. Land use succession provides a way to address the phenomenon of increased intensity of urban use as the urban area grows and encroaches on previously rural land, and as older urban areas change in character over time. A study of the Pearl River delta region of China suggests that this conversion is driven by the high returns from built-up land vis-à-vis the returns from farmland and forested lands (30 times higher return) (Dai et al. 2005). However, in Europe farmers have developed agrotourism and other strategies to increase the economic return of their farmland, producing high quality organic foods and linking consumers to farmers in personal bonds of trust and reciprocity (Holloway et al. 2006).

Residential use may displace small agricultural producers or open space, while commercial land use may outbid urban residences for desirable urban locations. Scale of change is associated with migration into cities, rapid development, and new regional roles that lead to changes in scale or at a given sector. Given the need for environmental social science to be spatially explicit, location is an important dimension in urban ecology. Contagion and other approaches to proximity analysis can be used to understand how adjacent development affects areas such as parks and rural areas (Attwell 2000; Bryant 2006).

The pattern of development can describe variations in the clustering or dispersed nature of structures and their relations to roads and other types of infrastructure.

There are choices to be made between high density urban dwellings and dispersed ones, notions of status and how it is displayed, and patterns of crime and social control that lead to suburban flight from the urban core area. How different households respond to urban growth is a dynamic, complex process that takes multiple forms and affects different social groups in diverse ways.

Studies in urban ecology have come up with surprising findings, such as those near New York City that found exotic earthworm species in forested lands near the city, higher levels of nitrogen deposition, and higher nitrogen turnover than in forests in rural areas (Cadenasso et al. 2006). There has been a growing interest in the biodiversity in and around cities (Adams et al. 2005). Part of the richness of some urban areas derives from the patchy or mosaic nature of habitats, their varying size, shape, and character (Young and Jarvis 2001). These mosaics of habitats can improve quality of life in the city and serve important educational functions (Savard et al. 2000). The engagement of local institutions and user groups ensures the protection of green areas and their biodiversity, as for example in the case of Stockholm's National Urban Park (Barthel et al. 2005). Grimm and colleagues (2000) as well as Pickett et al. (2001) have noted that urban ecosystems are strikingly heterogeneous and scale dependent, and can provide habitats for a rich variety of species. These urban ecosystem dynamics have become better understood thanks to the focused work of urban long-term ecological research sites (Redman et al. 2004), discussed in the next section.

THE URBAN LTERS

The first two urban LTER projects started in 1997 with support from the National Science Foundation: a study of the Baltimore watershed and a study of the central Arizona region around Phoenix (Luck and Wu 2002; Kinzig et al. 2005; Keys et al. 2007). The latter represents urban areas characterized by rapidly growing young cities in arid and semiarid ecosystems. The emphasis in these systems is not on redevelopment of the inner city—as it might be in older urban areas like Baltimore—but on rapid conversion of agricultural and natural open spaces into suburbanization (Keys et al. 2007). Accelerated urbanization in Phoenix has increased the fragmentation and structural complexity of the desert landscape (Jenerette and Wu 2001). Plant diversity in Phoenix varies by neighborhood, with higher plant diversity in wealthier neighborhoods due to exotics contained in home gardens, thereby increasing variation in plant genetic composition (Hope et al. 2006). These studies bring to bear the full panoply of bioecological measurements, including primary production, population and community characteristics (human and nonhuman), storage and dynamics of carbon and organic matter, energy and materials flow, patterns of disturbance (redevelopment, fire, flood), and succession (see Grove et al. 2006a for the methods used in studying vegetation in the Baltimore LTER). Socioeconomic dimensions are studied, in particular the process of how land use decisions feed back into shaping ecological characteristics such as species abundance and distribution, hydrology, land cover, and patchiness. In Baltimore, Grove and colleagues (2006b) found that lifestyle behavior was the best predictor of vegetation cover on private lands (and not simply income and education).

Given that cities in the desert Southwest such as Tucson and Phoenix are growing in excess of 10 percent per year, understanding the multiple effects these migrants have on the ecological patchiness of this water-limited ecosystem is of considerable interest to the future of desert metropolitan areas, as well as to an understanding of the process of human impacts as a whole. For example, by bringing water from the Colorado River and by using urban irrigation to construct a culturally desirable landscape of plants and flowers around homes, urbanites and suburbanites have increased the populations of plants (and land cover) and the insects and anthropods that make their homes in the plants. The counterintuitive outcome that species diversity would increase with urbanization is interesting in itself, and raises many other questions about human impacts in desert ecosystems.

The new urban ecology represented by the urban LTERs of Phoenix and Baltimore go beyond accounting for the flow of energy and materials by undertaking spatially explicit analysis using GIS data layers. These data layers are then incorporated into hierarchical models at distinct spatial scales. At local scales, patch models relate patch characteristics, (such as size, shape, and boundary conditions of ecological variables) to each other in statistical fashion. These are used to parameterize coarser scale models at the landscape level. At a landscape scale, models can be built that include multiple patch types that differ in species composition, density, and other features. These can be further upscaled to regional scale models of the entire rural-urban area around Phoenix, for example, and consider explicitly the spatial heterogeneity of processes across different scales of space and time. Readers may wish to check in at the Phoenix website for research updates and progress in this urban LTER: www.caplter.asu.

Research in LTERs has advanced our modeling approaches by pointing out that existing models, based largely on unmanaged and agricultural ecosystems, work poorly in urban ecosystems. Urban ecosystem models need to consider human biogeochemical controls such as impervious surface proliferation, engineered aqueous flow paths, landscaping choices, and human demographic trends to adequately represent the stocks and flows of the urban systems (Kaye et al. 2006). Some research has used complexity theory to point out that urban ecosystems have emergent properties and derive from local-scale and dynamic interactions between the physical world and the socioeconomic systems (Alberti et al. 2003).

FINAL REMARKS

In contrast to 1975, when only 37 percent of the world's population lived in urban settlements, as of 2005 over 50 percent of the population lived in urban areas (Lima Bezerra and Fernandes 2000:39). There are notable regional differences. In Latin

America, the urban population was already 61 percent in 1975 and 77 percent in 2000; Brazil is over 81 percent urban (Lima Bezerra and Fernandes 2000:39). The challenge will be even greater in high-growth areas, especially China, India, Indonesia, and Pakistan. In China, new cities are being built each year (Seto 2005). Cities like Bombay, Delhi, Peking, Calcutta, and Karachi are currently unable to provide adequate infrastructure for their vast populations. African cities are projected to experience explosive growth in the next two decades (UN Population Fund 2007). The risk, of course, is that cities will become increasingly vulnerable to unhealthy conditions, crime, and destruction of natural resources and cultural patrimony, which will undermine social well-being. This becomes even more likely with the prospect of global warming and climate change (Bulkeley and Betsill 2003).

Urban areas will need to overcome the natural physical degradation associated with rapid growth and crowding, as well as the social injustices associated with distancing between residents of urban areas. For decades vast numbers of people have lived in squalor in slums, while others live with an excess of material goods in palatial homes. In Rio de Janeiro and São Paulo, for example, the poor constitute 84 percent and 63 percent of the urban population respectively (Lima Bezerra and Fernandes 2000:44). Contemporary cities are increasingly characterized by illegal occupation of public lands for human settlements, a reduction of green areas, growing impermeabilization of the surface through paving and construction, a mismatch between the number of vehicles and the road infrastructure in place, difficulties in managing urban garbage, inadequate systems of removing waste water and human waste from the urban area and maintaining water quality, air and water pollution, and rising crime. European cities offer examples of how to address these challenges and maintain a high quality of life with less dependence on the automobile, greener cities, and less sprawl.

More hopeful is the situation of small and medium-size urban areas, if they can avoid the mistakes made by the large metropolises. The temptation to grow is enormous, despite the evident problems that it brings. Small urban areas have lost population to large metropolises in many cases due to limited employment opportunities, but in some areas they have begun modest growth attracting people from large cities with the promise of cleaner air, less crime, and greater well-being. In a world increasingly connected by computers, those with careers that permit them to work from home (telecommuting) are choosing to reside in small urban areas with a high quality of life, like college towns. If employers become comfortable with this solution, it may provide relief from the pressure to move to large cities. However, this solution still leaves those whose work is not information-driven in the overcrowded cities with few options.

The adaptability of our species to life in an increasingly urban world should inspire more research. Air and water pollution are no less challenging to our species than cold or low biological productivity. Crime, crowding, and traffic jams are no less important in how we choose our settlements or location than is proximity to good soils. The complexity of urban ecosystems has in the past discouraged ecological scientists, who preferred to measure "natural" systems to the human constructed urban ones. This neglect shows signs of ending with the development of urban LTERs. We now recognize that even natural systems were hardly ever pristine and that the human imprint on all of the earth's systems is far from negligible. Our cities are embedded in the natural systems and have a direct impact on those systems.

A synthesis of the past, present, and future of human adaptability research concluded that there are a number of important new directions (Ulijaszek and Huss-Ashmore 1997). Among the major questions for the future: What are the limits of our flexibility as a species? What are the effects of perception and cognition on adaptability? And what changes in the twenty-first century will most significantly impact our species? Addressing these questions will require researchers to broaden their perspective beyond biological considerations and socioeconomic surveys to include concerns about meaning, perception of resources, and modern economics. New perspectives will have to include concern with the social and psychological concerns of populations and not merely their fitness. Research will need to be multiscale, linking households to communities and national and international considerations. The goals of research must be examined critically, with due consideration for the relevance of the research and a more activist stand by researchers and their responsibility to the study community. This will mean a more active role, and participation, by the local community in the research—and empowering them with research skills and data so that they can make active use of it for their own purposes. The question, Who benefits from the research that you are carrying out? is commonly asked of researchers—and rightly so. Understanding human adaptability to a changing environment matters to our quality of life and well-being. It represents a quest in which we are all jointly engaged in as a species living in local and increasingly urban communities, and as members of the global human family.

SUGGESTED READINGS AND USEFUL WEBSITES

Urban ecology and sustainability have been the focus of several research centers and institutes affiliated with academic institutions. The Center for Urban and Regional Ecology at Georgia Institute of Technology (www.cure.gatech.edu) is affiliated with several other universities in Georgia (University of Georgia, Georgia State University).

The Center for Urban Restoration Ecology (www.i-cure.org), a collaboration between Rutgers University and the Brooklyn Botanical Garden, is working to restore previously used urban areas, such as landfills and former industrial sites. Restoration and urban ecology also are emphasized at the Restoration Institute at Clemson University (http://restoration.clemson.edu/htm/urban_ecology.htm; also see http://restoration.clemson.edu). Urban Ecology at the Campus and Community Ecology at Washington State University (www.campusecology.wsu.edu/index.htm) specifically focuses on campus sustainability. Also see their Urban Ecology page here: www.campusecology.wsu.edu/page_012.htm.

Books exploring urban development and sustainability include *Urban Place: Reconnecting with the Natural World* by Bartlett (2005); *Nature of Cities: Ecocriticism and Urban Environments* edited by Bennett and Teague (1999); *The Ecology of Place: Planning for Environment, Economy, and Community* by Beatley and Manning (1997); and *People in Cities: The Urban Environment and Its Effects* by Krupat (1985). The book *The Politics of Air Pollution: Urban Growth, Ecological Modernization, and Symbolic Inclusion* by Gonzalez (2006) specifically discusses the role of pollution in urban development, while the book *In the Nature of Cities: Urban Political Ecology and the Politics of Urban Metabolism* edited by Heynen et al. (2006b) looks at the interconnections between social, economic, political, and environmental factors in urban areas. Also see the book *Urban Ecosystems: A New Frontier for Science and Education* edited by Berkowitz et al. (2003) for information on the role of urban systems in environmental science and education.

Sustainability research and education is also the primary focus of the Center for Urban Ecology and Sustainability at the University of Minnesota (www.entomology .umn.edu/cues), while the Urban Ecology Institute, affiliated with Boston College (www.bc.edu/bc_org/research/urbaneco; www.urbaneco.org), educates students to increase their understanding of urban ecology and sustainability. This institute also works with other research centers at universities and colleges in the Boston area, such as the Center for the Environment at Mount Holyoke College (www.mtholyoke .edu/ce). Also see the Hixon Center for Urban Ecology at Yale University (www.yale .edu/hixon) and the Program in Urban Ecology at the Ecological Research Center of the University of Memphis (http://cas.memphis.edu/erc/pue/index.htm). In Canada, the Institute of Urban Ecology at Douglas College in British Columbia (www.douglas .bc.ca/iue) also works on education and community programs to maintain biodiversity in urban environments.

More general books on urban sustainability include *Cities and Climate Change: Urban Sustainability and Global Environmental Governance* by Bulkeley and Betsill (2003); *Sustainable Cities and Energy Policies* by Capello et al. (1999); and *Ecological City: Preserving and Restoring Urban Biodiversity* edited by Platt et al. (1994). Sustainability in New Orleans has been the focus of several books, especially following Hurricane Katrina, including *An Unnatural Metropolis: Wresting New Orleans from Nature* by Colten (2005) and *River and Its City: The Nature of Landscape in New Orleans* by Kelman (2003). The books *Land of Sunshine: An Environmental History of Metropolitan Los Angeles* edited by Deverell and Hise (2005); and *Hazardous Metropolis: Flooding and Urban Ecology in Los Angeles* by Osri (2004) specifically explore urban ecology and sustainability in Los Angeles, while *Concrete and Clay: Reworking Nature in New York City* by Gandy (2002) discusses urban issues in New York City; and *Shock Cities: The Environmental Transformation and Reform of Manchester and Chicago* by Platt (2004) explores environmental topics in Chicago and Manchester, UK.

Urban ecology and sustainability has been a funding priority through the NSF Program of Integrative Graduate Education and Research Training (IGERT, www.igert.org/index.asp) at several American universities, including the University of Washington (www.urbanecology.washington.edu) and Arizona State University (http://sustainability.asu.edu/igert). Other IGERT programs that deal with issues in urban ecology include the Sustainable Futures program at Michigan Technological University and Southern University at Baton Rouge, LA (www.sustainablefutures .mtu.edu/IGERT), the Water in the Urban Environment program at the University of Maryland (www.umbc.edu/cuere/igert), the Population and Environment program at the University of North Carolina-Chapel Hill (www.cpc.unc.edu/training/ igert_announce.html), and the Urban Environmental Sustainability program at the University of Southern California (www.cfr.washington.edu/research.urbaneco).

Some useful books discussing urban ecology include *Urban Ecology: An International Perspective on the Interaction Between Humans and Nature* by Marzluff et al. (in press); *Urban Ecology* by D. P. Smith (2007); *Urban Ecology* by Breuse et al. (1998); and *Urban Ecology as the Basis of Urban Planning* by Sukopp et al. (1995). Also see the papers "Future Directions in Urban Ecology" by Shochat et al. (2006a) and "Urban Ecology and Special Features of Urban Ecosystems" by Rebele (1994). Wildlife management in urban areas is discussed in *Urban Wildlife Management* by Adams et al. (2005), while the books *Urban Forestry: Planning and Managing Urban Greenspaces* by Miller (1997); and *Urban Forest Landscapes: Integrating Multidisciplinary Perspectives* by Bradley (1995) discuss management of forests in urban areas. Additional useful management and planning books are *Urban Environmental Planning: Policies, Instruments, and Methods in an International Perspective* edited by Miller and de Roo (2005); and *Sustainable Urban Design: An Environmental Approach* edited by Thomas (2003).

The University of Washington also is home to several research centers and programs dedicated to urban ecology and sustainability, including the Urban Ecology Research Laboratory (www.urbaneco.washington.edu) and the Urban Ecology Lab for Urban Design and Planning (www.caup.washington.edu/udp/urbanecology.html).

Sustainability in urban areas of the developing world is the subject of focus for several books, including *Managing Urban Futures: Sustainability and Urban Growth in Developing Countries* edited by Keiner et al. (2005); *Environmental Strategies for Sustainable Development in Urban Areas: Lessons from Africa and Latin America* edited by Fernandes (1998); *Rapid Urban Environmental Assessment: Lessons from Cities in the Developing World: Methodology and Preliminary Findings,* vol. 1, by Leitmann (1994); and *Consuming Cities: Urban Environment in the Global Economy after the Rio Declaration* by Low et al. (1999).

The Urban Ecology Collaborative is a database and resource network for urban ecology information in several cities (www.urbanecologycollaborative.org/uec). The Urban Forestry South Expo (www.urbanforestrysouth.org) specifically addresses forest resources in urban environments of the southern United States. Urban ecology also comprises several sites within the Long-Term Ecological Research (LTER) network, including the Central Arizona-Phoenix LTER (http://caplter.asu.edu/home/

index.jsp) and the Baltimore Ecosystem Study (www.beslter.org). Also see the website of urban ecology at the Institute of Ecosystem Studies (www.ecostudies.org/IES _urban_ecology.html, www.ecostudies.org). For the Washington, DC, area, the National Park Service (NPS) established the Center for Urban Ecology, detailing natural resource needs in and around the Washington, DC, area (www.nps.gov/cue). They also published an Urban Ecology book series in the 1970s about the ecology and urban development of the Washington, DC, region (www.nps.gov/history/ history/online_books/urban/index.htm).

Within architecture and urban planning, sustainability has been a driving goal of various research programs and centers, including the Urban Ecology Studio at Columbia University, a research and training site for architects and engineers in developing sustainable cities (www.seas.columbia.edu/earth/studio/default.htm), Urban Ecology (www.urbanecology.org), a nonprofit group of architects for developing sustainable urban planning, the Yale School of Forestry and Environmental Design at Yale University (http://environment.yale.edu/index.html), including the program in Urban Ecology and Environmental Design (http://environment.yale.edu/doc/554/ urban_ecology_and_environmental_design), and Ecology and Urban Planning, University of Helsinki, Finland (www.helsinki.fi/~niemela/ECOPLAN.html), which seeks to integrate ecological knowledge into urban planning. The UrbanSim website describes this new modeling software for sustainable urban planning and management (www.urbansim.org).

Several books that discuss urban sustainability in light of urban and municipal planning include *Urbanism, Health, and Human Biology in Industrialized Countries* edited by Schell and Ulijaszek (2007); *Cities and the Environment: New Approaches for Eco-Societies* edited by Inoguchi et al. (2005); *Ecological Networks and Greenways: Concept, Design, Implementation* edited by Jongman and Pungetti (2004); *Taking Sustainable Cities Seriously: Economic Development, the Environment, and Quality of Life in American Cities* by Portney (2003); *Eco-City Dimensions: Healthy Communities, Healthy Planet* by Roseland (1997); and *Landscape Ecology Principles in Landscape Architecture and Land-Use Planning* by Forman et al. (1996). Also see the paper "Ecological Urban Dynamics: The Convergence of Spatial Modeling and Sustainability" by Deal (2001) for more information on modeling sustainability in urban systems.

Books on sustainability and development in cities include *Evaluating Sustainable Development* by Brandon and Lombardi (2005); *Ecology and Economics: New Frontiers and Sustainable Development* edited by Barbier (2004); *Cities and Natural Process: A Basis for Sustainability* by Hough (2004); *Sustainable Cities* by Haughton and Hunter (2003); and *How Green Is the City? Sustainability Assessment and the Management of Urban Environments* edited by Devuyst et al. (2001). Also see the article "Bridging the Divide in Urban Sustainability: From Human Exemptionalism to the New Ecological Paradigm" by McDonald and Patterson (2007).

In the United Kingdom, the Trust for Urban Ecology serves as a nonprofit organization for creating new nature parks (www.urbanecology.org.uk), while the website of

Urban Nature: Ecology of the Living City at the University of Salford, UK, describes this research group dedicated to understanding the interaction between people and their built environment (www.els.salford.ac.uk/urbannature/index.htm). The Centre for Urban Regional Ecology (CURE) at the University of Manchester also deals with urban ecology (www.sed.manchester.ac.uk/research/cure). Urban ecology is a focus of research and education at Lincoln University in New Zealand (www.lincoln .ac.nz/story10335.html) and within a graduate and postgraduate research program for training on urban ecology at the University of Berlin in Germany: Perspectives on Urban Ecology Phase I (www.stadtoekologie-berlin.de/phase1/index_e.html), Perspectives on Urban Ecology Phase II: Shrinking Cities (www.stadtoekologie -berlin.de; English version: www.stadtoekologie-berlin.de/Englisch/index_e.html). Other urban ecological research think tanks in Germany are included as part of the Goethe Institute of German Think Tanks (www.goethe.de/wis/fut/prj/for/nch/ enindex.htm).

Also see the website of the Australian Research Centre for Urban Ecology (http://arcue.botany.unimelb.edu.au) and the CSIRO Sustainable Ecosystems (www.cse.csiro.au/research/urbanecosystems.htm; also www.cse.csiro.au/research/ urban) for information about urban ecology in Australia. At the United Nations (UN), the United Nations Education, Scientific, and Cultural Organization (UNESCO) Man and Urban Biology Group addresses urban ecosystems research (www.unesco.org/mab/ecosyst/urban.shtml), along with the UN Environment Program's (UNEP) World Conservation Monitoring Centre (www.unep-wcmc.org).

The page on Ecosustainable Links (www.ecosustainable.com.au/links.htm) at the Ecosustainable Hub (www.ecosustainable.com.au) lists websites for organizations, government agencies, research centers, and other programs on urban sustainability. The National Water Quality Assessment Program of the USGS Portal for Urban Ecology Studies (http://co.water.usgs.gov/nawqa/urbanPortal/html/ecology_urban .html) also lists resources about the aquatic environment in urban areas.

Water resources and availability are an increasing issue in urban development. Books that discuss water resources include *Integrated Urban Water Resources Management* edited by Hlavinek et al. (2006); *Urban Groundwater Management and Sustainability* by Tellam et al. (2006); and *Land Use: The Interaction of Economics, Ecology, and Hydrology* by O'Callaghan (1996).

GLOSSARY

Adaptation, Genetic or Evolutionary: Changes at the population level due to changes in gene frequencies that confer reproductive advantage to the population in a particular environment.

Adaptive Strategy: Conscious or unconscious, explicit or implicit plans of action carried out by a population in response to either external or internal conditions.

Adjustment, Acclimatory: Modest, reversible physiological adjustments to an environmental change or stress.

Adjustment, Cultural: The learned knowledge that people acquire as members of society. It is their most important means of coping as a species. Cultural adjustments permit the human species to respond quickly to changes in the environment.

Adjustment, Developmental: Nonreversible physiological and morphological changes resulting from organismic adaptation to environmental conditions during the individual's growth and development.

Adjustment, Regulatory: An organism's relatively rapid physiological and behavioral responses to changes in its environment.

Adobe: Building material formed from natural clays, sun-dried, and used in construction.

Advanced Very High Resolution Radiometer (AVHRR): A sensor in NOAA's weather satellites that covers the entire earth twice each day (temporal resolution of 12 hours) and that yields data with a spatial resolution of 1.1 by 1.1 kilometer. It is widely used for weather forecasting and for globally scaled analyses such as El Niño forecasts, famine early-warning systems, and applications require that scale of temporal or spatial resolution.

Affinal Relations: Kinship relations created by marriage.

Age-Area Concept: A notion developed by C. Wissler to arrive at the relative age of a cultural trait from its spatial distribution. Traits found at the edge of an area would be the oldest since they had diffused farthest from their origin.

Age Distribution: The proportion of a population found in each age class.

Albedo: Reflection of solar light from a surface of the earth.

Alfisols: *See* Soils.

Allele: Abbreviation for allelomorph. Refers to any one of the alternative forms of a gene.

Alluvial Fans: Deposits of sandy, loamy, or other light soils carried from their point of origin by water runoff and deposited in lower level, flat fans as the water is slowed down.

Amino Acid: Building units from which proteins are constructed. Twenty-two amino acids have been conclusively demonstrated to be constituents of plant proteins.

Anemia: A blood condition characterized by a decrease in the number of circulating red blood cells, hemoglobin, or both. Anemia may result from a variety of causes: deficient dietary iron, hemorrhage, lack of vitamin B_{12}, or intestinal diseases.

Aquifer: A stratum of rock able to hold water in its mass (for example, chalk, limestone, and sandstone). Aquifers get charged with water by exposure at some point to the ground surface—near a range of hills, for example.

Aridisols: *See* Soils.

Arterial (Blood) Pressure: A measurement of the force of the blood on the arterial walls as it leaves the heart. May be increased by movement to higher altitudes, reduction of arterial dimensions by deposits of fatty materials, or changes in blood viscosity.

Basal Area: The cross-sectional area of a tree trunk measured at a standardized DBH. It is usually represented by the area of the trunk in relation to another area. Total basal area is usually reported in square meters per hectare or as square centimeters per square meter. Basal area can be calculated for individual trees, individuals of a species, size classes, or the whole community of tree individuals.

Basal Metabolic Rate (BMR): The amount of energy needed to maintain body functions when a person is at digestive, physical, and emotional rest. BMR is expressed as calories per square meter of body surface per hour.

Bergmann's Rule: Describes body size increase in mammals, as environmental temperature decreases. Based on the relation between body volume and surface area.

Bilateral Descent: Reckoning descent through both mother and father.

Biomass: Total mass of living organisms present at a given moment in a population or area. It may be expressed in terms of kilocalories or in weight units per unit area. It may also refer to a portion of the total biomass, as in plant biomass, domestic livestock biomass, and so on.

Biome: A broad ecological unit, characterized by a set of climatic parameters and types of floral and faunal associations. The term is sometimes used to refer to distinctive life zones.

Biota: The flora and fauna of a region or ecosystem.

Biotic Community: The biological components in a given ecosystem, which are mutually interdependent and sustaining and which transfer, utilize, and give off energy.

Birth Rate: Number of births per 1,000 persons per year.

Body Core, Body Shell: Terms used in studies of human thermoregulation. The core is the internal part of the body and consists of the brain, lungs, heart, liver, and viscera. The shell is said to be the skin, muscles, subcutaneous fat, and extremities. Core temperature is measured rectally, while shell temperature is measured at the skin.

Brown Adipose Tissue: The primary tissue responsible for chemical heat production or nonshivering thermogenesis. It is found only in mammals and primarily in the cervical, interscapular, axillary, and abdominal regions.

Capillary: One of the microscopic blood vessels that join the arterial to the venous blood supply.

Carbohydrate: Compounds of carbon, hydrogen, and oxygen that form one of the three major groups of organic substances of which living matter is composed. (The others are proteins and fats.)

Carnivore: Meat-eating animals. Sometimes they are referred to as second- or third-order consumers.

Carrying Capacity: The number of individuals a habitat can support. *See* Population Pressure.

Cation Exchange Capacity: The sum total of exchangeable cations that a soil can absorb. Cation absorption refers to the adhesion of substances to the surfaces of solids (especially colloids). It may be referred to also as total exchange capacity or base-exchange capacity. It is expressed in milliequivalents per 100 grams of soil. *See also* Ion.

Circadian Rhythm: Daily rhythm that characterizes a species. The rhythm is set by environmental synchronizers among which light is the most important.

Circannual Rhythm: Yearly biological rhythm that reflects seasonal changes in the environment. Light, temperature, social interaction, and other factors may be implicated in these annual biological fluctuations in an organism.

Climax Community: The plant community that is at the end of secondary succession. The dominant plants of the climax bring about no further modifications in the physical environment and are said to be in equilibrium with prevailing conditions. Nonequilibrium and chaos theory have led to a critique of concepts like climax, viewed as emphasizing stasis and equilibrium.

Closed System: One that is bounded for heuristic reasons and treated as if it were not affected by forces outside the system. A closed system is maintained by internal cycling and negative feedback.

Colloid: Refers to both organic and inorganic matter characterized by small particle size and large surface/mass ratio.

Comparative Approach: An approach to the study of human societies in which a sample of societies or features of each are compared. It is evolutionist in its objectives and, through the use of the human relation area files, increasingly quantitative.

Consanguineal Relations: Relations based on common biological descent only, as in parental or sibling relationships.

Constraints: Intervening variables, present in the environment, that may alter the effects of a process, flow, or state. The effect may be positive or negative, but it is commonly used synonomously with limiting factors.

Consumers: Organisms that eat plants (for example, herbivores) and other animals (for example, carnivores) to survive. Consumers are dependent on producers to convert dispersed solar energy into biomass energy.

Correlation: The degree to which statistical variables vary together. It is measured by the correlation coefficient, which has a value from zero (that is, no correlation between the variables) to plus or minus one (that is, perfect positive or negative correlation between the variables).

Counterurbanization: The process of people leaving their urban residence in favor of less dense settlements in suburban and rural areas, including a return to growing their own food (but not necessarily).

Cultivators: Populations that rely on agriculture for subsistence.

Cultural Ecology: The study of how human adaptation to the environment takes place by way of cultural mechanisms. Defined by Julian Steward in very specific ways; see discussion in Chapter 2.

Culture: Learned knowledge, used to interpret experience and to generate behavior. It is the primary means of adaptation for *Homo sapiens*.

Cushion Plants: Plant forms common in cold, dry, or frost-prone areas. Plants are low and compact, with growth organs below or near ground level. This form minimizes exposure, maintains internal warmth, and preserves moisture.

Cybernetic System: A system that maintains control and adaptability by the process of information feedback.

Death Rate: Number of deaths per 1,000 persons per year.

Decomposers: Microscopic fungi and bacteria that reduce dead organic material to its elemental forms, thus making possible the cycling of matter.

Decomposition: Metabolic breakdown of organic materials. The result is heat energy and both simple organic and inorganic compounds.

Desert: Areas of less than 100 millimeters of rainfall per year, which usually lie in latitudes exposed to drying trade winds, subtropical high pressure belts, on lee side of mountains, or near cold ocean currents. Their primary productivity is low; they have little ground cover and high surface evaporation.

Determinism: A theoretical stance that is reductionist in its approach and seeks basic causes for phenomena. Environmental or geographic determinism was an important intellectual tradition up to and into the twentieth century. Current efforts at explanation opt for a more probabilistic (as opposed to an absolute) approach.

Diachronic: Refers to studies with a historical or evolutionary time dimension.

DBH (Diameter at Breast Height): A basic measurement of tree vegetation. It is used to estimate biomass, sometimes in combination with the total height of the tree. Adjustment is sometimes necessary in the case of trees with buttresses, or in the case of measuring the biomass of palms and bamboo, whose physiognomy differs from that of most tree species.

Diapause: Temporary interruption of growth associated with a period of dormancy.

Diffusion, Cultural: Refers to the tendency of human groups to share their cultural knowledge with others they encounter.

Diversification: An adaptive strategy that minimizes risk through the use of multiple resources.

Dormant: Being in a period of reduced biological activity—for example, hibernation or estivation.

Drought: A general condition of water shortage. Commonly a drought is so defined only when the shortage has an economic impact on populations.

Ecological Anthropology: The multidisciplinary study of how human populations cope with problems in their environment. Term is associated with the ecosystem concept and Rappaport's critique of cultural ecology.

Ecology: The study of the interaction between living and nonliving components of the environment. *See also* Cultural Ecology, Ecological Anthropology, and Ethnoecology.

Ecosystem: The assemblage of living and nonliving components in an environment together with their interrelations. As a unit of study, it may be defined broadly or narrowly, according to how the research problem is defined by the investigator.

Ecotone: A transitional zone between two distinct biomes; an "edge" habitat in which species from both biomes are found in a gradation from one biome to another.

Edaphic: The factors or features that deal with the influence of soils and climate on living things, especially on plants.

Efficiency, Energetic: The maximization of output per unit of energy input.

Electrolytes: A chemical compound that in solution dissociates by releasing ions (ionization). *See also* Ion.

Endemic: Restricted in distribution to a certain region or area.

Endogamy: Marriage practice in which individuals within a single kin group, community, or region tend to marry others included in this delimited population. *See also* Exogamy.

Energy: The capacity to do work (and carry information). May be chemical, nuclear, radiant, electrical, or mechanical in form. It is neither created nor destroyed, buy may be changed from one form to another. *See also* Thermodynamics.

Energy Flow: The changes in energy form and its rate in a system as it moves from one component of a system to another. Also a manner of modeling systems, associated with H. T. Odum in particular.

ENSO (El Niño Southern Oscillation): Fluctuations in oceanic temperatures across the Indo-Pacific region that lead every four to six years to notable global impacts on temperature and precipitation.

Entropy: Increased disorder in a system due to loss of potential energy (degradation).

Environmental Anthropology: The environmental approach in anthropology includes topics as diverse as primate ecology, paleoecology, human adaptability, ethnoecology, agrarian ecology, pastoral ecology, GIS, landscape ecology, and a number of other interdisciplinary areas concerned with human interactions with the physical environment, and with understanding how we can best meet the challenges of global and local environmental change.

Environmental Degradation: A loosely defined concept used to convey the notion of lowered soil quality, which in turn lowers floral and faunal productivity and diversity; a state in which an ecosystem cannot reach it climax stage. Precipitating factors may be overgrazing, salinization, overcropping without replacement of the lost soil nutrients, erosion, or, in general, mismanagement.

Epiphyte: A plant that grows on another living plant without taking anything from it (that is, it is not parasitic).

Equilibrium, Dynamic: The maintenance of properties essential to the continued existence of the system. Many ecological factors can influence the position of the equilibrium: evolutionary rates, barriers to dispersal, productivity levels, habitat heterogeneity, predation, and feedback processes. Dynamic equilibrium takes into account both negative and positive feedback processes.

Equilibrium, Static: Deals only with the processes of negative feedback that help maintain the system at a given level of existence.

Estivation: The reduction of biological activity by an organism, particularly during hot, dry periods.

Ethnoecology: The study of a population's ecological folk knowledge.

Ethnology: The comparative study of human societies.

Ethnopedology: The study of the folk knowledge of soils used by a population.

Ethology: The study of animal behavior, especially in its natural habitat. Ethologists try to understand why an animal behaves the way it does and what selective pressures have influenced the development of observed patterns.

Eutrophication: Process of nutrient concentration in an ecosystem. This accelerated enrichment may be the result of agriculture, urban waste, mining, or industrial activities. Eutrophication of aquatic ecosystems leads to changes in species composition and, in its extreme forms, to the death of most of the species valued by the human population.

Evapotranspiration: The total water loss from a plant surface by the processes of evaporation and plant transpiration (that is, respiration). Since it is difficult to separate these two aspects of water loss, the term *evapotranspiration* is used to more accurately describe this double water loss.

Evolution, Biological: The changes in the hereditary makeup of populations over time as populations interact with their environments.

Exchange Network: A system of trading, gift exchange, or barter, regulated by systems of mutual obligation. Such networks may provide for transfer of needed goods from one population to another or between regions having different sets of resources or may help maintain networks of mutual assistance.

Exogamy: A marriage practice in which individuals must marry outside of their own group. This may be defined as a kin group (for example, lineage), a community, a caste, or a region. It seems to be associated with social organizational features that aim at expanding the network of social cooperation.

Extractivism: Refers to a system of management that relies on the periodic exploitation of removable natural resources without efforts at reinvestment in the region to assure its long-term productivity or development. Extractive economic systems are found most often in frontier and colonial situations. However, one does find systems in which extractivists are engaged in intensive management of products, as with the case of açaí (see Brondizio, 2007).

Family, Extended: A unit to which members other than those of the nuclear group are added. These may include affinal, consanguineal, or fictive kin, who tend to reside in the same immediate surroundings or dwelling and cooperate economically and socially.

Family, Nuclear: Group composed of male and female mates and their children, who tend to occupy the same dwelling and rear their offspring as a group. Also referred to as *family of origin, orientation,* or *procreation.*

Feedback: A flow of information (energy) from one component to another in a system, which allows for its return to a previous equilibrium state (negative feedback) or a readjusting and reorganization of the system along new lines (positive feedback).

Fertility Rate: The number of births per 1,000 females of child-bearing age (fifteen to forty-five).

Fictive Kin: *See* Quasi-Kin.

Fire Management: The conscious or unconscious use of fire to bring about desired changes in vegetational cover. Fire eliminates litter and speeds its conversion into usable nutrients in forests, eliminates woody growth in grasslands, and encourages young grass growth preferred by grazing animals.

Fitness: Commonly refers to reproductive success of a population. The more fit a species the greater will be its ability to reproduce in a given territory.

Functionalism: A type of analysis used in the sciences that attempts to explain phenomena in terms of the functions they perform in the system.

Gene: General name given to a unit of heredity. Genes are located within the cell nucleus of chromosomes. Changes in genes (mutations) occur with a very low frequency and give rise to different forms of the same gene (alleles). Genes control the formation of the enzyme systems that determine the structure and function of organisms.

Gene Flow: Exchange of genetic traits between populations.

Genetic Plasticity: The ability of an organism to find expression for its genotypic qualities in a variety of physical expressions, all of which may represent various levels of adaptability to different forms of environmental stress. The more specific a genetic adaptation is to an environment, the less generalized the species and the less its genetic plasticity.

Genotype: The genetic contribution of an organism or its hereditary potential. Together with the environment, they produce the phenotype. The genotype may mask traits, as in the suppression of a recessive gene, or its potential may be unexpressed due to environmental conditions.

Georeferencing: The process of relating any data to a cartographic base and assigning coordinate information to the data so that it becomes spatially explicit.

GIS (Geographic Information Systems): A suite of techniques for spatially explicit analyses. It involves layering data (for example, soils, topography, roads) in a georeferenced database.

GPS (Global Positioning Systems): A system of twenty-four satellites originally launched to assist global navigation in the oceans. GPS receivers are widely used today for locating any physical feature on the earth by triangulating its position by use of several satellites relative to the location of the GPS receiver. Submeter accuracies are possible, but more commonly accuracies for most civilian GPS are 1–5 meters.

Grassland: A transitional biome between arid and humid zones. It is characterized by 10–30 millimeters of rainfall per year and is dominated by *Graminae* vegetation (grasses). Grasslands are characterized by rolling to flat terrain, periodic droughts, and high evapotranspiration in summer. They often occur in areas with a high water table. *See also* Savanna.

Groundwater: Water flowing or stored underground. It is a product of extraregional sources of water and may be stored below the surface in water-bearing rocks, aquifers, or other storage areas.

Group Fissioning: Splitting up villages or kin groups and reestablishing them in smaller, independent units. Used as a strategy to lower population pressure and reduce interpersonal conflict.

Habitat: Place where a plant or animal lives. It is often characterized by either dominant plant forms or physical characteristics (for example, grassland habitat).

Hardpan: A hardened soil layer resulting from the cementation of soil particles with organic matter, silica oxides, calcium carbonate, and so forth.

Hectare: A metric unit of surface area. It is equal to 10,000 square meters or 2.471 acres.

Herbivore: Any plant-eating animal.

Heterozygous: An individual that has inherited two different alleles at one more corresponding gene loci in a pair of chromosomes. As a result it does not breed true to character.

Historical Possibilism: An approach to the study of human society in which historical circumstances are given a predominant role is shaping observable phenomena. Associated with the work of Franz Boas and his followers.

Histosols: *See* Soil.

Homeostasis: The maintenance of constant internal conditions in the face of a varying environment.

Homozygous: An individual that has inherited two identical, rather than different, alleles at one or more corresponding gene loci. It breeds true for a particular character.

Horizon, Soil: A layer of soil with distinctive characteristics resulting from processes of soil formation.

Humus: Product of decomposition of organic matter, found in soils, usually black in color. In many soils, the top layer is known as the "humic horizon" and is of great importance for most domesticated plants.

Hunter-Gatherers: A human group characterized by the exploitation of wild food sources. Hunter-gatherers live in small bands or camps, are fairly mobile, and exploit relatively extensive territory with rather simple tools. They tend to maintain a mode of subsistence whereby males exploit local animal resources and females gather wild vegetative and other materials, which are shared by members of the group. Groups tend to be egalitarian, highly fissionable, and possess few items of personal property.

Hydromorphic: Soils formed under conditions of poor drainage in marshes, swamps, or flat zones.

Hyperventilation: Excessively high and rapid intake of oxygen, following stress or low oxygen (that is, hypoxic) conditions of high altitude areas. Excessive hyperventilation results in low carbon dioxide levels in the blood, or hypocapnia.

Hypothermia: A state of lowered body temperature. As the core temperature approaches 33°C, there is increased danger of malfunction in the thermoregulatory system.

Hypothesis: A statement of a causal or correlational relationship between two variables, X and Y; usually stated in a declaratory form. The magnitude and the direction of the relation are also indicated in a form that can be tested.

Hypoxia: Condition of low oxygen pressure, either in the atmosphere (at high altitudes) or in the bloodstream (for example, as a result of demanding exercise by an athlete).

Importance Value (IV): A measure of relative dominance, frequency, and density of vegetation.

Inceptisols: *See* Soils.

Information: Knowledge that is transferred. There is evidence that an evolutionary trend toward increased frequency of and dependence on the communication of information exists. The transmission of information is particularly sophisticated in *Homo sapiens*.

Intercropping: The practice of planting several crop species in one field simultaneously or of multilevel planting of species of varying heights. Provides cover for erosion prevention and protection of more tender crops. Minimizes risk of crop loss and increases land productivity.

Interfluve: An area of land between two rivers or water courses.

International Biological Program (IBP): A multinational research venture that was launched in 1964 and ended in 1974. Its goal was to study the biological basis of productivity and human welfare.

International Geosphere Biosphere Program (IGBP): An international scientific project dedicated to studying global environmental change. It was dominated initially by the atmospheric and earth sciences, but evolved to include other sciences, including the social sciences. It has several joint projects with the IHDP (see below).

International Human Dimensions Program (IHDP): The social sciences equivalent of the IGBP, studies the causes, consequences, and responses to global change by human societies. It has several projects, some by itself such as institutions and global environmental change, and others jointly with IGBP such as the Global Land Project.

Ion: A molecular constituent of one or more atoms that is free in a solution. An ion may carry a positive (cation) or a negative (anion) charge.

Kilocalorie: The amount of heat required to raise one kilogram of water one degree centigrade. The energy content of matter is measured by igniting a material in the presence of oxygen in a bomb calorimeter.

Lactase Deficiency: The hereditary inability to produce the intestinal enzyme lactase, which breaks down the milk sugar, lactose. The ingestion of lactose-containing milk by persons so affected creates symptoms of gastrointestinal cramps, flatulence, and diarrhea. It is most common in populations without long dairying histories, such as the Inuit. Using acidified milk or yogurt (nonlactose) prevents these symptoms.

Landsat: A series of US satellites operated by NASA that collect multispectral data of the earth systematically. For Landsat TM the temporal resolution is every sixteen days.

Laterite: A general term to refer to reddish brown iron and aluminum oxide-rich soils. When exposed to air, the layer may turn to hardpan irreversibly. Because the term has been used too loosely to refer to tropical soils of reddish coloration, the term *plinthite* has now replaced *laterite* in the soil science literature.

Leaching: The removal of soluble mineral salts from the upper layers of a soil by the movement of water through the horizons.

Lee Side: The protected side of a mountain or island away from the direction of prevailing winds. Opposite of "windward" side.

Legume: Members of the *Leguminosae* family. They have the property of fixing atmospheric nitrogen in the soil.

Levirate: A marriage custom that obligates a man to marry his deceased brother's widow.

Lineage, Segmentary: A lineage characterized by internal divisions or sects that may result in the emergence of new and separate descent groups. Its flexible form of organization is particularly appropriate to pastoral nomadic populations.

Litter: Fallen organic (plant) matter that accumulates on the surface of the soil. It forms a natural mulch and, if decomposed, humus. Litterfall is used as a measure of productivity in forest ecosystems.

Management: The plan of action, whether conscious or not, of a population in its utilization of social and environmental resources. Used synonymously with *strategy* and *behavioral adjustment*.

Matter: Anything that has the properties of mass (weight) and occupies space. May be in solid, liquid, or gaseous states.

Matter, Cycles of: The cyclical movements of all physical elements from complex organic to inorganic forms and back again. Examples include oxygen cycle, water cycle, and nutrient cycle.

Microclimate: The climatic condition, especially the temperature, nearest to an individual (for example, inside a dwelling or inside clothing). Refers to creation of environmental conditions different from those in the general area.

Migration: A short-term mechanism for dispersion of people or animals. May mean a permanent relocation but is distinguished from cyclical nomadism. *Seasonal migration* is subsumed under *transhumance*. May be considered an adaptive strategy of populations.

Model: A simplified representation of the interactions and components of a system. May elicit speculations about the processes that would explain or produce the observed facts of the system.

Mollisols: *See* Soils.

Monoculture (Monocropping): Cultivation of a single crop species in large fields, usually as an export commodity with market value. Often associated with plantation systems or intensive forms of food production requiring major inputs of energy and technology.

Mulching: Process of organic matter accumulation for maintaining soil moist (and, secondarily, nutrients) by covering the surface of the soil with live decomposing plant material. Mulching helps prevent erosion and soil heating from solar radiation and reduces evaporation from the soil surface.

MSS (Multispectral Scanner): A sensor that collects data for the same area of the earth at different wavelengths of the electromagnetic spectrum. Also refers to a sensor in Landsats 1 to 3 with 80 meters of spatial resolution and four spectral bands.

Mutualistic: A symbiotic relationship in which both species benefit from their intimate association.

Niche: All the components of the environment with which the organism or population interacts.

Nitrification: The biochemical oxidation of ammonium to nitrate. The process is essential to the provisioning of usable nutrients by plants.

Nomadism: An adaptation of cyclical human mobility to the scattered (and diverse) resources of a region, resulting in a lack of permanent settlements.

Open Systems: One that requires constant input from outside the system for maintenance. It includes considerations of positive feedback.

Oxisols: *See* Soils.

Parent Material (Bedrock): The underlying hard rock material under any soil profile, from which the soil horizons have originated. May be referred to as the C horizon.

Pastoralists: Persons who subsist by herding large groups of domesticated animals, opportunistic agriculture, and trade with more sedentary peoples. The pastoralist mode of production tends to be utilized in biomes that are marginal to agriculture and where pastures are scattered.

Pathogen: A bacterium, virus, or other disease-causing agent.

Peripheral Blood Flow: A physiological adjustment found in populations habitually exposed to cold in the extremities. It refers to the spontaneous rewarming of fingers and toes during cold exposure in a cyclical pattern of vasoconstriction and dilation. It is also known as *cold-induced vasodilation.*

pH: The scale along which acidity and alkalinity of a solution is measured. Acid solutions have a smaller pH and alkaline solutions a greater pH within a range from zero to fourteen.

Phenotype: The physical manifestation of the hereditary potential of an organism. The visible phenotype may express genetic traits most appropriate to the current environmental conditions.

Photosynthesis: The conversion of light energy into chemical energy in green plant cells.

Pixel: The smallest unit of spatial resolution in a photo or remotely sensed digital image. A satellite image may be composed of millions of pixels. Pixel size varies with the type of sensor used (for example, 80 meter spatial resolution for Landsat MSS versus 30 meter for Landsat TM).

Plinthite: *See* Laterite.

Population: A group of individuals of the same species that occupy a given area and interbreed.

Population Pressure: The demands of a population on the resources of its ecosystem. Refers to the relationship between population size and the ability of the ecosystem to sustain it.

Primary Production: Refers to either the assimilation of energy and nutrients by green plants *(gross primary production)* or to its accumulation and transformation into biomass *(net primary production).*

Producers: Ecological term that refers to organisms capable of converting solar energy into biomass. The most notable are green plants and blue-green algae.

Quasi-Kin or **Fictive Kin:** Treating those who are not related by consanguineal or affinal ties as if they were so connected. Often associated with adaptive forms of exchange, protection, and cooperation and established by ritual actions and the use of kinlike terms of address.

Raster Data: Data from satellites are stored in raster format or pixels (as opposed to polygons or vector data).

Recovery, Rate of: Refers to regeneration of plant or animal species following a period of biological degradation of an ecosystem.

Regression Coefficient: The rate of change of a dependent variable with respect to an independent variable.

Reproductive Success: The essential concept of the theory of natural selection. Helps explain how species have evolved, become extinct, or become dominant. The more "adapted" a species is in its environment, the greater the opportunity for individuals of the population to survive and reproduce and thus to occupy the territory. Also known as the theory of *natural selection.*

Resource Base: An environment's group of organic and inorganic resources upon which a population habitually depends for its subsistence.

Respiration: The metabolic process by which oxygen is assimilated and combined with nutrients and water to produce energy (calories) for body maintenance and work. By this same process the waste products of metabolism are returned to the environment.

Rhizobium: A soil bacterium able to utilize atmospheric nitrogen to build organic compounds (that is, nitrogen fixation). These bacteria are often found in special structures of legumes and other plants and aid plants in their nutrition. In turn, the rhizobia obtain sugars from the plant.

Savanna: A tropical grassland environment.

Secondary Growth: The process of vegetational succession in an ecosystem. Also known as *secondary succession.*

Semiarid Areas: Regions varying from 150–250 to 250–500 millimeters of rainfall per year. Dry land farming in diffuse areas is possible, but not always reliable. Pastoral nomadism and forms of oasis agriculture are often found in these areas.

Simulation: A technique of solving and studying problems by following the changes over time of a dynamic model of a system. A simulation model built from a series of sections whose relationship to one another can be stated mathematically, but which permits their simultaneous solution.

Slash-and-Burn: *See* Swidden Agriculture.

Social Organization: Distinguished by Firth from social structure as that aspect of a social system which refers to the systematic ordering of social relation. The existing forms of social organization are guided by precedents and rules set in the social structure. These rules delimit a range of socially possible acceptable behavior and imply the role of the social group in coordinating individual behaviors.

Social Structure: Principles according to which social features are organized. Includes kinship relation patterns, technoeconomic organization, belief systems, and political structure.

Socialization: The process of learning a culture through a lifelong process of internalization. May also be termed *enculturation.* Includes both institutional and informal learning processes.

Soil Profile: A cross-section that includes all the layers or horizons in a soil. A sample that expresses the type of processes experienced by the soil. Also used to determine its present characteristics and future potential.

Soil Structure: The arrangement of soil particles, such as granular, blocky, or columnar forms. Types of soil structure are characterized by differences in size and shape, and by degree of distinctness.

Soil Texture: Determined by the proportion of different sizes of soil particle, such as sand, gravel, silt, and clay. Soil texture is an important criterion in the classification of soils and is used by populations in evaluating the potential uses of a land area.

Soils: The portions of the earth's surface resulting from the weathering of rock and which support plant life. Soils can be categorized according to their current characteristics into ten orders: (1) *alfisols* are soils with argillic subsurface horizons, good supply of bases, and adequate moisture for plant growth; (2) *aridisols* are soils usually dry in all horizons and never moist for ninety consecutive days; (3) *entisols* lack horizon development; (4) *histisols* are characterized by high levels of organic matter, for example, bog soils and muck soils; (5) *inceptisols* have one or more diagnostic horizons that are believed to form quickly, but not as a result of leaching or weathering; (6) *mollisols* are characterized by a thick, dark mineral surface horizon and are associated with soils of grassland regions; (7) *oxisols* are soils of the tropics and subtropics characterized by the presence of an oxic horizon (a horizon from which most of the silica has been removed by weathering, leaving oxides of iron and aluminum); (8) *spodisols* are soils with accumulation of amorphous materials in subsurface horizons; (9) *ultisols* are soils with argillic subsurface horizons and low supply of bases; (10) *vertisols* are soils with swelling clays that develop deep, wide cracks during dry periods.

Sororate: A marriage custom that obligates a man to marry the sister of his deceased wife.

Spatially Explicit: Giving data precise coordinate location on a cartographic base to understand change over time in space.

Spectral: Refers to characteristics of the light spectrum captured by sensors off the earth's surfaces.

State Variables: Refers to the components of a system (for example, producers, consumers, and so forth).

Stoma: Tiny leaf pores that allow for carbon dioxide/oxygen exchange in the respiratory/photosynthetic processes of green plants.

Strategy: An adjustment by an organism or population to environmental or social conditions. Strategies may involve physiological or behavioral change.

Stress: A force or extreme situation in the environment of an organism or population that produces a deviation from homeostasis. Unless positive feedback responses can head the system away from the stress, death or disruption will tend to occur.

Subsistence: A broad term that includes the study of a form of production (that is, production for use); it may also mean what is essential for survival (that is, the food supply). Subsistence production characterizes many populations where the units of production are small, where a variety of food sources are grown or captured, and where reciprocity is utilized as a chief mechanism of exchange.

Succession: The process by which plant communities sequentially succeed one another as they proceed to a stable or climax community—or to maximum biomass possible in that biome.

Sucrase Deficiency: Lack of the intestinal disaccharide enzyme sucrase. It may produce a variety of gastrointestinal problems due to inability to digest the sugar sucrose.

Swidden Agriculture: Also known as *shifting agriculture, slash-and-burn, milpa,* and *citemene.* A system in which fields are cropped for fewer years than they are allowed to remain fallow. Often characterized by regrowth of the secondary species during fallow and by reliance on the slash-and-burn method of clearing fallow fields in preparation for planting.

Synchronic: Refers to studies at one point in time.

Systems Theory, General: Refers to a body of systematic theoretical constructs that deal with the general relationships in the empirical world. It attempts to develop theories with applicability to more than one discipline. Also can be used as a framework for developing theory.

Taiga: Zone of subarctic boreal coniferous forests.

Taxonomy: Systems of classification (by any group) that are predicated on the notion of distinctive features, which are used to separate distinct items into categories of like items. A way of ordering knowledge, which then provides a standard by which to interpret and categorize new phenomena.

Telecommuting: Connecting to one's workplace through a computer at home, in lieu of commuting to work by car or public transportation.

Thematic Mapper (TM): Landsat satellites launched after 1984 with seven spectral bands, 30 meter spatial resolution, and full earth coverage every sixteen days (temporal resolution). In 1999 an Enhanced Thematic Mapper sensor (ETM+) was successfully launched by NASA on Landsat 7. See Table 4.1 in this volume for a list of other satellites available and their spectral, spatial, and temporal resolutions.

Thermodynamics, Laws of: First law: Energy is neither created nor destroyed; Second law: part of energy used in work is lost as heat, leading to degradation of energy and increase in entropy, or disorder.

Thermogenesis: Refers to the types of mechanisms that initiate heat production in the body. For example, nonshivering thermogenesis is a chemical form associated with the presence of brown adipose tissue.

Thermo-Neutral Temperature: When environmental temperatures are between 25° and 27°C, humans are said to be in thermal equilibrium.

Transhumance: Seasonal migration of domesticated livestock and herders in order to exploit the semiarid grasslands.

Transition Matrix: A processing technique that compares georeferenced data sets representing different dates and computes measures of change between dates. The computation would determine the change in land cover class between two dates for a given area representing the same point in space.

Trophic Levels: Levels of feeding relationships from primary plant consumers to the most distant and complex member of the food chain. The trophic level defines the species' position in the food chain depending on the number of energy transfers associated with feeding habits. At the bottom are the food producers, then herbivores, followed by consumers.

Tropical Rain Forest: One of the oldest existing ecosystems, which is characterized by high ambient humidity and temperature and by diversity and complexity of life forms.

Tundra: The northernmost frontier of vegetation, which is treeless and alpinelike. A transitional ecotone between the tree line and permanent snow areas. Subvarieties include bushes, grasses, and desert tundras.

Upwelling: Vertical movements of water currents near coasts that bring nutrients from the ocean bottom to the surface. Rich fish and sea mammal populations are found in these coastal areas.

Vapor Pressure: Gaseous molecules, constantly in random motion, that at an equilibrium point between condensation and evaporation exert pressure. The magnitude of this vapor pressure depends on the bonding nature of the liquid and its temperature. Water, with strong internal bonding forces, has a low vapor pressure at room temperature. At higher ambient temperatures, vapor pressure is increased, and warm air can hold greater quantities of water, or humidity. Warm and dry air causes rapid liquid gas exchange, or evaporation.

Vasoconstriction and Vasodilation: Process of opening and narrowing of capillaries to restrict or permit greater blood flow from core to shell.

Vegetative Reproduction: Plant reproduction by grafts, cuttings, leaf sections, and so forth, rather than by production of seeds.

Wadi: A dried-up desert watercourse, except after rains, when it may become a roaring torrent or flash flood.

Work (or Aerobic) Capacity: Refers to the ability of the body to deliver oxygen to the tissues per unit of ventilatory or heart rate.

Worldview: Body of beliefs about the nature, structure, and parts of the world shared by members of a society. Such views may be expressed in myths, ceremonies, social interactional patterns, and attitudes toward nature.

Xerophytic Vegetation: Plants able to grow in extremely dry regions. They are characterized by physical features that minimize loss of water and leaf exposure to drying air and make more effective use of water.

BIBLIOGRAPHY

Aber, J. D., and J. M. Melillo
1991   Terrestrial Ecosystems. Philadelphia: Sanders.
Abu-Eshy, S. A., M. A. Abolfotouh, and Y. M. Al-Naggar
2001   Endemic Goitre in Schoolchildren in High and Low Altitude Areas of Asir
        Region, Saudi Arabia. Saudi Medical Journal 22(2):146–149.
Achtnich, W., and B. Homeyer
1980   Protective Measures Against Desertification in Oasis Farming as Demonstrated
        by the Example of the Oasis Al Hassa, Saudi Arabia. *In* Desertification in Ex-
        tremely Arid Environments. W. Meckelein, ed. Stuttgart: Geographisches In-
        stitut der Universitat.
Adams, C. E., K. J. Lindsey, and S. J. Ash
2005   Urban Wildlife Management. Boca Raton, FL: CRC Press.
Adams, J. B., and A. R. Gillespie
2006   Remote Sensing of Landscapes with Spectral Images: A Physical Modeling
        Approach. New York: Cambridge University Press.
Adams, R. M.
1966   The Evolution of Urban Society. Chicago: Aldine.
Adams, R. N.
1973   Energy and Structure. Austin: University of Texas Press.
1974   The Implications of Energy Flow Studies on Human Populations for the Social
        Sciences. *In* Energy Flow in Human Communities: Proceedings of a Work-
        shop. P. L. Jamison and S. M. Friedman, eds. University Park, PA: US Interna-
        tional Biological Program (IBP) and Social Science Research Council (SSRC).
Adolph, E. F.
1947   Physiology of Man in the Desert. London: Interscience.
Aide, T. M., J. K. Zimmerman, M. Rosario, and H. Marcano
1996   Forest Recovery in Abandoned Cattle Pastures Along an Elevational Gradient
        in Northeastern Puerto Rico. Biotropica 28(4):537–548.
Alavi, S. M. Z.
1965   Arab Geography in the Ninth and Tenth Centuries. Aligarh, India: Aligarh
        Muslim University, Department of Geography.

Alberti, M., J. M. Marzluff, E. Shulenberger, G. Bradley, C. Ryan, and C. Zummbrunnen
2003   Integrating Humans into Ecology: Opportunities and Challenges for Studying Urban Ecosystems. BioScience 53:1169–1179.

Alcamo, J. R., R. Leemans, and E. Kreileman
1998   Global Change Scenarios of the 21st Century. Results from IMAGE 2.4 Model. Oxford: Elsevier.

Aldashey, A., and R. Naeije, eds.
2007   Problems of High Altitude Medicine and Biology: Proceedings of the NATO Advanced Research Workshop on Problems of High Altitude Medicine and Biology, Issyk-Kul, Kyrgyz Republic, 5–6 June 2006. New York: Springer.

Alegre, J. C., D. K. Cassel, D. Bandy, and P. A. Sanchez
1986   Effect of Land Clearing on Soil Properties of an Utisol and Subsequent Crop Production in Yurimaguas, Peru. *In* Land Clearing and Development in the Tropics. R. Lal et al., eds. Rotterdam: A. A. Balkema.

Al-Farraj, A., and A. M. Harvey
2000   Desert Pavement Characteristics on Wadi Terrace and Alluvial Fan Surfaces: Wadi Al-Bih, UAE and Oman. Geomorphology 35(3–4):279–297.

Allan, N. J., G. W. Knapp, and C. Stadel
1988   Human Impact on Mountains. Totowa, NJ: Rowman & Littlefield.

Allan, W.
1965   The African Husbandman. Edinburgh: Oliver & Boyd.

Alland, A.
1973   Evolution and Human Behavior. 2nd ed. Garden City, NY: Doubleday-Anchor.
1975   Adaptation. Annual Review of Anthropology 4:59–73.

Alland, A., and B. McCay
1973   The Concept of Adaptation in Biological and Cultural Evolution. *In* Handbook of Social and Cultural Anthropology. J. Honigmann, ed. Chicago: Rand McNally.

Allen, E. B., ed.
1988   Reconstruction of Disturbed Arid Lands: An Ecological Approach. Boulder: Westview.

Allen, R. R., and C. R. Fenster
1986   Stubble-Mulch Equipment for Soil and Water Conservation in the Great Plains. Soil and Water Conservation 41:11–16.

Allen, T., and T. Starr
1982   Hierarchy. Chicago: University of Chicago Press.

Amin, A. A.
2004   The Extent of Desertification on Saudi Arabia. Environmental Geology 46(1): 22–31.

Amundson, R.
2001   The Carbon Budget in Soils. Annual Review of Earth and Planetary Sciences 29:535–562.

Ananda, J., and G. Herath
2005   Evaluating Public Risk Preferences in Forest Land-Use Choices Using Multiattribute Utility Theory. Ecological Economics 55(3):408–419.

Andersen, A. N., G. D. Cook, and R. J. Williams, eds.
2003   Fire in Tropical Savannas: The Kapalga Experiment. New York: Springer.

Andersen, S., G. Mulvad, H. S. Pedersen, and P. Laurenberg
2004   Gender Diversity in Developing Overweight over 35 Years of Westernization in an Inuit Hunter Cohort and Ethno-Specific Body Mass Index for Evaluation of Body-Weight Abnormalities. European Journal of Endocrinology 151(6): 735–740.

Anderson, A., ed.
1990   Alternatives to Deforestation. New York: Columbia University Press.

Anderson, A., P. May, and M. Balick
1991   The Subsidy from Nature. New York: Columbia University Press.

Anderson, D. G.
2002   Identity and Ecology in Arctic Siberia: The Number One Reindeer Brigade. New York: Oxford University Press.

Anderson, L. O., Y. E. Shimabukuro, R. S. DeFries, and D. Morton
2005   Assessment of Land Cover and Land Use Changes in the Brazilian Amazon Using Multitemporal Fraction Images Derived from Terra MODIS: Examples from the State of Mato Grosso. IEEE Geoscience and Remote Sensing Letters 2(3):315–318.

Andreae, M. O., and D. S. Schimel, eds.
1989   Exchange of Trace Gases Between Terrestrial Ecosystems and the Atmosphere. New York: Wiley-Interscience.

Angerbjoern, A., M. Tannerfeldt, and S. Erlinge
1999   Predator-Prey Relationships: Arctic Foxes and Lemmings. Journal of Animal Ecology 68(1):34–49.

Aoki, M.
1967   Optimization of Stochastic Systems. New York: Academic.

Aporta, C., and E. S. Higgs
2005   Satellite Culture: Global Positioning Systems, Inuit Wayfinding, and the Need for a New Account of Technology. Current Anthropology 46(5):729–753.

Aranibar, J. N., L. Otter, S. A. Macko, P. R. Dowty, H. H. Shugart, C. J. W. Feral, H. E. Epstein, F. Eckardt, and R. J. Swap
2004   Nitrogen Cycling in the Soil-Plant System Along a Precipitation Gradient in the Kalahari Sands. Global Change Biology 10(3):359–373.

Arima, E.
1975   A Contextual Study of the Caribou Eskimo Kayak. Ottawa: National Museum of Man.

Arndt, S. K., C. Arampatsis, A. Foetzki, Z. XiMing, L. XiangYi, and Z. FanJiang
2004   Contrasting Patterns of Leaf Solute Accumulation and Salt Adaptation in Four Phreatophytic Desert Plants in a Hyperarid Desert with Saline Groundwater. Journal of Arid Environments 59(2):259–270.

Aronoff, S.
2005   Remote Sensing for GIS Managers. Redlands, CA: ESRI Press.

Aschmann, H.
1962   Evaluations of Dry Land Environments by Societies at Various Levels of Technical Competence. *In* Civilizations in Desert Lands. R. Woodbury, ed. Salt Lake City: University of Utah Press.

Asner, G. P., A. J. Elmore, R. E. Martin, and L. P. Olander
2004   Grazing Systems, Ecosystem Responses, and Global Change. Annual Review of
        Environment and Resources 29:261–299.
Asner, G. P., and K. B. Heidenbrecht
2005   Desertification Alters Regional Ecosystem-Climate Interactions. Global
        Change Biology 11(1):182–194.
Åstrand, P., and K. Rodahl
1986   Textbook of Work Physiology: Physiology Bases of Exercise. 3rd ed. New York:
        McGraw-Hill.
Attwell, K.
2000   Urban Land Resources and Urban Planning: Case Studies from Denmark.
        Landscape and Urban Planning 52:145–163.
Avery, T. E., and G. L. Berlin
1992   Fundamentals of Remote Sensing and Airphoto Interpretation. 5th ed. New
        York: Macmillan.
Aw, D., and G. Diemer
2005   Making a Large Irrigation Scheme Work: A Case Study from Mali. Washing-
        ton, DC: World Bank.
Awogbade, M. O.
1983   Fulani Pastoralism: Jos Case Study. Zaria, Nigeria: Ahmadu Bello University
        Press.
Axelrod, R.
1997   The Complexity of Cooperation: Agent-Based Models of Competition and
        Collaboration. Princeton, NJ: Princeton University Press.
Badcock, B.
1984   Unfairly Structured Cities. Oxford: Blackwell.
Bailey, R. C., and T. Headland
1992   The Tropical Rain Forest: Is It a Productive Environment for Human Foragers?
        Human Ecology 19(2):261–285.
Bajema, C. J., ed.
1971   Natural Selection in Human Populations: The Measurement of Ongoing Ge-
        netic Evolution in Contemporary Societies. New York: Wiley.
Baker, H.
1970   Evolution in the Tropics. Biotropica 2(2):101–111.
Baker, P. T.
1966   Ecological and Physiological Adaptations in Indigenous South Americans. *In*
        The Biology of Human Adaptability. P. T. Baker and J. S. Weiner, eds. Oxford:
        Clarendon.
1968   Human Adaptation to High Altitude. *In* High Altitude Adaptation in a Peru-
        vian Community. P. T. Baker, ed. Occasional Papers in Anthropology, no. 1.
        University Park: Pennsylvania State University.
1969   Human Adaptation to High Altitude. Science 163:1149–1156.
1976a   Evolution of a Project: Theory, Method, and Sampling. *In* Man in the An-
        des. P. T. Baker and M. Little, eds. Stroudsburg, PA: Dowden, Hutchinson
        & Ross.
1976b   Work Performance of Highland Natives. *In* Man in the Andes. P. T. Baker and
        M. Little, eds. Stroudsburg, PA: Dowden, Hutchinson & Ross.

Baker, P. T., ed.
1968   High Altitude Adaptation in a Peruvian Community. Occasional Papers in Anthropology, no. 1. University Park: Pennsylvania State University.
1978   The Biology of High Altitude Populations. Cambridge: Cambridge University Press.

Baker, P. T., and J. S. Dutt
1972   Demographic Variables as Measures of Biological Adaptation: A Study of High Altitude Human Populations. *In* The Structure of Human Populations. G. A. Harrison and A. J. Boyce, eds. Oxford: Clarendon.

Baker, P. T., and M. Little, eds.
1976   Man in the Andes. US/IBP Synthesis Series, no. 1. Stroudsburg, PA: Dowden, Hutchinson & Ross.

Baker, P. T., and J. S. Weiner, eds.
1966   The Biology of Human Adaptability. Oxford: Clarendon.

Baker, T.
1976   Child Care, Child Training, and Environment. *In* Man in the Andes. P. T. Baker and M. Little, eds. Stroudsburg, PA: Dowden, Hutchinson & Ross.

Baldanzi, G.
1959   Efeitos da Queimada sobre a Fertilidade do Solo. Pelotas, Rio Grande do Sul, Brazil: Instituto Agronômico do Sul.

Balée, W.
1989   The Culture of Amazonian Forests. Advances in Economic Botany 7:1–21.
1994   Footprints of the Forest: Ka'Apor Ethnobotany: The Historical Ecology of Plant Utilization by an Amazonian People. New York: Columbia University Press.

Balée, W., ed.
1998   Advances in Historical Ecology. New York: Columbia University Press.

Balée, W., and C. Erickson, eds.
2006   Time and Complexity in Historical Ecology: Studies in the Neotropical Lowlands. New York: Columbia University Press.

Balée, W., and D. Posey, eds.
1989   Natural Resource Management by Indigenous and Folk Societies of Amazônia. Monograph Series, no. 7. New York: New York Botanical Garden.

Balikci, A.
1968   The Netsilik Eskimos: Adaptive Processes. *In* Man the Hunter. R. B. Lee and I. DeVore, eds. Chicago: Aldine.
1970   The Netsilik Eskimo. Garden City, NY: Natural History Press.

Baltaxe, R.
1980   The Application of Landsat Data to Tropical Forest Surveys. Rome: FAO.

Bamforth, D. B.
1988   Ecology and Human Organization on the Great Plains. New York: Springer.

Bandi, H. G.
1969   Eskimo Prehistory. London: Methuen.

Barbier, E. B., ed.
2004   Ecology and Economics: New Frontiers and Sustainable Development. New York: Springer.

Barclay, G.
1958   Techniques of Population Analysis. New York: Wiley.

Barker, G.
2005   The Archeology of Foraging and Farming at Niah Cave, Sarawak. Asian Perspectives 44(1):90–106.
Barker, J., ed.
1985   The Politics of Agriculture in Tropical Africa. Beverly Hills, CA: Sage.
Barkey, N. L., B. C. Campbell, and P. W. Leslie
2001   A Comparison of Health Complaints of Settled and Nomadic Turkana Men. Medical Anthropology Quarterly 15(3):391–408.
Barlett, P.
1977   The Structure of Decision-Making in Paso. American Ethnologist 4(2):285–308.
Barnard, A., ed.
2004   Hunter-Gatherers in History, Archaeology, and Anthropology. Oxford: Berg.
Barnes, B. V., D. R. Zak, S. R. Denton, and S. H. Spurr
2001   Forest Ecology. 4th ed. New York: Wiley.
Barnes, R. F. W.
2002   The Bushmeat Boom and Bust in West and Central Africa. Oryx 36(3):236–242.
Baron, J. S., ed.
2002   Rocky Mountain Futures: An Ecological Perspective. Washington, DC: Island.
Baron, J. S., M. D. Hartman, T. G. F. Kittel, L. E. Band, D. S. Ojima, and R. B. Lammers
1998   Effects of Land Cover, Water Redistribution, and Temperature on Ecosystem Processes in the S. Platte Basin. Ecological Applications 8(4):1037–1051.
Baron, J. S., N. L. Poff, P. L. Angermeier, C. N. Dahm, P. H. Gleick, N. G. Hairston Jr., R. B. Jackson, C. A. Johnston, B. D. Richter, and A. D. Steinman
2002   Meeting Ecological and Societal Needs for Freshwater. Ecological Applications 12(5):1247–1260.
Barrera-Bassols, N., and J. A. Zinck
2000   Ethnopedology in a Worldwide Perspective: An Annotated Bibliography. ITC Publication, no. 77. Enschede, Netherlands: ITC.
Barrera-Bassols, N., J. A. Zinck, and E. Van Ranst
2006   Symbolism, Knowledge, and Management of Soils and Land Resources in Indigenous Communities: Ethnopedology at Global, Regional, and Local Scales. Catena 65(2):118–137.
Barrett, G. W., J. D. Peles, and E. P. Odum
1997   Transcending Processes and the Levels-of-Organization Concept. BioScience 47(8):531–535.
Barry, R. G., and R. J. Chorley
1970   Atmosphere, Weather, and Climate. New York: Holt, Rinehart & Winston.
Barth, F.
1956   Ecologic Relationships of Ethnic Groups in Swat, North Pakistan. American Anthropologist 58:1079–1089.
1961   Nomads of South Persia. Boston: Little, Brown.
1969   Ethnic Groups and Boundaries: The Social Organization of Cultural Difference. Boston: Little, Brown.
1972   Ethnic Processes on the Pathan-Baluch Boundary. *In* Directions in Socio-Linguistics. J. Gumperz and D. Hymes, eds. New York: Holt, Rinehart & Winston.

Barth, H. J.
1999   Desertification in the Eastern Province of Saudi Arabia. Journal of Arid Environments 43(4):399–410.

Barthel, S., J. Colding, T. Elmqvist, and C. Folke
2005   History and Local Management of a Biodiversity-Rich, Urban, Cultural Landscape. Ecology and Society 105(2):10.

Bartholomew, W. V., J. Meyer, and H. Laudelout
1953   Mineral Nutrient Immobilization Under Forest and Grass Fallow in the Yangambi (Belgian Congo) Region. Institut National pour L'Etude Agronomique du Congo Serie 57:1–27.

Bartlett, P. F.
2005   Urban Place: Reconnecting with the Natural World. Cambridge, MA: MIT Press.

Barton, H.
2005   The Case for Rainforest Foragers: The Starch Record at Niah Cave, Sarawak. Asian Perspectives 44(1):56–72.

Basamba, T. A., E. Barrios, E. Amézquita, I. M. Rao, and B. R. Singh
2006   Tillage Effects on Maize Yield in a Colombian Savanna Oxisol: Soil Organic Matter and P Fractions. Soil & Tillage Research 91(1–2):131–142.

Baskin, Y.
1994   Ecologists Dare to Ask: How Much Does Diversity Matter? Science 254:202–203.

Bass, R.
2005   Caribou Rising: Defending the Porcupine Herd, Gwich-'in Culture, and the Arctic National Wildlife Refuge. Berkeley: University of California Press.

Basso, E.
1973   The Kalapalo Indians of Central Brazil. New York: Holt, Rinehart & Winston.

Bates, D. G.
2001   Human Adaptive Strategies: Ecology, Culture, and Politics. 3rd ed. Boston: Allyn & Bacon.

Bates, D. G., and S. H. Lees, eds.
1996   Case Studies in Human Ecology. New York: Plenum.

Bates, H. W.
1982   The Naturalist on the River Amazons. London: Murray.

Bates, M.
1953   Human Ecology. *In* Anthropology Today. A. L. Kroeber, ed. Chicago: University of Chicago Press.
1960   The Forest and the Sea. New York: Vintage.

Bateson, G.
1963   The Role of Somatic Change in Evolution. Evolution 17:529–539.
1972   Steps to an Ecology of Mind. New York: Ballantine.

Batistella, M.
2001   Landscape Change and Land Use/Land Cover Dynamics in Rondônia, Brazilian Amazon. CIPEC Dissertation Series, no. 7. Bloomington: Indiana University, Center for the Study of Institutions, Population, and Environmental Change.

Batistella, M., C. Criscuolo, E. E de Miranda, and A. L. Filardi
2004   Satélites de Monitoramento. Campinas: Embrapa Monitoramento por Satélite, 2004. Disponível em: www.sat.cnpm.embrapa.br.

Batistella, M., and E. F. Moran
2007   A Heterogeneidade das Mudanças de Uso e Cobertura das Terras na Amazônia: Em Busca de um Mapa da Estrada. *In* Dimensões Humanas da Biosferatmosfera na Amazônia. W. M. da Costa, B. K. Becker, and D. S. Alves, eds. São Paulo: Editora da Universidade de São Paulo.

Batistella, M., E. F. Moran, and D. S. Alves, eds.
In prep. Ambiente e Sociedade na Amazônia: Contribuições de LBA e outras perspectivas. São Paulo: EDUSP

Batterbury, S. P. J., and A. Bebbington
1999   Environmental Histories: Access to Resources and Landscape Change. Land Degradation and Development 10:279–289.

Bazzaz, F. A.
1998   Tropical Forests in a Future Climate: Changes in Biological Diversity and Impact on the Global Carbon Cycle. *In* Potential Impacts of Climate Change on Tropical Forest Ecosystems. A. Markham, ed. Dordrecht: Kluwer Academic.

Beall, C. M.
2000   Tibetan and Andean Patterns of Adaptation to High-Altitude Hypoxia. Human Biology 72(1):201–228.
2001   Adaptations to Altitude: A Current Assessment. Annual Review of Anthropology 30:423–456.
2006   Andean, Tibetan, and Ethiopian Patterns of Adaptation to High Altitude Hypoxia. Integrative and Comparative Biology 46(1):18–24.

Beall, C. M., M. J. Decker, G. M. Brittenham, I. Kushner, A. Gebremedhin, and K. P. Strohl
2002   An Ethiopian Pattern of Human Adaptation to High-Altitude Hypoxia. Proceedings of the National Academy of Sciences 99(26):17215–17218.

Beall, C. M., and M. Goldstein
1982   A Comparison of Chest Morphology in High Altitude Asian and Andean Populations. Human Biology 54:145–163.
1987   Hemoglobin Concentration of Pastoral Nomads Permanently Resident at 4,850–5,450 Meters in Tibet. American Journal of Physical Anthropology 73:433–438.

Beamont, P.
1989   Environmental Management in Drylands. New York: Routledge.

Beatley, T.
2000   Green Urbanism: Learning from European Cities. Washington, DC: Island.

Beatley, T., and K. Manning
1997   The Ecology of Place: Planning for Environment, Economy, and Community. Washington, DC: Island.

Beaver, P. D., and B. L. Purrington, eds.
1984   Cultural Adaptation to Mountain Environments. Athens: University of Georgia Press.

Becker, A., and H. Bugmann
1999   Global Change and Mountain Regions–Initiative for Collaborative Research. Stockholm, Sweden: IGBP Mountain Research Initiative.

Beckerman, S.
1979   The Abundance of Protein in Amazônia: A Reply to Gross. American Anthropologist 81:533–560.

1980   Fishing and Hunting by the Barí of Colombia. *In* Working Paper on South American Indians. Vol. 2. R. Hames, ed. Bennington, VT: Bennington College.

1989   Hunting and Fishing in Amazônia: Hold the Answers; What Are the Questions? Paper presented at Wenner-Gren Conference Amazonian Synthesis, Nova Friburgo, Rio de Janeiro, June 2–10, 1989.

Beckwith, C.
1987   The Tibetan Empire in Central Asia. Princeton, NJ: Princeton University Press.

Begon, M., C. Townsend, and J. L. Harper
2005   Ecology: From Individuals to Ecosystems. Oxford: Blackwell.

Behrens, C.
1989   The Scientific Basis for Shipibo Soil Classification and Land Use. American Anthropologist 91:83–100.

1990   Applications of Satellite Image Processing to the Analysis of Amazonian Cultural Ecology. Conference Proceedings. Applications of Space Age Technology in Anthropology. John C. Stennis Space Center, MS: NASA.

1994   Recent Advances in the Regional Analysis of Indigenous Land Use and Tropical Deforestation. Special Issue. Human Ecology 22(3):243–247.

Behrens, C., M. Baksh, and M. Mothes
1994   A Regional Analysis of Bari Land Use Intensification and Its Impact on Landscape Heterogeneity. Human Ecology 22:279–316.

Behrens, C., and T. Sever, eds.
1991   Applications of Space-Age Technology in Anthropology. John C. Stennis Space Center, MS: NASA.

Bell, R. R., and C. A. Heller
1978   Nutrition Studies: An Appraisal of the North Alaskan Eskimo Diet. *In* The Eskimo of Northwestern Alaska: A Biological Perspective. P. L. Jamison, S. L. Zegura, and F. A. Milan, eds. Stroudsburg, PA: Dowden, Hutchinson & Ross.

Belnap, J., S. L. Phillips, and M. E. Miller
2004   Response of Desert Biological Soil Crusts to Alterations in Precipitation Frequency. Oecologia 141(2):306–316.

Beniston, M.
1994   Mountain Environments in Changing Climates. London: Routledge.

2000   Environmental Change in Mountains and Uplands. Geneva: University of Geneva Press.

Bennett, J.
1969   Northern Plainsmen. Chicago: Aldine.

1973   Adaptive Strategy in the Canadian Plains. Canadian Plains Studies 1:181–199.

1976   The Ecological Transition. London: Pergamon.

1992   Of Time and the Enterprise: North American Family Farm Management in a Context of Resource Marginality. Minneapolis: University of Minnesota Press.

Bennett, M., and D. W. Teague, eds.
1999   Nature of Cities: Ecocriticism and Urban Environments. Tucson: University of Arizona Press.

Bentley, G. R.
1985   Hunter-Gatherer Energetics and Fertility: A Reassessment of the !Kung San. Human Ecology 13(1):79–109.

Bergman, R. W.
1980   Amazon Economics: The Simplicity of Shipibo Indian Wealth. Dell Plain Latin American Studies, no. 6. Syracuse: Syracuse University, Department of Geography.

Berke, P. R., J. MacDonald, N. White, M. Holmes, D. Line, K. Oury, and P. Ryznar
2003   Green Development to Protect Watersheds: Does New Urbanism Make a Difference? Journal of the American Planning Association 69:397–413.

Berkes, F.
1999   Sacred Ecology: Traditional Ecological Knowledge of Resource Management. Philadelphia: Taylor & Francis.

Berkes, F., ed.
1989   Common Property Resources: Ecology and Community-Based Sustainable Development. London: Bellhaven.

Berkes, F., and D. Jolly
2002   Adapting to Climate Change: Social-Ecological Resilience in a Canadian Western Arctic Community. Conservation Ecology 5(2):18.

Berkowitz, A. R., C. H. Nilton, and K. S. Hollweg, eds.
2003   Understanding Urban Ecosystems: A New Frontier for Science and Education. New York: Springer.

Berlin, B.
1992   Ethnobiological Classification. Princeton, NJ: Princeton University Press.

Bermingham, E., C. W. Dick, and C. Moritz, eds.
2005   Tropical Rainforests: Past, Present and Future. Chicago: University of Chicago Press.

Berner, J., C. Symon, L. Arris, and O. W. Heal
2005   Arctic Climate Impact Assessment. New York: Cambridge University Press.

Bernhardt, E. S., and M. A. Palmer
2007   Restoring Streams in an Urbanizing World. Freshwater Biology 52:738–751.

Berry, A., ed.
2002   Infinite Tropics. New York: Verso.

Berry, B. J.
1990   Urbanization. *In* The Earth as Transformed by Human Action. B. L. Turner II et al., eds. New York: Cambridge University Press.

Bertolini, L., and F. le Clercq
2003   Urban Development Without More Mobility by Car? Lessons from Amsterdam, A Multimodal Urban Region. Environment and Planning A 35(4):575–589.

Bicchieri, M. G., ed.
1972   Hunters and Gatherers Today: A Socio-Economic Study of Eleven Such Cultures in the Twentieth Century. New York: Holt, Rinehart & Winston.

Bierregaard, R. O., C. Gascon, T. Lovejoy, and R. Mesquita, eds.
2001   Lessons from Amazônia: The Ecology and Conservation of a Fragmented Forest. New Haven, CT: Yale University Press.

Biersack, A.
1999   From the New Ecology to the New Ecologies. American Anthropologist 101:5–18.

Billings, W. D.
1974   Arctic and Alpine Vegetation: Plant Adaptations to Cold Summer Climates. *In* Arctic and Alpine Environments. J. D. Ives and R. G. Barry, eds. London: Methuen.

Binford, L. R.
1985   Human Ancestors: Changing Views of Their Behavior. Journal of Anthropological Archeology 4:292–327.

Binford, M., A. Kolata, M. Brenner, J. Januseu, M. Seddon, M. Abbott, and J. Curtis.
1997   Climate Variation and the Rise and Fall of an Andean Civilization. Quaternary Research 47:235–248.

Binnema, T.
2001   Common and Contested Ground: A Human and Environmental History of the Northwestern Plains. Norman: University of Oklahoma Press.

Birdsell, J. B.
1953   Some Environmental and Cultural Factors Influencing the Structure of Australian Aboriginal Populations. American Naturalist 87:171–207.

Bishop, C. A.
1970   The Emergence of Hunting Territories Among the Northern Ojibwa. Ethnology 9:1–15.

Bishop, M. P., and J. F. Shroder
2004   Geographic Information Science and Mountain Geomorphology. New York: Springer.

Bjerregaard, P. E., E. Dewailly, T. K. Young, C. Blanchet, R. A. Hegele, S. E. O. Ebbesson, P. M. Risica, and G. Mulvad
2003   Blood Pressure Among the Inuit Populations in the Arctic. Scandinavian Journal of Public Health 31(2):92–99.

Bjerregaard, P. E., M. E. Jorgensen, K. Borch-Johnsen, and the Greenland Population Study
2004   Serum Lipids of Greenland Inuit in Relation to Inuit Genetic Heritage, Westernisation and Migration. Atherosclerosis 174(2):391–398.

Blaikie, P., and H. Brookfield
1987   Land Degradation and Society. London: Methuen.

Blanchet, C., E. Dewailly, P. Ayotte, S. Bruneau, O. Receveur, and B. J. Holub
2000   Contribution of Selected Traditional and Market Foods to the Diet of Nunavik Inuit Women. Canadian Journal of Dietetic Practice and Research 61(2):50–59.

Bliss, L. C.
1975   Devon Island, Canada. *In* Structure and Function of Tundra Ecosystems. T. Rosswall and O. W. Heal, eds. Stockholm: Swedish Natural Science Research Council.

Bliss L. C., G. M. Courtin, D. L. Pattie, R. R. Riewe, and W. A. Whitfield
1973   Arctic Tundra Ecosystems. Annual Review of Ecology and Systematics 4:359–399.

Bliss, L. C., O. W. Heal, and J. J. Moore
1981   Tundra Ecosystems: A Comparative Analysis. New York: Cambridge University Press.

Bliss, L. C., G. H. R. Henry, J. Svoboda, and D. I. Bliss
1994   Patterns of Plant Distribution within Two Polar Desert Landscapes. Arctic and Alpine Research 26(1):77.

Blom, D. E., J. E. Buikstra, L. Keng, P. D. Tomczak, E. Shoreman, and D. Stevens-Tuttle
2005   Anemia and Childhood Mortality: Latitudinal Patterning Along the Coast of Pre-Columbian Peru. American Journal of Physical Anthropology 127(2):152–169.

Blurton-Jones, N., and M. Konner
1976   !Kung Knowledge of Animal Behavior. *In* Kalahari Hunter-Gatherers. R. B. Lee and I. DeVore, eds. Cambridge, MA: Harvard University Press.

Boas, F.
1896   The Limitations of the Comparative Method of Anthropology. Science (New Series) 4:901–908.
1963   The Mind of Primitive Man. New York: Greenwood. Reprint.
1964   The Central Eskimo. Lincoln: University of Nebraska Press. (Originally published in 1888 by the Smithsonian Institution Press.)

Bobylev, L. P., K. Y. Kondratyev, and O. M. Johannessen
2003   Arctic Environment Variability in the Context of Global Change. New York: Springer.

Bodenhorn, B.
2000   It's Traditional to Change: A Case Study of Strategic Decision-Making. Cambridge Anthropology 22(1):24–51.

Bodmer, R. E., J. F. Eisenberg, and K. H. Redford
1997   Hunting and the Likelihood of Extinction of Amazonian Mammals. Conservation Biology 11(2):460–466.

Boecken, B., and M. Schachak
1994   Desert Plant Communities in Human-Made Patches: Implications for Management. Ecological Applications 4:702–716.

Boetsch, G., and E. Rabino-Massa
2005   Anthropological Research on Mountain Ecosystems: Biodemographic, Prehistoric Archeological and Genetic Aspects. International Journal of Anthropology 20(3):151–154.

Bogin, B.
1988   Patterns of Human Growth. Cambridge Studies of Biological Anthropology. Cambridge: Cambridge University Press.

Bogue, D.
1969   Principles of Demography. New York: Wiley.

Bohlen, J., F. Milan, and F. Halberg
1970   Circumpolar Chronobiology. Proceedings of the Ninth International Congress of Anatomists, Leningrad.

Boken, V. K., A. P. Cracknell, and R. L. Heathcoate
2005   Monitoring and Predicting Agricultural Drought: A Global Study. New York: Oxford University Press.

Bollig, M.
2006   Risk Management in a Hazardous Environment: A Comparative Study of Two Pastoral Societies. New York: Springer.

Bolstad, P.
2005   GIS Fundamentals: A First Text of Geographic Information Systems. 2nd ed. White Bear Lake, MN: Eider Press.

Bolton, R.
1973   Aggression and Hypoglycemia Among the Qolla: A Study in Psychological Anthropology. Ethnology 12:227–257.

Bonan, G. B., H. H. Shugart, and D. L. Urban
1990   The Sensitivity of Some High Latitude Boreal Forest to Climate Change Parameters. Climate Change 16:9–29.

Bonell, M., M. M. Hufschmidt, and J. S. Gladwell
1993   Hydrology and Water Management in the Humid Tropics: Hydrological Research Issues and Strategies for Water Management. Cambridge: Cambridge University Press.

Bonnema, J.
1977   Soils. *In* Ecophysiology of Tropical Crops. P. Alvim and T. Kozlowski, eds. New York: Academic.

Bookchin, M.
1979   Ecology and Revolutionary Thought. Antipode 10(3):21–32.

Booth, W.
1989   Monitoring the Fate of Forests from Space. Science 243:1428–1429.

Borowiec, A.
2003   Taming the Sahara: Tunisia Shows a Way While Others Falter. Westport, CT: Praeger.

Boserup, E.
1965   The Conditions of Agricultural Growth. Chicago: Aldine.

Boster, J.
1983   A Comparison of the Diversity of Jivaroan Gardens with That of the Tropical Forest. Human Ecology 11:69–84.
1984   Inferring Decision-Making from Preferences and Behavior: An Analysis of Aguaruna Jivaro Manioc Selection. Human Ecology 12(4):343–358.

Botkin, D. B., and C. E. Beveridge
1997   Cities as Environments. Urban Ecosystems 1:3–19.

Boudon, R.
2003   Beyond Rational Choice Theory. Annual Review of Sociology 29:1–21.

Bourliére, F., ed.
1983   Ecosystems of the World. Vol. 13, Tropical Savannas. Amsterdam: Elsevier.

Bourn, D.
2001   Environmental Change and the Autonomous Control of Tsetse and Trypanosomiasis in Sub-Saharan Africa: Case Histories from Ethiopia, the Gambia, Kenya, Nigeria and Zimbabwe. Oxford: Environmental Research Group.

Bousquet, F., O. Barreteau, P. D'Aquino, M. Etienne, S. Boissau, S. Aubert, C. LePage, D. Babin, and J. C. Castella
2002   Multi-Agent Systems and Role Games: Collective Learning Processes for Ecosystem Management. *In* Complexity and Management. M. A. Janssen, ed. Northampton, MA: Edward Elgar.

Bowen, M.
2005   Thin Ice: Unlocking the Secrets of Climate i+n the World's Highest Mountains. New York: Henry Holt.

Bowman, D., and L. D. Prior
2004   Impact of Aboriginal Landscape Burning on Woody Vegetation in Eucalyptus Tetrodonta Savanna in Arnhem Land, N. Australia. Journal of Biogeography 31(5):807–817.

Boyd, R., and P. Richerson
1985   Culture and the Evolutionary Process. Chicago: University of Chicago Press.

Bradley, G. A.
1995   Urban Forest Landscapes: Integrating Multidisciplinary Perspectives. Seattle: University of Washington Press.

Bradley, R., ed.
1989   Global Changes of the Past. Boulder: UCAR, Office of Interdisciplinary Earth Studies.

Bramwell, A.
1989   Ecology in the 20th Century: A History. New Haven, CT: Yale University Press.

Brandon, P., and P. Lombardi
2005   Evaluating Sustainable Development. Oxford: Blackwell Science.
Braudel, F.
1973   The Mediterranean and the Mediterranean World in the Age of Philip II. 2 vols. New York: Harper & Row.
Braund, S., S. Stoker, and J. Kruse
1988   Quantification of Subsistence and Cultural Need for Bowhead Whales by Alaskan Eskimos. Anchorage: International Whaling Commission.
Brecher, H., and L. Thompson
1993   Measurement of the Retreat of Qori Kalis Glacier in the Tropical Andes of Peru by Terrestrial Photogrammetry. Photogrammetric Engineering and Remote Sensing 59:1017–1022.
Breuse, J., H. Feldmann, and O. Uhlmann
1998   Urban Ecology. Berlin: Springer.
Breymeyer, A. I., ed.
1990   Ecosystems of the World: Managed Grasslands. Amsterdam: Elsevier.
1996   Global Change: Effects on Coniferous Forests and Grasslands. SCOPE Report, no. 56. New York: Wiley.
Briggs, L. C.
1975   Environment and Human Adaptation in the Sahara. *In* Physiologica Anthropology. A. Damon, ed. New York: Oxford University Press.
Briggs, M.
1996   Riparian Ecosystem Recovery in Arid Lands: Strategies and References. Tucson: University of Arizona Press.
Broll, G., and B. Keplin
2005   Mountain Ecosystems: Studies in Treeline Ecology. New York: Springer.
Bromley, D., ed.
1992   Making the Commons Work. San Francisco: Institute for Contemporary Studies.
Brondizio, E. S.
1996   Forest Farmers: Human and Landscape Ecology of Caboclo Populations in the Amazon Estuary. Ph.D. diss. Bloomington: Indiana University, Environmental Science Program, School of Public and Environmental Affairs.
2005   Intraregional Analysis of Land-Use Change in the Amazon. *In* Seeing the Forest and the Trees. E. F. Moran and E. Ostrom, eds. Cambridge, MA: MIT Press.
2007   The Amazonian Caboclo and the Açaí Palm: Forest Farmers in the Global Market. New York: New York Botanical Garden Press.
Brondizio, E. S., S. McCracken, E. F. Moran, A. Siqueira, D. Nelson, and C. Rodriguez-Pedraza
2002   The Colonist Footprint: Towards a Conceptual Framework of Deforestation Trajectories Among Small Farmers in Frontier Amazônia. *In* Patterns and Processes of Land Use and Forest Change in the Amazon. C. H. Wood and R. Porro, eds. Gainesville: University of Florida Press.
Brondizio, E. S., and E. F. Moran
In prep. Amazonian Deforestation: Why Taking a Closer Look Makes a Difference.
Brondizio, E. S., E. F. Moran, P. Mausel, and Y. Wu
1994   Land Use Change in the Amazon Estuary: Patterns of Caboclo Settlement and Landscape Management. Human Ecology 22(3):249–278.

1996   Land Cover in the Amazon Estuary: Linking of Thematic with Historical and Botanical Data. Photogrammetric Engineering and Remote Sensing 62(8):921–929.

Brondizio, E. S., and A. D. Siqueira

1997   From Extractivists to Forest Farmers: Changing Concepts of Caboclo Agroforestry in the Amazon Estuary. Research in Economic Anthropology 18:233–279.

Bronson, B.

1972   Farm Labor and the Evolution of Food Production in Population Growth: Anthropological Implications. B. Spooner, ed. Cambridge, MA: MIT Press.

1975   The Earliest Farming: Demography as Cause and Consequence. *In* Population, Ecology and Social Evolution. S. Polgar, ed. The Hague: Mouton.

Brookfield, H. C., and P. Brown

1963   Struggle for Land: Agriculture and Group Territories Among the Chimbu of the New Guinea Highlands. Melbourne: Oxford University Press.

Brooks, M. L.

2003   Effects of Increased Soil Nitrogen on the Dominance of Alien Annual Plants in the Mojave Desert. Journal of Applied Ecology 40(2):344–353.

Brosius, J. P.

1997   Endangered Forest, Endangered People. Human Ecology 25:47–69.

1999   Green Dots, Pink Hearts: Displacing Politics from the Malaysian Rain Forest. American Anthropologist 101:36–57.

Browder, J.

1989a   Public Policy and Deforesting the Brazilian Amazon. *In* Public Policies and the Misuse of Forest Resources. R. Repetti and M. Gillis, eds. Washington, DC: World Resources Institute.

Browder, J., ed.

1989b   Fragile Lands of Latin America. Boulder: Westview.

Browman, D. L.

1974   Pastoral Nomadism in the Andes. Current Anthropology 15:188–196.

1984   Pastoralism and Development in High Andean Lands. Journal of Arid Environments 7:313–328.

Browman, D. L., ed.

1987   Arid Land Use Strategies and Risk Management in the Andes. Boulder: Westview.

Brown, G. W., ed.

1968 and 1972 Desert Biology. 2 vols. New York: Academic.

Brown, J., P. Miller, L. Tieszen, and F. Bunnell, eds.

1980   An Arctic Ecosystem. Stroudsburg, PA: Dowden, Hutchinson & Ross.

Brown, J. C., and M. Purcell

2005   There's Nothing Inherent about Scale: Political Ecology, the Local Trap, and the Politics of Development in the Brazilian Amazon. Geoforum 36(5):607–624.

Brown, J. K., and J. K. Smith

2000   Wildland Fire in Ecosystems: Effects of Fire on Flora. Ft. Collins, CO: USDA, Forest Service Rocky Mountain Research Station.

Brown, L.

1971   The Biology of Pastoral Man as a Factor in Conservation. Biological Conservation 3(2):93–100.

Brown, P., and A. Podolefsky

1976   Population Density, Agricultural Intensity, Land Tenure and Group Size in the New Guinea Highlands. Ethnology 15:211–238.

Brown, S.
1993   Tropical Forests and the Global Carbon Cycle: The Need for Sustainable Land-Use Patterns. Agriculture, Ecosystems & Environment 46(1–4):31–44.
1996   Mitigation Potential of Carbon Dioxide Emissions by Management of Forests in Asia. Ambio 25(4):273–278.

Brown, S., A. S. Charles, W. Knabe, J. Raich, M. C. Trexler, and P. Woomer
1993   Tropical Forests: Their Past, Present, and Potential Future Role in the Terrestrial Carbon Budget. Water, Air, & Soil Pollution 70(1–4):71–94.

Browne, J.
2007   Darwin's Origin of Species: A Biography. Washington, DC: Atlantic Monthly Press.

Bruemmer, F.
1971   Seasons of the Eskimo. Greenwich, CT: New York Graphic Society.

Brush, S.
1975   The Concept of Carrying Capacity for Systems of Shifting Cultivation. American Anthropologist 77:799–811.
1976   Man's Use of an Andean Ecosystem. Human Ecology 4(2):128–132;147–166.
1977   Mountain, Field and Family: The Economy and Human Ecology of an Andean Valley. Philadelphia: University of Pennsylvania Press.
1982   The Natural and Human Environment of the Central Andes. Mountain Research and Development 2(1):19–38.

Brush, S., and D. Guillet
1985   Small-Scale Pastoral Production in the Central Andes. Mountain Research and Development 5(1):19–30.

Brush, S., J. Heath, and Z. Huaman
1981   The Dynamics of Andean Potato Agriculture. Economic Botany 35:70–88.

Brush, S., and D. Stabinsky
1997   Valuing Local Knowledge: Indigenous People and Intellectual Property Rights. Washington, DC: Island.

Brutsaert, T. D., E. Parra, M. Shriver, A. Gamboa, J. Palacios, M. Rivera, I. Rodriguez, and F. León-Velarde
2004   Effects on Birthplace and Individual Genetic Admixture on Lung Volume and Exercise Phenotypes of Peruvian Quechua. American Journal of Physical Anthropology 123(4):390–398.

Bryant, M. M.
2006   Urban Landscape Conservation and the Role of Ecological Greenways at Local and Metropolitan Scales. Landscape and Urban Planning 76:23–44.

Bryant, R. L., and S. Bailey
1997   Third World Political Ecology. London: Routledge.

Buck, S., and D. Brown
1964   Mortality from Lung Cancer and Bronchitis in Relation to Smoke and SO_2 Concentration. Research Paper, no. 7. England: Tobacco Research Council.

Buckley, W.
1967   Sociology and Modern Systems Theory. Englewood Cliffs, NJ: Prentice-Hall.

Buckley, W., ed.
1968   Modern Systems Research for the Behavioral Scientist. Chicago: Aldine.

Buckman, H., and N. Brady
1969   The Nature and Properties of Soils. 7th ed. New York: Macmillan.

Budd, G. M.
1974 Physiological Research at Australian Stations in the Antarctic and the Sub-antarctic. *In* Human Adaptability to Antarctic Conditions. E. K. E. Gunderson, ed. Washington, DC: American Geophysical Union.

Bulkeley, H., and M. M. Betsill
2003 Cities and Climate Change: Urban Sustainability and Global Environmental Governance. London: Taylor & Francis.

Bullard, R. D., A. O. Torres, and G. S. Johnson
2000 Sprawl City: Race, Politics, and Planning in Atlanta. Washington, DC: Island.

Bunker, S.
1985 Underdeveloping the Amazon. Urbana: University of Illinois Press.

Bunnell, F. L., S. F. MacLean, and J. Brown
1975 Barrow, Alaska, U.S.A. *In* Structure and Function of Tundra Ecosystems. T. Rosswall and O. W. Heal, eds. Stockholm: Swedish Natural Science Research Council.

Burch, E., and L. Ellanna
1994 Key Issues in Hunter-Gatherer Research. Oxford: Berg.

Burch, E. S.
1975 Eskimo Kinsmen: Changing Family Relationships in Northwest Alaska. American Ethnological Society Monograph, no. 59. New York: West.
1981 The Traditional Eskimo Hunter of Port Hope, Alaska: 1800–1875. Barrow: North Slope Burrough.
1983 People of the Arctic. Illustrated map. Washington, DC: National Geographic Society.
1985 Subsistence Production in Kivalana, Alaska: A Twenty-Year Perspective. Technical Paper, no. 128. Alaska Department of Fish and Game.

Burch, E. S., and T. C. Correll
1972 Alliance and Conflict: Inter-Regional Relations in Northern Alaska. *In* Alliance in Eskimo Society. L. Guemple, ed. Seattle: University of Washington Press.

Burchard, R.
1976 Myths of the Sacred Leaf: Ecological Perspectives on Coca and Peasant Bio-cultural Adaptation in Peru. Ph.D. diss. Indiana University, Department of Anthropology.

Bureau of Indian Affairs (BIA)
1971 A Study of the Impact of the Proposed Trans-Alaska Pipeline on the Alaska Native Population. Arlington, VA: Educational Systems Resources Corporation.

Burgess, E. W.
1925 The Growth of the City. *In* The City. R. E. Park et al., eds. Chicago: University of Chicago Press.

Burgess, E. W., and D. J. Bogue, eds.
1964 Contributions to Urban Sociology. Chicago: University of Chicago Press.

Burling, R.
1964 Cognition and Componential Analysis: God's Truth or Hocus-Pocus? American Anthropologist 66:20–28.

Burton, A. C., and O. G. Edholm
1955 Man in a Cold Environment. London: Edward Arnold.

Buskirk, E.
1976 Work Performance of Newcomers to the Peruvian Highlands. *In* Man in the Andes. P. T. Baker and M. Little, eds. Stroudsburg, PA: Dowden, Hutchinson & Ross.

Butzer, K.

1976   Early Hydraulic Civilization in Egypt: A Study in Cultural Ecology. Chicago: University of Chicago Press.

1990   A Human Ecosystem Framework for Archeology. *In* The Ecosystem Approach in Anthropology: From Concept to Practice. E. F. Moran, ed. Ann Arbor: University of Michigan Press.

Cadenasso, M. L., S. Pickett, and M. Grove

2006   Integrative Approaches to Investigating Human-Natural Systems: The Baltimore Ecosystem Study. Natures Sciences Sociétés 14:4–14.

Cain, S., and G. M. de Oliveira Castro

1959   Manual of Vegetation Analysis. New York: Hafner.

Caldwell, J. C., A. G. Hill, and V. J. Hull, eds.

1988   Micro-Approaches to Demographic Research. New York: Kegan Paul International.

Callaghan, T. V., L. O. Björn, Y. Chernov, T. Chapin, T. R. Christensen, B. Huntley, R. A. Ims, M. Johansson, D. Jolly, S. Jonasson, N. Matveyeva, N. Panikov, W. Oechel, and G. Shaver

2004   Past Changes in Arctic Terrestrial Ecosystems, Climate and UV Radiation. Ambio 33(7):398–403.

Callaghan, T. V., and B. Maxwell, eds.

1995   Global Change and Arctic Terrestrial Ecosystems. Ecosystems Research Report 10. European Commission: Belgium.

Camargo, F. C.

1958   Report on the Amazon Region. *In* Problems of Humid Tropical Regions. Paris: UNESCO.

Camerer, C.

1998   Bounded Rationality in Individual Decision-Making. Experimental Economics 1:163–183.

2003   Behavioral Game Theory: Experiments in Strategic Interactions. Princeton, NJ: Princeton University Press.

Camerini, J. R.

2001   The Alfred Russel Wallace Reader: A Selection of Writings from the Field. Baltimore, MD: The Johns Hopkins University Press.

Campbell, B. M., and J. Sayer

2003   Integrated Natural Resource Management: Linking Productivity, the Environment, and Development. Wallingford, UK: CABI Publishers/CIFOR.

Campbell, D.

1984   Response to Drought Among Farmers and Herders in Southern Kajiado District, Kenya. Human Ecology 12(1):35–64.

Campbell, J. B.

1987   Introduction to Remote Sensing. New York: Guilford.

Campbell, J. M.

1968   Territoriality Among Ancient Hunters: Interpretations from Ethnography and Nature. *In* Archeology in the Americas. Washington, DC: Anthropological Society of Washington.

Campbell, J. M., ed.

1962   Prehistoric Cultural Relation Between the Arctic of Temperate Zones of North America. Technical Papers, no. 11. Arctic Institution of North America.

Cancian, F.
1972   Change and Uncertainty in a Peasant Economy. Stanford, CA: Stanford University Press.

Cane, S.
1987   Australian Aboriginal Subsistence in the Western Desert. Human Ecology 15(4):391–434.

Cantor, L.
1970   A World Geography of Irrigation. 2nd ed. Edinburgh: Oliver & Boyd.

Capello, R., P. Nijkamp, and G. Pepping
1999   Sustainable Cities and Energy Policies. Advances in Spatial Science Series. New York: Springer.

Cardon, Z. G., and D. J. Gage
2006   Resource Exchange in the Rhizosphere: Molecular Tools and the Microbial Perspective. Annual Review of Ecology, Evolution and Systematics 37:459–488.

Carlson, L. D., and A. C. L. Hsieh
1965   Cold. *In* The Physiology of Human Survival. O. G. Edholm and A. Bacharach, eds. London: Academic.

Carneiro, R. L.
1957   Subsistence and Social Structure: An Ecological Study of the Kuikuru. Ph.D. diss. University of Michigan, Department of Anthropology.
1961   Slash-and-Burn Agriculture: A Closer Look at Its Implications for Settlement Patterns. *In* Man and Culture. A. F. Wallace, ed. Fifth International Congress of Anthropological and Ethnological Sciences.
1970   The Transition from Hunting to Horticulture in the Amazon Basin. Eighth Congress of Anthropological and Ethnological Sciences 3:243–251.
1974   Slash-and-Burn Cultivation Among the Kuikuru and Its Implications for Cultural Development in the Amazon Basin. *In* Native South Americans. P. Lyon, ed. Boston: Little, Brown.

Carpenter, S. R., and P. R. Leavitt
1991   Temporal Variation in Palimnological Records Arising from a Trophic Cascade. Ecology 72:277–285.

Carson, R.
1962   Silent Spring. New York: Hougton Mifflin.

Carson, W., and S. Schnitzer, eds.
In press   Tropical Forest Community Ecology. Oxford: Blackwell Science.

Carter, W. E.
1969   New Lands and Old Traditions. Gainesville: University of Florida Press.

Casagrande, D. G.
2004   Conceptions of Primary Forest in a Tzetzal Maya Community: Implications for Conservation. Human Organization 63(2):189–202.

Cashdan, E.
1989   Hunter and Gatherers: Economic Behavior in Bands. *In* Economic Anthropology. S. Plattner, ed. Stanford: Stanford University Press.

Casimir, M., and A. Rao
1998   Sustainable Land Management and the Tragedy of No Man's Land: An Analysis of West Himalayan Pastures Using Remote Sensing Techniques. Human Ecology 26:113–134.

Castaglioni, A.
1958   A History of Medicine. 2nd ed. New York: Alfred A. Knopf.

Cavalli-Sforza, L., and M. Feldman
1981   Cultural Transmission and Evolution. Princeton, NJ: Princeton University Press.

Cernusca, A., U. Tappeiner, and N. Bayfield, eds.
2000   Land-Use Changes in European Mountain Ecosystems. Berlin: Blackwell Science.

Chagnon, N.
1968   Yanomamo: The Fierce People. New York: Holt, Rinehart & Winston.

Chance, N. A.
1966   The Eskimo of North Alaska. New York: Holt, Rinehart & Winston.
1990   The Inupiat and Arctic Alaska: An Ethnography of Modern Development. New York: Holt, Rinehart & Winston.

Chapin, F. S.
1992   Arctic Ecosystems in a Changing Climate. New York: Academic.
1995   Arctic and Alpine Biodiversity: Patterns, Causes, and Ecosystem Consequences. New York: Springer.

Chapin, F. S., W. Eugster, J. P. McFadden, A. H. Lynch, and D. A. Walker
2000   Summer Differences Among Arctic Ecosystems in Regional Climate Forcing. Journal of Climate 13(12):2002–2010.

Chapin, F. S., R. L. Jefferies, J. F. Reynolds, G. R. Shaver, and J. Svoboda, eds.
1991   Arctic Ecosystems in a Changing Climate: An Ecophysiological Perspective. San Diego, CA: Academic.

Chapman, G. P.
1992   Desertified Grasslands: Their Biology and Management. Linnean Society Symposium, no. 13. San Diego, CA: Academic.

Chapman, J. L., and M. J. Reiss
1998   Ecology: Principles and Applications. 2nd ed. Cambridge: Cambridge University Press.

Chapple, E.
1970   Culture and Biological Man. New York: Holt, Rinehart & Winston.

Charnon, E. L.
1976   Optimal Foraging: The Marginal Value Theorem. Theoretical Population Biology 9:129–136.

Chen, M., Y. P. Huang, L. Guo, P. Cai, W. Yang, G. Liu, and Y. Qui
2002   Biological Productivity and Carbon Cycling in the Arctic Ocean. Chinese Science Bulletin 47(12):1037–1040.

Cheng, X. L., S. Q. An, B. Li, J. Chen, G. Lin, Y. Liu, Y. Luo, and S. Liu
2006   Summer Rain Pulse Size and Rainwater Uptake by Three Dominant Desert Plants in a Desertified Grassland Ecosystem in Northwestern China. Plant Ecology 184(1):1–12.

Chernigovsky, V. N., ed.
1969   Problems of Space Biology: Adaptation to Hypoxia and the Resistance of an Organism. Washington, DC: NASA.

Chernov, Y. I.
1985   The Living Tundra. New York: Cambridge University Press.

Childe, V. G.
1951   Man Makes Himself. New York: New American Library.

Childs, G.
1998   A Cultural and Historical Analysis of Demographic Trends and Family Management Strategies Among the Tibetans of Nubri, Nepal. Ph.D. diss. Indiana University, Department of Anthropology.

Chorghade, G. P., S. Kanade, and C. H. D. Fall
2006   Why Are Rural Indian Women So Thin? Findings from a Village in Maharashtra. Public Health Nutrition 9(1):9–18.

Chorley, R. J.
1973   Geography as Human Ecology. *In* Directions in Geography. R. J. Chorley, ed. London: Methuen.

Chowdhury, R. R., and B. L. Turner
2006   Reconciling Agency and Structure in Empirical Analysis: Smallholder Land Use in Southern Yucatan, Mexico. Annals of the Association of American Geographers 96(2):302–322.

Christensen, N. B.
2003   Inuit in Cyberspace: Embedding Offline, Identities Online. Copenhagen: Museum Tusculanum Press, University of Copenhagen.

Churchill, S. A.
1995   Biodiversity and Conservation of Neotropical Montane Forests. New York: New York Botanical Garden Press.

Cincotta, R., Y. Zhang, and X. Zhou
1992   Transhumant Alpine Pastoralism in Northeastern Qinghai Province: An Evaluation of Livestock Population Response During China's Agrarian Economic Reform. Nomadic Peoples 30:3–25.

Clark, D. A.
2004   Sources or Sinks? The Responses of Tropical Forests to Current and Future Climate and Atmospheric Composition. Philosophical Transactions of the Royal Society of London. Series B–Biological Sciences 359(1443):477–491.

Clark, J. S., E. C. Grimm, J. J. Donovan, S. C. Fritz, D. R. Engstrom, and J. E. Almendinger
2002   Drought Cycles and Landscape Responses to Past Aridity on Prairies of the Northern Great Plains, USA. Ecology 83(3):595–601.

Clarke, K. C.
2001   Getting Started with Geographic Information Systems. 3rd ed. Upper Saddle River, NJ: Prentice Hall.

Clarke, W.
1966   From Extensive to Intensive Shifting Cultivation: A Succession from New Guinea. Ethnology 5:347–359.
1971   Place and People. Berkeley: University of California Press.
1976   Maintenance of Agriculture and Human Habitats within the Tropical Forest Ecosystem. Human Ecology 4(3):247–259.

Clay, J.
1988   Indigenous People and Tropical Forests. Cambridge, MA: Cultural Survival.

Clements, D., and A. Shrestha
2004   New Dimensions in Agroecology. Binghamton, NY: Food Products Press.

Clements, F. E.
1905   Research Methods in Ecology. Lincoln, NE: University Publishing.

1907   Plant Physiology and Ecology. New York: H. Holt.

1916   Plant Succession: An Analysis of the Development of Vegetation. Washington, DC: Carnegie Institution of Washington.

1920   Plant Indicators: The Relation of Plant Communities to Process and Practice. Washington, DC: Carnegie Institution of Washington.

1928   Plant Succession and Indicators: A Definitive Edition of Plant Success and Plant Indicators. New York: H. W. Wilson.

Clements, F. E., and R. W. Chaney

1936   Environment and Life in the Great Plains. Washington, DC: Carnegie Institution of Washington.

Cloudsley-Thompson, J. L.

1977   Man and the Biology of Arid Zones. London: Edward Arnold.

1984   Sahara Desert. Oxford: Pergamon. Key Environments Series.

Cochrane, M. A., and M. D. Schulze

1998   Fire as a Recurrent Event in Tropical Forests of the Eastern Amazon. Biotropica 31:2–16.

Cochrane, T. T. and P. Sanchez

1982   Land Resources, Soils and Their Management in the Amazon Region. *In* Amazônia: Agriculture and Land Use Research. S. Hecht, ed. Cali, Colombia: CIAT.

Cochrane, M. A., A. Alencar, M. D. Schulze, and C. M. Souza Jr.

1999   Positive Feedbacks in the Fire Dynamics of Closed Canopy Tropical Forests. Science 284:1832–1835.

Cohen, J.

1991   Trophic Topology. Science 251:686–687.

Cohen, Y., ed.

1968   Man in Adaptation: The Cultural Present. Chicago: Aldine.

Coimbra, C.E.A. Jr.

1988   Human Settlements, Demographic Pattern and Epidemiology in Lowland Amazônia: The Case of Chagas' Disease. American Anthropologist 90:82–97.

1989   From Shifting Cultivation to Coffee Farming: The Impact of Change on the Health and Ecology of the Suruí Indians in the Brazilian Amazon. Ph.D. diss. Bloomington: Indiana University, Department of Anthropology.

Coimbra, C. E. A. Jr., N. Flowers, F. M. Salzano, and R. Santos

2002   The Xavante in Transition: Health, Ecology, and Bioanthropology in Central Brazil. Ann Arbor: University of Michigan Press.

Cole, D. P.

1975   Nomads of the Nomads. Chicago: Aldine.

Coleman, D. C. Jr., D. A. Crossley, and P. F. Hendrix

2004   Fundamentals on Soil Ecology. San Diego, CA: Academic.

Colfer, C. J., and Y. Byron, eds.

2001   People Managing Forests: The Links Between Human Well-Being and Sustainability. Washington, DC: Resources for the Future.

Collier, J.

1973   Alaskan Eskimo Education. New York: Holt, Rinehart & Winston.

Collings, P.

2000   Aging and Life Course Development in an Inuit Community. Arctic Anthropology 37(2):111–125.

2001   If You Got Everything, It's Good Enough: Perspectives on Successful Aging in a Canadian Inuit Community. Journal of Cross-Cultural Gerontology 16(2): 127–155.

Colten, C.
2005   An Unnatural Metropolis: Wresting New Orleans from Nature. Baton Rouge: Louisiana State University Press.

Conant, F.
1978   The Use of Landsat Data in Studies of Human Ecology. Current Anthropology 19:382–384.
1990   1990 and Beyond: Satellite Remote Sensing and Ecological Anthropology. *In* The Ecosystem Approach in Anthropology. E. F. Moran, ed. Ann Arbor: University of Michigan Press.

Conant, R. T., K. Paustian, and E. T. Elliott
2001   Grassland Management and Conversion into Grassland: Effects on Soil Carbon. Ecological Applications 11(2):343–355.

Condon, R. G.
1987   Inuit Youth: Growth and Change in the Canadian Arctic. New Brunswick: Rutgers University Press.
1991   Birth Seasonality, Photoperiod and Social Change in the Central Canadian Arctic. Human Ecology 19(3):287.

Conklin, B., and L. Graham
1995   The Shifting Middle Ground: Amazonian Indians and Eco-Politics. American Anthropologist 97:695–710.

Conklin, H. C.
1954   An Ethnoecological Approach to Shifting Agriculture. Transactions of the New York Academy of Sciences 17(2):133–142.
1957   Hanunóo Agriculture. Rome: Food and Agricultural Organization.
1961   The Study of Shifting Cultivation. Current Anthropology 2:27–61.
1963   The Study of Shifting Cultivation. Washington, DC: Pan American Union.
1980   Ethnographic Atlas of Ifugao. New Haven, CT: Yale University Press.

Connell, J.
1978   Diversity in Tropical Rain Forests and Coral Reefs. Science 199:1302–1310.

Constanza, R., F. Sklar, and M. White
1990   Modelling Coastal Landscape Dynamics. BioScience 40:91–107.

Constanza, R., and A. Voivnov
2004   Landscape Simulation Modeling: A Spatially-Explicit, Dynamic Approach. New York: Springer.

Constanza, R., L. Wainger, C. Folke, and K. Maler
1993   Modelling Complex Ecological Economic Systems. BioScience 43(8):545–555.

Conway, D., and N. Heynen, eds.
2006   Globalization's Contradictions: Geographies of Discipline, Destruction and Transformation. New York: Routledge.

Cook, A. G., A. C. Janetos, and W. T. Hinds
1990   Global Effects of Tropical Deforestation: Towards an Integrated Perspective. Environmental Conservation 17(3):201–212.

Cook, D., and J. E. Buikstra
1980   Palaeopathology: An American Account. Annual Reviews in Anthropology 9:433–470.

Cooke, R. U.
1982   Urban Geomorphology in Drylands. New York: United Nations University/ Oxford University Press.

Coomes, O. T., B. L. Barham, and Y. Takasaki
2004   Targeting Conservation-Development Initiatives in Tropical Forests: Insights from Analyses of Rain Forest Use and Economic Reliance Among Amazonian Peasants. Ecological Economics 51(1–2):47–64.

Coomes, O. T., F. Grimard, and G. J. Burt
2000   Tropical Forests and Shifting Cultivation: Secondary Forest Fallow Dynamics Among Traditional Farmers of the Peruvian Amazon. Ecological Economics 32 (1):109–124.

Cooper, A., and J. Millspaugh
1999   The Application of Discrete Choice Models to Wildlife Resource Selection Studies. Ecology 80(2):566–575.

Coppock, L.
1985   Turkana Livestock Feeding Ecology and Nutritional Dynamics. Ph.D. diss. Colorado State University.

Cottrell, F.
1955   Energy and Society: The Relation Between Energy, Social Change and Economic Development. New York: McGraw-Hill.

Coughenour, M., J. Eclis, D. Swift, D. Coppock, K. Galvin, T. McCabe, and T. Hart
1985   Energy Extraction and Use in a Nomadic Pastoral Ecosystem. Science 230: 619–625.

Couzin, J.
2007   Opening Doors to Native Knowledge. Science 315:1518–1519.

Cowie, J.
2007   Climate Change. Cambridge: Cambridge University Press.

Cowles, H. C.
1899   The Ecological Relations of the Vegetation on the Sand Dunes of Lake Michigan. Botanical Gazette 4:27, 95–117, 167–202, 281–308, 361–388.

Cox, S. B., C. P. Bloch, R. D. Stevens, and L. F. Huenneke
2006   Productivity and Species Richness in an Arid Ecosystem: A Long-Term Perspective. Plant Ecology 186(1):1–12.

Cronon, W.
1991   Nature's Metropolis: Chicago and the Great West. New York: Norton.

Cronon, W., ed.
1995   Uncommon Ground: Toward Reinventing Nature. New York: Norton.

Crumley, C. L., ed.
1994   Historical Ecology: Cultural Knowledge and the Change landscapes. Santa Fe, NM: School of American Research Press.

Crutzen, P. J., and M. O. Andreae
1990   Biomass Burning in the Tropics: Impacts on Atmospheric Chemistry and Biogeochemical Cycles. Science 250:1669–1678.

Cuevas, E., and E. Medina
1986   Nutrient Dynamics within Amazonian Rainforest Ecosystems. Oecologia 68:466–472.

Cultural Survival
1995   Geomatics (Special Issue). Cultural Survival Quarterly. Winter.

Culver, W. E.

1959   Effects of Cold on Man: An Annotated Bibliography, 1938–1951. Physiological Reviews, vol. 39, supp. 3.

Cunfer, G.

2005   On the Great Plans: Agriculture and Environment. College Station: Texas A&M University Press.

Cyert, R. M., and J. G. March

1963   A Behavioral Theory of the Firm. Englewood Cliffs, NJ: Prentice-Hall.

Dahl, G., and A. Hjort

1976   Having Herds: Pastoral Herd Growth and Household Economy. Stockholm: University of Stockholm Studies in Social Anthropology.

Dai, E., S. H. Wu, W. Z. Shi, C. K. Cheung, and A. Shaker

2005   Modeling Change-Patterns-Value Dynamics on Land Use: An Integrated GIS and Artificial Neural Network Approach. Environment Management 36:576–591.

Dale, V. H., R. A. Houghton, and C. A. S. Hall

1991   Estimating the Effects of Land-Use Change on Global Atmospheric CO_2 Concentrations. Canadian Journal of Forestry Research 21:87–90.

Dale, V. H., R. V. O'Neill, M. Pedlowski, and F. Southworth

1993   Causes and Effects of Land Use Change in Central Rondônia, Brazil. Photogrammetric Engineering and Remote Sensing 67:997–1005.

Daley, P., and B. A. James

2004   Cultural Politics and the Mass Media: Alaska Native Voices. Urbana: University of Illinois Press.

Damas, D.

1968   The Diversity of Eskimo Societies. *In* Man the Hunter. R. B. Lee and I. DeVore, eds. Chicago: Aldine.

1969   Environment, History and Central Eskimo Society. *In* Contributions to Anthropology: Ecological Essays. D. Damas, ed. Ottawa: National Museums of Canada.

2002   Arctic Migrants/Arctic Villagers: The Transformation of Inuit Settlement in the Central Arctic. Montreal: McGill-Queen's University Press.

Dang, S., H. Yan, S. Yamamoto, X. Wang, and L. Zeng

2004   Poor Nutritional Status of Younger Tibetan Children Living at High Altitudes. European Journal of Clinical Nutrition 58(6):938–946.

Danjoy, W. A.

1984   Use of Remote Sensing for Monitoring and Control of Deforestation in the High Jungle of Peru. Proceedings of the 18th International Symposium of Remote Sensing of the Environment. Ann Arbor: Environmental Research Institute of Michigan.

Darling, F. F., and M. A. Farvar

1972   Ecological Consequences of Sedentarization of Nomads. *In* The Careless Technology. M. T. Farvar and J. P. Milton, eds. Garden City, NY: Natural History Press.

Darwin, C.

1859   On the Origin of Species by Means of Natural Selection. London: Murray.

Davis, K., and M. S. Bernstam, eds.

1990   Resources, Environment and Population: Present Knowledge, Future Options. (Population and Development Review, supp. to vol. 16). The Population Council. New York: Oxford University Press.

Dawoud, M. A., M. M. Darwish, and M. M. El-Kady
2005　GIS-Based Groundwater Management Model for Western Nile Delta. Water Resources Management 19(5):585–604.

Deadman, P. J.
1999　Modelling Individual Behavior and Group Performance in an Intelligent Agent-Based Simulation of the Tragedy of the Commons. Journal of Environmental Management 56(3):159–172.

Deadman, P. J., D. T. Robinson, E. F. Moran, and E. S. Brondizio
2004　Effects of Colonist Household Structure on Land Use Change in the Amazon Rainforest: An Agent Based Simulation Approach. Environment and Planning B: Planning and Design 31:693–709.

Deal, B.
2001　Ecological Urban Dynamics: The Convergence of Spatial Modeling and Sustainability. Building Research & Information 29:381–393.

Dean, W. R. J.
2004　Nomadic Desert Birds. New York: Springer.

De Angelis, D., and L. Gross, eds.
1992　Individual-Based Models and Approaches in Ecology. New York: Chapman & Hall.

De Angelis, D., and W. Mooij
2005　Individual-Based Modeling of Ecological and Evolutionary Processes. Annual Review of Ecology, Evolution, and Systematics 36(1):147–168.

Decker, E. H., S. Elliott, F. A. Smith, D. R. Blake, and F. S. Rowland.
2000　Energy and Material Flow Through the Urban Ecosystem. Annual Review of Energy and the Environment: 685–740.

De Grandi, G. F., P. Mayaux, J. P. Malingreau, A. Rosenqvist, S. Saatchi, and M. Simard
2000　New Perspectives on Global Ecosystems from Wide-Area Radar Mosaics: Flooded Forest Mapping in the Tropics. International Journal of Remote Sensing 21(6–7):1235–1249.

Deiber, E. J., E. French, and B. Huag
1986　Water-Storage and Use of Spring Wheat Under Conventional Tillage and No-Till in Continuous and Alternate Crop Fallow Systems in the Northern Great Plains. Soil and Water Conservation 41:53–58.

DeJong, G.
1968　Demography and Research with High Altitude Populations. *In* High Altitude Adaptation in a Peruvian Community. P. Baker, ed. Occasional Papers in Anthropology, no. 1. University Park, PA: Pennsylvania State University, Department of Anthropology.
2000　Expectations, Gender, and Norms in Migration Decision-Making. Population Studies 54(3):307–319.

Denbow, J. R., and E. N. Wilmsen
1986　Advent and Course of Pastoralism in the Kalahari. Science 234:1509–1514.

Denevan, W.
1973　Development and the Imminent Demise of the Amazon Rain Forest. Professional Geographer 25(2):130–135.
1986　The Cultural Ecology, Archeology and History of Terracing and Terrace Abandonment in the Colca Valley of Southern Peru. Technical report to the National Science Foundation and the National Geographic Society. University of Wisconsin, Department of Geography.

Denevan, W., and C. Padoch, eds.
1987   Swidden-Fallow Agroforestry in the Peruvian Amazon. Advances in Economic Botany 5. New York: New York Botanical Garden.

Derocher, A. E., N. J. Lunn, and I. Stirling
2004   Polar Bears in a Warming Climate. Integrative and Comparative Biology 44(2): 163–176.

Desfor, G., and R. Keil
2004   Nature and the City: Making Environmental Policy in Toronto and Los Angeles. Tucson: University of Arizona Press.

Dettwyler, K.
1994   Dancing Skeletons: Life and Death in West Africa. Prospect Heights, IL: Waveland.

Dettwyler, S.
1977   The Effects of Verticalization on Adaptation of New Guinea. Unpublished manuscript. Indiana University, Department of Anthropology.

Detwiler, R. P., and C. A. S. Hall.
1988   Tropical Forests and the Global Carbon Cycle. Science 239:42–47.

Deutch, B., H. S. Pedersen, and J. C. Hansen
2004   Dietary Composition in Greenland 2000, Plasma Fatty Acids, and Persistent Organic Pollutants. Science of the Total Environment 331(1–3):177–188.

Deverell, W., and G. Hise, eds.
2005   Land of Sunshine: An Environmental History of Metropolitan Los Angeles. Pittsburgh: University of Pittsburgh Press.

De Vries, D., P. W. Leslie, and J. T. McCabe
2006   Livestock Acquisition Dynamics in Nomadic Pastoralist Herd Demography: A Case Study Among Ngisonyoka Herders of South Turkana, Kenya. Human Ecology 34(1):1–25.

Devuyst, D., L. Hens, and W. De Lannoy, eds.
2001   How Green is the City? Sustainability Assessment and the Management of Urban Environments. New York: Columbia University Press.

Diamond, J.
2005   Collapse: How Societies Choose to Fail or Succeed. New York: Viking.

Diaz, H. F.
2003   Climate Variability and Change in High Elevation Regions: Past, Present and Future. Dordrecht: Kluwer Academic.

Di Castri, F.
1976   International, Interdisciplinary Research in Ecology: Some Problems of Organization and Execution, the Case of the Man and the Biosphere Program. Human Ecology 4(3):235–246.

Dice, L.
1955   Man's Nature and Nature's Man. Ann Arbor: University of Michigan Press.

Dickinson, J.
1972   Alternatives to Monoculture in the Humid Tropics of Latin America. The Professional Geographer 24(3):217–222.

Dickinson, R. E.
1989   Predicting Climate Effects. Nature 342:343–344.

Dickinson, R. E., ed.
1987   The Geophysiology of Amazônia: Vegetation and Climate Interactions: New York: Wiley.

Dickinson, R. E., and P. Kennedy
1992   Impact on Regional Climate of Amazon Deforestation. Geophysical Research Letter 19:1947–1950.

Dillehay, T. D., and A. L. Kolata
2004   Long-Term Human Response to Uncertain Environmental Conditions in the Andes. Proceedings of the National Academy of Sciences of the USA 101(12):4325–4330.

Dittmar, T., and G. Kattner
2003   The Biogeochemistry of the River and Shelf Ecosystem of the Arctic Ocean: A Review. Marine Chemistry 83(3–4):103–120.

D'Odorico, P., and A. Porporato, eds.
2006   Dryland Ecohydrology. New York: Springer.

Dolsak, N., and E. Ostrom, eds.
2003   The Commons in the New Millennium: Challenges and Adaptation. Cambridge, MA: MIT Press.

Dombrowski, K.
1993   Some Considerations for the Understanding of Small Herd Dynamics in East African Arid Zones. Human Ecology 21(1):23–50.

Doughty, P.
1968   Huaylas: An Andean District in Search of Progress. Ithaca, NY: Cornell University Press.

Dove, M. R., and C. Carpenter
In Press   Environmental Anthropology: A Historical Reader. Boston: Blackwell.

Downing, T., and M. Gibson, eds.
1974   Irrigation's Impact on Society. Anthropological Papers, no. 25. Tucson: University of Arizona Press.

Downs, A.
1998   The Big Picture: How America's Cities Are Growing. Brookings Review 16(4):8–11.

Downs, J., and R. Ekvall
1965   Animals and Social Types in the Exploitation of the Tibetan Plateau. *In* Man, Culture and Animals. A. Leeds and A. Vayda, eds. Washington, DC: American Association for the Advancement of Science.

Draper, H. H.
1977   The Aboriginal Eskimo Diet. American Anthropologist 79:309–316.

Dreier, P.
2000   Sprawl's Invisible Hand. The Nation (February 21):6–7.

Driel, A. V.
2001   Sharing a Valley: The Changing Relations Between Agriculturalists and Pastoralists in the Niger Valley of Benin. Leiden: African Studies Centre.

Dubos, R. J.
1968   So Human an Animal. New York: Scribners.

Dudgeon, D.
2000   The Ecology of Tropical Asian Rivers and Streams in Relation to Biodiversity Conservation. Annual Review of Ecology and Systematics 31:239–263.

Duffey, E., M. G. Morris, J. Sheail, L. K. Ward, and T. C. E. Wells
1974   Grassland Ecology and Wildlife Management. London: Chapman & Hall.

Dufour, D.
1987   Insects as Food: A Case Study from the Northwestern Amazon. American Anthropologist 89:383–397.
1988   Cyanide Content of Cassava Cultivars Used by Tukanoan Indians of Northwestern Amazônia. Economic Botany 42(2):255–266.
1990   Use of Tropical Rainforests by Native Amazonians. BioScience 40(9):652–659.

Durham, W.
1976   The Adaptive Significance of Cultural Behavior. Human Ecology 4(2):89–121.
1990   Advances in Evolutionary Culture Theory. Annual Review of Anthropology 19:187–210.

Durnin, J. V. G. A.
1975   Energy Expenditure in Humans. *In* Institute of Ecology (TIE) A Manual of Energy Flow Studies. Manuscript mimeo. Available from Institute of Ecology, Indianapolis, IN.

Dutt, J. S.
1976   Altitude, Fertility and Early Childhood Mortality: The Bolivian Example. American Journal of Physical Anthropology 44:175.

Dutta, A., K. Pant, P. Kumar, and R. P. Singh
2004   Impact of Agroclimatic and Socioeconomic Variability on the Nutritional Status of Inhabitants in the Garwhal Himalayas. Ecology of Food and Nutrition 43(5): 409–420.

Dwyer, P.
1990   The Pigs that Ate the Garden: A Human Ecology from Papua New Guinea. Ann Arbor: University of Michigan Press.

Dyson-Hudson, N.
1966   Karimojong Politics. Oxford: Clarendon.

Dyson-Hudson, R., and N. Dyson-Hudson
1969   Subsistence Herding in Uganda. Scientific American 220:76–89.

Dyson-Hudson, R., and T. McCabe
1985   South Turkana Nomadism: Coping with an Unpredictably Varying Environment. 2 vols. New Haven, CT: Human Relations Area Files.

Early, J. D., and J. F. Peters
1990   The Population Dynamics of the Mucajai Yanomama. New York: Academic.

Eden, M. J., and J. T. Parry, eds.
1986   Remote Sensing and Tropical Land Management. New York: Wiley.

Eder, J.
1977   Agricultural Intensification and the Returns to Labour in the Phillippine Swidden System. Pacific Viewpoint 19:1–21.
1987   On the Road to Tribal Extinction: Depopulation, Deculturation and Adaptive Well-Being. Berkeley: University of California Press.

Edgell, H. S.
2006   Arabian Deserts: Nature, Origin, and Evolution. Dordrecht: Springer.

Edgerton, R.
1965   Cultural vs. Ecological Factors in the Expression of Values, Attitudes and Personality Characteristics. American Anthropologist 67:442–447.
1971   The Individual in Cultural Adaptation. Berkeley, CA: University of California Press.

Edholm, O. G.
1967   The Biology of Work. New York: McGraw-Hill.
Edholm, O. G., and H. E. Lewis
1964   Terrestrial Animals in Cold: Man in Polar Regions. *In* Handbook of Physiology: Adaptation to the Environment. D. B. Dill, ed. Washington, DC: American Physiological Society.
Ehlers, E.
1980   The Drying Oases of Central Iran. *In* Desertification in Extremely Arid Environments. W. Meckelein, ed. Stuttgart: Geographisches Institut der Universitat.
Ehrenfeld, J. G., B. Ravit, and K. Elgersma
2005   Feedback in the Plant-Soil System. Review of Environment and Resources 30:75–115.
Ehrlich, P. R.
1968   The Population Bomb. New York: Ballantine.
Eicher, C.
1985   Agricultural Research for African Development: Problems and Priorities for 1985–2000. Bellagio Conference. February.
Eisenberg, J. F., and R. W. Thorington
1973   A Preliminary Analysis of a Neotropical Mammal Fauna. Biotropica 5(3): 150–161.
Ekblaw, W. E.
1927   The Material Response of the Polar Eskimo to Their Far Arctic Environment. Annals of the Association of American Geographers 27(4):147–198.
El-Ashry, M. T.
1995   Issues in Managing Water Resources in Semiarid Regions. GeoJournal 35(1):53–57.
El-Ashry, M. T., and D. C. Gibbons
1988   West in Profile. *In* Water and Arid Lands of the Western United States. New York: Cambridge University Press.
Eldredge, N.
2005   Darwin: Discovering the Tree of Life. New York: Norton.
El Gamri, T.
2004   Prospects and Constraints of Desert Agriculture: Lessons from West Omdurman. Environmental Monitoring and Assessment 99(1–3):57–73.
Ellanna, L.
1983   Bering Strait Insular Eskimo: A Diachromic Study of Ecology and Population Structure. Technical Paper, no. 77. Alaska Department of Fish and Game.
Ellen, R.
1982   Environment, Subsistence and System: The Ecology of Small-Scale Social Formations. Cambridge: Cambridge University Press.
1990   Trade, Environment and the Reproduction of Local Systems in the Moluccas. *In* The Ecosystem Approach in Anthropology. E. F. Moran, ed. Ann Arbor: University of Michigan Press.
Ellen, R., and K. Fukui, eds.
1996   Redefining Nature: Ecology, Culture, and Domestication. Oxford: Berg.
Ellenberg, H.
1979   Man's Influence in Tropical Ecosystems in South America. Journal of Ecology 67(2):401–416.

Ellis, J. E., and C. Jennings
1975   A Comparison of Energy Flow Among the Grazing Animals of Different Societies. *In* TIE, A Manual of Energy Flow Studies. Manuscript mimeo. Available from Institute of Ecology, Indianapolis, IN.

Emmons, L.
1990   Neotropical Rainforest Mammals: A Field Guide. Chicago: University of Chicago Press.

English, R.
1985   Himalayan State Formation and the Impact of British Rule in the Nineteenth Century. Mountain Research and Development 5(1):61–78.

Epstein, J. M., and R. Axtell
1996   Growing Artificial Societies: Social Science from the Bottom Up. Cambridge, MA: MIT Press/Brookings Institution.

Erlandson, J.
1994   Early Hunter-Gatherers of the California Coast. New York: Plenum.

Esslinger, G. L.
1998   Water Politics in Southern Mexico. *In* Water Resources Issues in New Mexico. New Mexico Journal of Science 38:83–103.

Estes, J., and M. J. Consention
1988   Remote Sensing of Vegetation. *In* Global Ecology: Towards a Science of the Biosphere. M. B. Ramble, L. Margulis, and R. Fester, eds. New York: Academic.

Etkin, N. L.
1994   Eating on the Wild Side: The Pharmacologic, Ecologic, and Social Implications of Using Noncultigens. Tucson: University of Arizona Press.
2006   Edible Medicines: An Ethnopharmacology of Food. Tucson: University of Arizona Press.

Euskirchen, E. S., A. D. McGuire, D. W. Kicklighter, Q. Zhuang, J. S. Clein, R. J. Dargaville, D. G. Dye, J. S. Kimball, K. C. McDonald, J. M. Melillo, V. E. Romanovsky, and N. V. Smith
2006   Importance of Recent Shifts in Soil Thermal Dynamics on Growing Season Length, Productivity, and Carbon Sequestration in Terrestrial High Latitude Ecosystems. Global Change Biology 12(4):731–750.

Evangelou, P.
1984   Livestock Development in Kenya's Maasai Land. Boulder: Westview.

Evans, D., and J. Thames
1980   Water in Desert Ecosystems. US/IBP Synthesis. Vol. 11. Stroudsburg, PA: Dowden, Hutchinson & Ross.

Evans, T., A. Manire, F. de Castro, E. Brondizio, and S. McCracken
2001   A Dynamic Model of Household Decision Making and Parcel-Level Land Cover Change in the Eastern Amazon. Ecological Modelling 143(1–2):95–113.

Evans, T., D. K. Munroe, and D. C. Parker
2005a   Modeling Land-Use/Land-Cover Change: Exploring the Dynamics of Human-Environment Relationships. *In* Seeing the Forest and the Trees: Human-Environment Interactions in Forest Ecosystems. E. F. Moran and E. Ostrom, eds. Cambridge, MA: MIT Press.

Evans, T., W. Sun, and H. Kelley
2006   Spatially Explicit Experiments for the Exploration of Land Use Decision-Making Dynamics. International Journal of Geographic Information Science 20(9):1013–1037.

Evans, T., L. VanWey, and E. F. Moran
2005b   Human-Environment Research, Spatially-Explicit Data Analysis, and Geographic Information Systems. *In* Seeing the Forest and the Trees, pp. 161–186. E. F. Moran and E. Ostrom, eds. Cambridge, MA: MIT Press.

Evans, T., and B. Winterhalder
2000   Modified Solar Insolation as an Agronomic Factor in Terraced Environments. Land Degradation and Development 11(3):273–287.

Evans-Pritchard, E. E.
1940   The Nuer. London: Oxford University Press.

Evelith, P. B., and J. M. Tanner
1976   Worldwide Variation in Human Growth. Cambridge: Cambridge University Press.
1990   Worldwide Variation in Human Growth. 2nd ed. Cambridge: Cambridge University Press.

Evenari, M., I. Noy-Meir, and D. Goodall, eds.
1985   Ecosystems of the World: Hot Deserts and Arid Shrublands. Vol. 12A. Amsterdam: Elsevier.

Evenari, M., L. Shanan, and N. Tadmor
1971   The Negev: The Challenge of A Desert. Cambridge, MA: Harvard University Press.

Ewel, J. J.
1986   Designing Agricultural Ecosystems for the Humid Tropics. Annual Review of Ecology and Systematics 17:245–271.

Fagan, B. M.
1995   Ancient North America: The Archeology of a Continent. New York: Thames & Hudson.

Falesi, I. C.
1974   Soils of Brazilian Amazon. *In* Man in the Amazon. C. Wagley, ed. Gainesville: University of Florida Press.
1976   Ecosistema de Pastagem Cultivada na Amazônia Brasileira. Boletim Técnico, no. 1. Belém: EMBRAPA/CPATU.

Falkner, F., and J. M. Tanner
1986   Human Growth: A Comprehensive Treatise. Vol. 3, Methodology. Ecological, Genetic, and Nutritional Effects on Growth. 2nd ed. New York: Plenum.

FAO/UNESCO (Food and Agriculture Organization of the United Nations)
1973   Irrigation, Drainage and Salinity. Paris: UNESCO.

Farnworth, E., and F. Golley, eds.
1974   Fragile Ecosystems: Evaluation of Research and Applications in the Neotropics. New York: Springer.

Farooque, N. A., B. S. Majila, and C. P. Kala
2004   Indigenous Knowledge Systems and Sustainable Management of Natural Resources in a High Altitude Society in Kumaun Himalaya, India. Journal of Human Ecology 16(1):33–42.

Fearnside, P. M.
1990   Fire in the Tropical Rain Forest of the Amazon Basin. *In* Fire in the Tropical Biota. J. Goldhammer, ed. Berlin: Springer.
1996   Amazonian Deforestation and Global Warming: Carbon Stocks in Vegetation Replacing Brazil's Amazon Forest. Forest Ecology and Management 80(1–3):21–34.
1997   Transmigration in Indonesia: Lessons from Its Environmental and Social Impacts. Environmental Management 21:553–570.

Fediuk, K., N. Hidiroglou, R. Madere, and H. V. Kuhnlein
2002   Vitamin C in Inuit Traditional Food and Women's Diets. Journal of Food Composition and Analysis 15(3):221–235.

Feeny, D., F. Berkesv, B. McCay, and J. Acheson
1990   The Tragedy of the Commons: Twenty-Two Years Later. Human Ecology 18(1):1–19.

Ferguson, M. A. D., R. G. Williamson, and E. Meisser
1998   Inuit Knowledge of Long-Term Changes in a Population of Arctic Tundra Caribou. Arctic 51(3):201–219.

Fernandes, E., ed
1998   Environmental Strategies for Sustainable Development in Urban Areas: Lessons from Africa and Latin America. Aldershot, UK: Ashgate.

Fernandez-Juricic, E.
2000   Avifaunal Use of Wooded Streets in an Urban Landscape. Conservation Biology 24:513–521.

Fernandez-Juricic, E., and J. Jokimani
2001   A Habitat Island Approach to Conserving Birds in Urban Landscapes: Case Studies from Southern and Northern Europe. Biodiversity and Conservation 10:2023–2043.

Ferndon, E.
1959   The Drying Oases of Central Iran. Southwestern Journal of Anthropology 15:1–19.

Fernea, R. A.
1970   Shaykh and Effendi. Cambridge, MA: Harvard University Press.

Fienup-Riordan, A.
1983   The Nelson Island Eskimo: Social Structure and Ritual Distribution. Anchorage: Alaska Pacific University Press.

Firey, W.
1945   Sentiment and Symbolism as Ecological Variables. American Sociological Review 10:140–148.

Fish, S., and P. Fish
1990   An Archaeological Assessment of Ecosystems in the Tucson Basin of Southern Arizona. *In* The Ecosystem Approach in Anthropology. E. F. Moran, ed. Ann Arbor: University of Michigan Press.

Fisher, J. F.
1986   Trans-Himalayan Traders: Economy, Society, and Culture in Northwest Nepal. Delhi: Motilal Banarsidass.

Fittkau, E. J.
1968   The Fauna of South America. *In* Biogeography and Ecology in South America. Vol. 2. E. J. Fittkau, J. Illies, H. Klinge, G. H. Schwabe, and H. Sioli, eds. The Hague: Junk.

Fittkau, E. J., J. Illies, H. Klinge, G. H. Schwabe, and H. Sioli, eds.
1968   Biogeography and Ecology in South America. 2 vols. The Hague: Junk.

Fittkau, E. J., and H. Klinge
1973   On Biomass and Trophic Structure of the Central Amazonian Rain Forest Ecosystem. Biotropica 5(1):2–14.

Fitzhugh, W., ed.
1994   Anthropology of the North Pacific Rim. Washington, DC: Smithsonian Institution Press.

Flannery, K.
1968   Archeological Systems Theory and Early Mesoamerica. *In* Anthropological Archeology in the Americas. B. Meggers, ed. Washington, DC: Anthropological Society of Washington.

Flannery, K., M. Joyce, and R. Reynolds
1989   The Flocks of the Wamani: A Study of Llama Herders on the Punas of Ayacucho, Peru. San Diego, CA: Academic.

Fleming-Moran, M., and C. Coimbra
1989   Blood Pressure Studies Among Amazonian Native Populations: A Review from an Epidemiological Perspective. Social Science and Medicine 31:593–601.

Floyd, B.
1969   Eastern Nigeria. New York: Praeger.

Fogg, G. E.
1998   The Biology of Polar Habitats. New York: Oxford University Press.

Foin, T., and W. Davis
1987   Equilibrium and Disequilibrium Models in Ecological Anthropology. American Anthropologist 89:9–31.

Foley, J., A. Botta, and M. T. Coe
2002   El Niño Southern Oscillation and the Climate, Ecosystems, and Rivers of Amazônia. Global Biogeochemical Cycles 16, 1132.

Folk, G. E. Jr.
1966   Introduction to Environmental Physiology. Philadelphia: Lea and Febiger.

Folke, C., S. Carpenter, B. Walker, M. Scheffer, T. Elmqvist, L. Gunderson, and C. S. Holling
2004   Regime Shifts, Resilience and Biodiversity in Ecosystem Management. Annual Review of Ecology, Evolution and Systematics 35:557–581.

Foody, G. M., R. M. Lucas, P. J. Curran, and M. Honzak
1997   Mapping Tropical Forest Fractional Cover from Coarse Spatial Resolution Remote Sensing Imagery. Plant Ecology 131(2):143–154.

Foote, D. C.
1970   An Eskimo-Sea Mammal-Caribou Hunting Economy: Human Ecology in Terms of Energy. Proceedings of 8th International Congress of Anthropology of Ethnological Science 3:262–267.

Ford, J.
1977   Interactions Between Human Societies and Various Trypanosome-Tsetse-Wild Fauna Complexes. *In* Human Ecology in the Tropics. 2nd ed. J. P. Garlick and R. W. J. Keay, eds. London: Taylor & Francis.

Ford, J., B. Smit, J. Wandel, and J. MacDonald
2006   Vulnerability to Climate Change in Igloolik, Nunavut: What We Can Learn from the Past and Present. Polar Record 42:127–138.

Forde, C. D.
1934   Habitat, Economy and Society. New York: Dutton.

Forman, R. T. T., and M. Godron
1986   Landscape Ecology. New York: Wiley.

Forman, R. T. T., J. D. Olson, and W. E. Dramstad
1996   Landscape Ecology Principles in Landscape Architecture and Land-Use Planning. Washington, DC: Island.

Forman, S., ed.
1994   Diagnosing America. Ann Arbor: University of Michigan Press.
Forminykh, L. A., and B. N. Zolotareva
2004   Ecological Peculiarities of Gleysols in the Russian Arctic. Eurasian Soil Science 37(2):122–130.
Forrester, J.
1961   Industrial Dynamics. Cambridge, MA: MIT Press.
1968   Principles of Systems. Cambridge, MA: Wright-Allen Press.
1968   Urban Dynamics. Cambridge, MA: MIT Press.
Forsberg, M. C.
1999   Protecting an Urban Forest Reserve in the Amazon: A Multi-Scale Analysis of Edge Effects, Population Pressure, and Institutions. Ph.D. diss. Bloomington: Indiana University, Environmental Science Program, School of Public and Environmental Affairs.
Forsyth, T.
2002   Critical Political Ecology: The Politics of Environmental Science. London: Routledge.
Fosberg, F. R., B. J. Garnier, and A. W. Kuchler
1961   Delimitation of the Humid Tropics. Geographical Review 51(3):333–347.
Foster, D., and J. Aber, eds.
2004   Forests in Time: The Environmental Consequences of 1000 Years of Change in New England. New Haven, CT: Yale University Press.
Foulks, E.
1972   The Arctic Hysterias of the North Alaskan Eskimo. Washington, DC: American Anthropological Association.
Fox, J., R. R. Rindfuss, S. J. Walsh, and V. Mishra, eds.
2003   People and the Environment: Approaches for Linking Household and Community Surveys to Remote Sensing and GIS. Norwell, MA: Kluwer Academic.
Frake, C.
1961   The Diagnosis of Disease Among the Subanum of Mindanao. American Anthropologist 63:113–132.
1962   Cultural Ecology and Ethnography. American Anthropologist 64(1):53–59.
Frank, D. A., and P. M. Groffman
1998   Ungulate vs. Landscape Control of Soil C and N Processes in Grasslands of Yellowstone National Park. Ecology 79(7):2229–2241.
Frank, D. A., S. J. McNaughton, and B. F. Tracy
1998   The Ecology of the Earth's Grazing System. BioScience 48(7):513–521.
Franke, R., and B. Chasin
1980   Seeds of Famine: Ecological Destruction and the Development Dilemma in the Western African Sahel. New York: Universe Books.
Fratkin, E.
1977   The Dual Camel-Cattle Economy of the Ariaal Rendille. Paper presented at seminar on Pastoral Societies of Kenya. Mimeo. Ethnographic Museum of Japan.
1991   Surviving Drought and Development: Arial Pastoralists of Northern Kenya. Boulder: Westview.
1997   Pastoralism: Governance and Development Issues. Annual Review of Anthropology 26:235–261.

Fratkin, E., K. A. Galvin, and E. A. Roth, eds.
1994   African Pastoralism Systems: An Integrated Approach. Boulder: L. Rienner.
Fratkin, E., M. Nathan, and E. A. Roth
1997   Health Consequences of Pastoral Sedentarization Among Rendille of Northern Kenya. *In* Poverty Matters: Rich and Poor Among Pastoralists in Eastern Africa. D. Anderson and V. Broch-due, eds. London: James Curry.
Fratkin, E., E. A. Roth, and M. A. Nathan
2004   Pastoral Sedentarization and Its Effects on Children's Diet, Health, and Growth Among Rendille of Northern Kenya. Human Ecology 32(5):531–559.
Freedman, R., ed.
1964   Population: The Vital Revolution. Garden City, NY: Doubleday.
Freeman, M.
1971   A Social and Ecologic Analysis of Systematic Female Infanticide Among the Netsilik Eskimo. American Anthropologist 73:1011–1018.
Fricke, T.
1986   Himalayan Households: Tamang Demography and Domestic Precesses. Ann Arbor, MI: UMI Research Press.
1989   Introduction: Human Ecology in the Himalaya. Human Ecology 17(2):131–145.
Fricke, T., A. Thornton, and D. Dahal
1990   Family Organization and the Wage Labor Transition in a Tamang-Community of Nepal. Human Ecology 18(3):283–314.
Friedman, J.
1974   Marxism, Structuralism and Vulgar Materialism. Man 9:444–469.
Frisancho, A. R.
1975   Functional Adaptation to High Altitude Hypoxia. Science 187:313–319.
1976   Growth and Morphology at High Altitude. *In* Man in the Andes. P. T. Baker and M. Little, eds. Stroudsburg, PA: Dowden, Hutchinson and Ross.
1993   Human Adaptation and Accommodation. Ann Arbor: University of Michigan Press.
Frisancho, A., and L. Greksa
1989   Developmental Responses in the Acquisition of Functional Adaptation to High Altitude. *In* Human Population Biology. M. Little and J. Haas, eds. New York: Oxford University Press.
Frisch, R., and J. McArthur
1974   Menstrual Cycles: Fatness as a Determinant of Minimum Weight Necessary for Their Maintenance or Onset. Science 185:949–951.
Fukui, K., and R. F. Ellen, eds.
1996   Redefining Nature: Ecology, Culture and Domestication (Explorations in Anthropology Series). New York: Berg.
Furgal, C. M., S. Innes, and K. M. Kovacs
2002   Inuit Spring Hunting Techniques and Local Knowledge of the Ringed Seals in Arctic Bay (Ikpiarjuk), Nunavut. Polar Research 21(1):1–16.
Futemma, C.
2000   Collective Action and Assurance of Property Rights to Natural Resources: A Case Study from the Lower Amazon Region, Santarem, Brazil. CIPEC Dissertation Series, no. 6. Bloomington: Center for the Study of Institutions, Population, and Environmental Change, Indiana University.

Futemma, C., and E. S. Brondizio
2003   Land Reform and Land Use Changes in the Lower Amazon: Implication for Agricultural Intensification. Human Ecology 31(3):369–402.

Gaines, S. W., and W. M. Gaines
2000   Impact of Small-Group Decision-Making in Reducing Stress Conditions. Journal of Anthropological Archeology 19(1):103–130.

Galaty, J. G., and D. L. Johnson
1990   The World of Pastoralism: Herding Systems in Comparative Perspective. New York: Guilford.

Galvin, K.
1988   Nutritional Status as an Indicator of Impending Food Stress Disasters 12:147.

Galvin, K., D. Coppock, and P. Leslie
1994   Diet, Nutrition and the Pastoral Strategy. *In* African Pastoralist Systems. E. Fratkin, K. Galvin, and E. Ruth, eds. Boulder: Westview.

Galvin, K. A., P. K. Thornton, R. B. Boone, and J. Sunderland
2001   Impacts of Climate Variability on East African Pastoralists: Linking Social Science and Remote Sensing. Climate Research 19(2):161–172.

Gandy, M.
2002   Concrete and Clay: Reworking Nature in New York. Cambridge, MA: MIT Press.

Gao, Y., G. Y. Qiu, H. Shimizu, K. Tobe, B. Sun, and J. Wang
2002   A 10-Year Study on Techniques for Vegetation Restoration in a Desertified Salt Lake Area. Journal of Arid Environments 52(4):483–497.

Gardner, G., and P. Stern
1996   Environmental Problems and Human Behavior. New York: Allyn & Bacon.

Garfinkel, H. L., and L. B. Brubaker
1980   Modern Climate-Tree Growth Relationship and Climatic Reconstructions in Sub-Arctic Alaska. Nature 286:872–873.

Garlick, J. P., and R. W. L. Keay, eds.
1977   Human Ecology in the Tropics. 2nd ed. London: Taylor & Francis.

Gash, J. H. C., C. A. Nobre, R. L. Victoria, and J. M. Roberts, eds.
1996   Amazonian Deforestation and Climate. New York: Wiley.

Gash, J. H. C., and W. J. Shuttleworth
1991   Tropical Deforestation: Albedo and the Surface-Energy Balance. Climate Change 19(1–2):123–133.

Gaur, M. K., and H. Gaur
2004   Combating Desertification: Building on Traditional Knowledge Systems of the Thar Desert Communities. Environmental Monitoring and Assessment 99(13):89–103.

Gautam, A. P., G. P. Shivakoti, and E. L. Webb
2004   Forest Cover Change, Physiography, Local Economy, and Institutions in a Mountain Watershed in Nepal. Environmental Management 33(1):48–61.

Gearin, E.
2004   Smart Growth or Smart Growth Machine? *In* Up Against the Sprawl: Public Policy and the Making of Southern California. J. Wolch, M. Pastor, Jr., and P. Dreier, eds. Minneapolis: University of Minnesota Press.

Geertz, C.
1963   Agricultural Involution. Berkeley: University of California Press.
1972   The Wet and the Dry: Traditional Irrigation in Bali and Morocco. Human Ecology 1:23–40.

Geist, H. J., and E. F. Lambin
2001   What Drives Tropical Deforestation? A Meta-Analysis of Proximate and Underlying Causes of Deforestation Based on Subnational Case Study Evidence. LUCC Report Series, no. 4. www.geo.ucl.ac.be.
2002   Proximate Causes and Underlying Forces of Tropical Deforestation. BioScience 52(2):143–150.

Gentry, A.
1990   Four Neotropical Forests. New Haven, CT: Yale University Press.

German, L.
2003   Historical Contingencies in the Co-Evolution of Environment and Livelihood: Contributions to the Debate on Amazonian Black Earth. Geoderma 111(3–4): 307–331.

Gezon, L.
1997   Political Ecology and Conflict in Ankarana, Madagascar. Ethnology 36:85–100.
1999   Of Shrimps and Spirit Possession: Toward a Political Ecology of Resource Management in Northern Madagascar. American Anthropologist 101:58–67.

Ghaddar, N., K. Ghali, and B. Jones
2003   Integrated Human Clothing System Model for Estimating the Effect of Walking on Clothing Insulation. International Journal of Thermal Sciences 42(6):605–619.

Giampietro, M.
2004   Multi-Scale Integrated Analysis of Agroecosystems. Boca Raton, FL: CRC Press.

Gibson, C. C., M. A. McKean, and E. Ostrom, eds.
2000a   People and Forests. Cambridge, MA: MIT Press.

Gibson, C. C., E. Ostrom, and T. Ahn
2000b   The Concept of Scale and the Human Dimensions of Global Change: A Survey. Ecological Economics 32(2):217–239.

Gigerenzer, G., and R. Selten, eds.
2002   Bounded Rationality: The Adaptive Toolbox. Cambridge, MA: MIT Press.

Gilbert, A.
1994   Third World Cities: Poverty, Employment, Gender Roles and the Environment During a Time of Restructuring. Urban Studies 31(4–5):605–633.

Gilbert, A., and A. J. Gugler
1992   Cities, Poverty and Development: Urbanization in the Third World. 2nd ed. Oxford: Oxford University Press.

Gimblett, H. R., ed.
2003   Integrating Geographic Information Systems and Agent-Based Modeling Techniques for Simulating Social and Ecological Processes. New York: Oxford University Press.

Gintzburger, G., H. N. Le Houérou, and K. N. Toderich
2005   The Steppes of Middle Asia: Post-1991 Agricultural and Rangeland Adjustment. Arid Land Research and Management 19(3):215–239.

Glacken, C.
1967   Traces on a Rhodian Shore. Berkeley: University of California Press.

Glantz, M.
1996   Currents of Change: El Niño's Impact on Climate and Society. Cambridge: Cambridge University Press.

Glantz, M., ed.
1977 Desertification: Environmental Degradation in and around Arid Lands. Boulder: Westview.
Glaser, B., L. Haumaier, G. Guggenberger, and W. Zech
2001 The 'Terra Preta' Phenomenon: A Model for Sustainable Agriculture in the Humid Tropics. Naturwissenschaften 88(1):37–41.
Gliessman, S. R.
2001 Agroecosystem Sustainability: Developing Practical Strategies. Boca Raton, FL: CRC Press.
Godoy, R. A.
2001 Indians, Markets, and Rain Forests: Theory, Methods, Analysis. New York: Columbia University Press.
Godwin, H.
1957 Sir Arthur George Tansley. Biographical Memoirs of Fellows of the Royal Society 3:227–246.
1958 Sir Arthur George Tansley, FRS 1871–1955. Journal of Ecology 46:1–8.
1977 Sir Arthur Tansley: The Man and the Subject. The Tansley Lecture, 1976. Journal of Ecology 65:1–26.
Goldenweiser, A.
1937 Anthropology. New York: Crofts.
Goldschmidt, W.
1971 Independence as an Element in Pastoral Social Systems. Anthropological Quarterly 44(3):132–142.
Goldstein, M. C.
1981 New Perspectives on Tibetan Fertility and Population Decline. American Ethnologist 8(4):721–729.
Goldstein, M., and C. Beall
1991 Change and Continuity in Nomadic Pastoralism on the Western Tibetan Plateau. Nomadic Peoples 28:105–122.
Goldstein, M. C., P. Tsarong, and C. Beall
1983 High Altitude Hypoxia, Culture and Human Fecundity/Fertility: A Comparative Study. American Anthropologist 85(1):28–50.
Goldstone, R., and M. Janssen
2005 Computational Models of Collective Behavior. Trends in Cognitive Sciences 9(9):424–430.
Golley, F.
1992 The Ecosystem Concept in Biology. New Haven, CT: Yale University Press.
1993 A History of the Ecosystem Concept in Ecology: More than the Sum of the Parts. New Haven, CT: Yale University Press.
Golley, P., and F. Golley, eds.
1972 Tropical Ecology, with an Emphasis on Organic Productivity. Athens, GA: International Society of Tropical Ecology.
Gomes, M. P.
1988 Os Índios e o Brasil. Petrópolis: Vôzes. Available in an English revised edition from the University of Florida Press.
Gómez-Pompa, A., C. Vazquez-Yanes, and S. Guevera
1972 The Tropical Rain Forest: A Non-Renewable Resource. Science 177:762–765.

Gonzalez, G. A.
2006   The Politics of Air Pollution: Urban Growth, Ecological Modernization, and Symbolic Inclusion. Albany: State University of New York Press.

Goodall, D. W., and R. A. Perry
1979   Arid Land Ecosystems: Structure, Functioning and Management. Cambridge: Cambridge University Press.

Goodchild, M.
2003   Geographic Information Science and Systems for Environmental Management. Annual Review of Environment and Resources 28:493–519.

Goodchild, M., and D. Janelle, eds.
2004   Spatially-Integrated Social Science. Oxford: Oxford University Press.

Goodland, R. J., and H. S. Irwin
1975   Amazon Jungle: Green Hell to Red Desert? Amsterdam: Elsevier.

Goodman, A., G. Armelagos, and J. Rose
1984   The Chronological Distribution of Enamel Hypoplaisa from Prehistoric Dickson Mounds Populations. American Journal of Physical Anthropology 65:259–266.

Goodman, A., D. Dufour, and G. Pelto
2000   Nutritional Anthropology: Biocultural Perspectives on Food and Nutrition. Mountain View: Mayfield.

Goodman, A., and T. Leatherman, eds.
1998   Building a New Biocultural Synthesis: Political-Economic Perspectives in Human Biology. Ann Arbor: University of Michigan Press.

Goodman, A., and J. Rose
1990   Assessment of Systemic Physiological Perturbations from Dental Enamel Hypoplasia and Associated Histological Structures. Yearbook of Physical Anthropology 33:59–110.

Goodman, A., R. B. Thomas, A. Swedlund, and G. Armelagos
1988   Biocultural Perspectives on Stress in Prehistoric, Historical and Contemporary Population Research. Yearbook of Physical Anthropology 31:169–202.

Gough, L., and S. E. Hobbie
2003   Responses of Moist Non-Acidic Arctic Tundra to Altered Environment: Productivity, Biomass, and Species Richness. Oikos 103(1):204–216.

Gould, S. J.
1977a   Ever Since Darwin. New York: Norton.
1977b   Ontogeny and Phylogeny. Cambridge, MA: Harvard University Press.
1980   The Panda's Thumb. New York: Norton.
1981   The Mismeasure of Man. New York: Norton.
1983   Hen's Teeth and Horse's Toes. New York: Norton.
1995   Dinosaur in a Haystack. New York: Harmony.
1998   Leonardo's Mountain of Clams and the Diet of Worms. New York: Harmony.
1999   Rocks of Ages: Science and Religion in the Fullness of Life. New York: Ballantine.
2000a   Crossing Over: Where Art and Science Meet. New York: Three Rivers.
2000b   The Lying Stones of Marrakech. New York: Harmony.
2002a   I Have Landed: The End of a Beginning in Natural History. New York: Harmony.
2002b   The Structure of Evolutionary Theory. Cambridge, MA: Harvard University Press.
2003a   The Hedgehog, the Fox, and the Magister's Pox. New York: Harmony.

2003b   Triumph and Tragedy in Mudville: A Lifelong Passion for Baseball. New York: Norton.

Goulding, M.
1980   The Fishes and the Forest. Berkeley: University of California Press.
1981   Man and the Fisheries on an Amazon Frontier. The Hague: Junk.
1990   Amazon: The Flooded Forest. New York: Sterling.

Goulding, M., M. L. Carvalho, and E. G. Ferreira
1988   Rio Negro: Rich Life in Poor Water. The Hague: SPB Academic.

Goulding, M., D. J. Mahar, and N. J. H. Smith
1996   Floods of Fortune: Ecology and Economy Along the Amazon. New York: Columbia University Press.

Grace, J., J. Lloyd, J. McIntire, A. Miranda, P. Meir, H. Miranda, J. Moncrieff, J. Massheder, I. Wright, and J. Gash
1995a   Fluxes of Carbon Dioxide and Water Vapor over an Undisturbed Tropical Forest in Southwest Amazônia. Global Change Biology 1:1–12.

Grace, J., J. Lloyd, J. McIntire, A. Miranda, P. Meir, H. Miranda, C. Nobre, J. Moncrieff, J. Massheder, Y. Mahli, I. Wright, and J. Gash
1995b   Carbon Dioxide Uptake by an Undisturbed Tropical Rain Forest in Southwest Amazônia. Science 270:778–780.

Graetz, R. D.
1991   Desertification: A Tale of Two Feedbacks. *In* Ecosystem Experiments. E. Medina, D. Schindler, E. Schulze, B. Walker, and H. Mooney, eds. Scope Report, no. 45. New York: Wiley.

Gragson, T.
1989   Time Allocation of Subsistence and Settlement in a Ciri Khonome Pume Village of the Llanos of Apure. Ph.D. diss. Pennsylvania State University.

Graham, P.
2002   Building Ecology: First Principles for a Sustainable Built Environment. Oxford: Blackwell Science.

Grainger, A.
1982   Desertification. London: International Institute for Environment and Development.
1983   Improving the Monitoring of Deforestation in the Human Tropics. *In* Tropical Rain Forest: Ecology and Management. S. Sutton, T. C. Whitmore, and A. Chadwick, eds. Oxford: Blackwell.

Grandin, B. E.
1988   Wealth and Pastoral Dairy Production: A Case Study from Maasailand. Human Ecology 16(1):1–23.

Grant, W., and T. Swannack
In press   Ecological Modeling: A Commonsense Approach to Theory and Practice. Boston: Blackwell.

Gray, G. M.
1973   Drugs, Malnutrition and Carbohydrate Absorption. American Journal Clinical Nutrition 26:121–124.

Green, G. M., C. M. Schweik, and J. C. Randolph
2005a   Linking Disciplines Across Space and Time: Useful Concepts and Approaches for Land Cover Change Studies. *In* Seeing the Forest and the Trees, pp. 61–80. E. F. Moran and E. Ostrom, eds. Cambridge, MA: MIT Press.

2005b   Retrieving Land Cover Change Information from Landsat Satellite Images by
          Minimizing Other Sources of Reflectance Variability. *In* Seeing the Forest and the
          Trees. E. F. Moran and E. Ostrom, eds. Cambridge, MA: MIT Press.

Green, G. M., and R. Sussman
1990   Deforestation History of the Eastern Rain Forest of Madagascar from Satellite
          Images. Science 248:212–215.

Green, K. M.
1983   Using Landsat to Monitor Tropical Forest Ecosystems: Realistic Expectations of
          Digital Processing Technology. *In* Tropical Rain Forest: Ecology and Manage-
          ment. S. Sutton, T. C. Whitmore, and A. Chadwick, eds. Oxford: Blackwell.

Greenberg, J., and T. Park
1994   Political Ecology. Journal of Political Ecology 1:1–12.

Greene, R. P., and J. B. Pick
2006   Exploring the Urban Community: A GIS Approach. Upper Saddle River, NJ:
          Pearson-Prentice Hall.

Greksa, L. P.
1990   Developmental Responses to High-Altitude Hypoxia in Bolivian Children of
          European Ancestry. American Journal of Human Biology 2:603–612.

Greksa, L. P., H. Spielvogel, and L. Paredes-Fernandez
1985   Maximal Exercise Capacity in Adolescent European and Amerindian High Al-
          titude Natives. American Journal of Physical Anthropology 67:209–210.

Griffith, B.
2001   The Gardens of Their Dreams: Desertification and Culture in World History.
          London: Zed.

Grimm, N., and C. L. Redman
2004   Approaches to the Study of Urban Ecosystems: The Case of Central Arizona-
          Phoenix. Urban Ecosystems 7:199–213.

Grimm, N., J. M. Grove, S. Pickett, and C. Redman
2000   Integrated Approaches to Long-Term Studies of Urban Ecological Systems.
          BioScience 50:571–584.

Grimm, V., T. Wyszomirski, D. Aikman, and J. Uchmanski
1999   Individual-Based Modelling and Ecological Theory: Synthesis of a Workshop.
          Ecological Modelling 115:275–282.

**Grimm, V., U. Berger, F. Bastiansen, S. Eliassen, V. Ginot, J. Giske, J. Goss-Custard,
T. Grand, S. K. Heinz, G. Huse, A. Huth, J. U. Jepsen, C. Jørgensen,
W. M. Mooij, B. Müller, G. Pe'er, C. Piou, S. F. Railsback, A. M. Robbins,
M. M. Robbins, E. Rossmanith, N. Rüger, E. Strand, S. Souissi, R. A. Still-
man, R. Vabø, U. Visser, and D. L. DeAngelis**
2006   A Standard Protocol for Describing Individual-Based and Agent-Based Mod-
          els. Ecological Modelling 198(1–2):115–126.

**Groffman, P. M., D. J. Bain, L. E. Band, K. T. Belt, G. S. Brush, J. M. Grove, R. V.
Pouyat, I. C. Yesilonis, and W. C. Zipperer**
2003   Down by the Riverside: Urban Riparian Ecology. Frontiers in Ecology and the
          Environment 1:315–321.

Gross, D.
1975   Protein Capture and Cultural Development in the Amazon Basin. American
          Anthropologist 77(3):526–549.

Gross, D., G. Eiten, N. Flowers, F. Leoi, M. Ritter, and D. Werner
1979   Ecology and Acculturation Among Native Peoples of Central Brazil. Science 206:1043–1050.

Grossman, L.
1977   Man-Environment Relationships in Anthropology and Geography. Annals of the Association of American Geographers 67(1):126–144.

Grove, J. M., A. R. Troy, J. P. M. O'Neil-Dunne, W. R. Burch, M. L. Cadenasso, and S. Pickett
2006a   Characterization of Households and Its Implications for the Vegetation of Urban Ecosystems. Ecosystems 9:578–597.

Grove, J. M., M. L. Cadenasso, W. R. Burch, S. Pickett, K. Schwarz, J. O'Neil-Dunne, M. Wilson, A. Troy, and C. Boone
2006b   Data and Methods Comparing Social Structure and Vegetation Structure of Urban Neighborhoods in Baltimore, Maryland. Society and Natural Resources 19:117–136.

Grover, R. F.
1974   Man Living at High Altitudes. *In* Arctic and Alpine Environments. J. D. Ives and R. G. Barry, eds. London: Methuen.

Gubser, N. J.
1965   The Nunamiut Eskimos: Hunters of Caribou. New Haven, CT: Yale University Press.

Guemple, L., ed.
1972   Alliance in Eskimo Society. *In* Proceedings of the American Ethnological Society. Seattle: University of Washington Press.

Guhardja, E.
2000   Rainforest Ecosystems of E. Kalimantan: El Niño, Drought, Fire, and Human Impacts. New York: Springer.

Guillermé, A. E.
1988   The Age of Water: The Urban Environment in the North of France, A.D. 300–1800. College Station: Texas A&M University Press.

Guillet, D.
1981   Land Tenure, Agricultural Regime, and Ecological Zone in the Central Andes. American Ethnologist 8:139–158.
1983   Toward a Cultural Ecology of Mountains: The Central Andean and the Himalayan Compared. Current Anthropology 24(5):561–574.
1987   Terracing and Irrigation in the Peruvian Highlands. Current Anthropology 28(4):409–430.
1992   Covering Ground: Communal Water Management and the State in the Peruvian Highlands. Ann Arbor: University of Michigan Press.

Gulliver, P. H.
1955   The Family Herds. London: Routledge & Keagan Paul.
1975   Nomadic Movements: Causes and Implications. *In* Pastoralism in Tropical Africa. T. Monod, ed. London: International African Institute.

Gupta, S., M. C. Porwal, and P. S. Roy
2004   Human Modification of the Tropical Rain Forest of Nicobar Islands: Indicators from Land Use/Land Cover Mapping. Journal of Human Ecology 16(3):163–171.

Gurri, F.
1997   Regional Integration and Its Effect on the Adaptability and Environment of Rural Maya Populations in Yucatan, Mexico. Ph.D. diss. Indiana University, Department of Anthropology.

Gurven, M.
2001   Reciprocal Altruism and Food Sharing Decisions Among Hiwi and Ache Hunter-Gatherers. Behavioral Ecology and Sociobiology 56(4):366–380.

Gussow, Z.
1960   Pibloktok Hysteria Among the Polar Eskimos. *In* Psychoanalytic Study of Society. W. Muensterberger, ed. New York: International University Press.

Gutman, G., A. C. Janetos, C. O. Justice, E. F. Moran, J. F. Mustard, R. R. Rindfuss, D. Skole, B. L. Turner II, and M. A. Cochrane, eds.
2004   Land Change Science: Observing, Monitoring and Understanding Trajectories of Change on the Earth's Surface. Dordrecht: Kluwer Academic.

Gutmann, M. P.
2000   Scaling and Demographic Issues in Global Change Research. Climatic Change 44:377–391.

Gutterman, Y.
1993   Seed Germination in Desert Plants. New York: Springer.
2002   Survival Strategies of Annual Desert Plants. New York: Springer.

Guyer, J., and E. Lambin
1993   Land Use in an Urban Hinterland: Ethnography and Remote Sensing in the Study of African Intensification. American Ethnologist 95:836–859.

Gwynne, M. D.
1977   Land Use by the Southern Turkana. Paper presented at seminar on Pastoral Societies of Kenya. Mimeo. Ethnographic Museum of Japan.

Haas, J.
1976   Prenatal and Infant Growth and Development. *In* Man in the Andes. P. T. Baker and M. Little, eds. Stroudsburg. PA: Dowden, Hutchinson & Ross.

Haberl, H.
2001   The Global Socioeconomic Energetic Metabolism as a Sustainability Problem. Energy 31(1):87–99.

Hadley, G.
1967   Introduction to Probability and Statistical Decision Theory. New York: Holden-Day.

Häfele, W.
1980   Energy in a Finite World. Cambridge, MA: Ballinger.

Haffer, J.
1969   Speciation in Amazonian Forest Birds. Science 165:131–137.

Haftka, R. T., R. I. Rosca, and E. Nikolaidis
2006   An Approach for Testing Methods for Modeling Uncertainty. Journal of Mechanical Design 128(5):1038–1049.

Hagen, J.
1992   An Entangled Bank: The Origins of Ecosystem Ecology. New Brunswick, NJ: Rutgers University Press.

Haggarty, J. M., Z. Cernovsky, M. Husni, K. Minor, P. Kermeen, and H. Merskey
2002   Seasonal Affective Disorder in an Arctic Community. Acta Psychiatrica Scandinavica 105(5):378–384.

Haining, R.
1993   Spatial Data Analysis in the Social and Environmental Sciences. Cambridge: Cambridge University Press.

Hames, R., and W. Vickers, eds.
1983   Adaptive Responses of Native Amazonians. New York: Academic.

Hamilton, C.
1997   The Sustainability of Logging in Indonesia's Tropical Forests: A Dynamic Input-Output Analysis. Ecological Economics 21(3):183–195.

Hammel, H. T.
1964   Terrestrial Animals in Cold: Recent Studies of Primitive Man. *In* Handbook of Physiology: Adaptation to the Environment. D. B. Dill, ed. Washington, DC: American Physiological Society.

Hammond, D. S.
2005   Tropical Forests of the Guiana Shield: Ancient Forests in a Modern World. Wallingford: CABI Publishing.

Hanna, J.
1968   Cold Stress and Microclimate in the Quechua Indians of Southern Peru. *In* High Altitude Adaptation in a Peruvian Community. P. T. Baker et al., eds. Occasional Papers in Anthropology, no. 1. University Park: Pennsylvania State University.
1976   Natural Exposure to Cold. *In* Man in the Andes. P. T. Baker and M. Little, eds. Stroudsburg, PA: Dowden, Hutchinson & Ross.

Hanna, J. M., and P. T. Baker
1974   Comparative Heat Tolerance of Shipibo Indians and Peruvian Mestizos. Human Biology 46:69–80.

Hannon, B., and M. Ruth
1997   Dynamic Modelling of Biological Systems. New York: Springer.

Hansen, M. C., R. S. DeFries, J. R. G. Townshend, L. Marufu, and R. Sohlberg
2002a   Development of a MODIS Tree Cover Validation Data Set for Western Province, Zambia. Remote Sensing of Environment 83(1–2):320–335.

Hansen, M. C., R. S. DeFries, J. R. G. Townshend, R. Sohlberg, C. DiMiceli, and M. Carroll
2002b   Towards an Operational MODIS Continuous Field of Percent Tree Cover Algorithm: Examples Using AVHRR and MODIS Data. Remote Sensing of Environment 83(1–2):303–319.

Hansen, Z. K., and G. D. Libecap
2003   Small Farms, Externalities, and the Dust Bowl of the 1930's. Cambridge, MA: National Bureau of Economic Research.

Hao, A. M., K. Yuge, Y. Nakano, and T. Haraguchi
2005   Effectiveness of Environmental Restoration Induced by Various Trials for Preventing Desertification in Horgin Arid Land, China. Journal of the Faculty of Agriculture, Kyushu University 50(2):821–828.

Hardin, G.
1968   The Tragedy of the Commons. Science 1962:1243–1248.

Harney, K.
2002   Tax Benefits Tilted to Aid Homeowners. Washington Post (February 9):H–1.

Harpham, T., T. Lusty, and P. Vaughn
1988   In the Shadow of the City: Community Health and the Urban Poor. New York: Oxford University Press.

Harris, D. R.
1980   Human Ecology in Savanna Environments. San Diego, CA: Academic.
Harris, M.
1968   The Rise of Anthropological Theory. New York: Crowell.
1974a   Why a Perfect Knowledge of All the Rules One Must Know to Act Like a Native Cannot Lead to the Knowledge of How Natives Act. Journal of Anthropological Research 30(4):242–251.
1974b   Cows, Pigs, Wars, and Witches. New York: Vintage.
1977   Cannibals and Kings. New York: Random House.
Harris, N. S., P. B. Crawford, Y. Yangzom, L. Pinzo, P. Gyaltsen, and M. Hudes
2001   Nutritional and Health Status of Tibetan Children Living at High Altitudes. New England Journal of Medicine 344(5):341–347.
Harris, O.
1981   Labor and Produce in an Ethic Economy, N. Potosi, Bolivia. In Ecology and Exchange in the Andes. D. Lehmann, ed. Cambridge: Cambridge University Press.
Harrison, G. A., and A. J. Boyce, eds.
1972   The Structure of Human Populations. Oxford: Clarendon.
Harrison, G. A., and J. B. Gibson, eds.
1976   Man in Urban Environments. Oxford: Oxford University Press.
Harrison, G. A., and H. Morphy, eds.
1998   Human Adaptation. New York: Berg.
Harrison, G. A., and J. C. Waterlow, eds.
1990   Diet and Disease in Traditional and Developing Societies. Cambridge: Cambridge University Press.
Harrison, G. A., J. S. Weiner, J. M. Tanner, and N. A. Barnicot
1977   Human Biology: An Introduction to Human Evolution, Variation, Growth, and Ecology. 2nd ed. Oxford: Oxford University Press.
Hart, J., T. Hart, and P. Murphy
1989   Monodominant and Species-Rich Forests of the Humid Tropics: Causes for Their Co-Ocurrence. American Naturalist 133:613–633.
Hartinger, S., V. Tapia, C. Carrillo, L. Bejarano, and G. Gonzales
2006   Birth Weight at High Altitudes in Peru. International Journal of Gynecology and Obstetrics 93(3):275–281.
Hartshorn, G. S.
1978   Tree Falls and Tropical Forest Dynamics Tropical Trees as Living Systems. P. B. Tomlinson and M. H. Zimmerman, eds. Cambridge: Cambridge University Press.
Harvey, A. M., A. E. Mather, and M. Stokes
2005   Alluvial Fans: Geomorphology, Sedimentology, Dynamics-Introduction. A Review of Alluvial-Fan Research. Geological Society, London, Special Publications 251:1–7.
Harvey, D.
1973   Social Justice and the City. London: Edward Arnold.
1996   Justice, Nature, and the Geography of Difference. Oxford: Blackwell.
Hassan, F. A.
1972   Population Dynamics and the Beginnings of Domestication in the Nile Valley. Paper presented at annual meeting. American Anthropological Association.

Hassol, S. J.
2004   Impacts of a Warming Arctic: Arctic Climate Impact Assessment. Cambridge: Cambridge University Press.

Hastings, M.
1998   The Brain, Circadian Rhythms, and Clock Genes. British Medical Journal 317:1704–1707.

Hatcher, J. D., and D. B. Jennings, eds.
1966   Proceedings of the International Symposium on the Cardiovascular and Respiratory Effects of Hypoxia. New York: Hafner.

Haughton, G., and C. Hunter
2003   Sustainable Cities. London: Taylor & Francis.

Havenith, G.
2001   Individualized Model of Human Thermoregulation for the Simulation of Heat Stress Response. Journal of Applied Physiology 90(5):1943–1954.

Havnevik, H.
1989   Tibetan Buddhist Nuns. Oslo: Norwegian University Press.

Hawkes, K., K. Hill, and J. O'Connell
1982   Why Hunters Gather: Optimal Foraging and the Ache of Eastern Paraguay. American Ethnologist 9:379–398.

Headland, T. N.
1987   The Wild Yam Question: How Well Could Independent Hunter/Gathers Live in a Tropical Rain Forest Ecosystem? Human Ecology 15(4):463–491.

Heady, H.
1994   Rangeland Ecology and Management. Boulder: Westview.

Hecht, S. B.
1982   Agroforestry in the Amazon Basin. Amazônia: Agriculture and Land Use Research. S. Hecht, ed. Cali, Colombia: CIAT.

Hecht, S. B., and A. Cockburn
1989   The Fate of the Forest: Developers, Destroyers and Defenders of the Amazon. London: Verso.

Hecht, S. B., R. B. Norgaard, and G. Possio
1988   The Economics of Cattle Ranching in Eastern Amazônia. Interciencia 13(5): 233–240.

Heer, D., ed.
1968   Readings on Population. Englewood Cliffs, NJ: Prentice-Hall.

Heijnen, L., and R. W. Kates
1974   Northeast Tanzania: Comparative Observations Along a Moisture Gradient. *In* Natural Hazards. G. White, ed. New York: Oxford University Press.

Heintzelman, O. H., and R. M. Highsmith
1973   World Regional Geography. 4th ed. Englewood Cliffs, NJ: Prentice-Hall.

Heizer, R.
1955   Primitive Man as an Ecologic Factor. Kroeber Anthropological Society Papers 13:1–31.

Helfert, M. R., and K. P. Lulla
1990   Mapping Continental-Scale Biomass Burning and Smoke Palls over the Amazon Basin as Observed from the Space Shuttle. Photogrammetric Engineering and Remote Sensing 56:1367–1373.

Helm, J.
1962   The Ecological Approach in Anthropology. American Journal of Sociology 67:630–639.

Henderson-Sellers, A.
1987   Effect of Change in Land Use on Climate in the Humid Tropics. *In* The Geophysiology of Amazônia. R. Dickinson, ed. New York: Wiley.

Henry, G. H. R., and U. Molau
1997   Tundra Plants and Climate Change: The International Tundra Experiment (ITEX). Global Change Biology 3:1–9.

Herbert, S.
2005   Charles Darwin, Geologist. Ithaca, NY: Cornell University Press.

Herrera, R.
1985   Nutrient Cycling in Amazonian Forests. *In* Key Environments: Amazônia. G. Prance and T. Lovejoy, eds. London: Pergamon.

Herrera, R., C. F. Jordan, H. Klinge, and E. Medina
1978   Amazon Ecosystems: Their Structure and Functioning with Particular Emphasis on Nutrients. Interciencia 3(4):223–231.

Herrick, J. E., B. T. Bestelmeyer, S. Archer, A. J. Tugel, and J. R. Brown
2006   An Integrated Framework for Science-Based Arid Lands Management. Journal of Arid Environments 65(2):319–335.

Herrick, J. E., J. W. Van Zee, K. M. Havstad, L. M. Burkett, and W. G. Whitford
2005   Monitoring Manual for Grassland, Shrubland, and Savanna. Tucson: University of Arizona Press.

Herskovits, M.
1926   The Cattle Complex in East Africa. American Anthropologist 28:230–272; 361–388; 494–528.

Hesse-Biber, S. N., and P. Leavy
2006   Emergent Methods in Social Research. Thousand Oaks: Sage.

Hessen, D. O.
2002   UV Radiation and Arctic Ecosystems. New York: Springer.

Heynen, N., H. A. Perkins, and P. Roy
2006a   The Political Ecology of Uneven Urban Green Space: The Impact of Political Economy on Race and Ethnicity in Producing Environmental Inequality in Milwaukee. Urban Affairs Review 42(1):3–25.

Heynen, N., M. Kaika, and E. Swyngedouw, eds.
2006b   In the Nature of Cities: Urban Political Ecology and the Politics of Urban Metabolism. London: Routledge.

Hilbert, D. W., B. Ostendorf, and M. Hopkins
2001   Sensitivity of Tropical Forests to Climate Change in the Humid Tropics of North Queensland. Australian Ecology 26(6):590–603.

Hildes, J. A.
1966   The Circumpolar People: Health and Physiological Adaptations. *In* The Biology of Human Adaptability. P. T. Baker and J. S. Weiner, eds. Oxford: Clarendon.

Hill, A. G., ed.
1985   Population, Health and Nutrition in the Sahel. London: Routledge & Kegan Paul.

Hill, K., and M. Hurtado
1996   Ache Life History: The Ecology and Demography of a Foraging People. New York: Aldine de Gruyter.

Hills, T. L., and R. E. Randall
1968   The Ecology of the Forest/Savanna Boundary. Montreal: McGill University Savanna Research Project, Department of Geography.

Himes, J. H.
1991   Anthropometric Assessment of Nutritional Status. New York: Wiley-Liss.

Hlavinek, P., T. Kukharchyk, J. Marsalek, and I. Mahrikova, eds.
2006   Integrated Urban Water Resources Management. NATO Security Through Science Series–C: Environmental Security. Dordrecht: Springer.

Hoeckstra, T. W., and M. Shachak, eds.
1999   Arid Lands Management: Toward Ecological Sustainability. Urbana: University of Illinois Press.

Hoff, C. J., and A. E. Abelson
1976   Fertility. *In* Man in the Andes. P. T. Baker and M. Little, eds. Stroudsburg, PA: Dowden, Hutchinson & Ross.

Hoffecker, J. F.
2004   A Prehistory of the North: Human Settlement of the Higher Latitudes. New Brunswick, NY: Rutgers University Press.

Hoffer, R., J. E. Hobbie, J. M. Melillo, B. Moore, B. J. Peterson, G. R. Shaver, and G. M. Woodwell
1986   Analysis of Multiple Incidence Angle SIR-B Data for Determining Forest Stand Characteristics. Second Spaceborne Imaging Radar Symposium. Pasadena, CA: Jet Propulsion Laboratory.

Holden, S. J., D. L. Coppock, and M. Asefa
1991   Pastoral Dairy Marketing and Household Wealth Interactions. Human Ecology 19(1):35–59.

Holling, C. S.
1973   Resilience and Stability of Ecological Systems. Annual Review of Ecology and Systematics 4:1–23.
1986   The Resilience of Terrestrial Ecosystems, Local Surprise and Global Change. *In* Sustainable Development of the Biosphere. W. C. Clark and R. E. Munn, eds. Cambridge: Cambridge University Press.
1992   Cross-Scale Morphology, Geometry and Dynamics of Ecosystems. Ecological Monographs 62(4):447–502.

Holloway, L., R. Cox, L. Venn, M. Kneafsey, E. Dowler, and H. Tuomainen
2006   Managing Sustainable Farmed Landscape Through Alternative Food Networks: A Case Study from Italy. Geographical Journal 172:219–229.

Holmberg, A.
1969   Nomads of the Long Bow. New York: Natural History Press.

Holmgren, M., and M. Scheffer
2001   El Niño as a Window of Opportunity for the Restoration of Degraded Arid Ecosystems. Ecosystems 4(2):151–159.

Homewood, K., and J. Lewis
1987   Impact of Drought on Pastoral Livestock in Baringo, Kenya, 1983–1985. Journal of Applied Ecology 24:615–631.

Homewood, K. M., and W. A. Rodgers
1984   Pastoralism and Conservation. Human Ecology 12(4):431–441.

Hope, D., C. Gries, D. Casagrande, C. Redman, N. Grimm, and C. Martin
2006   Drivers of Spatial Variation in Plant Diversity Across the Central Arizona-Phoenix Ecosystem. Society and Natural Resources 19:101–116.

Hopkins, D. M., ed.
1967   The Bering Land Bridge. Stanford, CA: Stanford University Press.
Hoppeler, H., and M. Vogt
2001   Muscle Tissue Adaptations to Hypoxia. Journal of Experimental Biology 204(18): 3133–3139.
Hornbein, T., and R. Schoene, eds.
2001   High Altitude: An Exploration of Human Adaptation. New York: Dekker.
Horowitz, M.
1990   Donors and Deserts: The Political Ecology of Destructive Development in the Sahel. African Environment 7:185–210.
Horowitz, M., and M. Salem-Murdock
1987   The Political Economy of Desertification in White Nile Province, Sudan. *In* Lands at Risk in the Third World. P. Little and M. Horowitz, eds. Boulder: Westview.
Hough, M.
2004   Cities and Natural Process: A Basis for Sustainability. New York: Routledge.
Houghton, R. A.
1994   The Worldwide Extent of Land-Use Change. BioScience 44(5):305–313.
Houghton, R. A., D. S. Lefkowitz, and D. L. Skole
1991   Changes in the Landscape of Latin America Between 1850 and 1985. Forest Ecology and Management 38(3–4):143–172.
Houston, C. S., D. E. Harris, and E. Zeman
2005   Going Higher: Oxygen, Man and Mountains. Seattle, WA: Mountaineer.
Howell, N.
1976   The Population of the Dobe Area. *In* Kalahari Hunter-Gatherers. R. B. Lee and I. DeVore, eds. Cambridge, MA: Harvard University Press.
Hoyt, H.
1939   The Structure and Growth of Residential Neighborhoods in American Cities. Washington, DC: Federal Housing Administration.
Huber, U. M., H. K. Bugmann, and M. A. Reasoner, eds.
2005   Global Change and Mountain Regions: An Overview of Current Knowledge. Dordrecht: Springer.
Huchman, E., G. Vitkon, R. Just, and D. Silberman
1985   The Dynamics of Agricultural Development in Sparsely Populated Areas: The Case of Arava. *In* Desert Development: Man and Technology in Sparse Lands. Y. Grading, ed. Dordrecht: D. Reidel.
Hulme, M., E. M. Barrow, N. Arnell, P. A. Harrison, T. E. Downing, and T. C. Johns
1999   Relative Impacts of Human-Induced Climate Change and Natural Climate Variability. Nature 397:688–691.
Humphrey, R.
1962   Range Ecology. New York: Ronald Press.
Humphreys, L. R.
1997   The Evolving Science of Grassland Improvement. New York: Cambridge University Press.
Hunt, E., and R. Hunt
1974   Irrigation, Conflict and Politics: A Mexican Case. *In* Irrigation's Impact on Society. T. Downing and M. Gibson, eds. Tucson: University of Arizona Press.

Hunter, M. L., ed.
1999   Maintaining Diversity in Forest Ecosystems. Cambridge: Cambridge University Press.

Huntington, E.
1915   Civilization and Climate. New Haven, CT: Yale University Press.

Huntington, H. P.
1999   Traditional Knowledge of the Ecology of Beluga Whales (Delphinapterus leucas) in the Eastern Chukchi and Northern Bering Seas, Alaska. Arctic 52(1): 49–61.

Hurtado, M.
1964   Animals in High Altitudes: Resident Man. *In* Handbook of Physiology: Adaptation to the Environment. D. B. Dill, ed. Washington, DC: American Physiological Society.

Hurtado, M., K. Hawkes, K. Hill, and H. Kaplan
1985   Female Subsistence Strategies Among Ache Hunter-Gatherers in Eastern Paraguay. Human Ecology 13(1):1–28.

Huss-Ashmore, R., and R. B. Thomas
1997   The Future of Human Adaptability Research. *In* Human Adaptability: Past, Present and Future. S. Ulijaszek and R. Huss-Ashmore, eds. Oxford: Oxford University Press.

Hutchinson, G. E.
1953   The Itinerant Ivory Tower: Scientific and Literary Essays. New Haven, CT: Yale University Press.
1957   A Treatise on Limnology. Vol. 1, Geography, Physics and Chemistry. New York: Wiley.
1967   A Treatise on Limnology. Vol. 2, Introduction to Lake Biology and the Limnoplankton. New York: Wiley.
1975   A Treatise on Limnology. Vol. 3, Limnological Botany. New York: Wiley.
1979   The Kindly Fruits of the Earth: The Development of an Embryo Ecologist. New Haven, CT: Yale University Press.
1993   A Treatise on Limnology. Vol. 4, The Zoobenthos. New York: Wiley.

Iizumi, S., and Y. Iwanami
1975   Effects of Burning in Grasslands. *In* Ecological Studies in Japanese Grasslands. M. Numata, ed. Tokyo: University of Tokyo Press.

Ikeya, K.
1996   Dry Farming Among the San in the Central Kalahari. *In* African Study Monographs, supp. iss., no. 2.

ILCA (International Livestock Center for Africa)
1985   Annual Report. ILCA.

Indriati, E., and J. E. Buikstra
2001   Coca Chewing in Prehistoric Coastal Peru: Dental Evidence. American Journal of Physical Anthropology 114(3):242–257.

Ingold, T.
1974   On Reindeer and Men. Man 9(4):523–538.

Ingram, D. L.
1977   Physiological Reactions to Heat in Man. *In* Human Ecology in the Tropics. 2nd ed. J. P. Garlick and R. W. J. Keay, eds. London: Taylor & Francis.

Ingram, D. L., and L. E. Mount
1975   Man and Animals in Hot Environments. New York: Springer.
Inoguchi, T., E. Newman, and G. Paoletto, eds.
2005   Cities and the Environment: New Approaches for Eco-Societies. Tokyo: United Nations University.
Inoue, Y.
2003   Synergy of Remote Sensing and Modeling for Estimating Ecophysiological Processes in Plant Production. Plant Production Science 6(1):3–16.
IPCC (Intergovernmental Panel on Climate Change)
1990   Climate Change: The IPCC Scientific Assessment. J. Houghton, G. Jenkins and J. Ephraums, eds. New York: Cambridge University Press.
Irons, W.
1971   Variation in Political Stratification Among the Yomut Turkmen. Anthropological Quarterly 44(3):143–156.
1972   Variation in Economic Organization: A Comparison of the Pastoral Yomut and the Basseri. *In* Perspectives on Nomadism. W. Irons and N. Dyson-Hudson, eds. Leiden: Brill.
1975   The Yomut Turkmen: A Study of Social Organization Among a Central Asian Turkic-Speaking Population. Anthropological Papers, no. 58. Ann Arbor: University of Michigan.
IRRI (International Rice Research Institute)
1973   Annual Report. Mimeo. Los Baños, Philippines.
Irving, L.
1972   Arctic Life of Birds and Mammals, Including Man. New York: Springer.
Irving, W., and C. Harrington
1973   Upper Pleistocene Radiocarbon-Dated Artifacts from the Northern Yukon. Science 179:335–340.
Ives, J. D.
1974   The Impact of Motor Vehicles on the Tundra Environments. *In* Arctic and Alpine Environments. J. D. Ives and R. G. Barry, eds. London: Methuen.
2004   Himalayan Perceptions: Environmental Change and the Well-Being of Mountain Peoples. New York: Routledge.
Ives, J. D., and B. Messerli
1989   The Himalayan Dilemma: Reconciling Development and Conservation. London: Routledge.
Ives, J. D., B. Messerli, and R. Rhodes
1997   Agenda for Sustainable Mountain Development. *In* Mountains of the World. B. Messerli and J. Ives, eds. New York: Parthenon.
Jacobsen, J., and J. Firor, eds.
1992   Human Impact on the Environment: Ancient Roots, Current Challenges. Boulder: Westview.
Jacobs, J.
1992   The Death and Life of Great American Cities. New York: Vintage. Original edition 1961.
Jaffe, A. J.
1951   Handbook of Statistical Methods for Demographers. Washington, DC: U.S. Bureau of the Census, Government Printing Office.
James, P.
1966   A Geography of Man. 3rd ed. New York: Wiley.

Jamison, P. L.
1978   Research Area and Populations. *In* The Eskimo of Northwestern Alaska: A Biological Perspective. P. L. Jamison, S. L. Zegura, and F. A. Milan, eds. Stroudsburg, PA: Dowden, Hutchinson & Ross.

Jamison, P. L., S. L. Zegura, and F. A. Milan, eds.
1978   The Eskimo of Northwestern Alaska: A Biological Perspective. US/IBP Synthesis. Vol. 8. Stroudsburg, PA: Dowden, Hutchinson & Ross.

Janes, R. R.
1983   Archeological Ethnography Among the McKenzie Basin Dene, Canada. Technical Paper, no. 28. Alberta, Canada: Arctic Institute of North America, University of Calgary.

Janick, J.
1974   Plant Science: An Introduction to World Crops. 2nd ed. San Francisco: W. H. Freeman.

Jansen, K.
1998   Political Ecology, Mountain Agriculture and Knowledge in Honduras. Amsterdam: Thela.

Janssen, M. A., M. L. Schoon, and K. Weimao
2006   Scholarly Networks on Resilience, Vulnerability, and Adaptation within the Human Dimensions of Global Environmental Change. Global Environmental Change: Human and Policy Dimensions 16(3):240–252.

Janusek, J. W.
2006   The Changing Nature of Tiwanaku Religion and the Rise of an Andean State. World Archeology 38(3):469–492.

Janzen, D.
1975   Tropical Agroecosystems. *In* Food: Politics, Economics, Nutrition and Research. P. Abelson, ed. Washington, DC: American Association for the Advancement of Science.

Jarosz, L.
2004   Political Ecology as Ethical Practice. Political Geography 23(7):917–927.

Jarvenpa, R.
1998   Northern Passage: Ethnography and Apprenticeship Among the Subarctic Dene. Prospect Heights, IL: Waveland.

Jarvenpa, R., and H. J. Brumbach
2006   Circumpolar Lives and Livelihood: A Comparative Ethnoarcheology of Gender and Subsistence. Lincoln: University of Nebraska Press.

Jenerette, G. D., and J. G. Wu
2001   Analysis and Simulation of Land-Use Change in the Central Arizona-Phoenix Region, USA. Landscape Ecology 16:611–626.

Jenerette, G. D., W. L. Wu, S. Goldsmith, W. A. Marussich, and W. J. Roach
2006   Contrasting Water Footprints of Cities in China and the United States. Ecological Economics 57:346–358.

Jensen, J.
1996   Introductory Digital Image Analysis: A Remote Sensing Perspective. Upper Saddle River, NJ: Prentice Hall.

2005   Introductory Digital Image Analysis: A Remote Sensing Perspective. Rev. ed. Upper Saddle River, NJ: Prentice Hall.

2007   Remote Sensing of the Environment: An Earth Resource Perspective. Upper Saddle River, NJ: Pearson-Prentice Hall.

Jochim, M.
1990   The Ecosystem Concept in Archaeology. *In* The Ecosystgem Approach in Anthropology. E. Moran, ed. Ann Arbor: University of Michigan Press.

Johnson, A.
1971   Sharecroppers of the Sertao. Stanford, CA: Stanford University Press.
1974   Ethnoecology and Planting Practices in a Swidden Agricultural System. American Ethnologist 1:87–101.
1977   The Energy Costs of Technology in a Changing Environment: A Machiguenga Case. *In* Material Culture. Proceedings of the American Ethnological Society. St. Paul, MN: West.
1982   Reductionism in Cultural Ecology: The Amazon Case. Current Anthropology 23(4):413–428.

Johnson, A., and T. Earle
1987   The Evolution of Human Societies. Stanford: Stanford University Press.

Johnson, A., and A. Taylor
1991   Prevalence of Chronic Diseases: A Summary of Data from the Survey of American Indians and Alaska Natives. Rockville, MD: United States Department of Health and Human Services, Public Health Service, Agency for Health Care Policy and Research; Springfield, VA: National Technical Information Service.

Johnson, B.
1995   Human Rights and the Environment. Human Ecology 23:111–123.

Johnson, C. D., T. A. Kohler, and J. A. Cowan
2005   Modeling Historical Ecology, Thinking about Contemporary Systems. American Anthropologist 107(1):96–108.

Johnson, S. R., and A. Bouzaher, eds.
2006   Conservation of Great Plains Ecosystems: Current Science, Future Options. New York: Springer.

Johnson, W., V. Stoltzfus, and P. Craumer
1977   Energy Conservation in Amish Agriculture. Science 198:373–378.

Johnston, F. E., ed.
1987   Nutritional Anthropology. New York: Alan R. Liss.

Johnston, J., and J. Newton
1997   Building Green: A Guide to Using Plants on Roofs, Walls, and Pavements. London: London Ecology Unit.

Jones, M. H., J. T. Fahnestock, D. A. Walker, M. D. Walker, and J. M. Welker
1998   Carbon Dioxide Fluxes in Moist and Dry Arctic Tundra During the Snowfree Season: Responses to Increases in Summer Temperature and Winter Snow Accumulation. Arctic, Anarctic and Alpine Research 30(4):373–380.

Jongman, R., and G. Pungetti, eds.
2004   Ecological Networks and Greenways: Concept, Design, Implementation. Cambridge: Cambridge University Press.

Jordan, C. F.
1985   Nutrient Cycling in Tropical Forest Ecosystems. Chichester, UK: Wiley.

Jordan, C. F., ed.
1987   Amazonian Rain Forest. New York: Springer.

Jordan, C. F., and R. Herrera
1981   Tropical Rain Forests: Are Nutrients Really Critical? American Naturalist 117:167–180.

Jorgensen, J.
1990   Oil Age Eskimos. Berkeley: University of California Press.
Jorgensen, M. E., P. Bjeregaard, and K. Borch-Johnsen
2002   Diabetes and Impaired Glucose Tolerance Among the Inuit Population of Greenland. Diabetes Care 25(10):1766–1771.
Junk, W. J.
1975   Aquatic Wildlife of Fisheries. *In* The Use of Ecological Guidelines for Development in the American Humid Tropics. Morges, Switzerland: International Union for Conservation of Nature and Natural Resources.
Kahn, J. R., and J. A. McDonald
1995   Third-World Debt and Tropical Deforestation. Ecological Economics (12)2: 107–123.
Kaika, M.
2005   City of Flows: Nature, Modernity and the City. New York: Routledge.
Kaimowitz, D., and A. Angelsenn
1998   Economic Models of Tropical Deforestation: A Review. Bogor, Indonesia: Center for International Forestry Research (CIFOR).
Kallio, P.
1975   Kevo, Finland. *In* Structure and Function of Tundra Ecosystems. T. Rosswall and O. W. Heal, eds. Stockholm: Swedish Natural Science Research Council.
Kamuanga, M.
2003   Socio-Economic and Cultural Factors in the Research and Control of Trypanosomiasis. Rome: Food and Agriculture Organization of the UN.
Kang, Z. J., H. Xue, and T. Y. Bong
2001   Modeling of Thermal Environment and Human Response in a Crowded Space for Tropical Climate. Building and Environment 36(4):511–525.
Kaplan, H., and K. Hill
1985   Food Sharing Among Ache Foragers: Tests of Explanatory Hypotheses. Current Anthropology 26(2):223–246.
Karlsson, P. S., and T. V. Callaghan, eds.
1996   Plant Ecology in the Sub-Arctic Swedish Lapland. Ecological Bulletin 45. Malden, MA: Blackwell Science.
Karsenty, A.
2000   Economic Instruments for Tropical Forests: The Congo Basin Case. London: International Institute for Environment and Development. Center for International Forestry Research. Centre de Coopération Internationale pour le Développement.
Katz, B., and J. Bradley
1999   Divided We Sprawl. Atlantic Monthly 284(6):26–42.
Katz, S. H.
1987   Food and Biocultural Evolution: A Model for the Investigation of Modern Nutritional Problems. *In* Nutritional Anthropology. F. E. Johnston, ed. New York: Alan R. Liss.
Kaufmann, J. B., D. L. Cummings, D. E. Ward, and R. Babbitt
1995   Fire in the Brazilian Amazon: 1. Biomass, Nutrient Pools, and Losses in Slashed Primary Forests. Oecologia 104(4):397–408.
Kawagley, A. O.
2005   A Yupiaq Worldview. 2nd ed. Prospect Heights, IL: Waveland.

Kaye, J. P., P. M. Groffman, N. Grimm, L. Baker, and R. Pouyat
2006   A Distinct Urban Biogeochemistry? Trends in Ecology and Evolution 21:192–199.
Keil, R.
2003   Urban Political Ecology. Urban Geography 24:723–738.
Keiner, M., M. Koll-Schretzenmayr, and W. A. Schmid, eds.
2005   Managing Urban Futures: Sustainability and Urban Growth in Developing Countries. Zurich: Ashgate.
Keiser, M. B.
1978   Housing: An Environment for Living. New York: Macmillan.
Keller, M., J. Gash, and P. S. Dias eds.
In press Amazônia and Global Change. San Francisco, CA: International Geophysical Union.
Keller, M., D. J. Jacob, S. C. Wofsy, and R. C. Harriss
1991   Effects of Tropical Deforestation on Global and Regional Atmospheric Chemistry. Climate Change 19(1–2):139–158.
Kellogg, C.
1959   Shifting Cultivation. Journal of Soil and Water Conservation in India 7:35–59.
Kelman, A.
2003   River and Its City: The Nature of Landscape in New Orleans. Berkeley: University of California Press.
Kemp, W.
1971   The Flow of Energy in a Hunting Society. Scientific American 224(3):104–115.
Kempton, W.
1991   Lay Perspectives on Global Climate Change. Global Environmental Change 1:183–208.
1993   Will Public Environmental Concern Lead to Action on Global Warming? Annual Review of Energy and Environment 18:217–245.
Kempton, W., J. Boster, and J. Hartley
1995   Environmental Values in American Culture. Cambridge, MA: MIT Press.
Kenney, W. L., D. W. DeGroot, and L. A. Holowatz
2004   Extremes of Human Heat Tolerance: Life at the Precipice of Thermoregulatory Failure. Journal of Thermal Biology 29(7–8):479–485.
Kepner, W. G.
2006   Desertification in the Mediterranean Region: A Security Issue. Dordrecht: Springer.
Kertzer, D., and T. Fricke, eds.
1997   Anthropological Demography: Toward a New Synthesis. Chicago: University of Chicago Press.
Keverenge-Ettyang, G. A., W. V. Lichtenbelt, F. Esamai, and W. Saris
2006   Maternal Nutritional Status in Pastoral Versus Farming Communities in West Pokot, Kenya: Differences in Iron and Vitamin A Status and Body Composition. Food and Nutrition Bulletin 27(3):228–235.
Keyfitz, N.
1968   Introduction to the Mathematics of Population. Reading, MA: Addison-Wesley.
Keyfitz, N., and W. Fliegler
1971   Population: Facts and Methods of Demography. San Francisco: W. H. Freeman.
Keys, E., and W. J. McConnell
2005   Global Change and the Intensification of Agriculture in the Tropics. Global Environmental Change: Human and Policy Dimensions 15(4):320–337.

Keys, E., E. Wentz, and C. Redman
2007 The Spatial Structure of Land Use from 1970–2000 in the Phoenix, Arizona, Metropolitan Area. Professional Geographer 59:131–147.

Khogali, M., and M. Awad El-Karim
1987 Working in Hot Climates. *In* Recent Advances in Occupational Health. J. M. Harrington, ed. Edinburgh: Churchill Livingstone.

King, J. A.
1973 The Ecology of Aggressive Behavior. Annual Review of Ecology and Systematics 4:117–138.

Kinzig, A., P. Warren, C. Martin, D. Hope, and M. Katti
2005 The Effects of Human Socioeconomic Status and Cultural Characteristics on Urban Pattern of Biodiversity. Ecology and Society 10(1):23.

Kister, C.
2005 Arctic Melting: How Global Warming is Destroying One of the World's Largest Wilderness Areas. Monroe, ME: Common Courage Press.

Klepp, K., P. Biswalo, and A. Talle
1994 Young People at Risk: Fighting AIDS in North Tanzania. Oslo: Scandinavian University Press.

Klinge, H., W. A. Rodrigues, E. Brunig, and E. J. Fittkau
1975 Biomass and Structure in a Central Amazonian Rain Forest. *In* Tropical Ecological Systems. Trends in Terrestrial and Aquatic Research. F. B. Golley and E. Medina, eds. New York: Springer.

Knapp, G.
1991 Andean Ecology: Adaptive Dynamics in Ecuador. Boulder: Westview.

Knodel, J.
1977 Breast-Feeding and Population Growth. Science 198:1111–1115.

Koch, A., K. Molbak, P. Homoe, P. Sorensen, T. Hjuler, M. E. Olesen, J. Pejl, F. K. Pedersen, O. R. Olsen, and M. Melbye
2003 Risk Factors for Acute Respiratory Tract Infections in Young Greenland Children. American Journal of Epidemiology 158(4):374–384.

Kohler, T. A., and C. Van West, eds.
2000 Dynamics in Human and Primate Societies: Agent-Based Modeling of Social and Spatial Processes. Santa Fe Institute Studies in the Sciences of Complexity. New York: Oxford University Press.

Kofinas, G., G. Osherenko, D. Klein, and B. Forbes
2000 Research Planning in the Face of Change: The Human Role in Reindeer/Caribou Systems. Polar Research 19(1):3–21.

Kolata, A.
1993 The Tiwanaku: Portrait of an Andean Civilization. Cambridge, MA: Blackwell.

Kormondy, E.
1976 Concepts of Ecology. 2nd ed. Englewood Cliffs, NJ: Prentice Hall.

Kormondy, K. E., and D. Brown
1998 Fundamentals of Human Ecology. London: Prentice Hall.

Körner, C.
2003 Alpine Plant Life: Functional Plant Ecology of High Mountain Ecosystems. New York: Springer.

Kotlyakov, V. M.
1991 The Aral Seabasin. A Critical Environmental Zone. Environment 33(1):4–9.

Kottak, C.
1999   The New Ecological Anthropology. American Anthropologist 101:19–35.
Kraenzel, C. F.
1955   The Great Plains in Transition. Norman: University of Oklahoma Press.
Kraus, M. E.
1973   Eskimo-Aleut. *In* Linguistics in North America. Current Trends in Linguistics. Vol. 10. T. A. Sebeok, ed. The Hague: Mouton.
Krause, T. G., B. V. Pedersen, S. F. Thomsen, A. Koch, J. Wohlfahrt, V. Backer, and M. Melbye
2005   Lung Function in Greenlandic and Danish Children and Adolescents. Respiratory Medicine 99(3):363–371.
Kreutzmann, H.
2000   Sharing Water: Irrigation and Water Management in the Hindukush, Karakokram, Himalaya. Karachi: Oxford University Press.
Krichner, J. C.
1989   A Neotropical Companion: An Introduction to the Animals, Plants, and Ecosystems of the New World Tropics. Princeton, NJ: Princeton University Press.
Kroeber, A.
1939   Cultural and Natural Areas of Native North America. Berkeley: University of California Press.
Krupat, E.
1985   People in Cities: The Urban Environment and Its Effects. Cambridge: Cambridge University Press.
Krupnick, I.
1985   The Male-Female Ratio in Certain Traditional Populations of the Siberian Arctic. Inuit Studies 9(1):115–140.
1990   Cultures in Contact: The Population Nadir in Siberia and North America. European Review of Native American Studies 4(1):11–18.
1993   Arctic Adaptations. Hanover: University Press of New England.
Kull, C. A.
2004   Isle of Fire: The Political Ecology of Landscape Burning in Madagascar. Chicago: University of Chicago Press.
Kumar, B. M., and P. K. R. Nair
2006   Tropical Homegardens: A Time-Tested Example of Sustainable Agroforestry. Dordrecht: Springer.
Kummer, D. M.
1991   Deforestation in the Postwar Philippines. Chicago: University of Chicago Press.
Kurland, J., and S. Beckerman
1985   Optimal Foraging and Hominid Evolution: Labor and Reciprocity. American Anthropologist 87(1):73–93.
Kvitkova, L. V., G. A. Ushakova, E. V. Shchetinina, M. Yu. Ogarkov, E. Yu. Cherniavskaia, O. M. Polikutina, Ya. V. Kazachek, and O. L. Barbarash
2005   Thyroid Diseases in Reproductive Age Women Living in Shoria Mountains. Terapevticheskii Arkhiv 77(1):31–34.
Kwaku, A.
2005   Trypanotolerant Livestock in the Context of Trypanosomiasis Intervention Strategies. Rome: Food and Agriculture Organization of the UN.

Lachenbruch, A. H., and B. V. Marshall
1986   Changing Climate: Geothermal Evidence from Permafrost in the Alaskan Arctic. Science 234:689–696.

Ladell, W. S. S.
1964   Terrestrial Animals in Humid Heat: Man. *In* Handbook of Physiology: Adaptation to the Environment. D. B. Dill, ed. Washington, DC: American Physiological Society.

Lal, R.
2000   Global Climate Change and Tropical Ecosystems. Boca Raton, FL: CRC Press.

Laland, K., and K. Williams
1998   Social Transmission of Maladaptive Information in the Guppy. Behavioral Ecology 9(5):493–499.

Lambin, E. F., and H. J. Geist, eds.
2006   Land Use and Land Cover Change: Local Processes and Global Impacts. IGBP Springer Book Series, no. 9. Heidelberg: Springer.

Lambin, E. F., H. J. Geist, and E. Lepers
2003   Dynamics of Land Use and Land Cover Change in Tropical Regions. Annual Review of Environment and Resources 28: 205–241.

Lamprey, H.
1983   Pastoralism Yesterday and Today: The Overgrazing Problem. *In* Ecosystems of the World. Vol. 13, Tropical Savannas. F. Bourliere, ed. Amsterdam: Elsevier.

Landy, D.
1985   Pibloktoq (Hysteria) and Inuit Nutrition: Possible Implication of Hypervitaminosis A. Social Science and Medicine 21(2):173–185.

Langton, C., ed.
1997   Artificial Life: An Overview. Cambridge, MA: MIT Press.

Lansing, S.
1991   Priests and Programmers. Chicago: University of Chicago Press.
2003   Complex Adaptive Systems. Annual Review of Anthropology 32:183–204.

Lantis, M.
1947   Alaskan Eskimo Ceremonialism. Monograph of the American Ethnological Society, no. 11. New York: J. J. Augustin.

Lasco, R. D.
1998   Management of Philippine Tropical Forests: Implications to Global Warming. World Resource Review 10(3):410–418.

Lasker, G. W., and C. G. N. Mascie-Taylor, eds.
1993   Research Strategies in Human Biology: Field Survey Studies. Cambridge Studies in Biological Anthropology, no. 13. Cambridge: Cambridge University Press.

Laughlin, W. S.
1963   Eskimos and Aleuts: Their Origins and Evolution. Science 142:633–645.
1966   Genetical and Anthropological Characteristics of Arctic Populations. *In* The Biology of Human Adaptability. P. T. Baker and J. S. Weiner, eds. Oxford: Clarendon.
1968a   Hunting: An Integrating Biobehavior System and Its Evolutionary Importance. *In* Man the Hunter. R. B. Lee and I. DeVore, eds. Chicago: Aldine.
1968b   The Demography of Hunters: An Eskimo Example. *In* Man the Hunter. R. B. Lee and I. DeVore, eds. Chicago: Aldine.

1972   Ecology and Population Structure in the Arctic. *In* The Structure of Human Populations. G. Harrison and A. Boyce, eds. Oxford: Clarendon.

1975   Aleuts: Ecosystem, Holocene History and Siberian Origin. Science 189:507–515.

Laurance, W. F., and R. O. Bierregaard, eds.

1997   Tropical Forest Remnants: Ecology, Management and Conservation of Fragmented Communities. Chicago: University of Chicago Press.

Laurance, W. F., S. G. Laurance, and P. Delamonica

1998   Tropical Forest Fragmentation and Greenhouse Gas Emissions. Forest Ecology and Management 110(1–3):173–180.

Laurence, W. F., and C. Peres, eds.

2006   Emerging Threats to Tropical Forests. Chicago: University of Chicago Press.

Lave, C., and J. March

1975   An Introduction to Models in the Social Sciences. New York: Harper & Row.

Lawes, M. J.

2004   Indigenous Forests and Woodlands in South Africa: Policy, People, and Practice. Scottsville, South Africa: University of Kwazulu-Natal Press.

Leach, E. R.

1954   Political Systems of Highland Burma. London: London School of Economics and Political Science.

1961   Pul Eliya. Cambridge: Cambridge University Press.

Leake, C.

1964   Perspectives of Adaptation: Historical Backgrounds. *In* Handbook of Physiology: Adaptation to the Environment. D. B. Dill, ed. Washington, DC: American Physiological Society.

Lean, J., and D. Warrilow

1989   Simulation of the Regional Climate Impact of Amazon Deforestation. Nature 342:411–412.

Leatherman, T.

1998   Illness, Social Relations and Household Production and Reproduction in the Andes of South Peru. *In* Building a New Biocultural Synthesis. A. Goodman and T. Leatherman, eds. Ann Arbor: University of Michigan Press.

2005   A Space of Vulnerability in Poverty and Health: Political Ecology and Biocultural Analysis. Ethos 33(1):46–70.

Le Bars, M., J. M. Attonaty, S. Pinson, and N. Ferrard

2005   An Agent-Based Simulation Testing of the Impact of Water Allocation on Farmers' Collective Behaviors. Simulation-Transactions of the Society for Modeling and Simulation International 81(3):223–235.

Lee, D. H. K.

1964   Terrestrial Animals in Dry Heat: Man in the Desert. *In* Handbook of Physiology: Adaptation to the Environment. D. B. Dill, ed. Washington, DC: American Physiological Society.

1968   Man in the Desert. *In* Desert Biology. G. W. Brown, ed. New York: Academic.

1969   Variability in Human Response to Arid Environments. *In* Arid Lands in Perspective. W. McGinnies and B. Goodman, eds. Washington, DC: American Association for the Advancement of Science.

Lee, R. B.

1968   What Hunters Do for a Living, or How to Make Out on Scarce Resources. *In* Man the Hunter. R. B. Lee and I. DeVore, eds. Chicago: Aldine.

1972   !Kung Spatial Organization: An Ecological and Historical Perspective. Human Ecology 1(2):125–147.

1976   !Kung Spatial Organization. *In* Kalahari Hunter-Gatherers. R. B. Lee and I. DeVore, eds. Cambridge, MA: Harvard University Press.

Lee, R. B., and I. DeVore, eds.

1968   Man the Hunter. Chicago: Aldine.

1976   Kalahari Hunter-Gatherers. Cambridge, MA: Harvard University Press.

Lee, S. E., M. C. Press, and J. A. Lee

2000   Observed Climate Variations During the Last 100 Years in Lapland, Northern Finland. International Journal of Climatology 20(3):329–346.

Lees, S.

1974   Hydraulic Development as a Process of Response. Human Ecology 2(3):159–175.

1976   Choice of Technology in Irrigated Agriculture: Paper presented at 7th Annual Meeting, American Anthropological Association.

Lees, S., and D. Bates

1977   The Role of Exchange in Productive Specialization. American Anthropologist 79(4):824–841.

1990   The Ecology of Cumulative Change. *In* The Ecosystem Approach in Anthropology. E. F. Moran, ed. Ann Arbor: University of Michigan Press.

Lehman, J., D. Kern, B. Glaser, and W. Woods, eds.

2003   Amazonian Dark Earth: Origin, Properties, Management. Dordrecht: Kluwer Academic.

Leibenstein, H.

1976   Beyond Economic Man. Cambridge, MA: Harvard University Press.

Leigh, E. G., Jr.

1975   Structure and Climate in Tropical Rain Forest. Annual Review of Ecology and Systematics 6:67–86.

1999   Tropical Forest Ecology: A View from Barro Colorado Island. New York: Oxford University Press.

Leithard, C. S., and A. R. Lind

1964   Heat Stress and Heat Disorders. London: Cassell.

Leitmann, J.

1994   Rapid Urban Environmental Assessment: Lessons from Cities in the Developing World: Methodology and Preliminary Findings. Vol. 1. Washington, DC: World Bank Publications.

Lenski, G. E.

2005   Ecological-Evolutionary Theory: Principles and Applications. Boulder: Paradigm.

Leonard, W., T. Leatherman, J. Carry, and R. B. Thomas

1990   Contributions of Nutrition Versus Hypoxia to Growth in Rural Andean Populations. American Journal of Human Biology 2:613–626.

Leonard, W., J. Snodgrass, and M. V. Sorensen

2005   Metabolic Adaptation in Indigenous Siberian Populations. Annual Review of Anthropology 34:451–471.

Leopold, A.

1949   A Sand County Almanac. New York: Oxford University Press.

Leppaeluoto, J., and J. Hassi

1991   Human Physiological Adaptations to the Arctic Climate. Arctic 44(2):139–145.

Levin, R. I., and C. A. Kirkpatrick
1975   Quantitative Approaches to Management. 3rd ed. New York: McGraw-Hill.
Levin, S.
1998   Ecosystem and the Biosphere as a Complex Adaptive System. Ecosystems
          1(5):431–436.
Levin, S. A., ed.
1974   Ecosystem Analysis and Prediction. Philadelphia: Society for Industrial and
          Applied Mathematics.
Levins, R.
1968   Evolution in Changing Environments. Princeton, NJ: Princeton University
          Press.
Levy, J.
1961   Ecology of the South Plains. American Ethnological Society Proceedings.
          Mimeo.
Lewis, D., J. P. Kaye, C. Gries, A. P. Kinzig, and C. L. Redman
2006   Agrarian Legacy in Soil Nutrient Pools of Urbanizing Arid Lands. Global
          Change Biology 12(4):703–709.
Lewis, J. K.
1970   Primary Producers in Grassland Ecosystems. *In* The Grassland Ecosystem: A
          Supplement. R. L. Dix and R. G. Beidelman, eds. Fort Collins: Colorado State
          University, Range Science Department.
Lewis, S. L., Y. Malhi, and O. L. Phillips
2004   Fingerprinting the Impacts of Global Change on Tropical Forests. Philosophi-
          cal Transactions of the Royal Society of London. Series B-Biological Sciences
          359 (1443):437–462.
Lewontin, R. C., ed.
1968   Population Biology and Evolution. Syracuse, NY: Syracuse University Press.
Li, F. Z., and L. Yi
2005   Effect of Clothing Material on Thermal Responses of the Human Body. Mod-
          elling and Simulation in Materials Science and Engineering 13(6):809–827.
Li, O., R. Ma, and J. Simpson
1993   Changes in the Nomadic Pattern and Its Impact on the Inner Mongolia Steppe
          Grassland Ecosystem. Nomadic Peoples 33:63–72.
Li, S. Z., C. Z. Zhu, and M. W. Feldman
2004   Gender Differences in Child Survival in Contemporary Rural China: A Coun-
          try Study. Journal of Biosocial Science 36(1):83–109.
Li, X. R., Z. S. Zhang, J. G. Zhang, X. P. Wang, and X. H. Jia
2004   Association Between Vegetation Patterns and Soil Properties in the Southeast-
          ern Tengger Desert, China. Arid Lands Research and Management 18(4):
          369–383.
Li, X. R., H. Y. Zhou, X. P. Wang, Y. Zhu, and P. J. O'Conner
2003   The Effects of Sand Stabilization and Revegetation on Cryptogram Species Di-
          versity and Soil Fertility in the Tengger Desert, Northern China. Plant and Soil
          251(2):237–245.
Likens, G. E., and F. G. Bormann
1975   An Experimental Approach to New England Landscapes. *In* Coupling of Land
          and Water Systems. A. D. Hasler, ed. London: Chapman & Hall.
1995   Biogeochemistry of a Forested Ecosystem. 2nd ed. New York: Springer.

Likens, G. E., F. H. Bormann, N. M. Johnson, D. W. Fisher, and R. S. Pierce
1970   Effects of Forest Cutting and Herbicide Treatment on Nutrient Budgets in the Hubbard Brook Watershed-Ecosystem. Ecological Monographs 40(1):23–47.

Lillesand, T. M., R. W. Kiefer, and J. W. Chapman
2004   Remote Sensing and Image Interpretation. 5th ed. New York: Wiley.

Lima Bezerra, M. C., and M. A. Fernandes, eds.
2000   Cidades Sustentáveis: Subsídios a Elaboração da Agenda 21 Brasileira. Brasília, DF: Ministério do Meio Ambiente.

Linares, O.
1976   Garden Hunting in the American Tropics. Human Ecology 4(4):331–349.

Lindblom, C.
1964   The Science of Muddling Through. *In* The Making of Decisions. W. J Gore and J. W. Dyson, eds. New York: Free Press.

Lindeman, R. L.
1942   The Trophic-Dynamic Aspect of Ecology. Ecology 23:399–418.

Lindgren, D. T.
1985   Land Use Planning and Remote Sensing. Dordrecht: Nijhoff.

Liniger, H., and G. Schwilch
2002   Enhanced Decision-Making Based on Local Knowledge: The WOCAT Method of Sustainable Soil and Water Management. Mountain Research and Development 22(1):14–18.

Linkola, M.
1973   The Snowmobile in Lapland: Its Economic and Social Effects. *In* Circumpolar Problems: Habitat, Economy and Social Relations in the Arctic. G. Berg, ed. Oxford: Pergamon.

Lisboa, P.
1997   Caxiuanâ. Belém: Museu Paraense Emilio Goeldi.

Little, M. A.
1968   Racial and Developmental Factors in Foot Cooling: Quechua Indians and U.S. Whites. *In* High Altitude Adaptation in a Peruvian Community. P. T. Baker, et al., eds. Occasional Papers in Anthropology, no. 1. University Park: Pennsylvania State University.
1976   Physiological Responses to Cold. *In* Man in the Andes. P. T. Baker and M. Little, eds. Stroudsburg, PA: Dowden, Hutchinson & Ross.

Little, M. A., and P. T. Baker
1976   Environmental Adaptations and Perspectives. *In* Man in the Andes. P. T. Baker and M. Little, eds. Stroudsburg, PA: Dowden, Hutchinson & Ross.

Little, M. A., and D. H. Hochner
1973   Human Thermoregulation, Growth and Mortality. Reading, MA: An Addison-Wesley Module in Anthropology, no. 36.

Little, M. A., and P. W. Leslie, eds.
1999   Turkana Herds of the Dry Savanna: Ecology and Bio-Behavioral Response of Nomads to an Uncertain Environment. Oxford: Oxford University Press.

Little, M. A., and G. Morren
1976   Ecology, Energetics and Human Variability. Dubuque, IA: William C. Brown.

Little, M. A., R. B. Thomas, R. B. Mazess, and P. T. Baker
1971   Population Differences and Developmental Changes in Extremity Temperature Responses to Cold Among Andean Indians. Human Biology 43:70–91.

Little, P.
1985   Adding a Regional Perspective to Farming Systems Research: Concepts and
         Analysis. Human Organization 44:331–338.
1992   The Elusive Granary: Herder, Farmer and State in Northern Kenya. Cam-
         bridge: Cambridge University Press.

Livingstone, F. B.
1968   The Effects of Warfare on the Biology of the Human Species. *In* War: The
         Anthropology of Armed Conflict. M. Fried et al., eds. New York: Doubleday.

Lizot, J.
1977   Population, Resources and Warfare Among the Yanomami. Man (new ser.)
         12:497–517.

Lo, C. P., and A. K. W. Yeung
2002   Concepts and Techniques in Geographic Information Systems. Upper Saddle
         River, NJ: Prentice Hall.

Loffler, J.
2000   High Mountain Ecosystems and Landscape Degradation in Northern Norway.
         Mountain Research and Development 20(4):356–363.

Logan, K. A., and L. L. Sweanor
2001   Desert Puma: Evolutionary Ecology and Conservation of an Enduring Carni-
         vore. Washington, DC: Island.

Lomnicki, A.
1999   Individual-Based Models and the Individual-Based Approach to Population
         Ecology. Ecological Modelling 115:191–198.

Longman, K. A., and J. Jenix
1987   Tropical Forest and Its Environment. 2nd ed. New York: Longman/Wiley.

Lopez-Zetina, J., H. Lee, and R. Friis
2006   The Link Between Obesity and the Built Environment: Evidence from an Eco-
         logical Analysis of Obesity and Vehicle Miles of Travel in California. Health
         and Place 12(4):656–664.

Loram, A., J. Tratalos, P. Warren, and K. Gaston
2007   Urban Domestic Gardens: The Extent and Structure of the Resource in Five
         Major Cities. Landscape Ecology 22:601–615.

Lorek, J., and M. Sonnenschein
1999   Modelling and Simulation Software to Support Individual-Based Ecological
         Modelling. Ecological Modelling 115:199–216.

Loris, V., and G. Damiano
2006   Mapping the Green Herbage Ratio of Grasslands Using Both Aerial and Satel-
         lite Derived Spectral Reflectance. Agriculture, Ecosystems and Environment
         115(1–4):141–149.

Loutan, L.
1985   Nutrition Amongst a Group of Wodaabe Pastoralists in Niger. *In* Population,
         Health and Nutrition in the Sahel. A. Hill, ed. London: Routledge & Kegan Paul.

Lovett, J. V., ed.
1973   The Environmental, Economic and Social Significance of Drought. Sidney,
         Australia: Angus & Robertson.

Low, N., I. Elander, and B. Gleeson, eds.
1999   Consuming Cities: Urban Environment in the Global Economy After the Rio
         Declaration. London: Routledge.

Lowenstein, F.
1968   Some Aspects of Human Ecology in South America. *In* Biogeography and Ecology in South America. E. J. Fittkau, et al., eds. The Hague: Junk.
1973   Some Consideration of Biological Adaptation by Aboriginal Man. *In* Tropical Forest Ecosystems in Africa and South America. B. Meggers, et al., eds. Washington, DC: Smithsonian Institution Press.

Lowie, R. H.
1917   Culture and Ethnology. New York: Peter Smith.

Lu, D., E. Moran, and P. Mausel
2002   Linking Amazonian Secondary Succession Forest Growth to Soil Properties. Land Degradation and Development 13:331–343.

Lubchenko, J.
1998   Entering the Century of the Environment: A New Social Contract for Science. Science 279:491–497.

LUCC (Land-Use and Land-Cover Change)
1999   Land-Use and Land-Cover Change Implementation Strategy. Stockholm: IGPB Secretariat.

Luck, M., and J. Wu
2002   A Gradient Analysis of Urban Landscape Pattern: A Case Study from the Phoenix Metropolitan Region. Landscape Ecology 17: 327–339.

Lugo, A., and S. Snedaker, eds.
1971   Readings in Ecological Systems. New York: MSS Educational.

Lugo, A. E.
1988   The Future of the Forest: Ecosystem Rehabilitation in the Tropics. Environment 30(7):16–20, 41–45.

Lugo, A. E., and S. Brown
1992   Tropical Forests as Sinks of Atmospheric Carbon. Forest Ecology and Management 54(1–4):239–255.

Lutz, W., B. C. O'Neill, and S. Scherbov
2003   Europe's Population at a Turning Point. Science 299(5615):1991–1992.

Lyon, P., ed.
1974   Native South Americans. Boston: Little, Brown.

Lyons, T., M. Inglis, and R. Hitchcock
1972   The Application of Space Imagery to Anthropology. *In* Proceedings of the Third Annual Conference on Remote Sensing in Arid Lands. Tucson: University of Arizona, Office of Arid Land Studies.

Ma, Q.
2004   Appraisal of Tree Planting Options to Control Desertification: Experiences from Three-North Shelterbelt Programme. International Forestry Review 6(3–4):327–334.

MAB/UNESCO
1973   Ecological Effects of Energy Utilization in Urban and Industrial Systems. Paris: UNESCO.

Mabberly, D. J.
1991   Tropical Rain Forest Ecology. New York: Chapman & Hall.

Mackay, D. M.
1968a The Informational Analysis of Questions and Commands. *In* Modern Systems Research for the Behavioral Scientist. W. Buckley, ed. Chicago: Aldine.

1968b   Towards an Information-Flow Model of Human Behavior. *In* Modern Systems Research for the Behavioral Scientist. W. Buckley, ed. Chicago: Aldine.

Mackay, J. R.
1969   Tundra and Taiga. *In* Vegetation, Soils and Wildlife. J. G. Nelson and M. J. Chambers, eds. Toronto: Methuen.

Macy, M. W., and R. Willer
2002   From Factors to Actors: Computational Sociology and Agent-Based Modeling. Annual Review of Sociology 28:143–166.

Mahar, D. J.
1989   Government Policies and Deforestation in Brazil's Amazon Region. Washington, DC: World Bank.

Maimbolwa, M. C., B. Yamba, V. Diwan and A. B. Ransjö-Arvidson
2003   Cultural Childbirth Practices and Beliefs in Zambia. Journal of Advanced Nursing 43(3):263–274.

Mainguet, M.
1999   Aridity: Drought and Human Development. New York: Springer.

Malhi, Y., and O. Phillips
2005   Tropical Forests and Global Atmospheric Change. New York: Oxford University Press.

Malingreau, J., and C. J. Tucker
1988   Large Scale Deforestation in the Southeastern Amazon Basin of Brazil. Ambio 17:49–55.

Mallory, M. L., H. G. Gilchrist, B. M. Braune, and A. J. Gaston
2006   Marine Birds as Indicators of Arctic Marine Ecosystem Health: Linking the Northern Ecosystem Initiative to Long-Term Studies. Environmental Monitoring and Assessment 113(1–3):31–48.

Maloney, J. P., and U. Broeckel
2005   Epidemiology, Risk Factors, and Genetics of High Altitude Related Pulmonary Disease. Clinics in Chest Medicine 26(3):395–404.

Mann, D. H., R. E. Reanier, D. M. Peteet, M. L. Kunz, and M. Johnson
2001   Environmental Change and Arctic Paleoindians. Arctic Anthropology 38(2): 119–138.

Mann, G.
1996   Faunistische Untersuchung von drei Dachbegriinungen in Linz. OKO-L 18(2):3–14.

March, J. G., and H. A. Simon
1958   Organizations. New York: Wiley.

Martin, C.
1991   The Rainforests of West Africa. Boston: Birkhauser Verlag.

Martin, P.
1976   Ideas for the Study of Ritual and Ecology Among the Early Historic Native Peoples. Unpublished manuscript. Indiana University, Department of Anthropology.

Martine, G.
2007   Unleashing the Potential of Urban Growth. UN Population Fund, State of the World Population.

Marzluff, J., E. Shulenberger, W. Endlicher, M. Alberti, G. Bradley, C. Ryan, U. Simon, and C. ZumBrunnen, eds.
In press Urban Ecology: An International Perspective on the Interaction Between Humans and Nature. New York: Springer.

Mason, A.
2002   The Rise of an Alaskan Native Bourgeoisie. Inuit Studies 26(2):5–22.

Mata-Gonzalez, R., T. McLendon, and D. Martin
2005   The Inappropriate Use of Crop Transpiration Coefficients (K c) to Estimate Evapotranspiration in Arid Ecosystems: A Review. Arid Land Research and Management 19(3):285–295.

Mathieu, R., C. Freeman, and J. Aryal
2007   Mapping Private Gardens in Urban Areas Using Object-Oriented Techniques and Very High Resolution Satellite Imagery. Landscape and Urban Planning 81:179–192.

Matveyeva, N. V., O. M. Parinkina, and Y. I. Chernov
1975   Maria Pronchitsheva Bay, USSR. *In* Structure and Function of Tundra Ecosystems. T. Rosswall and O. W. Heal, eds. Stockholm: Swedish Natural Science Research Council.

Maud, P. J., and C. Foster
2006   Physiological Assessment of Human Fitness. 2nd ed. Champaign, IL: Human Kinetics.

Mausel, P., Y. Wu, Y. Li, E. F. Moran, and E. S. Brondizio
1993   Spectral Identification of Successional Stages Following Deforestation in the Amazon. Geocarto International 8:61–71.

Mayr, E.
1942   Systematics and the Origin of Species. New York: Columbia University Press.
1991   One Long Argument: Charles Darwin and the Genesis of Modern Evolutionary Thought. Cambridge, MA: Harvard University Press.

Mazess, R.
1975   Human Adaptation to High Altitude. *In* Physiological Anthropology. A. Damon, ed. New York: Oxford University Press.

Mazess, R., and W. Mather
1978   Biochemical Variation: Bone Mineral Content. *In* The Eskimo of Northwestern Alaska: A Biological Perspective. P. L. Jamison, S. L. Zegura, and F. A. Milan, eds. Stroudsburg, PA: Dowden, Hutchinson & Ross.

Mazmanian, D., and M. Kraft, eds.
1999   Toward Sustainable Communities: Transitions and Transformations in Environmental Policy. Cambridge, MA: MIT Press.

Mbida, C. M., W. Van Neer, H. Doutrelepont, and L. Vrydaghs
2000   Evidence for Banana Cultivation and Animal Husbandry During the First Millenium BC in the Forest of Southern Cameroon. Journal of Archeological Science 27(2):151–162.

McCabe, J. T.
1983   Land Use Among the Turkana. Rural Africana 15–16:109–125.
1984   Livestock Management Among the Turkana: A Social and Ecological Analysis of Herding in an East African Population. Ph.D. diss. State University of New York at Binghamton, Department of Anthropology.
1990   Turkana Pastoralism: A Case Study Against the Tragedy of the Commons. Human Ecology 18(1):81–104.
2004   Cattle Bring Us to Our Enemies: Turkana Ecology, Politics, and Raiding in a Disequilibrium System. Ann Arbor: University of Michigan Press.

McCay, B.
1981   Optimal Foragers or Political Actions? Ecological Analyses of a New Jersey Fishery. American Ethnologist 8(2):356–382.

McCay, B., and J. Acheson, eds.
1987   The Question of the Commons: The Culture and Ecology of Communal Resources. Tucson: University of Arizona Press.

McClain, M. E., R. L. Victoria, and J. E. Richey, eds.
2001   The Biogeochemistry of the Amazon Basin. New York: Oxford University Press.

McCortney, A. P.
1980   The Nature of Thule Eskimo Whale Use. Arctic 33(3):517–541.

McCoy, R. M.
2005   Field Methods in Remote Sensing. New York: Guilford Press.

McCracken, S., E. S. Brondizio, D. Nelson, E. F. Moran, A. D. Siqueira, and C. Rodriguez-Pedraza
1999   Remote Sensing and GIS at Farm Property Level: Demography and Deforestation in the Brazilian Amazon. Photogrammetric Engineering and Remote Sensing 65(11):1311–1320.

McCracken, S., A. Siqueira, E. F. Moran, and E. Brondizio
2002   Land Use Patterns on an Agricultural Frontier in Brazil: Insights and Examples from a Demographic Perspective. *In* Deforestation and Land Use in the Amazon. D. Wood and R. Porro, eds. Gainesville: University Press of Florida.

McCulley, R. L., E. G. Jobaggy, W. T. Pockman, and R. B. Jackson
2004   Nutrient Uptake as a Contributing Explanation for Deep Rooting in Arid and Semi-Arid Ecosystems 141(4):620–628.

McDonald, G., and M. Patterson
2007   Bridging the Divide in Urban Sustainability: From Human Exemptionalism to the New Ecological Paradigm. Urban Ecosystems 10:169–192.

McDonnell, M. J., and S. T. A. Pickett
1990   The Study of Ecosystem Structure and Function Along Urban-Rural Gradients: An Unexploited Opportunity for Ecology. Ecology 71:1231–1237.

McGhee, R.
1974   The Peopling of Arctic North America. *In* Arctic and Alpine Environments. J. D. Ives and R. G. Barry, eds. London: Methuen.
2002   Ancient People of the Arctic. Vancouver: University of British Columbia Press.

McGranahan, G., P. Jacobi, J. Songsore, C. Surjadi, and M. Kjellén
2001   The Citizens at Risk: From Urban Sanitation to Sustainable Cities. London: Earthscan.

McGraw, K., R. Hoffman, C. Harker, and J. H. Herman
1999   The Development of Circadian Rhythms in a Human Infant. Sleep 22(3):302–310.

McGuire, A. D., F. S. Chapin III, J. E. Walsh, and C. Wirth
2006   Integrated Regional Changes in Arctic Climate Feedbacks: Implications for the Global Climate System. Annual Review of Environment and Resources 31:61–91.

McIntosh, R. P.
1985   The Background of Ecology: Concept and Theory. Cambridge: Cambridge University Press.

Meadows, D. H., D. L. Meadows, J. Randers, and W. Behrens III
1972   The Limits to Growth. New York: Universe Books.

Meckelein, W.
1980   Saharan Oases in Crisis. *In* Desertification in Extremely Arid Environments. W. Meckelein, ed. Eichert: Rechber Ystrasse.

Meggers, B.
1971   Amazônia. Chicago: Aldine.
1974   Environment and Culture in Amazônia. *In* Man and the Amazon. C. Wagley, ed. Gainesville: University of Florida Press.
1994   Archaeological Evidence for the Impact of Mega-Niño Events on Amazônia During the Past Two Millenia. Climate Change 28:331–338.

Meggers, B., E. S. Ayensu, and W. D. Ducksworth, eds.
1973   Tropical Forest Ecosystems in Africa and South America. Washington, DC: Smithsonian Institution Press.

Meher-Homji, V. M.
1991   Probable Impact of Deforestation on Hydrological Processes. Climate Change 19(1–2):163–173.

Meir, A.
1987   Comparative Vital Statistics Along the Pastoral Nomadism-Sedentism Continuum. Human Ecology 15(1):91–107.

Melillo, J., M. Bustamante, D. Alves, R. DeFries, C. Cerri, and M. Keller
In press   Agricultural Transitions in the Amazon Basin. Washington, DC: Island.

Merkt, J. R., and C. R. Taylor
1994   "Metabolic Switch" for Desert Survival. Proceedings of the National Academy of Sciences, USA 91(25):12313–12316.

Messer, E.
1996   Hunger Vulnerability from an Anthropologist's Food Systems Perspective. *In* Transforming Societies, Transforming Anthropology. E. F. Moran, ed. Ann Arbor: University of Michigan Press.

Messerli, B., and J. Ives, eds.
1997   Mountains of the World: A Global Priority. New York: Parthenon.

Meyer, W.
1996   Human Impact on the Earth. New York: Cambridge University Press.

Meyer, W., and B. L. Turner II
1992   Human Population Growth and Global Land-Use/Cover Change. Annual Review of Ecology and Systematics 23:39–61.
1994   Changes in Land Use and Land Cover: A Global Perspective. Cambridge: Cambridge University Press.

Michelson, W.
1976   Man and His Urban Environment: A Sociological Approach. Rev. ed. Reading, MA: Addison-Wesley.

Micklin, P. P.
2000   Central Asian and Caucasian Project: Managing Water in Central Asia. London: Royal Institute of International Affairs.

Milan, F. A.
1978   Multidisciplinary Research on Northwest Alaskan Eskimos. *In* The Eskimo of Northwestern Alaska: A Biological Perspective. P. L. Jamison, S. L. Zegura, and F. A. Milan, eds. Stroudsburg, PA: Dowden, Hutchinson & Ross.

Milesi, C., S. Running, C. Elvidge, J. Dietz, B. Tuttle, and R. Nemani
2005   Mapping and Modeling the Biogeochemical Cycling of Turf Grasses in the U.S. Environmental Management 36(3):426–438.

Miller, D., and G. de Roo, eds.
2005   Urban Environmental Planning: Policies, Instruments, and Methods in an International Perspective. Aldershot, UK: Ashgate.

Miller, E. K.
1993   Atmospheric Influences on the Biochemistry of High-Elevation Forests. Ph.D. diss. Hanover, NH: Dartmouth College.

Miller, G. J.
2005   The Political Evolution of Principal-Agent Models. Annual Review of Political Science 8:203–225.

Miller, G. T.
1975   Living in the Environment. Belmont, CA: Wadsworth.

Miller, R. W.
1997   Urban Forestry: Planning and Managing Urban Greenspaces. Upper Saddle River, NJ: Prentice Hall.

Millon, R.
1962   Variations in Social Responses to the Practice of Irrigation Agriculture. *In* Civilizations in Desert Lands. R. B. Woodbury, ed. Anthropological Papers. Salt Lake City: University of Utah.

Milton, K.
1984   Protein and Carbohydrate Resources of the Maku Indians of Northwestern Amazônia. American Anthropologist 86:7–27.
1996   Environmentalism and Cultural Theory: Exploring the Role of Anthropology in Environmental Discourse. New York: Routledge.

Minor, T.
2002   Political Participation of Inuit Women in the Government of Nunavut. Wicazo Sa Review 17(1):65–90.

Minshull, R.
1970   The Changing Nature of Geography. London: Hutchinson University Library.

Mishra, C. H., H. T. Prins, and S. E. Van Wieren
2003   Diversity, Risk Mediation, and Change in a Trans-Himalayan Agropastoral System. Human Ecology 31(4):595–609.

Mistry, J.
2000   World Savannas: Ecology and Human Use. New York: Prentice Hall.

Mistry, J., and A. Berardi, eds.
2006   Savannas and Dry Forests: Linking People with Nature. Aldershot, UK: Ashgate.

Mitman, G.
1992   The State of Nature: Ecology, Community, and American Social Thought, 1900–1950. Chicago: University of Chicago Press.

Mitsch, W., and J. Day
2004   Thinking Big with Whole Ecosystem Studies and Ecosystem Restoration: A Legacy of H.T. Odum. Ecological Modelling 178(1–2):133–155.

Moerman, D.
1998   Native American Ethnobotany. Portland, OR: Timber Press.

Moerman, M.
1968   Agricultural Change and Peasant Choice in a Thai Village. Berkeley: University of California Press.

Mohamed-Salih, M., J. Baker, and J. Baekers, eds.
1995　　The Migration Experience in Africa. Uppsala: Scandinavian Institute of African Studies.

Molion, L.
1987　　Micrometeriology of an Amazonian Rain Forest. *In* The Geophysiology of Amazônia. R. Dickinson, ed. New York: Wiley.

Moller-Leimkuhler, A. M.
2003　　The Gender Gap in Suicide and Premature Death or: Why Are Men So Vulnerable? European Archives of Psychiatry and Clinical Neuroscience 253(1): 1–8.

Monge, C.
1948　　Acclimatization in the Andes. Baltimore: Johns Hopkins University Press.

Montagnini, F., and C. F. Jordan
2005　　Tropical Forest Ecology: The Basis for Conservation and Management. New York: Springer.

Moore, C. W. E.
1966　　Distribution of Grasslands. *In* Grasses and Grasslands. C. Barnard, ed. New York: St. Martin's.

Moore, L. G.
2000　　Comparative Human Ventilatory Adaptation to High Altitude. Respiration Physiology 121(2–3):257–276.

Moore, L. G., S. Niermeyer, and S. Zamudio
1998　　Human Adaptation to High Altitude: Regional and Life Cycle Perspectives. American Journal of Physical Anthropology 27:25–64.

Moore, L. G., and J. G. Regensteiner
1983　　Adaptation to High Altitude. Annual Review of Anthropology 12:285–304.

Moran, E. F.
1973　　Energy Flow Analysis and Manihot esculenta Crantz. Acta Amazonica 3(3):28–39.
1976　　Agricultural Development in the Transamazon Highway. Bloomington: Indiana University/Latin American Studies Working Papers.
1979a　Human Adaptability. N. Scituate, MA: Duxbury. Reissued by Westview Press, 1982.
1979b　Criteria for Choosing Successful Homesteaders in Brazil. Research in Economic Anthropology 2:339–359.
1981　　Developing the Amazon. Bloomington: Indiana University Press.
1982a　Ecological, Anthropological and Agronomic Research in the Amazon Basin. Latin American Research Review 17:3–41.
1982b　The Evolution of Cape Verde's Agriculture. African Economic History 11:63–86.
1984　　Limitations and Advances in Ecosystems Research. *In* The Ecosystem Concept in Anthropology. E. F. Moran, ed. Washington, DC: American Association for the Advancement of Science.
1989　　Models of Native and Folk Adaptation in the Amazon. Advances in Economic Botany 7:22–29.
1993a　Deforestation and Land Use in the Brazilian Amazon. Human Ecology 21:1–21.
1993b　Through Amazonian Eyes: The Human Ecology of Amazonian Populations. Iowa City: University of Iowa Press.
2006　　People and Nature: An Introduction to Human Ecological Relations. Oxford, UK: Blackwell.

Moran, E. F., ed.
1990   The Ecosystem Approach in Anthropology: From Concept to Practice. Ann Arbor: University of Michigan Press.
1995   The Comparative Analysis of Human Societies: Toward Common Standards for Data Collection and Reporting. Boulder: L. Rienner.
1996   Transforming Societies, Transforming Anthropology. Ann Arbor: University of Michigan Press.

Moran, E. F., R. T. Adams, B. Bakoyema, S. Fiorini, and B. Boucek
2006   Human Strategies for Coping with El Niño Related Drought in Amazônia. Climatic Change 77:343–361.

Moran, E. F., and E. S. Brondizio
1998   Land-Use Change After Deforestation in Amazônia. *In* NRC People and Pixels: Linking Remote Sensing and Social Science. Washington, DC: National Academy Press.
2001   Human Ecology from Space: Ecological Anthropology Engages the Study of Global Environmental Change. *In* Ecology and the Sacred: Engaging the Anthropology of Roy A. Rappaport. E. Messer and M. Lambeck, eds. Ann Arbor: University of Michigan Press.

Moran, E. F., E. S. Brondizio, and P. Mausel
1994b   Secondary Succession. Research and Exploration 10(4):458–476.

Moran, E. F., E. S. Brondizio, P. Mausel, and Y. Wu
1994a   Integration of Amazonian Vegetation, Land Use and Satellite Data. BioScience 44:329–338.

Moran, E. F., E. S. Brondizio, and S. McCracken
2002a   Trajectories of Land Use: Soils, Succession and Crop Choice. *In* Deforestation and Land Use in the Amazon. C. Wood and R. Porro, eds. Gainesville: University Press of Florida.

Moran, E. F., E. S. Brondizio, J. M. Tucker, M. C. Silva-Forsberg, S. McCracken, and I. Falesi
2000   Effects of Soil Fertility and Land Use on Forest Succession in Amazônia. Forest Ecology and Management. 139(1):93–108.

Moran, E. F., E. S. Brondizio, and L. VanWey
2005   Population and Environment in Amazônia: Landscape and Household Dynamics. *In* Population, Land Use and Environment. B. Entwisle and P. Stern, eds. Washington, DC: National Academies Press.

Moran, E. F., and E. Ostrom, eds.
2005   Seeing the Forest and the Trees: Human-Environment Interactions in Forest Ecosystems. Cambridge, MA: MIT Press.

Moran, E. F., E. Ostrom, and J. C. Randolph
2002b   Ecological Systems and Multitier Human Organizations. *In* UNESCO/ Encyclopedia of Life Support Systems. Oxford: EOLSS.

Moran, E. F., A. Packer, E. S. Brondizio, and J. Tucker
1996   Restoration of Vegetation Cover in the Eastern Amazon. Ecological Economics 18:41–54.

Morgan, L.
1977   An Ancient Eskimo Nation Takes on New Life. Alaska 43(9):34–35, 86–89.

Morley, R. J.
2000   Origin and Evolution of Tropical Rain Forests. New York: Wiley.

Morren, G.
1986   The Miyanmin: Human Ecology of a Papau New Guinea Society. Ann Arbor: UMI Research Press.

Mortimore, M. J.
1989   Adapting to Drought: Farmers, Famines and Desertification in West Africa. New York: Cambridge University Press.
1998   Roots in the African Dust: Sustaining the Sub-Saharan Drylands. New York: Cambridge University Press.

Morton, D., R. DeFries, Y. Shimabukuro, L. Anderson, F. Espirito-Santo, M. Hansen, and M. Carroll
2005   Rapid Assessment of Annual Deforestation in the Brazilian Amazon Using MODIS Data. Earth Interactions 9(8):1–22.

Mosier, A., J. K. Syers, and J. Freney
2004   Agriculture and the Nitrogen Cycle: Assessing the Impacts of Fertilizer Use on Food Production and the Environment. Washington, DC: Island.

Mott, G. O., and H. Popenoe
1975   The Ecophysiology of Tropical Grasslands. Mimeo. Gainesville: University of Florida, Center of Tropical Agriculture.

Müller-Beck, J.
1967   On Migrations of Hunters Across the Bering Land Bridge in the Upper Pleistocene. *In* The Bering Land Bridge. D.M. Hopkins, ed. Stanford: Stanford University Press.

Müller-Wille, L.
1974   The Snowmobile, Lapps and Reindeer Herding in Finnish Lapland. *In* Arctic and Alpine Environments. J. D. Ives and R. G. Barry, eds. London: Methuen.

Mumford, L.
1961   The City in History: Its Origin, Its Transformation and Its Prospects. New York: Harcourt, Brace & World.

Mundel, T., J. King, E. Collacott, and D. A. Jones
2006   Drink Temperature Influences Fluid Intake and Endurance Capacity in Men During Exercise in a Hot, Dry Environment. Experimental Physiology 91(5):925–933.

Muniz, L., and A. Galindo
2005   Urban Form and the Ecological Footprint of Commuting: The Case of Barcelona. Ecological Economics 55:499–514.

Murdoch, W.
1971   Ecological Systems. *In* Environment: Resources, Pollution and Society. W. Murdoch, ed. Stamford, CT: Sinauer.

Murphy, N. J., C. D. Schraer, M. C. Theile, E. J. Boyko, L. R. Bulkow, B. J. Doty, and A. P. Lanier
1997   Hypertension in Alaska Natives: Association with Overweight, Glucose Intolerance, Diet and Mechanized Activity. Ethnicity and Health 2(4):267–275.

Murra, J.
1965   Herds and Herders in the Inca State. *In* Man, Culture and Animals. A. Leeds and A. P. Vayda, eds. Washington, DC: American Association for the Advancement of Science.
1972   El Control Vertical de un Máximo de Pisos Ecológicos en La Economía de las Sociedades Andinas. *In* Visita de la Provincia de Leon de Huanuco en 1562. J. Murra, ed. Huanuco, Peru: Universidad Nacional.

Mutuo, P. K., G. Cadish, A. Albrecht, C. Palm, and L. Verchot
2005   Potential of Agroforestry for Carbon Sequestration and Mitigation of Green-house Gas Emissions from Soils in the Tropics. Nutrient Cycling in Agro-ecosystems 71(1):43–54.

Mwalyosi, R. B.
1991   Population Growth, Carrying Capacity and Sustainable Development in South-western Masailand. Journal of Environmental Management 33(2):175–187.

Myers, H.
2000   Options for Appropriate Development in Nunavut Communities. Inuit Stud-ies 24(1):25–40.

Mymrin, N. I., and H. P. Huntington
1999   Traditional Knowledge of the Ecology of Beluga Whales (Delphinapterus leucas) in the Northern Bering Sea, Chukotka, Russia. Arctic-Montreal 52(1):62–70.

Nachman, B.
1969   Fits, Suicides, Beatings and Time-Out. Anchorage: US Public Health Service, Alaska Native Service.

Nagendra, H.
2001   Using Remote Sensing to Assess Biodiversity. International Journal of Remote Sensing 22(12):2377–2400.
2002   Tenure and Forest Conditions: Community Forestry in the Nepal Terai. Envi-ronmental Conservation 29:530–539.

Nam, C., ed.
1968   Population and Society: A Textbook of Readings. Boston: Houghton Mifflin.

Natani, K., and J. T. Shurley
1974   Sociopsychological Aspects of a Winter Vigil at South Pole Station. *In* Human Adaptability to Antarctic Conditions. E. K. E. Gunderson, ed. Washington, DC: American Geophysical Union.

Nathan, M., E. Fratkin, and E. Ruth
1996   Sedentism and Child Health Among Rendille Pastoralists of Northern Kenya. Social Science and Medicine 43(4):503–515.

National Science Board
1989   Loss of Biological Diversity. Washington, DC: National Scientific Board Com-mittee on International Science.

National Science Foundation (NSF)
1997   People and the Arctic: A Prospectus for Research in the Human Dimensions of the Arctic System. Washington, DC: NSF.
2003   Complex Environmental Systems: Synthesis for Earth, Life and Society in the 21st Century. Arlington, VA: NSF.

Nazarea, V. D.
1998   Cultural Memory and Biodiversity. Tucson: University of Arizona Press.
1999   Ethnoecology: Situated Knowledge/Located Lives. Tucson: University of Ari-zona Press.

Neel, J. V.
1974   A Note on Congenital Defects in Two Unacculturated Indian Tribes. *In* Congen-ital Defects. New Direction in Research. D. T. Janerich et al., eds. New York: Academic.

Nelson, M.
1973   The Development of Tropical Lands. Baltimore: Johns Hopkins University Press.

Nelson, R., and B. Holben
1986   Identifying Deforestation in Brazil Using Multi-Resolution Satellite Data. International Journal of Remote Sensing 7:429–448.

Nelson, R. K.
1969   Hunters of the Northern Ice. Chicago: University of Chicago Press.

Nepstad, D., A. Moreira, and A. Alencar
1999   Flames in the Rainforest: Origins, Impacts and Alternatives to Amazonian Fire. Washington, DC: World Bank.

Netting, R.
1968   Hill Farmers of Nigeria. Seattle: Washington University Press.
1974a   Agrarian Ecology. Annual Review of Anthropology 3:21–56.
1974b   The System Nobody Knows: Village Irrigation in the Swiss Alps. *In* Irrigation's Impact on Society. T. E. Downing and M. Gibson, eds. Tucson: University of Arizona Press.
1976   What Alpine Peasants Have in Common: Observations on Communal Tenure in a Swiss Village. Human Ecology 4(2):135–146.
1977   Cultural Ecology. Menlo Park, CA: Cummings. Reissued by Waveland.
1981   Balancing on an Alp. New York: Cambridge University Press.
1990   Links and Boundaries: Reconsidering the Alpine Village as an Ecosystem. *In* The Ecosystem Approach in Anthropology. E. F. Moran, ed. Ann Arbor: University of Michigan Press.
1993   Smallholders, Householders: Farm Families and the Ecology of Intensive Sustainable Agriculture. Stanford: Stanford University Press.

Netting, R., G. Stone, and P. Stone
1995   The Social Organization of Agrarian Labor. *In* The Comparative Analysis of Human Societies. E. F. Moran, ed. Boulder: L. Rienner.

Newman, M. T.
1960   Adaptations in the Physique of American Aborigines to Nutritional Factors. Human Biology 32:288–313.

Newman, P.
2006   The Environmental Impact of Cities. Environment and Urbanization 18:275–295.

Newman, R.
1975   Adaptation to Heat. *In* Physiological Anthropology. A. Damon, ed. New York: Oxford University Press.

Nguyen, V. K., and K. Peschard
2003   Anthropology, Inequality and Disease: A Review. Annual Review of Anthropology 32:447–474.

Nicholaides, J. J. III, D. E. Bandy, P. A. Sanchez, J. R. Benites, J. H. Villachica, A. J. Coutu, and C. S. Valverde
1985   Agricultural Alternatives for the Amazon Basin. BioScience 35:279–285.
1983   Crop Production Systems in the Amazon Basin. *In* The Dilemma of Amazonian Development. E. F. Moran, ed. Boulder: Westview.

Nicholaides, J. J. III, and E. F. Moran
1995   Soil Indices for Comparative Analysis of Agrarian Systems. *In* The Comparative Analysis of Human Societies. E. F. Moran, ed. Boulder: L. Rienner.

Nicholson, S.
1999   The Physical-Biotic Interface in Arid and Semi-Arid Systems. *In* Arid Lands Management. T. Hoeckstra and M. Shachak, eds. Urbana: University of Illinois Press.

Nickerson, N. H., N. H. Rowe, and E. A. Richter
1973   Native Plants in the Diet of North Alaskan Eskimos. *In* Man and His Foods. C. E. Smith, ed. Birmingham: University of Alabama Press.

Nietschmann, B.
1971   The Study of Indigenous Food Production Systems: Mere Subsistence or Merrily Subsisting? Revista Geografica 74:83–99.
1972   Hunting and Fishing Focus Among the Miskito Indians, Eastern Nicaragua. Human Ecology 1(1):41–67.
1973   Between Land and Water. New York: Seminar Press.

Nihoul, J. C., P. O. Zavialov, and P. P. Micklin, eds.
2004   Dying and Dead Seas: Climatic Versus Anthropic Causes. Dordrecht: Kluwer Academic.

Nobre, C., and N. Renno
1985   Droughts and Floods in South America Due to the 1982–83 ENSO Episode. Proceedings of the 16th Conference on Hurricanes and Tropical Meteorology. Houston: American Metereological Society.

Nobre, C., P. Sellers, and J. Shukla
1991   Amazonian Deforestation and Regional Climate Change. Journal of Climate 4: 957–988.

Norgrove, L., and S. Hauser
2002   Yield of Plantain Grown Under Different Tree Densities and Slash and Mulch Versus Slash and Burn Management in an Agricultural System in Southern Cameroon. Field Crops Research 78(2–3):185–195.

Norman, M. J. T., C. J. Pearson, and P. G. E. Searle
1995   The Ecology of Tropical Food Crops. Cambridge: Cambridge University Press.

Norum, E., and D. Zoldoske
1985   Design and Operation of Solar Powered Drip Irrigation Systems. *In* Arid Lands: Today and Tomorrow. E. Whitehead, C. Hutchinson, B. Timmerman, and R. Varady, eds. Boulder: Westview.

Noy-Meir, I.
1973   Desert Ecosystems: Environment and Producers. Annual Review of Ecology and Systematics 4:25–51.
1974   Desert Ecosystems: Higher Trophic Levels. Annual Review of Ecology and Systematics 5:195–214.

NRC (National Research Council)
1981   Health Effects of Exposure to Diesel Exhaust. Washington, DC: National Academy Press.
1989   Arctic Social Science. Washington, DC: National Academy Press.
1992   Global Environmental Change: Understanding the Human Dimensions. Washington, DC: National Academy Press.
1993a   Arctic Contributions to Social Science and Public Policy. Washington, DC: National Academy Press.
1993b   Sustainable Agriculture and the Environment in the Humid Tropics. Washington, DC: National Academy Press.
1994a   Rangeland Health: New Ways to Classify, Inventory, and Monitor Rangelands. Washington, DC: National Academy Press.
1994b   Science Priorities for the Human Dimensions of Global Change. Committee on the Human Dimensions of Global Change. Washington, DC: National Academy Press.

1997a   Environmentally Significant Consumption: Research Issues. Committee on the Human Dimensions of Global Change. Washington, DC: National Academy Press.

1997b   NOAA's Arctic Research Initiative: Proceedings of a Workshop. Washington, DC: National Academy Press.

1998a   People and Pixels: Linking Remote Sensing and Social Science. Committee on the Human Dimensions of Global Change. Washington, DC: National Academy Press.

1998b   Decade-to-Century-Scale Climate Variability and Change: A Science Strategy. Commission on Geosciences, Environment and Resources. Washington, DC: National Academy Press.

1999a   A Global Environmental Change: Research Pathways for the Next Decade. Committee on Global Change Research. Washington, DC: National Academy Press.

1999b   Making Climate Forecasts Matter. Washington, DC: National Academy Press.

2000   Grand Challenges in Environmental Sciences. Washington, DC: National Academy Press.

2005a   Population, Land Use and Environment: Research Directions. Committee on the Human Dimensions of Global Change. Washington, DC: National Academy Press.

2005b   Valuing Ecosystem Services: Toward Better Environmental Decision-Making. Washington, DC: National Academy Press.

2006   Toward an Integrated Arctic Observing Network. Washington, DC: National Academy Press.

Numata, M., ed.
1975   Ecological Studies in Japanese Grasslands: Productivity of Terrestrial Communities. Japan IBP Synthesis Volume. Tokyo: University of Tokyo Press.

Nuttall, M., and T. V. Callaghan, eds.
2000   The Arctic: Environment, People, Policy. Amsterdam: Harwood Academic.

Nye, P. H., and D. J. Greenland
1960   The Soil Under Shifting Cultivation. Technical Communication, no. 51. Harpenden, UK: Commonwealth Bureau of Soils.

1964   Changes in the Soil After Clearing a Tropical Forest. Plant and Soil 21:101–112.

Nyerges, A., and G. Green
2000   The Ethnography of Landscape: GIS and Remote Sensing in the Study of Forest Change in West African Guinea Savanna. American Anthropologist 102(2):271–289.

O'Brien, W. J., ed.
1992   Toolik Lake: Ecology of an Aquatic Ecosystem in Arctic Alaska. Dordrecht: Kluwer Academic.

O'Callaghan, J. R.
1996   Land Use: The Interaction of Economics, Ecology, and Hydrology. New York: Chapman & Hall.

Odum, E.
1971   Fundamentals of Ecology. 3rd ed. Philadelphia: Saunders. Originally published in 1959.

Odum, E. P., and G. W. Barrett
2004   Fundamentals of Ecology. 5th ed. Belmont, CA: Thomas Brooks/Cole.

Odum, H.
1971 Environment, Power and Society. New York: Wiley-Interscience.
1983 Systems Ecology: An Introduction. New York: Wiley.
2004 Environmental Accounting: Emergy and Environmental Decision Making. New York: Wiley.
Odum, H., and E. Odum
1976 Energy Basis for Man and Nature. New York: McGraw-Hill.
Odum, H., and F. Pigeon, eds.
1970 A Tropical Rain Forest. Springfield, VA: U.S. Department of Commerce/ Atomic Energy Commission.
Oechel, W. C., T. Callaghan, T. Gilmanov, J. I. Holten, B. Maxwell, U. Molau, and B. Sveinbjornsson, eds.
1996 Global Changes and Arctic Terrestrial Ecosystems. New York: Springer.
Ohtsuka, R., and T. Suzuki
1990 Population Ecology of Human Evolution: Bioecological Studies of the Gidra in Papua New Guinea. Tokyo: University of Tokyo Press.
Ojima, D. S., K. A. Galvin, and B. L. Turner II
1994 The Global Impact of Land-Use Change. BioScience 44(5):300–304.
Okabe, A.
2006 GIS-Based Studies in the Humanities and Social Sciences. Boca Raton, FL: CRC/Taylor & Francis.
Okuda, T.
2003 Pasoh: Ecology of a Lowland Rain Forest in Southeast Asia. Tokyo: Springer.
Olalla-Tarraga, M. A.
2006 A Conceptual Framework to Assess Sustainability in Urban Ecological Systems. International Journal of Sustainable Development and World Ecology 13:1–15.
Oldfield, M. L., and J. Alcorn, eds.
1991 Biodiversity: Culture, Conservation and Ecodevelopment. Boulder: Westview.
Oliveira, P., and R. Marquis, eds.
2002 The Cerrados of Brazil: Ecology and Natural History of a Neotropical Savanna. New York: Columbia University Press.
Oliver, S.
1962 Ecology and Cultural Continuity as Contributing Factors in the Social Organization of the Plains Indians. Berkeley: University of California Publications in American Archaeology and Ethnology.
Oliver-Smith, A.
1977 Traditional Agriculture, Central Places and Postdisaster Urban Relocation in Peru. American Enthnologist 4(1):102–116.
Openshaw, S.
1994 Computational Human Geography: Towards a Research Agenda. Environment and Planning 26:499–508.
1995 Human Systems Modeling on a Grand New Area in Science: What Happened to the Science in Social Science? Environment and Planning 27:159–164.
Or, U., N. Magal, K. Magal, and D. Hefer
1985 Jordan Valley Drip Irrigation Scheme–A Model for Developing Countries. *In* Arid Lands: Today and Tomorrow. E. Whitehead, C. Hutchinson, B. Timmerman, and R. Varady, eds. Boulder: Westview.

Orbaek, J. B., R. Kallenborn, I. Tombre, E. N. Hegseth, S. Falk-Petersen, and A. H. Hoel, eds.
2006 Arctic Alpine Ecosystems and People in a Changing Environment. New York: Springer.

Orlove, B.
1977 Integration Through Production: The Use of Zonation in Espinar. American Ethnologist 4(1):84–101.
1980 Ecological Anthropology. Annual Review of Anthropology 9:235–273.

Orlove, B., J. Chiang, and M. Cane
2000 Forecasting Andean Rainfall and Crop Yield from the Influence of El Niño on Pleiades Visibility. Nature 403:68–71.

Orlove, B., and D. Guillet
1985 Theoretical and Methodological Considerations on the Study of Mountain Peoples: Reflections on the Idea of Subsistence Type and the Role of History in Human Ecology. Mountain Research and Development 5(1):3–18.

Oron, G., and J. De Malach
1987 Reuse of Domestic Wastewater for Irrigation in Arid Zones. Water Resource Bulletin 23(5):777–783.

Osborne, P. L.
2000 Tropical Ecosystems and Ecological Concepts. Cambridge: Cambridge University Press.

Osburn, W. Jr.
1974 The Snowmobile in Eskimo Culture. *In* Arctic and Alpine Environments. J. D. Ives and R. G. Barry, eds. London: Methuen.

Osri, J.
2004 Hazardous Metropolis: Flooding and Urban Ecology in Los Angeles. Berkeley: University of California Press.

Ostendorf, B., and J. F. Reynolds
1998 A Model of Arctic Tundra Vegetation Derived from Topographic Gradients. Landscape Ecology 13(3):187–201.

Ostrom, E.
1990 Governing the Commons: The Evolution of Institutions for Collective Action. New York: Cambridge University Press.
1998 The Institutional Analysis and Development Approach. *In* Designing Institutions for Environmental and Resource Management. E. T. Loehman and D. M. Kilgour, eds. Cheltenham, UK: Edward Elgar.
2001 Self-Governance and Forest Resources. *In* Land Reform Revisited: Access to Land, Rural Poverty, and Public Action. A. de Janvry, J. Platteau, and E. Sadoulet, eds. Oxford: Oxford University Press.
2005 Understanding Institutional Diversity. Princeton, NJ: Princeton University Press.

Ostrom, E., J. Burger, C. B. Field, R. B. Norgaard, and D. Policansky
1999 Revisiting the Commons: Local Lessons, Global Challenges. Science 284(5412): 278–82.

Ostrom, E., R. Gardner, and J. Walker
1994 Rules, Games and Common Pool Resources. Ann Arbor: University of Michigan Press.

Oswalt, W. H.
1967   Alaskan Eskimos. San Francisco: Chandler.

Ottoson, H. W., and E. M. Birch
1966   Land and People in the Northern Plains Transition Area. Lincoln: University of Nebraska Press.

Overpeck, J., K. Hughen, D. Hardy, R. Bradley, R. Case, M. Douglas, B. Finney, K. Gajewski, G. Jacoby, A. Jennings, S. Lamoureux, A. Lasca, G. MacDonald, J. Moore, M. Retelle, S. Smith, A. Wolfe, and G. Zielinski
1997   Arctic Environmental Change of the Last Four Centuries. Science 278(5341): 1251–1256.

Ovuka, M.
2000   More People, More Erosion? Land Use, Soil Erosion, and Soil Productivity in Murang's District, Kenya. Land Degradation and Development 11(2):111–124.

Oyama, M. D., and C. Nobre
2003   Non-Recovery of Tropical Forests: A New Climate-Vegetation Equilibrium State for Tropical S. America. Geophysical Research Letters 30(23):2199.

Palerm, A.
1968   The Agricultural Basis of Urban Civilization in Mesoamerica. *In* Man in Adaptation. Y. Cohen, ed. Chicago: Aldine.

Palm, C. A., S. Vosti, P. Sanchez, and P. Ericksen, eds.
2005   Slash-and-Burn Agriculture: The Search for Alternatives. New York: Columbia University Press.

Pan American Health Organization
1966   Life at High Altitudes. Washington, DC: Pan American Health Organization.

Paoli, G. D., L. M. Curran, and D. R. Zak
2005   Phosphorus Efficiency of Bornean Rain Forest Productivity: Evidence Against the Unimodal Efficiency Hypothesis. Ecology 86(6):1548–1561.

Parish, R.
2002   Mountain Environments. New York: Prentice Hall.

Park, R. E.
1926   The Urban Community as a Spatial Pattern and a Moral Order. *In* The Urban Community. E. Burgess, ed. Chicago: University of Chicago Press.

Park, R. E., E. W. Burgess, and A. McKenzie, eds.
1925   The City. Chicago: University of Chicago Press.

Parker, D., S. Manson, M. Janssen, M. Hoffmann, and P. Deadman
2003   Multi-Agent Systems for the Simulation of Land Use and Land Cover Change: A Review. Annals of the Association of American Geographers 93(2):316–40.

Pars, T., M. Osler, and P. Bjerregaard
2001   Contemporary Use of Traditional and Imported Food Among Greenlandic Inuit. Arctic 54(1):22–31.

Pasternak, D., and A. Schlissel
2001   Combating Desertification with Plants. New York: Kluwer Academic/Plenum.

Patenaude, G., R. Milne, and T. P. Dawson
2005   Synthesis of Remote Sensing Approaches for Forest Carbon Estimation: Reporting to the Kyoto Protocol. Environmental Science and Policy 8(2):161–178.

Pati, A. K.
2004   Chronobiology: Implications of Circadian Rhythms. National Academy of Science Letters-India 27(7–8):233–248.

Patten, B. C., ed.
1971   Systems Analysis and Simulation in Ecology. Vol. 1. New York: Academic.
Peck, D. L.
1990   Our Changing Planet: The FY 1991 U.S. Global Change Research Program. Washington, DC: Office of Science and Technology Policy, Committee on Earth Sciences.
Pedlowski, M. A., V. Dale, E. Matricardi, and E. M. da Silva Filho
1997   Patterns and Impacts of Deforestation in Rondônia, Brazil. Landscape and Urban Planning 38:149–157.
Peet, R., and M. Watts
1994   Development Theory and Environmentalism in an Age of Market Triumphalism. Economic Geography 69:227–253.
Peet, R., and M. Watts, eds.
1996   Liberation Ecologies: Environment, Development, Social Movements. London: Routledge.
Pelly, D. F.
2001   Sacred Hunt: A Portrait of the Relationship Between Seals and Inuit. Vancouver: Greystone.
Pelto, P.
1973   The Snowmobile Revolution. Menlo Park, CA: Cummings.
Pennington, T., G. P. Lewis, and J. A. Ratter
2006   Neotropical Savannas and Seasonally Dry Forests: Plant Diversity, Biogeography, and Conservation. Boca Raton, FL: CRC/Taylor & Francis.
Pentikainen, J., ed.
1996   Shamanism and Northern Ecology. New York: Walter de Gruyter.
Peter, K. A.
1987   The Dynamics of Hutterite Society. Edmonton: University of Alberta Press.
Peterson, N.
1975   Hunter-Gatherer Territoriality: The Perspective from Australia. American Anthropologist 77:53–68.
Phillips, O. L.
1997   The Changing Ecology of Tropical Forests. Biodiversity and Conservation 6(2):291–311.
Phillips, S. J., P. W. Comus, and R. H. Daley
2000   A Natural History of the Sonoran Desert. Berkeley: University of California Press.
Phoenix, G. K., and J. A. Lee
2004   Predicting Impacts of Arctic Climate Change: Past Lessons and Future Challenges. Ecological Research 19(1):65–74.
Pickett, S., W. Burch Jr., S. Dalton, T. Foresman, J. Grove, and R. Rowntree
1997   A Conceptual Framework for the Study of Human Ecosystems in Urban Areas. Urban Ecosystems 1:185–199.
Pickett, S., M. Cadenasso, and J. M. Grove
2004   Resilient Cities: Meaning, Models and Metaphor for Integrating the Ecological Socio-Economic and Planning Realms. Landscape and Urban Planning 69:369–384.

Pickett, S., M. Cadenasso, J. M. Grove, C. H. Nilon, R. V. Pouyat, W. C. Zipperer, and R. Costanza
2001   Urban Ecological Systems: Linking Terrestrial Ecological, Physical, and Socioeconomic Components of Metropolitan Areas. Annual Review of Ecology and Systematics 32:127–157.

Picón-Reátegui, E.
1976   Nutrition. _In_ Man in the Andes. P. T. Baker and M. Little, eds. Stroudsburg, PA: Dowden, Hutchinson & Ross.

Pietsch, S., and H. Hasenauer
2002   Using Mechanistic Modeling within Forest Ecosystem Restoration. Forest Ecology and Management 159(1–2):111–131.

Pike, R. L., and S. R. Williams
2006   Incorporating Psychosocial Health into Biocultural Models: Preliminary Findings from Turkana Women of Kenya. American Journal of Human Biology 18(6):729–740.

Platt, H.
1991   The Electric City: Energy and the Growth of the Chicago Area, 1800–1930. Chicago: University of Chicago Press.
2004   Shock Cities: The Environmental Transformation and Reform of Manchester and Chicago. Chicago: University of Chicago Press.

Platt, R. H., R. A. Rowntree, and P. C. Muick, eds.
1994   The Ecological City: Preserving and Restoring Urban Biodiversity. Boston: University of Massachusetts Press.

Plattner, S., ed.
1974   Formal Methods in Economic Anthropology. Washington, DC: American Anthropological Association.

Plog, F.
1975   Systems Theory in Archaeological Research. Annual Review of Anthropology 4:207–224.

Plotkin, M. J.
1993   Tales of a Shaman's Apprentice. New York: Viking Penguin.

Plummer, M. V.
2004   Seasonal Inactivity of the Desert Box Turtle, _Terrapene ornata luteola_, at the Species' Range Limit in Arizona. Journal of Herpetology 38(4):589–593.

Polis, G. A., ed.
1991   The Ecology of Desert Communities. Tucson: University of Arizona Press.

Popenoe, H.
1960   Effects of Shifting Cultivation on Natural Soil Constituents in Central America. Ph.D. diss. University of Florida, Department of Agronomy.

Porter, P. W.
1965   Environmental Potentials and Economic Opportunities. American Anthropologist 67:409–420.

Porter, R., and R. Knight, eds.
1971   High Altitude Physiology. Edinburgh: C. Livingstone.

Portney, K. E.
2003   Taking Sustainable Cities Seriously: Economic Development, the Environment and Quality of Life in American Cities. Cambridge, MA: MIT Press.

Posey, D.
1982   Nomadic Agriculture in the Amazon. New York Botanical Garden 6(1):18–24.
1985   Indigenous Management of Tropical Forest Ecosystems: The Case of Kayapó Indians of the Brazilian Amazon. Agroforestry Systems 3:139–158.
Posey, D., and W. Balée, eds.
1989   Resource Management in Amazônia. Monograph Series, no. 7. New York: New York Botanical Garden.
Potkanski, T.
1993   Decollectivization of the Mongolian Pastoral Economy. Nomadic People 33:123–135.
Potter, C.
1999   Terrestrial Biomass and the Effects of Deforestation on the Global Carbon Cycle. BioScience 49:769–778.
Potter, C., E. Davidson, S. Kouster, D. Nepstad, G. de Negreiros, and V. Brooks
1998   Regional Application of an Ecosystem Production Model for Studies of Biogeochemistry in Brazilian Amazônia. Global Change Biology 4(3):315–334.
Potter, R., and S. Lloyd-Evans
1998   The City in the Developing World. London: Longmans.
Poulton, E. C.
1970   Environment and Human Efficiency. Springfield, IL: C. Thomas.
Powers, J. S. and W. H. Schlesinger
2002   Relationships Among Soil Carbon Distributions and Biophysical Factors at Nested Spatial Scales in Rain Forests of Northeastern Costa Rica. Geoderma 109(3–4):165–190.
Prance, G., and T. Lovejoy, eds.
1985   Key Environments: Amazônia. London: Pergamon.
Pratt, D. J., and M. D. Gwynne, eds.
1977   Rangeland Management and Ecology in East Africa. London: Hodder & Stoughton.
Primack, R. B., and R. Corlett
2005   Tropical Rain Forests: An Ecological and Biogeographical Comparison. Malden, MA: Blackwell.
Przybylak, R.
2003   The Climate of the Arctic. Dordrecht, Netherlands: Kluwer Academic.
Pucher, J., and C. Lefevre
1996   The Urban Transport Crisis in Europe and North America. London: Macmillan.
Pugh, A. L.
1970   Dynamo 2: Users Manual. Cambridge, MA: MIT Press.
Pugh, L. G. C.
1966   A Programme for Physiological Studies of High Altitude Peoples. *In* The Biology of Human Adaptability. P. T. Baker and J. S. Weiner, eds. Oxford: Clarendon.
Pullin, A. S.
2002   Conservation Biology. Cambridge: Cambridge University Press.
Putnam, R.
2000   Bowling Alone: The Collapse and Revival of American Community. New York: Simon & Schuster.

Pyke, G. H., H. Pulliam, and E. Charnov
1977   Optimal Foraging: A Selective Review of Theory and Tests. Quarterly Review of Biology 52(2):137–154.

Quammen, D.
2007   The Reluctant Mr. Darwin: An Intimate Portrait of Charles Darwin and the Making of His Theory of Evolution. New York: Norton.

Quandt, S. A., and C. Ritenbaugh
1986   Training Manual in Nutritional Anthropology. Washington, DC: American Anthropological Association.

Quinn, J. A.
1940   Topical Summary of Current Literature on Human Ecology. American Journal of Sociology 46:191–226.

Raiffa, H.
1968   Decision Analysis. Reading, MA: Addison-Wesley.

Raikes, P. L.
1981   Livestock Development and Policy in East Africa. Uppsala: Scandinavian Institute of African Studies.

Ranson, K. J., G. Sun, R. G. Knox, E. R. Levine, J. F. Weishampel, and S. T. Fifer
2004   Assessing Tundra-Taiga Boundary with Multi-Sensor Satellite Data. Remote Sensing of Environment 93(3):283–295.

Rapoport, A.
1967   Yagua, or the Amazon Dwelling. Landscape 16(3):27–30.
1969   House Form and Culture. Englewood Cliffs, NJ: Prentice Hall.

Rappaport, R.
1968   Pigs for the Ancestors. New Haven, CT: Yale University Press.
1971   The Flow of Energy in an Agricultural Society. Scientific American 224(3): 116–132.
1977   Ecology, Adaptation and the Ills of Functionalism. Michigan Discussions in Anthropology 2:138–190.
1984   Epilogue. Pigs for the Ancestors. Rev. ed. New Haven, CT: Yale University Press.
1993   The Anthropology of Trouble. American Anthropologist 95:295–303.

Rapport, D. J., and J. E. Turner
1977   Economic Models in Ecology. Science 195:367–373.

Rapport, D. J., and W. G. Whitford
1999   How Ecosystems Respond to Stress. BioScience 49(3):193–203.

Rath, R. G.
1998   Classifying the Boreal Forest Using Radar Imagery: Implications for Global Research. M.A. thesis. University of New Mexico.

Rawski, E. S.
1972   Agricultural Change and the Peasant Economy of South China. Cambridge, MA: Harvard University Press.

Rebele, F.
1994   Urban Ecology and Special Features of Urban Ecosystems. Global Ecology and Biogeography Letters 4:173–187.

Redford, K. H.
1991   The Ecologically Noble Savage. Cultural Survival Quarterly 15(1):46–48.
1992   The Empty Forest. BioScience 42(6):402–422.

Redford, K. H., and C. Padoch, eds.
1992   Conservation of Neotropical Forests: Working from Traditional Resource Use. New York: Columbia University Press.

Redman, C. L.
1999   Human Impact on Ancient Environments. Tucson: University of Arizona Press.

Redman, C. L., J. Grove, and L. Kuby
2004a   Integrating Social Science into the Long-Term Ecological Research Network: Social Dimensions of Ecological Change and Ecological Dimensions of Social Change. Ecosystems 7:161–171.

Redman, C. L., S. R. James, P. R. Fish, and J. D. Rogers, eds.
2004b   The Archeology of Global Change. Washington, DC: Smithsonian Press.

Rees, P. H.
1971   Factoral Ecology: An Extended Definition Survey and Critique of the Field. Economic Geography 47 (supplement):220–230.

Rees, R. M., I. J. Bingham, J. A. Baddeley, and C. A. Watson
2005   The Role of Plants and Land Management in Sequestering Soil Carbon in Temperate Arable and Grassland Ecosystems. Geoderma 128(1–2):130–154.

Refinetti, R.
2006   Circadian Physiology. Boca Raton, FL: CRC Press/Taylor & Francis.

Reich, P. B., B. A. Hungate, and Y. Luo
2006   Carbon-Nitrogen Interactions in Terrestrial Ecosystems in Response to Rising Atmospheric Carbon Dioxide. Annual Review of Ecology, Evolution, and Systematics 37:611–636.

Reichel-Dolmatoff, G.
1971   Amazonian Cosmos: The Sexual and Religious Symbolism of the Tukano Indians. Chicago: University of Chicago Press.
1976   Cosmology as Ecological Analysis: A View from the Rain Forest. Man 11:307–318.

Reid, R. S., C. J. Wilson, R. L. Kruska, and W. Mulatu
1997   Impacts of Tsetse Control and Land-Use on Vegetative Structure and Tree Species Composition in South-Western Ethiopia. Journal of Applied Ecology 34(3):731.

Rejnmark, L., M. E. Jorgensen, M. B. Pedersen, J. C. Hansen, L. Heickendorff, A. L. Lauridsen, G. Mulvad, C. Siggaard, H. Skjoldborg, T. B. Sorensen, E. B. Pedersen, and L. Mosekilde
2004   Vitamin D Insufficiency in Greenlanders on a Westernised Fare: Ethnic Differences in Calcitropic Hormones Between Greenlanders and Danes. Calcified Tissue International 74(3):255–263.

Reinert, E. S.
2006   The Economics of Reindeer Herding: Saami Entrepreneurship Between Cyclical Sustainability and the Powers of State and Oligopolies. British Food Journal 108(7):522–540.

Reining, P.
1973   ERTS Image Analysis of a Site North of Segon, Mali, W. Africa. Springfield, VA: NTIS.

Relethford, J.
1999   The Human Species: An Introduction to Biological Anthropology. 4th ed. Mountain View, CA: Mayfield.

Remmert, H.
1980   Arctic Animal Ecology. New York: Springer.
Rennie, D.
1978   Exercise Physiology. *In* The Eskimo of Northwestern Alaska: A Biological Perspective. P. L. Jamison, S. L. Zegura, and F. A. Milan, eds. Stroudsburg, PA: Dowden, Hutchinson & Ross.
Reynolds, J. F., and D. M. Stafford Smith
2002   Global Desertification: Do Humans Cause Deserts? Berlin: Dahlem University Press.
Reynolds, J. F., and J. D. Tenhunen
1996   Landscape Function and Disturbance in Arctic Tundra. New York: Springer.
Reynolds, S. G., and J. Frame, eds.
2005   Grasslands: Developments, Opportunties, Perspectives. Rome: Food and Agricultural Organization of the UN.
Rhoades, E. R.
2000   American Indian Health: Innovation in Health Care, Promotion and Policy. Baltimore, MD: Johns Hopkins University Press.
Rhoades, R.
1986   Farming on High. *In* Mountain People. M. Tobias, ed. Norman: University of Oklahoma Press.
1992   Thinking Globally, Acting Locally: Technology for Sustainable Mountain Agriculture. *In* Sustainable Mountain Development. N. S. Jodha, M. Banskota, and T. Purtap, eds. New Delhi: Oxford/IBH Publishing.
1997   Pathways Toward Sustainable Mountain Agriculture in the 21st Century. Kathmandu: International Centre for Integrated Mountain Development.
1999   Mountain Research and Development in the 21st Century: The Need for a New Paradigm. *In* Anthropology and Sociology of Nepal. R. B. Chhetri and O. M. Gurung, eds. Kathmandu: Sociological and Anthropological Society of Nepal (SASON).
2000   Integrating Local Voices and Visions into the Global Mountain Agenda. Mountain Research and Development 20(1):4–9.
2001   Development Indicators for Mountain Regions (comment on Kreutzmann). Mountain Research and Development 21(3):307–308.
Rhoades, R., and S. Thompson
1975   Adaptive Strategies in Alpine Environments: Beyond Ecological Particularism. American Ethnologist 2(3):535–551.
Richards, A.
1939   Land, Labour and Diet in Northern Rhodesia. London: Oxford University Press.
Richards, P. W.
1973   The Tropical Rain Forest. Scientific American 229:58–67.
Richardson, H. W.
1973   A Comment on Some Uses of Mathematical Models in Urban Economics. Urban Studies 10:259–270.
Richardson, H. W., M. Vipond and R. Furbey
1974   Dynamics of Tests of Hoyt's Spatial Model. Town Planning Review 45:401–414.
Ricklefs, R.
1973   Ecology. Portland, OR: Chiron.
1990   Ecology. 3rd ed. New York: W. H. Freeman.

Riebsame, W., W. J. Parton, K. A. Galvin, J. C. Burker, L. Bohren, R. Young, and E. Knop
1994   Integrated Modelling of Land Use and Cover Change. BioScience 44(5): 350–356.

Rigby, P.
1969   Cattle and Kinship Among the Gogo: A Semi-Pastoral Society of Central Tanzania. Ithaca: Cornell University Press.

Rinard, A.
2000   Economy Fuels Sprawl's Rise on Capitol Agenda. Milwaukee Journal Sentinel (January 30) A1–10.

Rindfuss, R., S. Walsh, V. Mishra, J. Fox, and G. Dolcemascolo
2003   Linking Household and Remotely Sensed Data: Methodological and Practical Problems. *In* People and the Environment: Approaches for Linking Household and Community Surveys to Remote Sensing and GIS. J. Fox, S. Walsh, and V. Mishra, eds. Dordrecht: Kluwer.

Risser, P., ed.
1992   Long-Term Ecological Research: An International Perspective. Chichester, UK: Wiley.

Rivera, M. A., A. C. Aufderheide, L. W. Cartmell, C. M. Torres, and O. Langsjoen
2005   Antiquity of Coca Leaf Chewing in the South Central Andes: A 3,000 Year Archeological Record of Coca Leaf Chewing from Northern Chile. Journal of Psychoactive Drugs 37(4):455–458.

Robbins, P.
2004   Political Ecology: A Critical Introduction. Oxford: Blackwell.

Robbins, P., A. Poderman, and T. Birkenholtz
2001   Lawns and Toxins: An Ecology of the Cities. Cities 18:369–380.

Robertson, W.
1820   History of America. London: J. Haddon. Originally written in 1777.

Robson, B. T.
1969   Urban Analysis. Cambridge: Cambridge University Press.

Rockwell, L. C., E. Vargas, and L. G. Moore
2003   Human Physiological Adaptation to Pregnancy: Inter- and Intra-Specific Perspectives. American Journal of Human Biology 15(3):330–341.

Rockwood, L. L.
2006   Introduction to Population Ecology. Malden, MA: Blackwell.

Rodin, M., K. Michaelson, and G. Britan
1978   Systems Theory in Anthropology. Current Anthropology 19(4):747–762.

Rodway, G. W., L. A. Hoffman, and M. H. Sanders
2003   High Altitude-Related Disorders. Part I: Pathophysiology, Differential Diagnosis and Treatment. Heart and Lung 32(6):353–359.

Roosevelt, A. C.
1989   Natural Resource Management in Amazônia Before the Conquest: Beyond Ethnographic Projection. Advances in Economic Botany 7:30–62.
1991   Moundbuilders of the Amazon: Geophysical Archeology on Marajó Island, Brazil. San Diego, CA: Academic.

Roosevelt, A. C., R. A. Housley, M. Imazo da Silveira, S. Maranca, and R. Johnson
1992   Eighth Millenium Pottery from a Prehistoric Shell Midden in the Brazilian Amazon. Science 254:1621–1624.

Rööst, M., S. Johnsdotter, J. Liljestrand, and B. Essén
2004   A Qualitative Study of Conceptions and Attitudes Regarding Maternal Mortal-
         ity Among Traditional Birth Attendants in Rural Guatemala. International
         Journal of Obstetrics and Gynecology 111(12):1372–1377.

Roseland, M.
1997   Eco-City Dimensions: Healthy Communities, Healthy Planet. Gabriola Island,
         BC: New Society.

Ross, E.
1978   Food Taboos, Diet and Hunting Strategy: The Adaptation to Animals in Ama-
         zon Cultural Ecology. Current Anthropology 19:1–36.

Rosser, J. B.
1991   From Catastrophe to Chaos: A General Theory of Economic Discontinuities.
         Amsterdam: Kluwer.

Rosswall, T., and O. W. Heal, eds.
1975   Structure and Function of Tundra Ecosystems. Stockholm: Swedish Natural
         Science Research Council. Ecological Bulletin, no. 20.

**Roth, W. T., A. Gomolla, A. E. Meuret, G. W. Alpers, E. M. Handke, and F. H.
Wilhelm**
2002   High Altitudes, Anxiety, and Panic Attacks: Is There a Relationship? Depres-
         sion and Anxiety 16(2):51–58.

Rowley-Conwy, P.
2001   Arctic Archaeology: Issue 3. London: Routledge.

Royer, T., and C. E. Grosch
2006   Ocean Warming and Freshening in the Northern Gulf of Alaska. Geophysical
         Research Letters 33(16):6.

Ruddle, K.
1973   The Human Use of Insects: Examples from the Yukpa. Biotropica 5(2):94–101.

Rudel, T. K.
2005   Tropical Forests: Regional Paths of Destruction and Regeneration in the Late
         20th Century. New York: Columbia University Press.

Rudel, T. K., M. Perez-Lugo, and H. Zichal
2000   When Fields Revert to Forest: Development and Spontaneous Reforestation in
         Post-War Puerto Rico. Professional Geographer 52(3):386–397.

Rudel, T. K., and J. Roper
1997   The Paths to Rainforest Destruction: Cross-National Patterns of Tropical De-
         forestation, 1975–90. World Development 25(1):53–65.

Rupert, J. L., and P. W. Hochachka
2001   Genetic Approaches to Understanding Human Adaptation to Altitude in the
         Andes. Journal of Experimental Biology 204(18):3151–3160.

Rusk, D.
1999   Inside Game Outside Game: Winning Strategies for Saving Urban America.
         Washington, DC: Brookings Institution Press.

Ruthenberg, H.
1971   Farming Systems in the Tropics. London: Oxford University Press.

Rutter, J., M. Reick, and S. L. McKnight
2002   Metabolism and the Control of Circadian Rhythms. Annual Review of Bio-
         chemistry 71:307–331.

Saatchi, S. S., D. Agosti, K. Alger, J. Delabie, and Y. J. Musinsky
2001   Examining Fragmentation and Loss of Primary Forest in the Southern Bahia Forest of Brazil with Radar Imagery. Conservation Biology 15(4):867–875.

Sachs, A.
2006   The Humboldt Current: Nineteenth-Century Exploration and the Roots of American Environmentalism. New York: Viking.

Safdie, M.
1997   The City After the Automobile: An Architect's Vision. Toronto: Stoddart.

Safriel, U. N.
1999   The Concept of Sustainability in Dryland Ecosystems. *In* Arid Lands Management. T. Hoekstra and M. Shackak, eds. Urbana: University of Illinois Press.

Sahlins, M.
1964   Culture and Environment: The Study of Cultural Ecology. *In* Horizons in Anthropology. S. Tax, ed. Chicago: Aldine.

Sahlins, M. D., and E. Service, eds.
1960   Evolution and Culture. Ann Arbor: University of Michigan Press.

Salati, E.
1985   The Climatology and Hydrology of Amazônia. *In* Key Environments: Amazônia. G. Prance and T. Lovejoy, eds. London: Pergamon.

Salati, E., and P. B. Vose
1984   Amazon Basin: A System in Equilibrium. Science 225:129–138.

Salih, M. A., T. Dietz, A. Ghaffer, and M. Ahmad, eds.
2001   African Pastoralism: Conflict, Institutions, and Government. London: Pluto.

Sanchez, P.
1976   Properties and Management of Soils in the Tropics. New York: Wiley-Interscience.
1999   Improved Fallows Come of Age in the Tropics. Agroforestry Systems 47(1–3): 3–12.
2000   Linking Climate Change Research with Food Security and Poverty Reduction in the Tropics. Agriculture, Ecosystems and Environment 82(1–3):371–383.

Sanchez, P., and J. Benites
1987   Low Input Cropping for Acid Soils of the Humid Tropics. Science 238: 1521–1527.

Sanchez, P., and S. W. Buol
1975   Soils of the Tropics and the World Food Crisis. Science 188:598–603.

Sanchez, P., C. E. Seubert, E. J. Tyler, C. Valverde, M. Nureña, and M. K. Wade
1974   Investigaciones en Manejo de Suelos Tropicales en Yurimaguas, Selva Baja del Perú. Paper presented at Seminario de Sistemas de Agricultura Tropical. Lima, Peru: June 1–8, 1974.
1982   Amazon Basin Soils: Management for Continuous Crop Production. Science, 216:821–827.

Sanford, R. L. Jr., J. Saldarriaga, K. Clark, C. Uhl, and R. Herrera
1985   Amazon Rain-Forest Fires. Science 227:53–55.

Sanford, S.
1983   Management of Pastoral Development in the Third World. New York: Wiley.

Sanjek, R.
1990   Urban Anthropology in the 1980s. Annual Review of Anthropology 19:151–186.

Santos, J. L., F. Perez-Bravo, E. Carrasco, M. Calvillan, and C. Albala
2001   Low Prevalence of Type 2 Diabetes Despite a High Average Body Mass Index in the Aymara Natives from Chile. Nutrition 17(4):305–309.

Santos, J. R., C. C. Freitas, L. S. Araujo, L. V. Dutra, J. C. Mura, F. F. Gama, L. S. Soler, and S. J. S. Sant'Anna
2003   Airborne P-Band SAR Applied to the Aboveground Biomass Studies in the Brazilian Tropical Rainforest. Remote Sensing of Environment 87(4):482–493.

Santos, J. R., M. S. P. Lacruz, L. S. Araujo, and M. Keil
2002   Savanna and Tropical Rainforest Biomass Estimation and Spatialization Using JERS–1 Data. International Journal of Remote Sensing 23(7):1217–1229.

Santos, R. V.
1991   Coping with Change in Native Amazônia: A Bioanthropological Study of the Gavião, Suruí, and Zoró, Tupí-Mondé Speaking Societies from Brazil. Ph.D. diss. Bloomington: Indiana University, Department of Anthropology.

Sargent, F., ed.
1974   Human Ecology. Amsterdam: North-Holland.

Sarmiento, G.
1984   The Ecology of Neotropical Savannas. Cambridge, MA: Harvard University Press.

Sassen, S., ed.
2002   Global Networks: Linked Cities. New York: Routledge.

Sato, S.
1977   The Camel Ecology of the Rendille. Paper presented at Seminar on Pastoral Societies of Kenya. Mimeo. Ethnographic Museum of Japan.

Sauer, C.
1958   Man in the Ecology of Tropical America. Proceedings of the Ninth Pacific Science Congress 20:104–110.

Savard, J., P. Clergeau, and G. Mennechez
2000   Biodiversity Concepts and Urban Ecosystems. Landscape and Urban Planning 48: 131–142.

Scanlon, B. R., D. G. Levitt, R. C. Reedy, K. E. Keese, and M. J. Sully
2005   Ecological Controls on Water-Cycle Response to Climate Variability in Deserts. Proceedings of the National Academy of Sciences (USA) 102(17): 6033–6038.

Scheinsohn, V.
2003   Hunter-Gatherer Archeology in South America. Annual Review of Anthropology 32:339–361.

Schell, L., and S. Ulijaszek, eds.
2007   Urbanism, Health and Human Biology in Industrialized Countries. Society for the Study of Human Biology, Symposium 39. Cambridge: Cambridge University Press.

Schenk, H. J., and R. B. Jackson
2002   Rooting Depths, Lateral Root Spreads and Below-Ground/Above-Ground Allometries of Plants in Water-Limited Ecosystems. Journal of Ecology 90(3):480–494.

Schlaiffer, R. O.
1967   Analysis of Decisions Under Uncertainty. New York: McGraw-Hill.

Schlesinger, W. H.
1997   Biogeochemistry: An Analysis of Global Change. San Diego, CA: Academic.

Schmidt-Nielsen, K.
1964   Desert Animals: Physiological Problems of Heat and Water. New York: Oxford University Press.
1984   Scaling: Why Is Animal Size So Important? Cambridge: Cambridge University Press.
1990   Animal Physiology: Adaptation and Environment. Cambridge: Cambridge University Press.

Schneider, H. K.
1957   The Subsistence Role of Cattle Among the Pakot in East Africa. American Anthropologist 59:278–300.
1970   The Wahi Wanyaturu: Economics in an African Society. Chicago: Aldine.
1974   Economic Man. New York: Free Press.

Schneider, W.
2002   Contemporary Reindeer Herders on the Seward Peninsula: Realists with a Sense of History. Anthropologie et Sociétés 26(2):161–177.

Schneider, W., K. Kielland, and G. Finstad
2005   Factors in the Adaptation of Reindeer Herders to Caribou on the Seward Peninsula, Alaska. Arctic Anthropology 42(2):36–49.

Scholnick, A., C. K. Taylor, V. Finch, and A. Bornt
1980   Why Do Bedouins Wear Black Robes in Hot Desert? Nature 283: 373–375.

Schreiber, K. J., and J. Lancho Rojas
2003   Irrigation and Society in the Peruvian Desert: The Puquios of Nasca. Lanham, MD: Lexington.

Schrire, C., and W. L. Steiger
1974   A Matter of Life and Death: An Investigation into the Practice of Female Infanticide in the Arctic. Man 9(2):161–181.

Schroth, G.
2004   Agroforestry and Biodiversity Conservation in Tropical Landscapes. Washington, DC: Island.

Schull, W. J., and F. Rothhammer, eds.
2006   The Aymará: Strategies in Human Adaptation to a Rigorous Environment. New York: Springer.

Schuur, E. A. G.
2003   Productivity and Global Climate Revisited: The Sensitivity of Tropical Forest Growth to Precipitation. Ecology 84(5):1165–1170.

Schwartz, H. H.
2000   Rationality Gone Awry? Decision-Making Inconsistent with Economic and Financial Theory. Westport, CT: Praeger.

Schweik, C.
1998   The Spatial and Temporal Analysis of Forest Resources and Institutions. CIPEC Dissertation Series, no. 2. Bloomington: Center for the Study of Institutions, Population and Environmental Change, Indiana University.

Schweik, C., H. Nagendra, and D. Sinha
2003   Using Satellite Imagery to Locate Innovative Forest Management Practices in Nepal. Ambio 32(4):312–319.

Schwinning, S., and J. R. Ehleringer
2001   Water Use Trade-Offs and Optimal Adaptations to Pulse-Driven Arid Ecosystems. Journal of Ecology 89(3):464–480.

Schwinning, S., and O. E. Sala
2004   Hierarchy of Responses to Resource Pulses in Arid and Semi-Arid Ecosystems. Oecologia 141(2):211–220.

Scott, R. E.
2006   The Law and Economics of Incomplete Contracts. Annual Review of Law and Social Science 2:279–297.

Secoy, F. R.
1953   Changing Military Patterns on the Great Plains. Monographs of the American Ethnological Society, no. 21. Locust Valley, NY: Augustin.

Seeger, A.
1982   Native Americans and the Conservation of Flora and Fauna in Brazil. *In* Socio-Economic Effects and Constraints in Tropical Forest Management. E. G. Hallsworth, ed. New York: Wiley.

Sehgal, A.
2004   Molecular Biology of Circadian Rhythms. Hoboken, NJ: Wiley-Liss.

Serreze, M. C., M. M. Holland, and J. Stroeve
2007   Perspectives on the Arctic's Shrinking Sea-Ice Cover. Science 315:1533–1536.

Seto, K. C.
2004   Urban Growth in South China: Winners and Losers of China's Policy Reforms. Petermanns Geographische Mitteilungen 148(5):50–57.
2005   Economies, Societies, and Landscapes in Transition: Examples from the Pearl River Delta, China and the Red River Delta, Vietnam. *In* Population, Land Use and Environment: Research Directions. Committee on the Human Dimensions of Global Change. Washington, DC: National Academy Press.
In press The Transformation of South China. *In* Our Changing Planet: A View from Space. M. King, R. Williams, and K. Parkington, eds. Cambridge: Cambridge University Press.

Seto, K. C., and R. Kaufmann
2003   Modeling the Drivers of Urban Land Use Change in the Pearl River Delta, China: Integrating Remote Sensing with Socioeconomic Data. Land Economics 79(1):106–121.

Seubert, C. E., P. A. Sanchez, and C. Valverde
1977   Effects of Land Clearing Methods on Soil Properties of an Utisol and Crop Performance in the Amazon Jungle of Peru. Tropical Agriculture 54:307–321.

Sever, T.
1998   Validating Prehistoric and Current Social Phenomena upon the Landscape of the Peten, Guatemala, pp. 145–163. National Research Council, People and Pixels: Linking Remote Sensing and Social Science. Washington, DC: National Academy Press.

Sghaier, M., and W. D. Seiwert
1993   Winds of Change and the Threat of Desertification: Case Study from the Tunisian Sahara. GeoJournal 31(1):95–99.

Shantzis, S. D. and W. W. Behrens
1973   Population Control Mechanisms in a Primitive Agricultural Society. *In* Toward Global Equilibrium. D. L. Meadows and D. H. Meadows, eds. Cambridge, MA: Wright-Allen.

Shaver, G., W. Billings, F. S. Chapin, A. Giblin, K. Nadel-hoffer, W. Oechel, and E. Rastetter
1992 Global Change and the Carbon Balance of Arctic Ecosystems. BioScience 42(6):433–441.

Shelford, V.
1963 The Ecology of North America. Urbana: University of Illinois Press.

Shell-Duncan, B., and W. O. Obiero
2000 Child Nutrition in the Transition from Nomadic Pastoralism to Settled Lifestyles: Individual, Household, and Community Level Factors. American Journal of Physical Anthropology 113(2):183–200.

Shepard, R. J.
1974 Work Physiology and Activity Patterns of Circumpolar Eskimos and Ainu: A Synthesis of International Biological Program Data. Human Biology 46:263–294.

Shepherd, A., and D. Wingham
2007 Recent Sea-Level Contributions of the Antarctic and Greenland Ice Sheets. Science 315:1529–1532.

Sheridan, T.
1988 Where the Dove Calls: The Political Ecology of a Peasant Corporate Community. Tucson: University of Arizona Press.

Shermer, M.
2006 In Darwin's Shadow: The Life and Science of Alfred Russel Wallace: A Biographical Study on the Psychology of History. Oxford: Oxford University Press.

Shiyomi, M., and H. Koizumi
2001 Structure and Function in Agroecosystem Design and Management. Boca Raton, FL: CRC Press.

Shochat, E., P. S. Warren, and S. H. Faeth
2006a Future Directions in Urban Ecology. Trends in Ecology and Evolution 21:661–662.

Shochat, E., P. S. Warren, S. H. Faeth, N. E. McIntyre, and D. Hope
2006b From Patterns to Emerging Processes in Mechanistic Urban Ecology. Trends in Ecology and Evolution 21:186–191.

Short, K. R., J. L. Vittone, M. L. Bigelow, D. N. Proctor, and K. S. Nair
2004 Age and Aerobic Exercise Training Effects on Whole Body and Muscle Protein Metabolism. American Journal of Physiology, Endocrinology, and Metabolism 286(1):E92–E101.

Shryock, H., and J. S. Siegel
1971 The Methods and Materials of Demography. 2 vols. Washington, DC: U.S. Bureau of the Census, Government Printing Office.

Shryock, H., J. S. Siegel, and E. Stockwell
1976 The Methods and Materials of Demography. Orlando: Academic.

Shukla, J., C. Nobre, and P. Sellers
1990 Amazon Deforestation and Climate Change. Science 247:1322–1325.

Siegel, J. S., and D. Swanson
2004 The Methods and Materials of Demography. 2nd ed. Amsterdam: Elsevier.

Sierra, R., and J. Stallings
1998 The Dynamics and Social Organization of Tropical Deforestation in Northwest Ecuador, 1983–1995. Human Ecology 26(1):135–161.

Silver, C. S.
1990   One Earth, One Future: Our Changing Global Environment. National Academy of Sciences. Washington, DC: National Academy Press.

Silverwood-Cope, P.
1972   A Contribution to the Ethnography of the Colombian Maku. Ph.D. diss. University of Cambridge.

Simmons, I. G.
1974   The Ecology of Natural Resources. New York: Wiley.

Sinclair, J., and L. Ham
2000   Household Adaptive Strategies: Shaping Livelihood Security in the Western Himalaya. Canadian Journal of Development Studies 21(1):89–112.

Sindiga, I.
1987   Fertility Control and Population Growth Among the Maasai. Human Ecology 15(1):53–65.

Singh, N. T.
2005   Irrigation and Soil Salinity in the Indian Subcontinent: Past and Present. Bethlehem: Lehigh University Press.

Siniarska, A., and F. Dickinson
1996   Annotated Bibliography in Human Ecology. Delhi, India: Kamla-Raj Enterprises.

Sioli, H.
1973   Recent Human Activities in the Brazilian Amazon Region and Their Ecological Effects. *In* Tropical Forest Ecosystems in Africa and South America. B. Meggers, E. Y. Ayensu, and W. D. Ducksworth, eds. Washington, DC: Smithsonian Institution Press.
1991   Introduction to the Symposium: Amazônia-Deforestation and Possible Effects. Forest Ecology and Management 38(3–4):123–132.

Simmers, I.
2003   Understanding Water in a Dry Environment: Hydrological Processes in Arid and Semi-Arid Zones. Lisse, Abingdon: A. A. Balkema.

Siqueira, A. D., A. O. D'Antona, M. F. D'Antona, and E. F. Moran
2007   Embodied Decisions: Reversible and Irreversible Contraceptive Methods Among Rural Women in the Brazilian Amazon. Human Organization 66(2):185–195.

Siqueira, A. D., S. McCracken, E. Brondizio, and E. F. Moran
2003   Women in a Brazilian Agricultural Frontier. *In* Gender at Work in Economic Life. G. Clark, ed. Walnut Creek, CA: AltaMira. Society for Economic Anthropology Monograph Series, no. 20.

Siskind, J.
1973   To Hunt in the Morning. New York: Oxford University Press.

Skole, D., and C. Tucker
1993   Tropical Deforestation and Habitat Fragmentation in the Amazon: Satellite Data from 1978 to 1988. Science 260:1905–1910.

Slobodkin, L. B.
1968   Toward a Predictive Theory of Evolution. *In* Population Biology and Evolution. R. C. Lewontin, ed. Syracuse, NY: Syracuse University Press.
1974   Mind, Bind and Ecology. Human Ecology 2:67–74.

Slotten, R. A.
2006   The Heretic in Darwin's Court: The Life of Alfred Russel Wallace. New York: Columbia University Press.

Slovic, P., H. Kunreuther, and G. White
1974   Decision Processes, Rationality and Adjustment to Natural Hazards. *In* Natural Hazards. G. White, ed. New York: Oxford University Press.

Smedberg, E., C. M. Morth, D. P. Swaney, and C. Humborg
2006   Modeling Hydrology and Silicon-Carbon Interactions in Taiga and Tundra Biomes from a Landscape Perspective: Implications for Global Warming Feedbacks. Global Biogeochemical Cycles 20(2):15.

Smil, V.
1984   The Bad Earth: Environmental Degradation in China. London: ZED.

Smith, A. B.
2005   African Herders: Emergence of Pastoral Traditions. Walnut Creek, CA: AltaMira.

Smith, C.
1996   Development and the State: Issues for Anthropologists. *In* Transforming Societies, Transforming Anthropology. E. F. Moran, ed. Ann Arbor: University of Michigan Press.

Smith, D. P.
2007   Urban Ecology. New York: Routledge.

Smith, E. A.
1983   Anthropological Applications of Optimal Foraging Theory. Current Anthropology 24(5):625–651.
1991   Inujjuamint Foraging Strategies: Evolutionary Ecology of an Arctic Hunting Economy. Chicago: Aldine.

Smith, E. A., and J. McCarter
1997   Contested Arctic: Indigenous Peoples, Industrial States, and the Circumpolar Environment. Seattle: University of Washington Press.

Smith, E. A., and B. Winterhalder, eds.
1992   Evolutionary Ecology and Human Behavior. Chicago: Aldine.

Smith, J. M.
1982   Evolution and the Theory of Games. Cambridge: Cambridge University Press.

Smith, K., C. B. Barrett, and P. W. Box
2001   Not Necessarily in the Same Boat: Heterogeneous Risk Assessment Among East African Pastoralists. Journal of Development Studies 37(5):1–30.

Smith, L.
1972   The Mechanical Dog Team: A Study of the Ski-Doo in the Canadian Arctic. Arctic Anthropology 9(1):1–9.

Smith, N.
1974   Agouti and Babassu. Oryx 22(5):581–582.
1982a   Rainforest Corridors. Berkeley: University of California Press.
1982b   Colonization Lessons from the Rainforest. Science 212:755–761.
1999   The Amazon River Forest: A Natural History of Plants, Animals and People. New York: Oxford University Press.

Smith, N., I. C. Falesi, P. de T. Alvim, and E. A. S. Serrão
1996   Agroforestry Trajectories Among Smallholders in the Brazilian Amazon: Innovation and Resiliency in Pioneer and Older Settled Areas. Ecological Economics 18(1):15–27.

Smith, N., J. H. Schultes, and R. Evans
1990   Deforestation and Shrinking Crop Gene-Pools in Amazônia. Environmental Conservation 17(3):227–234.
Smith, R. L.
1974   Ecology and Field Biology. 2nd ed. New York: HarperCollins.
Smith, R. M., K. Gaston, P. Warren, and K. Thompson
2005   Urban Domestic Gardens: Relationship Between Landcover Composition, Housing and Landscape. Landscape Ecology 20:235–253.
Smith, V.
1982   Microeconomic Systems as an Experimental Science. American Economic Review 72:923–955.
Smole, W.
1976   The Yanomama Indians: A Cultural Geography. Austin: University of Texas Press.
Soil Conservation Service
1960   After Soil Classification, a Comprehensive System. Revised 1964. Washington, DC: Soil Conservation Service.
Solbrig, O., and E. Medina, eds.
1996   Biodiversity and Savanna Ecosystem Processes: A Global Perspective. New York: Springer.
Sonnenfeld, J.
2002   Social Dimensions of Geographic Disorientation in Arctic Alaska. Inuit Studies 26(2):157–173.
Sonneveld, B., and M. A. Keyzer
2003   Land Under Pressure: Soil Conservation Concerns and Opportunities for Ethiopia. Land Degradation and Development 14(1):5–23.
Southwood, T.
1977   Habitat: The Template for Ecological Strategies? Journal of Animal Ecology 46:337–365.
Southworth, J., and C. Tucker
2001   The Roles of Accessibility, Local Institutions, and Socioeconomic Factors Influencing Forest Cover Change in the Mountains of Western Honduras. Mountain Research and Development 21(3):276–283.
Soutiere, S. E., and C. G. Tankersley
2001   Challenges Implicit to Gene Discovery Research in the Control of Ventilation During Hypoxia. High Altitude Medicine and Biology 2(2):191–200.
Sowell, J. B.
2001   Desert Ecology. Salt Lake City: University of Utah Press.
Sparks, D.
2002   Environmental Soil Chemistry. San Diego, CA: Academic.
Spehn, E. M., M. Liberman, and C. Körner, eds.
2006   Land Use Change and Mountain Biodiversity. Boca Raton, FL: CRC Press.
Spencer, J. E.
1966   Shifting Cultivation in Southeast Asia. Berkeley: University of California Press.
Spencer, P.
1965   The Samburu. London: Routledge & Keagan Paul.
1973   Nomads in Alliance. London: Oxford University Press.
1988   The Maasai of Matapato: A Study of Ritual and Rebellion. Bloomington: Indiana University Press.

Spencer, R. F.
1959   The North Alaskan Eskimo. Bulletin no. 171 of the Bureau of American Ethnology. Washington, DC: Smithsonian Institution.

Spiegelman, M.
1968   Introduction to Demography. Cambridge, MA: Harvard University Press.

Sponsel, L.
1986   Amazon Ecology and Adaptation. Annual Review of Anthropology 15:67–97.

Spooner, B.
1974   Irrigation and Society: The Iranian Plateau. *In* Irrigation's Impact on Society. T. E. Downing and M. Gibson, eds. Tucson: University of Arizona Press.

Spooner, B., ed.
1972   Population Growth: Anthropological Implications. Cambridge, MA: MIT Press.

Sprout, H., and M. Sprout
1965   The Ecological Perspective on Human Affairs. Princeton, NJ: Princeton University Press.

Squires, G. D., ed.
2002   Urban Sprawl: Causes, Consequences and Policy Responses. Washington, DC: Urban Institute Press.

Stahl, P. W., ed.
1995   Archaeology in the Lowland American Tropics: Current Analytical Methods and Recent Applications. Cambridge: Cambridge University Press.

Stark, N.
1969   Direct Nutrient Cycling in the Amazon Basin. *In* II Simposio y Foro de Biología Tropical Amazónica. Bogotá, Columbia: Editorial Pax.

Stearman, A. M.
1991   Making a Living in the Tropical Forest: Yuqui Foragers in the Bolivian Amazon. Human Ecology 19(2):245–259.

Steegman, A. T.
1967   Frostbite of the Human Face as a Selective Force. Human Biology 39:131–144.
1970   Cold Adaptation and the Human Face. American Journal of Physical Anthropology 32:243–250.
1975   Human Adaptation to Cold. *In* Physiological Anthropology. Albert Damon, ed. New York: Oxford University Press.

Steenwerth, K. L., L. E. Jackson, F. J. Calderon, M. R. Stromberg, and K. M. Scow
2002   Soil Microbial Community Composition and Land Use History in Cultivated and Grassland Ecosystems of Coastal California. Soil Biology and Biochemistry 34(11):1599–1611.

Steffen, W., A. Sanderson, P. Tyson, J. Jager, P. Matson, B. Moore III, F. Oldfield, K. Richardson, J. K. Schellnhuber, B. L. Turner II, and R. Wasson
2004   Global Change and the Earth System: A Planet Under Pressure. IGBP Synthesis Volume. Berlin: Springer.

Steila, D.
1976   The Geography of Soils. Englewood Cliffs, NJ: Prentice Hall.

Stein, R.
2004   New Perspectives on Environmental Justice: Gender, Sexuality, and Activism. New Brunswick: Rutgers University Press.

Steinberg, S. J., and S. L. Steinberg
2006   GIS: Geographic Information Systems for the Social Sciences: Investigating Space and Place. Thousand Oaks, CA: Sage.

Steiner, F.
2002   Human Ecology: Following Nature's Lead. Washington, DC: Island.
Steininger, K. W., and H. Weck-Hannemann, eds.
2002   Global Environmental Change in Alpine Regions: Recognition, Impact, Adaptation, and Mitigation. Cheltenham, UK: Edward Elgar.
Stenlund, P.
2002   Lessons in Regional Cooperation from the Arctic. Ocean and Coastal Management 45(11):835–839.
Stenning, D. J.
1957   Transhumance, Migratory Drift, Migration: Patterns of Pastoral Fulani Nomadism. Journal of the Royal Anthropological Institute 87:57–73.
Stephens, D. W., and J. R. Krebs
1986   Foraging Theory. Princeton, NJ: Princeton University Press.
Stern, P.
2005   Wage Labor, Housing Policy and the Nucleation of Inuit Households. Arctic Anthropology 42(2):66–81.
Stern, P. R., and L. Stevenson, eds.
2006   Critical Inuit Studies: An Anthology of Contemporary Ethnography. Lincoln: University of Nebraska Press.
Steward, J.
1936   The Economic and Social Basis of Primitive Bands. *In* Essays in Anthropology Presented to A. L. Kroeber. R. Lowie, ed. Berkeley: University of California Press.
1938   Basin-Plateau Aboriginal Sociopolitical Groups. Bulletin 120, Bureau of American Ethnology. Washington, DC: Smithsonian Institution.
1955a   The Theory of Culture Change. Urbana: University of Illinois Press.
1977   Evolution and Ecology. Urbana: University of Illinois Press.
Steward, J., ed.
1939–   Handbook of South American Indians. 7 vols. Washington, DC: Bureau of
  1946   American Ethnology, Smithsonian Institution.
1955b   Irrigation Civilizations: A Comparative Study. Social Science Monograph 1. Washington, DC: Pan American Union.
Stewart, O.
1956   Fire as the First Great Force Employed by Man. *In* Man's Role in Changing the Face of the Earth. W. L. Thomas, ed. Chicago: University of Chicago Press.
Stinson, S.
1992   Nutritional Adaptation. Annual Review of Anthropology 21:143–170.
Stone, B.
2004   Paving over Paradise: How Land Use Regulations Promote Residential Imperviousness. Landscape and Urban Planning 69:101–113.
Stone, T. A., I. F. Brown, and G. M. Woodwell
1991   Estimation, by Remote Sensing, of Deforestation in Central Rondônia, Brazil. Forest Ecology and Management 38(3–4):291–304.
Stonehouse, B.
1989   Polar Ecology. New York: Chapman & Hall.
Storey, K. B.
2001   Molecular Mechanisms of Metabolic Arrest: Life in Limbo. Oxford: BIOS.
2002   Life in the Slow Lane: Molecular Mechanisms of Estivation. Comparative Biochemistry and Physiology–Part A. Molecular and Integrative Physiology 133(3): 733–754.

Stott, P., and S. Sullivan, eds.
2000   Political Ecology: Science, Myth and Power. London: Arnold.
Strickon, A.
1965   The Euro-American Ranching Complex. *In* Man, Culture and Animals. A. Leeds and A. P. Vayda, eds. Washington, DC: American Association for the Advancement of Science.
Stromberg, M. R., J. D. Corbin, and C. M. D'Antonio, eds.
2007   California Grasslands: Ecology and Management. Berkeley: University of California Press.
Sturtevant, W.
1964   Studies in Ethnoscience. American Anthropologist 66(3) pt. 2:99–131.
Sukopp, H., M. Numata, and A. Huber
1995   Urban Ecology as the Basis of Urban Planning. The Hague: SPB Academic.
Sussman, R., G. M. Green, and L. Sussman
1994   Satellite Imagery, Human Ecology, Anthropology and Deforestation in Madagascar. Human Ecology 22(3):333–354.
Suttie, J. M., S. G. Reynolds, and C. Batello, eds.
2005   Grasslands of the World. Rome: Food and Agricultural Organization of the UN.
Suttles, W.
1968   Coping with Abundance. *In* Man the Hunter. R. B. Lee and I. DeVore, eds. Chicago: Aldine.
Sutton, M. Q., and E. N. Anderson
2004   An Introduction to Cultural Ecology. Walnut Grove, CA: AltaMira.
Svendsen, M.
2005   Irrigation and River Basin Management: Options for Governance and Institutions. Wallingford, UK: CABI Publications.
Sweet, L.
1965   Camel Pastoralism in Northern Arabia and the Minimal Camping Unit. *In* Man, Culture and Animals: The Role of Animals in Human Ecologic Adjustments. A. Leeds and A. P. Vayda, eds. Washington, DC: American Association for the Advancement of Science.
Swift, J.
1977   Sahelian Pastoralists: Underdevelopment, Desertification and Famine. Annual Review of Anthropology 6:457–478.
Szelenyi, I.
1978   Ecological Change and Residential Mix in Adelaide. *In* Proceedings of RGS Symposium on Residential Mix in Adelaide. D. U. Urlich and B. A. Badcock, eds. Royal Geographical Society of Australasia.
Takahashi, J. S., F. W. Turek, and R. Y. Moore, eds.
2001   Circadian Clocks. New York: Kluwer Academic/Plenum.
Tanaka, J.
1976   Subsistence Ecology of Central Kalahari San. *In* Kalahari Hunter-Gatherers. R. B. Lee and I. DeVore, eds. Cambridge, MA: Harvard University Press.
Taylor, G.
1951   Geography in the Twentieth Century. London: Methuen.
Tedrow, T. C. F.
1977   Soils of the Polar Landscapes. New Brunswick, NJ: Rutgers University Press.
2004   Polar Desert Soils in Perspective. Eurasian Soil Science 37(5):443–450.

Tellam, J. H., R. G. Israfilov, and M. O. Rivett, eds.
2006   Urban Groundwater Management and Sustainability. NATO Science Series IV. Earth and Environmental Science. Vol. 47. Berlin: Springer.

Temple, N. J., and T. Wilson, eds.
2006   Nutritional Health: Strategies for Disease Prevention. Totowa, NJ: Humana.

Terborgh, J.
1983   Five New World Primates: A Study in Comparative Ecology. Princeton, NJ: Princeton University Press.

Theodorson, G. A., ed.
1961   Studies in Human Ecology. New York: Harper & Row.

Thomas, F.
1925   The Environmental Basis of Society. New York: Century.

Thomas, L. G.
1986   Ranchers' Legacy. Edmonton: University of Alberta Press.

Thomas, P., and J. Packham
2007   Ecology of Woodlands and Forests: Description, Dynamics, and Diversity. Cambridge: Cambridge University Press.

Thomas, R., ed.
2003   Sustainable Urban Design: An Environmental Approach. London: Spon.

Thomas, R. B.
1973   Human Adaptation to a High Andean Energy Flow System. Department of Anthropology, Occasional Papers. University Park: Pennsylvania State University.
1976   Energy Flow at High Altitude. *In* Man in the Andes. P. T. Baker and M. Little, eds. Stroudsburg, PA: Dowden, Hutchinson & Ross.
1998   The Evolution of Human Adaptability Paradigms: Toward a Biology of Poverty. *In* Building a New Biocultural Synthesis. A. H. Goodman and T. L. Leatherman, eds. Ann Arbor: University of Michigan Press.

Thomas, R. B., and B. P. Winterhalder
1976   Physical and Biotic Environment of Southern Highland Peru. *In* Man in the Andes. P. T. Baker and M. Little, eds. Stroudsburg, PA: Dowden, Hutchinson & Ross.

Thompson, L., M. Davis, and E. Mosley-Thompson
1994   Glacial Records of Global Climate: A 1500-Year Tropical Ice Core Record of Climate. Human Ecology 22(1):83–96.

Thompson, L., E. Mosley-Thompson, M. Davis, P. Lin, T. Yao, M. Dyurgerov, and J. Dai
1993   Recent Warming: Ice Case Evidence from Tropical Ice Cores with Emphasis in Central Asia. Global and Planetary Change 7:145–156.

Thompson, S. A.
1988   Patterns and Trends in Irrigation Efficiency. Water Resource Bulletin 24(1): 57–63.

Thurstain-Goodwin, M.
2001   The Sustainable City: Urban Regeneration and Sustainability. Environment and Planning B 28:629–630.

Tian, H.Q., S. Q. Wang, J. Liu, S. Pan, H. Chen, C. Zhang, and X. Shi
2006   Patterns of Soil Nitrogen Storage in China. Global Biogeochemical Cycles 20(1):9 GB1001.

Tickell, A.
1998   On Critical Geography and Civil Society. Environment and Planning A 30:761–766.

Tillman, D.
1999   Ecological Consequences of Biodiversity: A Search for General Principles. Ecology 80:1455–1474.

Tinker, A.
2000   Women's Health: The Unfinished Agenda. International Journal of Gynecology and Obstetrics 70(1):149–158.

Tivy, J.
1971   Biogeography. London: Oliver & Boyd.

Tole, L.
1998   Sources of Deforestation in Tropical Developing Countries. Environmental Management 22(1):19–33.

Tomka, S.
1992   Vicuñas and Llamas: Parallels in Behavioral Ecology and Implications for the Domestication of Andean Camelids. Human Ecology 20(4):407–434.

Toniolo, M. A.
2004   The Role of Land Tenure in the Occurrence of Accidental Fires in the Amazon Region: Case Studies from the National Forest of Tapajós, Pará, Brazil. Ph.D. diss. Bloomington: Indiana University, Joint Program in Public Policy, Department of Political Science and School of Public and Environmental Affairs.

Topoliantz, S., J. F. Ponge, and S. Ballof
2005   Manioc Peel and Charcoal: A Potential Organic Amendment for Sustainable Soil Fertility in the Tropics. Biology and Fertility of Soils 41(1):15–21.

Townsend, C. R., M. Begon, and J. L. Harper
2002   Essentials of Ecology. Oxford: Blackwell.

Townsend, P. K.
2000   Environmental Anthropology: From Pigs to Policies. Prospect Heights, IL: Waveland.

Trawick, P. S.
2003   The Struggle for Water in Peru: Comedy and Tragedy in the Andean Commons. Stanford, CA: Stanford University Press.

Troll, C.
1958   Las Culturas Superiores Andinas y el Medio Geográfico. Lima, Perú: Instituto de Geografía, Universidad Nacional de San Marcos.

Tucker, C.
1999   Private vs. Communal Forests: Forest Conditions and Tenure in a Honduran Community. Human Ecology 27(2):201–230.

Tucker, C., and E. Ostrom
2005   Multidisciplinary Research Relating Institutions and Forest Transformations. *In* Seeing the Forest and the Trees. E. F. Moran and E. Ostrom, eds. Cambridge, MA: MIT Press.

Tucker, C., and J. Southworth
2005   Processes of Forest Change at the Local and Landscape Levels in Honduras and Guatemala. *In* Seeing the Forest and the Trees. E. F. Moran and E. Ostrom, eds. Cambridge, MA: MIT Press.

Tucker, J., E. Brondizio, and E. F. Moran
1998   Rates of Forest Regrowth in Eastern Amazônia and a Comparison of Altamira and Bragantina Regions. Pará State, Brazil. Interciencia 23(2):64–73.

Turner, B. L. II, W. C. Clark, R. W. Kates, J. F. Richards, J. T. Mathews, and W. B. Meyer, eds.
1990   The Earth as Transformed by Human Action. New York: Cambridge University Press.

Turner, B. L. II, D. R. Foster, and J. Geoghegan, eds.
2004   Integrated Land-Change Science and Tropical Deforestation in the Southern Yucatan: Final Frontiers. Oxford: Oxford University Press.

Turner, B. L. II, W. B. Meyer, and D. L. Skole
1994   Global Land Use/Land Cover Change: Toward an Integrated Program of Study. Ambio 23:91–95.

Turner, B. L. II, D. Skole, S. Sanderson, G. Fisher, L. Fresco, and R. Leemans
1995   Land Use and Land Cover Change: Science/Research Plan. IGBP Report no. 35 and HDP Report no. 7. Stockholm: IGBP.

Turner, I. M.
2001   The Ecology of Trees in the Tropical Rain Forest. New York: Cambridge University Press.

Turner, M. G.
2005   Landscape Ecology: What Is the State of the Science? 36:319–344.

Turner, M. G., V. H. Dale, and R. H. Gardner
1989   Predicting Across the Scales: Theory Development and Testing. Landscape Ecology 3:245–252.

Turner, R. K., D. W. Pearce, and I. Bateman
1993   Environmental Economics: An Elementary Introduction. Baltimore, MA: Johns Hopkins University Press.

Turner, W., T. Nakamura, and M. Dinetti
2004   Global Urbanization and the Separation of Humans from Nature. BioScience 54:585–590.

Uchmanski, J.
1999   What Promotes Persistence of a Single Population: An Individual-Based Model. Ecological Modelling 115:227–241.

Udehn, L.
2002   The Changing Face of Methodological Individualism. Annual Review of Sociology 28:479–507.

Uhl, C.
1982   Recovery Following Disturbances of Different Intensities in the Amazon Rain Forest of Venezuela. Interciencia 7(1):19–24.
1983   You Can Keep a Good Forest Down. Natural History 92:69–79.

Uhl, C., and C. Jordan
1984   Succession and Nutrient Dynamics Following Forest Cutting and Burning. Ecology 65:1476–1490.

Uhl, C., and J. B. Kauffman
1990   Deforestation, Fire Susceptibility, and Potential Tree Responses to Fire in the Eastern Amazon. Ecology 71(2):437–449.

Uhl, C., and P. Murphy
1981   Composition, Structure and Regeneration of a Tierra Firme Forest in the Amazon Basin of Venezuela. Tropical Ecology 22(2):219–237.

Uhl, C., D. Nepstad, R. Bushbacher, V. Clark, B. Kaufman, and S. Subler
1989   Disturbance and Regeneration in Amazônia: Lessons for Sustainable Land Use. The Ecologist 19(6):235–240.

Ulijaszek, S. J.
1993   Nutritional Anthropology: Prospects and Perspectives. London: Smith-Gordon.

Ulijaszek, S. J., and R. Huss-Ashmore, eds.
1997   Human Adaptability: Past, Present and Future. Oxford: Oxford University Press.

UNEP (United Nations Environmental Program)
1997   Global Environmental Outlook. Oxford: Oxford University Press and United Nations Environmental Programme.

Unruh, J.
1991   Nomadic Pastoralism and Irrigated Agriculture in Somalia. Geojournal 25(1):91–108.

Usher, P. J., and G. Wenzel
1987   Native Harvest Surveys and Statistics. Arctic 40(2):145–160.

Vallentine, J.
1975   Range Development and Improvements. Provo, UT: Brigham Young University Press.

Van den Berg, A. E., T. Hartig, and H. Staats
2007   Preference for Nature in Urbanized Societies: Stress, Restoration, and the Pursuit of Sustainability. Journal of Social Issues 63:79–96.

Van den Brink, R., D. Bromley, and J. Chavas
1995   The Economics of Cain and Abel: Afro-Pastoral Property Nights in Sahel. Journal of Developing Studies 31(3):373–399.

Van der Hammen, T.
1972   Changes in Vegetation and Climate in the Amazon Basin and Surrounding Areas During the Pleistocene. Geologie en Mijnbouw 51(6):641–643.

Vandermeer, J. H.
2003   Tropical Agroecosystems. Boca Raton, FL: CRC Press.

Vandermeer, J. H., and I. Perfecto
2005   Breakfast of Biodiversity: The Political Ecology of Rain Forest Destruction. New York: Food First Books.

Van der Westhuyzen, J., R. E. Davis, G. C. Icke, and T. Jenkins
1987   Thiamin Status and Biochemical Indices of Malnutrition and Alcoholism in Settled Communities of !Kung San. Journal of Tropical Medical Hygiene 90(6):283–289.

Van Gemerden, B. S., H. Off, M. P. E. Parren, and F. Bongers
2003   The Pristine Rain Forest? Remnants of Historical Human Impacts on Current Tree Species Composition and Diversity. Journal of Biogeography 30(9):1381–1390.

Van Heerden, P.
1968   The Foundation of Empirical Knowledge. Wassenaar, The Netherlands: N.V. Vitgeverij Wistik.

Van Liere, E. J., and J. C. Stickney
1963   Hypoxia. Chicago: University of Chicago Press.

Van Marken Lichtenbelt, W., A. J. Frijns, M. Ooijen, D. Fiala, A. Kester, and A. Steenhoven
2004   Effect of Individual Characteristics on a Mathematical Model of Human Thermoregulation. Journal of Thermal Biology 29(7–8): 577–581.

VanStone, J. W.
2000   Reindeer as Draft Animals in Alaska. Inuit Studies 24(20):115–138.
Van Wambeke, A.
1978   Properties and Potentials of Soils in the Amazon Basin. Interciencia 3(4): 233–242.
Van Wie, C. C.
1974   Physiological Responses to Cold Environments. *In* Arctic and Alpine Environments. J. D. Ives and R. G. Barry, eds. London: Methuen.
Vayda, A. P.
1968   Hypotheses about Functions of War. *In* War: The Anthropology of Armed Conflict and Aggression. Morton Fried et al., eds. New York: Doubleday.
1983   Progressive Contextualization: Methods for Research in Human Ecology. Human Ecology 11(3):265–281.
1974   Warfare in Ecological Perspective. Annual Review of Ecology and Systematics 5:183–193.
1976   Warfare in Ecological Perspective. New York: Plenum.
Vayda, A. P., and B. McCay
1975   New Directions in Ecology and Ecological Anthropology. Annual Review of Anthropology 4:293–306.
Vayda, A. P., and R. Rappaport
1976   Ecology, Cultural and Noncultural. *In* Human Ecology. P. Richerson and J. McEvoy, eds. North Scituate, MA: Duxbury.
Vayda, A. P., and B. Walters
1999   Against Political Ecology. Human Ecology 27(1):167–180.
Vedwan, N., and R. Rhoades
2001   Climate Change in the Western Himalayas of India: A Study of Local Perception and Response. Climate Change Research 19:109–117.
Veth, P. M., M. A. Smith, and P. Hiscock, eds.
2005   Desert Peoples: Archeological Perspectives. Malden, MA: Blackwell.
Vickers, W.
1975   Meat Is Meat: The Siona-Secoya and the Hunting Prowess-Sexual Reward Hypothesis. Latinamericanist 11(1):1–5. Gainesville: University of Florida Center for Latin American Studies.
1976   Cultural Adaptation to Amazonian Habitats: The Siona-Secoya of Eastern Ecuador. Ph.D. diss. University of Florida, Department of Anthropology.
1984   The Faunal Components of Lowland South American Hunting Kills. Interciência 9(6):366–376.
1988   Game Depletion Hypothesis of Amazonian Adaptation: Data from a Native Community. Science 239:1521–1522.
Virtanen, T., K. Mikkola, A. Nikula, J. H. Christensen, G. G. Mazhitova, N. G. Oberman, and P. Kuhry
2004   Modeling the Location of the Forest Line in Northeast European Russia with Remotely Sensed Vegetation and GIS-Based Climate and Terrain Data. Arctic, Antarctic, and Alpine Research 36(3):314–322.
Vitousek, P., H. Mooney, J. Lubchenco, and J. Melillo
1997   Human Domination of Earth's Ecosystems. Science 277:494–499.
Voget, F.
1975   A History of Ethnology. New York: Holt, Rinehart & Winston.

Vogt, E., ed.
1974   Aerial Photography in Anthropological Field Research. Cambridge, MA: Harvard University Press.

Volder, A., L. C. Bliss, and H. Lambers
2000   The Influence of Temperature and Nitrogen Source on Growth and Nitrogen Uptake of Two Polar Desert Species, *Saxifraga caespitosa* and *Cerastium alpinum*. Plant and Soil 227(1–2):139–148.

Von Bertalanffy, L.
1968   General Systems Theory. Rev. ed. New York: Braziller.

Vuille, M., and C. Ammann
1997   Regional Snowfall Patterns in the High, Arid Andes. Climatic Change 36(34): 413–423.

Wackernagel, M., J. Kitzes, D. Moran, S. Goldfinger, and M. Thomas
2006   The Ecological Footprint of Cities and Regions: Comparing Resource Availability with Resource Demand. Environment and Urbanization 18:103–112.

Wackernagel, M., and W. Rees
1996   Our Ecological Footprint: Reducing Human Impact on the Earth. New York: New Society.

Waddell, E.
1972   The Mound Builders. Seattle: University of Washington Press.

Wadhams, P., J. A. Dowdeswell, and A. N. Schofield, eds.
1996   The Arctic and Environmental Change. Amsterdam: Gordon & Breach.

Wagenaar, K. T., A. Diallo, and A. P. Sayers
1986   Productivity of Transhumant Fulani Cattle in the Inner Delta of Mali. Addis Abbaba: International Livestock Centre for Africa.

Wagley, C.
1953   Amazon Town. New York: Macmillan.
1969   Cultural Influences on Population: A Comparison of Two Tupi Tribes. *In* Environment and Cultural Behavior. A. P. Vayda, ed. New York: Natural History Press.
1977   Welcome of Tears: The Tapirapé Indians of Central Brazil. New York: Oxford University Press.

Wahaab, R. A., and M. I. Badawy
2004   Water Quality Assessment of the River Nile System: An Overview. Biomedical and Environmental Sciences 17(1):87–100.

Walker, B., W. Steffen, J. Canadell, and J. Ingram, eds.
1999   The Terrestrial Biosphere and Global Change: Implications for Natural and Managed Ecosystems. Cambridge: Cambridge University Press.

Walker, B. H., D. Ludwig, C. S. Holling, and R. M. Peterman
1981   Stability of Semi-Arid Savanna Grazing Systems. Journal of Ecology 69:473–498.

Walker, D. M., F. J. Perez-Barberia, and G. Marion
2006   Stochastic Modelling of Ecological Processes Using Hybrid Gibbs Samplers. Ecological Modelling 198:40–52.

Walker, R.
In press The Expansion of Intensive Agriculture and Ranching in Amazônia. In Amazônia and Global Change. M. Keller, J. Gash, and P. S. Dias, eds. San Francisco, CA: International Geophysical Union.

Walker, R., E. F. Moran, and L. Anselin
2000   Deforestation and Cattle Ranching in the Brazilian Amazon: External Capital and Household Processes. World Development 28(4):683–699.

Wallace, A. F. C.
1956   Revitalization Movements. American Anthropologist 58(2):264–281.
1960   An Interdisciplinary Approach to Mental Disorders Among the Polar Eskimos of Northwest Greenland. Anthropologica 2(2):1–12.

Waller, R.
1967   Bronchi and Lungs-Air Pollution. *In* The Prevention of Cancer. R. Raven and F. Col, eds. London: Butterworth.

Walsh, C., A. H. Roy, J. W. Feminella, P. D. Cottingham, P. M. Groffman, and R. P. Morgan
2005a   The Urban Stream Syndrome: Current Knowledge and the Search for a Cure. Journal of the North American Benthological Society 24:706–723.

Walsh, C., T. D. Fletcher, and A. R. Ladson
2005b   Stream Restoration in Urban Catchments Through Redesigning Storm Water Systems: Looking to the Catchment to Save the Stream. Journal of the North American Benthological Society 24:690–705.

Walsh, S., and K. Crews-Meyer, eds.
2002   Linking People, Place and Policy: A GIScience Approach. Boston: Kluwer.

Walsh, S., T. Evans, W. Welsh, B. Entwisle, and R. Rindfuss
1999   Scale Dependent Relationships Between Population and Environment in Northeastern Thailand. Photogrammetric Engineering and Remote Sensing 65(1):97–105.

Walter, H.
1973   Vegetation of the Earth. New York: Springer.

Ward, M.
1975   Mountain Medicine: A Clinical Study of Cold and High Altitude. New York: Van Nostrand Reinhold. 2nd ed., 1985.

Ward, M. P., J. S. Milledge, and J. B. West
1995   High Altitude Medicine and Physiology. 2nd ed. London: Chapman & Hall.

Wardle, D. A.
2002   Communities and Ecosystems: Linking the Aboveground and Belowground Components. Princeton, NJ: Princeton University Press.

Warren, R.
1998   The Urban Oasis: Guideways and Greenways in the Human Environment. New York: McGraw-Hill.

Waterbury, J.
2002   The Nile Basin: National Determinants of Collective Action. New Haven, CT: Yale University Press.

Watkinson, A. K., and S. J. Ormerod
2001   Grasslands, Grazing, and Biodiversity. Journal of Applied Ecology 38(2): 233–237.

Watson, R., M. Zinyowera, and R. Moss, eds.
1998   The Regional Impacts of Climate Change: An Assessment of Vulnerability. IPCC Working Group II Report. New York: Cambridge University Press.

Watt, K.
1968   Ecology and Resource Management. New York: McGraw-Hill.

Watts, M.
1983   Silent Violence. Berkeley: University of California Press.

Wätzold, F., M. Drechsler, C. W. Armstrong, S. Baumgärtner, V. Grimm, A. Huth, C. Perrings, H. P. Possingham, J. F. Shogren, A. Skonhoft, J. Verboom-Vasiljev, and C. Wissel
2006   Ecological-Economic Modeling for Biodiversity Management: Potential, Pitfalls, and Prospects. Conservation Biology 20(4):1034–1041.

Way, A.
1978   General Health. *In* The Eskimo of Northwestern Alaska: A Biological Perspective. P. L. Jamison, S. L. Zegura, and F. A. Milan, eds. Stroudsburg, PA: Dowden, Hutchinson & Ross.

Webb, W. P.
1931   The Great Plains. Boston: Ginn.

Webber, P. J.
1974   Tundra Primary Productivity. *In* Arctic and Alpine Environments. J. D. Ives and R. G. Barry, eds. London: Methuen.

Weber, W., L. J. T. White, A. Vedder, and L. Naughton-Treves, eds.
2001   African Rain Forest Ecology and Conservation: An Interdisciplinary Perspective. New Haven, CT: Yale University Press.

Wedel, W.
1961   Prehistoric Man on the Great Plains. Norman: University of Oklahoma Press.
1975   Some Early Euro-American Percepts of the Great Plains and Their Influence on Anthropological Thinking. *In* Images of the Plains. W. B. Boulet and M. P. Lawson, eds. Lincoln: University of Nebraska Press.

Weihe, W., ed.
1963   The Physiological Effects of High Altitude. Oxford: Pergamon.

Weiner, J. S., and J. A. Lourie, eds.
1969   Human Biology: A Guide to Field Methods. IBP Handbook, no. 9. Oxford: Blackwell.

Weinstein, K. J.
2005   Body Proportions in Ancient Andeans from High and Low Altitudes. American Journal of Physical Anthropology 128(3):569–585.

Weiss, J. L., and J. T. Overpeck
2005   Is the Sonoran Desert Losing Its Cool? Global Change Biology 11(12):2065–2077.

Weiss, M., and A. E. Mann
1991   Human Biology and Behavior. Glenview, IL: Scott Foresman.

Weitz, C. A., R. M. Garruto, C. T. Chin, J. C. Liu, R. L. Liu, and X. He
2000   Growth of Qinghai Tibetans Living at Three Different High Altitudes. American Journal of Physical Anthropology 111(1):69–88.
2002   Lung Function of Han Chinese Born and Raised Near Sea Level and at High Altitude in Western China. American Journal of Human Biology 14(4):494–510.
2004   Morphological Growth and Thorax Dimensions Among Tibetans Compared to Han Children, Adolescents, and Young Adults Born and Raised at High Altitude. Annals of Human Biology 31(3):292–310.

Wenzel, G.
1985   Resource Harvesting and The Social Structure of Native Communities. *In* Native People and Renewable Resource Management. J. Grun and J. Smith, eds. Edmonton: Alberta Society of Professional Biologists.

1999   Sharing, Money, and Modern Inuit Subsistence: Obligation and Reciprocity at Clyde River, Nunavut. *In* Social Economy of Sharing: Resource Allocation and Modern Hunter-Gatherers. G. W. Wenzel, G. Hovelsrun-Broda, and N. Kishigami, eds. Osaka: National Museum of Ethnology.

2000   Inuit Subsistence and Hunter Support in Nunavut. *In* Nunavut: Inuit Regain Control of Their Lands and Their Lives, J. Dahl, J. Hicks, and P. Jull, eds. IWGIA Document, no. 102. Copenhagen: International Work Group for Indigenous Affairs.

2004   From TEK to IQ: Inuit Qaujimajatuqangit and Inuit Cultural Ecology. Arctic Anthropology 41(2):238–250.

Werner, D.
1978   Trekking in the Amazon Forest. Natural History 87:42–55.

Werner, D., N. Flowers, D. Gross, and M. Ritter
1979   Subsistence Productivity and Hunting Effort in Native South America. Human Ecology 7:363–315.

Werner, P. A., ed.
1991   Savanna Ecology and Management: Australian Perspectives and Intercontinental Comparisons. London: Blackwell.

Wessels, K. J., E. F. Moran, R. S. DeFries, J. Dempewolf, L. O. Anderson, A. J. Hansen, and S. L. Powell
2004   Mapping Regional Land Cover with MODIS Data for Biological Conservation: Examples from the Greater Yellowstone Ecosystem, USA and Para State, Brazil. Remote Sensing of Environment 92:67–83.

Wessman, C.
1992   Spatial Scales and Global Change: Bridging the Gap from Plots to GCM Grid Cells. Annual Review of Ecology and Systematics 23:175–200.

West, J. B.
1998   High Life: A History of High-Altitude Physiology and Medicine. Oxford: Oxford University Press.

West, O.
1972   The Ecological Impact of the Introduction of Domestic Cattle into Wildlife and Tsetse Areas of Rhodesia. *In* The Careless Technology. M. T. Farvar and J. P. Milton, eds. Garden City, NY: Natural History Press.

Western, D., and V. Finch
1986   Cattle and Pastoralism: Survival and Production in Arid Lands. Human Ecology 14(1):77–94.

Weyant, J., W. Cline, S. Frankhauser, O. Davidson, H. Dowlatabadi, J. Edmonds, M. Grubb, R. Richels, J. Rotmans, P. Shukla, and R. Tol
1996   Integrated Assessment of Climate Change: An Overview and Comparison of Approaches and Results. *In* Climate Changes, 1995: Economic and Social Dimensions of Climate Change. J. P. Bruce, H. Lee, and E. F. Haites, eds. Contribution of Working Group III to the Second Assessment Report of the Intergovernmental Panel on Climate Change. New York: Cambridge University Press.

Weyer, E. M.
1932   The Eskimos: Their Environment and Folkways. New Haven, CT: Yale University Press.

Wheatley, P.
1971   The Pivot of the Four Quarters. Chicago: Aldine.
Wheeler, S. M.
2002   The New Regionalism: Key Characteristics of an Emerging Movement. Journal of the American Planning Association 68:268–278.
Whelan, R. J.
2004   The Ecology of Fire. Cambridge: Cambridge University Press.
Whelpton, P.
1954   Cohort Fertility. Princeton, NJ: Princeton University Press.
White, G., ed.
1974   Natural Hazards. New York: Oxford University Press.
White, L.
1943   Energy and the Evolution of Culture. American Anthropologist 45:335–356.
1949   The Science of Culture. New York: Free Books.
1959   The Evolution of Culture. New York: McGraw-Hill.
White, R., and J. Whitney
1992   Cities and Environment: An Overview. *In* Sustainable Cities: Urbanization and the Environment in International Perspective. R. Stren, R. White and J. Whitney, eds. Boulder: Westview.
Whitford, W. G., ed.
1986   Pattern and Process in Desert Ecosystems. Albuquerque: University of New Mexico Press.
2002   Ecology of Desert Systems. San Diego, CA: Academic.
Whitmore, T. C.
1975   Tropical Rain Forests of the Far East. Oxford: Clarendon.
1989   Forty Years of Rain Forest Ecology, 1948–1988, in Perspective. GeoJournal 19(4):347–360.
1990   An Introduction to Tropical Rain Forests. Oxford: Clarendon.
Whittaker, R. H.
1970   Communities and Ecosystems. New York: Macmillan.
Whittaker, R. H., and G. E. Likens
1975   The Biosphere and Man. *In* Primary Productivity of the Biosphere. H. Leith and R. H. Whittaker, eds. Berlin: Springer.
Wieder, R. K., and D. H. Vitt
2006   Boreal Peatland Ecosystems. New York: Springer.
Wielgolaski, F. E.
1997   Ecosystems of the World: Polar and Alpine Systems. Amsterdam: Elsevier.
Wiens, J. A., and M. R. Moss, eds.
2005   Issues and Perspectives in Landscape Ecology. Cambridge: Cambridge University Press.
Wild, A.
2003   Soils, Land, and Food. Cambridge: Cambridge University Press.
Wiley, A. S.
2004   An Ecology of High Altitude Infancy: A Biocultural Perspective. New York: Cambridge University Press.
Wilimovsky, N. J., and J. N. Wolfe, eds.
1966   Environment of the Cape Thompson Region, Alaska, PNE–481. Springfield, VA: National Technical Information Service.

Wilk, R.
1990   Household Ecology: Decision-Making and Resource Flows. *In* the Ecosystem Approach in Anthropology. E. F. Moran, ed. Ann Arbor: University of Michigan Press.

Wilkie, D.
1994   Remote Sensing Imagery for Resource Inventories in Central Africa: The Importance of Detailed Data. Human Ecology 22:379–404.

Williams, G.
1966   Adaptation of Natural Selection. Princeton, NJ: Princeton University Press.

Williams, M., Y. Shimabukuro, D. A. Herbert, S. Pardi Lacruz, C. Renno, and E. B. Rastetter
2002   Heterogeneity of Soils and Vegetation in an Eastern Amazonian Rain Forest: Implications for Scaling Up Biomass and Production. Ecosystems 5(7):692–704.

Williams, P. R.
2002   Rethinking Disaster-Induced Collapse in the Demise of the Andean Highland States: Wari and Tiwanaku. World Archeology 33(3):361–374.

Williams, S. E., E. E. Bolitho, and S. Fox
2003   Climate Change in Australian Tropical Rainforests: An Impending Environmental Catastrophe. Proceedings of the Royal Society of London. Series B-Biological Sciences 270(1527):1887–1892.

Williams, S. R.
1973   Nutrition and Diet Therapy, 2nd ed. St. Louis, MO: C. V. Mosby.

Willigan, J. D., and K. Lynch
1982   Sources and Methods of Historical Demography. New York: Academic.

Wilmsen, E.
1989   Land Filled with Flies: A Political Economy of the Kalahari. Chicago: University of Chicago Press.

Wilson, D. S.
2003   Darwin's Cathedral: Evolution, Religion, and the Nature of Society. Chicago: University of Chicago Press.

Wilson, E. O.
1967   The Theory of Island Biogeography. Princeton, NJ: Princeton University Press.
1979   On Human Nature. Cambridge, MA: Harvard University Press.
1992   The Diversity of Life. Cambridge, MA: Belknap Press, Harvard University Press.
2002   The Future of Life. New York: Knopf.
2006   The Creation: An Appeal to Save Life on Earth. New York: Norton.

Wilson, E. O., ed.
1988   Biodiversity. Washington, DC: National Academy Press.
2005   From So Simple a Beginning: Darwin's Four Great Books. New York: Norton.

Wilson, E. O., and W. Bossert
1971   A Primer of Population Biology. Sunderland, MA: Sinauer Associates.

Wilson, G. A., and M. Juntti, eds.
2005   Unraveling Desertification: Policies and Actor Networks in Southern Europe. Wageningen: Wageningen Academic.

Wilson, P. N., and R. H. Coupal
1990   Adopting Water-Conserving Irrigation Technology: The Case of Surge Irrigation in Arizona. Agricultural Water Management 18(1):15–28.

Wilson, T. E., J. Cui, R. Zhang, and C. G. Crandall
2006   Heat Stress Reduces Cerebral Blood Velocity and Markedly Impairs Orthstatic Tolerance in Humans. American Journal of Physiology-Regulatory Integrative and Comparative Physiology 291(5):R1443–1448.

WinklerPrins, A., and N. Barrera-Basols
2004   Latin American Ethnopedology: A Vision of Its Past, Present and Future. Agriculture and Human Values 21(2–3):35–52.

Winterhalder, B.
1981   Foraging Strategies in a Boreal Environment. An Analysis of Cow Hunting and Gathering. *In* Hunter-Gatherer Foraging Strategies. B. Winterhalder and E. Smith, eds. Chicago: University of Chicago Press.
1986   Diet Choice, Risk and Food Sharing in a Stochastic Environment. Journal of Anthropological Archaeology 5:369–392.
1994   Concepts in Historical Ecology: The View from Evolutionary Ecology. *In* Historical Ecology. C. Crumley, ed. Santa Fe, NM: School of American Research Press.

Winterhalder, B., R. Larsen, and R. B. Thomas
1974   Dung as an Essential Resource in a Highland Peruvian Community. Human Ecology 2(2):89–104.
1978   Geoecology of Southern Highland Peru: A Human Adaptation Perspective. Occasional Paper 27/MAB Project 6. Boulder: Institute of Arctic and Alpine Research.

Winterhalder, B., and E. A. Smith, eds.
1981   Hunter-Gatherer Foraging Strategies: Ethnographic and Archeological Analyses. Chicago: University of Chicago Press.

Wisloff, U., S. M. Najjar, Ø. Ellingsen, P. M. Haram, S. Swoap, Q. Al-Share, M. Fernström, K. Rezaei, S. J. Lee, L. G. Koch, and S. L. Britton
2005   Cardiovascular Risk Factors Emerge After Artificial Selection for Low Aerobic Capacity. Science 307:418–420.

Wissler, C.
1926   The Relation of Nature to Man in Aboriginal America. New York: Oxford University Press.

Wittfogel, K. A.
1956   The Hydraulic Civilizations. *In* Man's Role in Changing the Face of the Earth. W. L. Thomas, ed. Chicago: University of Chicago Press.
1957   Oriental Despotism. New Haven, CT: Yale University Press.

Wojtkowski, P. A.
2004   Landscape Agroecology. New York: Food Products Press.

Wolch, J.
2007   Green Urban Worlds. Annals of the Association of American Geographers 97(2):373–384.

Wolch, J., M. Pastor Jr., and P. Dreier, eds.
2004   Up Against the Sprawl: Public Policy and the Making of Southern California. Minneapolis: University of Minnesota Press.

Wolf, B., and G. H. Snyder
2003   Sustainable Soils: The Place of Organic Matter in Sustaining Soils and Their Productivity. New York: Food Products Press.

Wolf, E.
1982   Europe and the People Without History. Berkeley: University of California Press.
1999   Envisioning Power. Berkeley: University of California Press.

Wolf, E., and A. Palerm
1955   Irrigation in the Old Acolhua Domain. Southwestern Journal of Anthropology 11:265–281.

Wolf, J., and S. Mahmood
1997   Water Disinfection Project Addresses Aral Sea Crisis. Water Engineering and Management 144(10):18–20.

Wood, C., and D. Skole
1998   Linking Satellite, Census, and Survey Data to Study Deforestation in the Brazilian Amazon. *In* People and Pixels: Linking Remote Sensing and Social Science D. Liverman et al., eds. Washington, DC: National Academy Press.

Woodburn, J.
1968   An Introduction to Hadza Ecology. *In* Man the Hunter. R. B. Lee and I. DeVore, eds. Chicago: Aldine.

Woodin, S., and M. Marquiss
1997   Ecology of Arctic Environments: 13th Special Symposium of the British Ecological Society. Cambridge University Press. *Or*: Special Publication no. 13 of the British Ecological Society. Malden, MA: Blackwell Science.

Woodwell, G., R. A. Houghton, T. Stone, R. Nelson, and W. Kovalick
1987   Deforestation in the Tropics: New Measurements in the Amazon Basin Using Landsat and NOAA AVHRR. Journal of Geophysical Research 92:2157–2163.

Woodwell, G., R. A. Houghton, T. Stone, and A. Park
1986   Changes in the Areas of Forests in Rondônia, Amazon Basin, Measured by Satellite Imagery. *In* The Changing Carbon Cycle: A Global Analysis. J. Trabalka and D. Reichle, eds. New York: Springer.

Wooster, D., ed.
1984   History as Natural History: An Essay on Theory and Method. Pacific Historical Review 3:1–19.
1988   The Ends of the Earth: Perspectives on Modern Environmental History. Cambridge: Cambridge University Press.

Worster, D.
1994   Nature's Economy: A History of Ecological Ideas. 2nd ed. Cambridge: Cambridge University Press.

Worthington, E.
1975   The Evolution of the IBP. Cambridge: Cambridge University Press.

Wright, H. A., and A. W. Bailey
2004   Fire Ecology: United States and Southern Canada. New York: Wiley.

Wright, S. J.
2003   The Myriad Consequences of Hunting for Vertebrates and Plants in Tropical Forests. Perspectives in Plant Ecology, Evolution and Systematics 6(1–2):73–86.

Wu, T. Y.
2001   The Qinghai-Tibetan Plateau: How High Do Tibetans Live? High Altitude Medicine and Biology 2(4):489–499.

Wyndham, C. H.
1966   Southern African Ethnic Adaptation to Temperature and Exercise. *In* The Biology of Human Adaptability. P. T. Baker and J. S. Weiner, eds. Oxford: Clarendon.

Wynne-Edwards, V. C.
1965   Self-Regulating Systems in Populations of Animals. Science 147:1543–1548.
Xu, C. L., and Z. Z. Li
2002   Stochastic Ecosystem Resilience and Productivity: Seeking a Relationship. Ecological Modelling 156(2–3):143–152.
Yagoub, M. M.
2004   Monitoring of Urban Growth of a Desert City Through Remote Sensing: Al-Ain, UAE, Between 1976 and 2000. International Journal of Remote Sensing 25(6):1063–1076.
Yamazaki, F., and K. Hamasaki
2003   Heat Acclimation Increases Skin Vasodilation and Sweating But Not Cardiac Baroreflex Responses in Heat-Stressed Humans. Journal of Applied Physiology 95(4):1567–1574.
Yang, D. C.
2002   Kakuma, Turkana, Dueling Struggles: Africa's Forgotten Peoples. St. Paul, MN: Pangaea.
Yellen, J. E.
1972   Ecology, Nomadic Movement and the Composition of the Local Group Among Hunters and Gatherers: An East African Example and Its Implications. *In* Man, Settlement and Urbanism. P. Ucko et al., eds. Cambridge, MA: Schenkman.
1974   Warfare in Ecological Perspective. Annual Review of Ecology and Sistematics 5:183–193.
1976   Settlement Patterns of the !Kung. *In* Kalahari Hunter-Gatherers. R. B. Lee and I. DeVore, eds. Cambridge, MA: Harvard University Press.
1977   Archaeological Approaches to the Present. New York: Academic.
Yengoyan, A.
1968   Demographic and Ecological Influences on Aboriginal Australian Marriage Sections. *In* Man the Hunter. R. B. Lee and I. DeVore, eds. Chicago: Aldine.
1976   Structure, Event and Ecology in Aboriginal Australia: A Comparative Viewpoint. *In* Tribes and Boundaries in Australia. N. Petersen, ed. Canberra: Australian Institute of Aboriginal Studies.
Yoshimura, H., and J. S. Weiner, eds.
1966   Human Adaptability and Its Methodology. Tokyo: Japan Society for the Promotion of Sciences.
Young, C. H., and P. J. Jarvis
2001   Measuring Urban Habitat Fragmentation: An Example from the Black Country. Landscape Ecology 16:643–658.
Young, S. B.
1989   To the Arctic: An Introduction to the Far Northern World. New York: Wiley.
Zegura, S. L.
1978   The Eskimo Population System: Linguistic Framework and Skeletal Remains. *In* The Eskimo of Northwestern Alaska: A Biological Perspective. P. L. Jamison, S. L. Zegura and F. A. Milan, eds. Stroudsburg, PA: Dowden, Hutchinson & Ross.
Zegura, S. L., and P. L. Jamison
1978   Multidisciplinary Research: A Case Study in Eskimo Human Biology. *In* The Eskimo of Northwestern Alaska: A Biological Perspective. P. L. Jamison, S. L. Zegura and F. A. Milan, eds. Stroudsburg, PA: Dowden, Hutchinson & Ross.

Zhang, H., C. Huizenga, E. Arens, and T. Yu
2001 Considering Individual Physiological Differences in a Human Thermal Model. Journal of Thermal Biology 26(4–5):401–408.

Zhang, Q. F., C. O. Justice, and P. V. Desanker
2002 Impacts of Simulated Shifting Cultivation on Deforestation and the Carbon Stocks of the Forests of Central Africa. Agriculture, Ecosystems and Environment 90(2):203–209.

Zhuang, J. G., H. F. Zhu, and Z. Zhou
2002 Reserved Higher Vagal Tone Under Acute Hypoxia in Tibetan Adolescents with Long-Term Migration to Sea Level. Japanese Journal of Physiology 52(1): 51–56.

Ziker, J. P.
2002 Peoples of the Tundra. Prospect Heights, IL: Waveland.

Zimmerer, K. S., ed.
2006 Globalization and New Geographies of Conservation. Chicago: University of Chicago Press.

Zimmerer, K. S., and T. J. Bassett, eds.
2003 Political Ecology: An Integrative Approach to Geography and Environment-Development Studies. New York: Guilford.

Zubrow, Ezra
1975 Prehistoric Carrying Capacity: A Model. Menlo Park, CA: Cummings.

1976 Demographic Anthropology. Albuquerque: University of New Mexico Press.

Zucchi, A., and W. Denevan
1979 Campos Elevados e História Cultural Prehispánica en los Llanos Occidentales de Venezuela. Caracas: Universidad Católica Andrés Bello.

INDEX